W9-ABO-199

TRAGEDY: *Vision and Form*

"Everything in Nature is lyrical in its ideal essence, tragic in its fate, and comic in its existence."—SANTAYANA

"If only one issue in a lifetime compels the moderate man to take a heroic stand, that is the one moment that fixes his place in history as either a man or a nonentity."

—HENRY MYERS

"We live too variously to live as one."—J. ROBERT OPPENHEIMER

TRAGEDY
Vision and Form

Edited by

ROBERT W. CORRIGAN
New York University

CHANDLER PUBLISHING COMPANY

124 Spear Street
San Francisco, California 94105

Science Research Associates, Inc., 259 East Erie Street, Chicago, Illinois 60611
Distributors   A Subsidiary of IBM

Previously published and copyrighted materials are reprinted with the permission of authors, publishers, or copyright owners as listed below:

MAX SCHELER, "On the Tragic." Translated by Bernard Stambler. Published in *Cross Currents*, Vol. IV, 1954, pp. 178–191. Reprinted with permission of *Cross Currents* and Francke Verlag, Berne.

MURRAY KRIEGER, "Tragedy and the Tragic Vision." From *The Tragic Vision* by Murray Krieger. Copyright © 1960 by Murray Krieger. Reprinted by permission of Holt, Rinehart and Winston, Inc.

RICHARD B. SEWALL, "The Vision of Tragedy." From *The Vision of Tragedy* by Richard B. Sewall, 1959. Reprinted by permission of Yale University Press.

KARL JASPERS, "Basic Characteristics of the Tragic." From *Tragedy Is not Enough* by Karl Jaspers.

GEORGE SANTAYANA, "The Tragic Mask," is reprinted with the permission of Charles Scribner's Sons from *Soliloquies in England and Later Soliloquies* by George Santayana (1922).

SIDNEY HOOK, "Pragmatism and the Tragic Sense of Life." From the Proceedings and Addresses of the American Philosophical Association, October, 1960. Reprinted with permission of the author.

ALDOUS HUXLEY, "Tragedy and the Whole Truth." From *Collected Essays by Aldous Huxley*. Copyright 1931, 1959 by Aldous Huxley. Reprinted with the permission of Harper & Row, Publishers, Incorporated.

SUSANNE LANGER, "The Tragic Rhythm." Reprinted with the permission of Charles Scribner's Sons from *Feeling and Form* by Susanne Langer. Copyright 1953 Charles Scribner's Sons.

NORTHROP FRYE, "The Mythos of Autumn: Tragedy." Reprinted from *The Anatomy of Criticism*, by Northrop Frye. Copyright 1957 by Princeton University Press. All rights reserved.

GEORGE BOAS, "The Evolution of the Tragic Hero." First published in *The Carleton Drama Review*, Vol. I, No. 1 (1955–1956).

HENRY A. MYERS, "Heroes and the Way of Compromise." From *Tragedy: A View of Life* by Henry A. Myers. Copyright © 1956 by Cornell University. Used by permission of Cornell University Press.

W. H. AUDEN, "The Christian Tragic Hero." From *The New York Times Book Review*, December 16, 1945. Copyright © 1945 by The New York Times Company. Reprinted by permission of the author and publisher.

ARTHUR MILLER, "Tragedy and the Common Man." From the *New York Times*, February 27, 1949, Sec. 2, pp. 1, 3. Copyright 1949 by The New York Times Company. Reprinted by permission of Ashley Famous Agency, Inc., agents for Arthur Miller.

ROBERT WARSHOW, "The Gangster as Tragic Hero." From *The Immediate Experience* by Robert Warshow, 1962. Copyright 1954 by Josiah Goldberg as Trustee of the estate of Robert Warshow.

MAUD BODKIN, "Archetypal Patterns in Tragic Poetry." From *Archetypal Patterns in Poetry* by Maud Bodkin. Oxford University Press, 1963. Reprinted by permission of the publisher.

ELDER OLSON, "Modern Drama and Tragedy." From *Tragedy and the Theory of Drama* by Elder Olson. Copyright 1961 by The Wayne State University Press. Reprinted by permission of the publisher.

D. D. RAPHAEL, "Why Does Tragedy Please?" From *The Paradox of Tragedy* by D. D. Raphael. Indiana University Press, 1960. Reprinted by permission of the publisher.

ROY MORRELL, "The Psychology of Tragic Pleasure." From *Essays in Criticism*, Vol. VI, No. 1 (January, 1956), pp. 22–37. Reprinted by permission of the publisher.

ERIC BENTLEY, "Melodrama." From *The Life of the Drama* by Eric Bentley. Copyright © 1964 by Eric Bentley. Reprinted by permission of Atheneum Publishers.

JAMES L. ROSENBERG, "Melodrama." From *The Context and Craft of Drama*, edited by Robert W. Corrigan and James L. Rosenberg, copyright © 1964 Chandler Publishing Company. Reprinted by permission of the author.

ROBERT B. HEILMAN, "Tragedy and Melodrama." Reprinted from *The Texas Quarterly*, Summer, 1960, with permission of the author.

WYLIE SYPHER, "Aesthetic of Revolution: The Marxist Melodrama." Reprinted from *The Kenyon Review*, Vol. X, No. 3 (Summer, 1948), with permission of the author.

JOSEPH WOOD KRUTCH, "The Tragic Fallacy." From *The Modern Temper* by Joseph Wood Krutch, copyright, 1929, by Harcourt, Brace & World, Inc.; renewed, 1957, by Joseph Wood Krutch. Reprinted by permission of the publishers.

KENNETH BURKE, "On Tragedy." Reprinted from *Counter-Statement*, Hermes Publications, 1953, with permission of the author.

STANLEY EDGAR HYMAN, "Psychoanalysis and the Climate of Tragedy." First published as "Freud and the Climate of Tragedy," *Partisan Review*, Vol. XXIII, No. 2 (Spring, 1956). Reprinted by permission of the author.

ORRIN E. KLAPP, "Tragedy and the American Climate of Opinion." Reprinted from *Centennial Review of Arts and Sciences*, Vol. II (Fall, 1958). Reprinted with permission of the author and publisher.

WILLIAM ARROWSMITH, "The Criticism of Greek Tragedy." First published in *Tulane Drama Review*, Vol. III, No. 3 (March, 1959). Reprinted with permission of the author.

CLIFFORD LEECH, "The Implications of Tragedy." Reprinted from *Shakespeare's Tragedies and Other Studies in 17th Century Drama* by Clifford Leech, Chatto & Windus, Ltd., 1950. Reprinted by permission of Chatto and Windus.

LIONEL ABEL, "The Fate of Athaliah—and Racine." Reprinted from *Metatheatre: A New View of Dramatic Form* by Lionel Abel. Copyright © 1963 by Lionel Abel. Reprinted by permission of Hill and Wang, Inc.

ERICH HELLER, "Goethe and the Avoidance of Tragedy." Reprinted from *The Disinherited Mind* by Erich Heller, by permission of Farrar, Straus & Company, Inc. Published 1957 by Farrar, Straus & Co., Inc.

ROBERT W. CORRIGAN, "The Sun Always Rises: Ibsen's *Ghosts* as Tragedy?" Reprinted from *Educational Theatre Journal*, 1959. Used by permission of *Educational Theatre Journal*.

JOHN GASSNER, "The Possibilities and Perils of Modern Tragedy." First published in *Tulane Drama Review*, Vol. I, No. 3 (June, 1957). Reprinted with permission of the author.

ARISTOTLE, From *The Poetics*. From *Aristotle on the Art of Poetry*, an amplified version with supplementary illustrations. Translated and revised by Lane Cooper, Cornell University Press, 1947. Reprinted by permission of the publisher.

FRIEDRICH HEGEL, From "The Philosophy of Fine Art." From *The Philosophy of Fine Art* by Friedrich Hegel, translated by F. P. B. Osmaston, 1920. Used by permission of the publisher G. Bell & Sons, Ltd.

FRIEDRICH NIETZSCHE, From "The Birth of Tragedy." From *Birth of Tragedy and the Genealogy of Morals* by Friedrich Nietzsche, translated by Francis Golffing, Doubleday & Company, Inc. Reprinted by permission of the publisher.

SØREN KIERKEGAARD, "The Ancient Tragical Motif as Reflected in the Modern." From *Either/Or, A Fragment of Life*, Vol. I, by Søren Kierkegaard, translated by David and Lillian M. Swenson, Princeton University Press, 1944. Reprinted by permisson of the publisher.

For John Gassner, long a good friend, with thanks for the many kind things he has done for me.

Contents

Preface

The facts of tragedy have haunted the spirit of every man in all ages, and for this reason the subject of tragedy has usually interested those who feel the need for a more intelligent awareness of themselves and the world in which they live. This has always been true, but never more so than it is to-day when we feel that our lives are perched precariously on the brink of continual disaster. The number of books and articles on tragedy and the tragic written in the last two decades is overwhelming. (Indeed, more has been written on the subject since 1940 than in the century prior to the out-break of the war in 1939.) It is unlikely that anyone has read them all, but the very fact of their existence indicates that the conditions of our world have forced our imaginations to dwell once again on the facts of suffering, failure, and death. Until the second World War "tragedy" was a dirty word in public parlance (we destroyed its power by indiscriminately using it to describe any kind of painful experience), and in academic circles it had become an honorific term reeking with a musty nostalgia for past ages of glory. It was argued that tragedy, the great flower of aristocratic societies, was dead and all attempts to revive it in a democratic and equalitarian age were doomed to failure. Even the mighty Ibsen seemed small when placed next to Aeschylus, Sophocles, and Euripides or Marlowe, Shakespeare, Corneille, and Racine. So said the professors. On the surface the students agreed and they read their Sophocles with dutiful respect, but they really liked O'Neill no matter how tin his ear was supposed to have been. In fact, it is now clear that tragedy hadn't died at all, it just went underground for a couple of centuries. Dostoyevsky, Nietzsche, and Kierkegaard had told us so, but most people were not convinced. Dunkirk, Belsen, and Hiroshima changed all this, and once again tragedy has taken its place as a part of our common routine.

Looking back it is easy to see how and why the subversion of tragedy occurred. After the Restoration and on into the eighteenth century, England had a new deal in politics and religion; the emerging middle-class economy was burgeoning and creating a new prosperity; a growing confidence in the methods of empirical science tended to dispel personal doubts; and the bright flame of the Enlightenment cast its light on all that was heretofore dark and mysterious. Many may have been "Born but to die, and reasoning but to err . . ."; but as Pope went on, there was a plan for those who would but look.

> All nature is but Art, unknown to thee;
> All Chance, Direction, which thou canst not see;
> All Discord, Harmony not understood;
> All partial evil, universal Good. . . .

On the continent the romanticism of Rousseau and his followers had a similiar effect on popular attitudes about tragedy. The Curse of Adam was a social blight and not an innate quality of man. Individual man was born good and was then corrupted by his society. But society could be changed and it was the duty of all men of good will to work for its improvement. In reducing Evil to evils, catastrophe was institutionalized and therefore remediable. Thus by insisting that human suffering and failure are not so much the result of our essentially divided nature as they are the effects of impersonal and external social forces, Rousseaunian romanticism tended to dissolve tragic guilt, although it should be noted that it was also largely responsible for creating the psychology of victimization.

The nineteenth century was the century of progress and tragedy was given little place in official life or official art. The "Cult of Life" emerged victorious (in theory at least) and the tragic view of life was the great enemy which had to be suppressed at all costs. Victorianism, with its sturdy morality, its conservativism, its willingness to compromise, and its ability to assimilate alien views into its unique brand of optimism, was riding high on the crest of a wave of material expansion and unthought-of prosperity. The voices of doubt and dissent were there, of course, but they were seldom heard. And in America we were too busy getting the land settled to worry much about things like tragedy.

At the turn of the present century rumblings from the underground and occasional eruptions could be heard. The theatre, especially, began to change. We see it first in the later plays of Ibsen and the post-inferno plays of Strindberg; later in the frenzied works of the German Expressionists. Even a Fabian optimist like Shaw, who for so long had an answer for everything, began to come up with the most improbable solutions to the question of "What's to be done?" And as the final curtain descends with Saint Joan crying out: "O God that madest this beautiful earth, when will it be ready to receive Thy saints? How long, O Lord, how long?" We know the answer is "never!" So we entered the Age of the Bomb and all the debates about the possibility of the common man being tragic (invariably any discussion of tragedy will sooner than later evoke the question: "Is *Death of a Salesman* a tragedy?") are ample, if not always eloquent, testimony that tragedy is once more a central concern of many thoughtful people.

But here new problems arise. No sooner do we admit the possibility of tragedy, than we exclaim: "Where are they?" People turn feverishly to the giants of the past or to Aristotle's *Poetics* and bemoan the fact that while our world may certainly be tragic, it is nonetheless inhospitable to the nobility and grandeur of tragedy. This kind of thinking is, I believe, the result of a formalistic fallacy. It is based on the assumption that there are certain formal and structural characteristics which all tragedy of all ages must share in common. But where in the history of drama will one find such formal consistency? Certainly not in Classical Greek tragedy nor in Shakespeare! Is tragedy always about death? Not in Sophocles. People say that the hero is brought low because he has a "tragic flaw," but this idea doesn't hold up when we examine a number of tragedies. What is the flaw of Oedipus? Pride. What is the flaw of Antigone? Pride. What is the flaw of Lear? Pride. Are they all the same play? And after all, what difference does it make? Aristotle called Euripides "the most tragic of poets," but many of his plays end happily and attempts to compare them to those of Sophocles in terms of structure have been misleading and meaningless. The moment we try to establish a general definition of tragedy in terms of some set of formal characteristics we are sure to come a cropper. The constant in tragedy is the tragic view of life or the tragic spirit: that sense that life is, as Scott Fitzgerald once put it, "essentially a cheat and its conditions are those of defeat." This spirit can and does take many forms—both in drama and life— but it is always there as a backdrop to man's fate. Tragedy has always been both a celebration and a protest of this condition, and it is as possible in our day as it ever was. If only we'd stop looking for another Shakespeare or Sophocles we might discover that *Mother Courage* is as much a tragedy as is *Coriolanus* or *Ajax*, or that Düerrenmatt's *The Visit of the Old Lady* says more to our time about the tragic nature of our existence than *Oedipus the King*.

And this is the chief reason for this book. The fact that tragedy is being taught in more and more of our colleges and schools is a sign of our cultural maturity. But this growth brings with it a new responsibility: what ideas will be transmitted in the process? This is not just an academic quibble. I agree with Professor Heilman that a failure to understand what tragedy is about can have important and undesirable consequences for our grasp of reality; that confusion in this subject may result in our losing touch with certain ideas that are an indispensable means of contemplating and understanding and experiencing the human catastrophes that surround us everywhere. This book is an attempt to bring together a fairly large number of essays which deal with such catastrophes of body and spirit with clarity, understanding, and compassion.

Finally, I should like to acknowledge the help of those who did so much to make this book possible. As always, the permission editors of the various publishers with whom I have corresponded have been cooperative, and I appreciate their many kindnesses and considerations. I particularly want to thank my colleagues Eric Bentley, Robert Heilman, Wylie Sypher, Stanley Edgar Hyman, Orrin Klapp, William Arrowsmith, and one of the greatest of my teachers, George Boas, for their willingness to let me use their work. I have acknowledged my great respect for John Gassner elsewhere.

ROBERT W. CORRIGAN

A Note on Organization

The ten parts of this volume can be divided into two main groups. The first six are concerned with the nature of the tragic spirit and the elements of the tragic form, as well as with our response to it. The last four groups cannot be related in this way. The four essays on melodrama may be the most important ones in this book because each of them focusses in a different but equally meaningful way on those ideas which most often confuse our thinking about tragedy. There has been precious little written on this subject and most of what has—usually to be found in "introduction" to the theatre or drama texts and other handbooks of this kind—isn't worth the paper it is written on. We can be grateful that at last four of our finest critics have turned their attention to this vital subject. The section entitled "The Climates of Tragedy" is particularly concerned with the problems facing the writer of tragedy in our time, and Part IX is included to reveal how the great tragedies of the past have been re-evaluated by the critics of today. Finally, I have included excerpts from four of the great classics of tragic theory both for obvious practical purposes and also to provide a comparison to what is being written now or has been in the recent past. As I indicated earlier, the literature on the subject of tragedy is huge in its amount and wide in its scope, and no editor will be able to satisfy all of his readers, but I do believe my selection does bring together all of the cross currents of critical thought on this subject—several of them for the first time—which is so important to so many people.

R. W. C.

Autumn, 1964

TRAGEDY: *Vision and Form*

On the Tragic *

In the following we will speak of no particular art in which the tragic is portrayed. It is impossible to arrive at the phenomenon of the tragic through the art product alone, although the results of examining its extant forms might be most fruitful in discovering what it really is. The tragic is rather an essential element of the universe itself. The material made use of by the art product and the tragedian must contain beforehand the dark strain of this element. To determine what makes a tragedy genuine we must first have as precise a notion as possible of the phenomenon.

It is doubtful whether the tragic is essentially an esthetic phenomenon. We are speaking of life and history in general without placing ourselves in any particular esthetic circumstance, no matter how unusually full of tragic events and circumstances. The question of how the tragic works on our emotions or of how we come to "enjoy" the tragic in some art form we are purposely avoiding. These things can not tell us what the tragic is. The usual "psychological" method of observation, proceeding from the investigation of the experiences of one observing a tragic incident to its "objective understanding," tries to discover and describe the evocations of these experiences. Such a method avoids the issue rather than clarifies it.[1] It tells us only what the tragic does, not what it is. The tragic is above all a property which we observe in events, fortunes, characters, and the like, and which actually exists in them. We might say that it is given off by them like a heavy breath, or seems like an obscure glimmering that surrounds them. In it a specific feature of the world's makeup appears before us, and not a condition of our own ego, nor its emotions, nor its experience of compassion and fear. What goes on in the observer of the tragic as he feels this heavy

---

[1] Even the famous definition of Aristotle: The tragic is that which arouses pity and fear.

* Max Scheler, "On the Tragic," Bernard Stambler, tr., *Cross Currents*, Vol. IV (1954), pp. 178–191.

breath and sees this shimmering darkness that encircles the head of the
"tragic hero" is not related to his ability to understand this phenomenon
by using his own symbolical way of looking at this feature in the world's
makeup. There are people who are blind, or half blind, to the tragic—like
Raphael, Goethe, and Maeterlinck.[2] One must know what the tragic is to
depict this experience. Moreover, the experience is historically far more
variable than the tragic itself. A tragedy of Aeschylus arouses entirely different emotions today than in his time, although the tragic is just as perceptible to both ages.

The mental processes of understanding the tragic, the inner perception
of how it is brought to us, are to be distinguished from what one experiences
in observing the tragic. This is not the same as the "experience" theory
of the tragic. It has nothing to do with depicting the way it works on us
psychologically. However, the former places the problem close to the essence of the tragic and its essential manifestations. Consequently, it should
not be disregarded.

How then should we proceed? Should we indiscriminately gather together examples of the tragic, selecting those events that impress men as
being such, and then ask what they possess in common? This would be a
method of induction that would lend itself well to experimental support.
Yet this would bring us only to the observation of our own ego when the
tragic works upon us. What right have we to trust men when they call
something tragic? A plurality of opinion does not help here. Without
knowledge of what the tragic is, must we be forced to decide between the
opinions that have weight and those which do not? But even taking this for
granted, we would still have to justify ourselves. We would have a confused
mass that we would call tragic. What would the common element be that
would justify this judgment of ours? Nothing more than the fact that they
are all called tragic.

All induction would presuppose that one knows beforehand what the essence of the tragic is, and not just what events are tragic. Our method of
procedure will be different. The few examples and statements of others that
may be given are not to serve as the basis for abstracting by induction a
concept of the tragic. They will rather give us some rough draft in which to
see the basic use of the word and the phenomenon expressed therein, without
taking into account who uses the word and to what intent. They will provide the basis for seeing in what experience this phenomenon comes to its
given state. We do not assume that the examples are facts in which the
tragic adheres as a property. They are only something which will contain
the basic manifestations of the tragic. They will provide us with the oppor-

---

[2] Cf. Maeterlinck's *La Sagesse et la Destinée*.

tunity of searching out these manifestations and finally of arriving at the tragic itself. It is not a question here of proofs but of indications or signs.

One should also guard against treating the tragic as a phenomenon with its own metaphysical, religious, and otherwise speculative interpretations. The tragic is not the result of an interpretation of the world and the important events of the world. It is a fixed and powerful impression that certain things make and one which can itself be subjected to many different interpretations. Theories like that which Maeterlinck proposes, basically the theory of every Rationalism and Pantheism, are totally wrong. According to these theories the tragic is the result of a false and unstable interpretation of the world. The tragic is attributed to the ways of thinking in uncivilized times with uncontrolled emotions. Or it is a sort of sudden bewilderment in the face of the defects of the world against which one knows of no help, or— what is the simple consequence of this as stated by Maeterlinck—no helper is at hand, no helper to put the matter in order. They obscure rather than clarify the essence of the tragic; their own outlook and times prevent them from seeing it. We, however, reason that these interpretations of the world are wrong because they have no place for the undeniable fact of the tragic and that any age which does not perceive it is insignificant.

Metaphysical interpretations of the tragic are most interesting. But the phenomenon itself is taken for granted by them. Certain metaphysicians like Eduard von Hartmann make God Himself the tragic hero. Others think the tragic lies only on the surface of things and that underneath all tragedies lies an imperceptible harmony, into which they are finally resolved. But to know where the tragic has its source, whether in the basic structure of existence or in human passions and unrest, is to know already what the tragic is.

Every interpretation fails before the inflexibility of reality which reduces it to silence.

This question of the tragic is only one example of the importance of contrasting the changing whims of the times with the facts of reality.

THE TRAGIC AND VALUES

All that can be called tragic is contained within the realm of values and their relationships.

In a universe free of values, such as that constructed by mechanical physics, there are no tragedies.

Only where there is high and low, nobleman and peasant, is there anything like a tragic event.

The tragic is not a value like beautiful, ugly, good, or bad. The tragic appears in objects only through the interplay of their inherent values.

It is always founded on values or connected with values. To repeat, it is found only in that realm where there are objects of value and where these work in one way or another on each other.

Serenity, sadness, grandeur, and earnestness can be classified among the more tranquil values. The tragic is absent here. It appears in the realm of changing values and circumstances. Something must happen for it to appear. There must be a period of time in which something is lost or destroyed.

In empty space—Schiller notwithstanding—dwells much sublimity, but not the tragic. In a spaceless world the tragic might be possible, but never in a timeless world. In its basic connotations the tragic always implies a determined effectiveness in doing and in suffering. The tragic "character" remains such only as long as he has the necessary dispositions for tragic acting and suffering. Even a situation calling for opposition of forces or their reconciliation is only tragic as long as it contains this effectiveness. If the tragic is to appear, however, this effectiveness must take on a definite direction, a direction toward the annihilation of a positive value in a determined hierarchy. The strength which annihilates it must possess this value itself.

To belong to the category of the tragic some value must be destroyed. With regard to man it does not have to be his existence or his life. But at least something of his must be destroyed—a plan, a desire, a power, a possession, a faith. The destruction as such is not tragic. It is rather the course that an object of lower or equal positive values, never of higher values, is able to force upon it. We can hardly call it tragic for a good man to defeat and bring about the downfall of an evil man, nor for a nobleman to do the same to a peasant. Moral approval precludes a tragic impression here. This much is certain. It is also certain that it must be an object of high positive value that destroys a value. (Values such as the honest with respect to the wicked, the good with regard to the bad, and the beautiful compared to the ugly, are here called positive. All values have this opposition and duality, even excluding their degree of "higher" and "lower.") The tragic is apparent only where the strength to destroy a higher positive value proceeds from an object possessing this positive value. The manifestation is, moreover, purest and clearest where objects of equally high value appear to undermine and ruin each other. Those tragedies most effectively portray the tragic phenomenon in which, not only is every one in the right, but where each person and power in the struggle presents an equally superior right, or appears to fulfill an equally superior duty. If an object of higher positive value, let us take for example a good, just man, is overpowered by some insignificant evil object, the tragic is at once senseless and irrational. In place of arousing tragic pity, it arouses painful indignation. Tragic pity can never fall completely into the depths of pain and disgust, but must maintain some semblance of coolness and calmness.

The tragic is first of all a struggle that is occasioned in an object of high positive value, i.e., of a high moral nature, generally treating of the family, marriage, or the state. The tragic is a "conflict" which takes place between the positive value and the very object which possesses it. The great art of the tragedian is to set each value of the conflicting elements in its fullest light, to develop completely the intrinsic rights of each party.

ON THE TRAGIC AND GRIEF

It is true that in some way all tragic events are sad, but in a very definite sense. This is precisely what fate is, an event surrounded by this quality of sadness.[3] On the other hand it arouses sorrow in the feelings of men. It makes the soul sad.

Not all sad persons are tragic characters, however. Every death is sad and makes those left behind sad as well, but assuredly not every death is tragic. Let us disregard for a moment that type of grief that is produced in us independently of any perception of values, almost as if caused by a "neutral" feeling. We would rather consider the "grieved over something." The nature of a certain event arouses our sentiments and produces this feeling in us. It should not appear to be caused by our individual wishes or aims, but only by the worth of the object. The tragic grief has a double characteristic, one rooted in itself, the other in its subject.

This kind of grief is free from all indignation, anger, reproach, and that accompanying the desire "if it had only been otherwise." It is a calm, quiet fullness; a special kind of peace and composure is characteristic of it.

The atmosphere of tragic grief will be absent if we are aroused to do something about it. Once the event has been completed and brought to its climax, any indication of a compromise or of some chance to avert the catastrophe makes tragic grief impossible.

Tragic grief contains a definite composure. It is thus distinguished from all specifically personal griefs, those which come from a personal experience of being "sad about something." It comes to us from the outside through the soul; it is occasioned by events that are "tragic." The tragedies of Aeschylus show especially well how to awaken this atmosphere of grief in its utmost purity.

We will not point out the twofold characteristic feature of the tragic which causes this atmosphere. One is the very nature of the world's makeup; every individual sad event is thus determined. The other is based on the appearance of an uncompromising inevitability of the destruction of a value, a species of destruction which every tragedy must contain.

In every genuine tragedy we see more than just the tragic event. We see over and above it the permanent factors, associations, and powers which

---

[3] That the quality of the sad is definitely not a "feeling," nor a so-called "empathic feeling," cf. the essay, "Idole der Selbsterkenntnis."

are in the very makeup of the world. It is these which make such a thing possible.[4] In every tragic event we are directly confronted with a definite condition of the world's makeup without deliberation or any sort of "interpretation." This confronts us in the event itself; it does not result from what
it does to the things which brought it about. It is only momentarily connected with the event and is independent of the elements that make it up.
It is present in the form of a slight presentiment.

Every objective grief like that of a tragic event has its own depth. (I
take the word here in a transferred meaning like the "depth" of a room.)
It has its own immensity, too, which distinguishes it from a very limited,
determined event. The depth is brought about by the fact that its subject is
twofold. One is the element of the event that has been seen by us. The other
is that point in the world's makeup that is exemplified by the event and of
which the event is but an example. Grief seems to pour out from the event
into unlimited space. It is not a universal, abstract world-makeup that would
be the same in all tragic events. It is rather a definite, individual element of
the world's construction. The remote subject of the tragic is always the
world itself, the world taken as a whole which makes such a thing possible.
This "world" itself seems to be the object immersed in sorrow. In the foreground of this darkness of sorrow we see the specific event and fate standing out all the more clearly.

The element in the world's makeup which produces these situations
seems to do so without any warning. In producing them it ignores the
peculiarities of the causes of the event and even its normal effects. It is this
which causes the second essential element of the tragic, its inevitability.

We will clarify this later. Right now we are interested in the peculiar
atmosphere which it lends to the tragedy.

There is a whole category of feelings and affections that can be connected with the destroying of a value. Their essence is in being "preventa-
ble," even if in a particular case they may or may not have been prevented.
It doesn't matter what these feelings might be—dread, fear, anger, horror,
or the like; they all have in general the characteristic of "excitement."
Thinking about the possibility of its turning out otherwise, or even better,
causes this excitement. In men it is more frequently caused by the thought,
"If so and so had only acted differently." This excitement is able to take
hold of a man only because he is a practical being and, as it were, the
potential actor in any event.

It softens when the inevitability is seen as an impossibility. The grief
does not cease to be what it is, but it assumes the character of the feelings
of dissatisfaction, excitement, and pain. These are taken in the same narrow sense as the physical feelings of fear, horror, and the like.

[4] We mean "such a thing" in the sense of "a so-constituted value."

Tragic grief is pure, without physical arousement. In a certain sense even a feeling of "contentment" is joined with it.

There is no desire to do away with the event which led to the destruction of some value. This is abolished by seeing its inevitability.

We see that the tragic seems to have its ultimate roots in the essential makeup of the world itself. It is this which clears away all sense of culpability or responsibility. When we see this in the nature of the event a certain reconciliation takes place. It is a species of reconciliation which fills us with peace and rest and with resignation. This resignation banishes the weakness and pain that would come from contemplating a better-made world.

Thus the specific sadness of the tragic is really an objective character of the event itself. It is independent of the individual circumstances of the beholder. It is free from the feelings provoked by excitement, indignation, blame, and the like. It has a depth and immensity. It is not accompanied by physical feelings or by what can be called real pain. It has a definite resignation, contentment, and a species of reconciliation with the existence which it chances to have.

THE TRAGIC KNOT

We asserted previously that in the tragic a struggle takes place between two objects possessing high positive value and that one of them must be overcome. There is one case where this is fulfilled to the highest degree. It happens when the objects are not different events, persons, or things, but coincide in one event, person, or thing; even better, in one and the same quality, power, or ability.

It would be most tragic if the same power which has brought either itself or another object to a very high positive value becomes its destroyer—especially if this takes place in the very act of its achievement.

If we are observing a certain action which is realizing a high value, and then see in that same action that it is working towards the undermining of the very existence of the being it is helping, we receive the most complete and the clearest of tragic impressions.

The same tragic impression occurs when a special courage or boldness which permits a man to accomplish an heroic deed undermines him because it exposes him to a danger that a moderately prudent man would avoid—"If only I were prudent enough I would not be called Tell." Another example is the man with high ideals toward a spiritual goal who permits them to become shipwrecked on the little things of life. Everyone according to Madame de Staël's dictum has the mistakes of his virtue: the same traits of character which permitted a man to do his best have brought him to catastrophe.

We don't have to talk only of human beings here. An art gallery can be destroyed by the very fire that was kindled to preserve the picture. The event has a sharp tragic character. The flight of Icarus is tragic. The very wax which glued his wings to him melts in the same degree as he flies toward the sun.

The use of the phrase, "the tragic knot," is a pertinent metaphor. It illustrates the inner entanglement between the creation of a value and the destruction of a value as they take place in the unity of the tragic action and the tragic event.

Something else can be deduced from the aforesaid. It is not the relationship between values that constitutes the "stage" for the tragic event, nor is it the connection of causal events which it contains. It is rather a special reference of the value relationships to the causal relationships. It is an essential characteristic of our world—and thus of every world—that the course of the causal events disregards completely the value of things. The exigencies of values as they develop toward a unity or as they unfold themselves toward their ideal fulfillment is not taken into account by the causal series. The simple fact that the sun shines on the good and bad alike makes tragedy possible. At times it may happen that the causal relationships simultaneously coincide with an increase of the values. This is accepted as only accidental. It is not occasioned by intrinsic determination. Nor is it occasioned by a consideration of what the values need to reach their fulfillment or that the causality is at hand to produce them.

Without this basic condition there can be no tragedy.

There would be no tragedy in a world which operated on an established system of laws whereby each thing had the powers and capabilities commensurate with its values, and whereby its activity was directed only towards the exigencies of developing or unifying these values. Tragedy would likewise be impossible in a world operating on a system of laws whereby the powers would be directed against the exigencies of these values, purposely opposing them. The tragic would thrive in a satanic world as well as in a divine—a fact that Schopenhauer forgot in his discussion of the tragic.

We see the tragic only when in one glance we embrace both the causality of things and the exigencies of their immanent values. In this unified glance the mind tries to synthetize the conditions in which it finds these values so as to arrive at the unity it is trying to achieve. Then it follows the course of events in their causal sequence. The result is a clear insight into the independence of these two things. It is here that we may see the formal "background" of all tragedies.

Obviously, it is not in the mere knowledge of this circumstance that the tragic exists. The tragic comes into sight only when this independence of the two elements becomes embodied in a concrete event.

What has just been said casts new light on our definition. For never is our insight so clear and so concentrated as when we see that the same action may in some places produce a high value and in others—quite indifferently —destroy this value.

Here then—where we are able to see the unity of an action at a single glance and not by discursive connection, limb by limb—here is a circumstance known previously only by concept which has now come tangibly within our grasp.

What do we mean when we say that in the tragic the destruction of value is "necessary"? Surely not the destruction of causality in general!

Is the question then one of "causal" necessity or is it likely to be one of quite another kind of necessity? Here one might begin to discriminate and say that it is indeed causal necessity but of a particular kind, that is, "inner necessity," and consequently a necessity which depends not on influences breaking in from the outer world but rather on the eternal nature of things and men. Only as such can things and men undergo the tragic fate. Actually, this concept of the tragic—widely held though it may be—is not borne out by the facts.

When a man who seems destined for a certain fate, either by congenital disease or by any sort of natural predisposition, is brought low the first time that external circumstance has a chance to work upon him—such an event does not seem tragic to us even if the highest values inhered in him, values independent of this natural predisposition. Thus Ibsen, with all his artistic genius, has not succeeded in making of Oswald, in *Ghosts*, a tragic figure, since the worm of destruction gnawing at Oswald is the result of a disease he has inherited from his father. We miss here something that belongs to the essence of the tragic hero: that the evil which drives the hero to his downfall pertains to those against whom the struggle is being waged, and also that such a struggle be actually waged.

Both these requirements are missing in *Ghosts*. Nor is the tragic hero to be found in him who immediately surrenders to the inimical, and who at the first dismissive word, immediately abnegates and resigns himself. The "necessity" of which we are now speaking must rather be of such a kind as to take its course even after the performance of all the "free" actions that may be tried in an attempt at flight. When we see the catastrophe opposed by all free efforts of will and means, and can still trace its irruption as "necessary"; when we can even trace, through the turmoil and anguish of this struggle to avert the catastrophe, a species of transcendent necessity: then and then only do we have an example before us of tragic "necessity."

Tragic necessity is not the necessity of the course of nature, a necessity which lies beneath freedom and the power of the will and which may be conceived as the free essence which permits the best linking of events in nature. Rather is tragic necessity of such a kind that it lies *above* freedom: it is to be found only in the conclusion of free acts or of "free causes" in the total sphere of causality, in which may be found even "unfree causes," that is, those which are the results of prior causes.

Wherever men are presented as "milieu-defined," as completely determined by "relationships," as in the naturalist "drama," we have a much less likely source of the tragic than in the drama which gives us the impression that consciously free choices are clearly and conclusively driving the events of the play to its catastrophe. Consequently neither naturalism and determinism on the one hand nor the rationalistic thesis of a "freedom of the human will" limited only by the chances of nature can provide a comprehension of the tragic, or anything more than the beginning of such comprehension. Both these views of the world have no place for the tragic since they make no provision for essential necessity reaching out above the qualities of nature and free choice.

There is still another reason why it is inadequate to define as "inner" that species of necessity we are here discussing. Immanent cause is that which in a thing or in a person exists as latent predisposition, or capacity, or skill, which functions at the inception of true relationships to other things or situations or persons. Wherever we encounter a strictly defined predisposition to the decline of value we must recognize an absence of the true development, of the veridical renewal, of the inner historicity which is needed for the tragic event: in such a situation the catastrophe itself would be predictable if we had a firm and exact picture of the character. The tragic however contains this paradox that when we behold the destruction of value it seems completely "necessary" and at the same time completely "unpredictable." Though the catastrophe may come closer and closer, driven by all the contributory factors (whether free or not), and each new event is visibly pregnant with danger, yet there must still remain one moment when everything—even by ideal calculation—could still turn out quite differently: whereupon from all this complexity is brought forth a deed which resolves these lurking factors into the unity of one species of reality by a means not rationally predictable.

The seemingly "propitious turn of events" just before the catastrophe, which so many tragic poets have been fond of, is a special means to exclude from the audience even the slightest appearance of "predictability." Even the increase of tension, which every tragedy must arouse, would not be possible if the catastrophe did not seem to us to be well founded from the beginning in the latent inner qualities of the characters and their relationships. It is *concrete* causality, which has nothing to do with "natural law," which governs tragic events as it also governs the irreversible motions of the constellations in their consummation of causality—that species of causality which is rightly called the truly "historical." For this we must return to the assertion of Schopenhauer that tragedy never exhibits true "character development" but only "character revelation," revelation of what was previously latent as disposition and character.

Even the tragic transformation of a character, the alteration of disposition and mentality, the essential and latent diversion from the previous course of life—even this transformation is seldom either the catastrophe itself or even an important part of it. A specifically tragic phenomenon is to be seen in the interruption—even in the midst of external victories—of a course of life directed towards certain values as goals. Tragic necessity is to be seen above all in the essence and essential relations of the inevitability and inescapability of things founded in society.

Even these negative definitions indicate that the species of "necessity" we have been talking about becomes apparent only when every conceivable kind of skill seems to be brought into play to halt the destruction of value and to preserve the value in question. Consequently two species of value-destruction are essentially untragic: first, those instances which are tinged with guilt because someone has failed in a duty definitely assigned to him; second, those instances which might have been avoided by the use of available techniques and means. In general, then, the quality of the tragic is lacking when the question "Who is guilty?" has a clear and definite answer.

Only where no such answer can be given does the stuff of tragedy begin to appear. We may use the term "tragic" only when we feel that everyone concerned in the story has hearkened to the demands of his duty with the utmost of his capabilities, and yet the disaster has had to occur. The tragic consists—at least in human tragedies—not simply in the absence of "guilt" but rather in the fact that the guiltiness can not be localized. Wherever we can substitute, in place of a man who plays a role in the unfolding of a catastrophe, another man who is like the first but morally better—that is, one who has a finer sympathy for moral opportunities as well as a greater energy of the moral will—to the extent that we can perform such substitution the growth of a feeling of tragedy is stunted by the amount of blame we can pin on the responsible person.

In such an instance "necessity" is missing as a quality of the tragic phenomena. Consider, for example, the death of Christ; suppose we were able to have the idea that his death, instead of being an essential relationship between His divine purity and the profaneness and opposition of an obdurate "world," had been brought about by the particular moral laxity of Pontius

Pilate, or by the wickedness of an individual named Judas, or by the inimical deeds of the Jews. If we were then able to imagine Jesus of Nazareth surrounded not by these men but by a group morally "better," or if we could place him in a different historical context where he would come to higher recognition and repute—if we could do these things the impression of the tragic would vanish.

The death of Jesus is tragic only when it is presented—everywhere and forever—as the consistent adherence to the higher duty of all the parties concerned. An execution, for example, can never have a tragic culmination. The tragic appears when the idea itself of "justice" appears as leading to the destruction of higher value. An execution, if it is unavoidable, awakens deep sympathy; if it were avoidable it might arouse deep anger or irritation, but never tragic sympathy.[5]

If it is true that a disaster becomes tragic only when everyone has done his duty and, in the usual sense of the word, no one has incurred "guilt," it becomes part of the essence of tragic conflict that this conflict be guiltless and unavoidable even before judges who approach the ideal in wisdom and virtue. The tragic misdeed is even definable as that which silences all possible moral and legal powers of judgment; and, on the other hand, every conflict is essentially untragic when by moral and legal lights it is seen to be obvious and simple. Every essential confusion of the bounds of right and wrong, of good and evil, in the unity of action; every maze of threads, of motives, of views, of duties, so presented as to seem to lead equally well to a judgment of "right" or "wrong"; every complication which is not based on necessary moral and legal wisdom but which instead produces from the circumstances alone an absolute confusion of our moral and legal powers of judgment—every such complication pertains to the subjective side of tragic feeling and thereby transposes us completely from the realm of possible "right" and "wrong," from possible "accusation" and "indignation." "Tragic guilt" is of a kind for which no one can be blamed and for which no conceivable "judge" can be found.

Out of this error of our moral judgments, out of this pardonable search for a subject upon whom to pin this "guilt," a guilt which appears to us as such with crystal clarity—only out of this appears that specific tragic grief and tragic sympathy of which we have been speaking, along with its unique peace and reconciliation of the emotions. Now too the shifting of that which is to be feared to the cosmos itself appears as the essence of the reconciliation of the individual men and wills with the culminating deeds and events in which they have been taking part.

---

[5] It is for this reason that Aeschylus, in his *Eumenides*, furnishes the judges of the Areopagus with both black and white marbles to indicate the guilt or innocence of Orestes.

In this way, tragic guilt becomes something other than definable "right" and "wrong," or than "obeying obligation" or "defying obligation."

But individual men have quite different microcosms of values, dependent on the extent of their actual moral awareness and even on the extent of their possible moral awareness. Only on these bases can be measured their possible "duties" and areas of duty—quite independently of all the peculiarities of their empirical real situations. If every individual does his "duty," to the extent that he does this he behaves *morally;* not otherwise can he do something of equal *value* or *be* in any way of equal value. How deep his gaze thereby penetrates into the macrocosm of moral value, which contains the entire extent of the realm of possible good and evil, and how deep a hold he takes within this macrocosm, are in no way to be decided by the extent to which each individual dutifully produces the "best" of the realm of values with which he has been endowed. It is not duty and the performance of it that "ennoble"—as the Kantian, short-sighted ethic puts it—but rather "noblesse oblige": this is the original nobility of man, which establishes for him quite varied arrays of possible duties—duties which stand in varied relationships to the moral world and are variously "significant" for it.

It makes a difference whether the man doing his duty is a grocer or a noble king; the first one in a vague way obeys a few moral value-distinctions, doing his "duty" with a couple of poor concepts of choice, while the other, living in the fullness of manifold human and other moral relationships, with a finely articulated and higher realm of moral value-distinctions before his eyes, does his "duty" while he demonstrates the highest value given to him, and in will and deed realizes this value. The latter man in this action must conduct himself as occasionally opposed to duty, while the man blind to value blandly performs *his* "duty." If we were now to say that in a true tragic presentation everyone must do his "duty," or at least that it would be prudent so to do, and that—even if everyone has done his duty— the destruction of value and the consequent lessening of the total moral value of the world must nevertheless take place, we would thereby still not know how to exclude this quite different dimension of the moral value-distinction of the individual and of his being taking part in the tragedy. It is rather a quite different species of the tragic which, in this dimension of being, bruises "noble" individuals against the strongly articulated "duties" of the mob. And it appears to be a particular melancholy-ironic glory of this kind of tragedy that the noble individual should accept a moral guilt that his companions do not accept. To the extent that the noble person can more easily become "guilty" than the ignoble—in accord with his richer and higher realm of duties—he is susceptible to a moral "risk" which ever bears with it something potentially tragic, as this risk simultaneously praises and blames his noble nature. The Prometheus of technic, who stole fire from

Zeus, is a tragic figure; but even more tragic are the moral Prometheuses in whose eyes a moral world comes with the brilliance of lightning, a moral world that never previously existed. . . . While they are realizing values and acquiring duties which the vulgar do not yet know how to see as value or to feel as duty, the vulgar are themselves only doing their "duty" while the noble see as "evil" what may still be "good" for the vulgar. Here is one instance of the tragic "fall" for the "noble," in that his every eventual moral disapproval of the vulgar must necessarily remain silent—to the extent that only through "good consciences" can his sacred "duty" be accomplished.

We can now penetrate more deeply into "tragic guilt" if we are careful to remain clear on the matter of what, in such a case, is the completion of the duty of the noble. Let it be a proposition here—with no attempt at proof—that moral "good" is the relation by which we realize or tend to realize in a given action that a preference indicates a more highly conceived value.[6] To prefer the higher value is always equivalent to depreciating the lower value, that is, to discontinue the realization of this lower value. However, all "moral norms," i.e., all imperative rules of a general type, are only exercises in what to will and what to do, as suggested by the average levelling of values in any given epoch resulting from the "situations" which are typical of and regularly recurring in this epoch; still, even this levelling of values provides "higher" values which must be realized. Every material rule of morality contains the presuppositions of the particular positive world of good appropriate to its level of civilization. What happens then when the "noble" man perceives a value which is higher than the average, a value which is generally trodden under in the levelling of values, and accomplishes his advance in the moral cosmos of value, an advance that the vulgar are not yet ready to grasp? In such a case it must be obvious to him that what appears "good" and "dutiful" according to the ruling morality now becomes wicked and evil—and by the same token becomes for him "opposed to duty." And this realization is not avoidable but rather—to use a term of Kant's—a "necessary perception" ("*notwendiger Schein*"). And since everything that can be generally a "moral law"—even to the most complete codification and strongly logical presentation of these laws— inevitably exhibits the positive material world of values of the "time," the "time" itself being determined by the prevailing system of value-levelling— such a man must violate the prevailing moral precept and also violate everything in the moral world that comes into the orbit of such precepts. He must necessarily appear "guilty" even before the fairest judge, when he is in fact guiltless and is so seen by God alone. That this is so is not an irregularity but rather part of the essence of all moral development. Here I mean

---

[6] Cf. my book, *Der Formalismus in der Ethik und die materiale Wertethik*, vol. I, Niemeyer, Halle, 1914.

to point out the root of that necessary and "guiltless guilt," which has hitherto been expressed in this paradoxical form only with a feeling for the justice of it. What is essential here is the necessity of the deception into which the most just moralist must blunder when confronted with the "tragic hero." Although the tragic hero with moral awareness [7] is obviously essentially the opposite of a sinner, he can not be distinguished from a sinner by the age in which he lives. Only to the extent that his newly experienced value becomes established and becomes the prevailing "morality" can he be seen and known—and then only in historical retrospect—as a moral hero. And so there are no present tragedies—there are only tragedies of the past. The tragic man necessarily goes his way in his "present" quiet and speechless. He strides unrecognized through the mob; he may even be there considered a sinner. The error of an instance which separates genius from sinner is here not an accidental but a necessary error. Here, in this tragic fate of the moral genius we can perhaps grasp, in a single species and fashion, the nerve of fate, the complete unpredictability of moral development in man. And even in the absolutely inevitable "fate" and the related absolute loneliness of the moral genius we can see a moment of the type of the tragic, as it may have happened to Jesus in Gethsemane. Here likewise appears the total fate of the world as it appears compressed into the experience of one man, as though in this moment he were standing alone and yet in the "middle," in the center of all the forces that animate the universe. His experience is as though whole epochs of history occurred in him, yet with no one else being aware of his experience—as though everything lay unified in his hand. And perhaps through this something more may become clear: the tragic hero of this kind is not guilty of his guilt, but rather it "happens" to him: this justifiable circumlocution repeats a very characteristic moment of "tragic guilt." That is: that the "guilt" comes to him and not he to the guilt! . . . "*Ihr fuhrt ins Leben ihn hinein.* . . . "

Nevertheless this "fall" into guilt does not mean that the tragic hero, either through immoderate passion or through stress and a drive in one direction, is so moved that this drive becomes the central point of his ego and his will consequently is impelled in this same direction. This is also the case in the usual moral guiltiness—at least in great measure; and quantities cannot here serve as a basis for differentiation. Even in the midst of the most powerful stresses the will which "follows" such a direction remains a new action, an action not entirely determined by this stress! The tragic guilt into which the hero "falls" is much more accurately characterized by calling it a "guilty" doing or renunciation of doing which darkens the areas of his possible choices and so makes a certain kind of guilt unavoidable, since the choice of the "best" meaning is necessarily in error.

---

[7] We are speaking here only of this kind and not of the tragic hero in general.

Moral or "guilty guilt" is based on the act of choice; tragic or unguilty guilt is rather based on the sphere of choice! The act of choice is consequently for the tragic hero free of guilt—just the reverse of what obtains in moral guilt, in which the sphere of choice also entails objectively guiltless possibilities, and only the guilt of the act is important. And so the tragic hero "becomes guilty" while doing a guiltless thing.

The consequence of what has been said is the absurdity of the schoolmasters' theory that a moral guiltiness is to be sought in tragedies, and that the tragic poet instead of being a respectable performer of a tragic phenomenon is made into a moral judge over his heroes, whom he punishes for their deeds while at the same time he animates them to perform those deeds. Only total blindness for the phenomenon of tragedy could hatch out this silliest of all theories.

But we should also fall into error if we should try to make the correct concept of tragic guilt serve as the complete definition of the tragic phenomenon. However, since from its earliest presentations the tragic has been a universal phenomenon, not one specifically human or limited to static will, such a definition is self-destructive. However, note this: where a "tragic guilt" is actually portrayed—and it is not the deed of the hero which brings the guilt upon him or is involved in the "catastrophe," nor is his downfall the bearer of the tragic phenomenon, but rather the "guilt of error" itself, and consequently the fact that purity of will falls into guilt—here is the very bearer and root of the tragic.

In this way it is tragic that Othello falls into the guilt of having to kill his beloved, and that guiltless Desdemona should be killed by her beloved who loves her. In his own words, "For, in my sense, 'tis happiness to die," the death of Othello is not punishment for his deed, which as "punishment" must terminate a conscious evil; rather is it deliverance. Tragic guilt is therefore not a condition of the tragic phenomenon—which would indeed be a *circulus in demonstrando*, if the guilt had to be not any sort of "guilt" but only "tragic" guilt—but it is a species of the tragic itself, and to the extent that we are here dealing with moral value, it is therefore a species of absolute value—so to speak, the culminating point of the tragic. Neither death nor any other mischance but only his "fall into guilt" constitutes the tragic fate of the hero.

Tragedy and the Tragic Vision *

MURRAY KRIEGER

If there were no eternal consciousness in a man, if at the foundation of all there lay only a wildly seething power which writhing with obscure passions produced everything that is great and everything that is insignificant, if a bottomless void never satiated lay hidden beneath all—what then would life be but despair?
—SØREN KIERKEGAARD, Fear and Trembling

Now of course the tragic is not the only vision projected by our serious literature and philosophy, nor is it necessarily the profoundest vision. But it is surely the most spectacular, and the most expressive of the crisis-mentality of our time. Consequently, it has won for those works obsessed with it the excited attention of our most stimulating critical minds. Perhaps in their excitement over the individual work they have neglected to define in general terms what this vision is—which is probably as it ought to be with the practicing critic. In any case there does not seem to be a systematic effort to say what is meant by the phrase and what, given this meaning, it has meant to recent writing.

It must be granted that, as with all terms of this kind, any meaning imposed upon it must be an arbitrary one that may or may not command agreement. But, agreed upon or not, it is valuable critically as it throws a consistently clear albeit diffuse light upon a broad enough and deep enough area in our literature. I propose here to create for the term a tentative definition that I have found most illuminating of modern literature and the modern mind, and in the balance of this volume to use it to conduct exploratory operations on a certain few novels of the last hundred or so years in order to demonstrate its incisive powers. Since I have some idea about where I shall come out, I must admit that my explorations will have all too

* Murray Krieger, "Tragedy and the Tragic Vision," from *The Tragic Vision* (Holt, Rinehart and Winston, 1960), pp. 1–21. [The footnotes for this selection have been renumbered.]

much direction to them and that consequently they will somewhat mislead us about the total reality of the works in the interest of showing the widespread relevance of my definition. By way of defense I can plead only that the definition was empirical in its origin and that it followed my probings into the individual novels rather than the other way round; in other words, that the meaning I am trying to create for the term is one that in my reading of these novels I feel that I have discovered.

It is surely needless to add that the act of enclosing a number of literary works within the limits of a given definition hardly passes any judgment upon works on either side of the boundary. For a work not to qualify as an example of the tragic vision is hardly a mark against it. Indeed, in the eyes of many, it may be quite the contrary. Of course, the meaning I want to establish for the tragic vision—indeed, any that would be worth very much —will be far more restrictive than the general lay usage of "tragedy" or "the tragic," which somehow broadens out to synonymity with catastrophe, the sorrowful, that which stems from or leads to "pessimism." But how, if we limit ourselves to technical literary definition, can we find for the tragic any meaning beyond that of Aristotle? The answer is, by moving from formalistic aesthetics to what I would term "thematics."

Thus it becomes necessary first to determine the extent to which we want the meaning of "the tragic vision" entangled with that of "tragedy," surely a term well enough defined in our critical tradition. The most obvious difference I would mark between the two is also a crucial one: "tragedy" refers to an object's literary form, "the tragic vision" to a subject's psychology, his view and version of reality. It is more than a difference between two extant approaches to the tragic. Rather, the second has usurped the very possibility of the first after having been born side by side with it. Perhaps it would be more accurate to say that the tragic vision was born *in*side tragedy, as a part of it: as a possession of the tragic hero, the vision was a reflection in the realm of thematics of the fully fashioned aesthetic totality which was tragedy. But fearful and even demoniac in its revelations, the vision needed the ultimate soothing power of the aesthetic form which contained it—of tragedy itself—in order to preserve for the world a sanity which the vision itself denied.

It is for these reasons that the reader who as a modern is obsessed with notions of the tragic ought in a way to find himself disappointed on turning for the first time to Aristotle's celebrated definition in the *Poetics*. We have been so accustomed to doing this treatise deference—and rightfully so from a formalistic point of view—that we can no longer approach it freshly and feel the letdown that should be ours as we glance over its superficial formal prescriptions that are to pass as a description of so sacred and reverenced a literary genre. All this about magnitude and completeness and catharsis—are these to do justice to the profound complex of metaphysical and psychological forces which the tragic unleashes? Or so, at least, we ought as moderns to say superciliously. But probably we should have expected no more than this from the *Poetics*. Perhaps it was not for the Greek theoretical consciousness—even in as late a representative as Aristotle—to be as self-consciously aware of the disturbing implications of the tragic mentality as it was of the formal requirements which transcended, or rather absorbed, this mentality and restored order to the universe threatened by it.

The cathartic principle itself, in maintaining that pity and fear are not merely to be aroused but to be purged, is evidence of the need in tragedy to have dissonance exploded, leaving only the serenity of harmony behind. As has often been noted, the peace of cosmic reconciliation is most explicitly insisted upon in the concluding portion of the *Oresteia*—the sublime *Eumenides*—or in the magnificent end of Oedipus' story at *Colonus*. Here is the restorative spirit of superhuman purgation at its most refined. Even in the less exceptional tragedies which do not conclude in such thorough and profound tranquillity—in those, that is, which end more "tragically" in the lay sense—there is often the touch of transcendent grace which saves the cosmos for us in the midst of the irrevocable devastation of human resources. It may, on rare and splendid occasions, be the pure shining thing of *Lear;* it may more often be little more than the matter-of-fact re-establishment of political order—an order, however, that reflects and is sanctioned by the cosmic order—which may be one of the reasons that it is so helpful to have tragedy concern itself with the fortunes of ruling princes.

But even if there were none of these, so long as tragedy remained a defined literary form, the fearsome chaotic necessities of the tragic vision would have to surrender finally to the higher unity which contained them. It is perhaps in this sense that we can speak of the formally sustained literary work ultimately coming to terms with itself. And from the standpoint of the audience—or at least the trained and sophisticated audience—even if there were no thematic elements of release for the passions aroused by the tragic performers, the disciplining and restricting demands upon aesthetic contemplation made by the rounded aesthetic whole would effect the catharsis demanded by Aristotle. The purging of dangerously aroused emotions, following as it does upon the satisfaction, the soothing grace, bestowed upon wayward materials by aesthetic completeness, uses form to overcome the threat of these materials and, consequently, these emotions. This roundedness, this completeness, carrying "aesthetic distance" with it as it brings us the assurances of form, presents us its formal order as a token, a security—something given in hand—to guarantee the cosmic order beyond the turbulence it has conquered. Thus it is that the cathartic principle *is* ultimately a purely formalistic one, even as tragedy, despite its foreboding rumblings, can remain a force for affirmation through its formal powers alone. Thus it is too that in the *Poetics* Aristotle rightly limits himself to formal considerations, leaving to later and less solvent generations the thematic implications of the vision which, so long as it is aesthetically framed in tragedy, is denied in its very assertion.

It is finally Hegel who, after many centuries during which no radically new approaches are made to tragedy—or at least none that are relevant to my interests here—takes up the task of explaining tragedy and catharsis in the thematic terms that Aristotle could afford to take for granted. Although it must be conceded that Hegel's analysis is clearly indebted to his metaphysic and his general philosophic method and although he does not concern himself with purely formal considerations, it is just this notion of reconciliation, of a final uniting or reuniting, that he emphasizes as the conclusive power of tragedy.[1] His insistence on the absoluteness, the wholeness, the indivisibility of what A. C. Bradley translates as "the ethical substance" is clue to Hegel's attempt to create a metaphysical equivalent for the unity of the Greek world—the unity which, translated into form, allowed tragedy to overcome the heretical defiance of its hero.

For Hegel the *hamartia* that defines the tragic hero always arises from his exclusive identification with a single moral claim, a claim which, however just within its own sphere, is, from the view of a total morality—that is, the ethical substance—merely partial, a too-assertive particular. Thus the hero's vision is necessarily destructive of the unity of the moral world, threatening with its monomaniac tendencies to produce an anarchy of unsupported metonymic leaps. And in defense of its absolute claims, the ethical substance must justly assert its oneness by ensuring the defeat of the hero whose nature it is, "at once his greatness and his doom, that he knows no shrinking or half-heartedness, but identifies himself wholly with the power that moves him, and will admit the justification of no other power." [2]

But this assertion of the ultimate unity of the moral order is what for Hegel leaves Greek tragedy with a final affirmation that transcends the carnage, "an aspect of reconciliation" that authoritatively seals the moral universe for even the most harshly devastated of its sacrificial victims, the bearers of the tragic vision. Here is a significant attempt to account thematically for the catharsis principle, to bring tragedy—for all its deadly

---

[1] For Hegel on tragedy, see his *The Philosophy of Fine Art*, trans. F. P. B. Osmaston (London, 1920), I, 272–313; II, 213–215; IV, 295–303, 308–326, 330–342. A. C. Bradley's is of course a brilliantly succinct and, by now, a classical summary of the Hegelian view ("Hegel's Theory of Tragedy," *Oxford Lectures on Poetry* [London, 1909], pp. 69–95).

[2] Bradley, p. 72.

turbulence—to the very threshold of a Wordsworthian "tranquil restoration." And who is to say that this restoration is not part of what may seem to be implied by the Aristotelian concept of *dénouement*—a falling action which does not usually stop with the hero's final destruction but leads to a quiet beyond the grave: to a resettling of things in acceptance of this destruction?

Of course it is this final inhibition of the tragic vision, this imposition of formal and moral order upon that which threatens it, that allows these dramas to be properly called classical in the best sense. And when the embracing frame is lost, the romantic tragic vision bursts forth unencumbered —often in merely melodramatic splendor—in no longer reconcilable defiance of traditional aesthetic as well as ethical order. Thus it may seem that Hegel, in assuming the virtues of the Greek world to be those of his own philosophic construct, is hardly representative of the self-conscious modernism that has dominated the last century and a half of our psychological history; the modernism that is characterized by fragmentation rather than by the ever-uniting synthesis which Hegel tried valiantly, if vainly, to impose upon it as its salvation. Can his or can any all-resolving "ethical substance" have validity for us as an absolute and claim our allegiance accordingly? Can it now claim the all-commanding universality that justly, though ruthlessly, imposes itself on the subversive tragic hero in its midst? Or is the tragic hero, as modern, fulfilling a proper human function and even a proper human obligation in standing with his integrity as an individual outside the universal? Which is another way of suggesting that whatever universals we may be left with do not deserve the obedience of the most daring of us. Hegel created a system whose universals, like those of the Greek world or even of the Elizabethan world as we find it reflected in Shakespeare, have a metaphysical sanction; whose social and political institutions have a cosmic sanction. How accurate an account is this of the shabby, Babbitt-like arbitrary things that must—if anything does—pass with our world as universals, given our secularized, hand-to-mouth versions of the claims of religion, of politics, of social morality? Surely the absolute is not to be found immanently within such as these. Justice, then, has passed from the universal to the rebellious individual; accordingly, our appropriate spokesman on matters relating the individual to the universal and the absolute is not the anachronistic system builder, Hegel, but that heterodox and unprofessional wrecker of the Hegelian universe, Søren Kierkegaard.

Faith is precisely this paradox, that the individual as the particular is higher than the universal, is justified over against it, is not subordinate but superior—yet in such a way, be it observed, that it is the particular individual who, after he has been subordinated as the particular to the universal, now through the universal becomes the individual who as the particular is superior to the universal, for the fact that the individual as the particular stands in an absolute relation to the absolute.[3]

At what is for Kierkegaard the most crucial moment of man's existence—the moment of the leap to faith—the absolute is attainable only through the individual, the particular, the purely personal. It is denied to the universal. Here, unhappily enough perhaps, is the answer of modernism's "isolato" to the Hegelian attempt to restore the union of men within a congenial universe that sanctioned, indeed commanded, and fixed its divine blessing upon, this union. For Kierkegaard, the ultimate act—the act of faith—cannot be mediated, since only universals can mediate. Consequently, the paradox of faith is "inaccessible to thought" and cannot be verbally communicated, both thought and language—like reason, on which they largely depend—necessarily expressing universals. Further, it is the inaccessibility of faith to mediation that makes the Abraham who intended to sacrifice Isaac either a murderer or a "true knight of faith"—in my terminology, either a tragic visionary [4] or a religious visionary—but *not* the sacrificer of his individual self to the universal expressed in moral law. The latter individual would be the highest form of ethical man but, for Kierkegaard, something less than either visionary. And Kierkegaard's Abraham, whichever visionary he may be, repudiates the universal. Thus the "immediacy" of either the tragic or the religious vision eliminates the universal as a possible resting place for the errant, as a possible justification of what he has so privately dared to will. And we can never be sure which of the two visions he carries. Indeed, now beyond reason, how can he himself claim certainty? For the religious vision would be too easy for Kierkegaard if one could *know* its authenticity.

The categories which Kierkegaard can help us impose provide our insecure world with alternatives to the way of Greek tragedy as it is interpreted by Nietzsche as well as by Hegel. While Nietzsche is, like Kierkegaard, an unhappy epitome of modern man, an alienated creature who is close to being himself a tragic visionary, he is like Hegel in wistfully finding and admiring in early tragedy the elements of reconciliation that give order to elements of chaotic conflict. Nietzsche sees united in tragedy the Apollonian and Dionysian motives, appropriately named by him for their respective gods: the one the dreamlike, sublime, and gracefully measured order of the light principle, in the highest sense the civilizing principle; the other the primordial, orgiastic release of the natural principle—the "underground"

---

[3] *Fear and Trembling*, by Søren Kierkegaard, trans. Walter Lowrie (Princeton, N.J.: Princeton University Press, 1941), p. 82.

[4] In light of the shriveling of the tragic concept in the modern world and the reduction of a total view to the psychology of the protagonist, I believe that this protagonist is now more appropriately designated "tragic visionary" than he is "tragic hero."

reality probably related to Jung's "racial unconscious" or to Freud's "id"—the barbarizing principle.[5] Nietzsche sees these motives as akin to the forces represented by the creative and yet restrained Olympians and by the chaos-producing Titans, except, of course, that instead of the unreconcilable warfare between Olympians and Titans there is in Greek culture a perfect blending of the Apollonian and the Dionysian.

The Greek knew and felt the terror and horror of existence. That he might endure this terror at all, he had to interpose between himself and life the radiant dream-birth of the Olympians. . . . out of the original Titan thearchy of terror the Olympian thearchy of joy gradually evolved through the Apollonian impulse towards beauty. . . . How else could this people, so sensitive, so vehement in its desires, so singularly constituted for *suffering*, how could they have endured existence, if it had not been revealed to them in their gods, surrounded with a higher glory?

Thus the Apollonian can so transform Dionysian terror "that lamentation itself becomes a song of praise."

Here is another thematic rendering of the principle of catharsis. But in order to make the formula work properly, both motives have to be maintained and maintained in equal strength. The Dionysian must be there for the Apollonian to transform, so that Apollonian radiance can retain its brilliance only by continually illuminating the Dionysian abyss. But it is an abyss which must not be denied, indeed must be acknowledged for what it is. Without the Dionysian, the Apollonian would seem to reflect a shallow, unearned optimism, a misreading of life that leaves the inescapable terror out of it. Thus Nietzsche can scorn the bland interpretations of "the serious and significant idea of Greek cheerfulness": "no matter where we turn at the present time we encounter the false notion that this cheerfulness results from a state of unendangered comfort." For the Apollonian cannot sustain itself in isolation; it can exist only in counterposition to the Dionysian. Otherwise it becomes perverted—as Nietzsche tells us it was perverted through Euripides—into the merely "Socratic," that moralistic denier of the Dionysian and consequently the destroyer of tragedy.

But what if we should find the Dionysian without the Apollonian? Here we would have life unalleviated, endlessly and unendurably dangerous, finally destructive and self-destructive—in short, the demoniacal. In effect it would be like tragedy without that moment in which the play comes round and the cosmos is saved and returned to us intact. It would be, in other words, the tragic vision wandering free of its capacious home in tragedy.

---

[5] For this entire discussion, see "The Birth of Tragedy," trans. C. P. Fadiman, *The Philosophy of Nietzsche* (New York: Modern Library, n.d.), especially pp. 951–969, 992–1017. [See in this volume pp. 443–451.]

The therapy produced by catharsis, which allowed the subversive elements
to be healthily exposed and aesthetically overcome, would no longer be
available. And the alienated members, now unchallenged, would be free to
turn inward upon themselves to nourish their indignation in the dark underground. Nietzsche himself has told us:

The tradition is undisputed that Greek tragedy in its earliest form had for its sole
theme the sufferings of Dionysus, and that for a long time the only stage-hero was
simply Dionysus himself . . . until Euripides, Dionysus never once ceased to be
the tragic hero . . . in fact all the celebrated figures of the Greek Stage—Prometheus, Oedipus, etc.—are but masks of this original hero, Dionysus.

But picture a world into which Dionysus cannot be reabsorbed by way of
the Apollonian with its final assertion of Greek "cheerfulness" and aesthetic
form, a world in which the Apollonian and Dionysian—long since torn
asunder—must live in a lasting separation that causes each to pervert its
nature, the Apollonian becoming the superficial worship of happiness and the
Dionysian the abandoned worship of demonism. Our modern tragic vision is
the Dionysian vision still, except that the visionary is now utterly lost, since
there is no cosmic order to allow a return to the world for him who has
dared stray beyond.

   The Kierkegaardian spirit would rather characterize the tragic vision as
"despair," perhaps finally much the same thing. It is despair which for
Kierkegaard is both the most wretched and the most hopeful stage of man's
sub-Christian existence. With some interpolation and considerable simplification on my part, the phenomenological pattern one may draw from
Kierkegaard for the tragic visionary may be seen as something like the following sketch.[6] A man lives his day-to-day existence below the religious
level, either "aesthetically," as an amoral or submoral hedonist, or "ethically," by easily subscribing, consciously or unconsciously, but for the
most part automatically, to that hierarchy of moral values which enables
him comfortably to function. If he is a self-conscious moralist, he is concerned with the discovery of order in apparent disorder; concerned, that is,

---

   [6] In the interest of accuracy it must be acknowledged that Kierkegaard himself
explicitly defines what he calls the tragic hero very differently from the way I am
attributing to his view here. In Fear and Trembling he specifically claims that "the tragic
hero still remains within the ethical." He sees the tragic hero as allowing himself to be
embraced by the universal, his most cherished interests to be sacrificed to it. Perhaps
here, as in so many other instances, Kierkegaard finds himself borrowing from the very
Hegelianism he is bent on destroying. I believe that, as part of his dissatisfaction with
the aesthetic in general, he never took this matter of the tragic as seriously as he might
have taken it, that he never realized the revolutionary treatment of it that is promised by
his other philosophic claims. It is thus, I hope, in the Kierkegaardian spirit, that I use
Kierkegaard to support my own claims about the tragic though they run counter to his
own occasional declarations.

with universal principles, but principles that are discoverable in and referable to the world of human relations.

While the ethical level is certainly an advance over the mindless com-
placency in the midst of an unperceived chaos found on Kierkegaard's "aesthetic" [7] level, nevertheless this ethical level, because it sees values—and the
order constructed in terms of values—as immanent rather than as transcendent, must itself remain pragmatic in its dictates for action. The orderly and
abstract principles, bounded by the uses of this world and resting on
rationality, much resist the paradox or absurdity which for Kierkegaard
characterizes the immediacy and subjectivity of Christian consciousness.
Thus finally common-sense pragmatism must inhere in the ethical level.[8]
And our ethical man, assuming the validity of his abstract and universal
principles inasmuch as they are conducive to order, can make decisions
cleanly, can act in accordance with these principles—as if they were the
absolute—since they blink the possible existence of a true moral dilemma
characterized by endless ambiguity. This is the farthest reach of Hegelian
man.

But our man can undergo a cosmic "shock": he can one day, to use
Kafka's metaphor, wake up and find himself irrevocably arrested "without
having done anything wrong." Or an Ahab, living until then by the proper
laws of seamanship, can one day lose his leg to the leviathan; a Lord Jim,
living until then by a schoolboy's code of honor, can one day be paralyzed
into inaction and be made to play the coward's role. Melville's Pierre,
having dedicated himself at all costs to absolute righteousness, can discover
in his righteousness a lust that has led to incest; Conrad's Kurtz, having
dedicated himself through altruism to a missionary zeal, can discover in his

---

[7] Whenever I use this term in the very special way of Kierkegaard I shall set it in
quotation marks. Where it appears without them, it is being used in its common sense
that pertains primarily to works of art and to our proper and limited responses to them
as art.

[8] It is here, in his insistence that religion has dimensions beyond morality, that Kierkegaard strikes at the roots of that naturalistic humanism which would identify the two.
Of course one may claim that Kierkegaard rather overdoes their separation since for
him, it seems, the one (religion) can begin only where the other (morality) leaves off.
I must, however, make it clear that, whenever speaking here of Kierkegaard's concept
of religion, I mean only his version of Christianity. It must be conceded that in many
places he refers to a pre-Christian, almost naturalistic religion, one in which the absolute
is still immanent in the universal and which, consequently, still falls within the ethical.
But if this stoical kind of religion can produce "the knight of infinite resignation," in its
security it of course cannot begin to reach toward "the true knight of faith," who is
rather a product of the loneliness and daring, the absurdity and subjectivity of Christian
consciousness. It is only his notion of Christianity—defiant as it is of the ethical—to
which Kierkegaard attributes absolute value, so that, to simplify matters, I have felt
justified in speaking of it informally as his notion of religion in general, to the neglect
of his other, inferior kind of religion.

zeal a worship of self and of gold that has led to blood sacrifice. Perhaps this shattering seizure is precisely what ethical man has had coming for assuming, as fallible individual, his identification with an ethical absolute. For the ethical is, by definition, the universal. And, however well meaning, the individual may very well be doomed to pervert the absolute he claims to represent, since he comes to it as individual and particular, and thus as unsanctioned.

In any case, with the shock our man is jarred loose. For "aesthetic" man the oblivious evasions of hedonic existence will of course no longer do. And ethical man, confronted by a moral contradiction which resists the elimination of either pole as well as the synthesis of both, finds suddenly that the neatly ordered and easily enacted worldly rights and wrongs of his ethical assumptions are utterly inadequate to the data of his moral experience. Unless he yields to "infinite resignation" by blindly, if courageously, sacrificing himself to the implacable demands of ethical absoluteness—thus at all costs still remaining Hegelian man [9]—he must deny its authority forever. And then, hopelessly adrift from his or any other moorings, he can float into will-lessness and thus abdicate from tragic heroism, or he can surge toward the demoniac. If his rebellion has rendered him unfit for society and its necessary universals—its laws—it is because, at whatever price, he has seen beyond them. If his end, as tragic, must be condemned even as it is pitied by the trim categories of worldly morality, he may, prideful as he is, take further pride in the fact that he has defiantly looked upon those insoluble cosmic antinomies which have dictated his fall.

Someone like Conrad's Marlow, however—the sensible even if sensitive man—must, at whatever cost to his pride and his vision, finally rest in the ethical level, however sympathetic he may be to those who have renounced it to move into the realm of the tragic. Who is to say whether it is out of a "failure of nerve" or out of a special strength flowing from a profoundly tranquil vision, hardly known to us since the Greeks, that he has resisted the unmitigated tragic? It depends, very likely, on whether our view is Kierkegaard's or that of a less austere, less Protestant authority; on whether ours is the tragic vision or the classic vision.

On the other hand, our excommunicated ethical man, realizing the complete futility of human existence, cannot find a relationship with anything beyond it. His permanent forsaking of the universal seems to forbid it. This, the essence of the tragic vision, is "the sickness unto death," despair. It is the stage induced by the shock; the stage which, beyond the "aesthetic" and

---

[9] This is in effect Kierkegaard's own definition of the tragic hero. He allows him to go no further; and this admission on my part indicates how far beyond him I have without authorization moved using his tools.

the ethical, yet falls short of Kierkegaard's version of the Christian. An advance over the first two, it is yet much more treacherous and, if one remains in it continually, far more miserable. If one can attain a break-through—a bravely irrational one unmediated by universals—he can reach the glories of transcendence; if he fails, he must live in the contemplation of nothingness. Or, to put it more specifically, at best he can become a Kierkegaard, if we grant that Kierkegaard ever, or for very long, accomplished the leap of faith; if not, he must remain in the torments of the Zarathustrian Nietzsche or of a more consistent Heidegger who constantly and unblinkingly dares encounter the nothingness that has capriciously hurled him into momentary existence. But he can never again rest in the self-deceptions of our John Deweys: those of our insistent naturalists who, for all the hardheadedness of their religious disbelief, are yet naively optimistic believers in a structured social morality and in social progress. These are, from the Kierkegaardian standpoint, the men of little heart; those who, evading the atheist's existential obligation to confront nothingness and its frighteningly empty consequences, construct elaborate rational structures based on nothing else: who whistle in the dark as if all were light.

One may prefer to say that it represents a supreme act of human courage to create meaningful communal structures of value on a substructure of acknowledged nothingness. Perhaps, as humanists say, man's creating God *is* a more sublime act than God's creating man. Perhaps. But the honest existentialist—anxious to confront his ontological status—would see the naturalist's structure in the void as an evasive act of bravado, not a closing act of bravery.

In the Kierkegaardian universe, then, there are two authentic visions—those I have termed the tragic and the religious—that can be earned through crisis by being forged in what Dostoevsky spoke of as the "great furnace of doubt." The other I have referred to is in this sense an illusory one. For the cheerfully naturalistic vision, which, pampering its security, denies itself nothing despite the fearsome implications of its own metaphysical denials, which existentially shirks the void it must rationally insist upon, is a pre-crisis vision, an illusion of ethical man demanded by his comfort, but one the stricken man can no longer afford. Like Kurtz, the tragic visionary may at the critical moment search within and find himself "hollow at the core," but only because he has suddenly been seized from without by the hollowness of his moral universe, whose structure and meaning have until then sustained him. What the shock reveals to its victim—the existential absurdity of the moral life—explodes the meaning of the moral life, its immanent god and ground. And there can be no post-crisis meaning and god except in defiance of reason, in acknowledgment of the impossibly paradoxical nature of moral existence. But this is to go beyond the despair that defines the tragic

visionary and to make the leap to the transcendent subjectivity of the only
kind of religious vision that the Kierkegaardian Protestant world leaves to
the stricken.[10]

On the other hand, the tragic visionary, in taking the alternative of defiance and seizing upon nothingness, is alone bold enough to take the existential consequences of his godlessness; and he takes them with pride, the very
hybris that, in its sinfulness, moved him to godlessness rather than to transcendence. But he does not, like the naturalist, try to play both sides of the
street to earn the prize of an ungrounded something: a world philosophically
negated which is somehow made to yield the existential ease that would
come if there were a meaning and purpose to be grasped. Sick of his pre-
crisis delusion, the tragic visionary is God's angry man who will take only
the real thing. He will refuse any longer to fool himself with the comfort-
able communal halfway houses of good works as a substitute for the absolute dedication of a religious faith which his inherited skepticism, issuing its
curse, has denied him.

Of course, from a less severely Protestant point of view, other "authentic" visions would be sanctioned. One that concerned me earlier is what
I called the classic vision, a vision that is of the world without being crass,
that is universal and conducive to order without optimistically thinning
moral reality as the superficially ethical man would. This vision is the all-
embracing one of an older world and an older order. It is what I have tried
to talk about in discussing the formal and thematic triumph of tragedy over
the errant tragic vision it contained within it. It is as if the security of the
older order wanted to test the profundity of its assurances, its capacity to
account for the whole of human experience, and thus bred within itself the

---

[10] Although this issue may not seem germane to a discussion of the tragic vision, it
is worth adding—in order to expose another favorite illusion of our naturalistic and anti-
existential tradition—that the religious vision described here cannot in fairness be
reduced to any so-called "failure of nerve." This phrase the Kierkegaardian would
reserve for the ethical man who flees the impact of the shock, for the naturalist himself.
The shock may indeed cause our nerves to quake, but they fail only with the failure of
our inner strength to manage, from the depths of despair, the awesome leap that makes
"the true knight of faith"—no easy accomplishment and hardly a soothing one. The
earned religious vision must not be cheapened. It is a vision that runs quite counter to
that implied by the Philistine claim that there were "no atheists on Bataan." No matter
how devout the final protestations of these doomed souls, these protestations were all
simply too comforting in their urgency, from the Kierkegaardian point of view, to have
a claim to religious authenticity. Thus Kierkegaard comments on people who want to
make an easy, escapist thing of faith:

> . . . these caricatures of faith are part and parcel of life's wretchedness, and the
> infinite resignation has already consigned them to infinite contempt. . . . They
> would suck worldly wisdom out of the paradox. Perhaps one or another may suc-
> ceed in that, for our age is not willing to stop with faith, with its miracle of turning
> water into wine, it goes further, it turns wine into water. (*Fear and Trembling* , p. 50.)

tragic vision as its *agent provocateur*. And by having the rebellion incarnate in the tragic visionary finally succumb to a higher order which absorbs but never denies the "destructive element," by purifying itself through the cathartic principle, tragedy is asserting the argument a fortiori for the affirmation of its humanistic and yet superhumanistic values. Consequently, it can witness all that befalls its hero without sharing in his disavowal of the meaning of our moral life; without denying, with him, the sensibleness of the universe and of life despite the explosive terrors they can hold in store.

But human possibilities, reduced as they are by disintegrations within the world that produced a Kierkegaard as its spokesman, no longer can reach to so inclusive a vision. If the only appeal to universals, to order, is pre-religious as well as pre-tragic, then the path of the religious visionary is as solitary as the tragic visionary's. And the ethical once shattered, there is no higher return to community—although, of course, for the less daring there may always be a retreat. The tragic vision remains what it was, but it can no longer be made through tragedy to yield to an order and a shared religious vision. The ultimately absorbent power of tragedy, symbolic of the earned affirmation of universals, is gone, with the result that the solitary visionary is left unchallenged, except by the threats of uncomprehending and unsympathizing destruction at the hands of aroused ethical righteousness, the arm of social practicality. This is hardly the all-deserving antagonist the tragic vision once had, nor is it one that can command a satisfying aesthetic completeness any more than it can a moral-religious unity. Instead, in the Kierkegaardian universe, we now find for the aware and authentic existent an unresolvable disjunctive: either the way of nothingness or the way of transcendence, but both equally the way of utter solitude. The universals which must damn him have been left behind.

It is perhaps for these reasons that recent literature expressing an earned religious vision is hard to come by. For this kind of religious vision is primarily characterized by the fact that it cannot be shared. Equally subjective, the tragic as the demoniac vision can at least be dramatized by being contrasted to the ethical with which it is at war and which, in defense of society, must seek to punish it—for good reasons and for bad. We can be shown the ambiguous nature of the values at stake in this struggle: the need for the insights provided by the tragic to advance our understanding beyond the unaccommodating caution of social necessity as institutionalized in the ethical; and yet the need to strike out at the visionary, to cling to the props society provides, at whatever cost to insight, since, man being a social animal, his struggle through daily drudgeries is a crucial and ordering activity that must not be threatened.

To sustain a balance and, consequently, an aesthetic tension between these antagonists, the author must resist identifying himself too thoroughly either with the tragic visionary or with the representative of the ethical. If he becomes one with his ethical man, he must dismiss the tragic realm too summarily, without granting its power—however costly—of revealing the full density of moral experience and the shallowness of the reasonable order it has been forced to cast off. And he must sell the vision short as vision, however quick he is to see it as tragic, or anyway as doomed, if not as at worst merely execrable or at best pathetic. Or if, on the other hand, the author becomes one with his tragic visionary, he so cuts himself off from man's communal need that, in surrendering to moral chaos, he surrenders also the only possibility left him to impose aesthetic form. Further, he shows himself to be too sure of the vision to acknowledge it as really tragic, however quick he is—in contrast to our too ethical author—to grant its value as a vision. Only within the balance, and the mutual qualifications it provides, can the vision be maintained both as tragic and as a vision worthy of our concern and our wonder. Thus, at the one extreme, in *Heart of Darkness*, for example, Conrad, through his alter ego Marlow, rejects Kurtz— indeed is utterly offended by the man—only in continual acknowledgment that his rebellion against decency, however odious, renders him in some way superior even to Marlow. And, at the other extreme, close as Gide comes to embracing the reckless passions of his hero in *The Immoralist*, the classical artist in him maintains enough distance to reveal to us honestly, and even with some condemnation, their destructive and self-destructive consequences.

Even with the ethical and the tragic held in such balance, however, the ethical may seem finally to be treated superciliously and even as at least half blind to what really is going on. And since the tragic is from the ethical standpoint so dangerously evil, there would seem to be a need for some level beyond the ethical from which the tragic visionary would be judged absolutely—a level which would include his insight and with it soar beyond a parochial pragmatism, but one which would have passed beyond the rage of rebellion to a final, perhaps otherworldly affirmation. But this is to call once again for what we no longer have—for the transformations that only tragedy can perform. For how are we now to distinguish outwardly between the religious and the tragic, between the angelic and the demoniac, when both equally transgress the ethical and the universal? As Kierkegaard in such brilliant detail asks, how shall we tell the Abraham among us from the self-deceived, maddened infanticide? To stop short of the religious insight is of course to rest in demonism; yet to leap to the religious vision, itself a perilous undertaking, is not to deny the temporal and, of course, the dramatic validity of the tragic. In neither instance is a retreat to the ethical possible. And the balance of necessities between the tragic and the ethical must continue as the primary mode of dramatic conflict, with the inherent weaknesses of each—the moral failing of the one and the visionary failing of the other—poised against each other to create the unresolvable tension that must now replace tragedy's more sublime catharsis as the principle of aesthetic control.

By now I hope I have clarified the sense in which I have been speaking of the unrelieved tragic vision as a modern vision, which is to claim also that it is a Protestant vision and, in an obvious sense, a romantic vision. Further, in its seizing upon the particular and its denial of any totality it is an heretical vision; and in its defiance of all rational moral order it is a demoniac vision. Finally, in a very special sense it is a casuistic vision; and it is this characteristic, perhaps, that makes it especially accessible to literary portrayal. The tragic vision, a product of crisis and of shock, is an expression of man only in an extreme situation, never in a normal or routine one. Literature dealing with it frequently dwells on the exceptional man; and when it does choose a normal man it does so only to convert him, by way of the extremity he lives through, into the exceptional man. The tragic vision is, by my definition, a vision of extreme cases, a distillate of the rebellion, the godlessness which, once induced by crisis, purifies itself by rejecting all palliatives. And the tragic visionary, by the stark austerity of his ontological position and of his dramatic position in the fable, is the extremist who—despite his rich intermingling with the stuff of experience—finds himself transformed from character to parable.

The literary obsession with extremity, with the exceptional, may represent an attempt at realism ultimately more sincere and more authentic than the cultivation of the norm, of what Lionel Trilling celebrates as "the common routine." If one wishes to assume the Kierkegaardian version of the human predicament, he will insist that it does and that at all times it has represented the only authentic attempt at realism. Even without Kierkegaardian psychoanalysis, however, we must admit that, at least in our time, driven as it is by crises and "arrests" and blind as it is to the healing power and saving grace of tragedy, the tragic has come, however unfortunately, to loom as a necessary vision and—or so it seems to the sadder of us —as one that can be neither reduced nor absorbed. Or is it, perhaps, that the Kierkegaardian version is right and that our world has itself become the tragic visionary, in its unbelief using self-destructive crises to force itself finally to confront the absurdities of earthly reality—those which have always been there lurking beneath for the visionary who would dare give up all to read them? Which is to ask, fearfully and even unwillingly, whether we have not been beguiled by aesthetic satisfactions and whether the utterly stripped tragic vision may not after all be less illusory than the fullness which shines through tragedy.

The Vision of Tragedy *

RICHARD B. SEWALL

LEAR. *Why, thou wert better in thy grave than to answer with thy uncovered body this extremity of the skies. Is man no more than this? Consider him well. Thou owest the worm no silk, the beast no hide, the sheep no wool, the cat no perfume. Ha! here's three on 's are sophisticated; thou art the thing itself. Unaccommodated man is no more but such a poor, bare, forked animal as thou art.*—KING LEAR

When at the end of the *Symposium* Socrates insisted to his friends Aristophanes and Agathon that "the genius of comedy is the same as the genius of tragedy, and that the writer of tragedy ought to be a writer of comedy also," the friends, says Plato, were "compelled to assent, being sleepy, and not quite understanding his meaning." It had been a long night, with much wine, and the friends might well have agreed to almost anything. But whether they would have agreed under different circumstances, and just what Socrates' arguments were, are other questions. One would like to know precisely what he said. Or perhaps the affair was a bit of a paradox spun out for his own amusement. For it seems clear—at least it is the thesis of this book— that the genius of tragedy is not the same as the genius of comedy. As for Socrates' notion that every writer ought to be able to do both, there can be no objection. Some few have done both. What he had in mind, perhaps, was the undeniable truth that the highest comedy gains its power from its sense of tragic possibility, and the profoundest tragedy presents a full if fleeting vision, through the temporary disorder, of an ordered universe to which comedy is witness. Without a sense of the tragic, comedy loses heart; it becomes brittle, it has animation but no life. Without a recognition of the truths of comedy, tragedy becomes bleak and intolerable.

But since the Greeks first wrote what they called tragedies and comedies,

* Richard B. Sewall, "The Vision of Tragedy," from *The Vision of Tragedy* (Yale University Press, 1959), pp. 1–8. [Footnotes for this selection have been omitted.]

and Aristotle in the *Poetics* formulated some principles about them, writers have been conscious of the two modes—each with its own demands—as engaging them in different undertakings, involving them in different worlds. They have gauged their predilections and capacities against the demands of each and have deliberately chosen one or the other, or some calculated mixture. They have often been explicit about it. Shakespeare announced his plays as "tragedies" or "comedies," or, when he chose, mixed the modes with the recklessness of Polonius. Marlowe spoke his intention when in the prologue to *Tamburlaine* he asked his audience to view his hero in "the tragic glass." Ben Jonson ventured into tragedy in his own scholarly, methodical way, boasting to have discharged (in *Sejanus*) all the crucial "offices of a *Tragic* writer," which he got from Aristotle. Milton's choice of the tragic form to express his final mood was deliberate and especially significant in relation to the tragic undertones of *Paradise Lost*. Artists are free—but free to choose their own sort of bondage. It is they and not so much the critics who have worked to maintain the integrity of the forms. Their conscious, explicit choices show that in their eyes the forms are real and different and not merely an academic conspiracy. The phenomenon is a powerful example of the fruitful interaction of tradition and individual talent.

Tragedy, traditionally the most exalted of the forms, has exerted on artists of many generations, not only Greek and Elizabethan, a compelling influence. Its effect on the individual talent has sometimes been noble and often disastrous. It requires an independent, radical vision whose lack is as fatal as the lack of a sense of ultimate harmony is in comedy. Sophocles and Euripides, though building on Aeschylus' original insights and to this extent acting in imitation of him, used the form he had established to express their own individual and radical visions. The Elizabethans, whose nervous and independent force worked creatively on whatever form they chose, expanded and improvised to suit their own expressive needs. Since then, as writers not so vitally equipped have attempted to write tragedy, the sense of strain and artificiality is frequent.

The French at their best (Racine, for instance) embodied the true tragic vision in a finely disciplined form; but their next best shows how precarious is the balance between creation and imitation. Milton's vision in the masterful *Samson Agonistes* has been called only "spasmodically tragic." In lesser artists, who approached tragedy too analytically or (it would seem) for its prestige, the strain is painfully obvious. The English theater after the Restoration produced plays called tragedies which are informed, rather, by the moral or "heroic" vision. The romantic poets, great admirers though they were of the Greeks and the Elizabethans, showed how far their world actually was from the world of *Oedipus* and *Lear* (which Shelley described as "the deepest and sublimest of the tragic compositions") when they ventured into tragedy. Shelley's preface to *The Cenci* is an earnest little treatise on tragedy; but he tried the form only once. As his wife wrote, "the bent of his mind went the other way." So did Byron's and Tennyson's, although they both wrote what they called tragedies. Goethe was perhaps wisest when he said "the mere attempt to write tragedy might be my undoing."

In the nineteenth century certain of the novelists had the surest sense of the thing itself. Genuine and vital strains of Greek and Hebraic tragic traditions, intensified by the tragic insights of Christianity, appear impressively, for instance, in Hawthorne, Melville, and Dostoevski. Hawthorne, whose sense of kinship with Greek and Elizabethan tragedy he more than once indicated, invested Hester Prynne with some of the hard outlines of Antigone's character and with much of the passion and color of an Elizabethan. Melville shaped Ahab as "a mighty pageant figure, fit for noble tragedies" and had him chase his "Job's whale" to the far quarters of the globe. Both novels show clearly that their authors were sensitive to the problem of making the tragic vision real to nineteenth-century democratic America. Dostoevski opened up a vast new tragic area by his own peculiar synthesis of the basic insights of all the traditions. Ibsen and O'Neill, Conrad, Kafka, and Faulkner (to name only a few) have each in their own way explored the area which he plotted out. Whether they have written "tragedies" is not at present the point, but they seem closer to the tragic spirit than the Romantic and Victorian imitators.

But how can it be said that a novel by Kafka or Faulkner is more truly tragic than *The Cenci?* What is the "true" tragic spirit, the thing itself? Is it right to say that writers choose the form, or does the form in some subtle way choose them? Shelley chose the form—his wife tells how the idea of writing a tragedy had haunted him long before he encountered the story of *The Cenci*—but, quite clearly, he himself was not chosen. Shakespeare's tragedies are grouped in a period of his life when, as far as we can tell biographically, the "bent of his mind" seems to have been that way. Goethe never felt chosen. He realized that the tragic sense of the world and of man's destiny was not his, and he stayed away. There was nothing that he could not have mastered technically; indeed, Shelley showed how far a near-perfect executive form could be from the thing itself. But tragedy demands qualities of vision which neither of them had.

In general, the tragic vision is not a systematic view of life. It admits wide variations and degree. It is a sum of insights, intuitions, feelings, to which the words "vision" or "view" or "sense of life," however inadequate, are most readily applicable. The tragic sense of life, as Unamuno describes it, is a subphilosophy, or a prephilosophy, "more or less formulated, more or less conscious." It reaches deep down into the temperament, "not so much flowing from ideas as determining them." It is an attitude toward life with which some individuals seem to be endowed to high degree, others less, but which is latent in every man and may be evoked by experience. Unamuno finds it characteristic of some nations and not others. Horace Walpole's epigram, "this world is a comedy to those who think, a tragedy to those who feel," has only relative truth, but it is significant in showing how readily the terms become metaphors to describe a view of life, a cast of thought or temperament.

The tragic vision is in its first phase primal, or primitive, in that it calls up out of the depths the first (and last) of all questions, the question of existence: What does it mean to be? It recalls the original terror, harking back to a world that antedates the conceptions of philosophy, the consolations of the later religions, and whatever constructions the human mind has devised to persuade itself that its universe is secure. It recalls the original un-reason, the terror of the irrational. It sees man as questioner, naked, unaccommodated, alone, facing mysterious, demonic forces in his own nature and outside, and the irreducible facts of suffering and death. Thus it is not for those who cannot live with unsolved questions or unresolved doubts, whose bent of mind would reduce the fact of evil into something else or resolve it into some larger whole. Though no one is exempt from moments of tragic doubt or insight, the vision of life peculiar to the mystic, the pious, the propagandist, the confirmed optimist or pessimist—or the confirmed anything—is not tragic.

Nor is the tragic vision for those who, though admitting unsolved questions and the reality of guilt, anxiety, and suffering, would become quietist and do nothing. Mere sensitivity is not enough. The tragic vision impels the man of action to fight against his destiny, kick against the pricks, and state his case before God or his fellows. It impels the artist, in his fictions, toward what Jaspers calls "boundary-situations," man at the limits of his sovereignty—Job on the ash-heap, Prometheus on the crag, Oedipus in his moment of self-discovery, Lear on the heath, Ahab on his lonely quarterdeck. Here, with all the protective covering stripped off, the hero faces as if no man had ever faced it before the existential question—Job's question, "What is man?" or Lear's "Is man no more than this?" The writing of a tragedy is the artist's way of taking action, of defying destiny, and this is why in the great tragedies there is a sense of the artist's own involvement, an immediacy not so true of the forms, like satire and comedy, where the artist's position seems more detached.

The findings of the anthropologists about the origins of tragedy are not irrelevant here. Even though they cannot be verified historically, they seem psychologically true. The religious ritual out of which it is thought tragedy grew—the dance of mourning in the fall festival at the death of the old year or (as some think) the ritual sacrifice of propitiation—was in itself an action, a response to a condition, a kind of answer to the question of existence. It was an answer in terms of gesture and action rather than language, and represents, perhaps, man's first attempt to deal creatively with pain and fear. Any action at all was better than nothing. It was not until later, when man graduated from the condition of pain and fear to the condition of suffering—which is the condition of pain and fear contemplated and spiritualized—that the response was verbalized in some kind of art form, a dirge or lament. Even in the most sophisticated of forms, literary tragedy, the element of gesture and action is strong, but it is the contemplated and individual response to suffering rather than the instinctive and tribal. Unamuno's fine anecdote about Solon shows elements of both—the primitive response by gesture (weeping) and the comment from the depths of an anguished spirit. "Why do you weep for the death of your son," the skeptic asked Solon, "when it avails nothing?" "I weep," replied Solon, "precisely because it avails nothing."

It is this sense of ancient evil, of "the blight man was born for," of the permanence and the mystery of human suffering, that is basic to the tragic sense of life. It informs all literature of a somber cast—the dirge, the lament, the melancholy lyric or song, the folk ballad of betrayal and death. It colors many scenes in the great epics and hovers about the best comedy as an imminent possibility. The tragedies of the tradition, from Aeschylus to Dostoevski, say this about it: that by most men it must be learned—and learned through direct, immediate experience: that is, through suffering. So universal is this testimony that it can be taken as one of the constants of tragedy, and the starting point. All men must learn to feel what wretches feel. In the lives of many writers of tragedy there is abundant evidence of deep autobiographic meaning in this recurrent theme, a fact of relevance to the sense of innerness and involvement that tragedy possesses above other forms.

Pressing out from this initial phase of the tragic vision, the artist's action or response takes him beyond the lament or the melancholy lyric toward an increasingly complicated dialectic as he contemplates the thrust and counterthrust of man against destiny. Here his cause is one with the philosophers and theologians, the difference being that the artist's dialectic is not of ideas in the abstract but of ideas in action, ideas as lived. His dialectic is not so much with words as with lives, and his focus is not so much man thinking as man acting, man "on the way." Where the philosophers and moralists would generalize on experience, find unity in multiplicity, and reduce experience to viable categories and prescriptions, the tragic artist explores each experience directly, *de novo*, for whatever it may reveal about man's capacities and possibilities. He presses the "boundary-situation" for its total yield. Whatever he finds man capable of, in action and under extremest pressure, is to him the truth, whether it be abject and miserable or sublime and redeeming. This truth constitutes the "discovery" of tragedy.

Historically, literary tragedy has always appeared at the mature period of a culture, not at its beginning. Although it retains the primitive sense of terror at what Joyce called "the secret cause" of suffering, it is in another sense highly sophisticated. It puts to the test of action all the formulations of philosophy and religion. In the three major western cultures—Hebrew, Greek, and Christian—there have come times (our present era may be one of them) when for reasons internal and external, spiritual and sociological, the questions of ultimate justice and human destiny seem suddenly to have been jarred loose again. Often these critical periods, or "moments," come after a long period of relative stability, when a dominant myth or religious orthodoxy or philosophic view has provided a coherent and sustaining way of life. Suddenly the original terror looms close and the old formulations cannot dispel it. The conflict between man and his destiny assumes once more the ultimate magnitude. It appears to be not a matter of accident, a temporary and limited disturbance, but an essential change in the face of the universe. The whole of society is involved, and the stake is survival. Thus the sense of despair in the early chapters of Job's complaint, the sense of doom in Greek tragedy, Gloucester's fears in the first act of *Lear*, and the sense of disintegration in *The Brothers Karamazov*.

In such periods, and in such moods, artists confront the existential question all over again. They ask, like the elderly trader in Conrad's *Lord Jim*, "How to be?" and embody their answers, ambiguous and tentative, in their "boundary-situations." Each age has different tensions and terrors, but they open on the same abyss. If each new artist's primary source must be the data of his own experience and observation, he just as surely learns from his fellow artists who have stared into the same depths. What they came up with, the statement of their fictions, constitutes the tradition—a total evaluation expressed in a literary form. As the tradition guides the new vision, the vision tests it, alters its focus and direction or expands its compass. Direction and focus may change, but the vision is constant.

Part Two

CHARACTERISTICS
OF THE TRAGIC

―――――――――――――――――

Basic Characteristics of the Tragic *

KARL JASPERS

The tragic looms before us as an event that shows the terrifying aspects of existence, but an existence that is still human. It reveals its entanglement with the uncharted background of man's humanity. Paradoxically, however, when man faces the tragic, he liberates himself from it. This is one way of obtaining purification and redemption.

Breakdown and failure reveal the true nature of things. In failure, life's reality is not lost; on the contrary, here it makes itself wholly and decisively felt. *There is no tragedy without transcendence.* Even defiance unto death in a hopeless battle against gods and fate is an act of transcending: it is a movement toward man's proper essence, which he comes to know as his own in the presence of his doom.

Where awareness of the tragic has become fundamental to man's awareness of reality, we speak of tragic readiness.[1] But we must distinguish between awareness of the transitoriness of things and genuine awareness of the tragic.

When he thinks of transitoriness, man views the actual events leading up to death, as well as the ephemeral character of all life, as parts of the natural cycle of growth, decay, and renewed growth. He recognizes himself as within nature and identifies himself with it. Here man comes upon a secret that makes him tremble. What is the soul which, independent of the flux of time, knows itself to be immortal, although aware of the finiteness of its worldly existence, aware that it is doomed to pass away in death? Yet, nei-

---

[1] *Tragische Haltung.* This is the inner attitude of composure in the face of tragedy; it resembles Hamlet's "the readiness is all."

* Karl Jaspers, "Basic Characteristics of the Tragic," from *Tragedy Is Not Enough* (Beacon Press, 1952), pp. 41–56. [Translator's minor footnotes for this selection have been omitted and those remaining are renumbered.]

ther this fact of mortality nor this secret of the soul can rightly be termed tragic.

Genuine awareness of the tragic, on the contrary, is more than mere contemplation of suffering and death, flux and extinction. If these things are to become tragic, man must act. It is only then, through his own actions, that man enters into the tragic involvement that inevitably must destroy him. What will be ruined here is not merely man's life as concrete existence, but every concrete embodiment of whatever perfection he sought. Man's mind fails and breaks down in the very wealth of its potentialities. Every one of these potentialities, as it becomes fulfilled, provokes and reaps disaster.

A yearning for deliverance has always gone hand in hand with the knowledge of the tragic. When man encounters the hard fact of tragedy, he faces an inexorable limit. At this limit, he finds no guarantee of general salvation. Rather, it is in acting out his own personality, in realizing his selfhood even unto death, that he finds redemption and deliverance.

He may find this deliverance through his sheer strength to bear the unknown without question, and to endure it with unshakable defiance. This, however, is the mere seed of deliverance, its barest possible form. Or he may find deliverance by opening his eyes to the nature of the tragic process which, brought to light, can purify the mind. Finally, deliverance may already have preceded contemplation of the tragic process in the case where some faith has, from the outset, led life onto the road to salvation. Then, tragedy appears as overcome from the beginning as man transcends to the unseen, to God, the background of all backgrounds.

Ways of Interpreting Tragic Knowledge

The meaning of those tragedies that lie before us as the work of poets cannot possibly be reduced to a single formula. These works represent man's labor dealing with his knowledge of the tragic. Situations, events, social forces, religious beliefs, and types of character are the means through which man expresses the tragic.

Every one of the great poems has a meaning which cannot be exhausted by interpretation. They offer no more than directions for interpretation to pursue. Where complete rational interpretation is possible, poetry becomes superfluous—indeed, there has never been truly poetic creation from the very beginning. Where interpretation can make some elements stand out clearly, it heightens their accessibility precisely by virtue of a profound vision that is uncharted, that is not exhaustible by any analysis or interpretation.

In all poems the intellectual construction of the poet asserts itself. In proportion, however, as the thought emerges as such without being made incarnate in dramatic figures, poetry grows weaker. To that degree, then, the work is generated not by the power of tragic vision but by philosophical preference. This is not to say that thoughts in tragic poetry may not have crucial philosophical significance.

Now that we have reviewed tragic knowledge as a whole, our interpretation must give more searching answers to three problems:

1. What do the objective aspects of the tragic look like? What is the pattern of tragic existence and of a tragic course of events? How is it conceived in thought? Our interpretation of tragic subjects in poetry will yield the answer.

2. How do the subjective aspects of the tragic work themselves out? How does the tragic enter into consciousness? How is tragic knowledge achieved and, through it, deliverance and redemption?

3. What is the meaning of any fundamental interpretation of the tragic?

The Tragic as Subject of Poetry

Without trying to define the tragic, we visualize the stark immediacy of tragic events as they have achieved form and expression in poetry.

Our interpretation must hold fast to the content of the poet's original vision, to what already has been expressed and interpreted in his work. Interpretation adds to this vision the meaning which is or might be implied in it, whether or not the poet had explicitly thought of it.

In poetry, tragic consciousness gives body to its own thought: it is only through the tragic mood that we can sense tension and disaster in events affecting us directly or in the world as a whole. Tragedy shows up in battle, in victory and in defeat, in guilt. It is the measure of man's greatness in breakdown and failure. Tragedy reveals itself in man's unconditional will to truth. There it stands revealed as the ultimate disharmony of existence.

The Tragic Atmosphere

Life and death, the cycle of blossoming and withering away, the fact of transitoriness, do not yet establish in themselves any tragic atmosphere. The onlooker can calmly contemplate this process in which he is himself included and by which he is sheltered. The tragic atmosphere arises as the strange and sinister fate to which we have been abandoned. There is something alien that threatens us, something we cannot escape. Wherever we go, whatever we see, whatever we hear, there is something in the air which will destroy us, no matter what we do or wish.

This mood occurs in Indic drama as the vision of a world which is the setting of our life, a setting in which we have been abandoned without any protection. Thus, in *Kausika's Wrath:*

The whole world seems a carrion-ground,
A plain of corpses slain by Siva's servant, Time.
The firmament at dusk seems red
With blood of victims executed.
Like embers of a pyre
The feeble sun-disk glows; stars above
Seem but a boneyard in the sky;
And, like a skull bleached white,
Glares the pale moon . . .

Moods of horror dominate some works of Brueghel and Hieronymus Bosch, as well as Dante's *Inferno*. But this mood is nothing more than foreground. We must look for something deeper, but we cannot find it without first passing through these terrors.

The tragic atmosphere in Greek drama is not the mood of all nature. Rather it is related to particular events, particular human figures, perhaps as the tension that grips everything even prior to any specific deed or occurrence, the tension that warns of doom, though no one yet knows what form the doom will take. Aeschylus' *Agamemnon* gives us an example, and one of singular magnificence.

The tragic mood assumes the many shapes of so-called pessimism and its various pictures of this world, whether in Buddhism or in Christianity, in Schopenhauer or in Nietzsche, in the *Edda* or in the *Nibelungenlied*.

BATTLE AND COLLISION

Truth and reality split apart. In consequence of this split, men must support each other in community, and they must battle in collision. Tragic knowledge sees those battles which are unavoidable. The question for the tragic poet is precisely this: Who is battling whom, and what is really colliding with what?

Immediately, the battle which has found poetic expression is the battle of men against men, or of man against himself. Incompatible needs, duties, motives, and qualities of character are locked in combat. Psychological and sociological analysis seems to make these battles understandable in terms of fact. But the poet sees farther and deeper. It is his task to render tragic knowledge visible, and all these limited realities serve him merely as raw material. Through this raw material he points out what is truly at issue in this conflict. The conflict is now understood according to the interpretations of the antagonists, or of the poet and, through him, the spectator. These interpretations of the battle are themselves realities. For significance so uncovered has always generated the strongest motive power. This significance emerges in the plot of the tragedy.

Such interpretations, when embodied in the work of art itself, are either immanent or transcendent. Tragedy may be immanent, as in a battle between the individual and the universal, or as in a battle of different ways of life that succeed each other in history; or it may be transcendent, as in a battle between men and gods, or as in a battle between the gods themselves.

THE INDIVIDUAL AND THE UNIVERSAL

The individual is opposed to universal laws, norms, necessities: untragically, he represents mere willfulness opposing the law; tragically, he represents the genuine exception which, though opposing the law, yet has truth on his side.

General principles are concentrated in the forces of society, in social stratification, rules, and offices. Hence society may give rise to tragedy. On the other hand, general principles may be concentrated in human character as an imperative of eternal laws which run counter to the drives and the personality of the individual. Hence there are also tragedies that arise from character.

Commonly, tragic works based on such interpretations are poetically weak. Human drives which are entirely concrete, and general rules which are entirely abstract, can meet in conflicts that may be rationally developed. But they do not take visible shape as compelling visions of the depths of existence. The very transparency of these alternatives exhausts the problem. Where there is no sense of the infinite vastness of what is beyond our grasp, all we finally succeed in conveying is misery—not tragedy. This is the peculiar predicament of modern tragedy since the Enlightenment.

THE CLASH OF WAYS OF LIFE

A comprehensive philosophy of history should interpret the changes in man's condition as a meaningful succession of historical ways of life; in every epoch these ways of life account for the general situation and the prevailing patterns of action and thought. They do not replace each other suddenly. The old is still alive while the new unfolds itself. The mighty breakthrough of the new is bound at first to fail against the staying power and coherence of the old way of life not yet exhausted. Transition is the zone of tragedy.

According to Hegel, the great heroes of history are tragic figures in this sense. They embody the new idea, purely and uncompromisingly. They arise in sunlike splendor. Their real significance goes unnoticed at first, until the old way of life senses its danger and gathers all its forces to destroy the new in the form of its outstanding representative. Whether Socrates or Julius Caesar, the first victorious protagonist of the new principle becomes, at the same time, the victim at the border of two eras. The old is justified in asserting itself, for it still functions; it is still alive and proves itself through its rich and elaborate traditional patterns of life, even though the seed of decay has already begun its fatal germination. The new is justified also, but it is not yet protected by an established social order and culture. For the time being it is still functioning in a vacuum. But it is only the hero, the first great figure of the new way of life, whom the old, in a last frantic rally of all its forces, can destroy. Subsequent breakthroughs, now untragic, will succeed. Plato and Augustus Caesar are brilliantly triumphant; they realize the vision; they mold men through their works; they shape the future. But they live with their gaze fixed upon the first hero who was the victim.

This interpretation represents a particular philosophy of history. It sets out to speculate only about what is immanent in this world, but proceeds to assign substance and personality to historic units which actually cannot be verified. It ends by endowing historical patterns with quasi-demonic self-direction.

MEN AGAINST GODS

The battle takes place between the single individual and the "powers," between man and demons, between man and the gods. These powers are elusive. They escape man if he would grasp or just understand them. They are both there and not there. The same god is helpful and vicious.

Man does not know. Unknowingly and unconsciously he falls prey to the very powers that he wanted to escape.

Man rebels against the gods, as Hippolytus, the chaste youth in the service of Artemis, revolted against Aphrodite. He is overcome in battle with the unconquerable one.

GODS AGAINST ONE ANOTHER

The battle is a collision of the powers, of the gods themselves: man is only a pawn in these terrible games, or their scene, or their medium; but man's greatness consists precisely in his act of becoming such a medium. By this act, he becomes imbued with a soul and identical with the powers.

In the *Antigone* of Sophocles, the hidden gods of chthonic or political origin are basically such powers locked in mutual combat. But in Aeschylus' *Eumenides* the battles of the gods are quite manifest and in the foreground, determining the needs of men. In the *Prometheus* such battles are represented even without man's entering upon the scene.

Tragic world views always contain evidence of struggles. But is struggle tragic in and for itself? Or if not, what makes it tragic? To decide this question, we must explore further aspects of the tragic world view.

VICTORY AND DEFEAT

Who or what conquers in tragedy? Men and the powers are colliding. The outcome suggests decision in favor of the conqueror: the losers are wrong. But this is not true. Rather, we discover the following aspects of the tragic:

1. Victory is not his who triumphs but his who fails in defeat. In suffering failure, the loser conquers. The apparent victor is in truth inferior; his victory is fleeting and hollow.

2. *What conquers is the universal*, the world order, the moral order, the universal laws of life, the timeless—but the very recognition of such universality implies its rejection: the nature of the universal is such that it must crush this human greatness which opposes it.

3. *In reality nothing conquers.* Instead, everything becomes questionable, the hero as well as the universal. Compared with the *transcendent*, all is finite and relative, and therefore deserves to be destroyed, the particular as well as the universal, the exception as well as the rule. Both the exceptional man and the sublime order have their own limits, beyond which they break down. What conquers in tragedy is the transcendent—or rather even this does not conquer, for it makes itself felt only through the whole situation. It neither dominates nor submits; it simply exists.

4. In victory and in defeat, in the very process of achieving a solution, a new historical order is born, transitory in its turn. Its significance applies first to the particular knowledge of the tragic from which it arose. The rank of a tragic poet is then determined by the content which he draws from victory and defeat, and from their resolution.

GUILT

Tragedy becomes self-conscious by understanding the fate of its characters as the consequence of guilt, and as the inner working out of guilt itself. Destruction is the atonement of guilt.

To be sure, the world is full of guiltless destruction. Hidden evil destroys without being seen; it acts without being heard; no worldly authority so much as hears about it, any more than when someone was being tortured to death in the dungeon of a castle. Men die as martyrs without being martyrs, in so far as no one is present to bear witness or to learn of their martyrdom. Every day some defenseless creatures are being tortured and destroyed on this earth. Ivan Karamazov flies into a mad rage at the thought of the children killed for mere pleasure by the warring Turks. But this whole heart-rending, gruesome reality is not tragic, in so far as disaster is not the atonement of a guilt and is unconnected with the meaning of this life.

The question of guilt, however, is not limited to the actions and lives of individual men. Rather, it refers to humanity as a whole, of which every one of us is a part. Where are we to look for the guilt that is responsible for all this undeserved disaster? Where is the power that makes the innocent miserable?

Wherever men saw this question clearly, they conceived of the idea of complicity in guilt. All men are jointly committed and jointly liable. Their common origin and their common goal account for this. A token of this, though not an explanation, is that we feel shaken and perplexed at the following thought, which seems absurd to our limited understanding: I am responsible for all the evil that is perpetrated in the world, unless I have done what I could to prevent it, even to the extent of sacrificing my life. I am guilty because I am alive and can continue to live while this is happening. Thus criminal complicity takes hold of everyone for everything that happens.

We must therefore speak of guilt in the wider sense of a guilt of human existence as such, and of guilt in the narrower sense of responsibility for any particular action. Where our own guilt is not limited to certain specific wrongdoings but, in a deeper sense, is found in the very nature of human existence, there the idea of guilt becomes truly inclusive. Tragic knowledge, therefore, distinguishes these two kinds of guilt:

First: Existence is guilt. Guilt in the larger sense is identical with existence as such. The idea, already found in Anaximander, recurs in Calderón, although in a different sense—that man's greatest guilt is to have been born.

This is revealed also in the fact that my very existence causes misery. Indian thought has an image for this: with every step, with every breath, I destroy living beings. Whether I act or not, merely by existing I infringe upon the existence of others. Passive or active, I incur the guilt of existence.

A particular life is guilty through its origin. True, I did not desire this world nor my particular existence in it. But I am guilty against my will, simply because it is I myself who have this origin. My descent from guilty ancestors causes my own guilt.

Antigone is born contrary to the law as the daughter of Oedipus and his own mother. The curse of her descent is active within her. But her very exclusion from the norm of legitimate descent accounts for her singular depth and human feeling: she possesses the surest and most unshakable knowledge of the divine law. She dies because she is greater than the others, because her exceptional case embodies truth. And she dies gladly. Death to her means release; all along her road of action she is at one with herself.

A particular character is guilty because of what he is.[2] Character is itself

---

[2] This was the "Orphic" view of Rohde and Nietzsche, now generally abandoned on the basis of new manuscript evidence brought forward by Diels. See, e.g., Jaeger, *Theology*, pp. 34 ff.

a form of destiny—in so far as I detach myself from my own character and turn to look upon it.

What baseness there is in me, what desires to do evil, what unregenerate pride there is in my perversity—all this I myself have neither wanted nor created. Yet I am guilty of all this. And my guilt begets my destiny, whether I die unwillingly and unredeemed, or whether I am destroyed in trying to transcend my base nature by summoning up a deeper resource of my being—a resource which enables me to reject what I was, even though I cannot become what I long to be.

Second: Action is guilt. Guilt in the narrower sense is found in any distinct action I carry out freely in the sense that it need not occur and could also occur differently.

Guilty action may consist in flouting the law; it is personal arbitrariness consciously opposing the universal for no other reason than its own arbitrariness. It is the consequence of culpable ignorance, of half-conscious transpositions and concealments of motives. Nothing else is involved in such wilfulness beyond the misery of meanness and evil.

The situation is different when tragic knowledge recognizes the guilt of an action. Truthful and morally necessary action, although springing from the foundation of freedom, may entail failure. Man cannot escape his guilt through right and truthful conduct: guilt itself seems incurred guiltlessly. Man takes this guilt upon himself. He does not try to evade it. He stands by his guilt, not out of personal stubbornness, but for the sake of the very truth, which is destined for failure in his necessary sacrifice.[3]

MAN'S GREATNESS IN FAILURE

Tragic knowledge cannot be extended and deepened without seeing in man the quality of greatness over and above his atonement of guilt.

That man is not God is the cause of his smallness and undoing. But that he can carry his human possibilities to their extreme and can be undone by them with his eyes open—that is his greatness.

What we essentially learn from tragic knowledge, therefore, is what makes man suffer and what makes him fail, what he takes upon himself in the face of which realities, and in what manner or form he sacrifices his existence.

The tragic hero—man heightened and intensified—is man himself in good and evil, fulfilling himself in goodness and canceling out his own identity in evil.[4] In each case his existence is shipwrecked by the consistency with which he meets some unconditional demand, real or supposed.

His resistance, stubbornness, and pride drive him into the "greatness" of

---

[3] *Schuld des Soseins.* This is guilt, not of existence, origin, or action, but arising from the stubbornness and meanness in one's character.

[4] *Im Bösen, sich vernichtend.* This implies both physical and spiritual self-destruction.

evil. His endurance, his dauntlessness, his love, raise him up into the good. Always he grows in stature through the experience of life at its limits. The poet sees in him the bearer of something that reaches beyond individual existence, the bearer of a power, a principle, a character, a demon.

Tragedy depicts a man in his greatness beyond good and evil. The poet's view resembles that of Plato: "Or do you suppose that great crimes and unmixed wickedness spring from a slight nature and not from a vigorous one . . . while a weak nature will never be the cause of anything great, either for good or for evil?" It is from the most gifted type of man that "these spring who do the greatest harm to communities and individuals, and the greatest good . . . but a small nature never does anything great for a man or a city." [5]

---

[5] Plato, *Republic*, VI, 491 e, 495 b. Shorey translation (Loeb Classical Library).

The Tragic Mask *

GEORGE SANTAYANA

Masks are arrested expressions and admirable echoes of feeling, at once faithful, discreet, and superlative. Living things in contact with the air must acquire a cuticle, and it is not urged against cuticles that they are not hearts; yet some philosophers seem to be angry with images for not being things, and with words for not being feelings. Words and images are like shells, no less integral parts of nature than are the substances they cover, but better addressed to the eye and more open to observation. I would not say that substance exists for the sake of appearance, or faces for the sake of masks, or the passions for the sake of poetry and virtue. Nothing arises in nature for the sake of anything else; all these phases and products are involved equally in the round of existence, and it would be sheer wilfulness to praise the germinal phase on the ground that it is vital, and to denounce the explicit phase on the ground that it is dead and sterile. We might as justly despise the seed for being merely instrumental, and glorify the full-blown flower, or the conventions of art, as the highest achievement and fruition of life. Substance is fluid, and, since it cannot exist without some form, is always ready to exchange one form for another; but sometimes it falls into a settled rhythm or recognizable vortex, which we call a nature, and which sustains an interesting form for a season. These sustained forms are enshrined in memory and worshipped in moral philosophy, which often assigns to them a power to create and to reassert themselves which their precarious status is very far from justifying. But they are all in all to the mind: art and happiness lie in pouring and repouring the molten metal of existence through some such tenable mould.

Masks are accordingly glorious things; we are instinctively as proud of designing and wearing them as we are of inventing and using words. The blackest tragedy is festive; the most pessimistic philosophy is an en-

---

* George Santayana, "The Tragic Mask," in *Soliloquies in England and Later Soliloquies* (Charles Scribner's Sons, 1922), pp. 131–135.

thusiastic triumph of thought. The life which such expressions seem to arrest or to caricature would be incomplete without them; indeed, it would be blind and abortive. It is no interruption to experience to master experience, as tragedy aspires to do; nor is it an interruption to sink into its episodes and render them consummate, which is the trick of comedy. On the contrary, without such playful pauses and reflective interludes our round of motions and sensations would be deprived of that intellectual dignity which relieves it and renders it morally endurable—the dignity of knowing what we are doing, even if it be foolish in itself, and with what probable issue. Tragedy, the knowledge of death, raises us to that height. In fancy and for a moment it brings our mortal wills into harmony with our destiny, with the wages of existence, and with the silence beyond. These discoveries of reason have fixed the expression of the tragic mask, half horror and half sublimity. Such is the countenance of man when turned towards death and eternity and looking beyond all his endeavours at the Gorgon face of the truth. This is not to say that it is less human, or less legitimate, to look in other directions and to make other faces. But whether the visage we assume be a joyful or a sad one, in adopting and emphasizing it we define our sovereign temper. Henceforth, so long as we continue under the spell of this self-knowledge, we do not merely live but act; we compose and play our chosen character, we wear the buskin of deliberation, we defend and idealize our passions, we encourage ourselves eloquently to be what we are, devoted or scornful or careless or austere; we soliloquize (before an imaginary audience) and we wrap ourselves gracefully in the mantle of our inalienable part. So draped, we solicit applause and expect to die amid a universal hush. We profess to live up to the fine sentiments we have uttered, as we try to believe in the religion we profess. The greater our difficulties the greater our zeal. Under our published principles and plighted language we must assiduously hide all the inequalities of our moods and conduct, and this without hypocrisy, since our deliberate character is more truly ourself than is the flux of our involuntary dreams. The portrait we paint in this way and exhibit as our true person may well be in the grand manner, with column and curtain and distant landscape and finger pointing to the terrestrial globe or to the Yorick-skull of philosophy; but if this style is native to us and our art is vital, the more it transmutes its model the deeper and truer art it will be. The severe bust of an archaic sculpture, scarcely humanizing the block, will express a spirit far more justly than the man's dull morning looks or casual grimaces. Every one who is sure of his mind, or proud of his office, or anxious about his duty assumes a tragic mask. He deputes it to be himself and transfers to it almost all his vanity. While still alive and subject, like all existing things, to the undermining flux of his own substance, he has crystallized his soul into an idea, and more in pride than in sorrow he has offered up his life on the altar of the Muses. Self-knowledge, like any art or science, renders its subject-matter in a new medium, the medium of ideas, in which it loses its old dimensions and its old pace. Our animal habits are transmuted by conscience into loyalties and duties, and we become "persons" or masks. Art, truth, and death turn everything to marble.

That life should be able to reach such expression in the realm of eternal form is a sublime and wonderful privilege, but it is tragic, and for that reason distasteful to the animal in man. A mask is not responsive; you must not speak to it as to a living person, you must not kiss it. If you do, you will find the cold thing repulsive and ghastly. It is only a husk, empty, eyeless, brittle, and glazed. The more comic its expression the more horrible it will prove, being that of a corpse. The animal in man responds to things according to their substance, edible, helpful, or plastic; his only joy is to push his way victoriously through the material world, till a death stops him which he never thought of and, in a sense, never experiences. He is not in the least interested in picturing what he is or what he will have been; he is intent only on what is happening to him now or may happen to him next. But when the passions see themselves in the mirror of reflection, what they behold is a tragic mask. This is the escutcheon of human nature, in which its experience is emblazoned. In so far as men are men at all, or men of honour, they militate under this standard and are true to their colours. Whatever refuses to be idealized in this way, they are obliged to disown and commit to instant oblivion. It will never do for a mind merely to live through its passions or its perceptions; it must discern recognizable objects, in which to centre its experience and its desires; it must choose names and signs for them, and these names and symbols, if they are to perform their function in memory and intercourse, must be tightly conventional. What could be more unseemly than a fault in grammar, or in many a case more laughable and disconcerting? Yet any solecism, if it were once stereotyped and made definitely significant, would become an idiom: it would become a good verbal mask. What is not covered in this way by some abiding symbol can never be recovered; the dark flood of existence carries it down bodily. Only in some word or conventional image can the secret of one moment be flashed to another moment; and even when there is no one ready to receive the message, or able to decipher it, at least the poet in his soliloquy has uttered his mind and raised his monument in his own eyes; and in expressing his life he has found it.

Pragmatism and the Tragic Sense of Life *

SIDNEY HOOK

I

"What, if anything, has philosophy to tell us about the human condition, about the fate of man and his works?" This question in all its changes I have heard repeatedly on three major continents. It is asked mostly by philosophical laymen—by students and teachers and men of letters in search of a center, or at least a shelter, in a world become dark and insecure because of the shadows of totalitarianism and war. It is asked at interdisciplinary conferences; and by academic administrators in search of projects to recommend to foundations, projects which, to use an expression in wide use, "are not merely of technical philosophical concern."

The question: What saving message do philosophers bring their fellow-men? I have heard asked even by professional philosophers agonizing over the fact that they have a subject but no apparent subject-matter. It was heard at the XIIth International Congress of Philosophy at Venice—and there the Soviet philosophers undertook to answer it. It is raised periodically by voices in this country and in our own association as a protest against analytic philosophy. It was the central theme of the Third East-West Philosophers' Conference where for six weeks forty older and almost as many younger philosophers tried to discover what bearing philosophy had on social practice. At one point we were told to imagine that we had the ear of the statesmen of the world, and were challenged to give them counsel on how to put the world's affair in order. No one recalled Plato's experience at Syracuse or reflected upon the fact that as far as we can judge the only request Aristotle made of Alexander, when he had *his* ear, was that he

* Sidney Hook, "Pragmatism and the Tragic Sense of Life," from the Proceedings and Addresses of the American Philosophical Association, October, 1960, pp. 5–26.

send back fresh biological specimens from Asia. Indeed, it is not likely that with his views about the essential superiority of the Greeks to the rest of mankind that Aristotle would have given his blessings to Alexander's enlightened, if premature, attempt to establish a world culture or that he would even have been sympathetic to the purpose of the East-West Philosopher's Conference.

This question, with which I begin, is certainly a large one and may be deemed an appropriate theme for discussion in conjunction with John Dewey's centenary year.

II

For some time now philosophers have been disputing with each other about what philosophy should or should not be. They would be better occupied, it seems to me, doing each what he thinks philosophically worth while instead of objecting either to linguistic analysis or metaphysical speculation, as the case may be. The issue is not one of proper definition or even whether philosophy is a science or a body of knowledge of comparable objectivity, but rather whether it is worth doing, whether there is sufficient illumination and fun in pursuing certain themes, ignored by others, to justify continuing to do so. After all no one really believes that only science is a self-justifying enterprise. But since the subject has become moot and since there has developed a wide concern about what, if anything, philosophy has to say of general human concern, some remarks about it are in order.

As some of you are aware, I have for many years concerned myself with problems of social and political and legal philosophy, with "problems of men" as authentic as any of those recognized by thinkers who would reform modern philosophy. But I find myself increasingly out of sympathy with those who have impugned the whole philosophical enterprise because of its failure to serve as a beacon to mankind in distress. When I ask myself why I feel uncomfortable and at odds with those who attack philosophers because they have nothing of immediate, practical moment to say, I find that my conception of philosophy although stated sometimes in words similar to theirs, differs in important ways. Put most succinctly, although I believe that philosophy is a *quest* for wisdom, many of those who cite this phrase, too, speak and act as if they already had it. The difference may be only of nuance and emphasis but it has a profound bearing on one's conception of the appropriate role of the philosopher in the culture of his time. It is the difference between being a moralist and being a moralizer. The moralizer may be called "the shouting moralist," of whom Santayana somewhere says that he "no doubt has his place but not in philosophy." It is a difference, on the one hand, between *analyzing* specific and basic social problems and conflicts, and *clarifying* the issues in dispute with all the tools at one's command—and, on the other, *proclaiming* solutions and programs on the basis of antecedent commitments which one shares with some faction of his fellow-men. It is the difference between approaching problems of human experience in terms of one's vocation as a philosopher, which is to do intellectual justice to the varied and conflicting interests present or discovered, and one's vocation as a citizen limited by specific duties he must fulfill. It is the difference between intellectual concern which may or may not lead to programs of action and commitment to programs of action which by their very nature estops self-critical thought.

In the course of its history philosophy has been many things. But its distinctive concern at all times *has* been the quest for wisdom. Otherwise there would be no point in including thinkers like Descartes or Leibnitz in the history of philosophy in addition to the history of science or mathematics. What distinguishes the philosopher as a moralist from the philosopher as a mathematician, logician or natural scientist, and from the ordinary man as a philosopher, is his sustained reflective pursuit of wisdom. This means two things. The systematic study of the knowledge which is relevant to wisdom: and the analysis of the commitments we assume and rule out when knowledge is related to policy. All of us know that wisdom and knowledge are not the same thing but we sometimes mistakenly speak as if they are opposed. A man may have knowledge of many things and not be wise but a wise man cannot be ignorant of the things he is wise about. He must have knowledge of the nature and career of values in human experience; knowledge of the nature and history of the situations in which they develop and conflict; knowledge of the minds and emotions of the carriers of value; knowledge of the consequences of actions taken or proposed. The wise man is not one who merely recites moral principles and applies a ready-made schedule of moral obligations to the problems and perplexities of value conflict. He is one who on the basis of what he already knows, or believes he knows, makes fresh inquiry into the situations which define alternatives and exact their costs. "Only the conventional and the fanatical," observes Dewey, "are always immediately sure of right and wrong in conduct." This means that a philosopher must earn his title to be wise not by right of philosophical tradition or philology but by the hard work of acquiring relevant knowledge and by hard thinking about it.

Here lie important tasks for the philosopher. To be wise he must immerse himself in the actual subject matters (not necessarily experiences) out of which life's problems arise. To be wise about economic affairs he must study economics, to be wise about problems of law he must study law, to be wise about politics he must study history, sociology and other disciplines. To be wise about war and peace he must study military technology and the theory and practice of communism including its strategic exploitation of peace movements to disarm the free world. Indeed, these subjects are so interrelated that to be wise about any one of them he must study them all. And I might add, in view of some current writing, to be wise about education it is not enough merely to rebaptize the ends of the good life as ends of a good education, too, as if without operational application to concrete historical situations, they had any but a peripheral bearing on the great, current problems of education. One must study social history, the psychology of learning, the methods and techniques of pedagogy to achieve educational wisdom. To enumerate the ends of the good life is not enough. Nor is a primer on logical analysis which can serve as an introduction to the study of *any* subject, a primer to a philosophy of education.

All of these problems are of tremendous complexity because of the number of independent variables they contain, because they rarely permit of controlled experiment, and because the community must sometimes act upon them in desperate urgency before the analysis is complete. This should make for humility among philosophers even as they bring to the study of these problems the methodological sophistication, the arts and skills of analysis which are the hallmarks of their profession. This is what *I* mean by "the problems of men." It is philosophy not as a quest for salvation but as a pursuit of understanding of great cultural issues and their possible upshot. It does not start from a complete stock of philosophical wisdom which it dispenses to others with hortatory fervor but with an initial sense of concern to meet the challenge of the great unresolved problems of our time, offering analysis of these problems which will win the respect of the specialist and yet command the attention of everyman, e.g. how to preserve peace *and* freedom, achieve adequate production and meaningful vocations for all, design patterns of creative leisure, effect desegration if possible without coercion, establish a welfare state and a spirit of enterprise, preserve national security and the right to dissent. It is philosophy as *normative* social inquiry. And it is *not* social reform. How could philosophy be identified with social reform in view of the existence of many esteemed philosophers from Aristotle to Santayana whose judgments of wisdom were conservative, hostile to social reform? Such identification would be comparable to defining a physicist as one who was committed to a specific hypothesis in physics.

At this point my inner ear senses unspoken murmurs of surprise. "Surely," some of you must be saying, "this constitutes a repudiation of John Dewey's conception of philosophy, for, after all, does not Dewey call upon philosophers as philosophers to do precisely what is being urged they should not do? Does not Dewey call upon philosophers to play the role of social reformers?" My answer is: "Not as I understand him and not as he is to be understood in the light of all he has written."

Here is not the place to provide the documentation. I content myself merely with saying that Dewey has a very *complex* conception of philosophy. Philosophy is indeed concerned primarily with what I call normative problems of social inquiry. But its function is also to provide leading, speculative ideas in science—natural and social. And a third function is to weave together certain families of ideas into a philosophical synthesis. "There is a kind of music of ideas," he says, "which appeals, apart from any question of verification, to the mind of thinkers!" Nor is this all. The philosopher must bring some perspective or vision to bear upon the world which is related to issues of value and hence makes the analysis of normative problems of social inquiry more sensitive. "Philosophies," declares Dewey, "are different ways of construing life. . . ."

There is more, then, than problems of normative social inquiry which falls within the province of the philosopher's concern. There is the illuminating perspective in which they are seen which is metaphysics. "If philosophy be criticism," Dewey asks in *Experience and Nature*, "what is to be said of the relation of philosophy to metaphysics?" His answer briefly is that metaphysics is a description of those gross features of the world which constitute the backdrop of the theatre of human activity against which men play out their lives. The conduct of life and the analysis of its problems, however indirectly, will reflect what we believe to be the generic features of human experience in the world. In this sense, as ultimately related to the human scene and the adventure of human life, but not to ontology, metaphysics is "a ground map of the province of criticism establishing base lines to be employed in more intricate triangulations."

This brings me finally to my theme of the tragic sense of life as a feature of human experience which provides an illuminating perspective upon the analysis of man's problems. The juxtaposition of the expressions "pragmatism" and "the tragic sense of life" may appear bewildering to those who understand pragmatism as a narrow theory of meaning and "the tragic sense of life" as the hysterical lament that man is not immortal—the theme song of Unamuno's book of that title. To speak of pragmatism and the tragic sense of life is somewhat like speaking of "The Buddhism of John Dewey" or "The Dewey Nobody Knows."

I am not aware that Dewey ever used the phrase "the tragic sense of life" but I know that growing up in the shadow of the Civil War, he felt what I shall describe by it and that it is implied in his account of moral experience. At any rate nothing of moment depends upon whether the view is actually Dewey's or Hegel's or William James' or Nicolai Hartmann's in all of whom it can be found. I take the responsibility of the interpretation and its application. It is a perspective which seems to me to illumine the pragmatic view that problems of normative social inquiry—morals in the broad sense —are the primary—not exclusive—subject matter of philosophy, and that reason or scientific intelligence can and should be used to resolve them.

By the tragic sense of life I do not understand merely sensitivity to the presence of evil or suffering in the world although all tragic situations to some degree involve one or the other. And since I have mentioned Buddha I should like to say that the presence of the evils in the world which led Buddha to surrender his Kingdom in order to seek salvation for himself and mankind are not to me the realities fundamental to the tragic sense of life. There were three things in Buddha's experience, reflection upon which led him to a renunciation of his princely lot and a quest for liberation from desire and incarnate existence—sickness, old age and death. One can very well understand why in the world in which he lived and for many centuries thereafter until our own, these phenomena loomed so large in the over-populated and poverty-stricken areas of Asia. Nonetheless if we are to distinguish between the sense of the *pitiful* and the sense of the *tragic*—sickness, old age and even many forms of death, despite their numbing effect upon human sensibility, are not necessarily to be classified as tragic.

First, given the rapidly expanding horizons of knowledge in our age, there is nothing in the nature of things which requires that the sick, any more than the poor, must always be with us. If scientific medicine develops at the same pace in the next few hundred years as it has in the last century, it is not shallow optimism to anticipate that the most serious forms of sickness will disappear and not be replaced by others. Even where sickness is present it may be the occasion of tragedy but by itself is not an illustration of it. In relation to the forces of nature man's lot may appear pitiful. The tragic is a moral phenomenon.

What is true of sickness is true of old age. The aged arouse our compassion because of their feebleness and fragility—and the multiplicity of their aches and pains. When these are absent—and this, too, is a concern of scientific medicine—there is a chance for serenity, wisdom and beauty of spirit to manifest themselves. There is sometimes a grandeur and stateliness about an old tree which aged persons do not possess because the processes of physical degeneration, and the consequent weakening of the vital powers, make man pitiful. There is no tragedy in growing old biologically but only sorrow; the element of the tragic enters in the defeat of plans or hopes, in the realization that in much grief there is not much wisdom, and that we cannot count merely upon the passage of time alone to diminish our stupidities and cruelties.

But what of death—Buddha's third appalling discovery—preoccupation with which has become so fashionable today among some European existentialist philosophers that their philosophy seems to be more a meditation upon death than upon life? Is not death the ultimate source of whatever is tragic in life? I cannot bring myself to think so. Nor can I convince myself that its nature and significance in life waited to be discovered by Kierkegaard and Heidegger and their modern disciples.

It is the reflective attitude towards death not the popular attitude or the one displayed by those in its last agonies, which throws light on its nature and place in life. The attitude exhibited by Socrates in facing it seems wiser than that expressed by the contemnors of the rational life who not content with talking about what they find when they look into themselves inflate it into a universal trait of the human psyche. So Tolstoy who is quoted by existentialist writers, writes: "If a man has learned to think, no matter what he may think about, he is always thinking of his own death. All philosophers are like that. And what truth can there be, if there is death?" Logically, of course, this makes no more sense than the even more extreme statement of Sartre that "if we must die then our life has no meaning," which to those who solve some problems in life and therefore find some meaning, might be taken as a premise in a new short proof of human immortality. All this it seems to me expresses little more than a fear of death and a craving for immortality. It is a commonplace observation, however, that most human beings who desire immortality desire not unending life but unending youth or other desirable qualities which life makes possible. The fable of Juno and her lover in which Juno petitions the Gods to take back the gift of eternal life they had conferred upon a mortal indicates that the Greeks knew that a life without end could be a dubious blessing. In this respect the Hellenes were wiser than the Hebrews whose God drives Adam from Paradise after he had eaten of the fruit of the tree of knowledge to prevent him from eating of the fruit of the tree of eternal life. Agony over death strikes me as one of the unloveliest features of the intellectual life of our philosophic times—and certainly unworthy of any philosophy which conceives itself as a quest for wisdom. It has never been clear to me why those who are nauseated by life, not by this or that kind of life but any kind of life, should be so fearful of death.

Wisdom is knowledge of the uses of life and death. The uses of life are to be found in the consummatory experiences of vision and delight, of love, understanding, art, friendship and creative activity. That is why in a contingent world of finite men, vulnerable to powers they cannot control which sometimes robs them of the possibility of any justifying consummations, death has its uses, too. For it gives us some assurance that no evil or suffering lasts forever. To anyone aware of the multitude of infamies and injustices which men have endured, of the broken bodies and tortured minds of the victims of these cruelties, of the multiple dimensions of pain in which millions live on mattress graves or with minds shrouded in darkness, death must sometimes appear as a beneficent release, not an inconsolable affliction. It washes the earth clean of what cannot be cleansed in any other way. Not all the bright promises of a future free of these stains of horror can redeem by one iota the lot of those who will not live to see the dawn of the new day.

It is nobler to exist and struggle in a world in which there is always a vital option to live or die. The fear of death, the desire to survive at any cost or price in human degradation, has been the greatest ally of tyranny, past and present. "There are times," says Woodbridge, "when a man ought to be more afraid of living than dying." And we may add, there are situations in which because of the conditions of survival, the worst thing we can know of anyone is that he has survived. We have known such times and situations. They may come again.

Even in a world in which all injustices, cruelties and physical anguish have disappeared, the possibility of withdrawing from it makes the world insofar forth a better and a freer world. So long as we retain possession of our faculties, our decision to remain in the world indicates a participating responsibility on our part for those events within it which our continuance affects. If human beings were unable to die they would to that extent be unfree. Man shares a *conatus sui esse persevare* with everything else in the world or at least with all other sentient beings. But just because he can on rational grounds give up his being, choose not to be, he differentiates himself most strikingly from his fellow creatures in nature. I conclude therefore that death as such is not a tragic phenomenon and that its presence does not make the world and our experience within it tragic. It would be truer to call tragic a world in which men wanted to die but couldn't.

What, then, do I mean by the tragic sense of life and what is its relevance to pragmatism? I mean by the tragic sense a very simple thing which is rooted in the very nature of the moral experience and the phenomenon of moral choice. Every genuine experience of moral doubt and perplexity in which we ask: "What should I do?" takes place in a situation where good conflicts with good. If we already know what is evil the moral inquiry is over, or it never really begins. "The worse or evil," says Dewey, "is the rejected good" but until we reject it, the situation is one in which apparent good opposes apparent good. "All the serious perplexities of life come back to the genuine difficulty of forming a judgment as to the values of a situation: they come back to a conflict of goods." No matter how we resolve the opposition some good will be sacrificed, some interest, whose immediate craving for satisfaction may be every whit as intense and authentic as its fellows, will be modified, frustrated or even suppressed. Where the goods involved are of a relatively low order, like decisions about what to eat, where to live, where to go, the choice is unimportant except to the mind of a child. There are small tragedies as there are small deaths. At any level the conflict of values must become momentous to oneself or others to convey adequately the tragic quality. Where the choice is between goods that are complex in structure and consequential for the future, the tragic quality of the moral dilemma emerges more clearly. And when it involves basic choices of love, friendship, vocations, the quality becomes poignant. The very nature of the self as expressed in habits, dispositions and character is to some extent altered by these decisions. If, as Hobbes observes, "Hell is truth seen too late," all of us must live in it. No matter how justified in smug retrospect our moral decisions seem to have been, only the unimaginative will fail to see the possible selves we have sacrificed to become what we are. Grant that all regrets are vain, that any other choice would have been equally or more regretted, the selves we might have been are eloquent witnesses of values we failed to enjoy. If we have played it safe and made our existence apparently secure, the fascinating experience of a life of adventure and experience can never be ours, and every thought of a good fight missed will be accompanied by a pang. It is a poor spirit William James reminds us who does not sense the chagrin of the tardy Crillon, who arriving when the battle is over is greeted by Henry IV with the words: "Hang yourself, brave Crillon! We fought at Arques, and you were not there!" On the other hand, if we have scorned to put down our roots, hugged our liberty tightly to ourselves by refusing to give hostages to fortune, become crusaders or martyrs for lost causes, we have thrust from ourselves the warmth of sustained affection, and the comforting regularities which can best heal the bruised spirit.

There is a conflict not only between the good and the good but between the good and the right where the good is a generic term for all the values in a situation and the right for all the obligations. The *concepts* of good and right are irreducible to each other in ordinary use. We are often convinced we must fulfill a certain duty even when we are far from convinced to the same degree that the action or the rule it exemplifies will achieve the greatest good. The "good" is related to the reflective satisfaction of an interest: "the right" to the fulfillment of a binding demand or rule of the community. There is no moral problem when in doing the right thing we can see that it *also* leads to the greatest good or when striving for the greatest good conforms to our sense of what is right. But the acute ethical problems arise when in the pursuit of the good we do things which appear not to be right, as e.g., when in order to avoid the dangers of war a nation repudiates its treaty obligations or when in order to win a war non-combatants are punished who are in no way responsible for the actions of others. They also arise when in doing what is right our actions result in evil consequences, as e.g., when a dangerous criminal, set free on a legal technicality, kills again or when the refusal to surrender to the unjust claims of an aggressor results in wholesale slaughter. Many have been the attempts made to escape the antinomies between the right and the good by defining the good as the object of right or the right merely as the means to the good. All have failed. To act upon the right no matter what its consequences for human weal or woe seems inhuman, at times insane. The thirst for righteousness has too often been an angry thirst satisfied if at all by long draughts of blood. On the other hand, the attempt to do good by *any* means no matter how unjust, is subhuman and usually irrational.

As compared to traditional ethical doctrines, ideal utilitarianism reaches farthest in our quest for an adequate ethics but in the end it, too, must be rejected. And it was the pragmatist and pluralist, William James, long before Pritchard and Ross, who indicated why in the famous question he asked: "If the hypothesis were offered us of a world in which Messrs. Fourier's and Bellamy's and Morris' Utopia should all be outdone, and millions be kept permanently happy on the one simple condition that a certain lost soul on the far off edge of things should lead a life of lonely torture, what except a specific and independent sort of emotion can it be which would make us immediately feel . . . how hideous a thing would be its enjoyment when deliberately accepted as the fruit of such a bargain?" The situation is unaltered if we recognize that there are other goods besides happiness and that justice is itself a good, because in that case the conflict breaks out again between good and good. In this connection I would venture the statement that it is the failure to see the radical pluralism in the nature of the goods which are reckoned in the consequences of an action which accounts both for Moore's view that it is self-evident that it can *never* be right knowingly to approve an action that would make the world as a whole worse than some alternative action and for Kant's view that there are some duties that it would *always* be right to perform, even if the consequences of the action resulted in a worse world or in no world at all. No specific rule can be laid down as absolutely binding in advance either way. Nothing can take the place of intelligence; the better or the lesser evil in each situation can be best defined as the object of reflective choice. Even the decision in the stock illustration of the text-books whether to execute an innocent man or turn him over to be tortured in order to save the community from destruction—would depend upon a complex of circumstances. It is perfectly conceivable that an unjust act will sometimes produce the greater good or the lesser evil. It is sometimes necessary to burn down a house to save a village. Although when applied to human beings the logic seems damnable, few are prepared to take the position of Kant in those agonizing moral predicaments that are not uncommon in history, especially the history of oppressed minority peoples, in which the survival of the group can be purchased only at the price of the pain, degradation and death of the innocent. No matter how we choose, we must either betray the ideal of the greater good or the ideal of right or justice. In this lies the agony of the choice.

Many have been the attempts to escape the guilt of that choice. I cite one from the past. During the Middle Ages, Maimonides writing on the Laws of the Torah to guide his people discusses what a community is to do when it is beset by enemies who demand the life of one man with the threat to kill all if he be not turned over to them. Maimonides teaches that they are to refuse to turn over any man even if all must die in consequence, except if their enemies call out the name of a specific person. I had heard this teaching defended on the ground that if the community itself had to make the decision who was to die, it would be taking the guilt of an innocent man's death upon itself, which is impermissible. But if the enemy names the man, then he can be turned over because the guilt and sin fall now on *their* heads. By this miserable evasion it was thought that the tragic choice could be avoided. But it turns out that Maimonides has been misread. What Maimonides really taught is that only if the name of the person who has been called out is of one already under the death sentence for his crimes should he be surrendered. But never an innocent man. "Never," however, is a long time. It is problematic whether the Jews would have survived if they had always abided by Maimonides' injunction.

If anything, human beings are more readily inclined to sacrifice the right to the good than the good to the right especially in revolutionary situations which have developed because of grievances too long unmet. It can easily be shown that it was Lenin's conception of Communist ethics which implicitly defined the right action as consisting in doing *anything*—literally anything that would bring victory in the class struggle—which explains the transformation of a whole generation of idealists into hangmen. In fact the health of the revolution whether in the times of Robespierre or Castro never really requires the holocaust of victims offered up to it. But no revolution including our own has ever been achieved without injustice to someone. However the conflict between the principles of right and the values of good be theoretically resolved, in every concrete situation it leads to some abridgement of principle or some diminution of value.

The most dramatic of all moral conflicts is not between good and good, or between good and right, but between right and right. This in its starkest form is the theme of Sophoclean tragedy but the primary locus of the tragic situation is not in a play but in life, in law, and in history. Innocence in personal matters consists in overlooking the conflict of moral duties and obligations. Innocence in political matters, the characteristic of ritualistic liberalism, consists in failing to see the conflicts of rights in our Bill of Rights and the necessity of their intelligent adjustment. In our own country we have witnessed again and again the antinomy of rights revealed in divided loyalties, in the conflict between allegiance to the laws of the state and allegiance to what is called divine law or natural law or the dictates of conscience.

On the international scene it is expressed in the conflict of incompatible national claims, each with *some* measure of justification, as in the Israeli-Arab impasse.

One of the noteworthy features of moral intuitionism as illustrated in the doctrines of Ross is this recognition that *prima facie* duties conflict and that every important moral act exhibits at the same time characteristics which tend to make it both *prima facie* right and *prima facie* wrong so that although we may claim certainty about these *prima facie* duties, any particular moral judgment or action is at best only probable or contingent. As Ross says, "There is therefore much truth in the description of the right act as a fortunate act." From this the conclusion to be drawn, it seems to me, is that the most important *prima facie* duty of all in a situation requiring moral decision is that of *conscientiousness*, or reflective assessment of all the relevant factors involved, and the searching exploration of our own hearts to determine what we sincerely want, whether we really wish to do what is right in a situation or to get our own scheming way come what may. As much if not more evil results from confusion of our purposes and ignorance of our motives than from ruthless and clear-eyed resolve to ignore everyone's interests but one's own. This emphasis on the importance of reflective inquiry into the features of the situation which bear on the rightness of an action seems to me to be more important than Ross' conception or interpretation of the intuitive apprehension of our *prima facie* duties. It is easier to doubt that we have this faculty of infallible intuition than that our intelligence has the power to discover our conflicts and mediate between them.

Irony is compounded with tragedy in the fact that many of the rights we presently enjoy we owe to our ancestors who in the process of winning them for us deprived others of their rights. In some regions of the world the very ground on which people stand was expropriated by force and fraud from others by their ancestors. Yet as a rule it would be a new injustice to seek to redress the original injustice by depriving those of their possessions who hold present title to them. Every just demand for reparations against an aggressor country is an unjust demand on the descendants of its citizens who as infants were not responsible for the deeds of aggression. That is why history is the arena of the profoundest moral conflicts in which some legitimate right has always been sacrificed, sometimes on the altars of the God of War.

The Christian and especially the Buddhist ethics of purity which seeks to transcend this conflict and avoid guilt by refusal to violate anyone's right in such situations, can only do so by withdrawing from the plane of the ethical altogether. This may succeed in God's eyes but not in man's. The Buddhist saint or any other who out of respect for the right to life of man or beast refuses ever to use force, or to kill, even when this is the only method, as it sometimes is, that will save multitudes from suffering and death, makes himself responsible for the greater evil, all the more so because he claims to be acting out of compassion. He cannot avoid guilt whether we regard him as more than man or less than man. No more than we does he escape the tragic decision.

There are three generic approaches to the tragic conflicts of life. The first approach is that of history. The second is that of love. The third is that of creative intelligence in quest for ways of mediation which I call here the pragmatic.

The approach of history is best typified by Hegel precisely because he tries to put a gloss of reason over the terrible events which constitute so much of the historical process. Its upshot is woefully inept to its intent. It suggests not only that whatever cause wins and *however* it wins, is more just than the cause which is defeated, but that the loser is the more wicked and not merely the weaker. Further, it calls into question the very fact of tragic conflict from which it so perceptively starts. No one has seen more profoundly into the nature of the tragic situation than Hegel and its stark clash of equally legitimate rights. But his solution, expressed in Schiller's dictum *Die Weltgeschichte ist das Weltgericht*, as Hegel develops it, makes the philosophy of history a theodicy. It thereby vulgarizes tragedy. For it attempts to console man with a dialectical proof that his agony and defeat are not really evils but necessary elements in the goodness of the whole. The position is essentially religious. No monotheistic religion which conceives of God as both omnipotent and benevolent, no metaphysics which asserts that the world is rational, necessary and good has any room for genuine tragedy.

The approach of love is incomplete and ambiguous. It is incomplete because if love is more than a feeling of diffused sympathy but is expressed in action no *man* can love everyone or identify himself with every interest. Empirically love has produced as much disunity as unity in the world—not only in Troy but in Jerusalem. Injustice is often born of love, not only of self-love but of love of some rather than others. Love is not only incomplete but ambiguous. There are various kinds of love and the actions to which they lead may be incompatible. An order of distinction is required. A man's love for his family must be discriminatory: his love of mankind not. He cannot love both in the same way without denying one or the other. The quality of love is altered with the range of its generalization. In one sense love always shows a bias which reinforces some conflicting interest; in another it gives all conflicting values its blessing without indicating any specific mode of action by which conflict can be mediated. Love may enable a person to live with the burden of guilt which he assumes when he sacrifices one right to another. But it is no guide to social conflict as the last two thousand years have shown. Because the Lord loves man equally nothing follows logically about the equality of man before the Law. "The *Agape* quality of love," says Tillich, "sees man as God sees him." But what *man* can tell us how *God* sees man? "Agape," continues Tillich, "loves in everybody and through everybody love itself." Karl Barth speaks more simply and intelligibly, and with a basic brutality which is the clue to his crude neutralism, when he claims that such love has no bearing whatever for the organization of any human society.

Finally there is the method of creative intelligence. It, too, tries to make it possible for men to live with the tragic conflict of goods and rights and duties, to mediate not by arbitrary fiat but through informed and responsible decision. Whoever uses this method must find his way among all the conflicting claims. He must therefore give each one of them and the interests it represents tongue or voice. Every claimant therefore has a right to be heard. The hope is that as much as possible of each claim may be incorporated in some inclusive or shared interest which is accepted because the alternatives are less satisfactory. To this end we investigate every relevant feature about it, the conditions under which it emerged, its proximate causes and consequences, the costs of gratifying it, the available alternatives and *their* costs. Every mediation entails some sacrifice. The quest for the unique good of the situation, for what is to be done here and now, may point to what is better than anything else available but what it points to is also a lesser evil. It is a lesser evil whether found in a compromise or in moderating the demand of a just claim or in learning to live peacefully with one's differences on the same general principle which tells us that a divorce is better for all parties concerned than a murder. In every case the rules, the wisdom, the lessons of the past are to be applied but they have presumptive, not final, validity because they may be challenged by new presumptions. "The pragmatic import of the logic of individualized situations," says Dewey, "is to transfer the attention of theory from pre-occupation with general conceptions to the problem of developing effective methods of inquiry," and applying them. It is a logic which does not preach solutions but explores the suggestions which emerge from the analyses of problems. Its categorical imperative is to inquire, to reason together, to seek in every crisis the creative devices and inventions that will not only make life fuller and richer but tragedy bearable. William James makes essentially the same point as Dewey in the language of ideals. Since in the struggles between ideals "victory and defeat there must be, the victory to be philosophically prayed for is that of the more inclusive side—of the side which even in the hour of triumph will to some degree do *justice* to the ideals in which the vanquished interests lay. . . ." But prayer is not enough. He goes on: "*Invent some manner* of realizing your own ideals which will also satisfy the alien demands—that and that only is the path of peace." To which we must add, provided there is a reciprocal will to peace in the matter. And even then, your own or the alien demands or both must be curtailed.

As you may have gathered by this time, I have been concerned to show that this pragmatic approach to the moral problem can not only be squared with the recognition of tragic conflicts, of troubles, minor and grave, which dog the life of man in a precarious world, but that it gets its chief justification from this recognition. Intelligence may be optimistic when it deals with the control of things but the moral life by its very nature forbids the levity and superficiality which has often been attributed to the pragmatic approach by its unimaginative critics.

Indeed I make bold to claim that the pragmatic approach to tragedy is more serious, even more heroic, than any other approach because it doesn't resign itself to the bare fact of tragedy or take easy ways out at the price of truth. Where death does not result from the tragic situation, there are always consequences for continued living which it takes responsibly without yielding to despair. It does not conceive of tragedy as a pre-ordained doom, but as one in which the plot to some extent depends upon us, so that we become the creators of our own tragic history. We cannot then palm off altogether the tragic outcome upon the universe in the same way as we can with a natural disaster.

Contrast this attitude towards tragedy with the Hegelian fetishism of history which in the end is but the rationalization of cruelty. Contrast it with the Judaic-Christian conception which offers at the price of truth, the hope that the felicities of salvation will both explain and recompense human suffering. Contrast it with the attitude of Unamuno whose hunger for immortality is so intense that he sees in intelligence or reason the chief enemy of life, both in time and eternity. For him the joy and delight of life is the conflict of value and value no matter what the cost. "The very essence of tragedy," he tells us, "is the combat of life with reason." And since the Inquisitor is concerned with the eternal life of his victim's soul, the potential victim must defend the Inquisitor's place in society and regard him as far superior to the merchant who merely ministers to his needs. "There is much more humanity in the Inquisitor," he says. Crazed by this thirst for the infinite, Unamuno glorifies war as the best means of spreading love and knowledge. He illustrates the dialectic of total absurdity and caprice in thought which often prepares the way for atrocity in life. Here is no quest for the better, for the extension of reasonable controls in life and society, for peace in action.

To be sure, Unamuno is so horrified by the flux of things in which all things are ultimately liquefied that he expresses pity for the very "star-strewn heavens" whose light will some day be quenched. But this cosmic sentimentality is disdainful of the vexatious, unheroic daily tasks of mediating differences, even of mitigating the consequences of irreconcilable conflicts, of devising ways to limit human suffering whose ubiquitous presence is the alleged cause of spiritual agony.

No two thinkers seem so far removed from each other as Miguel de Unamuno and Bertrand Russell—and as philosophers they are indeed related as a foothill to a Himalayan peak. But this makes all the more significant the similarity of their attitude towards the arts of social control which require the extension of man's power over nature. For Russell, any philosophy, and particularly one like Dewey's, which interprets ideas as implicit guides to activity and behavior, and knowledge as dependent upon experimental reconstructive activity in the situation which provokes it, exhibits "the danger of what may be called cosmic impiety." It is an arrogant power-philosophy whose insolence towards the universe is hardly less objectionable when it stresses social power than individual power.

It is fortunate that Russell's attitude—in which he is not always consistent—towards scientific power and control of our natural environment has not prevailed, otherwise the whole of modern civilization including modern medicine would never have developed. The charge of megalomania against any view of knowledge just because it is not a pure spectator view is absurd. For the pragmatic view accepts the Spinozistic dictum that nature can be changed only by nature's means. The problem is to discover or devise these means. This cannot be intelligently done without experimental activity. According to Russell's own position, power itself is neither good nor bad but only the uses and ends of power. But since he also tells us that there is no such thing as a rational or irrational end, that intelligence or reason is helpless in determining what we should do with our power, one can argue with much better warrant that it is *his* view, *if acted upon*, that increases "the danger of vast social disaster" than the pragmatic view which believes that by changing nature and society, men can to some extent change themselves in the light of rationally determined ends. No humane person can read history without being moved more by man's failures to use the knowledge he has had to remove the evils and sufferings which were remedial than by his attempt to achieve too great a control or power over nature. It was not science which was responsible for the use of the atomic bomb. It was politics—a failure of politics to understand the true situation. The pitiful disparity at any particular time between what we know and don't know is sufficient to inspire a sense of humility in the most intellectually ambitious. But it is only in the most vulgarized sense of the term "pragmatism," a sense which Russell helped to popularize by flagrant misunderstandings, that the adequacy of a theory of knowledge, which regards activity or experiment as integral to the achievement of knowledge of fact, can be judged by its alleged social consequences.

I am more interested tonight in stating a position than establishing it. As I understand the pragmatic perspective on life, it is an attempt to make it possible for men to live in a world of inescapable tragedy,—a tragedy which flows from the conflict of moral ideals,—without lamentation, defiance or make-believe. According to this perspective even in the best of human worlds there will be tragedy—tragedy perhaps without bloodshed but certainly not without tears. It focuses its analysis on problems of normative social inquiry in order to reduce the costs of tragedy. Its view of man is therefore melioristic, not optimistic. Some philosophers belittle man by asking him to look at the immensities without: others belittle him by asking him to look at the perversities and selfishness within. Pragmatism denies nothing about the world or men which one truly finds in them but it sees in men something which is at once, to use the Sophoclean phrase, more wonderful and more terrible than anything else in the universe, viz., the power to make themselves and the world around them better or worse. In this way pragmatic meliorism avoids the romantic pessimism of Russell's free man, shaking his fist in defiance of a malignant universe, and the grandiose optimism of Niebuhr's redeemed man with his delusions of a cosmic purpose which he knows is there but knows in a way in which neither he nor anyone else can possibly understand.

To the meliorist the recognition of the gamut of tragic possibilities is what feeds his desire to find some method of negotiating conflicts of value by intelligence rather than war, or brute force. But this is not as simple as it sounds. There is no substitute for intelligence. But intelligence may not be enough. It may not be enough because of limitations of our knowledge, because of the limited reach of our powers of control. It may not be enough because of the recalcitrance of will—not merely the recalcitrance of will to act upon goods already known and not in dispute, but because of unwillingness to find out what the maximizing good in the situation is. And although we are seeking to settle conflicts of value by the use of intelligence rather than by force, is it not true that sometimes intelligence requires the use of force?

Let us take this last question first. Faced by a momentous conflict of values in which some value must give way if the situation is to be resolved, the rational approach is to find some encompassing value on the basis of some shared interest. This, as we have seen, involves willingness to negotiate—to negotiate honestly. The grim fact, however, is that there is sometimes no desire to reason, no wish to negotiate except as a holding action to accumulate strategic power, nothing but the reliance of one party or the other upon brute force even when other alternatives may exist. In such cases the moral onus rests clearly upon those who invoke force. Their victory no more establishes their claim to be right than a vandal's destruction of a scientists' instruments of inquiry has any bearing on the validity of his assertions, evidence for or against which, could have been gathered by the instrument destroyed. The intelligent use of force to *prevent* or crush the use of force where a healthy democratic process, equitable laws and traditions and customs of freedom make it possible to vent differences in a rational and orderly way, is therefore justifiable even if on prudential grounds one may forego such action. This means that tolerance always has limits—it cannot tolerate what is itself actively intolerant.

There is a tendency in modern philosophical thought which, in rejecting too sweeping claims for the role of intelligence in human affairs, settles for too little even when it does not embrace a wholesale skepticism. Of course, a man may know what is right and not do it just as he may know what is true and not publicly assert it. In neither case is this a ground for maintaining that we cannot know what action is more justified than another or what assertion is more warranted than another. The *refusal* to follow a rational method, to give good reasons is one thing: the claim that there are different rational methods, different *kinds* of good reasons each with its own built-in modes of validity, is something else again—and to me unintelligible. To be sure, the acceptance of rational method is not enough. Men must have some non-rational element in common. Hume is on unquestionably solid ground in asserting that reason must always *serve* a human need, interest or passion. But his mistake outweighed his insight when he contended that rational method could only be a servant or slave of what it served and that needs, interests and passions could not be changed or transformed by the use of intelligence. In our flights into space if we encounter other sentient creatures capable of communicating with us, it is more likely that their logical and mathematical judgment will be the same as ours than their ethical judgments, because we can more readily conceive creatures of different needs than of different minds.

At any rate the world we live in is one in which men do not share all their needs and interests and yet it is one in which they have sufficient needs and interests in common to make possible their further extension, and to give intelligence a purchase, so to speak, in its inquiry.

The most difficult of all situations is one in which even the common use of methods of inquiry seems to lead to conclusions which are incompatible with each other although each is objectively justified. There is always an open possibility of ultimate disagreement no matter how far and long we pursue rational inquiry. We can conceive it happening. In such situations we must resign ourselves to living with our differences. Otherwise we must fight or surrender. But it is simply a non-sequitur to maintain that because no guarantee can be given that there will not be ultimate disagreement, penultimate agreements cannot be validly reached and justified.

In any case we cannot in advance determine the limits of reason or intelligence in *human* affairs. So long as we don't know where it lies, it is sensible to press on, at the same time devising the means to curb the effects of the refusal to reason when it manifests itself. Above all, we must avoid oversimplifying the choice of evils and encouraging the hope that to be unreasonable will pay dividends.

We are moving into another period of history in which freedom once more is being readied for sacrifice on the altars of survival. The Munichmen of the spirit are at work again. The stakes are now for the entire world. Our task as philosophers is not to heed partisan and excited calls for action, but rather to think through the problems of freedom and survival afresh. In a famous pronouncement two years ago Bertrand Russell declared that if the Kremlin refused to accept reasonable proposals of disarmament, the West should disarm unilaterally "even if it means the horrors of Communist domination." Although he no longer believes this, there are many others who do. I know that common sense is at a discount in philosophy but in ethics it should not be lightly disregarded. A position like this obviously can have only one effect, viz., to encourage the intransigeance of those who wish to destroy the free world without which there cannot be a free philosophy. You cannot negotiate successfully by proclaiming in advance that you will capitulate if the other side persists in being unreasonable. Our alternatives are not limited to surrender and extinction of freedom, on the one hand, and war and the danger of human extermination on the other. There are other alternatives to be explored—all tragic in their costs but not equally extreme. The very willingness, if necessary, to go down fighting in defence of freedom may be the greatest force for peace when facing an opponent who makes a fetish of historical survival. On pragmatic grounds, the willingness to act on a position like Kant's *fiat justitia, pereat mundus* may sometimes—I repeat—sometimes—be the best way of preserving a just and free world—just as the best way of saving one's life is sometimes to be prepared to lose it. The uneasy peace we currently enjoy as a result of "the balance of terror" is tragic. But it may turn out that it is less so than any feasible alternative today. If it endures long enough and it becomes clear to the enemies of freedom that they cannot themselves survive war, they may accept the moral equivalents of war in the making. The pragmatic program is always to find moral equivalents for the expression of natural inpulses which threaten the structure of our values.

I have perhaps overstressed the sense of the tragic in human life in an effort to compensate for the distortions to which pragmatism has been subject. There is more in life than the sense of the tragic. There is laughter and joy and the sustaining discipline of work. There are other dimensions of experience besides the moral. There is art and science and religion. There are other uses for intelligence besides the resolution of human difficulties. There is intellectual play and adventure. But until men become Gods— which will never be—they will live with the sense of the tragic in their hearts as they go in quest for wisdom. Pragmatism, as I interpret it, is the theory and practice of enlarging human freedom in a precarious and tragic world by the arts of intelligent social control. It may be a lost cause. I do not know of a better one. And it may not be lost if we can summon the courage and intelligence to support our faith in freedom—and enjoy the blessings of a little luck.

Tragedy and the Whole Truth *

ALDOUS HUXLEY

There were six of them, the best and bravest of the hero's companions. Turning back from his post in the bows, Odysseus was in time to see them lifted, struggling, into the air, to hear their screams, the desperate repetition of his own name. The survivors could only look on, helplessly, while Scylla "at the mouth of her cave devoured them, still screaming, still stretching out their hands to me in the frightful struggle." And Odysseus adds that it was the most dreadful and lamentable sight he ever saw in all his "explorings of the passes of the sea." We can believe it; Homer's brief description (the too poetical simile is a later interpolation) convinces us.

Later, the danger passed, Odysseus and his men went ashore for the night, and, on the Sicilian beach, prepared their supper—prepared it, says Homer, "expertly." The Twelfth Book of the *Odyssey* concludes with these words: "When they had satisfied their thirst and hunger, they thought of their dear companions and wept, and in the midst of their tears sleep came gently upon them."

The truth, the whole truth, and nothing but the truth—how rarely the older literatures ever told it! Bits of the truth, yes; every good book gives us bits of the truth, would not be a good book if it did not. But the whole truth, no. Of the great writers of the past incredibly few have given us that. Homer—the Homer of the *Odyssey*—is one of those few.

"Truth?" you question. "For example, 2 + 2 = 4? Or Queen Victoria came to the throne in 1837? Or light travels at the rate of 187,000 miles a second?" No, obviously, you won't find much of that sort of thing in literature. The "truth" of which I was speaking just now is in fact no more than an acceptable verisimilitude. When the experiences recorded in a piece of literature correspond fairly closely with our own actual experiences, or

---

* Aldous Huxley, "Tragedy and the Whole Truth," from *Collected Essays* (Harper & Row, 1959), 96–103.

with what I may call our potential experiences—experiences, that is to say, which we feel (as the result of a more or less explicit process of inference from known facts) that we might have had—we say, inaccurately no doubt: "This piece of writing is true." But this, of course, is not the whole story. The record of a case in a textbook of psychology is scientifically true, in so far as it is an accurate account of particular events. But it might also strike the reader as being "true" with regard to himself—that is to say, acceptable, probable, having a correspondence with his own actual or potential experiences. But a textbook of psychology is not a work of art— or only secondarily and incidentally a work of art. Mere verisimilitude, mere correspondence of experience recorded by the writer with experience remembered or imaginable by the reader, is not enough to make a work of art seem "true." Good art possesses a kind of super-truth—is more probable, more acceptable, more convincing than fact itself. Naturally; for the artist is endowed with a sensibility and a power of communication, a capacity to "put things across," which events and the majority of people to whom events happen, do not possess. Experience teaches only the teachable, who are by no means as numerous as Mrs. Micawber's papa's favourite proverb would lead us to suppose. Artists are eminently teachable and also eminently teachers. They receive from events much more than most men receive, and they can transmit what they have received with a peculiar penetrative force, which drives their communication deep into the reader's mind. One of our most ordinary reactions to a good piece of literary art is expressed in the formula: "This is what I have always felt and thought, but have never been able to put clearly into words, even for myself."

We are now in a position to explain what we mean when we say that Homer is a writer who tells the Whole Truth. We mean that the experiences he records correspond fairly closely with our own actual or potential experiences—and correspond with our experiences not on a single limited sector, but all along the line of our physical and spiritual being. And we also mean that Homer records these experiences with a penetrative artistic force that makes them seem peculiarly acceptable and convincing.

So much, then, for truth in literature. Homer's, I repeat, is the Whole Truth. Consider how almost any other of the great poets would have concluded the story of Scylla's attack on the passing ship. Six men, remember, have been taken and devoured before the eyes of their friends. In any other poem but the *Odyssey*, what would the survivors have done? They would, of course, have wept, even as Homer made them weep. But would they previously have cooked their supper, and cooked it, what's more, in a masterly fashion? Would they previously have drunk and eaten to satiety? And after weeping, or actually while weeping, would they have dropped quietly off to sleep? No, they most certainly would not have done any of these things.

They would simply have wept, lamenting their own misfortune and the horrible fate of their companions, and the canto would have ended tragically on their tears.

Homer, however, preferred to tell the Whole Truth. He knew that even the most cruelly bereaved must eat; that hunger is stronger than sorrow and that its satisfaction takes precedence even of tears. He knew that experts continue to act expertly and to find satisfaction in their accomplishment, even when friends have just been eaten, even when the accomplishment is only cooking the supper. He knew that, when the belly is full (and only when the belly is full) men can afford to grieve, and that sorrow after supper is almost a luxury. And finally he knew that, even as hunger takes precedence of grief, so fatigue, supervening, cuts short its career and drowns it in a sleep all the sweeter for bringing forgetfulness of bereavement. In a word, Homer refused to treat the theme tragically. He preferred to tell the Whole Truth.

Another author who preferred to tell the Whole Truth was Fielding. *Tom Jones* is one of the very few Odyssean books written in Europe between the time of Aeschylus and the present age; Odyssean, because never tragical; never—even when painful and disastrous, even when pathetic and beautiful things are happening. For they do happen; Fielding, like Homer, admits all the facts, shirks nothing. Indeed, it is precisely because these authors shirk nothing that their books are not tragical. For among the things they don't shirk are the irrelevancies which, in actual life, always temper the situations and characters that writers of tragedy insist on keeping chemically pure. Consider, for example, the case of Sophy Western, that most charming, most nearly perfect of young women. Fielding, it is obvious, adored her (she is said to have been created in the image of his first, much-loved wife). But in spite of his adoration, he refused to turn her into one of those chemically pure and, as it were, focused beings who do and suffer in the world of tragedy. That innkeeper who lifted the weary Sophia from her horse—what need had he to fall? In no tragedy would he (nay, *could* he) have collapsed beneath her weight. For, to begin with, in the tragical context weight is an irrelevance; heroines should be above the law of gravitation. But that is not all; let the reader now remember what were the results of his fall. Tumbling flat on his back, he pulled Sophia down on top of him—his belly was a cushion, so that happily she came to no bodily harm—pulled her down head first. But head first is necessarily legs last; there was a momentary display of the most ravishing charms; the bumpkins at the inn door grinned or guffawed; poor Sophia, when they picked her up, was blushing in an agony of embarrassment and wounded modesty. There is nothing intrinsically improbable about this incident, which is stamped, indeed, with all the marks of literary truth. But however true, it is an incident which could never,

never have happened to a heroine of tragedy. It would never have been allowed to happen. But Fielding refused to impose the tragedian's veto; he shirked nothing—neither the intrusion of irrelevant absurdities into the midst of romance or disaster, nor any of life's no less irrelevantly painful interruptions of the course of happiness. He did not want to be a tragedian. And, sure enough, that brief and pearly gleam of Sophia's charming posterior was sufficient to scare the Muse of Tragedy out of *Tom Jones* just as, more than five and twenty centuries before, the sight of stricken men first eating, then remembering to weep, then forgetting their tears in slumber had scared her out of the *Odyssey*.

In his *Principles of Literary Criticism* Mr. I. A. Richards affirms that good tragedy is proof against irony and irrelevance—that it can absorb anything into itself and still remain tragedy. Indeed, he seems to make of this capacity to absorb the untragical and the anti-tragical a touchstone of tragic merit. Thus tried, practically all Greek, all French, and most Elizabethan tragedies are found wanting. Only the best of Shakespeare can stand the test. So, at least, says Mr. Richards. Is he right? I have often had my doubts. The tragedies of Shakespeare are veined, it is true, with irony and an often terrifying cynicism; but the cynicism is always heroic idealism turned neatly inside out, the irony is a kind of photographic negative of heroic romance. Turn Troilus's white into black and all his blacks into white and you have Thersites. Reversed, Othello and Desdemona become Iago. White Ophelia's negative is the irony of Hamlet, is the ingenuous bawdry of her own mad songs; just as the cynicism of mad King Lear is the black shadow-replica of Cordelia. Now, the shadow, the photographic negative of a thing, is in no sense irrelevant to it. Shakespeare's ironies and cynicisms serve to deepen his tragic world, but not to widen it. If they had widened it, as the Homeric irrelevancies widened out the universe of the *Odyssey*—why, then, the world of Shakespearean tragedy would automatically have ceased to exist. For example, a scene showing the bereaved Macduff eating his supper, growing melancholy, over the whisky with thoughts of his murdered wife and children, and then, with lashes still wet, dropping off to sleep, would be true enough to life; but it would not be true to tragic art. The introduction of such a scene would change the whole quality of the play; treated in this Odyssean style, *Macbeth* would cease to be a tragedy. Or take the case of Desdemona. Iago's bestially cynical remarks about her character are in no sense, as we have seen, irrelevant to the tragedy. They present us with negative images of her real nature and of the feelings she has for Othello. These negative images are always *hers*, are always recognizably the property of the heroine-victim of a tragedy. Whereas, if, springing ashore at Cyprus, she had tumbled, as the no less exquisite Sophia was to tumble, and revealed the inadequacies of sixteenth-century underclothing, the play would no longer be the *Othello* we know. Iago might breed a family of little cynics and the existing dose of bitterness and savage negation be doubled and trebled; *Othello* would still remain fundamentally *Othello*. But a few Fieldingesque irrelevancies would destroy it—destroy it, that is to say, as a tragedy; for there would be nothing to prevent it from becoming a magnificent drama of some other kind. For the fact is that tragedy and what I have called the Whole Truth are not compatible; where one is, the other is not. There are certain things which even the best, even Shakespearean tragedy, cannot absorb into itself.

To make a tragedy the artist must isolate a single element out of the totality of human experience and use that exclusively as his material. Tragedy is something that is separated out from the Whole Truth, distilled from it, so to speak, as an essence is distilled from the living flower. Tragedy is chemically pure. Hence its power to act quickly and intensely on our feelings. All chemically pure art has this power to act upon us quickly and intensely. Thus, chemically pure pornography (on the rare occasions when it happens to be written convincingly, by some one who has the gift of "putting things across") is a quick-acting emotional drug of incomparably greater power than the Whole Truth about sensuality, or even (for many people) than the tangible and carnal reality itself. It is because of its chemical purity that tragedy so effectively performs its function of catharsis. It refines and corrects and gives a style to our emotional life, and does so swiftly, with power. Brought into contact with tragedy, the elements of our being fall, for the moment at any rate, into an ordered and beautiful pattern, as the iron filings arrange themselves under the influence of the magnet. Through all its individual variations, this pattern is always fundamentally of the same kind. From the reading or the hearing of a tragedy we rise with the feeling that

> Our friends are exultations, agonies,
> And love, and man's unconquerable mind;

with the heroic conviction that we too would be unconquerable if subjected to the agonies, that in the midst of the agonies we too should continue to love, might even learn to exult. It is because it does these things to us that tragedy is felt to be so valuable. What are the values of Wholly-Truthful art? What does it do to us that seems worth doing? Let us try to discover.

Wholly-Truthful art overflows the limits of tragedy and shows us, if only by hints and implications, what happened before the tragic story began, what will happen after it is over, what is happening simultaneously elsewhere (and "elsewhere" includes all those parts of the minds and bodies of the protagonists not immediately engaged in the tragic struggle). Tragedy is an arbitrarily isolated eddy on the surface of a vast river that flows on majestically, irresistibly, around, beneath, and to either side of it. Wholly-Truthful art contrives to imply the existence of the entire river as well as of the eddy. It is quite different from tragedy, even though it may contain, among other constituents, all the elements from which tragedy is made. (The "same thing" placed in different contexts, loses its identity and becomes, for the perceiving mind, a succession of different things.) In Wholly-Truthful art the agonies may be just as real, love and the unconquerable mind just as admirable, just as important, as in tragedy. Thus, Scylla's victims suffer as painfully as the monster-devoured Hippolytus in *Phèdre;* the mental anguish of Tom Jones when he thinks he has lost his Sophia, and lost her by his own fault, is hardly less than that of Othello after Desdemona's murder. (The fact that Fielding's power of "putting things across" is by no means equal to Shakespeare's is, of course, merely an accident.) But the agonies and indomitabilities are placed by the Wholly-Truthful writer in another, wider context, with the result that they cease to be the same as the intrinsically identical agonies and indomitabilities of tragedy. Consequently, Wholly-Truthful art produces in us an effect quite different from that produced by tragedy. Our mood when we have read a Wholly-Truthful book is never one of heroic exultation; it is one of resignation, of acceptance. (Acceptance can also be heroic.) Being chemically impure, Wholly-Truthful literature cannot move us as quickly and intensely as tragedy or any other kind of chemically pure art. But I believe that its effects are more lasting. The exultations that follow the reading or hearing of a tragedy are in the nature of temporary inebriations. Our being cannot long hold the pattern imposed by tragedy. Remove the magnet and the filings tend to fall back into confusion. But the pattern of acceptance and resignation imposed upon us by Wholly-Truthful literature, though perhaps less unexpectedly beautiful in design, is (for that very reason perhaps) more stable. The catharsis of tragedy is violent and apocalyptic; but the milder catharsis of Wholly-Truthful literature is lasting.

In recent times literature has become more and more acutely conscious of the Whole Truth—of the great oceans of irrelevant things, events, and thoughts stretching endlessly away in every direction from whatever island point (a character, a story) the author may choose to contemplate. To impose the kind of arbitrary limitations, which must be imposed by anyone who wants to write a tragedy, has become more and more difficult—is now indeed, for those who are at all sensitive to contemporaneity, almost impossible. This does not mean, of course, that the modern writer must confine himself to a merely naturalistic manner. One can imply the existence of the Whole Truth without laboriously cataloguing every object within sight. A book can be written in terms of pure fantasy and yet, by implication, tell the Whole Truth. Of all the important works of contemporary literature not one is a pure tragedy. There is no contemporary writer of significance who does not prefer to state or imply the Whole Truth. However different one from another in style, in ethical, philosophical, and artistic intention, in the scales of values accepted, contemporary writers have this in common, that they are interested in the Whole Truth. Proust, D. H. Lawrence, André Gide, Kafka, Hemingway—here are five obviously significant and important contemporary writers. Five authors as remarkably unlike one another as they could well be. They are at one only in this: that none of them has written a pure tragedy, that all are concerned with the Whole Truth.

I have sometimes wondered whether tragedy, as a form of art, may not be doomed. But the fact that we are still profoundly moved by the tragic masterpieces of the past—that we can be moved, against our better judgment, even by the bad tragedies of the contemporary stage and film— makes me think that the day of chemically pure art is not over. Tragedy happens to be passing through a period of eclipse, because all the significant writers of our age are too busy exploring the newly discovered, or rediscovered, world of the Whole Truth to be able to pay any attention to it. But there is no good reason to believe that this state of things will last forever. Tragedy is too valuable to be allowed to die. There is no reason, after all, why the two kinds of literature—the Chemically Impure and the Chemically Pure, the literature of the Whole Truth and the literature of Partial Truth—should not exist simultaneously, each in its separate sphere. The human spirit has need of both.

The Tragic Rhythm *

SUSANNE LANGER

As comedy presents the vital rhythm of self-preservation, tragedy exhibits that of self-consummation.

The lilting advance of the eternal life process, indefinitely maintained or temporarily lost and restored, is the great general vital pattern that we exemplify from day to day. But creatures that are destined, sooner or later, to die—that is, all individuals that do not pass alive into new generations, like jellyfish and algae—hold the balance of life only precariously, in the frame of a total movement that is quite different; the movement from birth to death. Unlike the simple metabolic process, the deathward advance of their individual lives has a series of stations that are not repeated; growth, maturity, decline. That is the tragic rhythm.

Tragedy is a cadential form. Its crisis is always the turn toward an absolute close. This form reflects the basic structure of personal life, and therewith of feeling when life is viewed as a whole. It is that attitude—"the tragic sense of life," as Unamuno called it—that is objectified and brought before our eyes in tragedy. But in drama it is not presented as Unamuno presents it, namely by an intellectual realization of impending death which we are constitutionally unable to accept and therefore counter with an irrational belief in our personal immortality, in "immortalizing" rites and supernatural grace.[1] Irrationalism is not insight, but despair, a direct recognition of instincts, needs, and therewithal of one's mental impotence. A "belief" that defies intellectual convictions is a frantically defended lie.

---

[1] See his *The Tragic Sense of Life, passim.* Unamuno's feelings are strong and natural; his aphorisms are often poetic and memorable. With his philosophical assertions, however, one cannot take issue, because he prides himself on being inconsistent, on the ground that "life is irrational," "truth is not logical," etc. Consistency of statements he regards as a mark of their falsity. Like some exasperating ladies, who claim "a woman's right to be inconsistent," he cannot, therefore, be worsted in argument, but—also like them—he cannot be taken seriously.

* Susanne Langer, "The Tragic Rhythm," from *Feeling and Form* (Charles Scribner's Sons, 1953), pp. 351–366.

That defense may constitute a great tragic theme, but it is not itself a poetic expression of "the tragic sense of life"; it is actual, pathetic expression, springing from an emotional conflict.

Tragedy dramatizes human life as potentiality and fulfillment. Its virtual future, or Destiny, is therefore quite different from that created in comedy. Comic Destiny is Fortune—what the world will bring, and the man will take or miss, encounter or escape; tragic Destiny is what the man brings, and the world will demand of him. That is his Fate.

What he brings is his potentiality: his mental, moral and even physical powers, his powers to act and suffer. Tragic action is the realization of all his possibilities, which he unfolds and exhausts in the course of the drama. His human nature is his Fate. Destiny conceived as Fate is, therefore, not capricious, like Fortune, but is predetermined. Outward events are merely the occasions for its realization.

"His human nature," however, does not refer to his *generally* human character; I do not mean to say that a tragic hero is to be regarded as primarily a symbol for mankind. What the poet creates is a personality; and the more individual and powerful that personality is, the more extraordinary and overwhelming will be the action. Since the protagonist is the chief agent, his relation to the action is obvious; and since the course of the action is the "fable" or "plot" of the play, it is also obvious that creating the characters is not something apart from building the plot, but is an integral portion of it. The agents are prime elements in the action; but the action is the play itself, and artistic elements are always for the sake of the whole. That was, I think, what prompted Aristotle to say: "Tragedy is essentially an imitation [2] not of persons but of action and life, of happiness and misery. All human happiness or misery takes the form of action; the end for which we live is a certain kind of activity, not a quality. Character gives us qualities, but it is in our actions—what we do—that we are happy or the reverse. In a play accordingly they do not act in order to portray the Characters; they include the Characters for the sake of the action. So that it is the action in it, i.e. its Fable or Plot, that is the end and purpose of the tragedy; and the end is everywhere the chief thing." [3] This "end" is the work as such. The protagonist and all characters that support him are introduced that we may see the fulfillment of his Fate, which is simply the complete realization of his individual "human nature."

The idea of personal Fate was mythically conceived long before the relation of life history to character was discursively understood. The mythi-

---

[2] "Imitation" is used by Aristotle in much the same sense in which I use "semblance." I have avoided his word because it stresses similitude to actuality rather than abstraction from actuality.

[3] *De Poetica*, chap. 6, II (1450a), translation by W. R. Roberts.

cal tradition of Greece treated the fate of its "heroes"—the personalities springing from certain great, highly individualized families—as a mysterious power inherent in the world rather than in the man and his ancestry; it was conceived as a private incubus bestowed on him at birth by a vengeful deity, or even through a curse pronounced by a human being. Sometimes no such specific cause of his peculiar destiny is given at all; but an oracle foretells what he is bound to do. It is interesting to note that this conception of Fate usually centers in the mysterious predictability of acts someone is to perform. The occasions of the acts are not foretold; the world will provide them.

For the development of tragedy, such determination of the overt acts without circumstances and motives furnished an ideal starting point, for it constrained the poets to invent characters whose actions would issue naturally in the required fateful deeds. The oracular prophecy, then, became an intensifying symbol of the necessity that was really given with the agent's personality; the "fable" being just one possible way the world might elicit his complete self-realization in endeavor and error and discovery, passion and punishment, to the limit of his powers. The prime example of this passage from the mythical idea of Fate to the dramatic creation of Fate as the protagonist's natural, personal destiny is, of course, the *Oedipus Tyrannus* of Sophocles. With that tremendous piece of self-assertion, self-divination and self-exhaustion, the "Great Tradition" of tragedy was born in Europe.

There is another mythical conception of Fate that is not a forerunner of tragedy, but possibly of some kinds of comedy: that is the idea of Fate as the will of supernatural powers, perhaps long decreed, perhaps spontaneous and arbitrary. It is the "Fate" of the true fatalist, who takes no great care of his life because he deems it entirely in the hand of Allah (or some other God), who will slay or spare at his pleasure no matter what one does. That is quite a different notion from the "oracular" Fate of Greek mythology; the will of a god who gives and takes away, casts down or raises up, for inscrutable reasons of his own, is Kismet, and that is really a myth of Fortune.[4] Kismet is what a person encounters, not what he is. Both conceptions often exist side by side. The Scotsman who has to "dree his weird" believes nonetheless that his fortunes from moment to moment are in the hands of Providence. Macbeth's Weird Sisters were perfectly acceptable to a Christian audience. Even in the ancient lore of our fairy tales, the Sleeping Beauty is destined to prick herself—that is, she has a personal destiny. In Greek

---

[4] Cf. N. N. Martinovitch, *The Turkish Theatre*, p. 36: "According to Islamic speculation, man has almost no influence on the development of his own fate. Allah is sovereign, doing as he likes and accounting to no one. And the screen of the haial [the comic shadow theater] is the dramatization of this speculative concept of the world."

tradition, on the other hand, where the notion of "oracular Fate" was so generally entertained that the Oracle was a public institution, Fate as the momentary decree of a ruling Power is represented in the myth of the Norns, who spin the threads of human lives and cut them where they list; the Three Fates are as despotic and capricious as Allah, and what they spin is, really, Kismet.

Tragedy can arise and flourish only where people are aware of individual life as an end in itself, and as a measure of other things. In tribal cultures where the individual is still so closely linked with his family that not only society but even he himself regards his existence as a communal value, which may be sacrificed at any time for communal ends, the development of personality is not a consciously appreciated life pattern. Similarly, where men believe that Karma, or the tally of their deeds, may be held over for recompense or expiation in another earthly life, their current incarnation cannot be seen as a self-sufficient whole in which their entire potentialities are to be realized. Therefore genuine tragedy—drama exhibiting "the tragic rhythm of action," as Professor Fergusson has called it [5]—is a specialized form of art, with problems and devices of its own.

The word "rhythm," which I have used freely with respect to drama, may seem a question-begging word, borrowed from the realm of physiology —where indeed the basic vital functions are generally rhythmic—and carried over somewhat glibly to the realm of conscious acts, which, for the most part—and certainly the most interesting part—are not repetitive. But it is precisely the *rhythm* of dramatic action that makes drama "a poetry of the theater," and not an imitation (in the usual, not the Aristotelian sense) or make-believe of practical life. As Hebbel said, "In the hand of the poet, Becoming must always be a passage from *form* to *form* [von *Gestalt* zu *Gestalt*], it must never appear, like amorphous clay, chaotic and confused in our sight, but must seem somehow like a perfected thing." [6] The analysis and definition of rhythmic structure, given in Chapter 8 with reference to musical forms,[7] may be applied without distortion or strain to the organization of elements in any play that achieves "living" form.

A dramatic act is a commitment. It creates a situation in which the agent or agents must necessarily make a further move; that is, it motivates a subsequent act (or acts). The situation, which is the completion of a given act, is already the impetus to another—as, in running, the footfall that catches our weight at the end of one bound already sends us forward to land on the other foot. The bounds need not be alike, but proportional,

---

[5] In *The Idea of a Theater*, especially p. 18.
[6] Friedrich Hebbel, *Tagebücher*, collected in Bernhard Münz's *Hebbel als Denker* (1913). See p. 182.
[7] See pp. 126–129 [of *Feeling and Form*].

which means that the impetus of any specially great leap must have been prepared and gathered somewhere, and any sudden diminution be balanced by some motion that carries off the driving force. Dramatic acts are analogously connected with each other so that each one directly or indirectly motivates what follows it.[8] In this way a genuine rhythm of action is set up, which is not simple like that of a physical repetitive process (e.g. running, breathing), but more often intricate, even deceptive, and, of course, not given primarily to one particular sense, but to the imagination through whatever sense we employ to perceive and evaluate action; the same general rhythm of action appears in a play whether we read it or hear it read, enact it ourselves or see it performed. That rhythm is the "commanding form" of the play; it springs from the poet's original conception of the "fable," and dictates the major divisions of the work, the light or heavy style of its presentation, the intensity of the highest feeling and most violent act, the great or small number of characters, and the degrees of their development. The total action is a cumulative form; and because it is constructed by a rhythmic treatment of its elements, it appears to *grow* from its beginnings. That is the playwright's creation of "organic form."

The tragic rhythm, which is the pattern of a life that grows, flourishes, and declines, is abstracted by being transferred from that natural activity to the sphere of a characteristically human action, where it is exemplified in mental and emotional growth, maturation, and the final relinquishment of power. In that relinquishment lies the hero's true "heroism"—the vision of life as accomplished, that is, life in its entirety, the sense of fulfillment that lifts him above his defeat.

A remarkable expression of this idea of tragedy may be found in the same book from which I borrowed, a few paragraphs above, the phrase, "the tragic rhythm of action." Speaking of Hamlet, Professor Fergusson observes: "In Act V . . . he feels that his role, all but the very last episode, has been played. . . . He is content, now, to let the fated end come as it will. . . . One could say that he feels the poetic rightness of his own death. . . .

"However one may interpret it, when his death comes it 'feels right,' the only possible end for the play. . . . We are certainly intended to feel that Hamlet, however darkly and uncertainly he worked, had discerned the way to be obedient to his deepest values, and accomplished some sort of purgatorial progress for himself and Denmark." [9]

---

[8] An act may be said to motivate further acts indirectly if it does so through a total situation it helps to create; the small acts of psychological import that merely create personality are of this sort.

[9] *Op. cit.*, pp. 132–133. "To be obedient to his deepest values" is nothing else than to realize his own potentialities, fulfill his true destiny.

"The second scene of Act V," the critique continues, "with the duel between Hamlet and Laertes, shows the denouements of all the intrigues in the play. . . . But these events, which literally end the narratives in the play, and bring Claudius' regime to its temporal end, tell us nothing new but the fact: that the sentence, which fate or providence pronounced long since, has now been executed. It is the pageantry, the ceremonial mummery, in short the virtual character of this last scene which makes us feel it as the final epiphany. . . ." [10]

Tragic drama is so designed that the protagonist grows mentally, emotionally, or morally, by the demand of the action, which he himself initiated, to the complete exhaustion of his powers, the limit of his possible development. He spends himself in the course of the one dramatic action. This is, of course, a tremendous foreshortening of life; instead of undergoing the physical and psychical, many-sided, long process of an actual biography, the tragic hero lives and matures in some particular respect; his entire being is concentrated in one aim, one passion, one conflict and ultimate defeat. For this reason the prime agent of tragedy is heroic; his character, the unfolding situation, the scene, even though ostensibly familiar and humble, are all exaggerated, charged with more feeling than comparable actualities would possess.[11] This intensification is necessary to achieve and sustain the "form in suspense" that is even more important in tragic drama than in comic, because the comic denouement, not marking an absolute close, needs only to restore a balance, but the tragic ending must recapitulate the whole action to be a visible fulfillment of a destiny that was implicit in the beginning. This device, which may be called "dramatic exaggeration," is reminiscent of "epic exaggeration," and may have been adopted quite unconsciously with the epic themes of ancient tragedy. But that does not mean that it is an accidental factor, a purely historical legacy from an older poetic tradition; inherited conventions do not maintain themselves long in any art unless they serve its own purposes. They may have their old *raison d'être* in new art forms, or take on entirely new functions, but as sheer trappings—traditional requirements—they would be discarded by the first genius who found no use for them.

Drama is not psychology, nor (though the critical literature tends to make it seem so) is it moral philosophy. It offers no discourse on the hero's or heroine's native endowments, to let us estimate at any stage in the action

---

[10] *Op. cit.*, p. 138.

[11] As Robert Edmond Jones has put it: "Great drama does not deal with cautious people. Its heroes are tyrants, outcasts, wanderers. From Prometheus, the first of them all, the thief who stole the divine fire from heaven, these protagonists are all passionate, excessive, violent, terrible. 'Doom eager,' the Icelandic saga calls them." *The Dramatic Imagination*, p. 42.

how near they must be to exhaustion. The action itself must reveal the limit of the protagonist's powers and mark the end of his self-realization. And so, indeed, it does: the turning point of the play is the situation he cannot resolve, where he makes his "tragic error" or exhibits his "tragic weakness." He is led by his own action and its repercussions in the world to respond with more and more competence, more and more daring to a constantly gathering challenge; so his character "grows," i.e. he unfolds his will and knowledge and passion, as the situation grows. His career is not change of personality, but maturation. When he reaches his limit of mental and emotional development, the crisis occurs; then comes the defeat, either by death or, as in many modern tragedies, by hopelessness that is the equivalent of death, a "death of the soul," that ends the career.

It has been reiterated so often that the hero of tragedy is a strong man with one weakness, a good man with one fault, that a whole ethics of tragedy has grown up around the significance of that single flaw. Chapters upon chapters—even books—have been written on the required mixture of good and evil in his character, to make him command pity and yet make his downfall not repugnant to "our moral sense." Critics and philosophers, from Aristotle to Croce, have written about the spectator's acceptance of the hero's fate as a recognition of the moral order he has defied or ignored, the triumph of justice the hero himself is supposed to accept in his final "conciliation" or "epiphany." The restoration of the great moral order through suffering is looked upon as the Fate he has to fulfill. He must be imperfect to break the moral law, but fundamentally good, i.e. striving for perfection, in order to achieve his moral salvation in sacrifice, renunciation, death.

All this concern with the philosophical and ethical significance of the hero's sufferings, however, leads away from the *artistic* significance of the play, to discursive ideas about life, character, and the world. At once we are faced with the usual dilemma of the critic who sees art as a representation of actual life, and an art form as a *Weltanschauung:* not every work of the genre can really be said to express the *Weltanschauung* that is supposed to characterize it, nor to give us the same general picture of the world, such as the "moral order" in which justice is inevitably done or the amoral "cosmic order" in which man is a plaything of forces beyond his control. Then the critic may come to the despairing conclusion that the genre cannot be defined, but is really just a name that changes its essential meaning from age to age. No less an authority than Ashley Thorndike decided that tragedy is really indefinable; one can trace the historical evolution of each conception, but not the defining attribute that runs through them all and brings them justly under one name. The only features that he found common to all tragedies were representation of "painful and destructive actions," and "criticism of life." [12] Either of these could, of course, occur in other art forms, too. A. C. Bradley, in his excellent *Shakespearean Tragedy*, points out that Shakespeare did not, like the Greek tragedians, postulate a superhuman power determining men's actions and accidents, nor a special Nemesis, invoked by past crimes, belonging to certain families or persons; he claims, in fact, to find no representation of Fate in Shakespeare.[13] Even justice, he holds, is not illustrated there, because the disasters men bring upon themselves are not proportioned to their sins; but something one might call a "moral order," an order not of right and wrong, but at least of good and evil. Accident plays its part, but in the main the agents ride for the fall they take.[14] Edgar Stoll, exactly to the contrary, maintains that the action in Shakespeare's tragedies "does not at bottom develop out of character." [15] One could go on almost indefinitely in citing examples of contradiction or exception to the various standards of tragic action, especially the fatalistic standard.

The fallacy which leads to this crisscross of interpretations and opinions is the familiar one of confusing what the poet creates with what he represents. It is the fallacy of looking, not for the artistic function of everything he represents and the way he represents it, but for something that his representations are supposed to illustrate or suggest—something that belongs to life, not the play. If, then, tragedy is called an image of Fate, it is expected to illustrate the workings of Fate. But that is not necessary; it may just as well illustrate the workings of villainy, neurosis, faith, social justice, or anything else the poet finds usable to motivate a large, integral action. The myth of Fate often used in Greek tragedies was an obvious motif, as in later plays romantic love defying circumstance, or the vast consequences of a transgression. But one should not expect a major art form to be bound to a single motif, no matter in how many variations or

---

[12] "Any precise and exact definition is sure to lack in comprehensiveness and veracity . . . We seem forced to reject the possibility of any exact limitation for the dramatic species, to include as tragedies all plays presenting painful or destructive actions, to accept the leading elements of a literary tradition derived from the Greeks as indicating the common bonds between such plays in the past, but to admit that this tradition, while still powerful, is variable, uncertain, and unauthoritative." (*Tragedy*, p. 12.) At the end of the book he sets up, as the only common standard, "an unselfish, a social, a moral inquiry into life." (p. 376.)

[13] In a footnote on p. 30 he writes: "I have raised no objection to the use of the idea of fate, because it occurs so often both in conversation and in books about Shakespeare's tragedies that I must suppose it to be natural to many readers. Yet I doubt whether it would be so if Greek tragedy had never been written; and I must in candour confess that to me it does not often occur while I am reading, or when I have just read, a tragedy of Shakespeare."

[14] The discussion of justice (Lecture I, "The Substance of Tragedy," p. 5) is noteworthy especially for his recognition of the *irrelevance of the concept* to dramatic art.

[15] *Shakespeare and Other Masters*, p. 31.

even disguises; to reduce the many themes that may be found in tragedy, from Aeschylus to O'Neill, all to "the workings of Fate," and the many *Weltanschauungen* that may be read out of (or into) it to so many recognitions of a supernatural order, a moral order, or a pure causal order, leads only to endless sleuthing after deeper meanings, symbolic substitutions, and far-reaching implications that no playgoer could possible infer, so they would be useless in the theater.

Fate in tragedy is the created form, the virtual future as an accomplished whole. It is not the expression of a belief at all. Macbeth's fate is the structure of his tragedy, not an instance of how things happen in the world. That virtual future has the form of a completely individualized, and therefore mortal, life—a measured life, to be exhausted in a small span of time. But growth, efflorescence, and exhaustion—the prototype of Fate—is not what the play is about; it is only what the movement of the action is like. The play is about somebody's desires, acts, conflict, and defeat; however his acts are motivated, however his deeds undo him, the total action is his dramatic fate. Tragic action has the rhythm of natural life and death, but it does not refer to or illustrate them; it abstracts their dynamic form, and imprints it on entirely different matters, in a different time span—the whole self-realization may take place in days or hours instead of the decades of biological consummation—so the "tragic rhythm" stands clear of any natural occasion, and becomes a perceptible form.

The kind of art theory that measures the value of drama by the way it represents life, or by the poet's implied beliefs about life, not only leads criticism away from poetry into philosophy, religion, or social science, but also causes people to think of the protagonist as an ordinary fellow man whom they are to approve or condemn and, in either case, pity. This attitude, which is undoubtedly derived—whether rightly or mistakenly—from Aristotle, has given rise to the many moral demands on the hero's character: he must be admirable but not perfect, must command the spectators' sympathy even if he incurs their censure; they must feel his fate as their own, etc.[16]

In truth, I believe, the hero of tragedy must *interest* us all the time, but not as a person of our own acquaintance. His tragic error, crime, or other flaw is not introduced for moral reasons, but for structural purposes: it marks his limit of power. His potentialities appear on stage only as successful acts; as soon as his avowed or otherwise obvious intentions fail, or his

---

[16] Thorndike regarded tragedy as the highest art form, because, as he put it, "it brings home to us the images of our own sorrows, and chastens the spirit through the outpouring of our sympathies, even our horror and despair, for the misfortune of our fellows." (*Op. cit.*, p. 19.) Shortly before, he conceded that it might also give us—among other pleasures —"aesthetic delight in a masterpiece." (p. 17.)

acts recoil on him and bring him pain, his power has reached its height, he is at the end of his career. In this, of course, drama is utterly different from life. The moral failure in drama is not a normal incident, something to be lived down, presumably neither the doer's first transgression nor his last; the act that constitutes the protagonist's tragic error or guilt is the high-water mark of his life, and now the tide recedes. His "imperfection" is an artistic element: that is why a single flaw will do.

All persistent practices in art have a creative function. They may serve several ends, but the chief one is the shaping of the work. This holds not only for character traits which make a dramatic personage credible or sympathetic, but also for another much-discussed device in drama—so-called "comic relief," the introduction of trivial or humorous interludes in midst of serious, ominous, tragic action. The term "comic relief" indicates the supposed purpose of that practice: to give the audience a respite from too much emotional tension, let them have entertainment as well as "pity and fear." Here again traditional criticism rests too confidently, I think, on Aristotle's observations, which—after all—were not the insights of a playwright, but the reflections of a scientifically inclined man interested in psychology. Aristotle considered the comic interlude as a concession to human weakness; and "comic relief" has been its name ever since.

The humorous interludes in tragedy are merely moments when the comic spirit rises to the point of hilarity. Such moments may result from all sorts of poetic exigencies; the famous drunken porter in *Macbeth* makes a macabre contrast to the situation behind the door he beats upon, and is obviously introduced to heighten rather than relieve the tense secrecy of the murder.

But the most important fact about these famous touches of "comic relief" is that they always occur in plays which have a vein of comedy throughout, kept for the most part below the level of laughter. This vein may be tapped for special effects, even for a whole scene, to slow and subdue the action or to heighten it with grotesque reflection. In those heroic tragedies that are lowered by the incursion of farce, and not structurally affected by its omission, there is no integral, implicit comedy—no everyday life—in the "world" of the play, to which the clowning naturally belongs and from which it may be derived without disorganization of the whole.[17] In *Macbeth* (and, indeed, all Shakespearean plays) there is a large, social, everyday life of soldiers, grooms, gossips, courtiers and commoners, that provides an essentially comic substructure for the heroic action. Most of the time

---

[17] Thorndike points out that *Tamburlaine* is of this genre: "Originally," he says, "the play contained comic scenes, omitted in the published form and evidently of no value in structure or conception." (*Op. cit.*, p. 90.)
See also J. B. Moore, *The Comic and the Realistic in English Drama.*

this lower stratum is subdued, giving an impression of realism without any obvious byplay; but this realism carries the fundamental comic rhythm from which grotesque interludes may arise with perfect dramatic logic.

The fact that the two great rhythms, comic and tragic, are radically distinct does not mean that they are each other's opposites, or even incompatible forms. Tragedy can rest squarely on a comic substructure, and yet be pure tragedy.[18] This is natural enough, for life—from which all felt rhythms spring—contains both, in every mortal organism. Society is continuous though its members, even the strongest and fairest, live out their lives and die; and even while each individual fulfills the tragic pattern it participates also in the comic continuity.[19] The poet's task is, of course, not to copy life, but to organize and articulate a symbol for the "sense of life"; and in the symbol one rhythm always governs the dynamic form, though another may go through the whole piece in a contrapuntal fashion. The master of this practice is Shakespeare.

Did the stark individual Fate of the purest Greek tragedy rule out, by its intense deathward movement, the comic feeling of the eternally full and undulating stream of life? Or was the richness that the comic-tragic counterpoint creates in other poetic traditions supplied to Aeschylus and Sophocles by the choric dance which framed and embellished the play? The satyr play at the end of the long, tragic presentation may well have been necessary, to assure its truth to the structure of subjective reality by an exuberant celebration of life.

There is yet another factor in drama that is commonly, and I think mistakenly, treated as a concession to popular taste: the use of spectacle, pageantry, brilliant show. Many critics apparently believe that a playwright makes provision for spectacular effects quite apart from his own poetic judgment and intent, simply to lure the audience into the theater. Thorndike, in fact, asserts that the use of spectacle bespeaks "the double purpose, hardly separable from the drama and particularly manifest in the Elizabethan dramatists, the two desires, to please their audiences and to create literature." [20] Brander Matthews said bluntly that not only theater, but all art whatever is "show business," whatever it may be besides.[21]

---

[18] A striking example is J. M. Barrie's little tragedy dating from the first World War, *The Old Lady Shows her Medals*. Despite the consistently comic treatment one expects the inevitable (and wordless) last scene.

[19] There is also a genre known as "tragicomedy" (the Germans call it *Schauspiel*, distinguishing it from both *Lustspiel* and *Trauerspiel*), which is a comic pattern playing with the tragic; its plot-structure is *averted tragedy*, temporizing with the sense of fate, which usually inspires a tragic diction, little or no exuberance (humor), and often falls into melodrama. A study of its few artistic successes, and their precise relations to pure comedy and pure tragedy, might raise interesting problems.

[20] *Op. cit.*, p. 98.

[21] *A Book About the Theater*, pp. 8–9. Cf. *supra*, p. 320.

Art, and especially dramatic art, is full of compromises, for one possible effect is usually bought at the expense of another; not all ideas and devices that occur to the poet are co-possible. Every decision involves a rejection. And furthermore, the stage, the available funds, the capabilities of the actors, may all have to be considered. But no artist can make concessions to what he considers bad taste without ruining his work. He simply cannot think as an artist and accept inexpressive forms or admit an element that has no organic function in the whole. If, therefore, he wishes to present spectacular scenes, he must start with an idea that demands spectacular presentation.

Every play has its intended audience, and in that audience there is one pre-eminent member: the author. If the play is intended for, say, an Elizabethan audience, that honorary member will be an Elizabethan theater-goer, sharing the best Elizabethan taste, and sometimes setting its fashion. Our dramatic critics write as though the poets of the past were all present-day people making concessions to interests that have long spent themselves. But the poets who provided stage spectacles had spectacular ideas, and worked with them until their expressive possibilities were exhausted.

The element of pure show has an important function in dramatic art, for it tends to raise feeling, whatever the feeling is. It does this even in actual life: a splendid hall, an ornate table arrangement, a company in full dress, make a feast seem bigger and the gathering more illustrious than a plain table in a cafeteria, refectory, or gymnasium, with the guests in street dress. A splendid funeral, passing in procession behind chanting priests, is more solemn than a drab one, though perhaps no one at the spectacular service feels more sad than at the colorless one. In the theater, the element of show is a means of heightening the atmosphere, whether of gaiety or terror or woe; so it is, first of all, a ready auxiliary.

But in tragedy it has a more specialized and essential function, too. Tragedy, which expresses the consciousness of life and death, must make life seem worth while, rich, beautiful, to make death awesome. The splendid exaggerations of the stage serve tragic feeling by heightening the lure of the world. The beautiful world, as well as the emotional tone of the action, is magnified by the element of spectacle—by lighting and color, setting and grouping, music, dance, "excursions and alarums." Some playwrights avail themselves freely of this help; others dispense with it almost entirely (never quite; the theater is spectacular at any time), because they have other poetic means of giving virtual life the glory that death takes away, or despair—the "death of the soul"—corrupts.

Spectacle is a powerful ingredient in several arts. Consider what playing fountains can do for a courtyard or a square, and how a ceremonial procession brings the interior of a cathedral to visible life! Architectural design may be marvelously altered by a supplement of fortuitous spectacle. The Galata bridge over the Golden Horn in the middle of Istanbul, with thousands of people and vehicles passing over it, coming from steep hillsides on either hand, looks as though it were hung from the mosque-crowned heights above; without the pageantry of its teeming cosmopolitan traffic it shrinks to a flat thoroughfare across the river, between its actual bridgeheads. An esplanade without the movement of water below it would be utterly unimpressive; flooded with moonlight, which picks out the surface movement of the water, or standing immovable against a towering surf, it may become veritably an architect's dream.

But pure show, not assimilated to any art, does not constitute a "work." Acrobatics, tennis playing, some beautiful occupational rhythms such as hauling nets, swinging hammers, or the evolutions of boats in a race, are fascinating, aesthetically thrilling, so they hold the spectator in a joyful trance; but they are not art. For a work of art, this trance is only one requisite. Spectacle, however beautiful, is always an *element* in art. It may well be a major element, as it was in Noverre's ballets, and in the court masques, but even these largely spectacular products are rated as "works" because they had something else that motivated the display: an imaginative core, a "commanding form." A circus could be a work of art if it had some central feeling and some primary, unfailing illusion. As it is, the circus sometimes contains genuine little "works"—a riding act that is really an equestrian dance, a piece of clowning that rises to genuine comedy. But on the whole the circus is a "show," not a work of art, though it is a work of skill, planning and fitting, and sometimes copes with problems that arise also in the arts. What it lacks is the first requisite for art—a conception of feeling, something to express.

Because a dramatic work has such a core, everything in it is poesis. It is, therefore, neither a hybrid product pieced together at the demand of many interests, nor a synthesis of all the arts—not even of a more modest "several." It may have use for paint and plaster, wood and brick, but not for painting, sculpture, or architecture; it has use for music, but not for even a fragment of a concert program; it may require dancing, but such dancing is not self-contained—it intensifies a scene, often abstracts a quintessence of its feeling, the image of sheer powers arising as a secondary illusion in the midst of the virtual history.

Drama is a great form, which not only invites expression of elemental human feeling, but also permits a degree of articulation, complexity, detail within detail, in short: organic development, that smaller poetic forms cannot exhibit without confusion. To say that such works express "a concept of feeling" is misleading unless one bears in mind that it is the whole life of feeling—call it "felt life," "subjectivity," "direct experience," or what you will—which finds its articulate expression in art, and, I believe, only in art. So great and fully elaborated a form as (say) a Shakespearean tragedy may formulate the characteristic mode of perception and response, sensibility and emotion and their sympathetic overtones, that constitutes a whole personality. Here we see the process of art expression "writ large," as Plato would say; for the smallest work does the same thing as the greatest, on its own scale: it reveals the patterns of possible sentience, vitality, and mentality, objectifying our subjective being—the most intimate "Reality" that we know. This function, and not the recording of contemporary scenes, politics, or even moral attitudes, is what relates art to life; and the big unfolding of feeling in the organic, personal pattern of a human life, rising, growing, accomplishing destiny and meeting doom—that is tragedy.

The Mythos of Autumn: Tragedy*

NORTHROP FRYE

Thanks as usual to Aristotle, the theory of tragedy is in considerably better shape than the other three *mythoi*, and we can deal with it more briefly, as the ground is more familiar. Without tragedy, all literary fictions might be plausibly explained as expressions of emotional attachments, whether of wish-fulfilment or of repugnance: the tragic fiction guarantees, so to speak, a disinterested quality in literary experience. It is largely through the tragedies of Greek culture that the sense of the authentic natural basis of human character comes into literature. In romance the characters are still largely dream-characters; in satire they tend to be caricatures; in comedy their actions are twisted to fit the demands of a happy ending. In full tragedy the main characters are emancipated from dream, an emancipation which is at the same time a restriction, because the order of nature is present. However thickly strewn a tragedy may be with ghosts, portents, witches, or oracles, we know that the tragic hero cannot simply rub a lamp and summon a genie to get him out of his trouble.

Like comedy, tragedy is best and most easily studied in drama, but it is not confined to drama, nor to actions that end in disaster. Plays that are usually called or classified with tragedies end in serenity, like *Cymbeline*, or even joy, like *Alcestis* or Racine's *Esther*, or in an ambiguous mood that is hard to define, like *Philoctetes*. On the other hand, while a predominantly sombre mood forms part of the unity of the tragic structure, concentrating on mood does not intensify the tragic effect: if it did, *Titus Andronicus* might well be the most powerful of Shakespeare's tragedies. The source of

* Northrop Frye, "The Mythos of Autumn: Tragedy," from *The Anatomy of Criticism* (Princeton University Press, 1957), pp. 206–223.

99

tragic effect must be sought, as Aristotle pointed out, in the tragic *mythos* or plot-structure.

It is a commonplace of criticism that comedy tends to deal with characters in a social group, whereas tragedy is more concentrated on a single individual. We have given reasons in the first essay for thinking that the typical tragic hero is somewhere between the divine and the "all too human." This must be true even of dying gods: Prometheus, being a god, cannot die, but he suffers for his sympathy with the "dying ones" (*brotoi*) or "mortal" men, and even suffering has something subdivine about it. The tragic hero is very great as compared with us, but there is something else, something on the side of him opposite the audience, compared to which he is small. This something else may be called God, gods, fate, accident, fortune, necessity, circumstance, or any combination of these, but whatever it is the tragic hero is our mediator with it.

The tragic hero is typically on top of the wheel of fortune, halfway between human society on the ground and the something greater in the sky. Prometheus, Adam, and Christ hang between heaven and earth, between a world of paradisal freedom and a world of bondage. Tragic heroes are so much the highest points in their human landscape that they seem the inevitable conductors of the power about them, great trees more likely to be struck by lightning than a clump of grass. Conductors may of course be instruments as well as victims of the divine lightning: Milton's Samson destroys the Philistine temple with himself, and Hamlet nearly exterminates the Danish court in his own fall. Something of Nietzsche's mountain-top air of transvaluation clings to the tragic hero: his thoughts are not ours any more than his deeds, even if, like Faustus, he is dragged off to hell for having them. Whatever eloquence or affability he may have, an inscrutable reserve lies behind it. Even sinister heroes—Tamburlaine, Macbeth, Creon—retain this reserve, and we are reminded that men will die loyally for a wicked or cruel man, but not for an amiable backslapper. Those who attract most devotion from others are those who are best able to suggest in their manner that they have no need of it, and from the urbanity of Hamlet to the sullen ferocity of Ajax, tragic heroes are wrapped in the mystery of their communion with that something beyond which we can see only through them, and which is the source of their strength and their fate alike. In the phrase which so fascinated Yeats, the tragic hero leaves his servants to do his "living" for him, and the center of tragedy is in the hero's isolation, not in a villain's betrayal, even when the villain is, as he often is, a part of the hero himself.

As for the something beyond, its names are variable but the form in which it manifests itself is fairly constant. Whether the context is Greek, Christian, or undefined, tragedy seems to lead up to an epiphany of law, of that which is and must be. It can hardly be an accident that the two great developments of tragic drama, in fifth-century Athens and in seventeenth-century Europe, were contemporary with the rise of Ionian and of Renaissance science. In such a world-view nature is seen as an impersonal process which human law imitates as best it can, and this direct relation of man and natural law is in the foreground. The sense in Greek tragedy that fate is stronger than the gods really implies that the gods exist primarily to ratify the order of nature, and that if any personality, even a divine one, possesses a genuine power of veto over law, it is most unlikely that he will want to exercise it. In Christianity much the same is true of the personality of Christ in relation to the inscrutable decrees of the Father. Similarly the tragic process in Shakespeare is natural in the sense that it simply happens, whatever its cause, explanation, or relationships. Characters may grope about for conceptions of gods that kill us for their sport, or for a divinity that shapes our ends, but the action of tragedy will not abide our questions, a fact often transferred to the personality of Shakespeare.

In its most elementary form, the vision of law (*dike*) operates as *lex talionis* or revenge. The hero provokes enmity, or inherits a situation of enmity, and the return of the avenger constitutes the catastrophe. The revenge-tragedy is a simple tragic structure, and like most simple structures can be a very powerful one, often retained as a central theme even in the most complex tragedies. Here the original act provoking the revenge sets up an antithetical or counterbalancing movement, and the completion of the movement resolves the tragedy. This happens so often that we may almost characterize the total *mythos* of tragedy as binary, in contrast to the three part saturnalia movement of comedy.

We notice however the frequency of the device of making the revenge come from another world, through gods or ghosts or oracles. This device expands the conceptions of both nature and law beyond the limits of the obvious and tangible. It does not thereby transcend those conceptions, as it is still natural law that is manifested by the tragic action. Here we see the tragic hero as disturbing a balance in nature, nature being conceived as an order stretching over the two kingdoms of the visible and the invisible, a balance which sooner or later *must* right itself. The righting of the balance is what the Greeks called *nemesis*: again, the agent or instrument of *nemesis* may be human vengeance, ghostly vengeance, divine vengeance, divine justice, accident, fate or the logic of events, but the essential thing is that *nemesis* happens, and happens impersonally, unaffected, as *Oedipus Tyrannus* illustrates, by the moral quality of human motivation involved. In the *Oresteia* we are led from a series of revenge-movements into a final vision of natural law, a universal compact in which moral law is included and which the gods, in the person of the goddess of wisdom, endorse. Here *nemesis*

like its counterpart the Mosaic law in Christianity, is not abolished but fulfilled: it is developed from a mechanical or arbitrary sense of restored
order, represented by the Furies, to the rational sense of it expounded by
Athene. The appearance of Athene does not turn the *Oresteia* into a comedy,
but clarifies its tragic vision.

There are two reductive formulas which have often been used to explain
tragedy. Neither is quite good enough, but each is almost good enough,
and as they are contradictory, they must represent extreme or limiting views
of tragedy. One of these is the theory that all tragedy exhibits the omnipotence of an external fate. And, of course, the overwhelming majority of
tragedies do leave us with a sense of the supremacy of impersonal power
and of the limitation of human effort. But the fatalistic reduction of tragedy
confuses the tragic condition with the tragic process: fate, in a tragedy,
normally becomes external to the hero only *after* the tragic process has been
set going. The Greek *ananke* or *moira* is in its normal, or pre-tragic, form
the internal balancing condition of life. It appears as external or antithetical
necessity only after it has been violated as a condition of life, just as justice
is the internal condition of an honest man, but the external antagonist of the
criminal. Homer uses a profoundly significant phrase for the theory of
tragedy when he has Zeus speak of Aegisthus as going *hyper moron, beyond*
fate.

The fatalistic reduction of tragedy does not distinguish tragedy from
irony, and it is again significant that we speak of the irony of fate rather
than of its tragedy. Irony does not need an exceptional central figure: as a
rule, the dingier the hero the sharper the irony, when irony alone is aimed
at. It is the admixture of heroism that gives tragedy its characteristic
splendor and exhilaration. The tragic hero has normally had an extraordinary, often a nearly divine, destiny almost within his grasp, and the
glory of that original vision never quite fades out of tragedy. The rhetoric
of tragedy requires the noblest diction that the greatest poets can produce,
and while catastrophe is the normal end of tragedy, this is balanced by an
equally significant original greatness, a paradise lost.

The other reductive theory of tragedy is that the act which sets the tragic
process going must be primarily a violation of *moral* law, whether human or
divine; in short, that Aristotle's hamartia or "flaw" must have an essential
connection with sin or wrongdoing. Again it is true that the great majority
of tragic heroes do possess hybris, a proud, passionate, obsessed or soaring
mind which brings about a morally intelligible downfall. Such hybris is the
normal precipitating agent of catastrophe, just as in comedy the cause of
the happy ending is usually some act of humility, represented by a slave or
by a heroine meanly disguised. In Aristotle the hamartia of the tragic hero
is associated with Aristotle's ethical conception of *proairesis*, or free choice

of an end, and Aristotle certainly does tend to think of tragedy as morally, almost physically, intelligible. It has already been suggested, however, that the conception of catharsis, which is central to Aristotle's view of tragedy, is inconsistent with moral reductions of it. Pity and terror are moral feelings, and they are relevant but not attached to the tragic situation. Shakespeare is particularly fond of planting moral lightning-rods on both sides of his heroes to deflect the pity and terror: we have mentioned Othello flanked by Iago and Desdemona, but Hamlet is flanked by Claudius and Ophelia, Lear by his daughters, and even Macbeth by Lady Macbeth and Duncan. In all these tragedies there is a sense of some far-reaching mystery of which this morally intelligible process is only a part. The hero's act has thrown a switch in a larger machine than his own life, or even his own society.

All theories of tragedy as morally explicable sooner or later run into the question: is an innocent sufferer in tragedy (i.e., poetically innocent), Iphigeneia, Cordelia, Socrates in Plato's *Apology*, Christ in the Passion, not a tragic figure? It is not very convincing to try to provide crucial moral flaws for such characters. Cordelia shows a high spirit, perhaps a touch of wilfulness, in refusing to flatter her father, and Cordelia gets hanged. Joan of Arc in Schiller has a moment of tenderness for an English soldier, and Joan is burned alive, or would have been if Schiller had not decided to sacrifice the facts to save the face of his moral theory. Here we are getting away from tragedy, and close to a kind of insane cautionary tale, like Mrs. Pipchin's little boy who was gored to death by a bull for asking inconvenient questions. Tragedy, in short, seems to elude the antithesis of moral responsibility and arbitrary fate, just as it eludes the antithesis of good and evil.

In the third book of *Paradise Lost*, Milton represents God as arguing that he made man "Sufficient to have stood, though free to fall." God knew that Adam would fall, but did not compel him to do so, and on that basis he disclaims legal responsibility. This argument is so bad that Milton, if he was trying to escape refutation, did well to ascribe it to God. Thought and act cannot be so separated: if God had foreknowledge he must have known in the instant of creating Adam that he was creating a being who would fall. Yet the passage is a most haunting and suggestive one nonetheless. For *Paradise Lost* is not simply an attempt to write one more tragedy, but to expound what Milton believed to be the archetypal myth of tragedy. Hence the passage is another example of existential projection: the real basis of the relation of Milton's God to Adam is the relation of the tragic poet to his hero. The tragic poet knows that his hero will be in a tragic situation, but he exerts all his power to avoid the sense of having manipulated that situation for his own purposes. He exhibits his hero to us as God exhibits Adam to the angels. If the hero was not sufficient to have stood, the mode is purely ironic; if he was not free to fall, the mode is purely romantic, the story of an invincible hero who will conquer all his antagonists as long as the story is about him. Now most theories of tragedy take one great tragedy as their norm: thus Aristotle's theory is largely founded on *Oedipus Tyrannus*, and Hegel's on *Antigone*. In seeing the archetypal human tragedy in the story of Adam, Milton was, of course, in agreement with the whole Judaeo-Christian cultural tradition, and perhaps arguments drawn from the story of Adam may have better luck in literary criticism than in subjects compelled to assume Adam's real existence, either as fact or as a merely legal fiction. Chaucer's monk, who clearly understood what he was doing, began with Lucifer and Adam, and we may be well advised to follow his example.

Adam, then, is in a heroic human situation: he is on top of the wheel of fortune, with the destiny of the gods almost within his reach. He forfeits that destiny in a way which suggests moral responsibility to some and a conspiracy of fate to others. What he does is to exchange a fortune of unlimited freedom for the fate involved in the consequences of the act of exchange, just as, for a man who deliberately jumps off a precipice, the law of gravitation acts as fate for the brief remainder of his life. The exchange is presented by Milton as itself a free act or *proairesis*, a use of freedom to lose freedom. And just as comedy often sets up an arbitrary law and then organizes the action to break or evade it, so tragedy presents the reverse theme of narrowing a comparatively free life into a process of causation. This happens to Macbeth when he accepts the logic of usurpation, to Hamlet when he accepts the logic of revenge, to Lear when he accepts the logic of abdication. The discovery or *anagnorisis* which comes at the end of the tragic plot is not simply the knowledge by the hero of what has happened to him —*Oedipus Tyrannus*, despite its reputation as a typical tragedy, is rather a special case in that regard—but the recognition of the determined shape of the life he has created for himself, with an implicit comparison with the uncreated potential life he has forsaken. The line of Milton dealing with the fall of the devils, "O how unlike the place from whence they fell!", referring as it does both to Virgil's *quantum mutatus ab illo* and Isaiah's "How art thou fallen from heaven, O Lucifer son of the morning," combines the Classical and the Christian archetypes of tragedy—for Satan, of course, like Adam, possessed an original glory. In Milton the complement to the vision of Adam on top of the wheel of fortune and falling into the world of the wheel is Christ standing on the pinnacle of the temple, urged by Satan to fall, and remaining motionless.

As soon as Adam falls, he enters his own created life, which is also the order of nature as we know it. The tragedy of Adam, therefore, resolves, like all other tragedies, in the manifestation of natural law. He enters a world in which existence is itself tragic, not existence modified by an act, deliberate or unconscious. Merely to exist is to disturb the balance of nature. Every natural man is a Hegelian thesis, and implies a reaction: every new birth provokes the return of an avenging death. This fact, in itself ironic and now called *Angst*, becomes tragic when a sense of a lost and originally higher destiny is added to it. Aristotle's hamartia, then, is a condition of being, not a cause of becoming: the reason why Milton ascribes his dubious argument to God is that he is so anxious to remove God from a predetermined causal sequence. On one side of the tragic hero is an opportunity for freedom, on the other the inevitable consequence of losing that freedom. These two sides of Adam's situation are represented in Milton by the speeches of Raphael and Michael respectively. Even with an innocent hero or martyr the same situation arises: in the Passion story it occurs in Christ's prayer in Gethsemane. Tragedy seems to move up to an *Augenblick* or crucial moment from which point the road to what might have been and the road to what will be can be simultaneously seen. Seen by the audience, that is: it cannot be seen by the hero if he is in a state of hybris, for in that case the crucial moment is for him a moment of dizziness, when the wheel of fortune begins its inevitable cyclical movement downward.

In Adam's situation there is a feeling, which in Christian tradition can be traced back at least to St. Augustine, that time *begins* with the fall; that the fall from liberty into the natural cycle also started the movement of time as we know it. In other tragedies too we can trace the feeling that *nemesis* is deeply involved with the movement of time, whether as the missing of a tide in the affairs of men, as a recognition that the time is out of joint, as a sense that time is the devourer of life, the mouth of hell at the previous moment, when the potential passes forever into the actual, or, in its ultimate horror, Macbeth's sense of it as simply one clock-tick after another. In comedy time plays a redeeming role: it uncovers and brings to light what is essential to the happy ending. The subtitle of Greene's *Pandosto*, the source of *The Winter's Tale*, is "*The Triumph of Time*," and it well describes the nature of Shakespeare's action, where time is introduced as a chorus. But in tragedy the *cognitio* is normally the recognition of the inevitability of a causal sequence in time, and the forebodings and ironic anticipations surrounding it are based on a sense of cyclical return.

In irony, as distinct from tragedy, the wheel of time completely encloses the action, and there is no sense of an original contact with a relatively timeless world. In the Bible the tragic fall of Adam is followed by its historical repetition, the fall of Israel into Egyptian bondage, which is, so to speak, its ironic confirmation. As long as the Geoffrey version of British history was accepted, the fall of Troy was the corresponding event in the history of Britain, and, as the fall of Troy began with an idolatrous misapplication of an apple, there were even symbolic parallels. Shakespeare's most ironic play, *Troilus and Cressida*, presents in Ulysses the voice of worldly wisdom, expounding with great eloquence the two primary categories of the perspective of tragic irony in the fallen world, time and the hierarchic chain of being. The extraordinary treatment of the tragic vision of time by Nietzsche's Zarathustra, in which the heroic acceptance of cyclical return becomes a glumly cheerful acceptance of a cosmology of identical recurrence, marks the influence of an age of irony.

Anyone accustomed to think archetypally of literature will recognize in tragedy a mimesis of sacrifice. Tragedy is a paradoxical combination of a fearful sense of rightness (the hero must fall) and a pitying sense of wrongness (it is too bad that he falls). There is a similar paradox in the two elements of sacrifice. One of these is communion, the dividing of a heroic or divine body among a group which brings them into unity with, and as, that body. The other is propitiation, the sense that in spite of the communion the body really belongs to another, a greater, and a potentially wrathful power. The ritual analogies to tragedy are more obvious than the psychological ones, for it is irony, not tragedy, that represents the nightmare or anxiety-dream. But, just as the literary critic finds Freud most suggestive for the theory of comedy, and Jung for the theory of romance, so for the theory of tragedy one naturally looks to the psychology of the will to power, as expounded in Adler and Nietzsche. Here one finds a "Dionysiac" aggressive will, intoxicated by dreams of its own omnipotence, impinging upon an "Apollonian" sense of external and immovable order. As a mimesis of ritual, the tragic hero is not really killed or eaten, but the corresponding thing in art still takes place, a vision of death which draws the survivors into a new unity. As a mimesis of dream, the inscrutable tragic hero, like the proud and silent swan, becomes articulate at the point of death, and the audience, like the poet in *Kubla Khan*, revives his song within itself. With his fall, a greater world beyond which his gigantic spirit had blocked out becomes for an instant visible, but there is also a sense of the mystery and remoteness of that world.

If we are right in our suggestion that romance, tragedy, irony and comedy are all episodes in a total quest-myth, we can see how it is that comedy can contain a potential tragedy within itself. In myth, the hero is a god, and hence he does not die, but dies and rises again. The ritual pattern behind the catharsis of comedy is the resurrection that follows the death, the epiphany or manifestation of the risen hero. In Aristophanes the hero, who often goes through a point of ritual death, is treated as a risen god, hailed as a new Zeus, or given the quasi-divine honors of the Olympic victor. In New Comedy the new human body is both a hero and a social group. The Aeschylean trilogy proceeds to the comic satyr-play, which is said to have affinities with spring festivals. Christianity, too, sees tragedy as an episode in the divine comedy, the larger scheme of redemption and resurrection. The sense of tragedy as a prelude to comedy seems almost inseparable from anything explicitly Christian. The serenity of the final double chorus in the St. Matthew Passion would hardly be attainable if composer and audience did not know that there was more to the story. Nor would the death of Samson lead to "calm of mind, all passion spent," if Samson were not a prototype of the rising Christ, associated at the appropriate moment with the phoenix.

This is an example of the way in which myths explain the structural principles behind familiar literary facts, in this case the fact that to make a sombre action end happily is easy enough, and to reverse the procedure almost impossible. (Of course we have a natural dislike of seeing pleasant situations turn out disastrously, but if a poet is working on a solid structural basis, our natural likes and dislikes have nothing to do with the matter.) Even Shakespeare, who can do anything, never does quite this. The action of *King Lear*, which seems heading for some kind of serenity, is suddenly wrenched into agony by the hanging of Cordelia, providing a conclusion which the stage refused to act for over a century, but none of Shakespeare's tragedies impresses us as a comedy gone wrong—*Romeo and Juliet* has a suggestion of such a structure, but it is only a suggestion. Hence while of course a tragedy may contain a comic action, it contains it only episodically as a subordinate contrast or underplot.

The characterization of tragedy is very like that of comedy in reverse. The source of *nemesis*, whatever it is, is an *eiron*, and may appear in a great variety of agents, from wrathful gods to hypocritical villains. In comedy we noticed three main types of *eiron* characters: a benevolent withdrawing and returning figure, the tricky slave or vice, and the hero and heroine. We have the tragic counterpart to the withdrawn *eiron* in the god who decrees the tragic action, like Athene in *Ajax* or Aphrodite in *Hippolytus;* a Christian example is God the Father in *Paradise Lost*. He may also be a ghost, like Hamlet's father; or it may not be a person at all but simply an invisible force known only by its effects, like the death that quietly seizes on Tamburlaine when the time has come for him to die. Often, as in the revenge-tragedy, it is an event previous to the action of which the tragedy itself is the consequence.

A tragic counterpart to the vice or tricky slave may be discerned in the soothsayer or prophet who foresees the inevitable end, or more of it than the hero does, like Teiresias. A closer example is the Machiavellian villain of Elizabethan drama, who, like the vice in comedy, is a convenient catalyzer of the action because he requires the minimum of motivation, being a self-starting principle of malevolence. Like the comic vice, too, he is something of an *architectus* or projection of the author's will, in this case for a tragic conclusion. "I limned this night-piece," says Webster's Lodovico, "and it was my best." Iago dominates the action of *Othello* almost to the point of being a tragic counterpart to the black king or evil magician of romance. The affinities of the Machiavellian villain with the diabolical are naturally close, and he may be an actual devil like Mephistopheles, but the sense of awfulness belonging to an agent of catastrophe can also make him something more like the high priest of a sacrifice. There is a touch of this in Webster's Bosola. *King Lear* has a Machiavellian villain in Edmund, and Edmund is contrasted with Edgar. Edgar, with his bewildering variety of disguises, his appearance to blind or mad people in different roles, and his tendency to appear on the third sound of the trumpet and to come pat like the catastrophe of the old comedy, seems to be an experiment in a new type, a kind of tragic "virtue," if I may coin this word by analogy, a counterpart in the order of nature to a guardian angel or similar attendant in romance.

The tragic hero usually belongs of course to the *alazon* group, an impostor in the sense that he is self-deceived or made dizzy by hybris. In many tragedies he begins as a semi-divine figure, at least in his own eyes, and then an inexorable dialectic sets to work which separates the divine pretence from the human actuality. "They told me I was everything," says Lear: " 'tis a lie; I am not ague-proof." The tragic hero is usually vested with supreme authority, but is often in the more ambiguous position of a *tyrannos* whose rule depends on his own abilities, rather than a purely hereditary or *de jure* monarch (*basileus*) like Duncan. The latter is more directly a symbol of the original vision or birthright, and is often a somewhat pathetic victim, like Richard II, or even Agamemnon. Parental figures in tragedy have the same ambivalence that they have in all other forms.

We found in comedy that the term *bomolochos* or buffoon need not be restricted to farce, but could be extended to cover comic characters who are primarily entertainers, with the function of increasing or focussing the comic mood. The corresponding contrasting type in tragedy is the suppliant, the character, often female, who presents a picture of unmitigated helplessness and destitution. Such a figure is pathetic, and pathos, though it seems a gentler and more relaxed mood than tragedy, is even more terrifying. Its basis is the exclusion of an individual from a group, hence it attacks the deepest fear in ourselves that we possess—a fear much deeper than the relatively cosy and sociable bogey of hell. In the figure of the suppliant pity and terror are brought to the highest possible pitch of intensity, and the awful consequences of rejecting the suppliant for all concerned is a central theme of Greek tragedy. Suppliant figures are often women threatened with death or rape, or children, like Prince Arthur in *King John*. The fragility of Shakespeare's Ophelia marks an affinity with the suppliant type. Often, too, the suppliant is in the structurally tragic position of having lost a place of greatness: this is the position of Adam and Eve in the tenth book of *Paradise Lost*, of the Trojan women after the fall of Troy, of Oedipus in the Colonus play, and so on. A subordinate figure who plays the role of focussing the tragic mood is the messenger who regularly announces the catastrophe in Greek tragedy. In the final scene of comedy, when the author is usually trying to get all his characters on the stage at once, we often notice the introduction of a new character, generally a messenger bearing some missing piece of the *cognitio*, such as Jaques de Boys in *As You Like It* or the gentle astringer in *All's Well*, who represents the comic counterpart.

Finally, a tragic counterpart of the comic refuser of festivity may be discerned in a tragic type of plain dealer who may be simply the faithful friend of the hero, like Horatio in *Hamlet*, but is often an outspoken critic of the tragic action, like Kent in *King Lear* or Enobarbus in *Antony and Cleopatra*. Such a character is in the position of refusing, or at any rate resisting, the tragic movement toward catastrophe. Abdiel's role in the tragedy of Satan in *Paradise Lost* is similar. The familiar figures of Cassandra and Teiresias combine this role with that of the soothsayer. Such figures, when they occur in a tragedy without a chorus, are often called chorus characters, as they illustrate one of the essential functions of the tragic chorus. In comedy a society forms around the hero: in tragedy the chorus, however faithful, usually represents the society from which the hero is gradually isolated. Hence what it expresses is a social norm against which the hero's hybris may be measured. The chorus is not the voice of the hero's conscience by any means, but very seldom does it encourage him in his hybris or prompt him to disastrous action. The chorus or chorus character is, so to speak, the embryonic germ of comedy in tragedy, just as the refuser of festivity, the melancholy Jaques or Alceste, is a tragic germ in comedy.

In comedy the erotic and social affinities of the hero are combined and unified in the final scene; tragedy usually makes love and the social structure irreconcilable and contending forces, a conflict which reduces love to passion and social activity to a forbidding and imperative duty. Comedy is much concerned with integrating the family and adjusting the family to society as a whole; tragedy is much concerned with breaking up the family and opposing it to the rest of society. This gives us the tragic archetype of Antigone, of which the conflict of love and honor in Classical French drama, of *Neigung* and *Pflicht* in Schiller, of passion and authority in the Jacobeans, are all moralized simplifications. Again, just as the heroine of comedy often ties together the action, so it is obvious that the central female figure of a tragic action will often polarize the tragic conflict. Eve, Helen, Gertrude, and Emily in the *Knight's Tale* are some ready instances: the

structural role of Briseis in the *Iliad* is similar. Comedy works out the
proper relations of its characters and prevents heroes from marrying their
sisters or mothers; tragedy presents the disaster of Oedipus or the incest of
Siegmund. There is a great deal in tragedy about pride of race and birthright, but its general tendency is to isolate a ruling or noble family from the
rest of society.

The phases of tragedy move from the heroic to the ironic, the first three
corresponding to the first three phases of romance, the last three to the last
three of irony. The first phase of tragedy is the one in which the central
character is given the greatest possible dignity in contrast to the other
characters, so that we get the perspective of a stag pulled down by wolves.
The sources of dignity are courage and innocence, and in this phase the
hero or heroine usually is innocent. This phase corresponds to the myth of
the birth of the hero in romance, a theme which is occasionally incorporated
into a tragic structure, as in Racine's *Athalie*. But owing to the unusual difficulty of making an interesting dramatic character out of an infant, the
central and typical figure of this phase is the calumniated woman, often a
mother the legitimacy of whose child is suspected. A whole series of tragedies based on a Griselda figure belong here, stretching from the Senecan
Octavia to Hardy's *Tess*, and including the tragedy of Hermione in *The
Winter's Tale*. If we are to read *Alcestis* as a tragedy, we have to see it as a
tragedy of this phase in which Alcestis is violated by Death and then has
her fidelity vindicated by being restored to life. *Cymbeline* belongs here too:
in this play the theme of the birth of the hero appears offstage, for Cymbeline was the king of Britain at the time of the birth of Christ, and the hal-
cyon peace in which the play concludes has a suppressed reference to this.
An even clearer example, and certainly one of the greatest in English
literature, is *The Duchess of Malfi*. The Duchess has the innocence of
abundant life in a sick and melancholy society, where the fact that she has
"youth and a little beauty" is precisely why she is hated. She reminds us too
that one of the essential characteristics of innocence in the martyr is an unwillingness to die. When Bosola comes to murder her he makes elaborate
attempts to put her half in love with easeful death and to suggest that death
is really a deliverance. The attempt is motivated by a grimly controlled
pity, and is roughly the equivalent of the vinegar sponge in the Passion.
When the Duchess, her back to the wall, says "I am the Duchess of Malfi
still," "still" having its full weight of "always," we understand how it is
that even after her death her invisible presence continues to be the most
vital character in the play. *The White Devil* is an ironic parody-treatment
of the same phase.
The second phase corresponds to the youth of the romantic hero, and is in

one way or another the tragedy of innocence in the sense of inexperience, usually involving young people. It may be simply the tragedy of a youthful life cut off, as in the stories of Iphigeneia and Jephthah's daughter, of Romeo and Juliet, or, in a more complex situation, in the bewildered mixture of idealism and priggishness that brings Hippolytus to disaster. The simplicity of Shaw's Joan and her lack of worldly wisdom place her here also. For us however the phase is dominated by the archetypal tragedy of the green and golden world, the loss of the innocence of Adam and Eve, who, no matter how heavy a doctrinal load they have to carry, will always remain dramatically in the position of children baffled by their first contact with an adult situation. In many tragedies of this type the central character survives, so that the action closes with some adjustment to a new and more mature experience. "Henceforth I learn that to obey is best," says Adam, as he and Eve go hand in hand out to the world before them. A less clear cut but similar resolution occurs when Philoctetes, whose serpent-wound reminds us a little of Adam, is taken off his island to enter the Trojan war. Ibsen's *Little Eyolf* is a tragedy of this phase, and with the same continuing conclusion, in which it is the older characters who are educated through the death of a child.

The third phase, corresponding to the central quest-theme of romance, is tragedy in which a strong emphasis is thrown on the success or completeness of the hero's achievement. The Passion belongs here, as do all tragedies in which the hero is in any way related to or a prototype of Christ, like *Samson Agonistes*. The paradox of victory within tragedy may be expressed by a double perspective in the action. Samson is a buffoon of a Philistine carnival and simultaneously a tragic hero to the Israelites, but the tragedy ends in triumph and the carnival in catastrophe. Much the same is true of the mocked Christ in the Passion. But just as the second phase often ends in anticipation of greater maturity, so this one is often a sequel to a previous tragic or heroic action, and comes at the end of a heroic life. One of the greatest dramatic examples is *Oedipus at Colonus*, where we find the usual binary form of a tragedy conditioned by a previous tragic act, ending this time not in a second disaster, but in a full rich serenity that goes far beyond a mere resignation to Fate. In narrative literature we may cite Beowulf's last fight with the dragon, the pendant to his Grendel quest. Shakespeare's *Henry V* is a successfully completed romantic quest made tragic by its implicit context: everybody knows that King Henry died almost immediately and that sixty years of unbroken disaster followed for England— at least, if anyone in Shakespeare's audience did not know that, his ignorance was certainly no fault of Shakespeare's.

The fourth phase is the typical fall of the hero through hybris and hamartia that we have already discussed. In this phase we cross the boundary line from innocence to experience, which is also the direction in which the hero falls. In the fifth phase the ironic element increases, the heroic decreases, and the characters look further away and in a smaller perspective. *Timon of Athens* impresses us as more ironic and less heroic than the better known tragedies, not simply because Timon is a more middle-class hero who has to buy what authority he has, but because the feeling that Timon's suicide has somehow failed to make a fully heroic *point* is very strong. Timon is oddly isolated from the final action, in which the breach between Alcibiades and the Athenians closes up over his head, in striking contrast with the conclusions of most of the other tragedies, where nobody is allowed to steal the show from the central character.

The ironic perspective in tragedy is attained by putting the characters in a state of lower freedom than the audience. For a Christian audience an Old Testament or pagan setting is ironic in this sense, as it shows its characters moving according to the conditions of a law, whether Jewish or natural, from which the audience has been, at least theoretically, redeemed. *Samson Agonistes*, though unique in English literature, presents a combination of Classical form and Hebrew subject-matter that the greatest contemporary tragedian, Racine, also reached at the end of his life in *Athalie* and *Esther*. Similarly the epilogue to Chaucer's *Troilus* puts a Courtly Love tragedy into its historical relation to "payens corsed olde rites." The events in Geoffrey of Monmouth's British history are supposed to be contemporary with those of the Old Testament, and the sense of life under the law is present everywhere in *King Lear*. The same structural principle accounts for the use of astrology and other fatalistic machinery connected with the turning wheels of fate or fortune. Romeo and Juliet are star-crossed, and Troilus loses Criseyde because every five hundred years Jupiter and Saturn meet the crescent moon in Cancer and claim another victim. The tragic action of the fifth phase presents for the most part the tragedy of lost direction and lack of knowledge, not unlike the second phase except that the context is the world of adult experience. *Oedipus Tyrannus* belongs here, and all tragedies and tragic episodes which suggest the existential projection of fatalism, and, like much of the Book of Job, seem to raise metaphysical or theological questions rather than social or moral ones.

Oedipus Tyrannus, however, is already moving into the sixth phase of tragedy, a world of shock and horror in which the central images are images of *sparagmos*, that is, cannibalism, mutilation, and torture. The specific reaction known as shock is appropriate to a situation of cruelty or outrage. (The secondary or false shock produced by the outrage done to some emotional attachment or fixation, as in the critical reception of *Jude the Obscure* or *Ulysses*, has no status in criticism, as false shock is a disguised resistance to the autonomy of culture.) Any tragedy may have one or more shocking scenes in it, but sixth-phase tragedy shocks as a whole, in its total effect. This phase is more common as a subordinate aspect of tragedy than as its main theme, as unqualified horror or despair makes a difficult cadence. *Prometheus Bound* is a tragedy of this phase, though this is partly an illusion due to its isolation from the trilogy to which it belongs. In such tragedies the hero is in too great agony or humiliation to gain the privilege of a heroic pose, hence it is usually easier to make him a villainous hero, like Marlowe's Barabas, although Faustus also belongs to the same phase. Seneca is fond of this phase, and bequeathed to the Elizabethans an interest in the gruesome, an effect which usually has some connection with mutilation, as when Ferdinand offers to shake hands with the Duchess of Malfi and gives her a dead man's hand. *Titus Andronicus* is an experiment in Senecan sixth-phase horror which makes a great deal of mutilation, and shows also a strong interest, from the opening scene on, in the sacrificial symbolism of tragedy.

At the end of this phase we reach a point of demonic epiphany, where we see or glimpse the undisplaced demonic vision, the vision of the *Inferno*. Its chief symbols, besides the prison and the madhouse, are the instruments of a torturing death, the cross under the sunset being the antithesis of the tower under the moon. A strong element of demonic ritual in public punishments and similar mob amusements is exploited by tragic and ironic myth. Breaking on the wheel becomes Lear's wheel of fire; bear-baiting is an image for Gloucester and Macbeth, and for the crucified Prometheus the humiliation of exposure, the horror of being watched, is a greater misery than the pain. *Derkou theama* (behold the spectacle; get your staring over with) is his bitterest cry. The inability of Milton's blind Samson to stare back is his greatest torment, and one which forces him to scream at Delilah, in one of the most terrible passages of all tragic drama, that he will tear her to pieces if she touches him.

Part Four

THE TRAGIC HERO

George Boas
THE EVOLUTION OF THE TRAGIC HERO

Henry A. Myers
HEROES AND THE WAY OF COMPROMISE

W. H. Auden
THE CHRISTIAN TRAGIC HERO

Arthur Miller
TRAGEDY AND THE COMMON MAN

Robert Warshow
THE GANGSTER AS TRAGIC HERO

The Evolution of the Tragic Hero *

GEORGE BOAS

Let me say at the outset that I am not going to play that ancient game of trying to define the indefinable. Names of literary *genres* are but tags for works of art which have certain historical relations, but there is no more reason to believe that *Hamlet* and the *Eumenides* have a common essence than there is to insist that Louis Capet and Louis Philippe have a common essence, or that the Lever Building in New York and Lincoln's log cabin have a common essence. People have been trying for years to give satisfactory definitions of such terms as "tragedy," "comedy," "novel," even "poetry," and they have never succeeded. The reason for their failure is clear enough. Words have a history. When they are first used, it is likely that they are unambiguous, but as time goes on, they are applied to more and more different things. Even invented names, like *Kodak*, come to broaden their extension and at one time the Eastman Company had to run an advertisement announcing, "If it isn't an Eastman, it isn't a Kodak." This does not deny the obvious fact that probably everything can be found to have something in common, if only the character of being talked about. So all things made by man have a common trait—they are human artifacts. But the reason why we are interested in a play or a poem or a picture or building or musical composition is not its similarity to all other plays, poems, pictures, buildings, and musical compositions, for most of the time we do not even perceive that similarity. There must be thousands of Frenchmen, living and dead, who have enjoyed a performance of Racine's *Phèdre* without seeing its similarity to either Euripides's or Seneca's *Hippolytus*. Our interest in a work of art is to be sure intensified if we can locate it in the tradition to which it belongs, but one does not have to be a literary

* George Boas, "The Evolution of the Tragic Hero," *The Carleton Drama Review*, Vol. I, No. 1 (1955–1956), pp. 5–21. [Footnotes in this selection have been renumbered.]

historian to be moved by a novel, poem, or play. Fortunately we are not all as yet Ph.D.'s, and it is devoutly to be hoped that we shall never all have that sad distinction. The history of ideas, like the history of taste, is a very important subject which illuminates obscure passages and thus makes it possible for us to understand works of art which seemed opaque at first sight. But at the same time it must be admitted that some works of art are dead, or so close to it that they can be kept alive only in an oxygen tent of footnotes and explanatory introductions. That this is so is a clear indication that the universality and eternality of great literature is an illusion, for even the greatest books require constant re-editing and thus re-interpretation. Homer, Lucretius, Dante, Shakespeare, even Goethe would lie unopened on the dusty back shelves of libraries without the work of editors.

Lest I be thought to be too dictatorial, we shall consider for a moment the remaining Greek tragedies. We all know from reading Aristotle's *Poetics* what they are supposed to have in common, from their high serious-ness to their cathartic effect on the baser emotions. To add another interpre-tation of what Aristotle actually said, or even of what he was trying to say, would be cruel and unusual punishment on a captive audience. I should prefer to rescue these dramatic poems from the Aristotelians, most of whom upon scrutiny turn out to be disciples of Horace or of St. Thomas Aquinas, and to look at them afresh. We have seven plays of Aeschylus, seven of Sophocles, and nineteen of Euripides. The total is but a small frac-tion not merely of all the tragedies written for the Theatre of Dionysus, but also of those written by our three authors. For Aeschylus wrote be-tween eighty and ninety plays, Sophocles over one hundred and twenty, Euripides over ninety. We have less than ten percent of the plays of these three men to go on and we have no way of knowing how representative our remaining plays are or even if they are what modern taste would call the best of all that were written. Consequently it should always be borne in mind that any generalization made about Greek tragedy has to be based on a very imperfect sample.

Using this sample, we can make the following statements, for what they are worth. First, Greek tragedy was built around certain plots which were supposed to be historical. There is the plot of the returned hero who like Agamemnon comes back from the wars to find conditions at home some-thing less than satisfactory. In his case he discovers his wife adulterously joined to her lover Aegisthus. Or there is the plot of the person who is the unwitting instrument of divine plans, like Oedipus and his daughters. Or there is the glorification of a recent historical event such as the victory of the Greeks over the Persians at Salamis; or the spectacular presentation of an ancient myth, such as that of the culture-hero Prometheus or of the daughters of Danaus. The one generalization which one can make about these plots, or subject-matters, is that they were all well known to the audience, much as the story of the Passion or the Fall of Man or the assassination of Lincoln would be to American audiences. Clearly in such cases the element of surprise was bound to be lacking. One could no more have Antigone decide for some reason or other not to bury Polyneices than one could have one of the Rover Boys appear in Ford's Theatre and knock the pistol out of Booth's hand just as he was about to shoot the President. We can not say that the hero does what he does because of Fate, or that the outcome is always determined by an oracle, or that the main character possesses a tragic flaw, or anything of that sort. But we can say that the audience could not be taken by surprise at the outcome. Today we are unaccustomed to his technique. We say that we prefer suspense, though musical audiences love to hear the same old pieces played over and over again and children are very exigent in their demand for accurate repetition of stories. We say that we do not approve of plays in which the *dénouement* can be seen as soon as the drama begins; we want it to be concealed. In fact, in some cases such as the short stories of O. Henry, we do not know until the last sentence what is going to happen. Apparently this demand was not characteristic of the Athenians.

In the second place, the very familiarity which the audience had with the plots made their development seem logical. There are Greek tragedies in which the hero or heroine tells the audience that he has to make a choice and that the result of the choice is already known to him. Thus even *Prometheus Bound*, which is almost like an oratorio, in that nothing takes place except the presentation of what Professor Kitto has called a situation, opens with the announcement of Prometheus's crime, the crime of having disobeyed the command of Zeus. And despite the taunts of Force, that one named *Forethought* should have known the consequence of his acts, Prometheus replies in his opening speech,

> Whatever comes,
> Stands clear before my vision. I can suffer
> Nothing that I foreknew not. I must bear
> All that is doomed, as best I may; well knowing
> None can do battle with Necessity.[1]

Similarly in *Antigone*, Sophocles has his heroine state clearly her course of action and her knowledge of what will happen if she pursues it. Sometimes, as in the Oedipus legend, the choice is only half-real, and consists in trying

---

[1] All translations, unless otherwise indicated, are by F. L. Lucas, as published in his *Greek Drama for Everyman*, London (J. M. Dent and Sons, Ltd.), by permission of the translator and publisher.

desperately to avoid the web which has been woven by the Fates and foretold by the oracle. But even here the hero knows what the oracle has said,
though the sting of the tragedy is his inability to so choose as to refute the
oracle, he makes every attempt to do so. This simply means that certain
causes have certain effects and that when a causal series is initiated, nothing
can be done to divert it from its natural course. Zeus alone is free; the
world is governed by Necessity. It is only in a few plays, such as Euripides's
Orestes, that there exists a hint of divine intervention in the affairs of men,
for whereas in Homer the gods are always interfering in one way or another
to protect their favorites—or defeat each other—in the tragic dramatists
they seem to stay pretty well in the background. In *The Eumenides* of
Aeschylus the final decision about the fate of Orestes is determined by a
vote of Athena but it is interesting to observe that the struggle otherwise is
an even one, though Apollo resorts to curious physiological theories to
prove that murdering his mother was less evil than revenging his father.[2] Regardless of the theories, the causes of the Furies and that of Apollo are
evenly balanced until the last moment. *Hippolytus* may similarly be interpreted as a symbolic statement of Olympian quarrels. But the rival claims
of Artemis and Aphrodite are presented at the beginning and end of the
play as prologue and epilogue. The goddesses themselves do not interfere
in the action, for after all Aphrodite does not try—to say nothing of succeed—to change Hippolytus's mind; and Phaedra dies, in spite of her cult
of the goddess, and so does Hippolytus in spite of his cult of her rival
divinity. What happens is the logical outcome of a choice of conduct.

When I say "logical," I use the term loosely. The analogy between cause
and effect and premise and conclusion is far from strict. There is no logic, it
might be said, in any effect's following from any cause. It is no more logical
that a man pay for his sins with death than it would be if he paid for them
with prosperity. But when we are sufficiently habituated to seeing certain
effects following certain causes, we attribute to the succession of events a
kind of compulsive force, as if nothing else could possibly happen. The difference between causal and logical necessity may be hard to grasp but it is a
real difference nevertheless. That is why it is worth pointing out.

This brings us to a third characteristic of the remaining Greek tragedies.
Whether the heroes have to make a choice between two equally legitimate
courses of action, as Hegel seemed to think, or not, they have to make a
choice and the usual result of it is self-defeat. I say "usual" for here again
the generalization will not hold up in all cases. In *The Persians* there is
nothing to come out badly, no self-defeat possible except for the enemy. In
Prometheus Bound we have but one part of a trilogy and do not really know

---

[2] Orestes himself does this in Euripides.

what took place in the last part. But we have some reason to believe that after the liberation of the Titan things took a turn for the better, as far as he was concerned. This at any rate is the orthodox view. Readers of Hesiod will recall another version of the myth according to which little good came to mankind with the introduction of fire into their lives. And in fact there will always be dispute about just what "badly" means. A person's death may with some justice be thought of as self-defeat, especially if he is responsible for it. But on the other hand, in what sense of the word does *Antigone* come out badly or result in self-defeat, since the heroine herself chose to do what she did? Her death may even be called self-fulfillment, as it seems to be in Anouilh's version of the play. With the exception of a few plays, one can conclude that the tragedies usually ended with the death of the hero.

There is still another characteristic of the Greek tragedies which we must not overlook. I refer to the Chorus. The role of the Chorus has been as hotly disputed as everything else in this domain. I have even heard it suggested that it existed for comic relief. It behaves like a thermometer, rising and falling with the temperature of the scene. It shifts its point of view without rhyme or reason, seeming to say that everyone is right. And in fact in a logical universe everyone is right. In such a world right and wrong are eternal principles which in themselves are really unintelligible. They become the premises from which everything flows. In the Oresteia revenge is of unquestioned importance, just as it seems to be in *Hamlet*. But so also is respect for a mother. The premises do not form a logical system at all but frequently are in contradiction with one another. Electra and her brother have only to decide whether the crime of leaving a father's murder unavenged is worse than that of matricide. That a person is more closely related to his father than to his mother, as Euripides makes Orestes argue, as if he had Aristotle's *De generatione animalium*, is the excuse for the matricide, though it naturally turns out to be a poor excuse. And the Chorus is not slow to point this out. If it had been a good excuse, there would have been no tragedy. Again, the constant harping on the privileges of royal blood presumably did not seem bizarre to the democratic Athenians; they accepted this apparently as an immutable principle. The various immutable principles are often presented to us by the Chorus as if it were important for the audience to know what the plays are really about. The laws are what matter, not the desires of individuals. That this principle was significant even outside the theatre appears in Plato's *Apology*. But there happens to be conflict between some of the laws themselves. I think that one sees this most clearly in *Antigone*, where the ethics of obedience comes head-on into collision with practical action. It would seem to me, though in this I am probably in the minority, that one of the main functions of the Chorus is to comment upon or to expound this philosophy, setting forth the poet's own ideas, or at least those ideas which he believes his public to share. Often the long choral passages are purely lyrical, like hymns; often they take the form of prayers. There are passages in *Agamemnon* which might be lifted out of context and read as philosophical meditations. But these Theban elders, Corinthian matrons, Trojan women, Greek sailors, usually do nothing except comment. For instance, in the long narrative that follows the sentinel's opening speech in *Agamemnon* we find the Chorus saying,

> Zeus, whoever He may be
> By that name on Him I call
> (If 'tis thus He would be known),
> Though I weigh infinity,
> Naught my thought may grasp at all,
> Save Him alone,
> To lift away this load of pain
> Burdening my soul in vain . . .
>
> He hath shown man wisdom's ways,
> He hath made His ordinance plain
> Unto all—"By suffering learn!"
> Sleepless still, the sinner pays:
> Dark memories, drop by drop, return,
> Till stubborn hearts are schooled by pain.
> So the stern Gods give their grace,
> Holding in Heaven the helmsman's place.

This is surely more likely to be the opinion of Aeschylus than that of a group of senile Argives. At times, however, the Chorus acts simply as an audience for one of the characters, but an audience which presumably re-acts as would be fit and proper for the public itself. It does not further the movement of the drama, but comments on it. It is as if the audience were brought upon the stage and made articulate. It is in these cases that the Chorus voices such conventional philosophy, though it is also possible that when, as is true of Euripides, the dramatist was unconventional in his philosophic and religious ideas, the Chorus was too. It appears to tell the real audience what to think or, if one prefer, it voices the opinions as well as the emotions of the dramatist. But whatever it does, it obviates the ne-cessity of our modern dramatists for pretending that the stage is real life. No Athenian dramatist had to go to extremes of ingenuity which a man like Ibsen, to say nothing of Eugène Scribe, had to employ to tell the audience what it was supposed to know. He seems to have realized that he was pre-senting a play in a theatre, and not photographing scenes from real life, and hence if he wanted something conveyed to the audience, he could make the Chorus do it.

It should also be pointed out that the heroes of all Greek tragedies were either gods or princes. This was erected into a rule by Aristotle and transmitted to us by the Renaissance theorists. We see its observance both in the French imitators of Greek tragedy and in Shakespeare even when he had a non-Hellenic subject. The Marxists have much of this. To them it is evidence that the dramatists identified themselves with the ruling class, even though in Athens the ruling class was not a hereditary aristocracy. It should be noted that if the plots of these spectacles were to be taken from history, there would be no way of avoiding the use of princes as protagonists. Ancient history says next to nothing about the common people and even the most unpleasant characters come from the nobility—indeed sometimes from Olympus. For that matter, whoever has found a permanent place in literature, identified by his name, and not merely as Second Citizen or Nurse or Messenger, is bound to develop into a nobleman as tradition grows. Even Ethan Allen—at least in Vermont—has turned into a sort of nobleman. People seem to prefer that their heroes have no vulgar streaks. But be that as it may, the fact is established, and the theory grew out of it that noblemen were tragic, common people comic.

But once again it must be said that the evil ones are as noble as the good ones. Agamemnon may be the victim, but his assassins are just as princely as he is; neither Orestes nor Pylades is less or more princely than their victims; and both Eteocles and Polyneices are brothers. It is thus impossible to distribute moral qualities on what the Marxists would call a class-basis. On the contrary, since the tragic situation is man against fate, man against law, man against the gods, man against necessity, social rank must count for nothing and the best way of reducing it to nonentity is to put all the characters on the same social level. Moreover, the situations are such that only divine beings or men descended from divine beings could be caught in them. For the old stories, hallowed by tradition, were reinterpreted morally and one might as well object to the princely character of Agamemnon and Oedipus as to the similar position of Abraham, Isaac, and Jacob. There emerge in all cultures certain figures who for one reason or another captivate the imagination of the people of that culture. These figures become national heroes, symbols of virtue, friendship, courage, self-sacrifice, wisdom. What is particularly interesting about these Greek heroes is their tragic fate. No tragedy has survived in which Deucalion and Pyrrha are the main characters. Nor have we anything resembling the Book of Job.

Finally, the distinction between villain and hero is impossible to draw in the remaining Greek tragedies. It is true that Menelaus shows up pretty badly according to our standards in Euripides's *Andromache*. But that may be because he stands for Sparta and the author's feelings about Sparta are clearly expounded in Andromache's famous tirade against its inhabitants.

But it is also true that Menelaus is none too heroic in *Orestes* either. But compared with Iago or Lady Macbeth, he is a mild villain indeed. It seems safe to conclude that in general the conflict in Greek Tragedy is not between people so much as within individuals. It is that element which probably has given them such power over the modern mind. For even when an ancient hero is doomed by fate, as Oedipus was, to commit a crime, one sees him in the struggle against the inevitable. The outcries against the gods, which are so characteristic of the speeches in Euripides, though Prometheus on his rock does not hesitate to give his frank opinion of Zeus, are again evidence that the tragic hero is made to feel himself caught in a situation over which he has little control but in which he must make some decision, however futile. But the unhappy outcome always emerges from his decision. He must choose and cannot choose well.

The tragedy of *Antigone* is the stock example of this. To us this drama is a drama of the conscientious objector. The girl is faced with the choice of obeying the law of the state or the law of the gods. If she obeys one law, she must perforce violate the other. In essence this choice is not different from that which faces Orestes and Electra, for they too have to choose between two apparently equal crimes. It is clear in the case of Antigone that she is free to choose, as her sister is too, at least as free as Adam and Eve were. But she is not free to avoid committing a crime. Moreover, though Creon in this play is far from being sympathetic to the modern reader, he is not the villain in the sense that he makes her violate the law of the state. He meets a tragic fate too and the second half of the play is given over to that. There is no condemnation of his decree in this play; he is the king and he has issued a law and the law must be obeyed. It is true that burial rites may not seem very important to some modern sceptics, though there are plenty of religious people who would be horrified if they are not observed. The point is, however, not what we think of the special circumstances of the decree; it is rather the greater conflict within a conscience. It is easy enough to say flatly that civil disobedience is always wrong, but people who say that overlook the possibility of the law itself being wrong. Suppose that Antigone were living in our own time; what analogue could we find for her dilemma? We might choose the conflict between the religious law which is said to hold life sacred—though neither church nor state has ever held all life sacred—and statute law which commands one to kill. If a religious girl were asked by her brother who was trying to evade the draft to shelter him from the police, what should she do? If the answer is that she should dash to the telephone and notify the police to come and get him, then why do we condemn those children in Germany who were said to have denounced their anti-Nazi parents and brothers to the Gestapo? I hope that none of you will ever be put in such a situation, but we are not too far from it when we are asked to denounce our friends for supposed subversive activities. I remember the case of a French father who refused to give up two American aviators to the Germans even though his refusal he knew meant the slaughter of his innocent fourteen year old son. He made his choice—on what grounds I do not know—but he made it. I also recall the pleas of people charged with being collaborators that their collaboration bought the lives of their compatriots. But for that matter, one has only to go back to the story of St. Mary the Egyptian who sold her chastity in order to cross the river into Jerusalem. That there is a conflict between God and Caesar is surely nothing new. We resolve the conflict, as we usually resolve such problems, by closing our eyes to it. But the conflict is there nevertheless, unless we deny the rights of one law or the other. As Sophocles makes Antigone say,

> It was not God that gave me such commandments,
> Nor Justice, consorts of the Lords of Death,
> That ever laid on men such laws as these.
> Nor did I hold that in your human edicts
> Lay power to override the laws of God,
> Unwritten yet unshaken—laws that live
> Not from to-day, nor yet from yesterday,
> But always—though none knows how first made known.

What I wish to emphasize in these words is not merely Antigone's choice, but the inevitable tragedy of it. Here there is no way out, no manner of reasoning to what one might call a happy ending. Her death is no solution and even if she had been snatched up to Heaven by some god and put among the stars, the conflict would not have been resolved. When then we say that in some Greek tragedies we have situations presented, that is what we mean. We have first to admit that there are some problems which are insoluble, conflicts which cannot be reconciled. To protest is to wail over the insolubility of the problem of squaring the circle or doubling the cube. But this is precisely what is expected, paradoxically enough, in a logical universe. Reason rests, as we have suggested, on unproved premises. We have to choose our premises; we do not demonstrate them. We may choose them because of revelation, authority, faith, tradition, common-sense, what you will. But when they are chosen, certain things follow from them and when they are translated into action, the resultant acts cannot be reversed or modified. Perhaps that is why Antigone rejects her sister's attempt to share her guilt. It is she, Antigone, whose life is part and parcel of the deed known as the burial of Polyneices, and the consequent civil disobedience. How much of this was accepted overtly by Sophocles, I shall not pretend to say, but that it is there is clear enough. The very improbability of the stories lends support to this view. For the only way to make them probable is to

humanize the characters, as Euripides is supposed to have done, and by
that very process to lessen the tragic effect.

One sees this at work in such a tragedy as *Andromache*. In Euripides this
is ostensibly the story of a mother's attempt to frustrate plots against her
child's life, of the rivalry between a wife and a concubine, of the hatred between two states, Sparta and Athens, in fact, a confusion of conflicts from
which scarcely any clear and single conflict can be untangled. The simplicity
of *Antigone* has gone for the very reason that Euripides is beginning to see
people as people, with all their jealousies, cowardice, and self-assertion.
To a Greek perhaps the situation was different. The characters were historical, the story well known. The individuals may have emerged from the
poetry as each upholding some moral principle, but to us they seem to be
more real, more flesh and blood, and for that reason less significant morally
than Antigone, Ismene, and Creon. The most one can do to clarify what
goes on is to read into Hermione a woman's jealousy of her rival, and into
Menelaus a father's interest in giving his daughter satisfaction, however
ignoble her desires might be. The trick which Menelaus plays on Andromache is simply a melodramatic incident which displays the Spartans'
treachery and nothing more. Andromache is given a speech in which she
proclaims that her choice lies between buying her life with her child's
death or his with hers. She exclaims against the unfairness of the choice in
that it was not she who chose to be the slave and concubine of Neoptolemus,
but the fortunes of war which put her in that position. The conflict which
set *Antigone* in motion was a choice between two profound moral claims on
the individual's conscience. In *Andromache* the conflict is that between
two people. The history of this plot through Seneca to Racine would be
well worth analysis, but in the time we have, we shall simply leap to
Racine.

In the French writer's *Andromaque*, the situation is frankly accepted as an
erotic duel. It is the psychology of love as a violent passion which pulls the
strings. Whereas in Euripides the man in the case, Neoptolemus, does not
even appear on the scene, in Racine he not only appears but becomes the
pivot on which everything turns. He is in love with Andromache who is
really faithful to the memory of Hector but who is supposed by her rival
Hermione to be in love with Pyrrhus, that is Neoptolemus. Everybody
misunderstands everybody else's motives, with the result that Hermione,
for the sole purpose of revenging herself on Pyrrhus, promises to marry
Orestes who is in love with her, if he will kill Pyrrhus. And then when he
has killed him, she bursts into a magnificent and, it must be confessed psychologically true, tirade telling him that he should have known that she was
driven to the idea by jealousy and that he should not have taken her seriously.

Ah! falloit-il en croire une amante insensée?
Ne devois-tu pas lire au fond de ma pensée?
Et ne voyois-tu pas, dans mes emportements,
Que mon coeur démentoit ma bouche à tous moments?
Quand je l'aurois voulu, falloit-il y souscrire?
N'as-tu pas dû cent fois te le faire redire?

This sort of thing is probably more to our taste than Euripides's drama, for our drama has become the conflict of persons, not of moral claims. The mythological status of the characters in the classical tragedy, the crystallization of their histories through tradition, made it next to impossible for a dramatist to introduce innovations of this type into his plays. They fell into a pattern established as a ritual. By drawing their characters down from the skies, the modern dramatist turned them into something resembling human beings.

We see the transformation almost completed in Shakespeare. It may be possible to interpret the plots of Shakespeare's tragedies as moral struggles, but I confess to never having seen such an interpretation which made much sense. Given the chivalric notion of honor and the need of revenging a father's death, I suppose that one can rewrite *Hamlet*, if one wishes, in the light of that concept. But what is one to make of *King Lear*, of *Julius Caesar*, of *Othello?* In all these cases it is the individual's personal psychology which determines the issue. Though the jealousy of Hermione in *Andromaque* seems to me to be more plausible than that of Othello, in both cases the individuals are victims of their own states of mind. There is nothing either in the situation or in any law of nature which compels them to act as they do. Granting that monsters such as Othello and Iago can exist, and your generation has grown accustomed to the existence of even worse psychological monsters, the emotional impact of their lines rests on their realism, an appearance heightened by the poetry. Now one can trace the history of the idea of personal psychology from Aristotle down and find that step by step it moves in the direction of giving more and more individuality to the person. Aristotle's *Nichomachean Ethics*, for instance, like his *Politics*, is based on the assumption that all men are alike—rational animals—though they may differ in their accidental traits. His pupil Theophrastus in the opening of his famous *Characters* raises the question "why it is that, while all Greece lies under the same sky and all the Greeks are educated alike, it has befallen us to have characters so variously constituted." His answer is that men fall into certain types or characters: The Flatterer, the Complaisant Man, the Surly Man, the Arrogant Man, the Ironical Man, and so on. The idea was backed up by the Humoralist School of Medicine which taught that a man's temperament was determined by the predominance of one of the four humors, from which we get the Sanguine man, the Melancholy man, the

Choleric man, and the Phlegmatic man. This idea and its derivatives prevailed for centuries. The Horatian principle of consistency of character was
accepted all through the Renaissance and we see it in satirical form in
Molière's comedies of the Miser, the Hypocrite, the Misanthrope, the
Hypochondriac, and I imagine, though I do not know for certain, that it is
behind the *commedia dell'arte* with its set of stock characters all behaving in
a ritualistic manner. I sometimes wonder whether the composition of the
nineteenth century repertory companies, with their juvenile leads, their
heavies, their comic figures, so faithfully reproduced in the English novel
of the same period, did not arise out of the same idea. At any rate it is not
until we come to Proust with his theory of the *intermittances du coeur* that the
notion of consistency of character finally disappears. But naturally when
this happens, behaviour becomes less explicable rationally, and the absurdity of behaviour in such writers as Cocteau—or perhaps even Gide—
and later Sartre and the other existentialists, is a natural outcome of this
more realistic view of human conduct.

The result of all this for tragedy is that whereas the tragic writer still
sees tragedy as self-defeat, each self acts in its own way, and no motive is
too absurd to be a real motive, a motive not merely real, but taken seriously
by both audience and author. We get a glimpse of this in some bits of
medieval Christian legend, such as that of the Jongleur of Notre Dame,
where the motive of the juggler saves him though what he actually does is
trivial. Thus both self-defeat and self-salvation come from within the individual himself. Hamlet, Lear, Othello, and their companions all bring
about their own destruction, though aided and abetted by external circumstances—if a wife and friend can be called external. The human problem
gradually becomes that of conquering the environment and of asserting one's
superiority to all those forces which might end in one's annihilation. The
importance of self-preservation, in the psychological sense of that term,
has grown since the rise of popular government and the industrialization of
production. For the threats to personal independence have also grown. We
may submit to these forces of annihilation or we may fight against them.
In our own country we have those who preach conformity to the general
rule of living and those who struggle to find some way of saving the individual who is forced to live in a system which is becoming more and more
corporate. Thus on the one hand we have the prophets who preach *esprit de
corps*, school spirit, being one of the gang, dressing, eating, talking, believing, fighting, playing exactly as everyone else does, in short, being perfectly
normal. The press, the radio, the advertising geniuses, of all sorts, spend
their energies in homogenizing society. On the other hand, from Emerson
and Thoreau down to William James, we have had our prophets who preach
self-reliance, leadership, primacy, originality. If the former establish so-

cieties and clubs for all purposes, the latter set up fellowships and prizes for outstanding services or accomplishments. How a youngster ever succeeds in understanding the situation escapes one of my generation. If he strives for primacy, then he is not one of the boys; if he becomes one of the boys, then he must abandon those interests which the boys do not share. Clearly, if what I say makes sense, our dramas will involve the individual going down to defeat by submitting to the group or going down to defeat by fighting against the group. The main difference between our tragedies and those of the seventeenth century will be that our heroes sometimes gladly accept the premises of their ultimate defeat.

The clearest case of this sort of tragedy is the famous play of Arthur Miller, *Death of a Salesman*. This play was called according to its publishers, —"a usually well-informed source—" "one of the finest dramas in the whole range of the American theatre"; "something to make strong men weep and think," though whether the connection is causal or not we are not told; "so simple, central and terrible that the run of playwrights would neither care nor dare to attempt it . . . touched with the tragic sense of life"; "a poignant, shattering and devastating drama"; a play which "has majesty, sweep and shattering dramatic impact"; a play "in which all is right and nothing is wrong." But if I continue, the very accumulation of praise will become too comic to be borne. Now all this is supposed to say that *Death of a Salesman* roused the critics, usually pretty *blasés*, to a high pitch of enthusiasm. But perhaps the most telling comment on this drama was that of Mr. John Mason Brown, duly reprinted by the Book-of-the-Month Club, "Mr. Miller's play is a tragedy modern and personal, not classic and heroic." It is indeed modern, not merely in the chronological sense, but also in the cultural sense and it is personal, in that a human being, not a cause or a moral issue, is the centre of the tragedy. But the tragedy itself consists in the hero's glad acceptance of the conditions of life which will lead to his own annihilation.

These conditions are the competitive activities of commercial life. A salesman is presented as a man who, whether he believes that what he sells is worth selling or not, must nevertheless consider it his mission in life to sell it. He is a man, as one of the characters says, "way out there in the blue, riding on a smile and a shoeshine." His life becomes invested with an aura of romance and one is given to understand that perhaps the very triviality of the enterprise is what gives it its inherent value. For it is a life which of course is instrumental to the making of money for someone else; but for the salesman himself, it, like virtue, is its own reward. Where so many of the Greek heroes bewail their fate which entangles them in a web of disaster, Willy Loman, the hero of this piece, voices no complaints whatsoever. He is like a knight errant pursuing a goal whose importance he never stops to consider. In fact, he himself does not even consider the money he earns his reward. If a fellow is impressive and well liked, that is enough. Mr. Miller makes this crystal clear, this pathetic yearning to be popular, to win friends and influence people. Here is one of his most poignant comments on the situation, the ability of the American commercial hero to idealize a sordid job. And the catastrophe seems to consist in Willy's final waking up to the bitter fact that the only person whom he impresses and by whom he is well liked is his wife, to whom he has been unfaithful. His sons have turned their back on his ideal, his neighbors and relatives see through him, his employer discharges him now that his usefulness as a salesman is over. The shoeshine was worn off, the smile has become a set grimace—he is out in the blue on nothing and for nothing.

In this play the individual's personality is no longer his own creation; it is the fiction of the society in which he lives and works. It is no longer Willy Loman who has made himself, but forces over which he presumably has no control have done this job of creating a self for him. We are not told why he chose this life—we find him in it and the intimation, if not the overt assertion, of the play is that he has no choice. Even his son, Biff, who tries to escape, seems unable to. It was not of course an oracle which foretold this, no malignant deity, but just as Oedipus was wrecked by Apollo's decree and forced to commit crimes which he was deliberately trying to avoid committing, so Willy Loman is presented as a man whose destiny was planned by beings remote from his wishes and ideas. One never knows how far an author means to extend the theme of his play and it may be unfair to Mr. Miller to say that this one is a comment on the totality of our civilization. But one rather imagines that the enthusiastic comments of the critics arose from their feeling that it was a picture typical of our "American way of life." Judging from the propaganda in the press and on the radio, there is reason to believe that the salesman is the typical American. "To sell" has become a verb whose object may now be not merely consumer goods in the literal sense of the word, but also ideas and people. One sells a religious creed, a philosophic theory, oneself. It would be hopelessly superficial to say that one makes the sale simply for the sake of the money which one receives in exchange. If that were true, there might be at least some common-sense in it. On the contrary, one sells an idea, one sells oneself for the sheer love of selling. This may have become the one mode of expressing our will to power which is left to us. We have reached the end of the dialectical road; or as the popular phrase has it, we have come full circle. For once again, we are faced with the possibility of tragedy in the sense in which *Antigone* is tragic. Whatever choice she makes will lead to defeat. If Willy Loman had refused to sell, he would have been a failure in the eyes of

American society; if he chose to sell, as he did, he must also end a worn-out heap of protoplasm muttering the gibberish of ideals which have no realization.

The love of horror seems essential to the Western soul. The myths of Greece are full of it; the stories of martyrdom and self-immolation color the whole of Christian literature; when the intellectuals of Europe in the eighteenth century went rationalistic, they developed the Gothic novel, the passion for ruins, the interest in decay; the Romantic movement, as we find it in Hugo, Poe, and Hoffmann meandered through the same old ruined castles inhabited by ghosts and other monsters; the later nineteenth century and the twentieth developed the novel of crime and detection; and we are now faced with a new crop of horror in the work of the Existentialists. Meanwhile, the non-literary world does its best to satisfy our craving for horror by doing horrible things: wars on a scale never before dreamt of, weapons which may well exterminate the whole race, genocide, torture, political persecution and, as far as our own country is concerned, crime on a gigantic scale which seems to have become a sport, engaged in for its own sake. We live in a world of horror and in our spare moments we amuse ourselves by reading about it. At the same time, organized religion flourishes as it has never flourished before, charitable foundations give away millions to fight disease, crime, and ignorance and we delude ourselves into thinking that never has man enjoyed a higher standard of living. And if the height of our standard of living is measured by our ability to sit back in comfort with a bottle of Coca-Cola by our sides watching television make clear the venality of our legislators and the timidity of our leaders, then it is very high indeed. But what else can we expect of a society in which salesmanship is the goal of every man's ambition? The tragedy of Willy Loman may be ignoble as compared to that of Prometheus or Antigone; we might nevertheless pause and ask ourselves whether in essence it is not the tragedy of every one of us, whether we know it or not.

Heroes and the
Way of Compromise[*]

HENRY A. MYERS

In a brief and pointed imaginary conversation between Frederick the Great and the utopian pacifists of his own time, William James once epitomized the almost comic clash between the attitude of the hero and that of the extreme advocates of moderation. " 'Dogs, would you live forever?' shouted Frederick the Great. 'Yes,' say our utopians, 'let us live forever, and raise our level gradually.' "

History in the making today offers to the student of human affairs another chapter, already half-written, in the ancient conflict between extremism and moderation. We are perhaps too close to our world to determine the prime cause, if indeed there be one only, of its division into warring camps. One clue, however, is to be found in the events leading up to World War II: the worship of half-truths which made some peoples seek the heroic life as a national ideal while others sought to live by compromise alone.

Frederick, in spite of his fierce scorn, must have been clever enough to see how much he owed to the moderate men of his own time, who served him as foils. Looking back on the events of the past thirty years, we can see that our own Fredericks owed much of their success in enthralling the spirit of great nations to the fortune which made them loom large against a pale background of peoples who seemed to have lost the courage to face the fact that a willingness to die is sometimes the price of a life worth the living. The hero is always dramatic; the moderate is colorless by contrast, and especially so when he loudly proclaims his revulsion from every form of the heroic spirit.

---

[*] Henry A. Myers, "Heroes and the Way of Compromise," from *Tragedy: A View of Life* (Cornell University Press, 1956).

What happens to a world in which the lines are sharply drawn between extremists and moderate men? Part of the answer is already written. First, the extremist forces his way of life upon his fellows. In the pursuit of his goal, whatever it may be, life is a bright coin which he is willing, at any moment, to exchange for glorious death; he scorns those who believe that a long and peaceful life is the only reasonable goal. In dealing with him, moderate men discover that compromise is not true compromise, but appeasement. Those who make this discovery have a choice between two equally extreme courses of action. Either they may themselves take heroic measures against the fanatic who will not compromise or they may persist in the error of appeasement until it becomes nihilism, the denial of the heroic in life which men sometimes pay for by losing their freedom and even their lives.

Living witnesses to this process, all the great nations were committed during World War II to the heroic way of life. Each was determined to fight on to victory or to death. Some sincerely believed that the moderate way of compromise is the only true way for men and for nations; but first, before they could think of ideal procedures, there was a job to be done, someone to be blotted out, someone with whom compromise was impossible.

After World War II, what? Freed from the menace of some of the new Fredericks, the moderates will presumably go back to the business of raising their level gradually. For some time they will have a new respect for *some* heroes, for those who successfully led them against the would-be world conquerors; but this new respect may easily vanish in the inevitable reaction against "blood, sweat, and tears." Will our utopians increase the power and menace of the remaining Caesars by again insisting that the way of compromise is always the best way of life?

We cannot correct the past mistakes which brought Caesarism into our world. The generation which turned moderation itself into a new form of extremism by refusing to find a place in their scheme of things for the heroic human spirit has done its work. But it is never too late to bring the lessons of experience to bear upon the future. A better understanding of human nature may yet save us from repeating old mistakes.

II

Dramatic poetry is a wonderful storehouse of the lessons of experience and possibly the best source of information concerning heroes and the heroic spirit. By an apparent paradox of intellectual history, the doctrine of the Superman, which exalts intensity of experience, and the philosophy of moderation, which aims chiefly at a long and complete life, were both derived from a study of the tragic hero. In the *Poetics* Aristotle described the extremism of the tragic hero as an error, a failure to find the moderate way, which causes his downfall. In *The Birth of Tragedy* Nietzsche concluded that only as an aesthetic phenomenon is life eternally justified, a conclusion which he expanded in his later writings into the view that life is worth the living only for the Superman, only for the tragic hero who lives dangerously, who risks all to gain all, who touches the heights and depths of experience.

The Birth of Tragedy was Nietzsche's first book. In tragedy he discovered the apparent explanation of his youthful admiration for Richard Wagner's heroic music; from a study of tragedy he derived the conclusions that have strongly influenced so many movements in modern society, movements ranging in intensity from the violence and brutality of the Nazi party to the relatively mild "strenuous life" advocated by Theodore Roosevelt.

According to his own account, Nietzsche at first undertook his study of tragedy to answer a question which seemed more likely to interest the scholars and philologists among whom he moved than to unsettle the world of affairs. Did their interest in tragedy indicate that the Greeks were a pessimistic or decadent people? Nietzsche decided, on the contrary, that tragedy represents the highest degree of affirmation and acceptance of life. In the years which saw the production of the great Attic tragedies the Greeks were a strong people, capable of facing reality at its worst without flinching.

In seeking the answer to his question Nietzsche contracted a raging fever of hero worship. The question of Greek pessimism widened out in his mind into the more important question of whether life is worth living. Most spectators of a great tragedy leave with a sense of reconciliation, with the feeling that life, though terrible, is just. On this point Nietzsche made an important reservation. Life is worth living, he decided, only for the extremist, only for the hero who reaches the heights and depths of feelings. Upon completing his study of tragedy, the future prophet of the Superman was prepared with the outlines of his message. Do you wish to make life worth living? Then love your fate; live dangerously and on the heights; be an extremist, a hero, a superman.

Nietzsche was fascinated by the intensity of the hero's experience, but Aristotle was more deeply impressed by its brevity. The simple fact revealed by tragedy is that heroes always live dangerously and usually do not live long. A comparison of Aristotle's remarks on the tragic hero in the *Poetics* with his theory of the golden mean in the *Nichomachean Ethics* shows the important influence of his study of dramatic poetry on his doctrine of moderation. Since heroes usually do not live long, the extremism which brings about their end is an error of judgment, a tragic failure in conduct. It is an error and a failure because happiness is not to be found in intensity of feeling but only in full self-realization, which requires a long and complete life. "For one swallow does not make a summer, nor does one day; and so too one day, or a short time, does not make a man blessed and happy." Virtue is the very opposite of the error of the tragic hero; it lies in the habit of choosing a mean between extremes, in the moderation which usually secures length of life.

Individual temperament is probably the only explanation for the paradoxical manner in which Aristotle and Nietzsche drew opposite conclusions from the same evidence. Quite clearly, one placed the highest value on the duration and completeness of experience, and the other placed it on intensity. The tragic hero, whose experience is intense, narrow, and brief, is a failure in the eyes of Aristotle and the ideal man in the eyes of Nietzsche.

The opposition between the cult of hero worship, which leads to Caesarism, and the philosophy of moderation, when it is carried to the extreme of nihilism, turns on the question of which quality of experience—intensity or duration—is more desirable. Aristotle himself never carried his doctrine of moderation to the extreme of nihilism. At the risk of inconsistency, he admitted that the virtuous man will sometimes prefer a swallow to a summer: "It is true of the good man too that he does many acts for the sake of his friends and his country, and if necessary dies for them . . . since he would prefer a short period of intense pleasure to a long one of mild enjoyment, a twelve-month of noble life to many years of humdrum existence, and one great and noble action to many trivial ones." The whole truth about human nature, as an answer to this question, can be derived from the same evidence from which the contradictory half-truths of hero worship and nihilism have been derived.

III

The tragic hero has enough in common with other men to make his fate significant to them, and at the same time is unusual enough to excite and hold their interest. His difference, which is the secret of his dramatic interest, is his intensity, which is first manifest in his unyielding purpose. The first quality which distinguishes the hero is the will to do or die, the uncompromising spirit which makes him pay any price, even life itself, for his object. It is this quality which Wolfe at Quebec has in common with Marlowe's Tamburlaine, which Stonewall Jackson shares with Melville's Captain Ahab. In itself it is without moral significance, for the unyielding hero may be either a saint or a sinner in the eyes of the spectator. But unyielding character is the spring from which heroic and dramatic actions flow.

The hero's attitude toward life is that of Ahab toward the whale; not even the gods can swerve him from his purpose. "Over unsounded gorges, through the rifled hearts of mountains, under torrents' beds, unerringly I rush! Naught's an obstacle, naught's an angle to the iron way!" Such intensity demands concentration, and Ahab's purpose is centered on a single object, Moby Dick. "Ay, ay!" he cries, "and I'll chase him round Good Hope, and round the Horn, and round the Norway Maelstrom, and round perdition's flames before I give him up." And so it always is with heroes: each has his favorite phantom, always something specific, never an abstraction. The hero does not die for love, or for power, or for success, or for revenge: he dies for Juliet, or for Abbie, or for Rautendelein, or for Desdemona; he dies to be Duncan's successor or for "infinite riches in a little room"; he dies to climb the tower that he has built. The hero is indeed always a monomaniac to some extent, but he is different from his fellow men only in degree, not in kind, only in the intensity with which he pursues his object.

In life and in drama the heroic is marked by an uncompromising will; in both, moreover, the difference between the simplest and the greatest is that the greatest brings the widest range of feeling and the highest intellectual power to bear upon his inflexible purpose. Such is the difference between Grant in the Wilderness and Lincoln in the White House, between Tamburlaine and Hamlet. Grant's determination to fight it out on one line is as firm as Lincoln's will to carry through the war, but Lincoln adds to fundamental determination an intellectual power made manifest in his brooding on the meaning of events, as in the Gettysburg and Second Inaugural addresses, and a wide range of feeling which carries him into the hearts of all the actors in the national tragedy. His acts of kindness to delinquent soldiers, his concern for the point of view of his opponents, his letter to Mrs. Bixby—make more pointed, more heroic, more valuable his determination to save the Union. We rightly value the heroic according to its cost to the hero; and a Hamlet, to whom the cost is so great as to make him seem at times weak in will, displays a richer heroism in one moment of tortured struggle than can be found in all the thoughtless, insensate fury of a Tamburlaine.

IV

Such is the nature of the hero; what are its inevitable consequences? If we may trust the testimony of all serious drama, the outstanding consequence is that the hero lives intensely but not long. Life is the price we must all pay for experience; most of us dole it out in little sums over a long period of time; the hero gladly pays in a lump sum.

A more profoundly significant consequence is that the hero always gets what he wants—and always pays the full price. Oedipus finds the unknown murderer, at a cost; Wolfe takes Quebec, but falls in the moment of victory; Ahab throws the harpoon, and dies; Romeo comes back to Juliet, in death. The hero can have anything he wants, for a price; but not even a hero can get something for nothing.

Drama reveals these consequences in many ways—by showing that the hero falls as far as he rises or that he is brought down by the very forces which bring him to the top. The great turn of the wheel of fortune which carries the hero to the extremes of joy and grief, often in one moment of dazzling intensity, is the dramatic symbol of the endless little ups and downs, the little sorrows and joys, of ordinary men. The hero's great moment contains within itself rise and fall, fortune and misfortune, triumph and disaster. As Ahab at last faces the white whale alone, he cries: "Oh, now I feel my topmost greatness lies in my topmost grief." Othello's fate is wonderfully balanced in the moment of his discovery of Desdemona's innocence. For him this discovery means sheer exaltation; and yet this exaltation must come to him balanced by the horror of his own crime. Joy and sorrow are balanced with a terrible nicety, that wonderful balance which Edgar in *King Lear* notes in speaking of the death of his father:

> his flaw'd heart,—
> Alack, too weak the conflict to support!—
> 'Twixt two extremes of passion, joy and grief,
> Burst smilingly.

All these qualities suit the hero to the purposes and necessities of dramatic poetry. Some attempts have been made to dispense with the hero in serious drama. Maeterlinck says in a famous essay on tragedy:

I have grown to believe that an old man, seated in his armchair, waiting patiently, with his lamp beside him . . . I have grown to believe that he, motionless as he is, does yet live in reality a deeper, more human, and more universal life than the lover who strangles his mistress, the captain who conquers in battle, or "the husband who avenges his honor."

That the old man is as tragic as the hero, no one should question: he too has his moments; he too pays for what he gets. If it were not so, if he were not tragic in this sense, then the hero of tragic drama could have no universal significance. The trouble with the old man in the armchair is that he is tragic but not dramatic. His life has meaning but lacks every other dramatic quality; intensity, suspense, surprise, reversal, heightened diction, power to excite basic feelings—all are missing. When we think of the tragic in terms of the two-sided nature of feeling which is the basis of the common destiny of men, one man is as good an illustration as another, but only the intense hero makes drama possible, and makes it possible for it to end within two hours.

After we have looked at enough heroes, we can readily understand Aristotle's reaction to their way of life. He sees the hero for what he is, if the ultimate standard of conduct is length and completeness of life: a man not "eminently good and just, yet whose misfortune is brought about not by vice or depravity, but by some error or frailty." No doubt this tragic flaw is simply the essential nature of the hero—his extremism. No hero ever chose the golden mean in a critical moment; no hero would ever sacrifice his purpose or any part of the "iron way" to the dictates of the kind of reason and virtue which bring length of life.

V

Great drama itself is not an adverse criticism of the way of heroes. Only confirmed Aristotelians believe that it is. Through his hero the dramatist is enabled to present the essence of life; and from the character of the hero and his fate we may draw our own conclusions. One famous exception is Ibsen's *Brand*, which was deliberately intended to be an attack on the heroic way of life. Brand, the fanatic priest, demands of all those about him, of his family and of his parishioners, the same heroic devotion to God and negation of the world which he himself seeks to practice. These demands result ultimately in the ruin of his family, the revolt of his flock, and his own death. But Ibsen is able to make the case neither better nor worse for the hero than have all great tragedies. Particularly interesting about the play, however, is what Ibsen, as a great dramatist, thought about the nature of the hero. This is revealed in two phrases, one positive, the other negative. "All or nothing," says Brand again and again to his followers in demanding their devotion. And warning them ever and again of evil, he repeats: "The devil is compromise."

From *Brand* we might conclude that Ibsen ascribed the woes of mankind to the iron way of heroes. But in *Peer Gynt*, his poetic satire on the Norwegian character, he wrote an even more impressive criticism of the way of compromise. The play was written out of the depths of Ibsen's indignation with Norway for her failure to ally herself with Denmark in the Danish-Prussian war. Peer Gynt is the opposite of Brand. "Enough," is his motto, not "all or nothing." His method is to go around obstacles and to abandon projects, ideals, and objectives when they seem to demand the ultimate risk. Since, in following this method, he wanders over the face of the earth, he seems to have led a richer life than Brand, who fights it out with the devil of compromise within the narrow confines of his parish. In the end, however, Peer is revealed as one who stands for nothing, a man without principles or character, a nonentity. Like the objects of Thoreau's pity, he has frittered away his life in detail. One could say to him, as to the little mouse who was granted his wish to have wings: "You're nothing but a nothing; you're not a thing at all."

All drama reminds us that it is a serious mistake to underestimate the power of the heroic or to assume that people see only the unpleasant consequences of the way of heroes and none of its compensations. The reverse is more often true. "Hero worship" is a familiar term, but there is no similar familiar term to denote reverence for the moderate man. Great drama excites not only pity and terror, but also awe and admiration, and other feelings that lie so deep that we cannot easily name them. Most of the power of the dramatic to excite deep feeling rests in the hero. In him we see ourselves on a larger scale, often ourselves as we should like to be, for who would not like to be firmer of purpose, more intent intellectually, capable of deeper feeling? While we hunger for more of life, we cannot resist the appeal of the hero's intensity. We necessarily have our moments when Aristotle's golden mean seems to be indeed a kind of "golden meanness," a doctrine for the half-hearted who shrink from the farther reaches of experience, a prescription for a long life and a dull one, a guiding principle for a world of old men dozing in armchairs.

VI

Powerful indeed is hero worship. If drama were possible only in the form of tragic poetry, one might agree with Plato in ruling poets out of the ideal state. Tragedy by itself is an incomplete picture of life; since it presents only heroes to us, it needs comedy as an antidote to the unbridled hero worship which at times it might otherwise cause. Comedy, which teaches us to know a fool when we see one, teaches us also that not any fool can be a hero. The ordinary man, taking his stand on a trivial issue in his efforts to ape the hero, succeeds in being merely sullen. Or if he is, like Nietzsche, a gentle and serious young scholar, an intuitive but humorless philologist, too long fed on a diet of tragic poetry and Wagnerian music, he goes forth as a prophet to trouble the world with dreams of life aesthetically justified by a race of tragic heroes and to bring himself to madness.

To go with Oedipus, we need the Dionysos of *The Frogs;* to go with Hamlet, we need Falstaff; to go with the Cid, we need Orgon. A main effect of *The Frogs* is to show what happens to Dionysos, a sturdy but moderate middle-class soul who sets out to play the part of Hercules, a hero. If the point sinks in, we think twice before aping the way of heroes. As for Falstaff—he is neither a hero nor a fool: he knows how his kind of person should behave on a battlefield; and so, without shame, he lies down to play dead until the heroes have done their work. Orgon *is* a fool, who would never escape the machinations of Tartuffe were it not for the intervention of the king's officer. His folly, which takes the form of worship of the extreme forms of piety, makes him an ideal dupe for a hypocrite.

We may thank the comic spirit for deflating the pseudoheroic in life, and enlist it always in our service against the triumph of the simplest kind of hero, who has intensity of purpose without a correspondingly great capacity for thought and feeling. Such heroes, who are always without humor themselves, flourish in the absence of laughter. Meredith long ago pointed out that the comic spirit is an enemy of the sentimental, of the puritanical, and of the bacchanalian: it is even more strongly the sworn foe of the pseudoheroic and of the kind of hero whose brutality is the result of a will unguided by thought and feeling.

VII

Between great science, which seeks to show us *nature as it is*, caring nothing for what *it should be*, and great poetry, which has always shown us *human nature as it is*, caring nothing for what the reader thinks *it should be*, there can be no quarrel. But science in its beginnings had to contend with the pretensions of poets in the realm of nature; and today men neglect the solid realities of poetry for the vaporings of rhapsodists, who rest their dreams of progress toward Utopia upon their faith in the ability of science to do the impossible. It pleases us to smile at the pretensions of the philosopher-poet, Heraclitus, who thought that a new sun is born each day in the heavens. We see the folly of trying to make poetry do the work of mathematics. But the rhapsodists of our world are not poets who seek to take over the province of science; rather they are the pseudo scientists who, either in ignorance of or in defiance of the storehouse of wisdom to be found in poetry, would persuade us that the changes which man has been able to effect in his environment foreshadow even more wonderful changes in human nature itself. We have much to learn from both science and poetry. Science has taught us that the same old sun rises daily; the ancient wisdom of poetry is that it shines, and will always shine, upon the same old race of men—upon moderate men, heroes, and fools alike.

On one point Nietzsche was truly inspired: he saw that there is no place in a culture for tragic poetry once men have convinced themselves that they can change the basic conditions of their lives. For tragic poetry steels us to face evil as an inevitable aspect of experience; and it has no place in our culture if we believe that science and technology can free us from evil. Tragic poetry teaches us that each man pursues his own specific good, and that all too often the desire of two or more men for the same object makes conflict a brute fact in human affairs. Of what use is tragic poetry if we are bemused by the Socratic dream of a universal good acceptable to all and sharable by all? Tragic poetry teaches us that fanatics who seek an absolute good for mankind bring down upon men, by an inevitable recoil, their deepest sufferings. Of what use is tragic poetry, if madmen, lusting for personal power, convince us that paradise on earth will be possible once we have submitted ourselves to their wills?

This is the ancient wisdom of poetry which history today confirms: human nature is unchanging, and heroes, fools, and moderate men are always with us. Each of us, indeed, may be fated to play all of these roles in turn.

and sometimes more than one role at once. There is often a comic view of even the admirable hero: the Socrates of *The Clouds*, snub-nosed, bald, homely as a gargoyle, absent-minded and absurd in his reasoning, is based upon life, as is the Socrates of the Dialogues. The world has decided that Plato has given us the truer measure of the man, but we should not forget the other portrait. Such twin portraits are often possible. When Rostand sought to follow Hugo's injunction to create heroes who would exhibit the contrast of the sublime and grotesque to be found in life itself, he wrote *Cyrano de Bergerac*, calling it a "heroic comedy" in order to point out that the heroic and the comic can in unusual instances go hand in hand. Cyrano, who says that he seeks "to be always admirable in all things," is a hero to outdo the ordinary hero, who is extreme in one thing only. "Everything to excess," a principle that is fantastic yet heroic, guides Cyrano's every act. When he fights, he fights a hundred men; when he is generous, he gives away all his money; when he is witty, he composes a ballade while fighting a duel. Spectators are so carried away by a blend of laughter and admiration that at the end no one can say which symbol is truer to the man, the grotesque, huge nose which makes him comic in appearance or the heroic plume which he wears in his hat, carrying it in death still unsmirched.

VIII

Are all men likely ever to agree that either intensity or duration is the higher value in experience? Not until the past is a completely false guide to the future; not until tragic poetry is completely out of touch with human nature. Since we have no grounds on which to predict the coming of a new kind of man, except the say-so of those romantic utopians who mistake science for magic, we must continue to think in terms of men as they are. In a world in which the fanatical extremist is a hardy perennial, always to be reckoned with, we must fortify ourselves with wisdom for the moment when our turn may come to play, as best we can, the part of heroes.

Since most men prefer a long life even at the expense of stretches of dullness, the Aristotelian golden mean points to the sensible course for men and nations most of the time. But if only one issue in a lifetime compels the moderate man to take a heroic stand, that is the one moment that fixes his place in history as either a man or a nonentity.

The trick is to know the right time and the right issue. No rule is possible. The simple hero is driven on by inflexible character. The fool mistakes the time and is merely sullen over trifles.

The moment when moderate men take a stand is always grave, but it is not a time for despair. All is not lost. What is lost is the delusion that men can live by compromise alone. This delusion is an empty and negative form of extremism. It is nihilism—the heroic negation of the heroic in life. If we were to follow it consistently, we should become zeroes and tempt others to take our places. The world of human nature abhors a vacuum. When some men shrink altogether from the heroic, others are tempted to use it in its worst form.

Finally, in order to act wisely we must free ourselves from the half-truths designed to prove that the justice of our individual fate depends upon our choice between moderation and heroic action. All universal meaning in tragic poetry depends upon our recognition that in respect to justice the fate of the tragic hero is the same as that of the moderate man. Nietzsche was wrong in assuming that life can be justified only by living intensely. On the other hand, it is the tender sentimentalist, never the hero himself, who shrinks from the grand reversals which turn life into drama and history; and Aristotle was right in recognizing the compensations of heroic deeds, even if that recognition does invalidate his general criticism of the tragic hero. The Ahabs and Lincolns, the Cordelias and Antigones, accept their fate because they know its inner reality, the exaltation which accompanies suffering or dying for principles. The death of the hero is an affirmation of the unalterable conditions of life, a memorable symbol for multitudes who show their own acceptance by living.

There is justice in life for both the hero and the moderate man. The very surface of events points to it. What the hero gains in intensity, he usually loses in duration. What the moderate man gains in duration, he usually loses in intensity. But there is a deeper reality which unites heroes and moderate men in a common destiny. Both are subject to the fixed conditions whereby sorrow is the price of joy. Through the two-sided nature of human feeling, with its poles of good and evil, each pays for what he gets. The hero takes all, gives all, in one grand moment. The moderate man pays a little, lives to doze in his chair, and pays a little more. The choice between intensity and duration cannot upset the just equation whereby men pay with their lives for experience.

The Christian Tragic Hero: Contrasting Captain Ahab's Doom and Its Classic Greek Prototype*

W. H. AUDEN

Moby Dick is at once an heroic epic like the *Iliad*, an heroic tragedy like the *Oresteia*, an heroic quest like the legend of the *Golden Fleece*, and an allegorical religious quest like *Pilgrim's Progress;* it is also a nineteenth century American novel. Even if it were not the great book it is, it would therefore be of unusual interest to the critic who would compare the values believed in and the attitudes held at different stages in Western civilization. I propose in this article to consider only one of them, the concept of the Tragic Hero in Greece and in Christendom. Most of the characteristics one observes in Melville's hero can also be seen in, say, the heroes of Shakespeare's tragedies, but Melville's choral asides make them more explicit in his own case.

To sum up in advance, the conclusions I shall try to demonstrate are these: first, Greek tragedy is the tragedy of necessity; i.e., the feeling aroused in the spectator is "What a pity it had to be this way"; Christian tragedy is the tragedy of possibility, "What a pity it was this way when it might have been otherwise"; secondly, the hubris which is the flaw in the Greek hero's character is the illusion of a man who knows himself strong and believes that nothing can shake that strength, while the corresponding Christian sin of Pride is the illusion of a man who knows himself weak but

---

*W. H. Auden, "The Christian Tragic Hero," from *The New York Times Book Review*, December 16, 1945, pp. 1, 21.

believes he can by his own efforts transcend that weakness and become strong.

In using the term Christian I am not trying to suggest that Melville or Shakespeare or any other author necessarily believed the Christian dogmas, but that their conception of man's nature is, historically, derived from them.

As an example of Greek tragedy let us take *Oedipus Rex*. As a young man, Oedipus learns from a prophecy that he is fated to murder his father and marry his mother. Believing that his foster parents are his real parents he leaves Carthage [*sic*]. He meets an old man on the road; they quarrel about who shall give way to the other, and Oedipus kills him. He comes to Thebes, saves it from a monster, and is rewarded by the hand of its Queen, Jocasta. Thebes is stricken with plague, and the Oracle declares the cause to be the undetected presence of a criminal. Oedipus undertakes an investigation and discovers that the criminal is himself. In expiation of his crime he puts out his eyes, and Jocasta hangs herself.

A modern reader, accustomed to the tragedy of possibility, instinctively asks, "Where and when did he make the wrong choice?" and as instinctively answers, "He should not have listened to the prophecy in the first place, or, having done so, then he should never have struck the old man or anyone else and should never have married Jocasta or anyone else." But such thoughts would never have occurred to Sophocles or his audience. Macbeth and Captain Ahab are wrong to listen to the prophecies about them, because they are equivocal, and each reads into his a possibility he is wrong to desire; the prophecy Oedipus hears is not only unequivocal but something he is right to wish to avoid. When he kills the old man he feels no guilt, neither is he expected to feel any, and when he marries Jocasta there is nothing the matter with the relation as such. It is only when it turns out that, as a matter of fact, the former was his father and the latter is his mother that guilt begins.

The tragedy is that what had to happen happened, and if one asks what was wrong with Oedipus, that such a terrible fate should be assigned to him, one can only say that it is a punishment for a hubris which was necessarily his before he learnt of the prophecy at all; i.e., had he not had such a character, the prophecy would never have been made.

Other Greek heroes are faced with the tragic choice between two evils: Agamemnon must either sacrifice his daughter or fail in his duty to the Greek Army; Antigone must be false either to her loyalty to her brother or to her loyalty to her city.

The tragic situation, of learning that one is a criminal or of being forced to become one, is not created by the flaw in the hero's character, but is sent him by the gods as a punishment for having such a flaw.

The pessimistic conclusion that underlies Greek tragedy seems to be this: that if one is a hero, i.e., an exceptional individual, one must be guilty of hubris and be punished by a tragic fate; the only alternative and not one a person can choose for himself is to be a member of the chorus, i.e., one of the average mass; to be both exceptional and good is impossible.

How does "Moby Dick" compare with this?

The hero, Captain Ahab, far from being exceptionally fortunate, is at the beginning, what in a Greek tragedy he could only be at the end, exceptionally unfortunate. He is already the victim of what the modern newspaper, which is Greek in this respect, would call a tragedy; a whale has bitten off his leg. What to the Greeks could only have been a punishment for sin is here a temptation to sin, an opportunity to choose; by making the wrong choice and continuing to make it, Ahab punishes himself. To say that a character is tempted means that it is confronted by possibility, that it is not a fixed state but a process of becoming: the possibilities are not infinite; i.e., Ahab cannot become Starbuck or Pip or Ishmael or anyone else except Ahab, but the possibilities are eternal; the past is irrevocable but always redeemable now.

Thus we can at every moment answer the question, "What should Ahab do now?" Before the story opens he has suffered and made his first wrong choice. He was not wrong to make Moby Dick into a symbol of all the inexplicable suffering in the world; on the contrary, the capacity to see the universal in the particular is the mark of human greatness, and it is only Flask, the Philistine trimmer, who says, "A whale is only a whale"; he was wrong, however, to insist on his own explanation, that the motive behind the whale's act and behind all suffering is personal malevolence. Once he has done so, he can still be saved, but he has made his salvation a much harder task, for he is now required to forgive the whale personally, in contrast, for instance, to Captain Boomer, who, like Ahab, has been deprived of a limb by Moby Dick, but in his pragmatic English way explains the whale's ferocity as mere clumsiness which is easier to forgive than malice.

In Greek tragedy are two kinds of characters, the exceptional hero and the average chorus, and neither can become the other; in Christian tragedy there is not only an infinite variety of possible characters, varying all the way from Ahab, the captain, who defiantly insists on being absolutely unique, down to Pip, the cabin boy, who is too afraid to claim even his own name, but overshadowing them all is the possibility of each becoming both exceptional and good; this ultimate possibility for hero and chorus alike is stated in Father Mapple's sermon, and it is to become a saint—i.e., the individual who of his own free will surrenders his will to the will of God. In this surrender he does not become a ventriloquist's doll, for the God who acts through him can only do so by his consent; there always remain two wills, and the saint, therefore (unlike the late Greek conception of the un-dramatic Sage who is good by necessity because he knows), never ceases to be tempted to obey his own desires.

Of this possibility Ahab's career is at every point a negative parody.

The saint does not ask to be one, he is called to become one, and assents to the call. The outward sign that Ahab is so called, is the suffering which is suddenly intruded into his life. What he is called to become, we do not, of course, know for certain—all we know for certain is that he rejected it—but we can guess that he was called to give up hunting whales—i.e., the normal cannibalistic life of this world, a life which is permitted, for instance, to Queequeg (who, though sinless, is not a saint, but the innocent man be-fore the fall) but no longer to Ahab once he has been made uniquely con-scious of the suffering it inflicts. Of the others, less is required: of Starbuck that he face evil instead of superstitiously avoiding it, of Stubb that he face his fears instead of whistling in the dark; but of Ahab alone is required, be-cause he alone has the necessary heroic passion, to become a real and not a merely respectable Quaker.

Ahab is not deaf; he hears the call and refuses it with all the passion with which he might have accepted it; like the saint he wills one thing—to kill Moby Dick. For this he leaves his wife and child; for this his first act in the book is to throw away his pipe, his last physical addiction, his last relation with the element of earth; for this he destroys the ship's quadrant, its rela-tion to the element of air so that the Pequod can only know the universe through compass and line in terms of the dualistic antagonism of fire and water.

The saint, knowing his will to be weak, may express his external resolve by a temporal or bodily ritual act, but his vow and his act concern his own will alone. Ahab attempts to use ritual as a magical means of compelling the wills of others, as when he forces the crew to swear on their harpoons, and finally even to compel lifeless things, as when he baptizes a harpoon itself.

Just as the saint never ceases to be tempted to forsake his calling, so, vice versa, Ahab is never free from the possibility of renouncing his refusal. Divine grace offers itself, now in the nostalgic beauty of fine weather, now as Gabriel, the mad idolater of the whale, an unlovely reflection of himself, and finally, in its strongest and least disguised form, as the cry for help of a friend in distress when the Pequod meets the Rachel, and it is only after he has refused this last offer that his doom becomes necessary. Melville por-trays this decisive change with great subtlety. For it is at this point that Ahab places the idiot Pip in his cabin and, in a grotesque parody of the saint as the servant of servants, takes for himself the humble position of lookout on the mast which is the negative image of the martyr's cross. Instead of gaining a martyr's crown, however, his hat, the badge of his authority, is snatched from his head by the Jovian eagle, and from this moment Fedallah, the slave, the projection of Ahab's will, seems suddenly to have taken charge of his creator, or rather his summoner. Fedallah is clearly intended by Melville, I think, to represent the demonic, i.e., that which (unlike Ahab, who is tempted by suffering) tempts itself and denies for the sake of denying, and about which, therefore, nothing historic can be said; we are only told his religion.

So Ahab, refusing life, goes unrepentant, like all of Shakespeare's tragic heroes, to the unnecessary death he has chosen, dragging with him all his companions, and the only survivor is, as in Greek tragedy, the Chorus, the spectator, Ishmael. But Ishmael is not, like the Greek Chorus, the eternal average man, for he isn't a character at all. To be a character one must will and act, and Ishmael has no will, only consciousness; he does not act, he only knows, and what he knows is good *and* evil, i.e., possibility. He cannot die because he has not yet begun to live, and he ends the book as a baby, reborn from the sea in Queequeg's coffin, thrust back into life as an orphan with his first choice still to make.

Tragedy and the Common Man[*]

ARTHUR MILLER

In this age few tragedies are written. It has often been held that the lack is due to a paucity of heroes among us, or else that modern man has had the blood drawn out of his organs of belief by the skepticism of science, and the heroic attack on life cannot feed on an attitude of reserve and circumspection. For one reason or another, we are often held to be below tragedy—or tragedy above us. The inevitable conclusion is, of course, that the tragic mode is archaic, fit only for the very highly placed, the kings or the kingly, and where this admission is not made in so many words it is most often implied.

I believe that the common man is as apt a subject for tragedy in its highest sense as kings were. On the face of it this ought to be obvious in the light of modern psychiatry, which bases its analysis upon classic formulations, such as the Oedipus and Orestes complexes, for instances, which were enacted by royal beings, but which apply to everyone in similar emotional situations.

More simply, when the question of tragedy in art is not at issue, we never hesitate to attribute to the well-placed and the exalted the very same mental processes as the lowly. And finally, if the exaltation of tragic action were truly a property of the high-bred character alone, it is inconceivable that the mass of mankind should cherish tragedy above all other forms, let alone be capable of understanding it.

As a general rule, to which there may be exceptions unknown to me, I think the tragic feeling is evoked in us when we are in the presence of a character who is ready to lay down his life, if need be, to secure one thing— his sense of personal dignity. From Orestes to Hamlet, Medea to Macbeth, the underlying struggle is that of the individual attempting to gain his "rightful" position in his society.

---

[*] Arthur Miller, "Tragedy and the Common Man," *New York Times*, February 27, 1949.

148

Sometimes he is one who has been displaced from it, sometimes one who seeks to attain it for the first time, but the fateful wound from which the inevitable events spiral is the wound of indignity, and its dominant force is indignation. Tragedy, then, is the consequence of a man's total compulsion to evaluate himself justly.

In the sense of having been initiated by the hero himself, the tale always reveals what has been called his "tragic flaw," a failing that is not peculiar to grand or elevated characters. Nor is it necessarily a weakness. The flaw, or crack in the character, is really nothing—and need be nothing, but his inherent unwillingness to remain passive in the face of what he conceives to be a challenge to his dignity, his image of his rightful status. Only the passive, only those who accept their lot without active retaliation, are "flawless." Most of us are in that category.

But there are among us today, as there always have been, those who act against the scheme of things that degrades them, and in the process of action everything we have accepted out of fear or insensitivity or ignorance is shaken before us and examined, and from this total onslaught by an individual against the seemingly stable cosmos surrounding us—from this total examination of the "unchangeable" environment—comes the terror and the fear that is classically associated with tragedy.

More important, from this total questioning of what has previously been unquestioned, we learn. And such a process is not beyond the common man. In revolutions around the world, these past thirty years, he has demonstrated again and again this inner dynamic of all tragedy.

Insistence upon the rank of the tragic hero, or the so-called nobility of his character, is really but a clinging to the outward forms of tragedy. If rank or nobility of character was indispensable, then it would follow that the problems of those with rank were the particular problems of tragedy. But surely the right of one monarch to capture the domain from another no longer raises our passions, nor are our concepts of justice what they were to the mind of an Elizabethan king.

The quality in such plays that does shake us, however, derives from the underlying fear of being displaced, the disaster inherent in being torn away from our chosen image of what and who we are in this world. Among us today this fear is as strong, and perhaps stronger, than it ever was. In fact, it is the common man who knows this fear best.

Now, if it is true that tragedy is the consequence of a man's total compulsion to evaluate himself justly, his destruction in the attempt posits a wrong or an evil in his environment. And this is precisely the morality of tragedy and its lesson. The discovery of the moral law, which is what the enlightenment of tragedy consists of, is not the discovery of some abstract or metaphysical quantity.

The tragic right is a condition of life, a condition in which the human personality is able to flower and realize itself. The wrong is the condition which suppresses man, perverts the flowing out of his love and creative instinct. Tragedy enlightens—and it must, in that it points the heroic finger at the enemy of man's freedom. The thrust for freedom is the quality in tragedy which exalts. The revolutionary questioning of the stable environment is what terrifies. In no way is the common man debarred from such thoughts or such actions.

Seen in this light, our lack of tragedy may be partially accounted for by the turn which modern literature has taken toward the purely psychiatric view of life, or the purely sociological. If all our miseries, our indignities, are born and bred within our minds, then all action, let alone the heroic action, is obviously impossible.

And if society alone is responsible for the cramping of our lives, then the protagonist must needs be so pure and faultless as to force us to deny his validity as a character. From neither of these views can tragedy derive, simply because neither represents a balanced concept of life. Above all else, tragedy requires the finest appreciation by the writer of cause and effect.

No tragedy can therefore come about when its author fears to question absolutely everything, when he regards any institution, habit or custom as being either everlasting, immutable or inevitable. In the tragic view the need of man to wholly realize himself is the only fixed star, and whatever it is that hedges his nature and lowers it is ripe for attack and examination. Which is not to say that tragedy must preach revolution.

The Greeks could probe the very heavenly origin of their ways and return to confirm the rightness of laws. And Job could face God in anger, demanding his right and end in submission. But for a moment everything is in suspension, nothing is accepted, and in this stretching and tearing apart of the cosmos, in the very action of so doing, the character gains "size," the tragic stature which is spuriously attached to the royal or the highborn in our minds. The commonest of men may take on that stature to the extent of his willingness to throw all he has into the contest, the battle to secure his rightful place in his world.

There is a misconception of tragedy with which I have been struck in review after review, and in many conversations with writers and readers alike. It is the idea that tragedy is of necessity allied to pessimism. Even the dictionary says nothing more about the word than that it means a story with a sad or unhappy ending. This impression is so firmly fixed that I almost hesitate to claim that in truth tragedy implies more optimism in its author than does comedy, and that its final result ought to be the reinforcement of the onlooker's brightest opinions of the human animal.

For, if it is true to say that in essence the tragic hero is intent upon claiming his whole due as a personality, and if this struggle must be total and without reservation, then it automatically demonstrates the indestructible will of man to achieve his humanity.

The possibility of victory must be there in tragedy. Where pathos rules, where pathos is finally derived, a character has fought a battle he could not possibly have won. The pathetic is achieved when the protagonist is, by virtue of his witlessness, his insensitivity or the very air he gives off, incapable of grappling with a much superior force.

Pathos truly is the mode for the pessimist. But tragedy requires a nicer balance between what is possible and what is impossible. And it is curious, although edifying, that the plays we revere, century after century, are the tragedies. In them, and in them alone, lies the belief—optimistic, if you will, in the perfectibility of man.

It is time, I think, that we who are without kings, took up this bright thread of our history and followed it to the only place it can possibly lead in our time—the heart and spirit of the average man.

The Gangster as Tragic Hero*

ROBERT WARSHOW

America, as a social and political organization, is committed to a cheerful view of life. It could not be otherwise. The sense of tragedy is a luxury of aristocratic societies, where the fate of the individual is not conceived of as having a direct and legitimate political importance, being determined by a fixed and supra-political—that is, non-controversial—moral order or fate. Modern equalitarian societies, however, whether democratic or authoritarian in their political forms, always base themselves on the claim that they are making life happier; the avowed function of the modern state, at least in its ultimate terms, is not only to regulate social relations, but also to determine the quality and the possibilities of human life in general. Happiness thus becomes the chief political issue—in a sense, the only political issue—and for that reason it can never be treated as an issue at all. If an American or a Russian is unhappy, it implies a certain reprobation of his society, and therefore, by a logic of which we can all recognize the necessity, it becomes an obligation of citizenship to be cheerful; if the authorities find it necessary, the citizen may even be compelled to make a public display of his cheerfulness on important occasions, just as he may be conscripted into the army in time of war.

Naturally, this civic responsibility rests most strongly upon the organs of mass culture. The individual citizen may still be permitted his private unhappiness so long as it does not take on political significance, the extent of this tolerance being determined by how large an area of private life the society can accommodate. But every production of mass culture is a public act and must conform with accepted notions of the public good. Nobody seriously questions the principle that it is the function of mass culture to maintain public morale, and certainly nobody in the mass audience objects

* Robert Warshow, "The Gangster as Tragic Hero," from *The Immediate Experience* (Doubleday, 1954), pp. 127–133.

to having his morale maintained.[1] At a time when the normal condition of the citizen is a state of anxiety, euphoria spreads over our culture like the broad smile of an idiot. In terms of attitudes towards life, there is very little difference between a "happy" movie like *Good News*, which ignores death and suffering, and a "sad" movie like *A Tree Grows in Brooklyn*, which uses death and suffering as incidents in the service of a higher optimism.

But, whatever its effectiveness as a source of consolation and a means of pressure for maintaining "positive" social attitudes, this optimism is fundamentally satisfying to no one, not even to those who would be most disoriented without its support. Even within the area of mass culture, there always exists a current of opposition, seeking to express by whatever means are available to it that sense of desperation and inevitable failure which optimism itself helps to create. Most often, this opposition is confined to rudimentary or semi-literate forms: in mob politics and journalism, for example, or in certain kinds of religious enthusiasm. When it does enter the field of art, it is likely to be disguised or attenuated: in an unspecific form of expression like jazz, in the basically harmless nihilism of the Marx Brothers, in the continually reasserted strain of hopelessness that often seems to be the real meaning of the soap opera. The gangster film is remarkable in that it fills the need for disguise (though not sufficiently to avoid arousing uneasiness) without requiring any serious distortion. From its beginnings, it has been a consistent and astonishingly complete presentation of the modern sense of tragedy.[2]

In its initial character, the gangster film is simply one example of the movies' constant tendency to create fixed dramatic patterns that can be repeated indefinitely with a reasonable expectation of profit. One gangster film follows another as one musical or one Western follows another. But this rigidity is not necessarily opposed to the requirements of art. There have been very successful types of art in the past which developed such specific and detailed conventions as almost to make individual examples of the type interchangeable. This is true, for example, of Elizabethan revenge tragedy and Restoration comedy.

For such a type to be successful means that its conventions have imposed themselves upon the general consciousness and become the accepted vehicles

---

[1] In her testimony before the House Committee on Un-American Activities, Mrs. Leila Rogers said that the movie *None But the Lonely Heart* was un-American because it was gloomy. Like so much else that was said during the unhappy investigation of Hollywood, this statement was at once stupid and illuminating. One knew immediately what Mrs. Rogers was talking about; she had simply been insensitive enough to carry her philistinism to its conclusion.

[2] Efforts have been made from time to time to bring the gangster film into line with the prevailing optimism and social constructiveness of our culture; *Kiss of Death* is a recent example. These efforts are usually unsuccessful; the reasons for their lack of success are interesting in themselves, but I shall not be able to discuss them here.

of a particular set of attitudes and a particular aesthetic effect. One goes to
any individual example of the type with very definite expectations, and
originality is to be welcomed only in the degree that it intensifies the expected experience without fundamentally altering it. Moreover, the relationship between the conventions which go to make up such a type and the
real experience of its audience or the real facts of whatever situation it pretends to describe is of only secondary importance and does not determine
its aesthetic force. It is only in an ultimate sense that the type appeals to its
audience's experience of reality; much more immediately, it appeals to previous experience of the type itself: it creates its own field of reference.

Thus the importance of the gangster film, and the nature and intensity of
its emotional and aesthetic impact, cannot be measured in terms of the place
of the gangster himself or the importance of the problem of crime in American life. Those European movie-goers who think there is a gangster on
every corner in New York are certainly deceived, but defenders of the
"positive" side of American culture are equally deceived if they think it
relevant to point out that most Americans have never seen a gangster. What
matters is that the experience of the gangster *as an experience of art* is universal to Americans. There is almost nothing we understand better or react to
more readily or with quicker intelligence. The Western film, though it
seems never to diminish in popularity, is for most of us no more than the
folklore of the past, familiar and understandable only because it has been
repeated so often. The gangster film comes much closer. In ways that we
do not easily or willingly define, the gangster speaks for us, expressing that
part of the American psyche which rejects the qualities and the demands of
modern life, which rejects "Americanism" itself.

The gangster is the man of the city, with the city's language and knowledge, with its queer and dishonest skills and its terrible daring, carrying his
life in his hands like a placard, like a club. For everyone else, there is at
least the theoretical possibility of another world—in that happier American
culture which the gangster denies, the city does not really exist; it is only a
more crowded and more brightly lit country—but for the gangster there is
only the city; he must inhabit it in order to personify it: not the real city,
but that dangerous and sad city of the imagination which is so much more
important, which is the modern world. And the gangster—though there are
real gangsters—is also, and primarily, a creature of the imagination. The
real city, one might say, produces only criminals; the imaginary city produces the gangster: he is what we want to be and what we are afraid we
may become.

Thrown into the crowd without background or advantages, with only
those ambiguous skills which the rest of us—the real people of the real city
—can only pretend to have, the gangster is required to make his way, to

make his life and impose it on others. Usually, when we come upon him, he has already made his choice or the choice has already been made for him, it doesn't matter which: we are not permitted to ask whether at some point he could have chosen to be something else than what he is.

The gangster's activity is actually a form of rational enterprise, involving fairly definite goals and various techniques for achieving them. But this rationality is usually no more than a vague background; we know, perhaps, that the gangster sells liquor or that he operates a numbers racket; often we are not given even that much information. So his activity becomes a kind of pure criminality: he hurts people. Certainly our response to the gangster film is most consistently and most universally a response to sadism; we gain the double satisfaction of participating vicariously in the gangster's sadism and then seeing it turned against the gangster himself.

But on another level the quality of irrational brutality and the quality of rational enterprise become one. Since we do not see the rational and routine aspects of the gangster's behavior, the practice of brutality—the quality of unmixed criminality—becomes the totality of his career. At the same time, we are always conscious that the whole meaning of this career is a drive for success: the typical gangster film presents a steady upward progress followed by a very precipitate fall. Thus brutality itself becomes at once the means to success and the content of success—a success that is defined in its most general terms, not as accomplishment or specific gain, but simply as the unlimited possibility of aggression. (In the same way, film presentations of businessmen tend to make it appear that they achieve their success by talking on the telephone and holding conferences and that success *is* talking on the telephone and holding conferences.)

From this point of view, the initial contact between the film and its audience is an agreed conception of human life: that man is a being with the possibilities of success or failure. This principle, too, belongs to the city; one must emerge from the crowd or else one is nothing. On that basis the necessity of the action is established, and it progresses by inalterable paths to the point where the gangster lies dead and the principle has been modified: there is really only one possibility—failure. The final meaning of the city is anonymity and death.

In the opening scene of *Scarface*, we are shown a successful man; we know he is successful because he has just given a party of opulent proportions and because he is called Big Louie. Through some monstrous lack of caution, he permits himself to be alone for a few moments. We understand from this immediately that he is about to be killed. No convention of the gangster film is more strongly established than this: it is dangerous to be alone. And yet the very conditions of success make it impossible not to be alone, for success is always the establishment of an *individual* pre-eminence that must be imposed on others, in whom it automatically arouses hatred; the successful man is an outlaw. The gangster's whole life is an effort to assert himself as an individual, to draw himself out of the crowd, and he always dies *because* he is an individual; the final bullet thrusts him back, makes him, after all, a failure. "Mother of God," says the dying Little Caesar, "is this the end of Rico?"—speaking of himself thus in the third person because what has been brought low is not the undifferentiated *man*, but the individual with a name, the gangster, the success; even to himself he is a creature of the imagination. (T. S. Eliot has pointed out that a number of Shakespeare's tragic heroes have this trick of looking at themselves dramatically; their true identity, the thing that is destroyed when they die, is something outside themselves—not a man, but a style of life, a kind of meaning.)

At bottom, the gangster is doomed because he is under the obligation to succeed, not because the means he employs are unlawful. In the deeper layers of the modern consciousness, *all* means are unlawful, every attempt to succeed is an act of aggression, leaving one alone and guilty and defenseless among enemies: one is *punished* for success. This is our intolerable dilemma: that failure is a kind of death and success is evil and dangerous, is—ultimately—impossible. The effect of the gangster film is to embody this dilemma in the person of the gangster and resolve it by his death. The dilemma is resolved because it is *his* death, not ours. We are safe; for the moment, we can acquiesce in our failure, we can choose to fail.

Part Five

THE LANGUAGE
OF TRAGEDY

Maud Bodkin

ARCHETYPAL PATTERNS IN TRAGIC POETRY

Elder Olson

MODERN DRAMA AND TRAGEDY

Archetypal Patterns in Tragic Poetry*

MAUD BODKIN

I

In an article, "On the Relation of Analytical Psychology to Poetic Art," [1] Dr. C. G. Jung has set forth an hypothesis in regard to the psychological significance of poetry. The special emotional significance possessed by certain poems—a significance going beyond any definite meaning conveyed— he attributes to the stirring in the reader's mind, within or beneath his conscious response, of unconscious forces which he terms "primordial images," or archetypes. These archetypes he describes as "psychic residua of numberless experiences of the same type," experiences which have happened not to the individual but to his ancestors, and of which the results are inherited in the structure of the brain, *a priori* determinants of individual experience.

It is the aim of the present writer to examine this hypothesis, testing it in regard to examples where we can bring together the recorded experience and reflection of minds approaching the matter from different standpoints. It is hoped that, in this way, something may be done towards enriching the formulated theory of the systematic psychologist through the insight of more intuitive thinkers, while at the same time the intuitive thinker's results may receive somewhat more exact definition.

My first illustration I shall take from an essay by Professor Gilbert Murray,[2] where the effect of great poetic drama is described in language some-

---

[1] Included in *Contributions to Analytical Psychology*, trans. H. G. and C. F. Baynes (Kegan Paul, 1928).

[2] "*Hamlet* and *Orestes*," in *The Classical Tradition in Poetry* (Oxford, 1927).

* Maud Bodkin, "Archetypal Patterns in Tragic Poetry," from *Archetypal Patterns in Poetry* (Oxford University Press, 1963). [The footnotes in this selection have been renumbered.]

what similar to that of Jung. Gilbert Murray has been comparing the tragedies of *Hamlet* and of *Orestes*, noting the curious similarities between them,
and how the theme that underlies them seems to have shown an "almost
eternal durability." When such themes as stirred the interest of primitive
man move us now, he says, "they will tend to do so in ways which we recognize as particularly profound and poetical" (p. 238). Gilbert Murray apolo-
gizes for the metaphor of which he cannot keep clear when he says that such
stories and situations are "deeply implanted in the memory of the race,
stamped as it were upon our physical organism." We say that such themes
"are strange to us. Yet there is that within us which leaps at the sight of
them, a cry of the blood which tells us we have known them always"
(p. 239). And again: "In plays like *Hamlet* or the *Agamemnon* or the *Electra*
we have certainly fine and flexible character-study, a varied and well-
wrought story, a full command of the technical instruments of the poet and
the dramatist; but we have also, I suspect, a strange, unanalysed vibration
below the surface, an undercurrent of desires and fears and passions, long
slumbering yet eternally familiar, which have for thousands of years lain
near the root of our most intimate emotions and been wrought into the fabric
of our most magical dreams. How far into past ages this stream may reach
back, I dare not even surmise; but it seems as if the power of stirring it or
moving with it were one of the last secrets of genius" (pp. 239–240).

We have here an expression, itself somewhat imaginative and poetical,
of an experience in presence of poetry which we may submit to closer examination—and this in two ways. We may study the themes that show this
persistence within the life of a community or race and may compare the
different forms which they assume; also we may study analytically in different individuals the inner experience of responding to such themes.

The inquiry is plainly of subtlety and complexity apt to discourage at
the outset those who prefer to avoid all questions that cannot be investigated
in accordance with a strict technique. There is little possibility here for experiment, since the kind of emotional experience which it is desired to investigate cannot be commanded at will under test conditions. A profound
response to great poetic themes can be secured only by living with such
themes, dwelling and brooding upon them, choosing those moments when
the mind seems spontaneously to open itself to their influence. We must
take where we can find it the recorded experience of those who have such
acquaintance with poetry.

To the present writer it appears, however, that it is by the study of such
deeper experience that psychology at the present time particularly needs
enrichment. We might almost say that academic psychologists have been
routed by the attack of those medical writers who claim access to the deeper
layers of the mind, just because the demand for exact verifiable results has

held academic psychologists to the mere outworks or surface of the mind they set out to study. If inexactness of thought or one-sided emphasis has characterized the medical writers, this can be established only by following them along the obscure paths they have opened into the concrete human psyche, and bringing to bear, if possible, a wider ranging interest and a more exact and cautious scrutiny.

The student who seeks to explore the imaginative response of present-day minds to the great themes of poetry may profit by considering the work not only of the medical psychologists, but also of the anthropologists who have attempted to study scientifically the reactions of more primitive minds. In studying the reception by a people of new cultural elements anthropologists have made use of the term "cultural pattern" to designate the pre-existing "configuration," or order of arrangement, of tendencies which determine the response of members of the group to the new element. In discussing the value for our "conceptual explorations" of "the culture pattern concept," Goldenweiser [3] has noted its relation to the concept of form and system in the arts and cultural disciplines; and L. L. Bernard, in the same work, has undertaken a classification of different kinds of environment, distinguishing the psycho-social environment, which includes such systems of symbols as are preserved in books, and in which he says "psychic processes reach the highest type of their objectified development." Such stored symbolic content can at any time become effective in activating the corresponding patterns in the minds of members of the group whose collective product and possession the symbols are.

It is within the general field of anthropology or social psychology that I conceive the inquiry to lie which I am here attempting to pursue. I shall use the term "archetypal pattern" to refer to that within us which, in Gilbert Murray's phrase, leaps in response to the effective presentation in poetry of an ancient theme. The hypothesis to be examined is that in poetry —and here we are to consider in particular tragic poetry—we may identify themes having a particular form or pattern which persists amid variation from age to age, and which corresponds to a pattern or configuration of emotional tendencies in the minds of those who are stirred by the theme.

In Jung's formulation of the hypothesis, and in the more tentative metaphorical statement of Gilbert Murray, it is asserted that these patterns are "stamped upon the physical organism," "inherited in the structure of the brain"; but of this statement no evidence can be considered here. Jung believes himself to have evidence of the spontaneous production of ancient patterns in the dreams and fantasies of individuals who had no discoverable

---

[3] *The Social Sciences and Their Interrelations*, edited by W. F. Ogburn and Alexander A. Goldenweiser (Allen & Unwin, 1928).

access to cultural material in which the patterns were embodied. This evidence is, however, hard to evaluate; especially in view of the way in which certain surprising reproductions, in trance states, of old material, have been subsequently traced to forgotten impressions of sense in the lifetime of the individual.

Of more force in the present state of our knowledge is the general argument that where forms are assimilated from the environment upon slight contact only, predisposing factors must be present in mind and brain. Whoever has experienced and reflected upon the attempt to convey an idea, especially an idea of intimate and emotional character, to a mind unprepared to receive it, will have realized that it is not mere contact with an idea's expression that secures its assimilation. Some inner factor must co-operate. When it is lacking, the experienced futility of attempted communication is the most convincing proof that it is, as Mr. F. C. Bartlett has said, "not fanciful to hold" that for the capture of objects complete, by the assimilative imagination, there must stir within us "larger systems of feeling, of memory, of ideas, of aspirations." Such systems may be cultural patterns confined to a particular group at a certain time, or may characterize a particular individual; but there are others of much wider range. Our question is whether there are some whose "almost eternal durability," in Gilbert Murray's phrase, justifies us in applying to them the term archetypal, and renders them of special interest and importance to the student of psychology and of literature.

II

We come nearer to our particular subject in raising the question: What is the distinctive advantage of having recourse to poetry for the study of these patterns?

Such a theme as that discussed by Gilbert Murray existed as a traditional story in ancient Greece before Aeschylus, and in Northern Europe before Shakespeare handled it. In that form it was already, as A. C. Bradley says of another traditional theme, "an inchoate poem": "such a subject, as it exists in the general imagination, has some aesthetic value before the poet touches it"; "it is already in some degree organized and formed." [4] Enriched by the poet's touch, the traditional story lives on in our imagination, a memory with aesthetic value, but fading into formlessness, when, as perhaps now in the mind of the reader, the reference to Orestes or to Hamlet excites only a faint recollection of what was once a vivid poetic experience. When, therefore, we desire to examine psychologically the emotional

---

[4] *Oxford Lectures on Poetry* (Macmillan, 1909), pp. 11–12.

pattern corresponding to a poetic theme, we may sometimes avail ourselves of references to the mere tales recalled in outline, but for closer examination there is need that the actual poetic experience be recovered, since it is in the imaginative experience actually communicated by great poetry that we shall find our fullest opportunity of studying the patterns that we seek—and this from the very nature of poetic experience.

In the writings of Professor Spearman, which have had so much influence in the determining of psychological method, there are references to imagination—one particularly to imagination as exercise in poetry [5]—in which he asserts that imagination in its intellectual aspect does not differ essentially from any other logical process in which new content may also be said to be generated, as when, from a given term, say "good," and a knowledge of the nature of verbal opposition, we pass to the term, "bad." Such a treatment of imagination illustrates the kind of abstraction that makes psychology, to some thinkers, appear so unreal and empty a study. A student who is interested in imaginative activity as exercised in poetry cannot accept the view that its intellectual aspect can be separated from its emotional nature and covered by any such logical formula as Spearman proposes.

Of the three laws of cognition which Professor Spearman formulates it would seem to be the first which most nearly concerns the poetic imagination. This law is stated: "Any lived experience tends to evoke immediately a knowing of its characters and experiences." A note adds: "The word 'immediately' means here the absence of any mediating process." [6] It is perhaps within this mediating process, denied by Spearman, that we may find a distinctive place for imagination as exercised in poetry.

When psychologists have raised the question: How does lived experience come to awareness? they have usually been content to assert that it happens through introspection, and to leave to philosophers any further investigation of the question. It is here that difficulty has arisen between the academic and the medical psychologists; since the latter believe themselves to have discovered large ranges of lived experience, of conative character, of which introspection can give no account—a discovery that seems surprising to those who believe that in introspection we have direct access to the nature of our desires.

Professor S. Alexander,[7] examining the question as a philosopher, concludes that lived experience, which is of conative character—as distinct from sensations and images, the objects of the mind—can only be "en-

---

[5] *The Nature of Intelligence and the Principles of Cognition* (Macmillan, 1927), pp. 334-336.

[6] *Op. cit.*, p. 48.

[7] *Space, Time, and Deity* (Macmillan, 1920).

joyed"; it cannot be contemplated. Introspection, he says, is "enjoyment" lived through, together with "a whole apparatus of elaborated speech" (p. 18), which causes the elements of the experience enjoyed to stand out in "subtly dissected form" (p. 19). "It is small wonder," he adds, "that we should regard our introspection as turning our minds into objects, seeing how largely the language which expresses our mental state has been elaborated in pursuit of practical interests and in contact with physical objects."

If this view is accepted, we see that the mediating process necessary before lived experience can come to awareness is the linking of such experience with actions and objects that affect the senses and can be contemplated, and with words that recall these objects in all their variety of human perspective. It is in the process of fantasy that the contemplated characters of things are broken from their historical setting and made available to express the needs and impulses of the experiencing mind. The recent study of dreams appears to have made it certain that the bewildering sequence of the images thrown up by the sleeping mind is due to processes of interaction between emotional dispositions lacking the customary control. In individual waking fantasy, and in myth and legend, we have other sequences of images which emotional patterns determine, and which seem to us strange as dreams, when, repeating them in the words used also for the results of logical reflection, we are led to contrast these incompatible renderings of experience.

When a great poet uses the stories that have taken shape in the fantasy of the community, it is not his individual sensibility alone that he objectifies. Responding with unusual sensitiveness to the words and images which already express the emotional experience of the community, the poet arranges these so as to utilize to the full their evocative power. Thus he attains for himself vision and possession of the experience engendered between his own soul and the life around him, and communicates that experience, at once individual and collective, to others, so far as they can respond adequately to the words and images he uses.

We see, then, why, if we wish to contemplate the emotional patterns hidden in our individual lives, we may study them in the mirror of our spontaneous actions, so far as we can recall them, or in dreams and in the flow of waking fantasy; but if we would contemplate the archetypal patterns that we have in common with men of past generations, we do well to study them in the experience communicated by the great poetry that has continued to stir emotional response from age to age. In studying such poetry here, we are not asking what was in the mind of Aeschylus or of Shakespeare when he fashioned the figure of Orestes or of Hamlet, nor do we ask how these figures affected a Greek or an Elizabethan audience. The question is between the writer and the reader of this book: what do the figures of

Orestes and Hamlet stand for in the experience communicated to us, as we see, read, or vividly recall the Greek or Shakespearian tragedy?

III

A preliminary difficulty, already touched on, must be considered in more detail. How can we secure that the experience communicated by a great play shall be present to us with such completeness and intensity that we can make adequate study of it?

A parallel question has been discussed by Percy Lubbock [8] in regard to the study of the form of a novel. Critical perception, he says, is of no use to us if we cannot retain the image of a book, and the book reaches us as a passage of experience never present in its completeness. The task of the reader, before he can criticize, is to refashion the novel out of the march of experience as it passed. The procession "must be marshalled and concentrated somewhere" (p. 15).

In watching a play adequately interpreted upon the stage, we find, perhaps more readily than in the silent reading of a novel, that the procession of experience is marshalled and concentrated at certain points; so that, recalling the images of these, we can look back upon the whole play as a living unity. The powerful emotional impression thus attained may persist while the play is read and recurred to again and again, and the individual impression clarified by comparison with the reflective results of critics and scholars. Central passages, while the play is thus lived with, grow ever richer in meaning, becoming intertwined with the emotional experience of one's own life.

Some such experience of *Hamlet* I must presume in the reader, since I cannot afford space to recall the play at all fully. I will venture, however, to refer to that passage in which for me the significance of the whole play seems most concentrated.

From the experience of seeing *Hamlet* performed some thirty years ago, there has remained with me the memory of the strange exaltation and wonder of beauty that attended the words of the dying Hamlet to Horatio:

> If thou didst ever hold me in thy heart,
> Absent thee from felicity awhile,
> And in this harsh world draw thy breath in pain,
> To tell my story.

This is one of the passages chosen by Matthew Arnold [9] as "touch-

---

[8] *The Craft of Fiction* (The Travellers' Library, 1926).
[9] "The Study of Poetry," *Essays in Criticism*, 2nd series, 1889.

stones" for poetry—passages possessing both in style and substance supreme poetic quality, the Aristotelian high truth and seriousness, beyond that of history or ordinary speech. I would suggest that this "high truth" of which Matthew Arnold speaks—like that character attributed by Lascelles Abercrombie to great poetry, "a confluence of all kinds of life into a single flame of consciousness"—belongs to the lines not as isolated, but as grown familiar in their setting—the unified experience of the play converging upon them and the incantation of their music carrying them ever deeper into the secret places of the mind that loves them.

One may make some attempt to analyse that "incantation," [10] or enchantment in which rhythm and sound of words evidently play a part. It seems to me that the enchantment of the line, "Absent thee from felicity awhile," is heightened by the later echoing of its sounds in the lines spoken by Horatio:

> Good night, sweet prince,
> And flights of angels sing thee to thy rest!

Against this music of heaven we feel more poignantly the contrast of the words, "in this harsh world draw thy breath in pain," that move, labouring, toward their goal in the words, "to tell my story." Through their power of incantation these words, as they fall in their place, seem to gather up all the significance of that struggle of a powerful impulse to action against an obscure barrier, all the impotent anger and perplexity, and longing for justification and release, that make up the story of Hamlet as Shakespeare tells it, and make also of Hamlet, and of these lines, a symbol for whatever such struggle and longing has tortured the mind that is responding to Hamlet's words.

IV

Before attempting to compare, with reference to underlying emotional pattern, *Hamlet* and the plays concerned with Orestes, we may consider briefly the study made of *Hamlet* by Dr. Ernest Jones.[11]

Dr. Jones, in exploring the nature of Hamlet's conflict, has to some extent followed the same line of inquiry that I am pursuing here. For what is it that the critic is actually doing when he traces the motives of a character in a play?

In projecting the figure of a man of a certain disposition and analysing the forces behind his behaviour, the critic is inevitably using the emotional experience which he himself undergoes in living through the play. Having

---

[10] Cf. Lascelles Abercrombie, *The Idea of Great Poetry*, 1925, p. 19.

[11] "A Psycho-Analytic Study of *Hamlet*," included in *Essays in Applied Psychoanalysis*, 1923.

experienced, as communicated by the speeches of Hamlet, a certain psychological movement in which a strong impulse to action is aroused, and again and again sinks back into apathy and despair—a movement which, while imaginatively experiencing it, the reader imputes to the fictitious speaker—afterwards, in reviewing the total impression so received, with analysis and synthesis of its successive movements, the critic discerns, so far as his thought does not deceive him, within the fictitious personality of Hamlet, the reflected pattern of the emotional forces that have operated within his own imaginative activity.

To Dr. Jones the conflict of Hamlet appears an example of the working of the Oedipus complex. Hamlet cannot whole-heartedly will the slaying of his uncle, because "his uncle incorporates the deepest and most buried part of his own personality." The repressed desire for the death of his father and the sexual enjoyment of his mother, persisting unconsciously from infancy, has produced an unwitting identification by Hamlet of himself and his guilty uncle, so that only at the point of death, "when he has made the final sacrifice . . . is he free . . . to slay his other self" (p. 57).

This psychological hypothesis, contributed by Freud and elaborated by Dr. Jones, has been welcomed by certain literary critics. Herbert Read, referring to the view of J. M. Robertson, that *Hamlet* is "not finally an intelligible drama as it stands"—that Shakespeare could not make a psychologically consistent play out of his barbaric plot and supersubtle hero—urges that however baffling to critics the play may have proved, nevertheless in experiencing it we are aware of a personal intensity of expression, a *consistent* intensity, giving the play a unity which the older academic critics lacked means to explore.[12] Dr. Jones's hypothesis, he considers, does serve to explain this acceptance by our feeling of any difficulties and incoherence which our thought may find. Using the terms I have suggested, we might say that the hypothesis of the Oedipus complex—i.e. of a persistent unconscious wish, hostile to the father and dishonouring to the mother, in conflict with the sentiment of filial love and loyalty—offers to our thought an emotional pattern which does correspond to the play of feeling stimulated during a full imaginative participation in the drama. Professor Bradley has spoken of *Hamlet* as deserving the title of "tragedy of moral idealism," [13] because of the intensity, both of idealizing love and of horror at betrayal of love, that we feel in Hamlet's speeches. He dwells upon the shock to such a moral sensibility as Hamlet's of witnessing the faithlessness of his mother and uncle; yet there seems a discrepancy between the horror and disgust that a sensitive mind might naturally feel at such faithlessness in others and the

---

[12] Herbert Read, *Reason and Romanticism* (Faber & Gwyer), p. 101.
[13] *Shakespearian Tragedy* (Macmillan, 1912), p. 113.

overwhelming disgust that Hamlet feels, at himself, his whole world and
his attempted action, unless we realize that he feels the treachery of his
mother and uncle echo within himself, and within the sentiment of loyal love
to his father that is his strongest conscious motive. If, in reviewing the experience communicated by the play, we conceive a loyal love undermined,
as it were, by a bewildered sense of treachery within as well as without, we
must, I think, agree that the Freudian hypothesis does throw some light
upon that intimate immediate experience which is the final touchstone of
critical theory.

V

Perhaps the most important contribution that has been made by the
Freudian theory of dream interpretation to the understanding of the emotional symbolism of poetic themes is that concerned with the "splitting"
of type figures. In comparing the Hamlet story with the story of Oedipus,
Dr. Jones asserts that both are variants of the same *motif*, but in one the father figure remains single, while in the other it is "split into two"—the
father loved and revered, and the hated tyrannical usurper.

This assertion involves two elements of hypothesis:

1. The fundamental assumption—implied also in the statements of Jung
and Gilbert Murray, with which this discussion opened—that these ancient
stories owe their persistence, as traditional material of art, to their power
of expressing or symbolizing, and so relieving, typical human emotions.

2. That the emotion relieved is in this case the two-sided—ambivalent—
attitude of the son towards the father. Let us examine this latter hypothesis
more closely.

It appears to be characteristic of the relation between father and son that
the father should excite in the son both feelings of admiration, love, and
loyalty, and also impulses of anger, jealousy, and self-assertion. The more
the son learns to "idolize" his father, developing what Shand has called the
"conscience of the sentiment," so that any muttering of jealousy or hostile
criticism is suppressed as disloyal, the more acute will become the tension
of the inner attitude. It is such an attitude that can find relief in imaginative
activity wherein both the love and the repressed hostility have play. In the
story of Oedipus, according to the Freudian hypothesis, a repressed persistent impulse to supplant the father and enjoy the mother finds expression
in the first part of the action; then in the latter part, in the hero's remorse
and suffering, appears the expression of the sentiment of respect and loyalty.
In the Hamlet legend—as it appears, e.g. in the Amleth Saga—combined
fear and hostile self-assertion against the father find expression through all
the incidents of simulated stupidity, and secret bitter word-play, and at last
in the achievement of the plotted slaying of the usurper; while at the same

time the sentiment of love and loyalty is triumphantly expressed in that same act of filial vengeance. It is Shakespeare only who appears to have brought into the rendering of the ancient story the subtle factor of the division and paralysis of the will of the hero, by the intuitive apprehension that the impulse that drove his uncle against his father was one with that present in himself.

The story of Orestes may be considered as another example of the imaginative expression of the ambivalent attitude of child toward parent. In this story, as presented by the three great Attic tragedians, there is a wealth of material illustrating the manner in which inner forces of emotion may, through shapes created by imagination, become palpable to sense. But we must be content here to consider briefly only the outline of the story.

Considered as a variant of the Hamlet theme, its distinctive note is that the usurper upon whom the son's fierce self-assertion and craving for vengeance strike is not alone the male kinsman, but also the queen-mother, who has betrayed, and with her own hands murdered the father. Therefore the moment of triumphant self-assertion, when the son has proved his manhood, and vindicated his loyalty upon his father's enemies, is also the moment when there awakens the palpable, pursuing horror of the outraged filial relation—since this enemy was also a parent, the mother of the slayer.

The conflict presented in the Orestes dramas is plainly concerned not directly with sex, but with combined love and hate of either son or daughter converging upon a parent figure which may be either father or mother. It is the enduring conflict between the generations which continues to find expression in the story, when more temporary questions—such as that between patriarchy and mother-right, which may have been present in Athenian minds—are no longer urgent. That this theme of conflict between the generations had great significance within the sensibility that found expression in Shakespeare's plays, is evident from the tragedy of *King Lear*.

In this drama the emotional conflict between the generations is communicated from the standpoint of the old man, the father who encounters in separate embodiment in his natural successors, the extremes of bestial self-seeking, and of filial devotion. Bradley has noted how the play illustrates "the tendency of imagination to analyse and subtract, to decompose human nature into its constituent factors." [14] This mode of thought, he suggests,[15] is responsible for "the incessant references to the lower animals" which occur throughout the play. Thus Goneril is likened to a kite, a serpent, a boar, a dog, a wolf, a tiger. This analysing work of the imagination, separating the bestial and the angelic in human nature and giving them distinct

[14] *Shakespearian Tragedy*, p. 264.
[15] *Ibid.*, p. 266.

embodiment, in the wicked daughters and Cordelia (and again in Edmund and Edgar, the cruel and the loyal sons of Gloucester), presents another instance of what we have already observed in the "splitting" of the father figure. The splitting in this play is from the point of view of the parent; as, in the Orestes or Hamlet story, it is from the point of view of the child. As, to the feeling of the child, the parent may be both loved protector and unjustly obstructing tyrant, and these two aspects find their emotional symbolism in separate figures in the play; so, to the feeling of the parent, the child may be both loving support of age and ruthless usurper and rival, and these two aspects find expression in separate figures, such as the tender and the wicked daughters of Lear.

VI

We have considered, so far, the emotional pattern corresponding to a particular theme—the conflict between the generations—which, though a recurring one, is by no means co-extensive with the realm of tragic drama. Can we identify an archetypal pattern corresponding to tragedy itself—its universal idea or form?

Gilbert Murray, taking the "essential tragic idea" to be that of "climax followed by decline, or pride by judgement," and attempting a closer analysis of this sequence, maintains that what is "really characteristic" of the tragic conflict is "an element of mystery derived ultimately from the ancient religious concepts of *katharsis* and atonement." [16] The death or fall of the tragic hero has in some sense the character of a purifying or atoning sacrifice.

In considering this conception we may first remedy an inadequacy that the reader has probably noticed in the previous discussion of the dramas of Hamlet and Lear, Orestes and Oedipus. We have so far ignored the royal status of the father and son concerned in the tragic conflict. Yet the kingly status has great significance for the feeling expressed in the play.

Consider, for instance, the tragedy of *King Lear*. "The master movement of the play," says Granville-Barker, is Lear's passing "from personal grievance to the taking upon him, as great natures may, of the imagined burden of the whole world's sorrow." [17] It is Lear's royal status that helps to make this movement possible. King Lear is at once "a poor, infirm, weak, and despised old man"—a father broken to tears and madness by his daughters' cruelty, and also in his sufferings a superhuman figure—one who can bid the "all shaking thunder strike flat the thick rotundity of the world" in vengeance for his wrongs. It is in part the associations with which history,

---

[16] *Op. cit.,* "Drama," p. 66.
[17] H. Granville-Barker, *Prefaces to Shakespeare* (1927), 1st series, p. 171.

and pre-history, has invested the name and image of king that make it possible for us, under the spell of Shakespeare's verse, to accept the figure of Lear as in this way exalted in his agony beyond human stature. His madness, his pitiful humanity, appear, according to that comment which Shakespeare puts into the mouth of an attendant, on behalf of all onlookers, "a sight . . . past speaking in a king." The word "king" is here, through its position in the play, loaded with a significance for the sources of which we must go far back in the story of the race and of the individual.

It is probably because, to the mind of the young child, the father appears of unlimited power that in the life-history of the individual imagination the figures of father and king tend to coalesce. Legends and fairy stories that reflect the feelings of more primitive people towards their king are interpreted by the child in the light of his own earlier feelings towards his father. In the case both of the child and of the primitive individual the same process seems to take place—an emerging of the consciousness of self from out a matrix of less differentiated awareness, which may be called collective or group-consciousness. The figures of both father and king tend to retain within those deeper levels of the mind to which poetry may penetrate, something of the *mana* that invested the first representative of a power akin to, but vastly beyond, that of the individual emerging into self-consciousness.

It is this supernatural aspect which the father-king of tragic drama has for the kindled imagination that is of importance when we try to understand the element of religious mystery which is characteristic of tragedy—plainly in the past, and, as Gilbert Murray holds, in some subtler fashion still in our experience to-day.

Upon this character of tragedy and the tragic hero it is possible, I think, to gain a certain fresh light from a consideration of the conclusions at which Dr. Jung has arrived through his study of fantasy figures appearing in personal analysis.

In *The Psychology of the Unconscious*, in the chapter entitled "The Sacrifice," he examines the symbol of the dying hero as it appears in individual fantasy, representing, according to his interpretation, an inflated infantile personality—a childish self that must be sacrificed, if the libido is to move forward into active life—and in a later work he discusses, under the title of the "Mana Personality," [18] a hero figure which he finds appearing with a richer content at late stages of analysis.

It is especially at times when barriers of personal repression are removed and images of "cosmic" character are arising freely, that the fantasy figure

---

[18] *Two Essays on Analytical Psychology*, 1928, trans. by H. G. and C. F. Baynes, Essay II, ch. iv.

may appear of some great prophet or hero who tends to assume control of the personality.[19] If the conscious or practical personality is poorly developed there is the greater likelihood that it will be overwhelmed when such powerful images rise from the unconscious.

As a literary example of such a case, parallel to actual ones within his experience, Jung accepts H. G. Wells's story of Preemby,[20] "a small, irrelevant, fledgling of a personality," to whom is presented in dream and fantasy the figure of Sargon, King of Kings, in such compelling fashion that he is led to identify himself with it. Jung observes that here "the author depicts a really classical type of compensation," [21] and we may compare it with the type of compensation which occurs in connexion with what we have already considered as the ambivalent attitude towards a parent.

If, within the conscious life, in relation to a parent, only reactions of admiration and affection are recognized, while other reactions, of hostile character, excited within the brain, are repressed, it is these latter that tend to present in dreams a parent figure as object of violence or contempt. Similarly, if within the conscious life the personal self comes to be known only as "an onlooker, an ineffective speechless man," utterly insignificant; while yet, within the life that animates that particular brain, strong reactions are excited of sympathetic exultation and delight at imaginative representations of human achievement—as the little Preemby of Wells thrilled at "the mystery of Atlantis and of the measurements of the Pyramids"—then there may arise, as compensatory to the belittled self, the figure of a hero-self, or *mana* personality, fashioned, as it were, from the stuff of these imaginative reactions; just as the figure of the hated father was fashioned from the energy of the repressed hostility, in compensation for the over-idealizing love.

The Preemby of Wells's story is saved from his delusion, after many sufferings, by learning to think of his vision as of the spirit of man and its achievements—an inheritance belonging no more to him personally than to every other man. In the same manner every individual in whose fantasy such mighty ghosts arise, with their superhuman claims and relationships, must learn to distinguish such claims from those of the personal self; while yet the personal self may be enriched through the conscious experience of its relation to the great forces which such figures represent.

In this way, according to the view of Jung—by interpreting and giving

---

[19] An interesting autobiographical account of this condition may be found in the writings of E. Maitland (*The Story of Anna Kingsford and Edward Maitland and of the New Gospel of Interpretation*, 1st ed., 1893). See especially the passage where he describes the first arrival of the authoritative "presence," and the voice distinctly heard: "at last I have found a man through whom I can speak."

[20] *Christina Alberta's Father*, 1925.

[21] *Op. cit.*, p. 193.

conscious direction to the "pure nature-process" [22] of fantasy in which compensatory images arise—such fantasy can become instrumental to the purging of the individual will and its reconciliation with itself. Is it in some such fashion as this that tragic drama, deeply experienced, now or in the past, exercises the function of purgation or atonement in relation to the passions of the spectator? With this question in view, we may examine a little further the nature of the emotional experience of tragic art, still using the examples of *Hamlet* and of *King Lear*.

Professor Bradley, in examining the experience of tragedy, cites these dramas as examples of tragedies at whose close we feel pain mingled with something like exultation. There is present, he declares, "a glory in the greatness of the soul," and awareness of an "ultimate power" which is "no mere fate," but spiritual, and to which the hero "was never so near . . . as in the moment when it required his life." [23]

I quote these statements of Bradley, not, of course, as universally acceptable, but as the attempt of one eminent critic to render his own deeply pondered experience of tragic drama. The experience is rendered in terms rather of philosophy or religion than of psychology. Can we translate it into any more psychological terms? What is this spiritual power, akin to the characters, and, in some sense, a whole of which they are "parts, expressions, products"? [24] I would propose (following the view set forth by F. M. Cornford) the psychological hypothesis that this power is the common nature lived and immediately experienced by the members of a group or community—"the collective emotion and activity of the group." [25] This common nature can, in Alexander's phrase, be enjoyed, but never directly contemplated. As unfathomable to introspection, it is termed by Jung the Collective Unconscious—the life-energy that in its spontaneous movement toward expression generates alike the hero figures of myth and legend and the similar figures that, appearing in individual fantasy, may overwhelm the personal consciousness.

According to Bradley, the tragic exultation that we feel at the close of *Hamlet* is connected with our sense that the spiritual power of which Hamlet is in some manner the expression or product, is receiving him to itself. It would be this same sense that, as Bradley observes,[26] demands, and is satisfied by, the words of Horatio, introducing, against Shakespeare's custom, the reference to another life: "flights of angels sing thee to thy rest." If, as I suggest, the spiritual power, which the philosopher analysing his poetic

[22] *Op. cit.*, p. 258.
[23] *Oxford Lectures on Poetry*, p. 84.
[24] *Shakespearian Tragedy*, p. 37.
[25] F. M. Cornford, *From Religion to Philosophy* (Arnold, 1912), p. 78.
[26] *Op. cit.*, p. 147.

experience is constrained to represent, be conceived psychologically as the awakened sense of our common nature in its active emotional phase, then our exultation in the death of Hamlet is related in direct line of descent to the religious exultation felt by the primitive group that made sacrifice of the divine king or sacred animal, the representative of the tribal life, and, by the communion of its shed blood, felt that life strengthened and renewed. Hamlet, though he dies, is immortal, because he is the representative and creature of the immortal life of the race. He lives, as he desired to live, in the story with which he charged Horatio—and us who, having participated in that story, descend from the poetic ecstasy to draw breath again in the harsh world of our straitened separate personalities.

The insight of Nietzsche, who knew at once the intoxication of the artist and the analytic urge of the philosopher, discerned the essential nature of tragedy as a vision generated by a dance.[27] The dance of rhythmical speech, like the dance of the ancient chorus, excites the Dionysian ecstasy wherein arises, serene and clear, the Apollonian vision of the imaged meanings the dancing words convey.

The painful images within the vision are at once intimately known and felt, and also "distanced" like the objects in a far stretching landscape, "estranged by beauty." So far as the memory material used by the imaginative activity comes from personal experience, it has undergone "separation . . . from the concrete personality of the experiencer" and "extrusion of its personal aspects"; [28] but experience is also used which has never been connected with the personal self—as when, in *King Lear*, Shakespeare causes the actor to "impersonate Lear and the storm together," [29] and in the storm "it is the powers of the tormented soul that we hear and see." [30] Here, dramatist, actor, and spectator are using experience which was never personal, but shaped through previous apprehension of physical storms into which was imaginatively projected that same impersonal emotional energy from which the daemonic figure of the hero is now fashioned.

To the impersonal, "distanced," vision corresponds, in Schopenhauer's phrase, "a Will-free subject," one indifferent to the aims and fears of the ego—not held to its private perspective.[31]

---

[27] See *The Birth of Tragedy*, Section 8.
[28] E. Bullough, "Distance as an Aesthetic Principle," *Brit. J. of Psychol.* v. part 2, p. 116.
[29] Granville-Barker, *Prefaces to Shakespeare*, p. 142.
[30] A. C. Bradley, *Shakespearian Tragedy*, p. 270.
[31] This character of the aesthetic experience is vividly expressed, in imaginative form, in the lines of De la Mare:

> When music sounds, all that I was I am
> Ere to this haunt of brooding dust I came.

Here we have the felt contrast between the subject of the aesthetic experience—"all that I was I am"—and the self that is bounded in space and time by the bodily organism—"this haunt of brooding dust."

This felt release, and Dionysian union with a larger whole, would seem to constitute that element of religious mystery—of purgation and atonement —traditionally connected with the idea of tragedy.

VII

If now, summing up our results, we recur to the question: what determining emotional pattern corresponds to the form of tragedy? We may answer first, in accordance with our earlier discussion, that the pattern consists of emotional tendencies of opposite character which are liable to be excited by the same object or situation, and, thus conflicting, produce an inner tension that seeks relief in the activity either of fantasy, or of poetic imagination, either originally or receptively creative. The nature of the opposed tendencies that find relief through diverse renderings of the essential tragic theme, the death or fall of a hero, it is not easy to describe at once with conciseness and adequacy. But we may attempt this through the concept of an ambivalent attitude toward the self.

In the gradual fashioning and transforming, through the experience of life, of an idea of the self, every individual must in some degree experience the contrast between a personal self—a limited ego, one among many—and a self that is free to range imaginatively through all human achievement. In infancy and in the later years of those who remain childish, a comparatively feeble imaginative activity together with an undisciplined instinct of self-assertion may present a fantasy self—the image of an infantile personality—in conflict with the chastened image which social contacts, arousing the instinct of submission, tend to enforce. In the more mature mind that has soberly taken the measure of the personal self as revealed in practical life, there remains the contrast between this and the self revealed in imaginative thought—well-nigh limitless in sympathy and aspiration.

Within what McDougall calls the self-regarding sentiment these contrasting images, and the impulses that sustain and respond to them, may bring about persistent tension. The experience of tragic drama both gives in the figure of the hero an objective form to the self of imaginative aspiration, or to the power-craving, and also, through the hero's death, satisfies the counter movement of feeling toward the surrender of personal claims and the merging of the ego within a greater power—the "community consciousness."

Thus the archetypal pattern corresponding to tragedy may be said to be a certain organization of the tendencies of self-assertion and submission. The self which is asserted is magnified by that same collective force to which finally submission is made; and from the tension of the two impulses and their reaction upon each other, under the conditions of poetic exaltation, the distinctive tragic attitude and emotion appears to arise.

The theme of the conflict between the generations—considered earlier, in relation to Hamlet and Orestes, as corresponding to an ambivalent attitude toward a parent figure—is plainly related to this more general theme and pattern; since, as we saw, the same underlying emotional associations cling to the images of father and of king. In experiencing imaginatively the conflict of the generations, the spectator is identified with the hero both as son, in his felt solidarity with the father and revolt against him, and again, when, making reparation for the "injustice" against his predecessor, he gives place to a successor, and is reunited with that whole of life whence he emerged.[32]

One or two points in regard to the argument may be briefly reviewed.

The question is sometimes asked whether the creative activity of the poet and the imaginative response of the reader are sufficiently alike, psychologically, to be considered together. Here I have been concerned primarily with imaginative response, and have not attempted to consider the distinctive activity of original composition. In so far, however, as the poet's work, e.g. a play of Shakespeare, does reveal his imaginative response to material communicated to him by others and by him to us, I have of course been concerned with the poet's experience.

The concept of racial experience enters the present essay in two ways: (1) all those systems or tendencies which appear to be inherited in the constitution of mind and brain may be said to be due to racial experience in the past. It is not necessary for our purpose to determine exactly the method of this "biological inheritance" from our ancestors. Of more importance for our purpose is the question concerning (2) the racial experience which we may "enjoy" in responding to that "social inheritance" of meanings stored in language which also comes to us from our ancestors, and wakens into activity the potentialities of our inherited nature. In such racial or collective experience as we have discussed in relation to tragic poetry, so far as there is reference to an experiencer, this seems to be not an individual, but rather that larger whole from which what we know as the individual, or personal, self has been differentiated, and which remains with us as the sense, either latent or active, of a greater power.

---

[32] Cf. the mystic saying of Anaximander, concerning the cycle of birth and death, wherein things "give reparation to one another and pay the penalty of their injustice," and the discussion of it by F. M. Cornford, *op. cit.* See especially pp. 8, 147, 176.

Modern Drama and Tragedy[*]

ELDER OLSON

It is impossible to look at modern drama—by which I mean drama from Ibsen's day to the present—without being struck by its richness and variety. There have been other periods of expansion in the history of drama, but I do not think it can be claimed that the Age of Elizabeth or the *Siglo de Oro*, for instance, produced plays of such diversity as the modern period. In the latter we find an immense and rapid proliferation of forms, coupled with the discovery and successful employment of new devices and techniques. There is a swift and steady expansion of the subject matter of drama; new materials are introduced, a fresh significance is found in old ones, and both are handled to produce the most subtle differentiations of effect. There are many evidences, along with all this, of basic reconceptions of the drama—of what the "dramatic" consists in, of the ends and effects of drama, even of the very nature of the theatre itself.

The gains are obvious. Are there any losses? I think we must admit there have been. If modern drama exhibits a remarkable expansion, there has also been a certain contraction. Verse has practically disappeared from modern drama; despite certain notable exceptions, it is a prose drama. And the prose—again with certain exceptions—is no greatly varied prose. On the contrary, it has shown a tendency to become more and more like ordinary speech, or rather, more and more like the ordinary speech of the man who is a little less than the ordinary. The drama has increasingly sought to be articulate in the language of the inarticulate; and because it has done so, it has had to confine itself to such subject matter as its language might permit. The language of the inarticulate does not permit the expression of subtle or profound thought or emotion; consequently drama has had to forego the subtler and profounder thoughts and emotions. And since language and thought and emotion enter into the subtler expressions of character, drama has had to forego the latter as well.

---

[*] Elder Olson, "Modern Drama and Tragedy," from *Tragedy and the Theory of Drama* (Wayne State University Press, 1961), pp. 237–260.

You may test these statements very easily. Open an anthology of Elizabethan drama and leaf through. You will quickly see that there are great
differences between the styles of Marlowe, Shakespeare, Webster, Tour-
neur, and Middleton. You will notice a very extensive vocabulary and
greatly diversified grammatical constructions. Read almost any of the plays;
you will find that the major characters, at least, have their distinctive manners of speaking and that different social classes speak differently. Read a
speech of any length by a major character; you will usually find that you are
told a great deal about what he is thinking and feeling, what sort of person
he is, and sometimes even what is going on in the remoter corners of his
mind. Now pick up an anthology of modern drama, and repeat the process.
The case will now be abundantly clear to you. If not, push the experiment
a step farther: try to identify dramatists, plays, and characters *simply by
reference to the language*. I think you will succeed in this far better with the
Elizabethans than with the moderns.

I do not want to insist on the *necessity* for drama of a great variety of
styles, though that variety is obviously useful. The French Classical dramatists exhibit a far narrower range of styles than the Elizabethans, but they
exhibit language of very great *flexibility*. And, if you are to have any really
wide variation of fine drama, you must have stylistic variety or stylistic
flexibility. You cannot play Beethoven's Opus 111 on a child's five-note
piano; and you cannot display the full range of character, thought, and passion in a language founded upon what the ordinary man thinks, feels, and
says in an ordinary situation. Humanity simply will not translate into such
sub-Basic English. The problems of translating Aeschylus are nothing by
comparison.

Modern drama has evolved, as I said, an immense variety of devices and
techniques; but even here the critic who is willing to be sufficiently captious
(as I, for one, happen to be) can protest that there is some restriction. Almost all of these devices have the same general tendency to decrease the
distance between actors and audiences, to give a greater impression of
immediacy or a greater continuity of the drama with life or—in a word—
to commit the drama to greater and greater realism.

That realism, now that we have tracked it down, lies at the bottom of
most dramatic construction. I am afraid that it is a very narrow realism. It
takes as the model of reality the common probabilities of everyday life, as
that life is lived by persons much like ourselves. It has developed, of course,
out of the naturalism and realism of the nineteenth century, the "cup and
saucer realism," "the slice of life." That naturalism grew out of a protest
against certain artificialities in drama and fiction, and proclaimed itself, in
contrast, an exponent of truth. From the very first, of course, it has had to
depart from that "truth." No playgoer or novel-reader is so imbecile as to
pay for the privilege of observing what he may witness at any time, free of

charge, by sitting in a park, walking up a back stair, or poking his head out of a window. The unusual had to be introduced, for the plain reason that the usual is likely to be uninteresting. The characters had to be seen at a time of crisis, and the audience had to have a view of them which ordinary life does not usually afford at such a time—the view, as H. L. Mencken once put it, through "the terrifying key-hole." People like the Alvings and Gablers and Helmers do not often exhibit their anguish in public.

As a program for new art, realism was undoubtedly fruitful: it would take us a long time to read the roll-call of the great fiction and drama which came out of it. As a program for new art, moreover, it extended the arts of fiction and drama. But it was never intended as, and cannot possibly serve as, a program for all art. Nevertheless, that is the role it is gradually coming to fill—quietly, unofficially, as a matter of assumption and custom rather than of rational decision. In this role it may become quite as tyrannical for drama as the conventions it was devised to attack.

We can see something of its stringency in two ways: we can ask to what extent it is actually commensurate with life, and we can ask to what extent it is commensurate with art. I do not think it can be claimed that modern drama as a whole—I have in mind not merely American contemporary drama, but European as well, and that from Ibsen onward—has managed to catch anything like a total image of life. Wonderfully as it has caught particular aspects, aspects never caught and never seen so before, I find that it has not caught certain others of high importance. I shall leave that matter, however, to your decision. It involves the question of what life is, and there are so many different conceptions of that, no doubt, that the matter is hardly arguable. But the extent to which modern drama is commensurate with art is a simple matter; we have only to look at what has been done in the past that might still be valuable and ask ourselves whether we are still doing it. Such a look will establish at once that we are not doing quite a lot of valuable things that have been done in the past. One that particularly interests me is this: we are not producing tragedy.

Tragedy involves characters who are, as Aristotle says, "better than we are"—better than the ordinary man. He meant *morally—of greater worth;* but the notion of superiority naturally associated itself, in societies which drew sharp and extreme distinctions not merely between persons but between the kinds of lives they were permitted to lead, with the notion of superiority of rank; and this association was turned into rigid rule by theorists like Donatus, who laid down the pattern of the theory of tragedy which was to be transmitted through the Middle Ages to the Renaissance. Even in the Renaissance, however, there sprang up a species of domestic tragedy, a "tragedy of the ordinary man," the leading examples of which are *The Yorkshire Tragedy* and *Arden of Feversham.* This species came to particular prominence and popularity later in the plays of George Lillo and others, and our contemporary tragedies of the ordinary man are descendants of this line.

These domestic tragedies had, and continue to have, the very great value of exhibiting the seriousness even of humble life, and the far greater value of extending the range of our sympathy—that is, of engaging our sympathies for someone with whom we might not otherwise have sympathized. The older forms patterned themselves for the most part upon high tragedy, except that they dealt with persons of lower station, and had to make various adjustments accordingly. The plots are general analogs of those of high tragedy; but character, motive, and circumstance are altered. *The Fatal Curiosity*, for example, turns on one of the stock forms of tragic deed, the killing of a stranger who is subsequently discovered to be a relative; only here the father murders for money, under the extreme pressure of poverty. Later forms depend, for their effect, on other elements of the serious. A play like Arthur Miller's *Death of a Salesman* achieves its seriousness through the fact that Willy Loman's situation is representative of, or at any rate analogous to, the situation of so many people. Tennessee Williams' plays depend for their power upon extremity of suffering and the invention of characters particularly sensitive and vulnerable to a particular kind of torment. Yet others—like Miller's *The Crucible*, which I think is one of the closest modern approximations to tragedy—achieve their effect through the importance of the moral issues involved.

It seems, in a way, ridiculous to talk about the dangers of such forms. Any artistic endeavor must involve its dangers; tragedy can turn into bombastic fustian, comedy into inanity or vulgarity. The excellent artist will do excellent things, and the bad one will do bad things, in any case. On the other hand, modern serious drama seems, at times, almost innocent of the dangers to which it is particularly liable; and we may as well consider what they are. It is concerned with the ordinary man, and primarily with the suffering of the ordinary man; and in order to make that suffering important, it must intensify the anguish of its protagonist. In its endeavor to obtain sympathy it can readily fall into sentimentality or morbidity. There is no special merit in displaying or observing suffering. After the rebellion of Spartacus, six thousand persons, men, women, and children, were crucified along both sides of the Appian Way, extending far out into the suburbs of Rome; and the Romans took little sightseeing trips with their families, to watch anguish which must have been acute. I do not think there was anything very meritorious in this behavior of the Romans. And I do not think there would be anything very meritorious in our walking into a cancer ward or a lunatic asylum, where people are suffering the absolutes of physical or mental torture, simply so that we might observe their agony and sympathize with it. To return to drama: unless the dramatist can give us a significant perception —one that evokes in us a response of some merit—he had better not show us the suffering at all. It can only be painful to us, or, if not painful, pleasurable in a way that is worse for us than the pain would be.

Another danger is violence. Stringent realism of dialog—particularly when it is the language of the inarticulate—does not allow of the expression of intense or deep emotion, as I have said; consequently we must see dreadful things done physically to the characters, or emotion must exhibit itself in violent physical action. What can characters of this sort do to show their rage or their suffering, except to slam doors and smash crockery and beat their fists upon wall or table, what can they do except rant in the clichés of common speech?

Put it this way: by all means let us have the ordinary man. But let us by no means have an ordinary view of the ordinary man; and even then, let us not suppose that there can be nothing else. Much of it is fine drama, and it is serious.

But I do not think it is of the highest seriousness; I do not think it is tragedy. . . .

Is tragedy possible in the present time?

A very common belief is that it is not, for the reason that kings and nobles have lost their aura of dignity. This seems to me utterly trivial. It is perfectly possible to make a person in ordinary, even low station in life into a tragic figure; and it is possible to load the stage with kings and nobles and not have tragedy. It is not the natural subject which makes tragedy or comedy, it is the conceived subject matter, the dramatic conception, and the kind of art which is exerted to realize it. Shakespeare makes *Othello* out of Cinthio's melodramatic tale—a mere crime story—not by altering the social status of Othello and Desdemona, but by altering their characters and the moral quality of their actions; and O'Neill fails to achieve tragedy in *Mourning Becomes Electra*, not because he transports the characters of the *Oresteia* to New England and strips them of their royal raiment and rank, but because he debases them. The conception of Shakespeare is elevated; the conception of O'Neill is not.

It is also often said that tragedy and similar forms are impossible in our age because we have lost our sense of standards, or have become so cynical that we cannot believe in moral elevation, or have become so divided in our beliefs that what is tragic for some is comic for others. These notions have been echoed back and forth for some decades now; it is time that we should say something which should have been said in the first place: *Produce the evidence.* An elaborate counter-argument might easily be provided, but I believe it is unnecessary. The mere fact that the great tragedies of the past continue to have their powerful effects upon us is sufficient to disprove all such hypotheses; for were these hypotheses true, such effect would be impossible.

Indeed, I can find no real reason why we should not have tragedy in our time, except that it fell into the hands of poets who were not dramatists and thus came into disrepute, while the dramatists themselves were both repelled by what the poets were doing and attracted by the possibilities of realistic drama in prose. The dramatists can hardly be blamed; a few pages of Stephen Phillips' *Aylmer's Secret* or *Ulysses* or Richard Le Gallienne's *Orestes* are enough to make one wish that neither poetry nor tragedy had ever been invented. But mis-handling does not obviate the possibility of good handling, as abuse does not preclude use.

If there is no reason why we should not have tragedy, is there any reason why we *should* have it? It is customary to become very eloquent in arguments of this sort and to make all sorts of extravagant claims. I do not really think that civilization will collapse because a given art is not being practised, or that man will forget the great dignity of man. Candidly, I can find only two reasons why the tragic art should be revived. Tragedy offers the dramatist greater scope for his genius; and it offers audiences a superior kind of pleasure, one which no other art can give. These are very simple reasons, but they seem to me quite enough.

Even so, I should want to qualify. I do not want all dramatists to drop what they are doing and take up tragedy; I merely want those who have a gift for tragedy to realize that there is no reason why they should not use it. I am not suggesting that they should model upon the great tragedies of the past, but that they should attempt to discover what may be great tragedy in the future. I am not suggesting that serious drama be bound by the past, but that it should be liberated from the immediate past. Far from calling for a new conservatism, I propose a new revolution; an extension, not a contraction, of the dramatic arts.

Would the new tragedy be poetic drama? Does poetry belong in the theatre? Does verse belong in it?

I think that this, too, requires a qualified answer. Poetry and verse belong in the theatre only when the play itself demands them, and when the dramatist is one who can supply them. The late Maxwell Anderson's plays never seemed to me to demand verse, and I cannot feel that the verse did anything whatsoever for them. The few specimens we have of George Bernard Shaw's dramatic verse convince me absolutely that he should always have written in prose.

And I think we have to be clear about what we mean by poetry and verse. Poetry is not made poetry by the fact that it involves poetic diction. The shoe is on the other foot: poetic diction is made poetic by the fact that it has been used to make a poem. It is generally thought that poetic diction consists of some special vocabulary of poetic words, or some special kind of style, or language involving the use of some special device such as metaphor, symbol, irony, paradox, or ambiguity. I shall not argue against these views; the history of poetry has done that for me. The history of poetry offers no evidence whatsoever that any word or style or device of language is *per se* inadmissible to poetry, or that any is *per se* constitutive of poetry. Good poetry has been written in every conceivable kind of diction; conversely, the mere use of a given diction has never been sufficient in itself to produce poetry. This is plain fact, whereas all the hypotheses about poetic diction are only hypotheses; and one fact nullifies absolutely any hypotheses to the contrary.

I should no more like to see the theatre invaded by bombast—on the pretext that it was "tragic" diction or "exalted style"—than I should like to see it invaded by another string of *Catos*, *Irenes*, or imitations of Shakespeare or the Greeks. Tragedy demands a high style, certainly; but the true high style is simply that which is appropriate to the tragic character—one, that is, which manifests his dignity. It is not bombast. The most affecting passages in the mature Shakespeare are composed in extremely simple language, elevated only by what they manifest to us.

Eliot seems to me to be right when he insists that if poetry is to enter the theatre, it can only be as useful to the drama. Only, this view does not go far enough; I should say it can only enter as useful to the drama *in the way in which it should be useful*. There is no doubt that the poetry in *Murder in the Cathedral* is useful; but it does more than it should; it assumes the main burden of the play.

The dominant characteristic of dramatic poetry is that it is uttered in very specifically determined circumstances, by a very specifically determined character; and its chief virtue is that it be absolutely subservient to dramatic demands. It should set before us—as vividly as possible—plot, character, and thought. The same considerations apply to verse. Verse has two chief functions in the theatre—the acoustical one, of making the words carry better (this is, I think, the real secret behind "Marlowe's mighty line"), and the dramatic function proper, of imitating as closely as possible the inflections, accents, and rhythms of speech, where these are signs of character, thought, or emotion. Verse gives the playwright much greater control over the actors than does prose. Shaw complained that whereas there was only one way of writing "Yes" or "No," there were fifty ways of saying one and five hundred ways of saying the other. A good poet does not have that difficulty. But verse should be used only when the dramatist has thought about his characters and their thoughts and emotions to the point where he must insist that their speeches be delivered in a particular way. Otherwise verse, and poetic diction too, will be useless appendages to the play, and perhaps hostile to its effect.

And, to wind the matter up: verse and diction are not essential to the theatre—in fact, we saw long ago that even language itself was not. But the greatest effects are impossible without them; and a drama which does not involve them must always fall short of those greatest effects.

Why Does Tragedy Please?*

D. D. RAPHAEL

Why does Tragedy please? An old question, asked in the old-fashioned way. If someone objects that the alleged paradox of the pleasure of Tragedy is, like other old-fashioned philosophical problems, created by the language used, that one does not take *pleasure* in Tragedy as in a dish of roast lamb, let him substitute some other word. Why does one receive *satisfaction* from seeing the representation of misery? Why should one *want* to see a tragic drama? Not everyone does. But many people do, myself among them, and even rate the 'pleasure' or 'satisfaction' of Tragedy higher than that of any other *genre* of literary art.

Every schoolboy knows that our question was first answered by Aristotle. And every undergraduate knows that scholars and literary critics have drowned in an ocean of ink the laconic remark that Tragedy 'effects through pity and fear the *catharsis* of such emotions'. I do not propose to analyse or advertise the doctrine of *catharsis*. There is little doubt that Aristotle was speaking in medical terms. Some may find spiritual purification in comparing the mind to the bowels. I should prefer to see aesthetics purged of physiological criticism. Aristotle's *Poetics*, as we have it, is a fragmentary work, and we do not know what he had to say in detail about Comedy; but there is good evidence for thinking that he regarded Comedy, too, as some sort of purge. I am reminded of the therapy practised in Molière's college of doctors at the conclusion of *Le Malade Imaginaire*. Whatever the disease, the prescription is always the same:

> *Clysterium donare,*
> *Postea seignare,*
> *Ensuita purgare.*
> (With a clyster deterge,

* D. D. Raphael, "Why Does Tragedy Please?" from *The Paradox of Tragedy* (Indiana University Press, 1960), pp. 13–36. [The footnotes in this selection have been renumbered.]

> Then let the blood splurge,
> And finally purge.)

We may leave the physiological critics to give Aristotle the four cheers that Molière's doctors give to their neophyte:

> *Bene, bene, bene, bene respondere.*
> *Dignus, dignus est intrare*
> *In nostro docto corpōre.*
> (Jolly, jolly, jolly, jolly fine oration.
> He's fit, he's fit to take his station
> In our learned corporation.)

Aristotle's followers could hardly do less, since for them 'the Philosopher' was the infallible President of *their* learned corporation. It is enough to reply, with Mr F. L. Lucas,[1] that 'the theatre is not a hospital', and to follow him in quoting Fontenelle's bow to those Aristotelian doctors and the queer aesthetic digestions of their patients:

'I have never understood how the passions are purged by the passions themselves; so I shall say nothing about that. If anyone is purged by this means, good luck to him; still, I do not quite see what is the good of being cured of pity.'[2]

Aristotle could have enlightened Fontenelle on the last point. The doctrine of *catharsis* is an answer to Plato's criticism of dramatic art in the *Republic*. Tragic drama calls forth pity for the distress of its heroes, and this, Plato thinks, will render us liable to self-pity, instead of endurance, when we meet misfortune ourselves. Pity is therefore antagonistic to virtue (as Plato understands virtue), and the attempt to control pity requires the banishment of the art that fosters it. Aristotle seeks to defend Tragedy while retaining Plato's criterion of justification. Harmful emotions must have some outlet; better to let them boil up at mere representations, and then the soul will be less troubled by them on real occasions of misfortune. Aristotle disagrees with Plato about the psychological effect of exciting emotion. In opposition to Plato's view (a sound one, in my opinion) that the capacity for emotion grows with exercise, Aristotle puts forward the specious doctrine that when our feelings are stirred we blow off steam and so are 'purged'. But he does not question Plato's ethical tenet that pity is a bad thing. The wonder is that men living in the tradition of Biblical ethics should have felt able to swallow Doctor Aristotle's medicine for the cure of compassion.

Plato speaks only of pity or sympathy. Why does Aristotle add fear? It is easier to answer that than to understand why so many people have accepted the addition. In his *Rhetoric* (Book II, Chapters 5 and 8), Aristotle

---

[1] *Tragedy*, London: Hogarth Press, 1927, p. 29.
[2] *Réflexions sur la Poétique*, xlv; original quoted by Lucas, p. 34.

regards pity and fear as near relations. It would be going too far to say that for Aristotle, as for Hobbes, pity *is* or always includes fear of similar calamities for ourselves (though when we criticize Hobbes, it is worth remembering that his error is simply an exaggeration of what he had found in Aristotle). Yet Aristotle does think, it seems to me, that one of the purposes of Tragedy is to make us fear for ourselves the distress we pity in others.[3]

It does not need much argument to refute the view that Tragedy is intended to arouse emotions concerning oneself. Classical and romantic tragedians alike place their characters at a distance of time, place, and status, in order to produce an impersonal contemplation. As someone has remarked, no member of Sophocles' audience was likely to suppose himself in any danger of murdering his father and marrying his mother through the extraordinary chances that brought such a fate to Oedipus. A modern playwright, Jean Anouilh, assures his audience that no disturbing emotions are stirred up by Tragedy; quite the contrary:

> Most of all, it's restful, is Tragedy, because you know that there is no more hope, dirty sneaking hope; that you are caught, caught at last like a rat in a trap. . . . And there is nothing more you can try; that's that![4]

He speaks with appropriate irony, no doubt, when he repeats, 'It's restful', but the disturbing effect of casting away all hope is not the disturbance of fear. Aristotle himself says that 'fear sets us thinking what can be done, which of course nobody does when things are hopeless'.[5]

Nor does it need much argument to show that Aristotle ties pity and fear too closely together. His doctrine rests on the fact that to be capable of pity we must be capable of imagining, and therefore of experiencing in ourselves, pain or evil such as that which we see affecting or threatening the person pitied. More generally, sympathy of any kind, since it includes the representation in imagination of another's feelings, presupposes experience of sufficiently similar feelings in ourselves. To pity another's pain I must know

---

[3] S. H. Butcher, in later editions of *Aristotle's Theory of Poetry and Fine Art*, is inclined to deny this (see 4th ed., London: Macmillan, 1907, p. 259, footnote on the phrase, φόβος δὲ περὶ τὸν ὅμοιον, 'fear concerns someone like ourselves', *Poetics*, xiii, 2). He says that, for Aristotle, 'the φόβος of tragedy is not, like the φόβος of the *Rhetoric* and of real life, a fear for ourselves'. He appears to overlook one passage in the *Rhetoric* (1383a 8 ff.), which not only recalls the phrase, φόβος δὲ περὶ τὸν ὅμοιον, of *Poetics*, xiii, but seems plainly to compare the orator's representation with the tragedian's: 'When it is advisable that the audience should be frightened, the orator must make them feel that they really are in danger of something, pointing out that *it has happened to others who were stronger than they are, and is happening, or has happened, to people like themselves* (τοὺς ὁμοίους), *at the hands of unexpected people, in an unexpected form, and at an unexpected time.*' (Quotations in English from the *Rhetoric* are taken from the Oxford translation by Rhys Roberts. The italics here are mine.)

[4] First speech of the Chorus in Anouilh's *Antigone*.

[5] *Rhetoric*, 1383a7.

what pain is. But though the prospect of pain to myself will arouse fear, it is not necessary, for the experience of pity, that one should experience or imagine fear. It is enough to imagine pain and to possess what I shall vaguely call 'fellow-feeling'. Now this 'fellow-feeling' is referred to by Aristotle himself in *Rhetoric*, Book II, Chapter 13 (1390a19), where he throws out, in passing, a distinction between the kind of pity felt by the young and that felt by the old. The young, he says, pity others from '*philanthropia*', while the old do so 'out of weakness, imagining that anything that befalls anyone else might easily happen to them, which, as we saw, is a thought that excites pity'.[6] Aristotle recognizes here that the semiselfish pity he has previously analysed is not the only kind there is, and we must agree with S. H. Butcher [7] that 'the tacit reference to self makes pity, as generally described in the *Rhetoric*, sensibly different from the pure instinct of compassion, the unselfish sympathy with others' distress, which most writers understand by pity'. Having admitted that, we might as well discard altogether Aristotle's doctrine that Tragedy relies on pity and fear as he understands them.

Chapter XIII of the *Poetics*, which says most about pity and fear in Tragedy, also makes two references to *philanthropia*. Aristotle is discussing the kind of character, and the kind of reversal of fortune, suitable for a tragic hero. The spectacle of a wholly good man brought low from prosperity to disaster, he says, is neither pitiful nor terrible but only shocking. That of a bad man raised up from adversity to success has 'none of the necessary tragic qualities; it is neither "philanthropic" nor pitiful nor terrible'. The downfall of a bad man will not do either, for while it is 'philanthropic' it does not arouse pity or fear. There remains only the moderately good man, brought to disaster not by vice but by some *hamartia* ('error', 'fault'), and he, in Aristotle's opinion, is the ideal tragic hero.

Perhaps we should not attach any significance to the primacy of position given to *philanthropia* in the list of three emotions necessary for the tragic effect. Still, the fact remains that it is added as a third emotion. Aristotle evidently sensed here that his restricted form of pity was not enough; the appeal of Tragedy includes the evincing of a generous sympathy, which Aristotle could feel only when he was young.

I have not quite finished with Aristotle. I have dismissed *catharsis* summarily as old game, and have concentrated my discussion on the doctrine of pity and fear, which still seems to be accepted as a matter of course by many writers on Tragedy. I must now say something about *hamartia*, not from any thought that this part of Aristotle's theory has been insufficiently criticized by others, but in order to bring out farther the confusion in his account of the tragic emotions.

---

[6] Cf. Butcher, *op. cit.*, p. 258, footnote 1.
[7] *Op. cit.*, pp. 257–8.

Aristotle distinguishes four possible subjects, and decides that only the last can be properly tragic. The first case, the downfall of a completely virtuous man, is rejected as unsuitable for Tragedy because it rouses neither pity nor fear but is shocking. One might well query Aristotle's conclusion about pity. (Fear certainly may be absent, but that is irrelevant, as I have already argued, and does not prevent the situation from being tragic.) It is commonly acknowledged that Aristotle is wrong to reject the downfall of virtue as a suitable subject for Tragedy. Both Antigone and Cordelia answer to it. Few of us will follow Hegel in judging Antigone morally culpable, or follow Gervinus in finding Cordelia to have been condemned to death by Shakespeare for the crime of leading a French army against England. We know that Dr Johnson 'could not bear to read the last scenes' of *King Lear* because he was 'so shocked by Cordelia's death', and preferred Tate's version with a happy ending. His experience confirms Aristotle's judgement that virtue come to grief is shocking. Let us leave that side of it for the moment. So far we have no sound evidence that this is not a fit subject for tragic pity, and we shall perhaps be more inclined to agree with W. Macneile Dixon [8] that the suffering of a blameless person is the *most* tragic type. Hegel indeed will not allow pity for Antigone, but then he will not allow pity for any tragic hero. Pity will do for your 'country cousins', he tells us; the heroes of Tragedy are too noble for that kind of thing—and too Hegelian, for they recognize the justice of their fate. But Sophocles did not think so when he caused Antigone to make her final exit with the words, 'I have given reverence where reverence is due', as her verdict on her 'crime'.

One can see why Aristotle could not allow that the misery of a saint inspires fear. He says, a little later in the chapter, that fear is aroused by the misfortune of a person like ourselves. Since an audience is a collection of average men, not saints, they will not fear the misfortunes of saints. What of pity? This, he says, is aroused by unmerited misfortune; and the misfortunes of the saint above all answer to that description. I suppose Aristotle would hold, not unreasonably, that the moral offensiveness of the situation is too strong for any emotions other than shock.[9] The representation of virtue come to grief offends our moral sense. Aristotle is right enough about that. But we shall debar such a subject from Tragedy only if we are convinced, as Dr Johnson certainly was, that God does not allow such things to happen.

Let us now turn to the fourth case, Aristotle's ideal tragic hero, a moderately good man who falls into misfortune not through vice but through some *hamartia*. Unlike the misfortune of the completely virtuous, Aristotle

[8] *Tragedy*, London: E. Arnold, 1924, p. 135.
[9] Cf. Butcher, *Aristotle's Theory of Poetry and Fine Art*, 4th ed., p. 309.

seems to argue, the fourth case is not morally offensive, because the disaster is the result of *hamartia*.

If we do not share the ethical views of Aristotle and his masters, we may wish to deny this. The cause of the hero's downfall is expressly stated to be not vice or depravity but 'error', and where, we may ask, is the justice of that? Still, we have to remember that the *Poetics* was written by Aristotle, not by a Christian. Those who do remind us of this when discussing the doctrine of *hamartia*, too often take it unquestioningly for granted that Plato and Aristotle speak for all Greeks. Macneile Dixon, for instance, who is in general almost as hard as I am on Aristotle's theory of Tragedy, excuses Aristotle's mistaken doctrine of *hamartia* as typically Greek: 'For the clear-eyed intellectualism of the Greeks error was sin and sin error, miscalculation, in short, a form of guilt, for which Nature had no forgiveness.' [10] To be sure, the Greek philosophers Socrates, Plato, and Aristotle, all held an intellectualist doctrine of ethics. Virtue is knowledge, the perfect life is the philosophic life of knowledge. But I am not convinced that most Greeks agreed with them, and I am certain that the tragedians did not.[11] The tragedians would have agreed that ignorance can bring unhappiness, but does this imply that ignorance is sin? There is a difference between recognizing a fact and accepting it as just and proper. We have all heard of Margaret Fuller's decision to accept the universe, and of Carlyle's 'Gad! she'd better!' Not everyone does. Anouilh makes his tragic heroine one who says 'No', who refuses to accept the universe. The universe promptly crushes her, of course. she'd have done 'better' to say yes—better from a prudential point of view. But the tragedian perhaps is not concerned wish the prudential view. He may, like Anouilh's Antigone, reject the way the world wags and the powers that wag it so. Euripides seems at times to take this attitude, and possibly Shakespeare when he wrote *King Lear*. Or the tragedian may, like Aeschylus and Sophocles, be merely puzzled and dissatisfied. What he does not do is to accept the world unquestioningly.

Let us look a little more closely into Aristotle's preference for the erring hero. Does the hero's error justify his fate, even on Aristotle's view? *Oedipus Rex* seems to have been Aristotle's favourite Tragedy. Oedipus certainly suffers from *hamartia*, as Aristotle says. He is over-confident and over-rash, and his failings contribute to his downfall. But are they the main cause of his sins? Before he was born, the gods had doomed him to kill his father and marry his mother. They endowed him with his failings of character in order to carry out their plan, but even then all sorts of marvels and coincidences had to be contrived for the prophecy to come true. Even if he is held responsible for his defects of character and knowledge, can we apply Plato's dic-

[10] *Tragedy*, p. 131.
[11] Cf. Macneile Dixon himself, for Aeschylus at least, on pp. 79–80 of his book.

tum,[12] 'the responsibility rests on his choice; Heaven is not to blame'? Oedipus did not choose; he was pushed into it. Much the same is true of the *hamartiae* of other tragic heroes. Aristotle is not justified in saying that the misfortune is the *consequence* of *hamartia* in such a sense as to take away any moral offensiveness from the hero's fate.

Besides, if the hero did deserve his fate, he could not, on Aristotle's view, be the subject of pity. For, it will be remembered, Aristotle insists that pity is aroused by *unmerited* misfortune. If, therefore, a hero's misfortune arises from *hamartia* and so does not shock the moral sense as would the misfortunes of the virtuous, it is not unmerited and so cannot arouse pity. If pity is justified, the hero's *hamartia* does not prevent his fate from being unmerited and thereby shocking the moral sense. Aristotle cannot have it both ways: if *hamartia* is responsible, there cannot be pity; and if pity is appropriate, *hamartia* cannot take the blame. Aristotle lands himself in inconsistency on the sole type of plot that he allows to be properly tragic. He is therefore left without any possible plot at all.

Fortunately the tragedians are not Aristotelians. They are able to use successfully three of his four types of plot. We have already noted instances of wholly virtuous heroes (or rather, heroines, a qualification not without interest). And it has often been pointed out that Shakespeare at least is able to use wicked men, like Macbeth and Richard III, as tragic heroes—so long as they exhibit, in Corneille's phrase, *grandeur d'âme*. *Greatness* of spirit; that is the essential quality of the tragic hero. Goodness, whether perfect or 'flawed', is not necessarily required, though it can certainly show itself to be a species of spiritual grandeur.

I have delayed too long over Aristotle, longer than his theory of Tragedy deserves. Little did he dream, poor man, that his scrappy remarks would be taken so seriously by later dramatists and critics. His fate at their hands is indeed unmerited, a fit object for our pity. It is the fashion among philosophers nowadays to praise Aristotle and belabour Aristotelians. Let us say, therefore, with a half measure of truth, that our over-long criticism is directed against the long line of his followers.

I do not intend to go through the theories of Tragedy proposed by later philosophers. There was a time when it would have been essential to discuss Hegel. But I think there is no need now to criticize Hegel's view of Tragedy, and unlike Aristotle he gets hisses from the fashionable first-nighters of the philosophical audience. The tale is told (I have got it from Mr F. L. Lucas) that Hegel used to greet the Sunday joint with the words, 'Come, let us fulfil its destiny'. We may therefore leave him to his own Promethean destiny of being devoured when he is not left to grow cold on the shelf, and

---

[12] *Republic*, Book X, 617c.

hope that he is able to acknowledge, with the Spartan resignation of his tragic hero, an eternal justice in his fate. Hegel did contribute something to the theory of Tragedy, as did Schopenhauer and Nietzsche. The trouble with all of them is that they approached their data with a ready-made metaphysics to which Tragedy had to be fitted willy-nilly.

The metaphysical problem from which they fashioned their Procrustean beds for Tragedy, is the problem of evil—by which I mean the existence of unmerited suffering. I have already allowed that a villain may be a tragic hero. Nevertheless, it seems to me, the poignancy of Tragedy comes out chiefly in the misery of innocence. All Tragedy deals with the presentation of evil, but some of the greatest works of tragic drama are concerned specifically with the metaphysical or theological problem of evil. If one already has some metaphysical theory of the world, some rational scheme into which all human experience is to be fitted, one approaches the problem of evil with an explanation ready made. The great tragedians do not inscribe evil under a prepared rubric. Sometimes they are groping their way to an explanation. Sometimes they seem to be denying that there is any explanation. Mostly, however, they are concerned simply to present the phenomenon of evil vividly before us, stamping it with a great question-mark and leaving us to answer the question as we can—if we can. Metaphysicians who already have their answer, be it optimistic like Hegel's or pessimistic like Schopenhauer's and Nietzsche's, distort the position of the tragic dramatist, whose first business is to express the disturbing character of the existence of evil, not to explain it or explain it away.

So far as I am aware, I have no ready-made solution to the problem of evil. I hope that the view of Tragedy which I shall put forward is derived from the evidence alone and not from a preconceived philosophy. I have little doubt, however, that preconceptions of *interest* have caused me to select certain aspects of tragic drama for emphasis, while a person whose main interests lay elsewhere would view Tragedy with a different focus. There is no single truth in philosophical generalization on matters of this kind. I shall be content if what I have to say succeeds in commending itself as *a* general truth about tragic drama.

Tragedy always presents a conflict. This proposition needs no defence. It is familiar enough. But a conflict between what? I suggest that it is a conflict between inevitable power, which we may call necessity, and the reaction to necessity of self-conscious effort. Tragic conflict differs from the conflicts presented by other forms of drama in that the victory always goes to necessity. The hero is crushed.

I have spoken of necessity, not fate. Writers on this subject often draw a distinction between classical Tragedy, which attributes human disaster to fate, and modern Tragedy, which attributes it to human character. For my purpose the distinction is irrelevant. In both cases, the cause of the disaster is necessity, whether external to the hero or inherent in his own character. For that matter, external necessity is not exhausted by fate or non-human powers. Antigone is in conflict with, and is crushed by, political power. (It is true that, in the same play, Creon opposes, and is in a different way struck down by, supernatural ordinance; but Antigone and her ordeal form the centre of interest.) In any event it is superficial to make the difference between classical and, say, Shakespearean Tragedy turn on a distinction between supernatural and psychological causes. Is Aeschylus' portrayal of Clytemnestra in the *Agamemnon* a study of the workings of supernatural fate or of human psychology? It is either or both.[13] And the same is true of Shakespeare's treatment of Macbeth. You may choose, if you wish, to regard the workings of character as embodying dark forces that transcend the individual. Or you may regard myths, that speak of supernatural forces, as vivid expressions of the effects of psychological traits. *King Lear* is agreed to be the most nearly classical of Shakespeare's Tragedies; yet it can be treated as a study of pride and ingratitude. On the other side, is the psychological interest of Euripides' *Medea* any less than that of *Othello* or *Phèdre*?

The conflict, then, is with necessity, inevitable power that is bound to defeat any opposition. The tragic hero, even though he be a villain like Macbeth, attracts our admiration because of some *grandeur d'âme*, a greatness in his effort to resist, and our pity for his defeat. Although he must be crushed in his conflict, since his adversary is necessity, yet he does not yield the victory on all counts:

> *Capta ferum victorem cepit.*

His *grandeur d'âme* is sublime and wins our admiration. Herein lies the satisfaction, the elevation, produced by Tragedy.

So far, I have not said anything particularly novel. Let me now proceed to characterize further the aesthetic satisfaction of Tragedy. Tragic beauty is a species of the sublime. What is felt to be sublime is something surpassingly great.[14] It may be physically great or spiritually great, 'the starry heavens above' or 'the moral law within'. Both these, said Kant, fill us with wonder and awe. Now I want to suggest that the reaction to the sublime need not always be wonder *and awe*. It may be admiration alone. The works of God or Nature, 'the chains of the Pleiades, the bands of Orion'—when

---

[13] Cf. Professor Kitto's account of the 'dual plane', discussed in §2 of the second essay in this book [*The Paradox of Tragedy*].

[14] Cf. A. C. Bradley, 'The Sublime', in *Oxford Lectures on Poetry*. London: Macmillan, 1909.

we feel these to be sublime, we feel wonder and awe. As A. C. Bradley says, our rapture goes along with self-surrender, with feelings of abasement no less than those of elevation. But what of the sublimity of human effort? When we see this, does our admiration include feelings of abasement? We may feel that we ordinary mortals could not rise to the heights of the tragic hero if we were in his place—though I shall try to show that the dramatist deliberately counters this by raising us in other ways above the characters in his play. At any rate, we do not feel that *man* is lowly, is dust and ashes, when confronted by the greatness of that which he opposes and by which he is crushed. He is defeated, but he remains great, sublime, in his fall. The greatness of his opponent is greatness of physical power. His own greatness is greatness of spirit. I suggest that at least some of the peculiar satisfaction of tragic drama comes from a feeling that the sublimity of the hero's spirit is superior to the sublimity of the power which overwhelms him. The dramatist stirs in us more admiration for the human spirit than awe for the powers of necessity.

Both Tragedy and Epic, as Aristotle says, elevate man in their representation of human action, while Comedy abases him. Both Tragedy and Epic achieve the elevation of a hero through triumph in a conflict. Tragedy differs from Epic in that the tragic conflict and its issue are complicated and paradoxical. On the natural plane, the hero is worsted by the strength of his adversary, which thus appears great and, in the necessity of its conquest, sublime in the sense of awe-inspiring. On the spiritual plane, the hero appears great in his necessarily futile struggle. The inevitability of his defeat on the natural plane is what gives sublimity to his reaction. The inner conflict of Tragedy is between the two forms of the sublime, the awe-inspiring strength of necessity and the *grandeur d'âme* which inspires admiration. Each triumphs on its own plane, but the triumph of the human spirit is the more elevating. And that is why the tragic fate of the hero gives us satisfaction.

Because Tragedy snatches a spiritual victory out of a natural defeat, it is nearer to the religious attitude than is Epic. In another way, however, Tragedy tends to be inimical to religion. It elevates man in his struggle with necessity, while the religious attitude is one of abasement before that which is greater than man, before the awe-inspiring sublime. This corollary of the sense of the tragic invites further discussion. Before pursuing it, we must return to pick up a thread left loose a short while ago.

The tragic hero, like the epic hero, Aristotle remarks, is given a nobility greater than that of life. As Anouilh says in his *Antigone*, futile reaction against necessity has no place in the life of ordinary men. 'It's a luxury (*C'est gratuit*). It's for kings.' Does it then follow that the audience of ordinary men feel themselves small before the grandeur of the superhuman heroes on the stage? No, it does not follow, for the dramatist employs his arts on the audience, too. He cannot give them superhuman nobility, such as he gives his hero, but in another way he raises them above his hero. A mark of the tragic hero is his limited knowledge, and the mark of tragic irony is the contrast between the hero's ignorance and the audience's knowledge, whereby statements that mean one thing to him have a *double entendre* for them. In his ignorance the tragic hero displays the finitude of man. The audience are free from this limitation. Within the universe of the play, they have the omniscience of the gods. A former colleague of mine, Mr D. H. Monro, in his book *Argument of Laughter*, speaks of the 'God's-eye view' of humanity presented in the Comedy of character. It is given in Tragedy, too. Indeed, in Greek Tragedy it is sometimes a view superior to that of a god. For if a god is brought upon the stage, the audience has a view embracing both the outlook of the god and that of the other characters. Even in *Prometheus Vinctus*, where Zeus never actually appears as a character on the stage, Aeschylus sets the audience above Zeus and Prometheus alike, for his aim is to seek a superior theology in which power and benevolence shall be combined, and in so far as he grasps and communicates such a 'God's-eye view' he places his audience at the vantage point from which that view may be obtained.

Tragedy is a form of art, and its pleasure is an aesthetic pleasure. We rarely, if ever, obtain from the so-called tragedies [15] of life the satisfaction that we gain from tragic drama. In life, we are on the same level as those who suffer, we are fellow human beings. Our sympathy for their disaster is usually too strong for feelings of satisfaction at any sublimity they may display. In the theatre, the way is cleared for the appreciation of sublimity by giving us the 'God's-eye view'. The scene is set in the past, so that we know what is going to happen; or, if not in the past, in a distant clime, so that we shall not be too disposed to identify ourselves in sympathy with the characters on the stage. The dramatist fails in his purpose if, like Phrynichus with *The Capture of Miletus*, he represents life close to his audience and inhibits admiration by excessive pity.

Yet the separation must not go too far; for we shall be able to admire the human quality of the characters only if we feel sympathy for them as human beings ourselves. The author of Comedy, especially of satiric Comedy, can sometimes allow the distance between audience and stage to cross the boundary separating the human from the non-human. For instance, by de-humanizing his characters, as Karel Čapek does in *The Insect Play*, he completes the temporary deification of the audience—for he does not want them to sympathize. When the play is done, and they are brought back from

---

[15] It is important to bear in mind the distinction between tragic drama and 'tragedy' in a looser sense. I mark it by writing the word with a capital initial letter when it has the first meaning, and not when it has the second.

divinity to humanity, they will see the beasts in themselves. The tragedian must raise his audience to the level of the God's-eye view, yet at the same time he must be careful not to deprive them of fellow-feeling with the characters on the stage.

He can succeed in this double purpose because the tragic hero is himself larger than life. The hero lacks the omniscience of his audience, but the gods who watch him, like the powers against whom he strives, fall below him in *grandeur d'âme*. Hero and adversary are balanced by their respective superiority in spiritual grandeur on the one side and natural power on the other. *Vis-à-vis* the audience, the spiritual grandeur of the hero is balanced by their godlike omniscience. Thus we can at the same time sympathize and admire. The hero is a man like us, showing human weaknesses from which the devices of art free us for the nonce; but though an object of our sympathy, he also seems sublime, for he outstrips us, and the superior powers whom he opposes, in greatness of spirit. And our sympathy for him as a fellow human being gives to his sublimity a stronger appeal than that exerted by the sublimity of the alien power with which he contends. By such devices Tragedy exalts man in our eyes. Its creed is humanistic.

The affinities of Tragedy with the sublime are emphasized by Mr Chu Kwang-Tsien in an interesting thesis whose scope is far wider than is indicated in its title, *The Psychology of Tragedy*.[16] He says (p. 11) that writers on aesthetics, with the possible exception of Burke, have 'never suspected' any close relation between the sense of the tragic and that of the sublime. This can hardly be true. A connection of some sort is too obvious to be overlooked, and perhaps writers on the subject have thought it too obvious to be mentioned. It may well be, however, that no one has previously explored the character of the connection, and this, as I hope my own suggestions have shown, is not so obvious or straightforward as one might suppose. Macneile Dixon uses the *word* 'sublime' at one or two points in his book on *Tragedy*, and no doubt others have done the same; but Macneile Dixon certainly does not develop any relation between Tragedy and the concept of the sublime. It is, I think, much to Mr Chu Kwang-Tsien's credit that he has done so, though I want to criticize the way in which he relates the two.

Chu Kwang-Tsien accepts the usual view that the sense of the sublime includes feelings of both admiration and awe, elevation and abasement. He suggests that the beauty of Tragedy is a species of the sublime, differing from other species in that the feelings which constitute the sense of the tragic include pity as well as admiration and awe. Putting his position in another way, he holds that Aristotle's addition of fear to Plato's pity is justified if

---

[16] Strasbourg: Librairie Universitaire d'Alsace, 1933.

one interprets fear as awe, and that wonder or admiration should probably be added, as suggested by Corneille, to Aristotle's two feelings of pity and fear.[17] Turning to the aesthetic descriptions of the objects of these states of mind, Chu Kwang-Tsien says that the object of aesthetic pity or sympathy is the graceful, which is usually tinged with a feeling of sadness; that the object of aesthetic admiration is grandeur, in the case of Tragedy heroic grandeur; and that the object of awe in Tragedy is the power of fate. (I find rather odd his linking of pity with the graceful, but I am not here concerned with the truth of that contention.) His general argument for including aesthetic fear or terror in the reaction to Tragedy, and therefore for classing the tragic with the sublime, runs as follows. Pity alone would give us the sense of sad gracefulness. This by itself is not tragic because not uplifting; it can be merely sentimental. We must add heroic grandeur, which arouses wonder and admiration. But if the heroic element predominates, the result will not be tragic; *Le Cid* is not tragic, while *Romeo and Juliet* is. To produce the sense of the tragic, the heroic element must be balanced by 'the element of terror'. 'The merely terrible is in its effect just opposite to the heroic, each possesses what the other lacks. The heroic inspires us without first thrilling us with an emotion of fear, whereas the merely terrible thrills us with fear without inspiring us. The tragic must produce both effects at once.' [18] The fear which we feel in Tragedy is not, however, fear for the tragic hero or for ourselves, as Aristotle thought. 'In every case, it is the fear before the cruel and capricious visage of the Moirae, who have wrought all these "old, unhappy far-off things".' [19] This fear is followed by elevation. 'It calls forth an extraordinary amount of vital energy to cope with an extraordinary situation. It makes us equal to a tremendous task which in actual reality we can hardly hope to accomplish.' The pleasure of Tragedy is 'a pleasure that always accompanies overflowing life and intense activity'.[20]

It will be observed that Chu Kwang-Tsien's account has some features in common with mine but diverges from it in other respects. Where we differ, the thread of his argument seems to me to show certain weaknesses.

(1) He says that pity alone does not constitute the tragic emotion; there must be added admiration of heroic grandeur. With this I agree. He then says that heroic grandeur alone will not do, either, for the effect of heroic poetry or drama is not the same as that of Tragedy; and therefore he feels justified in adding an element of fear. But this second step in his argument seems to overlook the presence of pity. The tragic hero differs from the epic hero in being the object of pity as well as of admiration. There is no

---

[17] *The Psychology of Tragedy*, pp. 80–97.
[18] *The Psychology of Tragedy*, p. 90.
[19] p. 95.
[20] p. 96.

need to add fear in order to distinguish the tragic from the merely heroic.

(2) Chu Kwang-Tsien proceeds to vindicate the introduction of fear on the ground that the effect of Tragedy is that of the sublime, and the sublime always involves fear or abasement as well as admiration of grandeur. My own account has questioned this last proposition. May not an epic hero be sublime, even though he is not thwarted by fate? Chu Kwang-Tsien goes on to describe the fear of Tragedy as a feeling of awe before the power of fate, and he compares it with the fear and abasement before God of which Eliphaz speaks in the *Book of Job*. He would agree that the sense of the sublime in the *Book of Job*, and elsewhere, is a feeling both of wonder and of awe at surpassing grandeur and power found together, in God, or in any other being or thing that is sublime in this commonly acknowledged sense. The qualities exciting wonder and awe belong to the one object, and the two feelings are consequently directed upon the one object as sublime. Now when he previously argued that Tragedy must include grandeur to stir wonder and admiration, he referred to the grandeur of the tragic *hero*. *This* grandeur does not produce awe. Chu Kwang-Tsien himself says that the 'fear' or awe of Tragedy is not directed upon the individual hero but on fate. It follows that his analogy with the effect of the sublime, as he understands the sublime, is faulty. In his sense of the sublime, a sublime object is both great and terrible, and its greatness is what makes it terrible. But in characterizing Tragedy as a mode of the sublime, he has located the greatness in one place, in the tragic hero, and the cause of terror in another, in fate. Clearly he ought to have said that *fate*, as it appears in Tragedy, is sublime because both great and terrible. What then will he say of the tragic hero? Is he or is he not sublime? If he is, we must admit that grandeur alone may be sublime. If he is not, then the requirement that Tragedy exhibit *heroic* grandeur is otiose. The combination of grandeur with the terrible or awe-inspiring is supplied by fate, and if that combination is all that is required for the sublimity of Tragedy, there is no need for grandeur in the characters.

(3) Finally, Chu Kwang-Tsien's account of tragic sublimity leaves him without any naturally ensuing explanation of the pleasure taken in Tragedy, and he has to resort to an *ad hoc* explanation which seems decidedly weak. He says that our fear of fate 'calls forth an extraordinary amount of energy to cope with an extraordinary situation'. The pleasure is 'a pleasure that always accompanies overflowing life and intense activity'. Well, the energy is called forth from the tragic hero more than from the audience. It is he, after all, not they, who has 'to cope with an extraordinary situation'. No doubt Chu Kwang-Tsien would say that we share the hero's energy by 'aesthetic sympathy' or empathy. Be it so. But it will be admitted that the energy communicated to us by the exercise of aesthetic imagination cannot be as great, or shall we say as real, as the energy which our imagination imitates. Then

if the energy which we receive through imagination gives us pleasure, because pleasure 'always accompanies overflowing life and intense activity', it follows that the tragic hero must experience greater, or a more real, pleasure in his exercise of energy to cope with his extraordinary situation. Do the dramatists think so? Does Lear feel pleased as the blows of fate are doubled and redoubled upon him, requiring greater and greater effort to bear them? Is Macbeth enjoying himself when he recognizes the force of necessity and faces it with words which undoubtedly give *us* enjoyment of the sublime?

> Tomorrow, and tomorrow, and tomorrow,
> Creeps in this petty pace from day to day,
> Until the last syllable of recorded time;
> And all our yesterdays have lighted fools
> The way to dusty death.

Chu Kwang-Tsien finds the distinction between the sublimity of Tragedy and other forms of sublimity purely in the fact that the tragic emotion includes pity. I have suggested that the peculiar mark of tragic sublimity is that Tragedy presents a conflict between two forms of the sublime and makes one of these, the sublimity of human heroism, appeal to us more than the other. I agree that tragic sympathy is important here, but I have tried to show how it is. Sympathy with the tragic hero causes us to appreciate his sublimity more warmly than that of the power which confronts him. Our pleasure arises from the feeling that one like us reaches the greater height. In my view, therefore, abasement has no place in the tragic emotion.

The Psychology of Tragic Pleasure*

ROY MORRELL

Mine is a hackneyed subject, and I should like to say at once that some obvious points which may appear heavily laboured in the first part of this paper, are included not in order to instruct, but to facilitate reference when I come to a psychoanalytical analogy at the end.

I have little room, in my theory, for the jargon of psychological pleasure terms such as Sadism and Masochism. The masochistic element in literature is familiar and it appears distinct from Tragedy. The Romantic mood which finds pleasure in "swooning to death" has, I know, been called tragic, but this is, I believe, a confusion. When Tragedy appears in nineteenth century literature, it seems alien and even shocking to the Romantic sensibility. The argument that the appeal of Tragedy is sadistic is likewise unconvincing: the critic argues—rightly, I think—that literature or drama which openly relishes cruelty repels those of us who are not sadists, yet those of us who are not sadists can find pleasure in Tragedy.

The argument in favour of sadism might, however, be pressed in a different way: it might be said that some "censorship" mechanism enables us to derive sadistic pleasure—those of us who deny that we are sadists—only from something not *too* sadistic, from something not recognizable as sadism. Psychologists do, in fact, extend the term sadism to include not only sexual violence or a relish in inflicting pain inexplicable except through some sexual analogy, but also a more general satisfaction in the discomfiture of others. At one time it seemed to me that tragic pleasure must be explicable in this way. Are not all but the best of men moved to envy the lot of their more energetic or more successful fellows? We may think we are unselfish, or good sports-

---

* Roy Morrell, "The Psychology of Tragic Pleasure," *Essays in Criticism*, Vol. VI, No. 1 (January, 1956), pp. 22–37.

men, rejoicing in our friend's success, his windfall, his prize in the sweep-stake—he bought only one ticket, lucky fellow, and we had bought ten—we may rejoice in his fat legacy. We cannot blame ourselves, we blame only him, when we quickly detect signs of "uppishness" in him; and we leave him to go his superior way. How quickly and virtuously, on the other hand, do we rally round with demonstrations of friendship and pity, refraining from the least mention of "poetic justice," should he lose his wealth as quickly as he acquired it. Nor is it entirely petty thus to wish for an assurance that Fate is not too unfair, that if she withholds from us her special favours, she does not deal us her worst blows. To see disaster befalling a great and fortunate person dwarfs our own worries and troubles, and makes them more easily bearable. Fate, great personages, disasters befalling them—these are the stuff of tragedy, and that pity should be seen as something related to envy, and therefore undesirable, perhaps indicates that Aristotle was thinking partly along these lines.

Reflection will show us, however, that any such theory is incomplete. It assumes a detachment on the part of the audience; it ignores the fact that most spectators and readers sympathize, or perhaps actually identify them-selves with the hero. We may be more sophisticated than the schoolboy who forgets that Jim Hawkins is not himself, but we sympathize with Oedi-pus, Lear, Othello, Tess and Hugo actively enough to wish to avert the disasters which await them. In short, tragic pleasure does not arise through the gratification of a wish, but in a wish's frustration. This reminder should prevent our toying with psychological pleasure terms, masochism or sad-ism, dilute them as we may, or with any conception of "poetic justice." Tragedy does not "please" in this sense; it does not please our palate, nor awaken pleasurable anticipation. On the contrary, we resist Tragedy, and try to avert it. The pleasure arises only afterwards, and no small part of the pleasure is the discovery that we have the strength to face a world which is larger than the mere creation of our wishes.

There remain the anthropologists' data of the magical origins of Tragedy. We all know that pain, mutilation, sacrifice, ritual burial, once implied re-newal, resurrection, the germination of the seed. But what have such things to do with us today? Having outgrown the magical view of the world, why have we not outgrown Tragedy? It is true that primitive impulses still move us unconsciously. Freud has shown that accidents, breakages and the like, are sometimes instinctive sacrifices, sops to Nemesis. We may not use the word *Hubris*, but we dislike and fear boasting; we touch wood, and hang up mistletoe; and in the same way the tragic experience, in which we suffer vicariously, may still be "good magic" and seem to appease the Fates.

The Fates indeed are merely projections of our anxieties, and if the Fates have gone, the anxieties remain. And it is in this way, I think, that we usually find the appeal of Tragedy defined today. If art is man's method of imposing a pattern on the disorderly material of life, Tragedy's function is to get under control life's most chaotic and difficult parts. Gilbert Murray said, "In its primitive form, drama was doing beforehand the thing you longed or dreaded to do; doing afterwards the thing that lived in your mind and could not be exorcised."

Modern warfare has shown that man has not outgrown this need for anticipating or exorcising. In Freud's account of war neuroses, he pointed out that the anxious individuals, whose imaginations pictured the horrors of battle in advance, were least liable to shell-shock. He also pointed out that recovery from shock was necessarily accompanied by dreams of the shocking experience. Attempts to cure the patient by diverting his mind always failed; his injured psyche was set on rehearsing and rehearsing the horror in daydreams and in sleep until gradually the experience was brought under control; and cures were accelerated not by removing the patients to the quiet of the country, trying to make them forget, but rather by reminding them of the battlefield, supplementing their imaginings by noises of bombardment and by additional shocks.

All this is well known, but it is interesting because, first, it suggests why surprise is unimportant in Tragedy. Indeed, as Mr. Lucas says, dramatic irony and suspense—with their hints of what is about to happen—far from detracting from the effect of tragedy only enhance the horror. We can, moreover, see a great tragedy again and again, without diminution of effect: it is, indeed, as if, within our own minds, Tragedy were never a performance, always a rehearsal. Second, Freudian psychology corroborates our previous impression that "Tragic Pleasure" is a phrase which can be used only with reserve, in inverted commas. We are not "pleased" by the destruction of the hero, any more than the soldier is "pleased" either by the shock which penetrates his illusions, or by the dreams by which he seeks to control or exorcise the terror. Pleasure there is indeed, but only afterwards, in the feeling of having gained control, partial or complete, over the chaotic experience.

In the book where Freud develops this theme—that certain human behaviour can be explained only by going, as the title puts it, "Beyond the Pleasure Principle," he analyses examples of play in children, where sometimes, by persistent repetition, the child's psyche obtains control over a painful experience. Freud then compares the psyche to a cell. He sees it as having a highly sensitive interior protected by a hard rind from the cruel shock-laden wind of the real world. Some objective reality may be absorbed into layers of the rind, and defences may be strengthened by marshalling energies from within to resist specific attacks—just as our soldier who was full of "horrible imaginings" before the battle, saved himself from shell-shock. Some adaptation is possible, but the psyche tries to "make do" with the simplest set of illusions which seems as if it might, with luck, work. Except that "work" is hardly the word: the psyche is essentially lazy, seeking to economize effort. Sooner or later, however, an unexpected disaster may break through these too simple defences, and the whole equilibrium of the psyche may be upset until the new experience has been absorbed and brought under control, and a more complex, a less dangerously sensitive, composition established.

There is nothing new in this: it is Gilbert Murray's theory of rehearsing and exorcising, in metaphor. But, as Freud explains, the metaphor of the cell economizing its energy in pursuit of a "pleasure principle" (its little labour-saving ideal home is really the home of the death instincts), but being forced to reorganize itself into more complex life—this metaphor refers these "unpleasure processes," of which the tragic experience is one, to the very principle of life itself. It is thus that the sperm forces the ovum to live, repeating in every individual the process by which organic life began. Whatever disturbances occurred during the cooling of the globe, one imagines life—not real life at first, but merely the potentiality of life—coming into being not once but many times, and fading out again, until some further disturbances intervened, enforcing a readjustment, a complication of the cell, the beginning of a cycle of life, before the simplicity of death could be re-attained.

In this view, then, there are two sets of impulses, one set which can be termed "death instincts," which are innate; and the other set, reacting to disturbing stimulation from the outside, which enable the individual to adapt and to reorganize and to live more complexly—Tragedy exciting the second set. I am simplifying, perhaps; for instance I omit the possibility of innate disturbances which may complicate the life of the psyche by fifth-column activity within. With Freud's name on one's lips one is not likely to forget such impulses as complicated the life of Oedipus, for example. But on the whole I am not misrepresenting Freud, for in this book he does make mention—a single passing mention, but unambiguous—of Tragedy.

By "death instincts" Freud explains that he doesn't mean "suicide instincts." Death is not their immediate, only their ultimate aim; their immediate aim is the preservation of the established life-cycle to death, with the least possible interference or tension. Tragedy's preoccupation with death indicates no alliance with these "death instincts" but rather a desire to rid us of the numbing effect of its terror. But there are obvious reservations to be made here: in many tragedies we are reminded that death is not the worst that can happen to the hero, and I hope to show later that his death has, in addition, a special function to perform.

For the moment the essential function of Tragedy would appear to be the complicating and strengthening of the psyche by means of shocks from outside: not, of course, violent and disorganizing shocks, but mild, preventive, reorganizing ones. The participation in "tragic conflicts" may be a part of such reorganizing; though I am thinking of a toughening less crude than that which some German philosophers have thought desirable. Theoretically it would, I suppose, be possible to present a tragedy so horrible that there resulted a real shock—like shell-shock—from which the patient would have to be cured. In practice, however, we can usually protect ourselves by recalling, if we are forced, that what is happening on the stage is not "real." There is probably a level of tragedy, involving not too drastic a reorganization of the psyche, at which tragedy is most effective.

But when we come to define this level, and to consider the mechanism by which the tragic experience is conveyed to the audience, it seems to me that we are inevitably defining characteristics in the tragic hero. In Elizabethan tragedy, we are at once aware of the hero's position—Faustus's, Hamlet's, Clermont's, Othello's—a step or so ahead of his age. He develops fine sensibilities at heavy cost; he suffers and fails. The audience follow the hero's aspirations, his explorations in new realms of feeling; they face the possibility that such noble struggles will be thwarted by the insensibility and evil of the men around them, by the weight of the past, by blind chance. Despite the hero's defeat, however, the experience is, for the audience, a reorganization from the old life to the new fuller one; the cell is hindered in its easy acceptance of the old instinctive life cycle, and compelled to live more complexly. I believe a great tragedy always has this effect of bringing the consciousness to a threshold between the old and the new, although it may have other methods of doing this than by representing the hero as thus stepping to a threshold or beyond. Nor is the representation of such a hero alone sufficient: the nobility of Clermont is not enough, for instance, to make a great tragedy out of *The Revenge of Bussy D'Ambois*.

None the less, a great hero—one human enough for the audience's sympathy, and remarkable enough to lift their imaginations—is important. It is mainly through the hero's thoughts and feelings that we judge the truth of the world which the dramatist asks us to accept, its "values," its relevance to the possibilities of our own existence. I have already said we feel more than a detached sympathy for the hero; we feel more than "there, but for the grace of God, go I"; we identify ourselves, and go, with him. The extent of the identification varies in different members of the audience, and with different types of Tragedy. Some identification occurs even in Comedy; but the essence of comedy is that identification is partial and temporary and that we are continually dissociating ourselves in laughter. Stephen Haggard and Athene Seyler tell us in *The Craft of Comedy* that actors recognize this, keeping slightly "outside" the parts, self-dramatizing and slightly over-characterizing, in comedy, but acting realistically and "straight," identifying themselves with their parts and trying to "live" them, empathizing—if I may use this word in a more limited sense than it is normally used in criticism—empathizing in the characters in a serious play. I used the word "realistically" inaccurately as a paraphrase of the actors' word "straight." In fact, too great a degree of realism with its reminders of the particular and commonplace can be distressing to the audience. If the audience too are to empathize in the hero, we should probably agree that a slightly stylized and remote production is more effective; indeed, this matter of "psychological distance" in drama has been explored by philosophers and critics.

My emphasis on the reality of the hero is unfashionable, and went out with Bradley. But although I am willing to defend this emphasis, I realise that the position has its dangers; particularly if adopted by actors. If an actor believes that a play exists for the sake of character, and for his acting of it, the result is frequently disastrous. Nothing repels an audience so much as finding that an actor, with a strong and perhaps highly mannered personality, has "got in" first. I am not arguing that personalities should dominate the play, least of all the personalities of actors. Such domination defeats the whole end of drama, which is not to give scope for actors or actresses (*pace* M Cocteau), nor to impress the audience, but to enable the audience to respond and react themselves. And they can only respond naturally and unselfconsciously if the actor has the tact to leave a little of the initiative to them, if he underacts a little, perhaps. And, needless to say, they can only respond if the whole play, the whole action, rings true. Only then can they also be convinced by the hero's part in it. I certainly do not believe that the play should be subordinated to character, none the less I do believe that for the full functioning—the purging—of Tragedy, our credulity, our four-dimensional acceptance, our ability to emphasize in the tragic hero, or bovarize—as Huxley and others have called it—is always relevant. I need hardly distinguish here between bad bovarism and good: if we are tempted to identify ourselves with some hero of less intelligence and capacity for living than ourselves, it is probably to satisfy some dream of affluence or success; in short, to escape. Empathy in a character of a different kind, with a mind and soul larger than our own, requires effort and imagination, and, apart from any ordeal, any adjustment to the harsher realities which may be forced upon us by the tragic development of the plot, the greater awareness into which we are led tallies with the experience we derive from other great art.

Before considering whether this is the whole truth, I should like to recapitulate briefly and add to what I've said about the tragic hero. We have argued that whatever pleasure-principle factors enter, the distinctive appeal of Tragedy can only be explained by going "beyond the pleasure principle"; we suffer an ordeal, face life at its most difficult and complex, but derive pleasure in the new readiness and power we have gained thereby. To enable us to live more complexly and to persuade us that what we are getting is true to life—for it is important that we should not feel that the dramatist is either cheating us or sparing us, treating us as children who cannot be told the truth—we are invited to empathize in a hero of a certain type. We feel more deeply and subtly, act more courageously, more passionately, in him, and all the time with the conviction that it is true to life, a fuller life than our own. We may add that as drama has to work quickly, superficial superiorities, such as those of rank and fortune mentioned by classical critics, may predispose some of us to empathize, though modern class-conscious audiences may prefer other qualities. Whatever else the tragic hero is, however, he should not be dull: some conscientiously proletarian modern writers make a mistake, I think, when they solemnly present a drab little hero—unless they succeed in making out of him a twentieth-century Everyman. That may be as successful occasionally as the great character who lifts our imaginations, and it may invite our empathy no less.

Edith Sitwell has remarked that Tragedy always opens on a question, "Who?"—Who is the tragic hero? What is his significance? The answer is seldom given as explicitly as in the closing lines of *The Great God Brown:* the Police Captain, you may remember, has given Cybel a few minutes alone the dying Brown to make him talk; he then comes in and asks, "Well, what's his name?" Cybel answers, "Man," and the Police Officer, his notebook open, asks "How d'yuh spell it?"

The spelling is not difficult: it is either "Everyman," ourselves, whose fate we must endure; or it is "Potential Man," whose powers of living it would be well for the species if we could assimilate.

Nothing of what I have said so far is new, and little, I hope, is controversial. But one point is unexplained: If Tragedy is, as I have described it, a vicarious ordeal, why is the unhappy ending essential? Why cannot the ordeal he provided by a serious and terrifying depiction of the sufferings of the hero, if he recovers from an almost mortal wound to live "happily ever after"? Death, as we know, is not essential. Oedipus lives on for a while; but in his despair, blood streaming from his eyesockets, he is a more terrible symbol of defeat than the hanged Jocasta. Defeat, the end of effective life, the end of hope for the hero—these are essential. His death, in fact, is convenient; but why?

It is true that the death of the hero is occasionally accompanied by the suggestion of a new start. Before the death of Henchard, some of our interest has been transferred to Elizabeth-Jane; Macbeth's death is followed by the coronation of Malcolm; there is even mention of the succession in *Hamlet*; but these are not "happy endings." Between the effect of *Hamlet* and that of *The Winter's Tale* there is a difference of kind not of degree: I know this difference depends not merely on the ending, but differences in the texture of the play throughout; and a key difference, in my view, is that in the Tragicomedy our sympathies are not centred to the same extent on a single person. In this, it seems to me there is a special propriety: that the audience should not be asked to empathize seriously and deeply in a hero who is going, not to die, but to live "happily ever after."

Still, there is this difference in texture and it would be fairer to compare the effect of *Villette* with that of *Jane Eyre*, or the two versions of a Shakespeare tragedy, before and after it had been doctored to "please" Restoration or eighteenth-century audiences. I don't think there can be serious doubt that, despite Aristotle's contrary opinion, the unhappy ending is indispensable for tragic effect, and the ordeal theory is incomplete. Indeed nothing would seem to fit the ordeal theory better than some modern crime fiction. Raymond Chandler does not spare his readers when he describes his hero being taught by some thug to mind his own business, but I have yet to encounter a critic who calls this literature tragic.

The effect of Tragedy is courage; not mere toughness, nor bravado, nor the will to display power, but simply calmness and readiness, the discovery that even in the harshest experiences there is, to quote Richards, "no difficulty"; the difficulty arises from the illusions and subterfuges by which we seek to dodge reality, and which we unconsciously fear are going to betray us.

But how does this change come about? How is it that for a time we are personally participating in the fears and difficulties of the hero, our need to dodge increased; and then that we are, almost suddenly sometimes, freed from these apprehensions, having achieved an impersonal objective attitude?

Freudian psychology helped us with a corroboration before, can it now provide us with an answer? We are again up against the difficulty of providing generalizations which are valid for all types of individuals—I recall a member of the Cambridge English Faculty who claimed that he had never experienced tragic catharsis: clearly my generalizations cannot include him. I put forward no chain of proof, tested at every link, only a kind of analogy which seems to me more plausible at some times than at others.

In pathological "fixations," when the psyche shrinks from developing into maturity, it often turns aside into a fantasy world comparable to the empathizing or bovarizing fantasies which we have been discussing. It is permissible to compare normal with pathological processes, for, as the example of Mme Bovary reminds us, no sharp line divides the two. It is a matter of better or of worse adjustment, and both possibilities are open to all of us.

At all events, with the conception of psychological fixation in mind, we can reframe our question thus, "Does Tragedy provide the individual in the audience with a means of expansion through empathy, through good 'bovarism,' and then, *but only in the destruction of the hero*, free the individual, break his empathy at the point where it is in danger of becoming a fixation, where his fantasies might otherwise usurp the energies required for real life?" If this question is framed correctly, we could say simply that the individual adjusts himself to real life because his fantasy life has died with the hero.

I do not know how general these fixation fantasies are, however, and I should like to establish an analogy between the tragic "empathy-ordeal-disaster" process and some more general fantasy process. But meanwhile one point is worth noting. Freud in dealing with fixations has concentrated mainly on infantile incest fantasies; the tragic function—of enabling one to grow and adjust oneself—might therefore be expressed as breaking free from a fixation, if one had no more to explain than *Oedipus Tyrannus*. But the main point hangs on Freud's reminder that an elaborate fantasy-living is *normal* in children. In their "endless imitation," they enter into fantasies, change them, discard them to meet the demands of real life, return to fantasy play at a moment's notice—they cease being soldiers or Red Indians and rush in to their real dinner, then rush out again to be pirates or shipwrecked mariners—doing safely, easily and normally what no adult can do without serious risk to his sanity. The explanation of this links up with what we said earlier about good and bad empathy: the whole principle of a child's life is growth, expansion; and his normal fantasies are informed inevitably with this expansion; they are, mainly, fantasies of growing up; and he is indeed growing minute by minute; except for the pathological case, the child with the infantile fixation, the child has no past, but only a future which he is constantly realizing. For the adult it is a different matter; every fantasy has the danger of becoming a fixation, a mental cancer growing inward when the normal expansive organic growth has slowed down, a step aside, a turn back to the past—unless, as we have suggested, the fantasy is of a special kind, derived from outside impact, demanding new effort, offering new opportunities of creative, imaginative, expansion.

But we were seeking in the realms of psychology for a more general type of fantasy, for comparison with tragic empathy. Is this not found in the artificially induced fantasy of the "transference," a part of the mechanism by which all psycho-therapeutic analysis was at one time attempted? An account of this mechanism is given in Jung's *Modern Man in Search of a Soul*. Jung describes the failure of Breuer's early therapeutic treatment, which Breuer with deliberate but, as it turned out, most unfortunate reference to Aristotle, called "Catharsis." Breuer's "Catharsis" was simply free confession aided by the probings of the physician, and Jung explains that it "consisted of putting the patient in touch with the hinterland of his mind." It failed because one of two kinds of fixation followed treatment and caused a relapse. In fact, though of course Breuer did not realize it at this stage, it did not purge effectively; the term "Catharsis" had been usurped.

Breuer's treatment seemed to promise success; the patient always improved at first; but then one of two things happened: in some cases, to use Jung's words, "The patient goes away apparently cured—but he is now so fascinated by the hinterland of his own mind, that he continues to practise catharsis to himself at the expense of his adaptation to life. He is bound to the unconscious—to himself." In other cases, as is well known, the patient develops a sense of complete dependence on the physician, and collapses if the connection is severed. Both reactions are in the nature of fantasy-fixations: in the first case, the patient's fantasies are self-contained, they are fantasies about himself; in the second case a fantasy of child-parent dependence—the patient is the child; the physician the parent—is set up, and persists. In short, all Breuer had discovered or rediscovered was the relief and comfort of confession, and the helpless dependence which followed it.

Freud's system of analysis which superseded Breuer's made use of a similar relationship of dependence—the dependence of child-patient on father-confessor-physician—in the preliminary stages, but strove to break this "transference" later. This break was always regarded, of course, as indispensable for a cure; and, when properly successful, it effected something much more in the nature of a real catharsis. The important difference between Freud's analytical "transference" and Breuer's was that Freud's did not merely bring to light a few repressed thoughts and impulses from the "hinterland of the patient's mind," it strove also to bring the patient face to face with some terror, forced him to experience in his fantasy something which had been evaded in the past, something which provided a key to later conduct with its evasions and suppressions. Only if the psycho-analyst is able to lead the patient to a climax of resistance ending in painful temporary collapse, does this treatment end successfully and lead to the eventual readjustment of the patient. This process is different from that of Tragedy mainly in the fact that the patient is led back to a point where a wrong turning had been taken in his past development, where he takes the hurdle he had evaded then, and leaves his old self behind; whereas in tragedy, the individual is led forward. But there are points of comparison too: there is the initial fantasy, there is the postponed and resisted pain, eventually faced either in the death of the hero, or in what may be regarded as the death of the old incomplete self; there is also that oft-discussed, perhaps essential tragic element, "recognition," the "anagnorsis" of Aristotle, which is akin to, perhaps leads to, self-revelation.

I had hoped to explain Tragedy in terms of psycho-analysis and instead find myself expressing the analytical process in terms of tragedy. We can, however, add a few more bricks which seem to fit into the wall of this circular argument. If the effect of tragedy depends, as I believe, upon the end, not merely upon any earlier ordeal; if, not indeed the death of the hero, but the end of what he stands for is essential to release the audience and enable them to adjust themselves to reality, if purgation depends not merely upon the intensity of the transference but indispensably also upon the way it is broken, then we might expect, as a result of empathizing in heroes who do not fail tragically, but instead live "happily ever afterwards," a pathological state of dependence similiar to the pathological condition of Breuer's patients. But this is not unlike Mme Bovary's state; and those people who, not making the mistake of Mme Bovary and attempting to live their day dreams, do none the less seek wish-fulfilment dreams in novels and films, are often called, with justice, film or fiction "addicts." Their first need after reading the average novel, or seeing the average film, seems to be to return to the cinema or the fiction library for another one. Whatever exciting or dangerous "ordeals" the addict has experienced vicariously, "purgation" is not one of them, and he attempts no adjustment but remains dependent on his fantasies. He could not continue to empathize in a person who is dead, but he is glad to do so in one who lives happily ever afterwards; and the more he gets from Hollywood or the bestseller-writer, the more dependent he becomes, upon his own fantasies, or upon the dispenser of them. I make the distinction because the tone of certain writers—talking down to the reader, flattering him, comforting him, encouraging his prejudices—has not escaped critical comment. It seems to me not impossible that a reader may get to the point of feeling that the favourite author knows him and his weaknesses and secrets so well that the author is almost in the reader's confidence; and as a sales device, ensuring the complete dependence of the reader upon the physician-confessor-guardian-parent of an author who continually dispenses absolution to the reader for not growing up, it is unrivalled.

Referring to *Hamlet* and *The Winter's Tale* earlier, I suggested that in a Tragicomedy there was a propriety in not inviting so deep and serious an empathy in the hero, as would be proper in Tragedy. The reason is implied in what I have just said: empathy does not break itself, and an author whose theme gives him no opportunity of breaking it, should not—if he intends to deal honestly with his public—invite it very deeply and intensely in the first place. Good Tragicomedy—and perhaps most of us would agree that Tragicomedy is not commonly entirely convincing—but the best Tragicomedy has some of the critical detachment of Comedy; or else it distributes the empathy amongst several characters.

Had I the time I should have liked to mention one or two other points. I

think, for instance, that those moments to which Mr. Eliot has called attention, when the hero dramatizes himself and his lonely struggle against the
Fates, find a place in my scheme. Such self-dramatization in real life is not
amiable; we forgive it, in moments of exceptional stress, in those we know
and love, but we take it as weakness. The heroes who do this kind of thing
continually from the rise of the curtain on Act I are, as serious tragic heroes,
intolerable. In great tragedy we forgive it, as we forgive it in ourselves and
in our friends; but the dramatic effect lies in the fact that at such moments,
when the audience know the limits of the hero's strength, the nearness of his
end, and the hero too knows it, but is desperately hiding the knowledge from
himself—at such moments our critical faculty is stirring to waken, and our
empathy is, as it were, being worked loose.

I should also have liked to discuss those tragedies which the audience approaches quite detachedly, their critical sense awake throughout. In my
view such Tragedies are a different species, and to regard them as the same
leads only to confusion in theatrical production and in criticism.

But it is possible here to offer only a brief summary.

Tragedy is man's rehearsal of the harsher realities of life; by it the
psyche's cell is forced out of its lethargy, its conservative instinctive life-
cycle where it is only delusively secure, and it adapts itself to a more complex readiness for life.

The tragic hero is usually, as Aristotle said, uncommonly great and alive:
only if he is great (but we mean by this not merely great in rank) does his
downfall impress us with the insignificance of our own petty anxieties and
mishaps; only if he is great—better than ourselves—does our attempt to
share his experiences increase our own capacity for living. The place of the
great hero is sometimes, however, successfully supplied by the figure of
"Everyman" or by the representative not of all mankind but of a large
group. Exceptionally our empathy may even be elicited by an idea, a
"cause," with the success of which the fates of numerous individuals are
bound up. This could be said not only of a few modern plays, but also of
Antigone. Character, or some figure or idea in which the audience can identify themselves exactly as in a great character, is indispensable to tragedy;
it must not dominate the action, but it is, despite Aristotle, as indispensable
as action. In certain modern plays—*A Streetcar Named Desire, Lottie Dundass*
and others—the action is adequate, the end is disastrous, but the persons are
not tragic characters: their place is not in drama, but in a psychoanalyst's
case-book; they are tawdry and second-rate persons with whom no audience
can with advantage identify themselves, and their failure, whatever else it
may be, is not tragic.

Finally, despite Aristotle, Mr. Lucas and others, the general seriousness
of the theme is not enough: the action must end in disaster. More than a

bare hint of the "rebirth" or renewal theme is dangerous. A production of *Macbeth*, for instance, which allowed all our sympathy for Macbeth to ebb before the desperate scenes in Acts IV and V, and encouraged us to identify ourselves and our interests in Malcolm, would transform the play into melo-drama. But in the tragic end of the hero, and of the hopes we had in him, there is nothing defeatist; for only in his failure is some connection, some "transference" between us and our fantasy life in the play, broken, and our own energies set free.

Melodrama*

ERIC BENTLEY

THE BAD NAME OF MELODRAMA

Some time ago I ran into a magazine article containing this comment on Joseph Conrad:

One word comes before long to haunt the mind of any persistent reader of Conrad's stories—the word Melodrama. Why does he do it? What has he got against life? What is the purpose of all these feuds, assassinations, revealing plottings, these fearful disasters and betrayals. . . .

Not long afterwards I met with that passage again—quoted by a critic who proffers this answer to its queries: finding it difficult either to invent or report, Conrad has to derive his narratives from other narratives. "To such a temperament," writes our critic, " 'drama' is an alternative to dramatic life." And an example is provided. It has recently come to seem highly likely that the young Conrad tried to kill himself, and for what might be called prosaic reasons—"depression, bad health, and a financial mess." Instead of reporting the drab sequence of events, Conrad made out of it a melodrama of love and honor. The struggle within himself became in fiction a fight between two distinct persons.

The question why Conrad "does it" and what he "has got against life" are in greater need of explanation, surely, than his procedure. Only under the influence of a narrow and philistine Naturalism can we ask why an artist shows life at a remove and in some established genre. The transposition of an inner struggle to a duel between persons does not even need a convention to carry it: such changes are made nightly by everyone in his dreams. If one can make of one's tussles with suicidal wishes a drama of love and honor, one has given to private and chaotic material a public and recognizable form.

---

* Eric Bentley, "Melodrama," from *The Life of the Drama* (Atheneum, 1964), pp. 195–218.

One has made art out of fantasy and pain. One has found the link between emotion and civilized values. One has achieved universality.

All this, of course, would have been readily granted by our two critics but for the particular vehicle (form, convention) which Conrad chose: melodrama. It has a bad reputation—and that is the worst thing a word can have in the literary world just as it is the worst thing a man can have in the social world.

Where did this bad reputation come from? It is, I think, substantially the bad reputation of popular Victorian melodrama. Now it is unfair to judge anything by its weakest link, but it is not unfair to ask: how weak is its weakest link? What is the least that anyone would ask of a melodrama? As apt an answer as any is: a good cry. The contempt implied in terms like sob stuff and tear jerker is not more interesting than the very wide appeal of the thing despised.

An inquiry into melodrama—the appeal of melodrama—can legitimately start with a thought or two about tears.

In Praise of Self-Pity

What does it mean: to weep? Laughter has engaged the attention of many brains, among them some of the best. A brief search in book indexes and library catalogues calls attention to an extensive literature. Tears are a relatively unexplored ocean.

One reason why laughter has had a better press must be the obvious one: that laughter is (or is held to be) pleasant, whereas weeping is (or is held to be) unpleasant. Laughter is also something one gets a good mark for. What tired orator does not expatiate on the benefits of a sense of humor? To weep, on the other hand, is something that little boys are assiduously taught not to do. Women are greater realists: they will speak of having a good cry. The phrase points to perhaps the commonest function of tears: they are a mechanism for working off emotion—commonly, quite superficial emotion. But there are tears and tears. Crying your heart out is a matter of deep emotion. Then there are tears of joy. "Excess of sorrow laughs," says Blake, "excess of joy weeps." Shaw put it this way:

Tears in adult life are the natural expression of happiness as laughter is at all ages the natural recognition of destruction, confusion, and ruin.

*   *   *

The tears shed by the audience at a Victorian melodrama come under the heading of a good cry. They might be called the poor man's catharsis, and as such have a better claim to be the main objective of popular melodrama than its notorious moral pretensions. Besides referring to superficial emotion, the phrase "having a good cry" implies feeling sorry for oneself. The pity is self-pity. But, for all its notorious demerits, self-pity has its uses. E. M. Forster even says it is the only thing that makes bearable the feeling of growing old—in other words, that it is a weapon in the struggle for existence. Self-pity is a very present help in time of trouble, and all times are times of trouble.

Once we have seen that our modern antagonism to self-pity and sentiment goes far beyond the rational objections that may be found to them, we realize that even the rational objections are in some measure mere rationalization. Attacks on false emotion often mask a fear of emotion as such. Ours is, after all, a thin-lipped, thin-blooded culture. Consider how, in the past half-century, the prestige of dry irony has risen, while that of surging emotion has fallen. This is a cultural climate in which a minor writer like Jules Laforgue can rate higher than a major one like Victor Hugo. Or think of our changed attitude to death. Would any age but this receive the death of admired persons "with quiet understatement"? We may think that Mr. Auden pours his heart out in his good poem on the death of Yeats, but just compare Mr. Auden's poem with the product of more old-fashioned culture, say, with Garcia Lorca's "Lament for the Death of Ignacio Mejias"! Would even Lorca's title be possible in English? Is lamenting something we can imagine ourselves doing? On the contrary we modernize the Greek tragedies by deleting all variants of "woe is me." If Christ and Alexander the Great came back to life, we would teach them to restrain their tears.

Once I did see death done justice to. An Italian actor came on stage to announce the death of a colleague. He did indeed lament. He shook, he wept, he produced streams of passionate rhetoric, until the audience shook, and wept, and lamented with him. Now that is self-pity, certainly. One is not sorry for a corpse; one is sorry for oneself, deprived; and in the background is the fear of one's own death. But so much the better for self-pity. The experience was had, not refused.

The point has some importance for mental health. Modern psychiatry begins with those *Studies on Hysteria* in which Freud and Breuer try to explain what happens when emotional impressions are not allowed to wear themselves out. The shock of pain craves to be relieved and released by cries and writhings and tears. Good little boys who keep still and quiet under a rain of blows may pay for their stoicism twenty years later on a therapist's couch. Their resentments, instead of being worn away by a natural process, have been hoarded in the Unconscious.

If you have dismissed tears and loud lamentation from your daily life, you might check whether they are equally absent from your dreams at night. You may be no more sentimental than the next man, and yet find you have many dreams in which you weep profusely and at the same time disport yourself like an actor in the old melodrama: throwing yourself on your knees, raising your arms plaintively to heaven, and so forth. For you, in that case, grandiose self-pity is a fact of life. As it can only be copied by the use of grandiose style, the grandiosity of melodrama would seem to be a necessity.

PITY AND FEAR

I have been defending melodrama in its weakest link, for certainly self-pity is only valuable up to a point in life and only tolerable up to a point on the stage. Pity for the "hero" is the less impressive half of melodrama; the other and more impressive half is fear of the villain. Pity and fear: it was Aristotle in his *Poetics* who coupled them, and tried to give an account of the total effect of tragedy in these terms. It seems an oversimplification. In tragedy, most of us now feel, more is involved. Is more involved in melodrama? Is not working on the audience's capacity for pity and fear the alpha and omega of the melodramatist's job? In his *Rhetoric*, Aristotle explains that pity and fear have an organic relation to each other. An enemy or object of terror is presupposed in both cases. If it is we who are threatened, we feel fear for ourselves; if it is others who are threatened, we feel pity for them. One might wish to carry this analysis a little further in the light of the fact that most pity is self-pity. We are identified with those others who are threatened; the pity we feel for them is pity for ourselves; and by the same token we share their fears. We pity the hero of a melodrama because he is in a fearsome situation: we share his fears; and, pitying ourselves, we pretend that we pity him. To rehearse these facts is to put together the dramatic situation of the characteristic popular melodrama: goodness beset by badness, a hero beset by a villain, heroes and heroines beset by a wicked world.

Pity represents the weaker side of melodrama, fear the stronger. Perhaps the success of a melodramatist will always depend primarily upon his power to feel and project fear. Feeling it should be easy, for fear is the element we live in. "We have nothing to fear but fear itself" is not a cheering slogan because fear itself is the most indestructible of obstacles. Therein lies the potential universality of melodrama.

Human fears are of two kinds. One belongs to the common-sense world: it is reasonable in the everyday sense to fear that one might slip on ice or that an airplane might crash. The other kind of fear—perhaps none too rationally—is called irrational. Savage superstitions, neurotic fantasies, and childhood imaginings spring to mind, and equally outside the bounds of common sense is the fear of God. Superstition and religion, neurosis and infantility are in the same boat.

Melodrama sometimes uses the "irrational" type of fear in such a direct form as that of Frankenstein's monster or Dracula. More often it lets irrational fear masquerade as the rational: we are given reasons to fear the villain, but the fear actually aroused goes beyond the reasons given. Talent in melodramatic writing is most readily seen in the writer's power to make his human villain seem superhuman, diabolical. Historically the villains in our tradition stem from the archvillain Lucifer, and a good deal of recent Shakespeare scholarship has been illustrating in detail the possible derivation of *Richard III* from the medieval Vice. The illustrations are nice to have; the principle was clear in advance. But where the villains stem from is relatively unimportant. What matters is whether a given writer can actually endow his villain with some of the original energy. We must catch a glimpse of hell flame, a whiff of the sulphur. This we do in even a comic work if the sense of horror is profound enough—as in Kleist's *The Broken Jug*. Among modern writers it must be admitted that the novelists—Melville or Emily Brontë—have been better diabolists than the playwrights. The stage villains, despite their reputation, have not been too monstrously evil. If their imprecations have seemed ludicrous, it is because the evil is not more than skindeep. A villain shouldn't have to work too hard at villainy.

Because the drama tends to concentrate its vision in a few persons, it will tend to embody evil in a few villains, and often in a single one. This is not to say that it has no other resource. Melodramatic vision is paranoid: we are being persecuted, and we hold that all things, living and dead, are combining to persecute us. Or rather, nothing is dead. Even the landscape has come to life if only to assault us. Perhaps one might sense something of this vision behind Birnam Wood's coming to Dunsinane in *Macbeth*, even though the playwright provides soldiers to carry it. For Emily Brontë, at any rate, the Yorkshire moors and the Yorkshire weather are "the very devil"—just as much as her villain, Heathcliffe. Popular Victorian melodrama made extensive use of bad weather and dangerous landscape. High seas and deep chasms threaten to swallow our hero up. The very fact that I describe such events as "swallowing up" shows that a little of the animism rubs off, even on a critic.

It is amazing what the nineteenth-century stage could do in the presentation of raging seas, mountains, glaciers, frozen lakes, and the like, yet there were always much narrower limits than in a novel, and the playwright had to reinforce the hostility of landscape with other hostilities. "Melodramatic" artifices of plot come under this head, and particularly that notorious device: outrageous coincidence. It is often by virtue of this feature that melodrama is differentiated from tragedy, the argument being that the melodramatic procedure is too frivolous. Yet there are some particularly gross examples in the supreme tragedies, and, in general, outrageous coincidence, when not frivolously used, has no frivolous effect. It intensifies the effect of paranoia. It enlists circumstances in the enemy's ranks—as Strindberg did in real life when several little incidents conspired to deprive him of his absinthe on several successive occasions. It represents a projection of "irrational" fear.

EXAGGERATION

The long arm of coincidence is a freakish thing. Mention it and within a minute someone will use the word exaggeration. This brings us back both to the prejudice against melodrama and to the essence of melodrama itself. Like farce, this genre may be said, not to tumble into absurdity by accident, but to revel in it on purpose. To question the absurd in it is to challenge, not the conclusion, but the premise. In both genres, the writer enjoys a kind of *Narrenfreiheit*—the fool's exemption from common sense—and what he writes must be approached and judged accordingly.

We are accustomed to acknowledge only a slight degree of exaggeration in the artistic reproduction of life—just enough, we tell ourselves, to sharpen an outline. The image in our minds is of portraits in which the painter renders the appearances much as we think we have seen them our-selves, though we permit him a ten per cent deviation because he's an artist. But suppose the deviation from common sense grows much greater? Is the picture necessarily getting worse all the time? No, but for exaggerations which are no longer slight but gross, we require another criterion. A dif-ference of degree turns into a difference of kind. Of a melodramatist whom we disapprove, we must not say: "You have exaggerated too much," but: "You have exaggerated awkwardly, mechanically." We might even have to say: "You have exaggerated too little," for in an age of Naturalism a writer's courage sometimes fails him and he tries to pass off a tame duck as a beast of the jungle.

The exaggerations will be foolish only if they are empty of feeling. In-tensity of feeling justifies formal exaggeration in art, just as intensity of feeling creates the "exaggerated" forms of childhood fantasies and adult dreams. It is as children and dreamers—one might melodramatically add: as neurotics and savages too—that we enjoy melodrama. Exaggeration of what? Of the facts as seen by the sophisticated, scientific, adult mind. The primitive, neurotic, childish mind does not exaggerate its own impressions.

What is a giant? A man, eighteen feet high. An exaggeration surely? Someone has multiplied by three. What is a giant? A grownup as seen by a baby. The baby is two feet high, the grownup, six. The ratio *is* one to three. There is no exaggeration.

There is a very fine French film, *Zero for Conduct*, in which school teachers are seen through children's eyes. They seemed enormous and dis-torted at times because the camera has been placed near their feet. People called the result stylization. The word suggests the sophisticated, the artificial, and the adult. What was done was naïve, natural, and infantile. The word "exaggeration" can be misleading.

There is something similar to say of the "grandiosity" of melodramatic acting. That we are all ham actors in our dreams means that melodramatic acting, with its large gestures and grimaces and its declamatory style of speech, is not an exaggeration of our dreams but a duplication of them. In that respect, *melodrama is the Naturalism of the dream life.* Nor is it only to our dreams that melodramatic acting corresponds. Civilization, as I have been saying, asks us to hide our feelings and even instructs us in the art of doing so. What feelings we cannot completely conceal we reduce to mere shadows of themselves. Hence the appositeness of the movie camera: it can see those minute movements of the features which is all that is left in civilized man of corporeal expression. When it enlarges them in close-ups ten or more feet high it is achieving the old melodramatic grandiosity in its own way and without the actors' assistance.

One of the principal emotions is Fear. What does it look like?

The heart beats wildly . . . there is a deathlike pallor; the breathing is labored; the wings of the nostrils are widely dilated; there is a gasping and convulsive motion of the lips, a tremor on the hollow cheek, a gulping and catching of the throat; the uncovered and protruding eyeballs are fixed on the object of terror; or they may roll restlessly from side to side. . . . The pupils are . . . enormously dilated. All the muscles of the body may become rigid or may be thrown into convulsive movements. The hands are alternately clenched and opened, often with a twitching movement. The arms may be protruded as if to avert some dreadful danger, or may be thrown wildly over the head.

What does Hatred look like?

. . . intense frowning; eyes wide open; display of teeth; grinding teeth and contracting jaws; opened mouth with tongue advanced; clenched fists; threatening action of arms; stamping with the feet; deep inspirations—panting; growling and various cries; automatic repetition of one word or syllable; sudden weakness and trembling of voice . . . convulsion of lips and facial muscles, of limbs and trunk; acts of violence to one's self, as biting fists or nails; sardonic laughter; bright redness of face; sudden pallor of face; extreme dilation of nostrils; standing up of hair on head. . . .

Now someone might suppose I have been quoting descriptions of melodramatic acting. We today have certainly never thought of anyone but a stage villain grinding his teeth or giving vent to fiendish hate in a sardonic laugh. Actually, the first of these quotations is from Charles Darwin's book on the emotions, and the second is from an old Italian manual on the same subject. William James used to read both passages to his classes at Harvard, and they are preserved, where I myself found them, in his *Principles of Psychology.* If these are fair accounts of emotion, then melodrama is not so much exaggerated as uninhibited.

LANGUAGE

Melodramatic dialogue has been the object of more mockery, perhaps, than even the plots and the characters and the acting. Naturally, vulgar melodrama is couched in vulgar rhetoric, but the joke against this rhetoric remains a poor one if the assumption is made, and it usually is, that plain, colloquial English should have been used, and not a heightened form of the language. An elevated rhetoric is a legitimate and indeed inexorable demand of melodrama. Ordinary conversation would be incongruous and anticlimactic.

In any case, the Victorian rhetoric that makes us smile was not a new thing, created by Victorian melodramatists. It was the lag-end—the rags and tatters, if you will—of something that had once been splendid. Few would call the dialogue of Victor Hugo's plays good tragic poetry. But it is good rhetoric, as is the dialogue of the German *Sturm und Drang* drama from which French Romantic drama derives. In England the postmedieval drama begins with the establishment of a melodramatic rhetoric in Marlowe's *Tamburlaine*, and melodramatic rhetoric subserved tragedy, or declined into bombast or banality, or merely served its natural purpose as the proper style of melodrama, until about 1850.

Almost exactly at that date we find the old melodramatic order confronting the new Naturalistic one in what should be a classic instance. Turgenev wrote a play about a woman and her stepdaughter both in love with the same man. This play—*A Month in the Country*—inaugurates the era of natural, unmelodramatic dialogue. Now the writing of *A Month in the Country* was possibly prompted by a play of Balzac's on the same theme, *The Stepmother*, in which some may be surprised to find the great "realist" still using the melodramatic method in general and the melodramatic rhetoric in particular. Turgenev's work ends with a quiet separation and an equally quiet departure by coach; Balzac's with poisonings, lifetime punishments, an appeal to God, and a hint of insanity:

STEPDAUGHTER   I have been told all. This woman is innocent of the crime she is accused of. Religion has made me realize that pardon cannot be obtained on high by those who do not leave it behind them here below. I took the key of her desk from Madame. I myself went in search of poison. I myself tore off this piece of paper to wrap it in; for I wanted to die.

STEPMOTHER   Oh! Pauline! take my life, take all I love . . . Oh! doctor, save her!

STEPDAUGHTER   Do you know why I come to pull you out of the abyss you are in? Because Ferdinand has just told me something which has brought me back from the tomb. He has such horror of being with you in life, that he is following me—me—into the grave, where we shall rest together, married by death.

STEPMOTHER   Ferdinand! . . . Ah! God Above! At what price am I saved?

FATHER   But, unhappy child, why are you dying? Am I not, have I ceased for one moment to be a good father? They say it is I who am guilty . . .

YOUNG MAN   Yes, General. And it is I alone who can solve the riddle for you, and make clear to you how you are guilty.

FATHER   You, Ferdinand, you to whom I offered my daughter, you who love her . . .

YOUNG MAN   My name is Ferdinand, Count of Marcandal, son of General Marc-andal . . . you understand?

GENERAL   Ah! Son of a traitor, you could bring under my roof only death and treachery! . . . Defend yourself!

YOUNG MAN   Will you fight, General, against a dead man?
(*He falls.*)

STEPMOTHER   (*rushes to the Young Man with a cry*)   Oh! (*She recoils before the father who advances toward his daughter; then she takes out a phial, but throws it away at once.*) Oh! No, I condemn myself to live for this poor old man! (*The father kneels beside his dead daughter.*) Doctor, what is he doing? . . . Could he be losing his reason? . . .

FATHER   (*stammering like a man who cannot find the words*) I . . . I . . . I . . .

DOCTOR   General, what are you doing?

GENERAL   I . . . I am trying to say a prayer for my daughter! . . .
(*The curtain falls.*)*

I have picked a passage from a great writer lest anyone be tempted to attribute the deficiencies of such writing to lack of talent. Another mistake would be to think that the advantage lies in every respect with Turgenev. In art, every advantage is also a disadvantage. The gentleness of muted strings and the majesty of the full orchestra cannot be presented concurrently. Turgenev and Chekhov achieved their special effects by foregoing others. Modern persons will tend to attribute Balzac's failure to the absurdity of the incidents: he piles on the agony till we smile. Yet this diagnosis cannot be correct—Shakespeare piles on as much agony and we do not smile. The failure is only one of a tired rhetoric that no longer gives to the events and situations sufficient support.

---

* I have translated this afresh because the only translation I could find was far more ponderous than the French. It renders "*coupable*" as "culpable," "*l'abîme où vous êtes*" as "the abyss which had engulfed you," etc. I have left out a couple of speeches, and given the characters appellations calculated to help those who do not know the play.

ZOLA AND AFTER

So, one could say, melodrama died with Balzac's generation, and Naturalism took its place in Turgenev's generation. As such generalizations go, it is not a bad one, but as such generalizations also go, it is misleading. What actually happened was both more curious and more complex. Naturalism did become the creed of the age. Its acceptance was indeed widespread, embracing most cultured people. It is a doctrine which I find present-day American students still regarding as the law of the Medes and Persians. The curious thing is that, while our age generally is dedicated to Naturalist principles, the outstanding writers of the age are forever protesting against them. The fact of the protest, and its frequency, proves the prevalence of the principles, right enough; but, going back over the record, it is amazing how *many* writers of how *many* different schools protested. It is even enlightening to learn what some of the champions of Naturalism actually did —and actually said.

Emile Zola, for instance, who is supposed to have killed melodrama and given birth to the Naturalistic philosophy. Hear him attack melodrama:

> I defy the romantics to put on a cloak and dagger drama; the medieval clanking of old iron, the secret doors, poisoned wines and all the rest of it would convince no one. Melodrama, that middle class offspring of the romantic drama, is even more dead and no one wants it any more. Its false sentimentality, its complications of stolen children, recovered documents, its brazen improbabilities, have all brought it into such scorn that our attempt to revive it would be greeted with laughter. . . .

Any wish one might feel to demonstrate the merit of plots about stolen children and recovered documents is checked by the knowledge that Zola spoke under provocation of a thousand bad works of art. And note what, in this same preface to *Thérèse Raquin*, he proposes to replace bad melodrama with:

> I made the one dark room the setting for the play so that nothing should detract from its atmosphere and sense of fate. I chose ordinary, colorless, subsidiary characters to show the banality of every-day life behind the excruciating agonies of my chief protagonists. . . .

"Banality," "colorlessness"—certainly these belong to the naturalistic conception as generally understood. But a "sense of fate"? "Excruciating agonies"? And the banality only a foil to these extremities? At this point, one remembers what had been the effect of removing "banalities" from the Victorian melodrama. It had been to reduce the spectator's anxiety by relieving him of contact with his own life. By such a reduction, melodrama was becoming ever more boring and silly. What Zola is really doing is recharging the battery of fear which had been allowed to run down. The substitution of a banal (that is, recognizable) milieu for a "romantic" (that is, unacceptable) milieu is to play on the spectator's anxieties. True, Zola regarded his view of environment as scientific, but in those days science was itself the supreme romance, and here we find him calling for a sense of fate —which is what his own depiction of environment, like Ibsen's and Strindberg's incidentally—bears witness to. Technically, Zola's accounts of the milieu differ from Melville's or Emily Brontë's. He goes through a certain rigmarole—or ritual—of sociobiology, but he arrives at similar results. He is melodramatic.

The most pointed and prolonged polemic ever conducted against melodrama is to be found in the works of Bernard Shaw, prefaces and plays alike. *The Devil's Disciple* is the obvious, crude example, but in the preface to *Saint Joan*, nearly thirty years later, Shaw is still hammering away at the same point and arguing that the merit of his new play lies in its avoidance of melodrama. Notably, he has changed the character of the historical Bishop Cauchon so that the latter will no longer remind anyone of a stage villain.

Now Shaw's Cauchon is certainly at some distance from the snarling, gloating, swaggering villain of vulgar melodrama, but, for all Shaw's propaganda against the idea of villains, is he not still a villain, and even a traditional one? It was scarcely a new idea to make the devil witty, genial, and sophisticated. Actors take to the role of Cauchon, just because, if they are experienced, they have played it many times before. One *may* smile and smile and be a villain: one often does.

If Shaw hated the morals of melodrama—the projection upon the world of our irresponsible narcissistic fantasies—he loved its manners. Maybe any man only parodies what he is secretly fond of; maybe he is envious of the parodied author's prowess; or maybe he thinks he could outdo him. In any case, Shaw did not rest content with parody. After firing salvos at melodrama, he went on to steal its ammunition. As well as illustrating the limitations of melodrama, *The Devil's Disciple* exemplifies its merits, and, in the critical writings of Shaw, though we do not find the *name* of melodrama held in honor, we find the melodramatic element honored under other names: such as opera.

Unlike most opera-goers of today, Shaw enjoyed opera as a form of theatre, rather than a kind of concert, and he entered enthusiastically into just those libretti which the twentieth century has decided are so much bosh —such as the libretti of *Rigoletto* and *Il Trovatore*. Nor is this enthusiasm extracurricular: Shaw's plays themselves call for the "exaggerated," sweeping movements of operatic (that is, melodramatic) performance. At one time Shaw had to stress and reiterate this point because his stage director,

Granville-Barker, leaned toward the Naturalistic use of both voice and body. A photograph survives of Shaw showing Barker a little swordplay in *Androcles and the Lion*. On the picture Barker has achieved only a "small," nervous attitude, while Shaw is striking a flamboyant pose with his feet set wide apart and his sword held high in the air. His advice to Barker about his own form of theatre in general—"Remember that it's Italian opera"—we can translate: "Play it as melodrama."

The furthest that Shaw's playwriting ever got from melodrama was, I suppose, the "pure dialogue" of the "Don Juan in Hell" scene from *Man and Superman*. The cast is made up of a hero, a heroine, a villain, and a clown, a drama quartet which is said to have become standard in the hands of the French playwright Pixerécourt a hundred years earlier. Pixerécourt is listed in the textbooks as the founder of popular melodrama.

Since *Man and Superman* (1903) we have had various modernist schools of drama and various individual departures or one-man schools. The result of action and reaction, they present themselves as battling factions of contrasting conviction, yet it is impossible to mention one innovator of the period who was not trying to reintroduce the melodramatic. German Expressionism can be interpreted as the search for a modern dress for melodrama, Brecht's Epic Theatre as an attempt to use melodrama as a vehicle for Marxist thought. Cocteau, Anouilh, and Giraudoux have put the Greek myths to melodramatic use. Of the three, the most concentratedly melodramatic is Cocteau, perhaps because fear of persecution is his strongest emotion; in his *Orpheus*, the maenads are the hostile world of all melodrama.

What of Eugene O'Neill? Some think he revived tragedy. Those who disagree have usually spoken only of a failure. But if he often failed to achieve tragedy, O'Neill succeeded as often in achieving melodrama.

What O'Neill's father had chiefly done for a living was play Edmond Dantès in the melodrama *Monte Cristo*. The young O'Neill was a rebel against Father and considered himself a rebel against *Monte Cristo*. It remains a question, though, whether the modern ideas he picked up in Greenwich Village are the backbone of his work or whether, like many rebels against Father, he was not really identified with Father. That the son of an actor should be a playwright is in itself interesting. It is as if the son wished to write the father's lines and "work" him like a marionette. However this may be, *Mourning Becomes Electra*, as it seems to many of us, fails where it is modern and intellectual, succeeds where it is Victorian melodrama.

It was the melodramatic touch that O'Neill brought to the American theatre already in the twenties, that Lillian Hellman and Clifford Odets brought to it in the thirties, and that Tennessee Williams and Arthur Miller brought in the late forties. In the nineteen fifties, one of the most striking new presences in world theatre was Eugène Ionesco. His play

The Lesson is about a mild-seeming teacher who murders forty pupils a day. Ionesco uses Grand Guignol as a vehicle for a vision of modern life. The same is true of the leading younger playwright in the German-language area, Friedrich Dürrenmatt. . . .

But I would not like to spoil the point by pushing it too far. The phrase "revival of melodrama" is far from covering all that is alive in modern drama, nor would I wish to call every play *a melodrama* in which there are melodramatic elements. On the contrary, I shall later propose the label *tragi-comedy* for some plays whose melodramatic qualities have been noted here. And of course there is no reason why the same play should not be seen, now as a melodrama, now as a tragi-comedy, now as something else again, if thereby its inherent qualities are brought out. Reality in this field, as in others, is various and variable, and each perspective on it has some peculiar advantage.

The Quintessence of Drama

As modern persons we are willy-nilly under the spell of Naturalism. However often we tell ourselves the contrary, we relapse into assuming the normal and right thing to be a subdued tone, small human beings, a milieu minutely reproduced. Indeed a tremendous amount of energy goes into keeping up this illusion of the monotonous mediocrity of everyday life: otherwise how could the genteel tradition have survived the discoveries of modern physics and the atrocities of modern behavior? I am arguing, then, up to a point, that melodrama is actually more natural than Naturalism, corresponds to reality, not least to modern reality, more closely than Naturalism. Something has been gained when a person who has seen the world in monochrome and in miniature suddenly glimpses the lurid and the gigantic. His imagination has been reawakened.

The melodramatic vision is in one sense simply normal. It corresponds to an important aspect of reality. It is the spontaneous, uninhibited way of seeing things. Naturalism is more sophisticated but Naturalism is not more natural. The dramatic sense is the melodramatic sense, as one can see from the play-acting of any child. Melodrama is not a special and marginal kind of drama, let alone an eccentric or decadent one; it is drama in its elemental form; it is the quintessence of drama. The impulse to write drama is, in the first instance, the impulse to write melodrama, and, conversely, the young person who does not wish to write melodrama, does not write drama at all, but attempts a nondramatic genre, lyric, epic, or what not. It should be clear, then, why in treating melodrama, farce, tragedy, comedy, I have put melodrama first.

In this chapter I have tried to break down a prejudice against melodrama, just as in previous chapters I tried to break down prejudices against plot and prejudices against type characters—and, *mutatis mutandis*, for the same reasons. At the same time, there has been a negative side to this chapter's argument. I have used the words "childish," "neurctic," "primitive," even the words "narcissistic" and "paranoid," and in this summing-up I have had to insert saving clauses like "up to a point" and "in a sense."

In *The Interpretation of Dreams* Freud says that neurotics, like children, "exhibit on a magnified scale feelings of love and hatred for their parents." The remark needs interpreting. What, for instance, is a nonmagnified scale of feeling, and who exhibits that? Sigmund Freud, when hating a father who humiliated himself before antisemites? Anna Freud, when dedicating her life to continuing the work of Sigmund Freud? I mean the *argumentum ad hominem* kindly; and it could be aimed at anyone. What I am saying is that any nonmagnified feelings represent an ideal standard, and what we all have are the magnified feelings of the child, the neurotic, the savage. Such feelings of course form the basis of melodrama, and are the reason for its manifold magnifications.

Though melodramatic vision is not the worst, it is also not the best. It is good "up to a point," and the point is childhood, neuroticism, primitivity. Melodrama is human but it is not mature. It is imaginative but it is not intelligent. If again, for the sake of clarity, we take the most rudimentary form of melodrama, the popular Victorian variety, what do we find but the most crass of immature fantasies? The reality principle is flouted right and left, one is oneself the supreme reality, one's innocence is axiomatic, any interloper is a threat and a monster, the ending will be happy because one feels that it has to be. In an earlier chapter I said theatre corresponded to that phase of a child's life when he creates magic worlds. I mean that that is where theatre comes from, not necessarily where it remains. Melodrama belongs to this magical phase, the phase when thoughts seem omnipotent, when the distinction between *I want to* and *I can* is not clearly made, in short when the larger reality has not been given diplomatic recognition.

Am I speaking now of all melodrama or just of the vulgar melodrama of Victorian popular theatres? It is hard to draw such a line, as it is hard to draw a line between melodrama and tragedy. Rather than separate blocks, the reality seems to be a continuous scale with the crudest melodrama at one end and the highest tragedy at the other. In tragedy the reality principle is not flouted, one is not oneself the sole reality to be respected, one's guilt is axiomatic, other people may or may not be threats or monsters, the ending is usually unhappy.

Yet the idea of such a scale is misleading if it suggests that tragedy is utterly distinct from melodrama. There is a melodrama in every tragedy, just as there is a child in every adult. It is not tragedy, but Naturalism, that tries to exclude childish and melodramatic elements. William Archer, a Naturalist, defined melodrama as "illogical and sometimes irrational tragedy." The premise is clear: tragedy is logical and rational. Looking for everyday logic and reasonableness in tragedy, Archer remorselessly drew the conclusion that most of the tragedy of the past was inferior to the middle-class drawing-room drama of London around 1910. Had he been consistent he would even have included Shakespeare in the indictment.

But tragedy is not melodrama minus the madness. It is melodrama plus something.

Melodrama*

JAMES L. ROSENBERG

I would like to defend a dirty word. Like a lot of dirty words, it is dirty, I feel, only through association—and mistaken association, at that.

The word is "melodrama."

It qualifies, I should say, as just about the dirtiest word in the lexicon of the modern critic of the drama—second only, perhaps, to "sentimental." In fact, it seems to have become a sort of universally applicable term of abuse; like "communism," roughly speaking, it seems to mean "bad."

Thus, when M. Ionesco wants to take a crack at M. Sartre, he calls him a writer of "political melodramas" (a masterpiece of ploymanship, combining two dirty words into a sort of portmanteau term of insult). One of the recurring and almost unceasing critical debates on the American dramatic scene has to do with the question of whether Arthur Miller and Tennessee Williams write melodramas or tragedies—with the clear assumption that to convict them of the former is to discredit them artistically. Mr. Kitto, in trying to come to prickly grips with that thorniest of dramatists, Euripides, finds himself forced—with every evidence of dismay— to conclude that a number of Euripides' plays can be described only as "melodramas"—and so much the worse for Euripides. (As Kitto says, of the *Iphigenia in Aulis*, "Now this is not a bad story, but it is not really tragic, and Euripides knows it." Not a bad story, but not really tragic—does this not sum up our critical attitudes, if they may be dignified by such a term, toward melodrama?)

What does the latest handbook of dramatic terms have to tell us? "Melodrama" is "a play wherein characters clearly virtuous or vicious are pitted against each other in sensational situations filled with suspense, until justice triumphs. The situations, not the characters, are exciting. . . . Melodrama is sometimes said to be tragedy with character left out." Another

---

* James L. Rosenberg, "Melodrama," in *The Context and Craft of Drama*, Robert W. Corrigan and James L. Rosenberg, eds. (Chandler, 1964), pp. 168–185.

book tells us that "melodrama . . . has always been regarded as the low-liest form of drama, fit only for the critic's scorn and laughter." And still another defines the opprobrious word as "A play which is sensational, im-plausible in characterization, dialogue, and situation, abounds in thrilling struggles between heroic and villainous figures, and ends happily in the romantic triumph of virtue."

In short, this form is so ludicrously bad one wonders how and why it has survived from Euripides to the present day. It is, as the King of Siam would say, a puzzlement. But Siamese puzzlement can, if pursued, become the beginnings of wisdom—or at least a gleam of insight.

For instance, do you feel, as I do, a faint uneasiness over the awareness that such plays as *Medea* and *Electra* and *Richard III* and *The Revenger's Tragedy* and *The White Devil* and *Cyrano de Bergerac* have all been pretty universally—and, I think, quite accurately—described as "melodramas"? Are these *really* "fit only for the critic's scorn and laughter"? Are they "tragedy with character left out"? Does any one of them "end happily in the romantic triumph of virtue"?

To make matters infinitely worse, some of the very same critics who speak so disparagingly of melodrama as a form are among those who label some of the foregoing plays as melodramatic.

It is all very well for Emerson to say that a foolish consistency is the hobgoblin of little minds, or for a Walt Whitman to bellow "Do I con-tradict myself? Very well, then, I contradict myself!" and go striding away to sweat perfume. Emerson was a Transcendentalist and Whitman a poet, which means, I suppose, that they are exempt from the laws of logic and lucidity. But a critic is not—or should not be. He works with terms—terms that should be rational and meaningful, not only to him but to his readers; and, if they are not, he is in the lunatic position of the mathematician who works with numbers which have no value. Criticism becomes—as, I suspect, modern drama criticism has become, to a great degree—a sort of Alice in Wonderland conversation around the Mad Hatter's tea table. Humpty Dumpty could make words mean whatever he wanted them to, because he was insane and in a lunatic world, but the critic who does so falsifies and betrays the very essence of his being and reason for his existence. Yet I submit that no one can read very far in the realms of more or less con-temporary dramatic criticism without becoming aware of the fact that our critical terminology has serious bugs in it. "Back to the old drawing board!" cries the cheerful little Peter Arno scientist as the experimental plane goes down in flames—and maybe it's not a bad idea for us.

Just how clear and workable are even our most hallowed and cherished generic terms? How many of us have been guilty—how often?—of prattling away glibly about "tragedy," invoking the ghost of Aristotle and handing down the tables of the law from the Sinai of the lecture platform, the desk, or the armchair? And yet how many of us, I wonder, have *really* looked at what Aristotle said (or reputedly said) and laid it alongside the general body of so-called "Greek tragedy"? If and when we do this, does it not strike us that not just some Greek tragedies, but most, do not conform to the standards for Greek tragedy? (I would be willing to argue that only one does—and how valuable is a critical term which refers to exactly one out of the millions of plays that have been written since the first actor crawled painfully out of the primeval ooze—never, some would say, to advance much further?) *Oedipus at Colonus* and the *Oresteia* end happily; it is not even clear who the tragic protagonist is in *Antigone* and *Philoctetes;* the heroine of *Medea* is a villain; the unities are cheerfully broken in a half dozen others one could mention.

And, as for "comedy"—! I have a standing offer of a pound of my flesh, which I will quite blithely bestow upon anybody who can give me a definition of comedy which will cogently and adequately embrace twenty or so "comedies" from Aristophanes to Ionesco (a disconcerting journey in itself, come to think of it).

And what one is to do with plays like *The Misanthrope* or *The Wild Duck* or *The Cherry Orchard*, I frankly don't know. Only the truly pedantic mind could put them into one of the pigeonholes labeled "tragedy" or "comedy" and feel satisfied with his choice. Maybe only the truly pedantic mind would *want* to.

I would like to submit that the first order of business today for those seriously interested in the drama as an art form rather than a branch of hucksterism is to start cleaning out our vocabularies and honing our definitions to a sharper edge. For working with critical terminology is like looking into a microscope: if the focus isn't razor sharp, you're wasting your time.

I'm afraid I have neither the time nor the ability to undertake the rehabilitation of such sweeping terms as "tragedy" and "comedy." But "melodrama" is a somewhat simpler and more glaring problem, and it is to this that I address myself, hopeful, if not of regaining lost ground, at least of raising questions in the minds of others who can perhaps set to work to do so.

What I have said so far should suggest, I hope, that we are in trouble when it comes to the word "melodrama." The word, as it is popularly defined, does not fit some of the most famous plays in the *genre*—just as in the case of "tragedy" and "comedy"—and its use as a generalized term of abuse certainly does not seem to conform to our experience in either the theatre or the library.

Why and how has this state of affairs come about?

Let's look a little more closely at the term. What seem to be the general objections to or misgivings about "melodrama," as they reveal themselves in nearly all the definitions we have considered? Are they not really two, mainly: (1) melodrama is inferior to tragedy—the other form of "serious" drama; and (2) melodrama "falsifies" life. (Notice the adjectives applied to it: "sensational," "thrilling," "romantic," "implausible." "Implausible," above all, is, I suspect, a key word.)

Well, suppose we start by trying to lay these two ghosts. "Melodrama is inferior to tragedy"—or, as one book put it, "Melodrama is . . . tragedy with character left out." An interesting observation, that, implying that Medea and Richard III and Vindice and Cyrano are somehow not very interesting as "characters"! But for the moment I am even more concerned with the supposition underlying this whole line of thinking, which is that melodrama is trying to be tragedy and not quite making it. And if you assume, as most critics seem to, that tragedy is *per se* the pinnacle of dramatic art, then any comparison with it becomes, by definition, an invidious one. But why must generic classification necessarily degenerate into a game of hierarchies? Is it not enough to perceive that there are various modes of perception—the tragic, the comic, the melodramatic, the farcical, the pastoral, the epic (I am beginning to sound, and feel, like Polonius!)—can we not perceive these various modes without lusting hotly after hierarchical arrangement? Tragedy is certainly "different from" melodrama; this fact does not necessarily make it "better than." Can we not be satisfied with saying that tragedy and comedy and melodrama and farce are different modes of perception, each with its own validity, none necessarily better or worse than the others? (Just in passing, I would like to insist, too, on these *genres* as modes of perception, not techniques of writing. Melodrama, like tragedy, is a way of seeing, not a trick of writing. You write a melodrama —a *good* melodrama—because you see the world that way, not because you think: "Today I think I'll write a melodrama.")

I would like, further, to italicize that adjective, *good*—for is it not noteworthy that nearly all discussions of "melodrama" are actually discussions about *bad* melodramas of the heroine-tied-to-the-railroad-tracks variety— but discussions *as though bad melodramas were the norm?* It's as though critics were to base all their considerations of tragedy on Jonson's *Sejanus* or Addison's *Cato*, or, let us say, their considerations of comedy on *Getting Gertie's Garter*—always with the unspoken assumption that these are outstanding and typical examples of the form. It is perfectly easy to dismiss melodrama as trash if you confine your examination of it to Kotzebue and Boucicault and their inferiors. But just how fair is this assumption? And is it really asking too much of the critic that he be, if not perceptive, at least fair? And that he have the intellectual rigor to question and examine the received terminology instead of, well, just receiving it? But how treacherously easy it is to just repeat the critical commonplaces of yesteryear without testing them for a heartbeat, and how painful and difficult it is to actually think through a set of terms.

But let us press on with this painful and difficult—but, I hope, ultimately rewarding—business. What of the somewhat more serious objection that melodrama falsifies life? This objection is based, of course, on another curious and revelatory presupposition: that it is the business of drama, and art generally, to deal "honestly" with life—to present it to us accurately. Here is where naturalism rears its ugly head once more, that odd Zolaesque disease that has spread like acne over the body dramatic for the past hundred years—and whose spread is not yet checked. Ravaged by this spiritual pink-eye, though, we seem to have lost sight of the fact that art, by its very etymology, never has been in any way concerned with this sort of technological verisimilitude. Art, if it involves anything, surely involves selection, arrangement, meaningful distortions and relocations of the data of experience, and the doctrine which would convict an art-form of falsifying or distorting "reality" would lead inevitably to an appreciation of a page of statistics or an accurate newspaper report (if I may be forgiven a contradiction in terms) as the highest art. Does the melodramatist "simplify" his characters and select certain character traits to emphasize? Of course he does. So does Ben Jonson. So does Molière. So does Shaw. So did the *commedia dell'arte*. With few exceptions, what playwright doesn't? Does he "arrange" the elements in his plot with an eye to theatrical effect? Naturally. Doesn't Sophocles? Or Shakespeare? Since when is it opprobrious to try to write a play that will be effective in the theatre? Would it not be even more questionable to try to write a play that would be *in*effective in the theatre? Clearly this line of thinking leads to an appreciation of an instruction manual on how to change a typewriter ribbon as the highest form of art (it's "real" and "true to life"), and—most importantly—it simply banishes imagination. And that, I submit, is what modern popular art has largely become: art without imagination, which is a little like life without love—the only form, I suppose, that a people numbed by fact and desensitized by quantity can adequately respond to.

This situation, if true, is melancholy, but it still does not mean that we, as defenders of the dramatic faith (and imagination), have merely to accede to it. I suggest that there is a positive therapeutic value in attempting to restore "melodrama" to respectability, and above all in trying to see that what are generally considered its weakest points are actually its strongest and most distinctive.

Before we can go very far in an examination of the nature of melodrama, though, it might be well to pause a moment and consider the over-all nature of drama and theatre. "Everything is what it is and not another thing," said Bishop Butler, in the eighteenth century—in one of those breathtakingly bare statements which seem almost childishly simple, like so many of Aristotle's precepts, but which, on closer examination, prove to contain a most profound and subtle truth. (I think particularly of Aristotle's observation that a play should have a beginning, a middle, and an end.) All right. What *is* a dramatic representation, a play as performed in the theatre? What distinguishes it from other forms of art? It employs language? All literature does. It is a narrative form? So is the novel, the short story, sometimes even the poem. It employs physical movement? So does ballet. The possible list of comparisons is almost endless, and mostly, I'm afraid, pretty fruitless.

Ultimately, there are, I believe, only two or three really distinguishing features which define a performed play:

(1) It is an event which occurs both in space (like a picture or a statue) and in time (like a poem or a symphony). Lessing has said about all there is to say about this in his *Laokoon;* the only point I want to make about it for the moment is that the performed drama is distinguished by a kind of *plenitude* which no other art form possesses. Its appeal is rich, varied, and immediate.

(2) The tense of drama is the perpetual present. A play is something which happens—right here and now—with all the illusion of unmediated spontaneity. It is, in the philosophical sense of the word, an accident rather than an essence, and all our experience shows us, I believe, that while we pay lip service to essence, we live by—and are interested in—accidents. See the front page of tonight's newspaper. Who can deny that part of the appeal of the theatre—subconscious, perhaps—is the awareness that at any moment you, as a member of the audience, may see a literal accident: an actor may blow his lines, a piece of scenery may fall. For all the rehearsals and preparations, which are attempts to bring the riotous accidentalism of the universe under man's rational control, the play is happening every time for the first time, and its future is unknown. Why else do we watch the baseball game by television, or the high-wire act at the circus? Isn't it true that somewhere in all of us there lurks the half-hidden hope that the aerialist may make a misstep, the star outfielder may drop a fly ball? And when they do, it's *exciting* (a word I would like now to smuggle into this discussion). For the real excitement of theatre lies in this accidental immediacy; it is like life in that the future is perpetually unknown, despite all our efforts to shape it. A certain actor in Act Two of a certain play may forget his lines or fall down, but no one knows—least of all, the actor himself!—whether he will or not until the precise second when the words emerge from his mouth.

For all the artificial arrangements of script and rehearsal, the living performance is always a universe of perpetual potentiality. A realm, in other
words, of excitement.

(3) The material of the theatre is the human form. (I do not overlook
the values of light and scenic background; I simply assume that they are
merely that—background and context for the human actor. In other words,
I assume that if the curtain rose and allowed us to gaze for two hours on a
set, we would not consider this a drama.) The material of the painter is
paint and canvas; of the sculptor, plaster and stone; of the composer, sound;
of the poet, words. But all these—with the exception of sound—are human
artifacts, they are impersonal, and can be brought under some fairly consistent sort of human control. But the human being, as material to work
with, is—I need scarcely tell any director—a highly volatile and uncon-
trollable chemical element. Again, we have the element of excitement, of
unpredictability, the constant contrast between the infinite variety and
malleability of the human organism and the rigid inflexibility of the forms
which surround him. (Bergson, in his famous theory of laughter, had hold,
I suspect, of an even larger idea.) The human form—flesh and blood—is the
very material of the theatre art. It's an interesting thought. Pope said:
"The proper study of mankind is man," but he might just as well have
amended it to: "The *only possible* study of mankind is man." For is it not
true that the one preeminently fascinating subject for us is ourselves—that,
indeed, we are properly speaking not even capable of dealing with anything
else? Why else do we anthropomorphize our gods and humanize our animals? We may, to be sure, study the cellular structure of leaves or the motions of the stars, but do we really understand the leafness of leaves and the
starness of stars, or do we just read ourselves and our human attitudes into
them?

Now, with these elements of the unique nature of theatre in mind, let me
shift the focus from the stage to the auditorium and inquire what it is that
draws us, as audience, to a theatrical representation. The excitement, the
fascination with the human, to be sure—but what does all this add up to?
What is this peculiar and potent magic which can draw people to sit
jammed together in a large room watching other people in a smaller room
move through rituals of imitative action? Is it not, in the final analysis, the
same magnetic force that draws people to the cathedral, the football stadium,
the beer tavern—in short, any place where life is expressing itself in a more
vivid and concentrated form than it does in the ordinary daily round of dull
routine?

In other words, what I am working toward here is a fairly simple
formula: We go to the theatre (as we do to the church, the athletic arena,
the social center) to be made more aware of our aliveness. Whether con-

sciously or not, this, I suspect, is the great drive of all human beings: To express Life. (In this we are like Camus's Caligula, who, bloody, beaten, dying, cries out, in the last line of the play: "I'm still alive!") Is this not the whole rhythm of human existence? Every day, every minute we are dying, and somehow we feel that we want to have made full use of the vital potentiality that was given us at the start instead of just letting it run through our fingers like water, as is the case, for example, with Chekhov's people. Most of us feel much of the time, I suspect, like Chekhov people: We are living at only about 10 percent of our capacities at best, and the dead hand of routine and boredom lays itself upon the organic vitality of our days, so that we soon find ourselves looking back over a wasteland of missed chances, empty hours, neglected opportunities. But up there on the stage all is different. There, everything matters; every moment is significant; nothing is wasted; there, life *really* burns with a hard gemlike flame—as it so rarely does on the other side of the footlights.

And—to return deviously and by indirection to my starting point—that everything matters is true above all of the melodramatic stage. There the central actors—Medea, Richard III, Vindice, Cyrano, Dick Dudgeon—are actors in every sense of the word: people who act, who do things, and also people who conceive of themselves consistently in histrionic terms, who stand back, as it were, observing and enjoying their own performances. Their doing so, incidentally, is theatricalism with a vengeance—for here the theatre becomes not merely an analogue of life, but simultaneously a kind of lens through which to see life. But, above all, it is the wonderful, frank, quite self-conscious *vitality* of these melodramatic heroes that delights us and that gives us a vicarious stimulation—for here surely are people living at about 101 percent of their vital capacity at any given moment, people living every minute of their lives at, in Gerard Manley Hopkins' fine phrase, "the highest pitch of stress."

And if this is the highest and truest function of theatre—indeed, of all art and of religion, as well—to put us in contact with some sort of electrical current of vitality, to recharge our spiritual batteries, to make us—in the fullest sense of the word—more meaningfully alive, then is not melodrama, in which stimulation and vitality and excitement are everything, is it not perhaps the highest, rather than the most contemptible, of dramatic forms?

A heretical notion, to be sure. But all the more reason for examining it. I suppose one of the first heretics was the first man who ate an oyster.

So, having pushed my theory from a tentative defense of melodrama to a flagrant claim for it as the highest form of drama—like a good melodramatist, I believe in nothing if not in excess—let me try now to push it even further.

Earlier, you will recall, I rejected hierarchies. Now, I am constructing

one of my own. I suppose it makes a difference whether you feel you are
on the defensive or are carrying the fight into the enemy camp. In any case,
swollen with *hubris* as I am, indulge me for a minute and let me move on
to an aggressive defense—or, at least, a tentative defense—of melodrama as
the highest form of dramatic art. Or, let's say, to put it a bit more precisely,
the *purest* form. (A good melodramatist should likewise be able to display
some fancy footwork from time to time in shifting his terms.)

Let me recall you to the auditorium once more and seat you out there in
the fourth row, center section. We have talked about the rewards which
theatre offers, the anticipatory excitement you may legitimately feel as the
house lights dim and the curtain rises. But what of the other side of the
coin? What are some of the drawbacks and problems which peculiarly distinguish theatre? You know some of them as well as I do. There are always
those first few moments of foot shuffling, seat banging and program rattling
in the auditorium, and there are always those members of the audience who,
as soon as the curtain goes up, begin, in the words of a famous critic, "to
strum their catarrhs." What is the result of all this? That generally we miss
the first few—often vital—moments of exposition. (With the result that
the experienced playwright usually gives his exposition, not once, but twice.
It makes for clumsy literature, but for sound theatre—and thereby hangs
a tale.)

Actually, the theatregoer out front is in one of the most difficult and im-
practical positions conceivable for a viewer or auditor of the arts. For one
thing, he is fixed; he cannot move his position in relation to the performance. For another, he must catch it all on the fly, as it were. If he misses a
line or a nuance, he cannot go back and retrieve it; it is lost forever. If he
wants to re-examine a passage, he cannot turn back the page and re-
read it. I have spoken earlier of the richness of theatre, but that same richness and plenitude can also be a drawback. It can be—and often is—a source
of confusion and muddle. Too much is going on in any play at almost any
time—too many simultaneous appeals to the ear and to the eye—for the
audience to give the play the same kind of intense and almost rapt attention
they can give a painting or a poem or a piece of music. Viewing a painting
in the stillness and relative solitude of an art gallery is quite a different matter from plunging into the noisy hurly-burly of a theatre. The viewer can
move about and view the painting from various angles, as he pleases; his ear
is not meanwhile being distracted by music or dialogue; and he can experience the art work at his own pace, in as leisurely a fashion as he desires.
He sets the rhythm of his perception—the work of art does not impose it
upon him. The same thing is true of the man sitting quietly in his library
reading a poem or a novel or a play; he can give the work his undivided
attention, free of all external distractions. (I am imagining, I confess, a

rather idyllic man, completely free of wife, children, dogs, television sets, neighbors, etc., etc. But, after all, this whole thing is pretty much an exercise in pure speculation.) Even the listener in the concert hall, while he suffers some of the limitations imposed upon the theatregoer, is asked to pay attention only with his ears, not his eyes. He may—many concertgoers do, I discover—actually close his eyes while listening, the better to avoid visual distraction and concentrate with the one sense that is being appealed to. But the poor theatregoer cannot close his eyes—nor his ears. All his senses must be brought into simultaneous operation; all are being appealed to—either directly or vicariously—and his attention becomes accordingly diffused.

Hence the frequent charge, especially by literary people, that the theatre is a coarse form. It is, of course—that is its nature—and almost any play will read rather barely and awkwardly, considered in purely literary terms, alongside almost any novel or lyric poem. But of course a play is not just a literary piece, a sort of chamber work designed only to be read; it is designed to be performed, under aesthetically adverse conditions—and thus the rather heavy-handed and awkward "plants" and repetitions in even the best of stage scripts, as compared to the much greater subtlety and complexity of the novel or the poem. But the play has its compensations, as we have already mentioned, in the tremendous immediacy and vividness of its physical impact, which no novel or poem can even approximate.

And, again, I would like to pick up this point—the grossness, the physical immediacy of the stage—and, applying it to melodrama, try to suggest that melodrama presents this better than any other dramatic form, and that this is to be seen, not as a shameful weakness, but as a positive virtue.

The theatre is a physical place. The stage is a place of objects—bodies, planes, solids, lines, colors, lights, etc. It is through these means that it expresses itself. Going to the theatre is not merely an intellectual or an abstractly aesthetic experience; it is above all a sensory experience.

This sensory quality means that the initial impact of a play—again, I would argue, of any work of art—is emotional, rather than intellectual. Or, if you find yourself suspicious of the intellectual-emotional dichotomy, as I do, let's try to sharpen the terminology once more by saying that the initial impact of a dramatic work in the theatre is visceral rather than cerebral. Pure perception precedes rationalization. And—granted that pure perception *without* rationalization amounts to nothing more than a kind of glandular reaction—it is also true that, without a powerful and stimulating initiating sense impression, the rationalizing mind has quite literally nothing to rationalize about. First things first, and "one world at a time, Waldo," as the dying Thoreau said.

And, I would maintain, the peculiar nature of theatre considered as an art

form is its ability to present us with these naked moments of pure perception
—distorted, heightened, vivified so as to carry outward into the dark neutrality of the auditorium and assault our senses as directly as the odor of a
rose or a slap in the face. The intellectualization of the experience—the inevitable second step if the experience is to be meaningful instead of random
—comes later. In the auditorium, we don't worry about whether or not
Oedipus has an Oedipus complex; we are confronted with a man caught in
the meshes of a dilemma. (In fact, is it not fair to say that every really good
play that has ever been written can be boiled down to this simple formula:
Man in a dilemma? Which is, in itself, the whole myth of human existence.)

"Everything is what it is and not another thing." Theatre is an art form
whose materials—flesh and blood—and whose means—public mimetic representation—endow it peculiarly with the power to present us with moments of direct, pure perception. Ergo, that theatrical form which presents
them best can be labeled the "best"—i.e., the purest—theatrical form, in
that it is the most conformable to the laws of its being. It is not, like the
theatre of naturalism, the theatre trying to be the novel, or, like much so-
called "poetic" drama, the theatre aspiring to the condition of lyric poetry.
It is the Theatre Theatrical, *das Ding an sich.*

And theatre at its most truly theatrical is melodrama.

Now, please note that I am not holding up for approbation a theatre of
sheer mindless excitement and Grand Guignol sensation. I cling firmly to
my demand for the intellectual nature of theatre—in fact, I'm afraid I must
say that I find the distinguishing mark of modern theatre, modern American
theatre, particularly, is an extraordinary lack of real intellectual rigor, as
compared to the fields of the novel or of lyric poetry. At times, the flabbiness
of Broadway's "thinking" is almost beyond belief. But I do say that there is
always and inevitably a time lag between perception and conceptualization,
that this is true above all of an art of such immediacy as theatre, and that
theatre ignores this basic law of its being at its own dire peril.

Is it not noteworthy that, in looking back over the history of the drama
for the last seventy-five to a hundred years—the Realists' reign of terror—
we see an art form consistently and coyly trying to pretend to be something
other than itself? What is the purpose of all these correctly furnished drawing rooms and dining rooms and kitchens, with *real* furniture and *real* rugs
and sometimes even, wonderful to relate, *real* water coming out of *real*
taps? What is the purpose of all this hugger-mugger except to pretend that
theatre is not actually theatre at all, but what we are pleased to call "real
life"? In other words, we are in on the deliberate detheatricalization of the
theatre, the emasculation of an art form, performed by its own high
priests.

The modern trend toward greater "theatricality" is, I think, an inevitable and long-delayed (and, I might add, healthy) reaction to this curious condition, and we find it everywhere we look today—in Brecht, in the absurdists, in Thornton Wilder, in Düerrenmatt and Frisch, in such very new young Americans as Jack Gelber and Edward Albee, in such groups as the Living Theatre and the Actors' Workshop. No art form can defy the very laws of its own being and go on living for very long; in fact, seventy-five years in a moribund state (a marvelous title, come to think of it, for a history of American drama)—this is a long time, even for an Edgar Allan Poe hero. It is high time, in every sense of the word, to pry open the coffin and release the barely living corpse.

You may have noticed that I have smuggled into the discussion a set of definitions and a frame of reference that are somewhat different from those we started with, and that I have now maneuvered melodrama into a corner and rendered it indistinguishable from "Theatre," with a capital "T."

But I announced at the outset that I proposed to redefine "melodrama," and I feel no sense of chicanery in having sneaked up on it in this fashion. Can one equate "melodramatic" with "theatrical"? I think so—and to the greater glory of both words. The whole mainstream of the drama, from Thespis to Arthur Kopit, has been, if you will, melodramatic rather than tragic or comic—and it's about time that we got over our curiously Victorian sense of shame in this matter.

The Greeks, with their chanting and dancing choruses and declaiming masked figures, were not afraid to be "theatrical" and—let's face it—"melodramatic." Nor were the *commedia dell'arte* performers. Nor were Shakespeare and his contemporaries. Nor Molière and his troupe. It is only somewhere along about the eighteenth or nineteenth centuries that the bourgeois sensibility begins to anesthetize the histrionic sensibility, and dramatists and actors begin to feel ashamed of behaving excessively and begin to lose sight of the fact that excess—the "fine excess" of Keats's fine phrase—is not only the nature of their being but the only reason for their existence. A good play should be a fever chart of life, and not a fever chart which has flattened out into a straight line, devoid of monstrous and drastic peaks and valleys, for such a one has—by definition—ceased to be a fever chart. It is simply a report of a normal—and therefore uninteresting—condition.

The function of the drama—of all art—is surely to put us in contact with the abnormal, the unusual, the extraordinary, perhaps to exhort us to aspire toward these peaks of unusualness ourselves, at least to make us more sensitive toward their occasional irruption into the dull and featureless normality of our own daily existence. And to condemn a playwright for writing melodramatically seems to me tantamount to criticizing a painter for using a bit too much color or a composer for writing a shade too melodically. Just as color and sound are the materials of the painter and the composer, so action is the material of the playwright—and to condemn him for using the materials most appropriate to his form is a curious line of criticism, to say the least.

The time, I think, is preeminently ripe for a rallying cry: "Melodramatists of the world, unite! You have nothing to lose but your inhibitions." The theatre, from its Dionysian beginnings, has never been a place of inhibitions—which were, after all, inventions of fairly modern times.

The time is ripe for a truly and greatly melodramatic drama, a drama which will assault us with visions of Man Alive in a Universe of Danger—again, a kind of formula-phrase which suggests the very archetype of Drama. Above all, though, Man Alive—alive and in action, and with Death always just offstage, waiting in the wings.

And this is melodrama. Simply the protoplasmic stuff of which great art has always been made. It is a dirty word only when its means and purposes become directed toward cheap or sentimental ends—as can be done with any art form. But, in the hands of the great melodramatists, like Euripides or Shakespeare, it needs no defense—from me or from anyone. It speaks for itself, powerfully, vividly, conclusively, with the energies of art, and tells us, as all great art does, about ultimate things.

Tragedy and Melodrama:
Speculations on Generic Form*

ROBERT B. HEILMAN

I

This essay grows out of my sense of a persistent confusion in the use of
the word *tragedy*. As critics, of course, we know that we can never expect to
agree on final definitions that will make possible a consistent criticism. But
the discrepancies which we can never finally eliminate, even in professional
usage, have got completely out of hand in popular usage. This fact is my
starting point, and in this sense, literary criticism merges with social criticism. The word *tragedy* means not only plays of a certain kind but almost all
kinds of painful experiences: an early death, an unexpected death by disease,
a financial failure, a suicide, a murder, an automobile accident, a train accident, an airplane accident, a successful military movement by a hostile
power, a sadistic act, a government error, almost any act of violence. I recall an accident in which a small plane, whose pilot had bailed out, crashed
into a building; the newspaper I was then reading headlined the story,
"Tragedy to Plane and Factory." This seemed to stretch the idea of tragedy
pretty far. The strain was increased by the fact, which was soon revealed,
that the factory was a cheese factory, for to many people cheese will not
seem the likeliest of tragic materials.

What I want to explore is the possibility of finding distinctions among
the host of disagreeable events lumped under the word *tragedy*. Note my
word *explore*. Such criticism is not logical demonstration; it is at best a form
of rhetoric. That is, it succeeds in so far as it persuades anyone else that it
is useful. The most the critic can hope for is to be partially persuasive.

An experiment in making distinctions should justify itself. However, I
want to note what seems to me to be an especial danger in that loose use of

* Robert B. Heilman, "Tragedy and Melodrama," *The Texas Quarterly*, Summer, 1960,
pp. 36–50.

245

the word *tragedy* that penetrates our whole society. I do not think we can simply rest in our knowledge that we have wide areas of bad usage. We need to make some effort to counter bad usage. For when a word is a catchall for many meanings only loosely related, it loses character. It tends to be used only for simple or wholesale or lump meanings. In fact, we can propose it as a law of language that when one word gains several meanings, the inferior meaning will tend to force the superior meaning out of circulation: I mean that the rougher, more general, looser, or lazier meaning will win out over the more exact or precise or demanding meaning. This is Gresham's law of semantic currency. When *tragedy* means the whole world of misfortune we cannot distinguish particular misfortunes in terms of their cause, nature, and meaningfulness. We lack the words for this; what is worse, we lack the concepts. What we do not distinguish, we do not understand; I will go a step further and suggest that if experiences are not understood, there is a sense in which they are not even experienced. This confusion extends beyond verbal haziness and begins to interfere with fundamental clarity of mind and therefore, I think, with sense of reality.

II

I believe that the word *tragedy* may suitably be applied to one form of catastrophic experience, and that this can be differentiated from all others. For a start, we may use Aristotle's definition of the tragic hero as the good man who gets into trouble through some error or shortcoming for which the standard term has become the tragic flaw. This I take to be a central, irreducible truth about tragic reality.

This assumption of mine has a number of consequences. The first is that the tragic character is essentially a divided character, and I shall regularly use *divided*, *dividedness*, and *division* as key words. The idea of goodness and the idea of the flaw suggest different incentives and different directions, a pulling apart, though not of pathological intensity, within the personality. The division in the hero may be of different sorts. In the first place, it may reflect the kind of division that seems inseparable from human community— from the fact that, in the ordering of life, we maintain different imperatives that correspond to different and perhaps irreconcilable needs. Hamlet and Orestes, those heroes so different from each other in time and place and yet so incredibly alike in the trials that visit them, cannot avenge their fathers, the victims of evil deeds, without themselves committing evil deeds. Antigone cannot be true to family duty and love, and to religious obligation, without contravening civil law; and Creon—who in some ways is really a better tragic hero than Antigone—cannot or at least does not maintain civil order without punitive decrees that profoundly violate human feelings and sense of justice. Yet none of these heroes could refrain from the course that leads to guilt without feeling intolerably acquiescent in a public evil.

Such heroes and heroines, if I do not misread them, incorporate the dividedness of a humanity whose values, because they naturally elude the confines of formal logic, create an apparently insoluble situation. In this situation the crucial actions of heroes, though they are exacted by a powerful sense of moral obligation, nevertheless become infused with guilt. For these heroes the two counterimperatives have so much authority that no observer can say with assurance, "It would be better if Hamlet or Antigone or Cordelia had done so and so." Nor could a fully aware person, caught between injunctions that are apparently incompatible, come out of such situations without damage; he could be safe only by canceling part of his awareness. This canceling would surely threaten the common order more than the ambiguous act does. Suppose Hamlet had decided that the ghostly exhortations that he heard were simply the product of tensions within himself, that he was worrying too much, that his best step was to get adjusted to the existent order and to stop brooding about evils which he couldn't help anyway and which might well be only imaginary. Or that Orestes had decided that his father deserved his fate, or Cordelia that she might just as well follow her sisters in applepolishing an eccentric elder. Maybe these would be safe courses, at least temporarily. But what diminished persons we would have, and what a shrunken sense of reality.

Of characters caught in the Hamlet and Orestes situation we may say that they are divided between "imperatives," that is, different injunctions, each with its own validity, but apparently irreconcilable. With another type of tragic hero the division may be said to be between "imperative" and "impulse," between the moral ordinance and the unruly passion, between mandate and desire, between law and lust. Tradition and community give an ordinance, but egotism drives one away from it. Macbeth seeks power through politics, Faustus through intellect; what makes them tragic, as ordinary power-grabbers are not, is that neither of them can ever, in yielding to impulse, force out of consciousness the imperatives that he runs against. Oedipus has the same division, but with a different alignment of forces: he wants to obey the imperative but is betrayed by the riotous impulse. Finally, there is a third representative tragic dividedness—the split between impulse and impulse, which I believe to be a characteristic situation in Ibsen. Rebecca West and Rosmersholm, for instance, are divided between what I will call the impulses of the old order and those of rationalist enlightenment, in a peculiarly modern tragic situation.

I have used the term *imperative* to denote the obligation of general validity, the discipline of self that cannot be rejected without penalty, whether it is felt as divine law or moral law or civil law, or, in a less codified but no less prescriptive way, as tradition or duty or honor. Imperative reflects a communal consciousness. By *impulse* I refer to the force that originates in or is rooted in or identified with the individual personality and is of an almost biological sort; though the specific feelings that impel the individual may be of the widest occurrence in humanity, they are felt as a need, or as a satisfaction, or as an aggrandizement of the individual, in almost a bodily way. Imperative tends toward the self-abnegatory, impulse toward the self-assertive. But I do not wish to labor this distinction. I have made it, and I have suggested three basic patterns of division, as a way of trying to make concrete the idea of dividedness in the tragic hero.

There are two other consequences of the idea of tragedy as the experience of the good man with the flaw. The first of these is that division means choice: there are alternatives, and man must select one or another. This idea is so familiar that I will limit myself to this bare statement of it. The second is that choice implies consciousness: alternatives are not really alternatives, at least in the dramatic substance, if they do not in some way, however indirectly or however tardily, live in the consciousness of the hero. The drama is a lesser one—it has less range—if the hero simply does not know what it is all about or never comes to know what it is all about. Willie Loman is a hero of such limited consciousness that, for many readers, he pushes *Death of a Salesman* into a lower order of excellence. Division, finally, is not only the occasion of self-awareness or self-knowledge, but the very material of self-knowing. It is the inconsistent and the contradictory that require the studious intelligence; the unified, the coherent, the harmonious dissolve the world of alternatives and render the customary strivings of self-understanding irrelevant.

III

To sum up: *tragedy* should be used only to describe the situation in which the divided human being faces basic conflicts, perhaps rationally insoluble, of obligations and passions; makes choices, for good or for evil; errs knowingly or involuntarily; accepts consequences; comes into a new, larger awareness; suffers or dies, yet with a larger wisdom.

Now this is quite different from popular or journalistic tragedy (here we come to the social dimension of the problem): young man drives fast, hits truck that drives out in front of him, and he and his fiancée are killed. This will almost invariably be called, "Tragedy on Highway 90," and for many people this is *all* of tragedy. The death-dealing truck might be a disease or a careless engineer or a defective airplane wing or an assailant; the essence of it is the shock of unprogrammed death. This is a rather long way from the tragic pattern that we are able to discern in the practice of the Greeks and

Elizabethans and at least in the intuitions of some moderns. Even in the most skillful journalism we would hardly be able to get inside the victims and see them as divided between options or struggling in a cloudy dilemma of imperative and impulse; they do not choose but are chosen; something just happens to them; consequences are mechanical, not moral; and most of all they do not grow into that deeper understanding, of themselves and of their fate, which is the dramatic heart of the experience. For in that sudden death there is little to understand; consciousness is not sharpened but is bluntly ended.

To use the term *tragedy* indiscriminately for what Oedipus does and experiences and learns, and for what happens to a car driver through his own or someone else's carelessness, I submit, is not a casual slip of the tongue or a laughable folk error, but a real confusion that can have undesirable consequences for our grasp of reality. For by our Gresham's law of semantic currency, the cheaper meaning forces out the meaning of precise value. Tragedy comes to mean *only* accidents and sudden death or anachronistic death. As a result we tend to lose touch with certain ideas that are an indispensable means of contemplating human catastrophe: the idea that calamity may come from divisions within human nature and within the ordering of life. The idea that man may choose evil. The idea that potential evil within him may overcome him despite resolution or flight. The idea that brutal events may come out of the normal logic of character. The idea that man is never safe from himself. The idea that the knowledge of such ideas is essential to the salvation of the individual and to the health of institutions. All these ideas are implicitly discarded if the word *tragedy* conveys to us only such a thing as a smashup on Highway 90. And what do we put in place of what is lost? The idea that the worst that can happen to us is an unexpected shortening of life. The idea that this cutting short is the work of causes outside ourselves. The idea that we are innocent victims. This is a fantastic loss of tools of understanding and, implicitly, an unhealthy oversimplification of reality.

Here you may want to argue that in using such a phrase as "only unhappy accidents" I am minimizing the extent, the influence, and the force of such events. Not at all. I do not deny the reality of accidents, the pain and anguish they cause, or their power to move us either in daily experience or in literary representation. I do not suppose that we can eliminate unhappy accidents, ignore them, forget them, deny their power over our actions and feelings, or discontinue making literature of them. All I am troubled by is calling them "tragedy," which I am hoping to persuade you is no trivial error. I have the greatest respect for the rare news editor who, instead of announcing "Tragedy on Highway 90," will say "Accident on Highway 90: Two Dead." There is the crux of the matter: putting experience into the right category. Now, for the category of event which is so widely called "Tragedy on Highway 90" the proper term, I suggest, is *disaster*. It is a sufficiently capacious term to include all kinds of fatal accidents, the mortal illnesses that strike (we think) ahead of time, the destructive blows of a nature not yet quite tamed, and all the murderous violence that comes directly or by ricochet from the envious, the hostile, and the mad. Its very etymology makes *disaster* an appropriate term: it implies an undoing by action of the stars, and thus it is a fitting metaphor for all the unhappinesses that seem to come from without, to have no meaningful causes, and to let us feel guiltless. From now on, then, instead of speaking of the two meanings of *tragedy*—the meaning implied in the literary examples that remain always alive, and the contemporary journalistic meaning that pervades all our speech—I shall use the terms *tragedy* and *disaster* to denote these areas of experience that may always be theoretically distinguished.

However much they may be interwoven in the concrete event, tragedy and disaster are two fundamentally different structures of experience; to confuse them will involve errors of three kinds—intellectual, emotional, moral. The intellectual error I have already described or implied: it is to seek the causes of evil always outside ourselves, to whitewash ourselves, to be always without responsibility for calamities. The loose use of the word *tragedy* also leads us to a concomitant error of feeling. For if tragedy is simply what happens to us, we are all victims; victims must be pitied; and we can soon ooze into a rich morass of self-pity. Obviously we don't want to pity ourselves, if we are well people; but the universalization of the disaster principle sneaks pity in the back door. Sometimes we can pity ourselves simply by pitying others: Othello is a case in point. Or, in glorifying the man who pities, we may reveal a desire to cuddle up under that sympathetic wing. The word *compassionate* has become a cliché of book reviewing; in our time it is almost an ultimate term of praise for a writer. It has become embarrassing. Is *compassion* the word that comes to mind when we think of Shakespeare's treatment of Lear or Sophocles' portrayal of Oedipus? Is it not rather completeness of understanding, insight into human division, a full sense of both excellence and flaw? Compare the Christopher Fry character who says, "I'm still remembering/I can give pain, and that in itself is loss/Of liberty." When we shift from feeling sorry for pain received to fear of pain given, we move from the sense of disaster toward the tragic sense.

The third error in taking disaster for tragedy is the moral one of adopting a single-standard quantitative view of life. Disaster centers in death: we are getting less life than we have coming to us. It is not necessary to quarrel with a universal disinclination to die, especially ahead of what looks like sound scheduling; but as a matter of clarity we should observe that in our day the quest for longevity is both more extensive and more passionate than it has ever been before. This appears in our obsession with disaster, the most forceful reminder of mortality. Disaster is the realm of quantity of life; tragedy, of quality of life. The inevitable fear of disaster can grow until it eliminates all issues of quality. I do not complain about fear of death, which is a fact of life; my point is only that the ending of life is not the sole imperfection of life, and that to act as though it is, is not healthful.

IV

In disaster, what happens comes from without; in tragedy, from within. In disaster, we are victims; in tragedy, we make victims, of ourselves or others. In disaster, our moral quality is secondary; in tragedy, it is primary, the very source of action.

In literature, the problem is that of distinguishing between tragedy and what I will call, for the time being, the literature of disaster, which is often called tragedy. I regard the two forms as generically different, though they look alike because they both depict suffering. The literature of disaster comprises all those pages in which we record what has been done to us by fire, famine, the sword, and unjust men; in which our role is that of Job, plagued by our own kind, by machines, and by nature. In tragedy, as an art form, we contemplate our own errors; in the literature of disaster we mark the errors of others and the imperfections of circumstance. In tragedy we act; in the literature of disaster we are acted upon.

In the literature of disaster we find victims of situations that range from very simple to very complex. Though I want to avoid little catalogues that are too neat, I will suggest that we can identify several basic types of the victims that artists have discerned—the victims of nature, the victims of society, the victims of evil individuals, and those who are victims of themselves. This last, of course, sounds very much like tragedy, and the distinction will have to be clarified later.

Since I do not have space for analysis of plays, I will have to be like the Oriental geometrician who stated a theorem, drew an illustrative figure, and substituted, for the steps of demonstration leading to a formal conclusion, simply the word *Behold!* I use Synge's *Riders to the Sea* as an example of the literature of disaster dealing with the victim of nature; this play is generally called a tragedy, but its core is pathos; we remain serene observers, sympathetic, sharing the sadness of death, but never drawn into the experience of division and of self-knowledge, for there is none. The victim of society, a familiar figure in post-Romantic sensibility, appears archetypally in Dr. Stockmann in Ibsen's *Enemy of the People*—an embarrassingly simple picture of a noble reformer done in by a crass community. Our emotional involvement here hardly approaches the adult level. The drama of disaster that deals with the victim of society is managed somewhat more complexly in Friedrich Duerrenmatt's *The Visit* (1955). In this play the townspeople, to gain a vengeful woman's gift of a billion marks, informally sentence to death and execute one of the town's leading citizens, the original seducer of the woman who gives the billion marks. Like various dramas of disaster, *The Visit* has a powerful impact because it devotes itself exclusively to demonstrating the infinitude of human venality. It gains power at the expense of depth and complication; it simply excludes any other human characteristic but vengefulness and corruptibility. It denies the division which is at the heart of tragedy; and so, I submit, it not only narrows the aesthetic experience but reduces us to shocked spectators of a crime. This is one of the two representative risks of the literature of disaster: at the popular extreme it may entice us into a stereotyped situation, ready-made for emotional wear; or, a , in *The Visit*, it may lock us out of a situation by making it so eccentric that to enter it would be suicide. That, too, is always a risk of expressionist drama, to which *The Visit* belongs: in such difficulties, as well as in other matters, we realize postrealist expressionism is very much like prerealist allegory.

The victim of the politically disordered society appears in *The Diary of Anne Frank*. Here again is a drama of disaster that offers simple and easy emotional experience, pity for victims; only at one point does it approach tragedy—at the point at which Mr. Frank says, of the tensions among the hiding victims of the Nazis, "We don't need the Nazis to destroy us. We're destroying ourselves." The victim of the evil individual is found in one of the great dramas of disaster in English—Webster's *The Duchess of Malfi*, in which a charming and innocent woman is tortured and destroyed by her cruel brothers. She is not presented tragically; she does not, like great tragic heroes, "earn" her fate. Her honorable conduct simply happens to run afoul of the purposes of her vicious brothers. Lear, on the contrary, has made Goneril and Regan efficacious in the world; they are projections of a part of his own divided nature. Lear has made his world in a way that the Duchess has not. Webster presents the evil brothers as autonomous—like a flood or holocaust that destroys. This is not to deny the existence of autonomous evil; it is simply to say that it is not the world of tragedy.

Finally, in Gorki's *Lower Depths* and O'Neill's *The Iceman Cometh* (two works with extraordinary similarities of plot and structure), we find plays that are concerned with the disaster of personality: that is, with that kind of collapse which makes the individual incapable of normal adult life. When we speak of the disaster of the self, however, we remember that the origin of the tragic situation is also within the self. At the risk of too epigrammatic a contrast we may say that the disaster of self has its origin in weakness, the tragedy of self in strength. In disaster, individuals are not up to traditional requirements; in tragedy, they are not held down by traditional requirements and eventually find themselves not up to the special rules they propose for themselves. One aesthetic leads to Mr. Zero, the other to Dr. Faustus; one character says, "Pity me," the other says, "I have sinned." In *The Duchess of Malfi* Bosola sums up the action with the phrase "Oh this gloomy world." In *Riders to the Sea* Maurya says, ". . . there isn't anything else the sea can do to me." In *The Iceman Cometh* Larry Slade concludes, "By God, there's no hope! . . . Life is too much for me." "This gloomy world"—what is done to me—what is too much for me: this is the realm of disaster—of what happens to the victims of nature, of societal power or war, of weakness before the exigencies of life, of disillusionment, of corruption, of evil men. The realm of actual disaster that is the raw material of literary art is a large one. We do not underestimate the immediacy or anguish of that realm, or fail in sympathy with those injured or betrayed by such events, if we say, once again, that such fates are something other than tragic, and that the drama portraying such fates is not of the tragic order.

For many things that are terrible are not tragic.

V

The term *literature of disaster* which I have so far used is a cumbersome term and a limiting term. I propose, as my final point, that the literature of disaster is really a subdivision of a larger literary type. To that type I will give the term *melodrama*.

I am aware that to take *melodrama*, which in casual contemporary usage is a derogatory term designating popular machine-made entertainments, and to apply it to a wide range of literature that includes sober work and somber tones may seem capricious to the point of scandal. I hasten to deny caprice and to explain that I use melodrama as a neutral descriptive term. I use it because I believe that what we call "popular melodrama" has reduced to stereotypes and thus has trivialized the basic structural characteristics of a form that can be serious as well as silly.

Let us look first at the popular sense of *melodrama*. Its nature is suggested by phrases such as these: pursuit and capture, imprisonment and escape, false accusation, cold-blooded villain, innocence beleaguered, virtue triumphant, eternal fidelity, mysterious identity, lovers reconciled, fraudulence revealed, enemies foiled; the whole realm of adventure; the realm of mystery from the supernatural to the whodunit; the realm of vice and crime from horror to detection to reform. It is the world of shock and thrill, of what is regularly called "gripping" and "poignant." But it is rarely devoid of ideas, however flat and hackneyed these may be. In a century and a half its color has been variously revolutionary, democratic, patriotic, antitotalitarian, reformist (anti-gambling, slavery, drinking, dope addiction, etc.). The form is represented with delightful amplitude in an early example, Thomas Morton's *Speed the Plough* (1798), which, along with various popular comic effects, contains upper-class injustice, *nouveau riche* snobbery, poor man's integrity, a lover who almost gives up the poor girl for the rich one, bigamy, economic threats, secret grief, irrational enmity, mysterious identity, old villainy disclosed in a bloodcurdling confessional, a castle fire and a rescue, and garnishings of patriotic sentiment.

When we are still not free from totalitarianism it may seem blasphemous to suggest that Lillian Hellman's *Watch on the Rhine*, an anti-Nazi play of 1941, offers us, even if a little more sophisticatedly, the same fare as *Speed the Plough*. There is a simple villain-hero structure: we have no choice but to hate the Nazi sympathizer and love everyone else, and everyone else is mostly delightful Americans.

Speed the Plough and *Watch on the Rhine* both have the stock devices of entertainment popular in their day. But beneath the standardized appeals there is a basic plot form—the conflict of villains and heroes, of what we nowadays laughingly call good guys and bad guys. Yet such a pattern of action should not be dismissed as the especial property of the simple-minded. For however dull or trite or grotesque the actions of these good and bad competitors may be, the plots are simply a debased popular form of a stable central structure that appears in all times and in trivial and sober plays alike: in this structure, man is pitted against some force outside of himself—a compact enemy, a hostile group, a social pressure, a natural event, an accident, or a coincidence. This is one of the persistent fundamental structures of literature, whether it appear in a silly or meretricious form in a cinema or television thriller or be elaborated with dignity and power in *The Trojan Women* or *Romeo and Juliet*. It draws upon permanent human attitudes, some perilous and some preserving, whether we disavow these when they become ludicrous in a Western or scarcely recognize them in some extraordinary struggle into which we have been drawn by artistic skill—the story of Annapurna, *Nigger of the Narcissus*, *War and Peace*, *Richard III*.

In the structure of melodrama, I suggest, man is essentially "whole"; this key word implies neither greatness nor moral perfection, but rather an absence of the kind of inner conflict that is so significant that it *must* claim our first attention. He is not troubled by motives that would distract him from the conflict outside himself. He may, in fact, be humanly incomplete; but his incompleteness is not the issue. In tragedy, man is divided; in melodrama, he has at least a quasi wholeness against besetting problems. In tragedy, the conflict is within man; in melodrama, it is between men, or between men and things.

We can find virtually "whole" or undivided characters in Ibsen's Dr. Stockmann, fighting community greed, and Lillian Hellman's Kurt Müller, fighting against Nazis. They are created by the same conception of character that appears in popular heroes pitted against cattle rustlers, holdup men, or racketeers. I say this not to disparage but to note the neutral fact of identity of character structure. If we rarely inspect the characters of heroes, we inspect those of victims even less. We find a virtually unified nature in Synge's Maurya, whose family is cut down by the sea; in the Franks, cut down by Nazi malice; in the Duchess of Malfi, cut down by her sadistic brothers. Villains are whole characters too—for instance, Duerrenmatt's citizenry that murders for money, and the Duchess of Malfi's murderous brothers. Even the wretched characters depicted by Gorki and O'Neill have a kind of wholeness: the wholeness of half-beings really cut off from any counterimpulses that would leave them split between retreat and participation. Wholeness, in other words, is a technical structure of character and personality; it is morally neutral; in goodness or badness, strength or weakness, the protagonist is in the main free from divergent impulses.

When we speak of the structure of a form we refer not only to its system of characterization and arrangements of characters but to its dynamics, or, in other terms, the structure of its action. We have seen how the popular thriller and the serious problem play, as we usually call it, are organized alike—on some variation of the villain-hero conflict. The final problem is to see how the drama of disaster also belongs to this pattern. In all these cases we have an essentially undivided protagonist facing an outer conflict. In this kind of situation only several types of outcome are possible—victory, or defeat, or perhaps a stalemate or compromise. Here is the *key* point. Disaster and the popular happy-ending play are not different formal entities but are simply the opposite extremes of the spectrum of melodrama: at one end, man, essentially whole, is beaten down by his antagonist; at the other, also essentially whole, he comes out on top. At the one end, man is victim; at the other, victor. The nature of the conflict is the same, the central structure is the same, but the artist chooses one point of view or another. He may see man vs. nature or political forces or society or other individuals, and he may see him as lost or as triumphant; there are scores of plays doing it one way or the other. The identifying mark of the melodramatic structure is not the particular outcome of the plot, but the conception of character and the alignment of forces. This identity we can always find beneath a considerable diversity of arrangements of action.

Finally, the melodramatic organization of experience has a psychological structure. It puts us into a certain posture which we find agreeable and that within limits has a certain utility. In most general terms, what it affords is the pleasure of experiencing wholeness—not the troubling, uneasy wholeness that exists when all the divergent elements of personality remain within the field of consciousness, or the rare integration of powers that may be earned by long discipline, but the sensation of wholeness that is created when one responds with a single impulse or potential and lets this function as a surrogate for the whole personality. In this quasi wholeness he is freed from the anguish of choice and from the pain of struggling with counterimpulses that inhibit and distort his single direct "action." If there is danger he is courageous; he is not distracted by fear, expediency, or the profit motive. Or he can be serene in adversity, unhampered by self-seeking, by impatience with the frailties of others, or by doubt about ends. Thus Kurt Müller in *Watch on the Rhine* and the stage version of Anne Frank's father: through them, melodrama affords a unity of desirable feeling—of the wisdom to bear troubles, of practical competence against evil. One is untroubled by psychic or physical fumbling, by indecisiveness, by weak muscles or strong counterimperatives. One is under the pleasant yoke of what I will call a monopathy: that single strong feeling that excludes all others and thus renders one whole. It may be a monopathy of hope or, for that matter, a monopathy of hopelessness; a monopathy of contempt for the petty, discontent with destiny, indignation at evil doing, or castigation of the guilt of others. Even in defeat and disaster, in being overwhelmed and victimized, I am convinced, the human being is able to find certain monopathic advantages.

Melodrama, in sum, includes the whole range of conflicts undergone by characters who are presented as undivided or at least without divisions of such magnitude that they *must* be at the dramatic center; hence melodrama includes a range of actions that extend from disaster to success, from defeat to victory, and a range of effects from the strongest conviction of frustration and failure that serious art can dramatize to the most frivolous assurance of triumph that a mass-circulation writer can confect. The issue here is not the reordering of the self, but the reordering of one's relations with others, with the world of people or things; not the knowledge of self, but the maintenance of self, in its assumption of wholeness, until conflicts are won or lost. There is a continuous spectrum of possibilities from the popular play in which the hostile force is always beatable to the drama of disaster in which the hostile force is unbeatable; at one extreme we view man in his strength, at the other, in his weakness. In structure of feeling the form is monopathic.

But the tragic hero is divided; he is in some way split between different forces or motives or values. His nature is dual or even multifold; the different elements are always present and dramatically operative; they are always realities that have to be reckoned with. In structure of feeling we may call tragedy "polypathic." The monopathic concentration may actually make melodrama in some ways more overwhelming, as in *The Duchess of Malfi*, where everything enlarges the sense of ruin; but tragedy, where impulses and options are double and multifold, where we are drawn now this way and now that, exacts a very much more complex and troubling awareness. One example: the spectacle of the aged Lear in the storm is overwhelming, too.

But it cannot inspire simply a monopathic pity, since we do not forget that in a sense Lear has created this storm himself. Profound pity for the victim, yes, but also acknowledgment of the paradoxical presence of justice, and sense of irony—all are present in a disturbing polypathic experience.

In melodrama, man is seen in his strength or in his weakness; in tragedy, in both his strength and his weakness at once. In melodrama, he is victorious or he is defeated; in tragedy, he experiences defeat in victory, or victory in defeat. In melodrama, man is simply guilty or simply innocent; in tragedy, his guilt and his innocence coexist. In melodrama, man's will is broken, or it conquers; in tragedy, it is tempered in the suffering that comes with, or brings about, new knowledge.

The pathological extreme of the tragic condition is schizophrenia—where normal dividedness is magnified into the split that is illness. The pathological extreme of the melodramatic condition is paranoia—in one phase, the sense of a hostile "they" who will make one their victim, and, in another phase, the sense of one's own grandeur and, implicitly, of the downfall of others. Melodrama has affinities with politics; tragedy, with religion. Pragmatic politics appears as a competition for power between good and evil; our side is "good," and the other side, "evil." In the religious view of man is a sense of his dividedness, of the co-presence of counterimpulses always striving for dominance, of the fact that throughout his life he is a dual creature with equal possibilities of coming to salvation or damnation. Melodrama leans toward the timely, tragedy toward the timeless; on the one hand we have the world of protest and problem plays; on the other, the world of meditation and myth.

So much for the efforts to pile up distinctions between two basic sets of habits and attitudes. We have described melodrama as monopathic, presenting man in defeat or victory, in guilt or innocence; as having affiliations with politics and history, drawn to the topics that change with time. We have described tragedy as polypathic, showing man's victory in defeat, his mingling of guilt and innocence; as having affiliations with religion and myth, seeking the constants that transcend change. I have meant to suggest rather than to insist. It would not be helpful to make absolute, unvarying boundary lines; in life and literature, as they exist, there are not many instances of pure types. The literary work or the human personality *leans* in one direction or the other; it rarely *plunges* toward an extreme. But one cannot judge the individual work, or the person's way of confronting reality—one cannot say that here is a melodramatic style with some moments of the tragic or that here is a tragic cast of mind that includes something of the melodramatic—without first distinguishing the theoretical poles of attraction. The test of these theoretical constructions is their helpfulness in identifying actual literary structures or in understanding the strategies of spirit that men devise to face an imperfect world.

Aesthetic of Revolution:
The Marxist Melodrama*

WYLIE SYPHER

The world of Dickens, we agree, is constructed upon a dualism of values that, aesthetically, are the values of melodrama: the good people and the bad, the proud and the humble, the hard and the soft, the simple and the devious, the rich and the poor. Edmund Wilson has remarked that the only complexity of which Dickens appears capable is to make one of his noxious characters wholesome or to turn one of his clowns into a serious person. The mechanism of the Dickens morality is the choice between extreme situations. The mechanism of the Dickens psychology is opposition and conversion—revolution within the psyche.

These Dickensian oppositions and conversions—the revolutionary choice between extremes—are, aesthetically, the mechanics of much of the art and thought of the 19th Century, which reaches its most determinate effects by means of polarities. The extremities of the 19th Century dilemma are inherent in the bourgeois situation. They are recognized by Dostoievsky's underground man, who observes, "Every day I keep discovering in myself elements of the most opposite order conceivable, and can feel them swarming within me." Thus the underground psyche, the psyche in the bourgeois world, behaves by revolutionary exclusions and leaps. Dostoievsky's sickness is, he confesses, his desperate situation between contradictory wills: "The more I have recognized what is good and what constitutes the great and the beautiful, the deeper I have plunged into the mire." This desperation is also the sickness of Baudelaire, who step by step descended to the hell of his own vices. The choice either/or in Kierkegaard or Dostoievsky is an archetypal pattern of 19th Century response. The same mechanism of either/or operates in the spasmodic decisions to which Browning and the

* Wylie Sypher, "Aesthetic of Revolution: The Marxist Melodrama," *The Kenyon Review*, Vol. X, No. 3 (Summer, 1948), pp. 431–444.

Brontës drive their characters, in Schopenhauer's will to power and will to passivity, in Carlyle's heroic codes for master and slave, in Nietzsche's satanic inversion of philistine ideals, and especially in the romantic antithesis of matter and spirit, and the iron laws of science that banished a personal deity from the universe and named God a gaseous vertebrate. The choice offered the Victorians was descent from Adam or descent from ape. The weaker 19th Century minds hovered near compromise. The stronger became revolutionary. The alternatives were too unequivocal to be unified or reconciled within the sensibility. The imagination was pressed away from the neutrality of the world toward overstatement.

The art of Dickens is of the coarser 19th Century texture in which the polarities are animated by picturesque instances that have the vitality of overstatement. The assurance of Macaulay, liberal historian and social critic, overcharges his opinions until they have little relevance beyond their rhetorical effects, their "style." A great deal of the 19th Century has style in this sense, a grossness of manner apparent in Hugo or Browning's imagery (where a tulip is a bubble of blood and a kiss is fresh as dewdrops from a wilding rose) or the brassy equations of Macaulay's prose:

This progress, having continued during many ages, became at length, about the middle of the eighteenth century, portentously rapid, and has proceeded, during the nineteenth, with accelerated velocity. In consequence partly of our geographical and partly of our moral position we have, during several generations, been exempt from evils which have elsewhere impeded the efforts and destroyed the fruits of industry. While every part of the Continent, from Moscow to Lisbon, has been the theatre of bloody and devastating wars, no hostile standard has been seen here but as a trophy. While revolutions have taken place all around us, our government has never once been subverted by violence.

The tension within this prose is the tension of extreme situations that we feel in the rhetoric of Newman, the infamies of Baudelaire, the hysteria of Carlyle, which is more grotesque, or the immoralism of Nietzsche, which is more lyrical. In Dickens the malaise is released by the prose-poem, the blank-verse interludes in the novels; in Browning the pitch is higher but less sustained. In Ruskin the surge of the prose lengthens to enormous tidal periods that lose, eventually, some of their energy in the decorative confusion of Pater's impressions and the loose ripple of Swinburne's metre.

The writers of the 19th Century have an eye for what Gertrude Stein called *the event*. Their narratives, even in the case of "realists" like Zola or George Eliot, culminate with symbolic acts or gestures. We do not forget the well-managed climax such as the putrescence of Nana's white flesh or the drowning of Maggie and Tom in the Floss, just as we do not forget the crises between Astarte and Manfred, Catherine and Heathcliff, Nora and Helmer, Roxane and Cyrano—variations upon the theme of beauty and the beast. Not in the beginning, but in the end, is the act, the gesture. The limit of the 19th Century imagination is the final expressive tableau, a stasis, a consummate act. The most casual arrangements in the painting of Degas and Manet are carefully arrested impressions having the air of rehearsal. The 19th Century drama was not performed within the legitimate theatre, but was diffused—adulterated—into prose fiction, history, philosophy, social criticism, music, and painting, which, in turn, were contaminated by "events." The event is not only drama. It is melodrama, too.

2.

The thesis that melodrama is a characteristic mode of 19th Century thought and art becomes clearer when we attempt to identify contrasting modalities in the 18th and 20th Centuries. Although the 18th Century played its own incidental melodrama, we may say that the characteristic mode of enlightened thought and art was the mental fiction—those abstract and summary concepts erected inside the mind and harmoniously adjusted to each other within the rationalized order of Nature. These mental fictions were the substructure of the distinctive 18th Century performances in every direction: the rights of man, the literary rules, the state of nature, the deistic world order, the coherent Newtonian universe with its fictions of absolute space and absolute time, the perfectibility of mankind, the theoretical codes of the encyclopedists, the generalizations of the heroic couplet, the regularity of the sonata, the balances of Augustan and Georgian architecture, the precise articulations of the formal garden, the nobility of the savage, the simple economic motives of enlightened self-interest. All these modes of the 18th Century mind could enlist the emotions, and often did; yet their substratum was the purely intellectual construct, the beautiful and coherent simplification that was not dramatized because it stood detached, without opposition or polarity, as an absolute assumption or idea, and because it was not animated or mythologized. The 18th Century sensibility moved freely and remotely in the clear atmosphere of the mental fiction.

Also in contrast to the 19th Century melodrama, the authentic 20th Century modality has abandoned the "event" and the theatrical act. We bear with us a sense of the conditional, of interrelationships, that the 19th Century did not. We cannot isolate events. Our interpretation is less personal. We are more scientific and sceptical. For us the universe is denser—a continuum, in fact, without the vacuums and intermissions necessary to distinguish the individual events. Our recognition of complexities is so involved that we cannot with assurance locate an event in its isolated status; we cannot separate it from its antecedents and contexts. Our novels have fewer emphatic moments and are devoted to close interconnections, uninterrupted impressions, multiple approaches. As Whitehead has put it, the whole is part of every event, and every event occurs only within the structure of the whole. Thus an event is for us a hypothetical occasion. Indeed, we have so far abandoned the melodramatic view that we have often withdrawn to impersonal, abstract representation of our perceptions. The disintegrations of cubism suggest our pictorial view. By a determined analysis or "destruction" of the object we reduce it to a study of intimate and manifold relationships, a fragmentation within a continuum of forms until the definition of the "subject" remains equivocal. In narrative the disintegration began as early as Chekhov, and has continued within Proust, Joyce, Stein, and Woolf. Melodrama has become, for us, an inappropriate and incredible modality.

If we may generalize upon the modalities of vision within the different periods: in the Middle Ages there was a modality of correspondences between the seen and the unseen which made available a scheme of parallels, symbols, allegories, and equivalents; in the Renaissance there was a modality of humanism, a view of man as free agent in a material universe adaptable to the liberated will and investigative mind of Leonardo, Machiavelli, Montaigne, Shakespeare, and Milton; in the 18th Century there was a modality of the intellectual fiction, the secular absolute existing as an assumption at some uncertain removal from the actuality it presumably interpreted; in the 20th Century there is a modality of relationships, a sense of the interdependencies within a continuum, pressures of environment and context, and the difficulty of isolating the event or determining its meaning.

3.

And for the 19th Century the modality is melodrama, the oversimplification into polarities and oppositions that may be animated by emphatic instances. To the 19th Century mind the very iron laws of science operate with melodramatic fatalism—the pressure of population against subsistence, the dynamics of supply and demand and the wages fund, the struggle for existence in a nature red in tooth and claw, the unalterable majestic course of matter and force mythologized by Hardy and the biologist Haeckel, the brooding malign policies of Egdon Heath and the awesome tyranny of power in geology and physics, with men and generations of men sealed within the grim and dusty hills of the Mongolian desert.

All this is melodrama, not tragedy; and certainly not science. The view of the world as a diagram of polar forces encourages not only a melodramatic ethics (the strong and the weak, the hard and the soft, the good and the bad) but also emotive history and emotive science, which, as Huxley confidently assumed, can satisfy the spiritual longings of man. Having done with a personal God, the 19th Century could now displace the drama in its mind into the universe itself by means of the laws of geology, biology, energy, and, more immediately, economics. By a confusion of categories the inevitabilities of matter and motion and political economy assume a moral sanction, just as in melodrama chance assumes the tenor of poetic justice, just as the impersonal "naturalism" of Zola and Ibsen always moves toward moral conclusions. The world becomes a theatre of tensions between abstractions. Melodrama has become social, if not cosmic.

The choices of the 19th Century are arbitrarily conceived and arbitrarily offered: the bourgeois or the blond beast, the slave or the master, democracy or aristocracy, the soiled woman or the pure, progress or poverty, free will or necessity, the Virgin or the Dynamo, God or Nature, bureaucracy or laissez-faire, poetry or science, culture or anarchy. The very attempt at "Victorian compromise," and its ineffectiveness—even in John Stuart Mill's scrupulous and tenacious indecisions—indicate how liable the 19th Century sensibility was to shift toward extreme situations, how ready it was to perform a "leap," a psychic revolution. Therefore the aesthetic category of melodrama becomes a modality of the 19th Century mind, which emancipated itself only with difficulty from oversimplified premises, a fatalism theatrically effective, and a displacement of moral responses into the universe. The declamatory language, the violent and symbolic gestures, the animation of polar opposites to the point of caricature are evidence of a psychic crisis. The social art of Forain, for instance, is not tragic or scientific, but given to the emphatic gesture, the picturesque event. Melodrama cannot admit exceptions, for they would immediately involve the action too deeply within the context of actuality and trammel the gesture. The types must behave with a decorum of extremes; the resolution must be vividly schematic. The tensions must concentrate toward a last overwhelming tableau, a final stasis beyond which one must not think. The aesthetic values of melodrama are the values of crisis, the event accepted as consummation. Simply because its situation is so precarious, the 19th Century mind is disposed to revolution—psychic revolution, at least.

According to the materialistic dialectic we should hardly expect that Marxism could wholly liberate itself from the archetypal behavior of 19th Century thought, the fallacy of melodrama, the revolutionary fallacy. To the 19th Century psyche, revolution is consummation. After our "revisions" of the 19th Century modality we now understand that revolution is not drama; that there are only events within revolutions. But these events are not revolutions. Revolution is not consummation.

4.

Theoretically the Hegelian dialectic—thesis, antithesis, and synthesis— is not liable to the melodramatic fallacy of sharp oppositions, choices between polarities, schematic exclusions, sudden flights from the relative to the absolute, from the complex to the simplified. Yet the tensions within bourgeois society represented many romantic choices between extreme situations. Dialectical materialism was an opportunity to check these romantic adventures, modulate the oppositions, and offer new and more discriminating structures to the 19th Century mentality of crisis. Engels, writing upon Feuerbach, said that the world is a complex of processes without final solutions or eternal truths; one must not be imposed upon by the old metaphysical antitheses between true and false, good and bad, necessary and accidental. "One knows that these antitheses have only a relative validity." Philosophically, then, the Marxist dialectic successfully utilizes the Hegelian strategy to penetrate further into the neutral process of reality and to level the melodramatic accents within the theatre of history, where the episodes do not converge upon a climax but extend into a complicated and minute internal relevance.

The mentality of crisis, however, had its effect upon Marx not in the philosophical but in the aesthetic category. A deep paradox within *Capital* is caused by a transposition from philosophic to aesthetic structures. Philosophically the work is not melodrama; aesthetically it is. And the aesthetic transvaluation here proves of the greatest consequence: in spite of the discriminations of his essentially undramatic dialectic Marx has yielded to the almost irresistible aesthetic temptation to prefigure the revolution as drama. This aesthetic transvaluation from dialectic to theatre has unexpected ethical and economic results. The mentality of crisis has always been favorable to poetry and symbolic action. A great deal of 19th Century poetry was written in prose. The Victorian novel has recently been appraised as poetry —*Wuthering Heights*, for example. History by Carlyle is no less poetic, like the philosophy of Nietzsche. In this sense *Capital* is a dramatic poem, or possibly a dramatic epic. Its great economic themes are treated chorally, with all the strophic progress of the ode and the almost rhythmic stress of an ironic injustice committed against the masses. If we are not distracted by the superficial diffusion of the book, its elaborate and energetic logic and its accumulation of evidence, we see that its concealed structure is mythical.

Perhaps *Capital* is archetypal 19th Century melodrama because it is, like the *Manifesto*, directed toward the final revolutionary act. In the bourgeois epoch tensions have converged until class antagonisms are simplified— oversimplified according to the canon of the dialectic itself. The social drama is on that account more rapid, more violent, more schematic than ever. In Kenneth Burke's phrase, the Marxist grammar of motive requires a terminology of action. But the culmination of the class struggle is the revolutionary stasis. The movement of history has been foreshortened toward the scene when the expropriators are expropriated. The dialectic is no longer a philosophic tactic; it is a program and Marx is writing the last episodes. History is no longer process; it is gesture. Archetypal melodrama, erupting into the materialistic dialectic, throws into question the status of the act—the revolution—within the Marxist system. The aesthetic mechanism, the transposition to myth, the theatrical climax have abbreviated the dialectic and may have damaged it irreparably.

Capital foreshortens the historical process by a dramatic structure—the beginning, middle, and end of capitalism. The opening is a juxtaposition of polarities figuratively arranged, a mythical opposition of forces: the free laborer confronting the capitalist. "One thing is clear," notes Marx: "Nature does not produce on the one side owners of money or commodities, and on the other men possessing nothing but their own labor-power. This relation has no natural basis, neither is its social basis one that is common to all historical periods." Only after the extinction of the older forms of social production—the passing of the saturnian economic reign—does the buyer of labor meet the seller of labor in the bourgeois *mise en scène*, the free and open market with its unalterable code of enlightened selfishness, supply and demand, and the sanctions of the acquisitive ego to truck, barter, and exchange. This complication of the economic drama "can only take place under certain circumstances that centre in this, viz., that two very different kinds of commodity-possessors must come face to face and into contact; on the one hand, the owners of money, means of production, means of subsistence, who are eager to increase the sum of values they possess by buying other people's labor-power; on the other hand, free laborers, the sellers of their own labor-power, and therefore the sellers of labor." The historical drama—in contrast to the historical dialectic—opens with this social re-arrangement, a fall into original capitalist sin. "And this one historical condition comprises a world's history." Or rather not the process of world's history but fateful dramatic absolute contradiction into which the dialectic has simplified itself by pressure and counter-pressure.

As the tensions narrow between counter-pressures, the dialectic of history becomes less flexible; the events become decisive. Severe and absolute contradiction determines the approaching reversal. In this conflict the proletarian, not the capitalist, appears to exercise freedom of will, and the relentless, undeviating motive of the exploiter, more histrionically realized than ever before in society, evokes the antagonistic response of the exploited—class-consciousness. There is no "recognition" or "discovery" for the capitalist, only for the worker. This "algebra of revolution" develops through "tendencies working with iron necessity towards inevitable results." As in melodrama, the actors become dehumanized: "here individuals are dealt with only in so far as they are the personifications of economic categories, embodiments of particular class-relations and class-interests." The impulses of the capitalist are rigidly conditioned by the role he has assumed. "The restless never-ending process of profit-making alone is what he aims at. This boundless greed after riches, this passionate chase after exchange-value, is common to the capitalist and the miser; but while the miser is merely the capitalist gone mad, the capitalist is a rational miser." Behavior has become symbolic; the *dramatis personae* react with the decorum of caricature. We have Marx's own annotation that "the characters who appear on the economic stage are but the personifications of the economical relations that exist between them." Melodrama has been superimposed upon the historical process. On the stage of the world "our friend Moneybags" is, for a while, lucky enough to find a class that can be bought and sold.

Clearly the melodrama does not exhaust the dramatic possibilities. Our friend Moneybags belongs in the Marxist social comedy, those Dickensian interludes in *Capital* full of grotesques like "the celebrated sophist and sycophant Edmund Burke" and Jeremy Bentham, "that insipid, pedantic, leather-tongued oracle of the ordinary bourgeois intelligence." There is also the parson Townsend, a lively ominous caricature, who argues, "It seems to be a law of nature that the poor should be to a certain degree improvident that there may always be some to fulfil the most servile, the most sordid, and the most ignoble offices in the community. The stock of human happiness is thereby much increased, whilst the more delicate are not only relieved from drudgery but are left at liberty without interruption to pursue those callings which are suited to their various dispositions." The 19th Century drama is ambiguous. In Dickens cruelty is extended to grotesque comedy. In Goya caricature is extended to savage hatred. In Dostoievsky farce extends to pathos. *Capital* is melodrama, comedy of humors, parody, and satire.

The primitive accumulation of capital having been accomplished and the mythos or action having been arranged, the shock of the class war mounts through a series of crises that are, in effect, a continuation of the Malthusian incident sketched in 1798.

The law, finally, that always equilibrates the relative surplus-population or industrial reserve army, to the extent and energy of accumulation, this law rivets the laborer to capital more firmly than the wedges of Vulcan did Prometheus to the rock. It establishes an accumulation of misery corresponding with accumulation of capital.

Social involvements progress by an intensely emotive dynamics with free play of sarcasm and a dialectic of temperament:

After capital had taken centuries in extending the working day to its normal maximum limit, and then beyond this to the limit of the natural day of 12 hours, there followed on the birth of mechanism and modern industry in the last third of the 18th century a violent encroachment like that of an avalanche in its intensity and extent. All bounds of morals and nature, age and sex, day and night were broken down. Capital celebrated its orgies.

Surely Marx has stood the Hegelian dialectic back on its head again, transforming the world by the demiurgos of his dramatic sense; if the world is not idea, at least the dramatic illusion plays over history. Lately it was argued that the test of a writer's achievement is his ability to transform the world by displacing his imagination far afield until he incorporates into his vision larger and larger areas of experience. If this is so, Marx displaced his imagination farther afield than any social dramatist of the 19th Century. His myth is more comprehensive, more fully realized, more totally displaced than the myths of Hegel, Taine, or Comte.

A unity of action sustains this diffused myth. The capitalist production must be continually and progressively revolutionized to increase the productivity of labor and the amount of surplus value. Thus the lazarus-layer of the proletarian is depressed further toward the condition of misery. Meanwhile, by a fatalism as somber as the system of Hardy's universe, the enormous power of the factories begets a feverish output—then a glut of markets, a crisis, and a sequence of collapses. Presently the theatre widens to include the entire scene of imperialism opening upon colonial perspectives. As the working day lengthens, the conflict over "the last hour" sets in, together with new cycles of production for profit, not for use. The "natural" cycle of exchange—Commodity-Money-Commodity—becomes distorted into the capitalist cycle of exchange for money—Money-Commodity-Money. Simultaneously the absolute general law of capitalist accumulation has been concentrating wealth until, by a dramatic foreshadowing, the expropriation of the exploiters is ironically begun.

This expropriation is accomplished by the action of the immanent laws of capitalistic production itself, by the centralization of capital. One capitalist always kills many.

The drama accomplishes its reversal. With the assurance of poetic justice Marx observes that "capitalist production begets, with the inexorability of a law of Nature, its own negation. It is the negation of negation." Were statistics ever so illuminated in the glaring light of the social theatre as in the mighty chapters on The Working Day and Machinery And Modern Industry, with their strophic declamations? "Capital is dead labor, that vampire-like, only lives by sucking living labor, and lives the more, the more labor it sucks." The outcome of these terrible strains between exploiter and exploited cannot be in doubt. As soon as the capitalist has engaged in the fratricidal policy of killing fellow capitalists and has condemned the masses to a condition of *la misère*, "from that moment new forces and new passions spring up in the bosom of society; but the old social organization fetters them and keeps them down. It must be annihilated; it is annihilated." The revolution is a mythical act; the negation of negation is final justice. "Centralization of the means of production and socialization of labor at last reach a point where they become incompatible with their capitalist integument. This integument is burst asunder. The knell of capitalist private property sounds. The expropriators are expropriated." In the end is the act. Revolution is consummation. As Engels commented, what is essential "is a social *act*." The dialectic has attained its final tableau by dislocating philosophy and history into drama—one of the greatest 19th Century leaps. It is necessary, because of the oversimplification of forces, that melodrama should end with a stasis so conclusive that it appears arbitrary; it is so in the Dickensian novel. It was apparently difficult for Marx to think beyond this final violent expropriation; it has remained difficult to do so because the revolution is theatre, not dialectic. The dialectic has been transvalued to a symbolic act, an apocalypse. The Marxist problem is to pass beyond this theatrical stasis. Lenin's theory of the withering of the state, the lower and higher socialism, is a somewhat ineffective and hasty motion to descend from apocalypse to dialectic, from drama to the process of history. There is, according to Lenin, "no shadow of an attempt on Marx's part to conjure up a Utopia, to make idle guesses about that which cannot be known." The course by which humanity proceeds to the higher communism "we do not and cannot know."

In its origin *Capital* was melodramatic—the undertaking to reverse the contemporary movement toward idealism and to stand the Hegelian system right side up by displacing the Hegelian idea into the actual world. Either system terminates in stasis—in Marx's case the "universal crisis," the revolution to end all revolutions, the consummate revolution within *and without* the psyche. The displacement of the dialectic into the material world was, of course, the achievement to secure for *Capital* a relevance beyond that of other melodramas. The Marxist melodrama is, at the very least, *about something*.

5.

The inclusive and damaging irony is this: melodrama is a notoriously bourgeois aesthetic. Here the dialectic has operated with its least expected fatalism—the Marxist revolution against the bourgeoisie is in itself an alarming symptom of the bourgeois malady.

To define its choices the 20th Century has often looked backward, particularly to Stendhal, Kierkegaard, Nietzsche, Dostoievsky—and Marx. Their definitions were usually made by emphatic instances enlarged to symbolic dimensions in Stendhal's romantic experimental man, Kierkegaard's anxious man, Nietzsche's superman, Dostoievsky's underground man, and Marx's revolutionary man. Our dilemmas can readily be suggested by the polarities and exclusions of melodrama. Yet melodrama, especially in its revolutionary stasis, is an aesthetic fallacy.

Part Eight

THE CLIMATES
OF TRAGEDY

Joseph Wood Krutch
THE TRAGIC FALLACY

Kenneth Burke
ON TRAGEDY

Stanley Edgar Hyman
PSYCHOANALYSIS AND THE CLIMATE OF TRAGEDY

Orrin E. Klapp
TRAGEDY AND THE AMERICAN CLIMATE OF OPINION

The Tragic Fallacy*

JOSEPH WOOD KRUTCH

Through the legacy of their art the great ages have transmitted to us a dim image of their glorious vitality. When we turn the pages of a Sophoclean or a Shakespearean tragedy we participate faintly in the experience which created it and we sometimes presumptuously say that we "understand" the spirit of these works. But the truth is that we see them, even at best and in the moments when our souls expand most nearly to their dimensions, through a glass darkly.

It is so much easier to appreciate than to create that an age too feeble to reach the heights achieved by the members of a preceding one can still see those heights towering above its impotence, and so it is that, when we perceive a Sophocles or a Shakespeare soaring in an air which we can never hope to breathe, we say that we can "appreciate" them. But what we mean is that we are just able to wonder, and we can never hope to participate in the glorious vision of human life out of which they were created—not even to the extent of those humbler persons for whom they were written; for while to us the triumphant voices come from far away and tell of a heroic world which no longer exists, to them they spoke of immediate realities and revealed the inner meaning of events amidst which they still lived.

When the life has entirely gone out of a work of art come down to us from the past, when we read it without any emotional comprehension whatsoever and can no longer even imagine why the people for whom it was intended found it absorbing and satisfying, then, of course, it has ceased to be a work of art at all and has dwindled into one of those deceptive "documents" from which we get a false sense of comprehending through the intellect things which cannot be comprehended at all except by means of a kinship of feeling. And though all works from a past age have begun in this way to fade there are some, like the great Greek or Elizabethan tragedies,

* Joseph Wood Krutch, "The Tragic Fallacy," *The Modern Temper* (Harcourt, Brace and World, 1957), pp. 115–143.

which are still halfway between the work of art and the document. They no longer can have for us the immediacy which they had for those to whom they originally belonged, but they have not yet eluded us entirely. We no longer live in the world which they represent, but we can half imagine it and we can measure the distance which we have moved away. We write no tragedies today, but we can still talk about the tragic spirit of which we would, perhaps, have no conception were it not for the works in question.

An age which could really "appreciate" Shakespeare or Sophocles would have something comparable to put beside them—something like them, not necessarily in form, or spirit, but at least in magnitude—some vision of life which would be, however different, equally ample and passionate. But when we move to put a modern masterpiece beside them, when we seek to compare them with, let us say, a *Ghosts* or a *Weavers*, we shrink as from the impulse to commit some folly and we feel as though we were about to superimpose Bowling Green upon the Great Prairies in order to ascertain which is the larger. The question, we see, is not primarily one of art but of the two worlds which two minds inhabited. No increased powers of expression, no greater gift for words, could have transformed Ibsen into Shakespeare. The materials out of which the latter created his works—his conception of human dignity, his sense of the importance of human passions, his vision of the amplitude of human life—simply did not and could not exist for Ibsen, as they did not and could not exist for his contemporaries. God and Man and Nature had all somehow dwindled in the course of the intervening centuries, not because the realistic creed of modern art led us to seek out mean people, but because this meanness of human life was somehow thrust upon us by the operation of that same process which led to the development of realistic theories of art by which our vision could be justified.

Hence, though we still apply, sometimes, the adjective "tragic" to one or another of those modern works of literature which describe human misery and which end more sadly even than they begin, the term is a misnomer since it is obvious that the works in question have nothing in common with the classical examples of the genre and produce in the reader a sense of depression which is the exact opposite of that elation generated when the spirit of a Shakespeare rises joyously superior to the outward calamities which he recounts and celebrates the greatness of the human spirit whose travail he describes. Tragedies, in that only sense of the word which has any distinctive meaning, are no longer written in either the dramatic or any other form and the fact is not to be accounted for in any merely literary terms. It is not the result of any fashion in literature or of any deliberation to write about human nature or character under different aspects, any more than it is of either any greater sensitiveness of feeling which would make us shrink from the contemplation of the suffering of Medea or Othello or of any greater optimism which would make us more likely to see life in more cheerful terms. It is, on the contrary, the result of one of those enfeeblements of the human spirit not unlike that described in the previous chapter of this essay, and a further illustration of that gradual weakening of man's confidence in his ability to impose upon the phenomenon of life an interpretation acceptable to his desires which is the subject of the whole of the present discussion.

To explain that fact and to make clear how the creation of classical tragedy did consist in the successful effort to impose such a satisfactory interpretation will require, perhaps, the special section which follows, although the truth of the fact that it does impose such an interpretation must be evident to any one who has ever risen from the reading of *Oedipus* or *Lear* with that feeling of exultation which comes when we have been able, by rare good fortune, to enter into its spirit as completely as it is possible for us of a remoter and emotionally enfeebled age to enter it. Meanwhile one anticipatory remark may be ventured. If the plays and the novels of to-day deal with littler people and less mighty emotions it is not because we have become interested in commonplace souls and their unglamorous adventures but because we have come, willy-nilly, to see the soul of man as commonplace and its emotions as mean.

II

Tragedy, said Aristotle, is the "imitation of noble actions," and though it is some twenty-five hundred years since the dictum was uttered there is only one respect in which we are inclined to modify it. To us "imitation" seems a rather naïve word to apply to that process by which observation is turned into art, and we seek one which would define or at least imply the nature of that interposition of the personality of the artist between the object and the beholder which constitutes his function and by means of which he transmits a modified version, rather than a mere imitation, of the thing which he has contemplated.

In the search for this word the estheticians of romanticism invented the term "expression" to describe the artistic purpose to which apparent imitation was subservient. Psychologists, on the other hand, feeling that the artistic process was primarily one by which reality is modified in such a way as to render it more acceptable to the desires of the artist, employed various terms in the effort to describe that distortion which the wish may produce in vision. And though many of the newer critics reject both romanticism and psychology, even they insist upon the fundamental fact that in art we are concerned, not with mere imitation, but with the imposition of some form upon the material which it would not have if it were merely copied as a camera copies.

Tragedy is not, then, as Aristotle said, the *imitation* of noble actions, for, indeed, no one knows what a *noble* action is or whether or not such a thing as nobility exists in nature apart from the mind of man. Certainly the action of Achilles in dragging the dead body of Hector around the walls of Troy and under the eyes of Andromache, who had begged to be allowed to give it decent burial, is not to us a noble action, though it was such to Homer, who made it the subject of a noble passage in a noble poem. Certainly, too, the same action might conceivably be made the subject of a tragedy and the subject of a farce, depending upon the way in which it was treated; so that to say that tragedy is the *imitation* of a *noble* action is to be guilty of assuming, first, that art and photography are the same, and, second, that there may be something inherently noble in an act as distinguished from the motives which prompted it or from the point of view from which it is regarded.

And yet, nevertheless, the idea of nobility is inseparable from the idea of tragedy, which cannot exist without it. If tragedy is not the imitation or even the modified representation of noble actions it is certainly a representation of actions *considered* as noble, and herein lies its essential nature, since no man can conceive it unless he is capable of believing in the greatness and importance of man. Its action is usually, if not always, calamitous, because it is only in calamity that the human spirit has the opportunity to reveal itself triumphant over the outward universe which fails to conquer it; but this calamity in tragedy is only a means to an end and the essential thing which distinguishes real tragedy from those distressing modern works sometimes called by its name is the fact that it is in the former alone that the artist has found himself capable of considering and of making us consider that his people and his actions have that amplitude and importance which make them noble. Tragedy arises then when, as in Periclean Greece or Elizabethan England, a people fully aware of the calamities of life is nevertheless serenely confident of the greatness of man, whose mighty passions and supreme fortitude are revealed when one of these calamities overtakes him.

To those who mistakenly think of it as something gloomy or depressing, who are incapable of recognizing the elation which its celebration of human greatness inspires, and who, therefore, confuse it with things merely miserable or pathetic, it must be a paradox that the happiest, most vigorous, and most confident ages which the world has ever known—the Periclean and the Elizabethan—should be exactly those which created and which most relished the mightiest tragedies; but the paradox is, of course, resolved by the fact that tragedy is essentially an expression, not of despair, but of the triumph over despair and of confidence in the value of human life. If Shakespeare himself ever had that "dark period" which his critics and biographers have imagined for him, it was at least no darkness like that bleak and arid despair which sometimes settles over modern spirits. In the midst of it he created both the elemental grandeur of Othello and the pensive majesty of Hamlet and, holding them up to his contemporaries, he said in the words of his own Miranda, "Oh, rare new world that hath *such* creatures in it."

All works of art which deserve their name have a happy end. This is indeed the thing which constitutes them art and through which they perform their function. Whatever the character of the events, fortunate or unfortunate, which they recount, they so mold or arrange or interpret them that we accept gladly the conclusion which they reach and would not have it otherwise. They may conduct us into the realm of pure fancy where wish and fact are identical and the world is remade exactly after the fashion of the heart's desire or they may yield some greater or less allegiance to fact; but they must always reconcile us in one way or another to the representation which they make and the distinctions between the genres are simply the distinctions between the means by which this reconciliation is effected.

Comedy laughs the minor mishaps of its characters away; drama solves all the difficulties which it allows to arise; and melodrama, separating good from evil by simple lines, distributes its rewards and punishments in accordance with the principles of a naïve justice which satisfies the simple souls of its audience, which are neither philosophical enough to question its primitive ethics nor critical enough to object to the way in which its neat events violate the laws of probability. Tragedy, the greatest and the most difficult of the arts, can adopt none of these methods; and yet it must reach its own happy end in its own way. Though its conclusions must be, by its premise, outwardly calamitous, though it must speak to those who know that the good man is cut off and that the fairest things are the first to perish, yet it must leave them, as *Othello* does, content that this is so. We must be and we are glad that Juliet dies and glad that Lear is turned out into the storm.

Milton set out, he said, to justify the ways of God to man, and his phrase, if it be interpreted broadly enough, may be taken as describing the function of all art, which must, in some way or other, make the life which it seems to represent satisfactory to those who see its reflection in the magic mirror, and it must gratify or at least reconcile the desires of the beholder, not necessarily, as the naïver exponents of Freudian psychology maintain, by gratifying individual and often eccentric wishes, but at least by satisfying the universally human desire to find in the world some justice, some meaning, or, at the very least, some recognizable order. Hence it is that every real tragedy, however tremendous it may be, is an affirmation of faith in life, a declaration that even if God is not in his Heaven, then at least Man is in his world.

We accept gladly the outward defeats which it describes for the sake of the inward victories which it reveals. Juliet died, but not before she had shown how great and resplendent a thing love could be; Othello plunged the dagger into his own breast, but not before he had revealed that greatness of soul which makes his death seem unimportant. Had he died in the instant when he struck the blow, had he perished still believing that the world was as completely black as he saw it before the innocence of Desdemona was revealed to him, then, for him at least, the world would have been merely damnable, but Shakespeare kept him alive long enough to allow him to learn his error and hence to die, not in despair, but in the full acceptance of the tragic reconciliation to life. Perhaps it would be pleasanter if men could believe what the child is taught—that the good are happy and that things turn out as they should—but it is far more important to be able to believe, as Shakespeare did, that however much things in the outward world may go awry, man has, nevertheless, splendors of his own and that, in a word, Love and Honor and Glory are not words but realities.

Thus for the great ages tragedy is not an expression of despair but the means by which they saved themselves from it. It is a profession of faith, and a sort of religion; a way of looking at life by virtue of which it is robbed of its pain. The sturdy soul of the tragic author seizes upon suffering and uses it only as a means by which joy may be wrung out of existence, but it is not to be forgotten that he is enabled to do so only because of his belief in the greatness of human nature and because, though he has lost the child's faith in life, he has not lost his far more important faith in human nature. A tragic writer does not have to believe in God, but he must believe in man.

And if, then, the Tragic Spirit is in reality the product of a religious faith in which, sometimes at least, faith in the greatness of God is replaced by faith in the greatness of man, it serves, of course, to perform the function of religion, to make life tolerable for those who participate in its beneficent illusion. It purges the souls of those who might otherwise despair and it makes endurable the realization that the events of the outward world do not correspond with the desires of the heart, and thus, in its own particular way, it does what all religions do, for it gives a rationality, a meaning, and a justification to the universe. But if it has the strength it has also the weakness of all faiths, since it may—nay, it must—be ultimately lost as reality, encroaching further and further into the realm of imagination, leaves less and less room in which that imagination can build its refuge.

III

It is, indeed, only at a certain stage in the development of the realistic intelligence of a people that the tragic faith can exist. A naïver people may have, as the ancient men of the north had, a body of legends which are essentially tragic, or it may have only (and need only) its happy and childlike mythology which arrives inevitably at its happy end, where the only ones who suffer "deserve" to do so and in which, therefore, life is represented as directly and easily acceptable. A too sophisticated society on the other hand—one which, like ours, has outgrown not merely the simple optimism of the child but also that vigorous, one might almost say adolescent, faith in the nobility of man which marks a Sophocles or a Shakespeare, has neither fairy tales to assure it that all is always right in the end nor tragedies to make it believe that it rises superior in soul to the outward calamities which befall it.

Distrusting its thought, despising its passions, realizing its impotent unimportance in the universe, it can tell itself no stories except those which make it still more acutely aware of its trivial miseries. When its heroes (sad misnomer for the pitiful creatures who people contemporary fiction) are struck down it is not, like Oedipus, by the gods that they are struck but only, like Oswald Alving, by syphilis, for they know that the gods, even if they existed, would not trouble with them, and they cannot attribute to themselves in art an importance in which they do not believe. Their so-called tragedies do not and cannot end with one of those splendid calamities which in Shakespeare seem to reverberate through the universe, because they cannot believe that the universe trembles when their love is, like Romeo's, cut off or when the place where they (small as they are) have gathered up their trivial treasure is, like Othello's sanctuary, defiled. Instead, mean misery piles on mean misery, petty misfortune follows petty misfortune, and despair becomes intolerable because it is no longer even significant or important.

Ibsen once made one of his characters say that he did not read much because he found reading "irrelevant," and the adjective was brilliantly chosen because it held implications even beyond those of which Ibsen was consciously aware. What is it that made the classics irrelevant to him and to us? Is it not just exactly those to him impossible premises which make tragedy what it is, those assumptions that the soul of man is great, that the universe (together with whatever gods may be) concerns itself with him and that he is, in a word, noble? Ibsen turned to village politics for exactly the same reason that his contemporaries and his successors have, each in his own way, sought out some aspect of the common man and his common life—because, that is to say, here was at least something small enough for him to be able to believe.

Bearing this fact in mind, let us compare a modern "tragedy" with one of the great works of a happy age, not in order to judge of their relative technical merits but in order to determine to what extent the former deserves its name by achieving a tragic solution capable of purging the soul or of reconciling the emotions to the life which it pictures. And in order to make the comparison as fruitful as possible let us choose *Hamlet* on the one hand and on the other a play like *Ghosts* which was not only written by perhaps the most powerful as well as the most typical of modern writers but which is, in addition, the one of his works which seems most nearly to escape that triviality which cannot be entirely escaped by any one who feels, as all contemporary minds do, that man is relatively trivial.

In *Hamlet* a prince ("in understanding, how like a god!") has thrust upon him from the unseen world a duty to redress a wrong which concerns not merely him, his mother, and his uncle, but the moral order of the universe. Erasing all trivial fond records from his mind, abandoning at once both his studies and his romance because it has been his good fortune to be called upon to take part in an action of cosmic importance, he plunges (at first) not into action but into thought, weighing the claims which are made upon him and contemplating the grandiose complexities of the universe. And when the time comes at last for him to die he dies, not as a failure, but as a success. Not only has the universe regained the balance which had been upset by what *seemed* the monstrous crime of the guilty pair ("there is nothing either good nor ill but thinking makes it so"), but in the process by which that readjustment is made a mighty mind has been given the opportunity, first to contemplate the magnificent scheme of which it is a part, and then to demonstrate the greatness of its spirit by playing a role in the grand style which it called for. We do not need to despair in *such* a world if it has *such* creatures in it.

Turn now to *Ghosts*—look upon this picture and upon that. A young man has inherited syphilis from his father. Struck by a to him mysterious malady he returns to his northern village, learns the hopeless truth about himself, and persuades his mother to poison him. The incidents prove, perhaps, that pastors should not endeavor to keep a husband and wife together unless they know what they are doing. But what a world is this in which a great writer can deduce nothing more than that from his greatest work and how are we to be purged or reconciled when we see it acted? Not only is the failure utter, but it is trivial and meaningless as well.

Yet the journey from Elsinore to Skien is precisely the journey which the human spirit has made, exchanging in the process princes for invalids and gods for disease. We say, as Ibsen would say, that the problems of Oswald Alving are more "relevant" to our life than the problems of Hamlet, that the play in which he appears is more "real" than the other more glamorous one, but it is exactly because we find it so that we are condemned. We can believe in Oswald but we cannot believe in Hamlet, and a light has gone out in the universe. Shakespeare justifies the ways of God to man, but in Ibsen there is no such happy end and with him tragedy, so called, has become merely an expression of our despair at finding that such justification is no longer possible.

Modern critics have sometimes been puzzled to account for the fact that the concern of ancient tragedy is almost exclusively with kings and courts. They have been tempted to accuse even Aristotle of a certain naïveté in assuming (as he seems to assume) that the "nobility" of which he speaks as necessary to a tragedy implies a nobility of rank as well as of soul, and they have sometimes regretted that Shakespeare did not devote himself more than he did to the serious consideration of those common woes of the common man which subsequent writers have exploited with increasing pertinacity. Yet the tendency to lay the scene of a tragedy at the court of a king is not the result of any arbitrary convention but of the fact that the tragic writers believed easily in greatness just as we believe easily in meanness. To Shakespeare, robes and crowns and jewels are the garments most appropriate to man because they are the fitting outward manifestation of his inward majesty, but to us they seem absurd because the man who bears them has, in our estimation, so pitifully shrunk. We do not write about kings because we do not believe that any man is worthy to be one and we do not write about courts because hovels seem to us to be dwellings more appropriate to the creatures who inhabit them. Any modern attempt to dress characters in robes ends only by making us aware of a comic incongruity and any modern attempt to furnish them with a language resplendent like Shakespeare's ends only in bombast.

True tragedy capable of performing its function and of purging the soul by reconciling man to his woes can exist only by virtue of a certain pathetic fallacy far more inclusive than that to which the name is commonly given. The romantics, feeble descendants of the tragic writers to whom they are linked by their effort to see life and nature in grandiose terms, loved to imagine that the sea or the sky had a way of according itself with their moods, of storming when they stormed and smiling when they smiled. But the tragic spirit sustains itself by an assumption much more far-reaching and no more justified. Man as it sees him lives in a world which he may not dominate but which is always aware of him. Occupying the exact center of a universe which would have no meaning except for him and being so little below the angels that, if he believes in God, he has no hesitation in imagining Him formed as he is formed and crowned with a crown like that which he or one of his fellows wears, he assumes that each of his acts reverberates through the universe. His passions are important to him because he believes them important throughout all time and all space; the very fact that he can sin (no modern can) means that this universe is watching his acts; and though he may perish, a God leans out from infinity to strike him down. And it is exactly because an Ibsen cannot think of man in any such terms as these that his persons have so shrunk and that his "tragedy" has lost that power which real tragedy always has of making that infinitely ambitious creature called man content to accept his misery if only he can be made to feel great enough and important enough. An Oswald is not a Hamlet chiefly because he has lost that tie with the natural and supernatural world which the latter had. No ghost will leave the other world to warn or encourage him, there is no virtue and no vice which he can possibly have which can be really important, and when he dies neither his death nor the manner of it will be, outside the circle of two or three people as unnecessary as himself, any more important than that of a rat behind the arras.

Perhaps we may dub the illusion upon which the tragic spirit is nourished the Tragic, as opposed to the Pathetic, Fallacy, but fallacy though it is, upon its existence depends not merely the writing of tragedy but the existence of that religious feeling of which tragedy is an expression and by means of which a people aware of the dissonances of life manages nevertheless to hear them as harmony. Without it neither man nor his passions can seem great enough or important enough to justify the sufferings which they entail, and literature, expressing the mood of a people, begins to despair where once it had exulted. Like the belief in love and like most of the other mighty illusions by means of which human life has been given a value, the Tragic Fallacy depends ultimately upon the assumption which man so readily makes that something outside his own being, some "spirit not himself"— be it God, Nature, or that still vaguer thing called a Moral Order—joins him in the emphasis which he places upon this or that and confirms him in his feeling that his passions and his opinions are important. When his instinctive faith in that correspondence between the outer and the inner world fades, his grasp upon the faith that sustained him fades also, and Love or Tragedy or what not ceases to be the reality which it was because he is never strong enough in his own insignificant self to stand alone in a universe which snubs him with its indifference.

In both the modern and the ancient worlds tragedy was dead long before writers were aware of the fact. Seneca wrote his frigid melodramas under the impression that he was following in the footsteps of Sophocles, and Dryden probably thought that his *All for Love* was an improvement upon Shakespeare, but in time we awoke to the fact that no amount of rhetorical bombast could conceal the fact that grandeur was not to be counterfeited when the belief in its possibility was dead, and turning from the hero to the common man, we inaugurated the era of realism. For us no choice remains except that between mere rhetoric and the frank consideration of our fellow men, who may be the highest of the anthropoids but who are certainly too far below the angels to imagine either that these angels can concern themselves with them or that they can catch any glimpse of even the soles of angelic feet. We can no longer tell tales of the fall of noble men because we do not believe that noble men exist. The best that we can achieve is pathos and the most that we can do is to feel sorry for ourselves. Man has put off his royal robes and it is only in sceptered pomp that tragedy can come sweeping by.

IV

Nietzsche was the last of the great philosophers to attempt a tragic justification of life. His central and famous dogma—"Life is good *because* it is painful"—sums up in a few words the desperate and almost meaningless paradox to which he was driven in his effort to reduce to rational terms the far more imaginative conception which is everywhere present but everywhere unanalyzed in a Sophocles or a Shakespeare and by means of which they rise triumphant over the manifold miseries of life. But the very fact that Nietzsche could not even attempt to state in any except intellectual terms an attitude which is primarily unintellectual and to which, indeed, intellectual analysis is inevitably fatal, is proof of the distance which he had been carried (by the rationalizing tendencies of the human mind) from the possibility of the tragic solution which he sought; and the confused, half-insane violence of his work will reveal, by the contrast which it affords with the serenity of the tragic writers whom he admired, how great was his failure.

Fundamentally this failure was, moreover, conditioned by exactly the same thing which has conditioned the failure of all modern attempts to achieve what he attempted—by the fact, that is to say, that tragedy must have a hero if it is not to be merely an accusation against, instead of a justification of, the world in which it occurs. Tragedy is, as Aristotle said, an imitation of noble actions, and Nietzsche, for all his enthusiasm for the Greek tragic writers, was palsied by the universally modern incapacity to conceive man as noble. Out of this dilemma, out of his need to find a hero who could give to life as he saw it the only possible justification, was born the idea of the Superman, but the Superman is, after all, only a hypothetical being, destined to become what man actually was in the eyes of the great tragic writers—a creature (as Hamlet said) "how infinite in capacities, in understanding how like a god." Thus Nietzsche lived half in the past through his literary enthusiasms and half in the future through his grandiose dreams, but for all his professed determination to justify existence he was no more able than the rest of us to find the present acceptable. Life, he said in effect, is not a Tragedy now but perhaps it will be when the Ape-man has been transformed into a hero (the Übermensch), and trying to find that sufficient, he went mad.

He failed, as all moderns must fail when they attempt, like him, to embrace the tragic spirit as a religious faith, because the resurgence of that faith is not an intellectual but a vital phenomenon, something not achieved by taking thought but born, on the contrary, out of an instinctive confidence in life which is nearer to the animal's unquestioning allegiance to the scheme of nature than it is to that critical intelligence characteristic of a fully developed humanism. And like other faiths it is not to be recaptured merely by reaching an intellectual conviction that it would be desirable to do so.

Modern psychology has discovered (or at least strongly emphasized) the fact that under certain conditions desire produces belief, and having discovered also that the more primitive a given mentality the more completely are its opinions determined by its wishes, modern psychology has concluded that the best mind is that which most resists the tendency to believe a thing simply because it would be pleasant or advantageous to do so. But justified as this conclusion may be from the intellectual point of view, it fails to take into account the fact that in a universe as badly adapted as this one to human as distinguished from animal needs this ability to will a belief may bestow an enormous vital advantage as it did, for instance, in the case at present under discussion where it made possible for Shakespeare the compensations of a tragic faith completely inaccessible to Nietzsche. Pure intelligence, incapable of being influenced by desire and therefore also incapable of choosing one opinion rather than another simply because the one chosen is the more fruitful or beneficent, is doubtless a relatively perfect instrument for the pursuit of truth, but the question (likely, it would seem, to be answered in the negative) is simply whether or not the spirit of man can endure the literal and inhuman truth.

Certain ages and simple people have conceived of the action which passes upon the stage of the universe as of something in the nature of a Divine Comedy, as something, that is to say, which will reach its end with the words "and they lived happily ever after." Others, less naïve and therefore more aware of those maladjustments whose reality, as least so far as outward events are concerned, they could not escape, have imposed upon it another artistic form and called it a Divine Tragedy, accepting its catastrophe as we accept the catastrophe of an *Othello*, because of its grandeur. But a Tragedy, Divine or otherwise, must, it may again be repeated, have a hero, and from the universe as we see it both the Glory of God and the Glory of Man have departed. Our cosmos may be farcical or it may be pathetic but it has not the dignity of tragedy and we cannot accept it as such.

Yet our need for the consolations of tragedy has not passed with the passing of our ability to conceive it. Indeed, the dissonances which it was tragedy's function to resolve grow more insistent instead of diminishing. Our passions, our disappointments, and our sufferings remain important to us though important to nothing else and they thrust themselves upon us with an urgency which makes it impossible for us to dismiss them as the mere trivialities which, so our intellects tell us, they are. And yet, in the absence of tragic faith or the possibility of achieving it, we have no way in which we may succeed in giving them the dignity which would not only render them tolerable but transform them as they were transformed by the great ages into joys. The death of tragedy is, like the death of love, one of those emotional fatalities as the result of which the human as distinguished from the natural world grows more and more a desert.

Poetry, said Santayana in his famous phrase, is "religion which is no longer believed," but it depends, nevertheless, upon its power to revive in us a sort of temporary or provisional credence and the nearer it can come to producing an illusion of belief the greater is its power as poetry. Once the Tragic Spirit was a living faith and out of it tragedies were written. Today these great expressions of a great faith have declined, not merely into poetry, but into a kind of poetry whose premises are so far from any we can really accept that we can only partially and dimly grasp its meaning.

We read but we do not write tragedies. The tragic solution of the problem of existence, the reconciliation to life by means of the tragic spirit is, that is to say, now only a fiction surviving in art. When that art itself has become, as it probably will, completely meaningless, when we have ceased not only to write but to *read* tragic works, then it will be lost and in all real senses forgotten, since the devolution from Religion to Art to Document will be complete.

On Tragedy*

KENNETH BURKE

Ambitious writers have selected the "death of tragedy" as an instance of science's destructive effect upon the highest poetry. Tragedy, they have observed, was developed out of a sense of theological or metaphysical stability; man was dignified; he had some direct or personal relationship with the forces of the cosmos; his problems were of vast importance in the universal scheme. But the "illusions" of tragedy are slain by the scientific point of view, which leaves us too humiliated for the noble, godlike posturings of tragedy, wherein man shares the "mystic participation" which M. Lévy-Bruhl attributes to the savage: that sense of the universe as being personally with him or against him. Tragedy is ruined, they say, when the "illusion" of man's personal connection with superhuman processes is lost, when he is looked upon as a mere species of animal that happens to inhabit a planet for a certain number of years between its birth and its extinction. This "death of tragedy" (and thus, the death of the very essence of poetry) is manifested already as an inability to write great tragedies—and in time it will even be manifested as an inability to appreciate the great tragedies already written. Such is, in essence, the position of those who hold to a fundamental opposition between poetry and science—and it has been stated with much fervour and fluency by Mr. Krutch in his volume *The Modern Temper*.

Mr. Krutch combines under his concept of tragedy both the tragic drama and the tragic spirit. Once a distinction is made between them, however, the issue may look less discouraging. The death of the tragic drama we should attribute to the crumbling of an ideology, as previously explained. The highly fluctuant nature of our thinking at the present time makes more naturally for the essayistic than the dramatic—and the death of tragedy is a natural corollary of this general situation. The question of "poetic illusions" need not enter.

---

* Kenneth Burke, "On Tragedy," *Counter-statement* (Hermes, 1953), pp. 252–255.

In the matter of the tragic spirit, however, there seems to be no essential abatement at all. For if tragedy is a sense of man's intimate participation in processes beyond himself, we find that science has replaced the older metaphysical structure with an historical structure which gives the individual man ample grounds to feel such participation. What science has taken from us as a personal relationship to the will of Providence, it has regiven as a personal relationship to the slow, unwieldy movements of human society. It is to the greatest credit of Nietzsche that he made this readjustment so thoroughly, turning from the "tragic dignity" of theology to the "tragic dignity" of history, and showing that if there was something "poetic" in the sense of a stable metaphysical structure personally concerned with the fate of man, there can be something equally "poetic" constructed out of the "illusion" or belief now current, the sense of the individual's place in an historical process. In another way the same readjustment was made by Pater in his *Marius the Epicurean*, where the "tragic fallacy" arises from our sense of Marius's close personal relationship to deep alterations in the mentality of peoples. Mr. Krutch himself, had he admitted a distinction between the tragic drama and the tragic spirit, would not have become involved as he does in the task of disproving his own thesis at the close of his book. For having said that tragedy is dead, and that it is dead because the new scientific "truths" have destroyed the tragic "illusions," he ends: "Some small part of the tragic fallacy may be said indeed to be still valid for us, for if we cannot feel ourselves as great as Shakespeare did, if we no longer believe in either our infinite capacities or our importance in the universe, we know at least that we have discovered the trick which has been played upon us and that whatever else we may be we are no longer dupes." He will accept the full responsibilities of this "truth," though the "truth" deprive him of something so edifying, so necessary to the most wholesome human expansiveness, as tragedy: "If death for us and our kind is the inevitable result of our stubbornness, then we can only say, 'So be it.' Ours is a lost cause and there is no place for us in the natural universe, but we are not, for all that, sorry to be human. We should rather die as men than live as animals." He pictures those of his kind watching simpler men who, through having gone less far in their thinking, enjoy certain vital advantages (high among which is "tragic importance"). But though recognizing the advantages that lie with the simple, those of his kind will follow their thoughts even to disaster. Such are Mr. Krutch's obdurate conclusions.

Now, tragedy as a mechanism is based upon a calamitous persistence in one's ways. It is "nobler" when the persistence is due to a moral stability on the part of the hero than when it is due to a mere misunderstanding. What, then, if not the formula for tragedy is this position of Mr. Krutch? He will take a personal stand in relation to a *historic* process (the historic process being in this instance the loss of certain magical or theological or meta-physical "illusions" based upon "non-scientific" systems of causality)—and in this stand he will persist at all hazards. It is good to have a writer display so well the basic machinery for a modern tragedy in a book heralding the death of all tragedy.

Psychoanalysis and the Climate of Tragedy*

STANLEY EDGAR HYMAN

Psychoanalysis and tragedy are not easy matters to discuss from a mere reading knowledge, with no experience either behind the footlights or on the couch. Yet if we take tragedy not as a subdivision of drama but as a larger complex of attitudes and actions found in many literary forms, and psychoanalysis as a cultural rather than a medical phenomenon, specialists have written little enough to our purpose, and the overlap between the two areas has been so inadequately discussed that a critic of literature may perhaps be pardoned for stepping in brashly where theater people and analysts hesitate to tread.

Tragedy as we know it had its first and greatest flowering in fifth-century Athens, in the plays of Aeschylus, Sophocles, and Euripides, and its fullest theoretical formulation in the *Poetics* of Aristotle. The forms of Attic tragedy, as Aristotle half knew from tradition, derived from the sacrificial rites of Dionysus, in which the god in bull or goat form was annually slain, dismembered, and resurrected. The plots of Attic tragedy came principally from Homer, and the bloody stories of incest and murder fit the ritual forms so well because the Homeric tales themselves, as Rhys Carpenter has shown most fully in *Folk Tale, Fiction and Saga in the Homeric Epics*, derive from similar rites far from Mount Olympus. Out of the *agon* or dramatic conflict between the god in human form and his antagonists evolved the ethical concepts of *hamartia* or shortcoming, the tragic flaw; and *hybris* or pride, the imperfect insight into man's true stature in relation to destiny and the gods. These defects motivated the action, and for the spectators, in Aristotle's

---

*Stanley Edgar Hyman, "Psychoanalysis and the Climate of Tragedy," *Partisan Review*, Vol. XXIII, No. 2 (Spring, 1956), pp. 198–214.

formulation, the tragic action aroused pity and terror and symbolically purged them through catharsis. The moral ingredients of tragedy are thus: the flawed protagonist swollen with pride; *peripeteia*, the sudden pitiable and terrifying change in his fortunes; and a cathartic climax that Herbert Weisinger in *Tragedy and the Paradox of the Fortunate Fall*, borrowing the phrase from Isaiah, has called the "small moment," that desperate awaiting of the fateful outcome when all seems in doubt.

Buried in the Old Testament there are tragic dramas, particularly the very Greek story of Saul and his "bloody house" in the books of Samuel, but the later priestly theology has imposed its institutional conception of the sacrificial animal without blemish on the earlier *hybris* stories, and revised such obvious tragedies as Jonah and Job, the former into a curious redemptive comedy that concludes on the parable of the gourd, the latter with an ending that begs all its questions and blandly returns all Job's earthly property twofold. On the basis of a theology where the only sins are disobeying God or worshiping rival gods, and the consequences of those are never in doubt, no agonistic form is possible, and the Judaic tradition has produced nothing like a tragic or dramatic literature.

Building on this tradition, Christianity too seems incompatible with a tragic literature, as Weisinger among others has shown. The great Christian drama of the Passion cannot be tragic because the perfection of Jesus eliminates *hybris* or any shortcoming, neither pity nor terror in Aristotle's sense is possible because of our inability to identify our own flawed human nature with the image of perfect goodness suffering absolute injustice, and the final victory is always certain. Drama with a human protagonist, insofar as it is Christian, cannot be tragic, since the issue has been settled once and for all by the victory of Jesus in His Incarnation, and His Atonement makes all subsequent private atonement unnecessary for the Christian,[1] who needs only some combination of Faith and Grace to participate in the antecedent act. Dante properly recognized this in identifying his great poetic drama as a divine comedy. When tragic possibility is reintroduced in Christian history it is invariably repudiated as heresy: the Manichean belief that the issue has not yet been finally settled, denying Incarnation its victory; or the Pelagian repudiation of Original Sin, obviating divine Atonement.

Nor have the great Oriental faiths produced anything we could properly call tragedy. Since their common sacrificial figure, as William Empson re-

---

[1] I am leaving this statement in as a curiosity. I cannot imagine what came over me when I wrote it, since I know better and knew better then. Actually, Christian orthodoxy insists that Christ's Atonement makes atonement by the Christian necessary, and in fact Christ's Atonement is the event that makes later atonement possible. Christ, in short, is the Christian's representative, not his substitute. My 1956 statement is not far from the Antinomian heresy, that justification by Grace exempts from the moral law. [1963]

minds us in *Some Versions of Pastoral*, is not the Western Dying God, typified by Jesus on the Cross, but an antithetical image of The Sincere Man at One With Nature, typified by the Buddha under the Bo tree, no Passion is possible, and there can be neither struggle nor victory. Lacking our characteristic Western philosophy of change, the great Oriental faiths seem to lock man in a permanent dualism, which does not become resolved in time, but has always been transcended in a higher unity pre-existent in the blinding moment of eternity.

I would submit that the great tragic literature of the modern world has escaped divine comedy by being only nominally Christian, and in fact deeply heretic at key points. Shakespeare may be Christian in *Measure for Measure* and *The Tempest*, but *Lear* and *Macbeth*, *Othello* and *Hamlet* are Christian only in their insistence on the radical imperfectibility of man. They exist in a Manichean and Pelagian universe where the Incarnation has never happened and the Atonement consequently did not occur. In this universe proud man is locked in mortal struggle with the inner forces of evil, and must win through to some private redemption and true-seeing by means of his own suffering, with no otherworldly allies. The great tragic novels like *Karamazov* and *Moby-Dick* are similarly Manichean and Pelagian, with Jesus appearing in person in the first to hear from the Grand Inquisitor the failure of His Incarnation, and Ahab in the second, striking through the mask of the Christian Atonement and finding his own sacrificial atonement, that of a Pelagian man-god, in the consubstantial mystery of immolation with the great whale.

The rise of rationalism, whether in its characteristic eighteenth-century form as mechanical determinism or its characteristic nineteenth-century form as optimistic perfectibility, killed the tragic possibility that had co-existed with Christianity in pagan survival and Christian heresy. Francis Fergusson has defined the tragic rhythm of action in *The Idea of a Theater* as the movement from "Purpose" through "Passion" to "Perception" (acknowledging his debt to Kenneth Burke's "*poiema*," "*pathema*," "*mathema*"). Taking, as Aristotle did, Sophocles' *Oedipus Tyrannus* as the archetypal tragedy, Fergusson has discussed later dramatic literature as the hypertrophy of one or another phase of the tragic rhythm. In his terms, the rationalist world of mechanical determinism would permit no Purpose because we can have no free will or choice, no Passion because suffering becomes meaningless where we "understand" all and forgive all, and no Perception because no increase of self-knowledge could come from the discovery that everything has been externally caused. In the Victorian world of optimistic perfectibility (to return to our earlier terms) *hybris* can be dissipated by a bracing daily cold bath, *peripeteia* waits only on improvements in the social machinery, and what small moment of terror, doubt, or despair could survive the splendid teleological faith that the Heavenly City is at this moment having its building plots laid out on earth?

It is my belief that the writings of Sigmund Freud once again make a tragic view possible for the modern mind. Insofar as psychoanalysis is a branch of clinical psychology aimed at therapy, it is optimistic and meliorative (although Freud, in such statements as "Analysis Terminable and Interminable," was far more pessimistic about the difficulties and ultimate limits of cure in biological "rock-bottom" than the majority of his followers). Insofar as it is a philosophic view of man and a body of speculative insights that can be turned on every area of culture (that is, what Freud called "applied" psychoanalysis), it is gloomy, stoic, and essentially tragic. Its basic recognition is the radical imperfectibility of man, a concept it derives not from the Christian Fall, but from the Darwinian Descent. Freudian man is an imperfectible animal, and, as the biological punishment for having risen in the scale beyond the microorganism, a dying animal. The first protoplasm "had death within easy reach," Freud observes in *Beyond the Pleasure Principle*. For Freud, the aim of human existence is the reclamation of some cropland of ego from the "Zuyder Zee" of id, and the limited victory in this bitter struggle is achieved primarily through the traditional philosophic means of self-knowledge. Man's animal nature is to be controlled and channeled in the least harmful direction possible, not changed or abolished, and cure lies not in extirpating animality but in facing it and living with it.

Human life "is hard to endure," Freud says in *The Future of an Illusion*, but we must learn "to endure with resignation." "If you would endure life," he recommends in "Thoughts for the Times on War and Death," "be prepared for death." In such essays as "An Apology of *Raymond Sebond*" and "That to Philosophie, is to Learn How to Die," Montaigne confronted death as nobly and resolutely as Socrates in Plato's *Phaedo*, but without Socrates' eloquent faith in individual resurrection and the afterlife. Since many of us are not Socratics but skeptics, and our problem to adjust not to the dying animal that will be sloughed off to free some eternal spirit but to the dying animal that becomes putrid meat and nothing else, we might do well to eschew the easy consolations of religion and turn to whatever grimmer satisfactions exist in Freud's stubbornly materialist view. Here we can find not only an Original Sin—the Freudian myth of the expulsion from the Eden of the womb added to the Darwinian myth of the origin of death—in which the modern mind can believe, but some terrestrial hopes for redemption and the good life.

In terms of Greek tragedy, the Oedipus complex is another phrasing of *hybris* (of King Oedipus' own *hybris*, in fact), the child's swollen pride that he is a fitter mate for his mother than the tall stranger. Libido, the blind energy of sexual impulses, is equivalent to the ancient Greek "wild Ate," the daughter of Zeus and Strife, the wrath or madness that seizes the hero and moves him to senseless violence, destruction, or self-destruction. Sublimation is the small moment, the reintroduction of possibility, the birth of art and all human culture out of filth. Sublimation allows St. Francis to create a life of goodness out of an impulse to bestiality, or Bach to compose for an organ that is not the one with which psychoanalysis is preoccupied. Even the curative procedure of analysis itself, the transference, is a scapegoat mechanism, and Freud in his whole life and work is a sacrificial figure, almost a Dying God, even without the benefit of such probably apocryphal anecdotes as the one of Freud dashing out of his office shouting, "Why must I listen to such swinishness!"

If the human condition is ultimately animal, even swinish, man is nevertheless capable of moral action and sometimes of a life of sacrificial good, as Freud himself was. In terms of Ruth Benedict's somewhat oversimple dichotomy between shame cultures and guilt cultures, the Freudian neuroses are our own guilty or introjected equivalents for the public shame of wrongdoing in Attic tragedy, and they motivate an internal symbolic action like the redemptive ritual on the stage. For Freud, the choice is a newer dialectic statement of the old dualism, truly "beyond the pleasure principle": destroy others or turn the destruction inward. The ancient Zoroastrian divinities Ormuzd and Ahriman that Mani brought into Christianity are still locked in mortal combat in Freud's "exquisitely dualistic conception of the instinctive life," now called Eros the life instinct and Thanatos the death instinct. "The death instinct turns into the destructive instinct" when it is directed outward to the external world, Freud writes in "Why War?" and he concludes the grandest of his philosophic works, *Civilization and Its Discontents*, with the extremely moderate hope:

Men have brought their powers of subduing the forces of nature to such a pitch that by using them they could now very easily exterminate one another to the last man. They know this—hence arises a great part of their current unrest, their dejection, their mood of apprehension. And now it may be expected that the other of the two "heavenly forces," eternal Eros, will put forth his strength so as to maintain himself alongside of his equally immortal adversary.

In essence, this prophetic statement, written as long ago as 1929, asks no more than the old horseplayer's reasonable prayer, "Lord, let me break even, I need the money."

If Freud produced a climate of opinion in which tragedy could again flourish, an important group of his followers in this country, the neo-Freudians or "revisionists," have done their best to dispel it as quickly as possible. In half a century of existence, psychoanalysis has raced through the whole religious cycle from revolutionary prophetic truth to smug Sunday sermon, and almost as soon as Freud's philosophy began to have an effect on our culture it was hushed up and denied in his name. The revisionists, principally the late Karen Horney, Erich Fromm, and the late Harry Stack Sullivan, along with a number of others of similar views, have put Freudian psychoanalysis into what Emerson called the "optative mood."

All began by publishing independently, but Horney and Fromm had had some contact in Berlin, where they had been influenced in varying degrees by Wilhelm Reich's "Freudo-Marxist" movement. Horney, who has written most extensively about the causes of her defection, has explained that she could not swallow either the views of feminine psychology Freud published in the *New Introductory Lectures* in 1933, or the death instinct, the former as a woman but the latter as a citizen. "Such an assumption," she writes of the death instinct in *New Ways in Psychoanalysis*, "paralyzes any effort to search in the specific cultural conditions for reasons which make for destructiveness. It must also paralyze efforts to change anything in these conditions. If man is inherently destructive and consequently unhappy, why strive for a better future?" In his more articulate strivings, befitting a social psychologist, Fromm found the gloomy fixities of biological instincts equally incompatible with hopes of improving the human condition by first making over society. Sullivan, from a very different background in clinical psychiatry, primarily with psychotics, came to similar conclusions. All three have influenced one another, first by their publications, later through direct discussion and a kind of uneasy collaboration. Their views and approaches, however, remain different enough so that one can choose to be a Horneyite, a Frommian, or a Sullivanite, and in some cases, like that of Clara Thompson, one can make several of these choices in succession.

The leading neo-Freudians, as well as their shifting followers, appear to be entirely sincere and dedicated psychoanalysts and psychiatrists, convinced by developments in the social sciences or by their own clinical experience that Freud was culture-bound, masculine-biased, cancer-morbid, or for some reason blind to what they can see. The result of their revisions has nevertheless, in my opinion, been not to improve or modernize psychoanalysis, but to abandon its key insights both as a science and as a philosophy. Their effect has been to re-repress whatever distasteful or tragic truths Freud dug out of his own unconscious or his patients', and to convert the familiar device of resistance into revisionist theory.

Freud always believed that "prudish America" would welcome his theories and water them down with equal enthusiasm, and his expectation has not been disappointed. The passion of Americans for constant reassurance that they live in the Garden of Eden (which Horney characteristically refers to as "the greater freedom from dogmatic beliefs which I found in this country") was in evidence as far back as 1912, when Jung wrote Freud from America that he was having great success in overcoming resistance to psychoanalysis by playing down sexuality, and Freud wrote back that he need not boast, since "the more he sacrificed of the hard-won truths of psychoanalysis, the less resistance he would encounter." Even predicting this American bowdlerization, however, Freud could hardly have imagined the extent to which it would be done in his name, in books worshipfully acknowledging his teaching or fulsomely dedicated to his memory. Paradoxically, with the aim of making psychoanalysis more scientific, the neo-Freudians have made it less so: where Freud was descriptive, they are hortatory; where he was the humble therapist, they are faith healers, inspirational preachers, be-glad-you're-neurotic Pollyannas.

The question of whether in fact Horney, Fromm, and Sullivan are Freudians or psychoanalysts at all seems to me of relatively minor importance, and is probably impossible to answer authoritatively anyway. In *The History of the Psychoanalytic Movement* in 1914, Freud reserved the right, as the founder of psychoanalysis, to say what it was and what it was not, but his various statements of the criteria involved shift disconcertingly. In the *History*, he calls the theory of "repression" in the unconscious the pillar on which the edifice rests, "really the most essential part of it," along with the empiric facts of "transference" and "resistance." "Every investigation which recognizes these two facts and makes them the starting-point of its work may call itself psychoanalysis," he writes, "even if it leads to other results than my own." Later in the book he describes the dream as "the shibboleth of psychoanalysis," and a few pages later declares that Jung's approach "no longer has the slightest claim to call itself psychoanalysis," apparently because it discards the sexual nature of the libido and the reality of the Oedipus complex. In other works, Freud makes the infantile sexual etiology of the neuroses the test of psychoanalysis, or remarks "a psychoanalytic, that is, genetic explanation."

If any investigation starting from the mechanisms of the unconscious may call itself psychoanalysis, the theories of Horney, Fromm, and Sullivan are probably psychoanalytic. They certainly recognize the existence of resistance and repression, and Horney even calls the concept of resistance "of paramount value for therapy." On the genesis of the neuroses from infantile sexuality, they are considerably less orthodox, since they recognize early sex frustrations as causative in some cases but insist that factors like "anxiety" or "the current life situation" are more relevant. They use the term "transference," but mean not a repetition of an infantile attachment, Freud's "cure through love," but, with Sullivan, a significant new sort of interpersonal relation, the first break in the patient's chain of "parataxic" distortions; or, with Horney, simply that human relationship of the patient's which is easiest to study, control, and explain to him. "As for the transference, it is altogether a curse," Freud wrote in a bleak letter to Pfister in 1910; it never occurred to him that he could solve the problem by a little Draconian redefinition.

If we take Freud's sexual concepts, so unattractive to Jung's American contacts in 1912, as basic, there is no likelihood of calling Horney, Fromm, and Sullivan Freudian psychoanalysts. I would take these basic concepts to be: *libido*, the volcanic sexual instinct; *id*, the caged beast of the unconscious ("a cauldron of seething excitement," Freud called it in a different metaphor); and the *Oedipus complex*, the destructive rivalry with one parent and attachment to the other. In varying degrees, the revisionists have denied all three or modified them out of recognition. For Horney, the libido concept is harmful nonsense suggesting discouraging limitations to therapy; the id is a "debatable doctrine" (what she keeps of Freud she calls "findings," what she rejects, "doctrines"); and the Oedipus complex does not exist in healthy adults, but is produced accidentally in neurotics, as Adler had suggested earlier, by parental sex-stimulation or parent-fostered anxiety. For Fromm, as for Jung, the sexual libido is simply an assumption "one does not share"; what Freud called id is largely eradicable drives produced by the culture; and the Oedipus complex is, Fromm agrees, the central phenomenon of psychology and the nucleus of all neuroses, but it is not a nasty sexual attraction to one parent and a murderous rivalry with the other, but merely a normal and healthy struggle against parental authority in the quest for freedom and independence. For Sullivan, sexual difficulties tend to be symptoms rather than causes, so that libido and id simply do not exist, and a variety of interesting interpersonal attachments take the place of the Oedipus complex.

The neo-Freudians insist on the importance of sociology and anthropology for knowledge of the ways in which the culture determines personality and character, or at least limits their possibilities. A good deal of their sociology, however, seems to be about as profound as Fromm's ingenious formulation "the most backward class, the lower middle class," and their anthropology is typified by Thompson's statement that Benedict has shown in the Kwakiutl or the Dobu "a whole society of psychically crippled and unproductive people," and that certain primitive cultures seem to be "predominantly destructive of man's best interests." If Fromm has read more modern anthropology than Freud, he has apparently been less affected by it, and cultural relativism has not laid a glove on him. In *The Sane Society*, Fromm equates all ethics with "Greco-Judaeo-Christian" ethics, a moral absolute, and remarks casually, "natural ethics, the Decalogue," with the engaging footnote: "Minus the first commandment, which bears on man's destiny and not on ethics."

The opportunity, vastly greater than Freud's, that the neo-Freudians have for acquiring some accurate information about the nature of man in society seems to have resulted only in cheerier illusions. Malinowski in *Sex and Repression in Savage Society* would appear to have confirmed the universality of the Oedipus complex by finding among his matriarchal Trobrianders an equivalent, the male child's rivalry with the culture's father surrogate, the mother's brother. The neo-Freudians have taken it instead to show that, in Horney's words, "the generation of such a complex depends on a whole set of factors operating in family life"; in other words, that all such unwholesome manifestations are socially produced and could be eliminated by social change. If Freud generalized a universal human psyche from an early practice consisting largely of neurotic Jewish middle-class women in turn-of-the-century Vienna, a reading of *The Golden Bough*, and his own self-analysis, all we can say is that the ingredients of that curious stew simmered down to more wisdom than all the resources of American industriousness have brought the neo-Freudians. Socrates sitting on a stone in the market place still knows more about the world than Alexander conquering it.

Ultimately, the differences of Horney, Fromm, and Sullivan with Freud reduce themselves to a contrasting view of human nature, to philosophic disagreement. The revisionists see man as fundamentally good, innocent, and unfallen; thus they inevitably have a different conception of human drives, relationships, and the aims of therapy. In Horney's view of the child frustration, sibling rivalry, the Oedipus complex, and similar factors are not ultimately determining; the important matters are "such parental attitudes as having real interest in a child, real respect for it, giving it real warmth," and "such qualities as reliability and sincerity." As for adults:

It is so much easier for a woman to think that she is nasty to her husband because, unfortunately, she was born without a penis and envies him for having one than to think, for instance, that she has developed an attitude of righteousness and infallibility which makes it impossible to tolerate any questioning or disagreement. It is so much easier for a patient to think that nature has given her an unfair deal than to realize that she actually makes excessive demands on the environment and is furious whenever they are not complied with.

Horney cannot countenance the Freudian view because it would allow "no liking or disliking of people, no sympathy, no generosity, no feeling of justice, no devotion to a cause, which is not in the last analysis essentially determined by libidinal or destructive drives."

The aim of therapy is not Freud's modest relief from neurotic difficulties, but "true happiness," to which most patients, she says, had never even dared aspire. "The enjoyment of happiness is a faculty to be acquired from within," she adds, and the end of analysis for the patient is "to give him the courage to be himself," or in another formulation, "by rendering a person free from inner bondages make him free for the development of his best potentialities." Horney never doubts that when the patient has the courage to be himself it will be a good self, or that he has best potentialities to develop, because she shares Rousseau's faith that "the spontaneous individual self" is born free and good but is everywhere in environmental chains. Beneath everything there is some sort of ultimate, absolute "genuineness" in the personality, and it is this that gives her her faith, against Freud's "disbelief in human goodness and human growth," that "man has the capacity as well as the desires to develop his potentialities and become a decent human being."

Fromm charges that Freud may have been inspired in his theorizing by "an unsolved problem in the relationship to his own mother," but nothing in Fromm's background has given him cause to doubt "the unconditioned love of the mother for her children *because they are her children*." The slogan of his "humanistic psychoanalysis" is "productive love," which enriches both parties and surpasseth understanding. Fromm's first book, *Escape From Freedom*, carries as its epigraph the unlovely Talmudic saying, "If I am not for myself, who will be for me?" His second book, inevitably entitled *Man for Himself*, explains how he got his key term ("Genuine love is rooted in productiveness and may properly be called, therefore, 'productive love' "). Since only a person genuinely capable of loving himself is capable of loving others, self-interest is a social good, as it was for Bernard Mandeville and Adam Smith. Fromm writes:

The failure of modern culture lies not in its principle of individualism, not in the idea that moral virtue is the same as the pursuit of self-interest, but in the deterioration of the meaning of self-interest; not in the fact that people are *too much concerned with their self-interest*, but that they are *not concerned enough with the interest of their real self; not in the fact that they are too selfish, but that they do not love themselves.*

Even the superego in *The Sane Society* is loving and productive, "a voice which tells us to do our duty, and a voice which tells us to love and to forgive—others as well as ourselves."

The aim of therapy is naturally to free this true self for its true productive loving self-interest. "Mental health is characterized by the ability to love and to create," he writes, and "creation" as an ideal is defined rather broadly: "an ever-increasing number of people paint, do gardening, build their own boats or houses, indulge in any number of 'do it yourself' activities." As for the nature of man, "we look upon human nature as essentially historically conditioned," and Freud's Manichean dualism becomes the Christian certainty of victory for God's Party: "the forward-going life instinct is stronger and increases in relative strength the more it grows." We know that our redeemers live, even if they are only people in the French

Communities of Work with "a resilient spirit of good will," "people who have said 'yes' to life"; not yet the truly "awakened ones" like "Ikhnaton, Moses, Kung Futse, Lao-tse, Buddha, Jesaja, Socrates, Jesus."

Sullivan's underlying philosophy seems essentially similar, although its expression is a good deal more rugged and considerably less inspirational. In *Conceptions of Modern Psychiatry*, Sullivan defines love as a "state of affectional rapport," which has "great adaptive possibilities" and produces "a great increase in the consensual validation of symbols." In *The Interpersonal Theory of Psychiatry*, he redefines it in even clammier terms:

Intimacy is that type of situation involving two people which permits validations of all components of personal worth. Validation of personal worth requires a type of relationship which I call collaboration, by which I mean clearly formulated adjustments of one's behavior to the expressed needs of the other person in the pursuit of increasingly identical—that is, more and more nearly mutual satisfactions, and the maintenance of increasingly similar security operations.

For Sullivan, perhaps because so much of his clinical experience was with psychotics rather than neurotics, the aim of therapy is less ambitious: better interpersonal relations, better communication, and a positive direction toward goals of collaboration and of mutual satisfaction and security. He is less impressed by the miraculous "unique individual self" that will flower than Horney and Fromm, and his vision of the nature of man is not so much Rousseau's uncorrupted innocent as a neutral network of interpersonal relations, as capable of good, bad, or indifferent functioning as a telephone switchboard. How far it is from a tragic vision we can see in such comments as: "When difficulties in the sex life are presented by a patient as his reason for needing psychiatric help . . . the patient's difficulty in living is best manifested by his very choice of this as his peculiar problem."

Other neo-Freudians show similar optimism. Franz Alexander, the head of the Chicago Psychoanalytic Institute, sponsors a shorter and more directed therapy, in line with his idea that the therapist is not dealing with the stubborn sexual libido, but with three basic human tendencies he has named: to receive or take, to retain, and to give or eliminate. Clara Thompson believes with Fromm in "creative productive love," as a consequence of which she sees the aim of therapy as "calm self-possession," the patient "free to develop his powers." Like Horney, Fromm, and Sullivan, she simply cannot believe in the existence of evil. Surely a child "in a perfectly benign environment" would not show "serious destructiveness," and any child warped by bad parents can be readily redeemed "if a teacher, a Boy Scout leader or some other hero of childhood presents a consistently different attitude." Bruno Bettelheim, the principal of the Orthogenic School at the University of Chicago, calls on psychoanalysis to emphasize "positive hu-

man emotions and motivations," and to interpret behavior in terms of
"inner freedom and human autonomy" and "man's inherent dignity." Beyond these, there are Fay B. Karpf's "Dynamic Relationship Therapy," and
what Patrick Mullahy, a Sullivanite trained in philosophy, describes as "the
sense of adequacy, competence, and power which comes from self-respect
and respect for others—a rational feeling of power." An inch or two further,
and we are lying down in green pastures beside Norman Vincent Peale.

The question is not what degree of therapeutic success these doctrines
give, since the evidence suggests that any internally consistent system of
interpretation accepted by the patient, from shamanism to the miraculous
grottos of Zurich, can cure,[2] but rather what happens to literature in a culture that has shaped them and is in turn somewhat shaped by them. If
tragedy requires Freud's stoic winning through to the perception of harsh
truth, and all the influence of our psychology goes directly against it, then
perhaps we should be content with comedy or even farce. Unfortunately, the
neo-Freudian doctrines could as readily be shown, I think, to be uncongenial
to art of any sort. Comedy and farce, like dreams, are the disguised fulfillment of repressed wishes. As the dream is organized in reaction to the commanding injunctions of the superego, so the comic arts get their structuring
from a similar ethical conflict, the opposition of accepted what-ought-to-be
to what-is. In the cultural determinism of the interpersonalists, where whatever happens is no individual's fault, comedy is as impossible as tragedy.

Lionel Trilling, who has been uniquely distinguished among modern
literary critics by his defense of Freudian orthodoxy against vulgarization
and revision,[3] has remarked that one of the greatest contributions of psychoanalysis to literature is its image of the mind as a kind of poetry-making
machine, so that it constitutes almost a science of tropes. Insofar as literary
or artistic form and dream form are the products of similar devices, and
operations analogous to condensation, displacement, and the rest shape the
poem, Freud has given us one of the great critical tools for literary analysis.
Where the revisionists deny genetic and dynamic factors and insist on "the
current life situation," here, as on so many occasions, they repudiate insight
and hobble art. Burke has written in *The Philosophy of Literary Form* that

---

[2] In *New Statesman* for January 7, 1956, Dr. H. J. Eysenck of the University of London
printed some disconcerting figures on psychoanalytic cure, based on a review of the
published material. Of neurotic patients treated by means of any kind of psychotherapy,
approximately two out of three recover. Of neurotics who receive no therapy whatsoever, approximately two out of three recover. In other words, two out of three is apparently the percentage of spontaneous recovery. Since then, none of the letters in *New
Statesman* taking issue with Dr. Eysenck's conclusions has challenged these figures.

[3] Since this was written, Trilling has published his 1955 Freud Anniversary Lecture,
Freud and the Crisis of Our Culture, with its bold and brilliant vision of Freud's biological
limitation as a sanctuary against the omnipotent tyranny of culture.

the poem consists of three aspects: dream, prayer, and chart. The neo-Freudian poem has for its dream, The validation of all components of personal worth; for its prayer, Help me to stop making excessive demands on the environment; for its chart, To thine own self-interest be true.

Perhaps a good measure of the fault lies in our country itself. In a paper, "Freud in America: Some Observations," read at the 1954 meeting of the American Psychological Association, Joseph Adelson discussed the resistance to Freud in terms of the deeply entrenched American idea of "the indefinite perfectibility of man" that Toqueville noted as early as 1835. Adelson writes:

American feeling is animated by a zest for freedom; it cries out against constraint. While men may vary in what they achieve, their destinies are open and infinite. We may fall into error or failure, yet we do so, not because of an inner taint, but through circumstance; and circumstance, the American feels, can be rectified. Original sin, even in its most secular versions, has not attracted our thought. In changing the external, in modifying situations, men, we feel, can make and re-make themselves. It is in the idea of man's perfectibility and in the vision of a tractable world that Americans find their way to life's meaning. Throughout its history American feeling has struggled against the concept of limitation and has been held by the attitudes of hope and optimismm.

Adelson summarizes Freud's contrary vision of human life, and adds:

The American mood is substantially different. We experiment enthusiastically, trying this and that, all of our efforts informed by a vigorous faith in the endless plasticity of the human organism. It is my impression that we tend to disregard the dark and archaic components of the personality; at the very least we deprive them, rhetorically, of their vigor. Think of how Freud expressed the intensity of the instincts or of the superego—"oceanic," "surging," "raging." American psychology uses much blander adjectives. We tend to emphasize the ego's resources, its ability, somehow, to drive its way to health. In fact, the systems of Rogers, Horney, and Sullivan have in common the explicit assumption that the organism autonomously moves forward to growth. We incline to see the therapeutic task, then, as involving the strengthening of ego capacities. A friend of mine puts it this way: "We don't try to kill the weeds; we feed the clover and hope that *it* will kill the weeds."

If Freud, *in conjunction with* other intellectual and social forces, succeeded in denting this Emersonian optimism in the period between the two world wars, many of his most articulate followers have since labored to hammer it back into shape. No one can say that any given work of art is affected by any given body of ideas, but we must assume in general that ideas have consequences. It is instructive to note how many important contemporary writers have followed their earlier tragic work with later mellowings. Hemingway is a classic example. Where *The Sun Also Rises* and *A Farewell to Arms*, if not masterpieces, are authentically tragic, moving from Purpose through Passion to Perception; such later novels as *For Whom the Bell Tolls* and *Across the River and Into the Trees* are merely bathetic; and if Robert Jordan or Colonel Cantwell commits *hybris*, the author seems no longer aware of it. Where "The Undefeated" was a truly cathartic work of art, its recent rewriting as *The Old Man and the Sea* is almost a Frommian parody ("If I am not for myself, who will be for me?"). Faulkner has moved similarly from a fiction of ritual tragedy in *The Sound and the Fury* and *Light in August* to optimistic comedy or fairy tale, as have Steinbeck, Caldwell, and so many others. Such dissimilar poets as Frost and Eliot traveled the same route from earlier bleak stoicism to such later chatty affirmations as *A Masque of Mercy* and *The Confidential Clerk*. If on the whole our poets have been less affected than the novelists by the retreat from tragic insight, it is perhaps only that not many of them were ever there to begin with.

We would all enthusiastically welcome the psychoanalytic good society, where every psyche was well and whole, and no one had impulses that could not or should not be gratified. To the extent that a good part of our literature depends on our being deeply and irremediably sick, renouncing it would be a small price to pay for general psychic health, just as Hegel was prepared to slough off art as an inferior form of communion when the stage of perfect communion was realized. Even within our limited experience at present, we can see how much our great literature depends on and is informed by the patterns of neurosis in our culture. To an unacculturated Cheyenne, King Lear would be simply an old man behaving very badly; to those gentle socialists the Mountain Arapesh, the whole disordered story of ungrateful children and rival claims to power and property would be meaningless. In real life, we are sure, Mr. and Mrs. Othello have no problem that a good marriage counselor couldn't clear up in ten minutes, and any of our clinics would give Iago some useful job around the grounds allowing him to work off his aggressions in some socially approved fashion.

Unfortunately, Mr. and Mrs. Othello do not exist in real life but in art, where their deadly misunderstanding is essential to our own well-being, and Iago is permanently out of the therapist's clutches. The psychoanalytic good society seems no nearer of achievement now than it did in Vienna in 1900, and to many of us it seems further off. Meanwhile all the Cheyenne are acculturated and apt to behave almost as badly as Lear, given similar provocation. If the Mountain Arapesh have not yet learned the joys of private property and early toilet training from our movies, they soon will, and one day they will all wear thin bow ties and know what bites sharper than the serpent's tooth. The trouble with the revisionist Freudians is not that they would give up art for the psychoanalytic good society, but that they pretend that it is already here, that we are well when we are in fact desperately ill, and they drive out art when it is almost the only honest doctor who will tell us the truth.

If Freud showed us that human life was nasty, brutish, and short, and had always been, he was only holding the mirror up to our own faces, saying what the great philosophers and the great tragic writers have always said. If we are serious, our reaction to this bitter truth is neither to evade it with one or another anodyne, nor to kill ourselves, but to set out humbly through the great tragic rhythm of pride and fall, so curiously alike in psychoanalysis and literature. At the end of this hard road we can see faintly beckoning that self-knowledge without which, we are assured on good authority, we live as meanly as the ants.

Tragedy and the American Climate of Opinion[*]

ORRIN E. KLAPP

> *America has always taken tragedy lightly. Too busy to stop the activity of their twenty-million-horse-power society, Americans ignore tragic motives that would have overshadowed the Middle Ages; and the world learns to regard assassination as a form of hysteria, and death as a neurosis, to be treated by a rest-cure. Three hideous political murders, that would have fattened the Eumenides with horror, have thrown scarcely a shadow on the White House.*—HENRY ADAMS

I

It has sometimes been remarked that Americans have a kind of armor against tragic experience. Courage, optimism, realism, the Pollyanna spirit —what should it be called? "Somehow missing from this land of plenty," says Norbert Wiener, is an awareness that "the world is not a pleasant little nest made for our protection, but a vast and largely hostile environment, in which we can achieve great things only by defying the gods; and that this defiance inevitably brings its own punishment."[1] We have our share of troubles, to be sure, but without the conviction that trouble is permanent and necessary; rather, it is an exceptional phenomenon that we must be good sports to face when it comes and work hard to eliminate as soon as possible. A poll would easily show that most Americans think of tragedy simply as fortuitous. Other typical attitudes support this general view: we should accentuate the positive and not dwell on the gloomy side, religion should make us happy,[2] stories should come out all right in the end. We are not, then (as Edith Hamilton said of the Greeks and Miguel Unamuno of the Spanish), a tragic people.

---

[1] *The Human Use of Human Beings* (New York: Houghton Mifflin, 1954), pp. 183–184.

[2] Paul Hutchinson, for instance, deplores the "cult of reassurance" that has so largely taken the place of the tragic conception of Christianity, in "Have We a 'New' Religion?,"

[*] Orrin E. Klapp, "Tragedy and the American Climate of Opinion," *Centennial Review of Arts and Sciences*, II (Fall, 1958), pp. 396–413.

Probably this is why, though such plays are part of our cultural inheritance, they cannot be said to have much popular appeal. You could watch movies and television continuously for a month and not see a single example of tragedy, properly speaking.[3] One student of the mass mind, Leo Gurko, claims, however, that the success now and then of movies like *Hamlet* or Broadway plays like *A Streetcar Named Desire* is proof of a hunger for mature art in the general public.[4] I would like to believe it but would be more convinced by his argument if the evidence of demand were clearer in the popular media. How many movie stars may be called tragedians?

The lack of tragedy in America is the more curious when we consider that it is a *pleasure* we are missing. Those who may claim to understand it say that it is one of the keenest joys of the spirit to see a man plunge into a course of suffering from which he does not choose to escape. Edith Hamilton, indeed, states the paradox that "the greater the suffering, the more terrible the events, the more intense our pleasure." This joy has been described by Joseph Wood Krutch as an *elation* based on confidence in the greatness of man, from having watched him pass through mighty passions with supreme fortitude; and by Shelley as an exalted *calm* in which there is neither censure nor hatred but only knowledge and self-respect. If calm and elation are the products of tragedy, then why does it not rank with tranquillizing pills as a commodity on the American market? The same needs that favored the vogue of "peace of mind" books should make it a popular art form. It should be on a par with westerns and musical comedies. It should sell soap on the radio theatre. It should play a prominent part in American religion. But it clearly does none of these things. The explanation must be that the needs served by tragedy are different from those served by comfort; that the words like joy, calm, and elation are perhaps inadequate to convey to our minds what tragic satisfaction consists of—that the difficulty is semantic and ultimately cultural. We simply do not have a culture in which tragedy makes much sense.

Two main questions, then, emerge. First, what difference does it make, after all, whether or not Americans understand tragedy? The other requires an explanation: what are the elements of culture, or, as Kurt Lewin calls it, social climate, that stand in the way of the proper appreciation of this kind of art and its hero?

Life, April 11, 1955, pp. 138 ff. See also Reinhold Niebuhr, *Beyond Tragedy* (New York: Charles Scribner's Sons, 1955).

[3] American movies, say Martha Wolftenstein and Nathan Leites, are shallow emotionally, however many great lovers and gunmen stalk the stage. Love is easily transferred and does not commit one to tragic consequences; crises take the form of external, not inner, conflict, in which winning is all-important and suffering is "pointless and unnecessary,"—*Movies, A Psychological Study* (Glencoe, Illinois: Free Press, 1950), pp. 94–99, 295–301.

[4] Leo Gurko, *Heroes, Highbrows and the Popular Mind* (Indianapolis: Bobbs-Merrill, 1953), pp. 198, 302–304.

II

As to whether it makes any difference, there is an impressive number of thinkers like C. E. M. Joad, Reinhold Niebuhr, Paul Hutchinson, and J. W. Krutch, to name a few, who are concerned about the moral implications of the lack of tragedy. They see an impoverishment of spirit inherent in the inability to see positive value in tragedy and its hero. Their concern, it need hardly be said, is not whether Americans will lose a pleasure, but whether they will sacrifice the hard-won maturity, wisdom, and religious understanding that seem somehow connected with the fate of the tragic hero. There is a political issue, too, best shown in novels like Huxley's *Brave New World* and Orwell's *Nineteen Eighty-Four;* that is, what kind of relation of man-to-man and state-to-man is implicit in an attitude lacking the tragic sense. Since tragedy is at the same time a check on pride and a testimony of human dignity, we may be fearful that without this perspective, leaders may act with too much assurance that they are right and with too little respect for the individuals under them.

It is to the underlying cultural and semantic problem, however, that I wish to give most attention here—to find out more about how and why the tragic hero is *misunderstood* in America. At the center of the problem, it seems to me, is the fact that the average American does not get the happiness—the sense of triumph, affirmation, and understanding—that experts say he should out of this kind of experience. So we may judge that he misinterprets it. And by looking at American culture and studying the reactions of audiences we may hope to see what it is that stands in the way of adequate understanding. My thesis is that there are three main reasons: (1) a stock of cultural images (social types) that displace or inhibit tragic perception; (2) an unfavorable climate of opinion and belief; and (3) an actual shrinkage that has occurred in the stature of the heroes being presented, making it easier to fail to see them as having the dignity necessary to be tragic.

On the score of competing cultural images, let us first look at some of the conceptions, the popular types, that stand in the way of tragic understanding. Because of their partial resemblance to the tragic figure, they may easily be assigned to any man who gets himself into serious trouble, and thus prevent people from seeing him in what may be called a deeper way. And because they are themselves appealing, they are interesting enough to steal the show from the tragic hero. One of these competing types is the *victim*, the sufferer of a disaster or wrong. While he gets plenty of sympathy, he is too innocent to be tragic: he lacks willful fault and inner conflict; he has not brought the trouble on himself; and so we feel only a melodramatic conflict between him and the villains or forces that have harmed him. The *soap opera heroine* suffers also, to be sure; but she also is melodramatic, rather like the victim, basically good, for whom in this case things work out well in the end. These features disqualify her as a tragic heroine. The *martyr*, too, suffers, but his is a willing and knowing sacrifice for a noble cause; he, too, is a melodramatic hero in conflict with villains; and on both counts he is too good, too "perfect," to be tragic. (On this reasoning, the death of Jesus is not a tragedy, strictly speaking,[5] nor is that of Joan of Arc, Nathan Hale, or any other noble soul who dies for a cause. They are simply too good in their crucial acts; they have not the flaws you find in an Othello, a Macbeth.) The *villain* suffers also; but he is not tragic because we are glad of what he gets, more or less; he is too bad to deserve much sympathy. When newspapers report that gangsters shoot one another, we are likely to say, not "tragic" but "so much the better." Yet many a man whom we write off as a villain might have been tragic if we had looked at him a little more closely. Still another figure competing with the tragic hero is the *daredevil*, who courts death and sometimes provides a morbid thrill at the curve of the racetrack. His smash-up is akin to disaster if it affects the audience, or to folly if the actor kills only himself. In the latter case, he is a fool, at a far pole from the tragic hero. Then there is the pathological *case*, a person who comes to ruin because of sickness or insanity. However horrible such an end may be, it has nothing of the essentially tragic, because, for one thing, it is not voluntary, and if we sympathize at all, it is as with a victim. Besides, if we see such a man as a crackpot or other kind of mental deviant, his abnormality works against tragic compassion; instead of sympathizing, more than likely we will be repelled. Finally, among all the other types competing with the tragic figure for popular interest and understanding must be mentioned the outright *fool*, who gets himself into absurd or disgraceful trouble; he suffers, to be sure, but usually receives more laughter than sympathy.[6]

With such a repertory of distracting types, it is small wonder that when a real tragic figure appears he is misunderstood. It is so easy to think of him in terms of these other types! How many times, for instance, has Hamlet been called a dreamer who couldn't make up his mind?—or psychoanalyzed to the point that he became a "case," and his tragic dignity disappeared into an Oedipus complex? Madame Bovary is strictly a tragic character, but

---

[5] "Jesus is, superficially considered, a tragic figure; yet not really so. Christianity is a religion which transcends tragedy. Tears, with death, are swallowed up in victory. The cross is not tragic but the resolution of tragedy. . . . Christianity's view of history is tragic insofar as it recognizes evil as an inevitable concomitant of even the highest spiritual enterprises. It is beyond tragedy insofar as it does not regard evil as inherent in existence itself but as finally under the dominion of a good God."—Reinhold Niebuhr, *Beyond Tragedy* (New York: Charles Scribner's Sons, 1937, 1955), pp. 155, x–xi.

[6] Viewed in terms of his social status, he is a ridiculed figure. See my "The Fool as a Social Type," *American Journal of Sociology*, LV (1949), 157–162; also Enid Welsford's excellent study, *The Fool, His Social and Literary History* (London, 1935).

many of us are tempted to classify her as either a very foolish or a very bad woman. Or, in the case of someone like Othello, we may lay all the blame on a villain who got him into trouble; we see him merely as a victim; and thus we deprive him of guilt and conflict. In other words, because we are used to thinking in terms like "villain," "fool," and other types with which our culture provides us, we easily miscast the tragic hero.

These misunderstandings may be of some help, however, in seeing, by contrast, what a tragic hero ought to be. He should be a complex figure, whose self-imposed punishment and conflict within challenge our compassion and understanding. He must (however foolish or wicked his course of action may superficially seem) keep his dignity and remain heroic. Any tendency to "write him off" as a fool, no-account, mental case, etc., is a sign of failure of understanding; so, also, is it to simplify him in the opposite way, to a point where he is all good, others are to blame, and he has no inner conflict.

If such are the miscastings likely to happen because of competing types in American culture, let us look at actual responses of audiences to tragedies, both in real life (news) and in art. By asking people what they think about a character and his fate, it is possible to analyze the main perceptual images and decide whether he is being understood or misunderstood, and in what ways.

First, an interpretation by a group of college students of news-stories of real life "tragedies," as they might be called in ordinary parlance. Two of these appeared on the same day in a local paper: one of a deserted husband who ran amok and killed his children; the other of a jealous ex-husband who dogged the life of his divorced wife, finally entered her apartment, and shot her, then himself. I discussed them with the group on the day they were reported. The interpretations were on the surface different. There was consensus that killer #1 was a poor fellow driven out of his mind by his wife's meanness; #2 was simply a villain and no sympathy was shown him. The main reason for this difference seems to have been the way the news was reported. An interview in the papers had brought out #1's point of view, telling how his wife had wronged him, showing her, in other words, as the villain, him as the victim. There had been no such interview, however, with the dead #2: only the external features of the crime were reported; so he remained a villain though his crime was somewhat less serious in terms of numbers of people injured. Did killer #1 become tragic, then, in escaping from the villain's part? On the contrary, *neither* of the interpretations could properly be called tragic. It was simply a case of locating the villain. I cite these cases to show how hard it is to develop—one might say manufacture —such a complex viewpoint toward reality without a favorable culture and suitable art form to, as it were, blow up the experience to bigger than life-size.[7] All of the elements of a classic tragedy—a *Hercules Distracted,* an *Othello*—were there, no doubt, if one could only see them. But under the perceptual conditions of American culture, it is so much easier to see the simpler types of villain, victim, fool, and so on. In case #1 (which came closer to being tragic), sympathy had merely shunted from the victims to the killer (as a sick man, who became another victim), and hatred and blame had transferred to his wife. The basic melodramatic pattern remained.

But, you may say, it is too much to expect of any audience that they will see in raw facts—especially such as can be gotten from news reports—the elements of tragedy well enough to get the right feeling. The important question is, what do they see in an ideal drama, where the meaning and impact have been heightened by an artist?

I have, in fact, also discussed classic tragedies with adult groups after a recent reading. My experience has been (and I wonder how many teachers of literature will agree with me) that when people know it is a classic they are talking about, they make an effort to understand it according to the approved literary formulas, but, when the amenities are done, they usually get around to finding fault with the hero. There seems to be a need to blame him as a villain, or to escape involvement with him by calling him a fool, or to see him as a victim and put the blame on somebody else. This reaction is entirely consistent, as I see it, with my remarks about the armor that Americans have against tragic experience.

To find out more about this, especially the ways in which they were interpreting the hero and the extent to which alienation from him might be felt, I made a thematic analysis of responses to tragedy, asking 134 college students to choose a play or story with which they were familiar from a list of twenty well-known ones,[8] ranging from Sophocles' *Oedipus* to mod-

---

[7] As Lord Chesterfield said, "Tragedy must be bigger than life, or it would not affect us." Behind this is the assumption that tragedy is not something that people just naturally grasp, but is a complex perception made possible by a set of cultural conditions and an invention—a device, an art form, for improving our perception of reality by enlarging certain aspects of it. So it is a contrived thing, unlikely to happen without the help of an artist. Since it is an invention, we do not expect a people to have tragedy, however hard their lot, unless they have borrowed or inherited it. This seems to accord with the fact that the distribution of tragedy is limited: the outlook of primitive peoples, judging by their tales and myths, is generally melodramatic; some advanced civilizations, such as India, are without the tragic sense; there have been only two great centers of tragic development, ancient Greece and Elizabethan England, both in the Western tradition.

[8] The heroes rated were: Willy Loman in *Death of a Salesman* by Arthur Miller, Blanche DuBois in *A Streetcar Named Desire* by Tennessee Williams, Romeo in *Romeo and Juliet*, Hamlet, Macbeth, Mio in *Winterset* by Sherwood Anderson, Emperor Jones in *Emperor Jones* by Eugene O'Neill, Clyde Griffiths in *An American Tragedy* by Theodore Dreiser, Captain Ahab in *Moby Dick* by Herman Melville, Mrs. Alving in *Ghosts* by Henrik Ibsen, Hedda Gabler in *Hedda Gabler* by Henrik Ibsen, Raskolnikov in *Crime and Punishment* by Dostoyevski, Brutus in *Julius Caesar* by Shakespeare, King Lear, Antigone in *Antigone* by Sophocles, Orestes in *Electra* by Sophocles, Medea in *Medea* by Euripides, and Phaedra in *Phaedra* by Racine.

ern ones by O'Neill, Dreiser, Anderson, Williams, and Miller. Twenty-five of the students had seen the J. Arthur Rank production of *Romeo and Juliet* within a week and chose this for interpretation.

Let us look first at the side which is favorable to the appreciation of tragedy. More than half said "a deeply significant and worthwhile experience" (61%); "symbolic of the experience of mankind" (53%). Somewhat less than half said "sympathize deeply with the hero" (43%); "a better-than-average person who displayed along with merits a serious fault or mistake" (44%). A third thought of the protagonist as "basically heroic" (30%); a fourth as "an admirable person" (25%). A fourth thought that the story had "a terrible but noble ending" (28%). Only a fifth thought the play demonstrated the "fortitude and dignity of the central character" (18%), and a sixth that it showed "the frailty of even strong or worthy people" (16%). These, of course, are not necessarily responses to tragedy as such, but they could be; they are [at] least oriented in that direction.

Much of this sympathy, however, is for that special kind of misunderstanding of tragedy that we have designated as martyrdom, for over a fourth saw the hero as "a kind of martyr for a social cause or value" (28%), and more sympathy is for the helpless victim, as shown below.

Many showed signs of missing the point and substituting an inadequate conception; for instance: "could have avoided trouble if he had used more sense" (53%) seems to imply that he is a fool and that the ending should have been happy (i.e., would have been but for his bungling). So does: "he brought it all on himself through mistakes or weaknesses" (40%). Throwing reproach on the hero tends to alienate the audience from him; he has spoilt the story as they expected it to work out. They leave him, so to speak, to stew in his own juice.

Very few, however, condemned him as an outright villain (7%). About half, on the contrary, "pitied him" (52%), as a "victim, helpless and not to blame for most of what happened" (45%). Some said "people took advantage of him or got him into trouble" (16%), or that he was "a good person injured by bad persons" (13%). These remarks excuse him, no doubt. But do they not do so by weakening him?

About one out of five were simply alienated by the story. It was: "something that shouldn't have happened" (20%), a "gloomy and unpleasant story" (19%), "a pointless catastrophe" (12%); it "would have been better if it had ended more happily" (11%). Nineteen percent were indifferent to or repelled by the hero.

As you see, many of these responses appear to fall short of a tragic interpretation. Those who are alienated or see the story as just something that shouldn't have happened fall into this category. So also do those who weaken the hero till he is only a victim or a fool, since they rob him of dignity and free will. Less than half would grant that he was a better-than-average person, showing that in the eyes of many the tragedy endowed the sufferer with no special stature—that his manner of bearing misfortune was no better than that of anybody else. Those who melodramatized him as a martyr (about a third) generated sympathy at the expense of tragic insight, since, as we have seen, the martyr concept tends to exonerate a person for his trouble and throw the blame on villains.

More specifically, the main ways a tragic hero can be misinterpreted seem to be as: (1) a melodramatic good guy who for some inexplicable reason has failed, (2) a villain, (3) a fool, or (4) a passive and pathetic victim.

I feel this shows how in some ways we Americans have difficulty doing justice to the tragic character, especially to his complexity and dignity. Even if sympathetic, we are inclined to reduce him to a simpler or an inferior type (the martyr is simpler though not inferior). Sympathy (as for a victim or martyr) is no guarantee of tragic understanding; yet we may suspect that if it were not for the artist's working skillfully to build up sympathy, most tragedies would be villainies or follies of one kind or another.

Why does this reduction occur? Aside from the usual limitations of the human mind (such as ignorance and laziness), I think a theory of short-circuiting by cultural images is called for. That is, people respond to an event in terms of their stock of available images. They are likely to go to the image that is closest and easiest, among those which seem at all to fit the situation. We may grope for a name to call Medea, and fall back upon something like "villainess!" This amounts to a displacement of complex and delicate interpretations by simpler ideas. The ease of short-circuiting will depend on the prominence, range, and availability of character types in the culture; for example, whether art and drama have favored the building up of certain types more than others. The ratio of tragic to non-tragic stories in our culture should be expected to affect our ability to make such interpretations. Our interpretations should depend, also, on current conditions, such as whether a "crisis" mentality exists. Crises apparently favor villains, and it is generally recognized that melodrama is the enemy of tragedy. So a culture that favors melodrama (with its happy endings) works against tragedy. Something like this might also be said for comedy. That is, though its "relief" function in tragedy is recognized, too much slapstick in popular media probably creates an atmosphere in which people find it hard to make serious interpretations—they are looking for the fool, not for dignity.

After all, so much is wrong with the tragic hero! To the superficial view he is plainly a failure. Willy Loman kills himself. What satisfaction are people supposed to get out of that? A tragic hero is asked to perform the paradoxical feat of lifting the human spirit while plunging it into the most appalling catastrophes. And this is to be symbolized by a character who is full of weakness and conflict (compared with a folk hero like Sigurd or some of the more primitive dragon-slayers). His very mistakes and flaws may alienate the audience to the point that they see him as a villain or fool. If he does not positively err, he may, like Hamlet with his hand suspended over the back of Claudius, be unable to deliver a fully satisfying blow. In any case, all that comes out of his downfall is a triumph obscurely implied.

Much depends, then, on a delicate set of conditions that would allow such a triumph to be perceived. Indeed, unless a culture were especially prepared to accept him, we might very well expect the tragic hero to be a total wash-out.

III

This brings our attention to the second main factor in American culture that makes it hard for the tragic hero to succeed: the climate of opinion, sometimes called the ethos. Some peoples seem to have an ethos that keeps them from seeing tragedy at all.[9] Ours is not so limiting as that, of course; but it does contain unfavorable perspectives or beliefs, three in particular that we shall try to analyze with the help of experts.[10]

One is the optimistic presumption that keeps us from appreciating the extent to which things—God, fate, history, nature—are not on our side. A vivid awareness of evil, says O'Connor, is essential to the idea of tragedy. Nietzsche said the same: "Banish evil, and it will go hard with the writers of tragedy." Now our age has managed to a great extent to banish evil by considering it not in the scheme of things. Characteristically, A. J. Cronin says, "If we think correctly and courageously, there is no misfortune inherent in human existence that we cannot turn to our ultimate advantage." Such a view is no doubt "healthy," but it is purely a presumption that the world is set up so that man can exploit it. Things should come out all right, says the optimistic presumption; but *this* did not come out all right; therefore something is wrong with it. So optimism must arm its hero with Excalibur, give him a horseshoe in his glove to guarantee success. One of these symbolic horseshoes in American life is the idea of progress. Another is the scientific optimism inherited from the eighteenth century. Another is the invincible belief in romantic marriage in spite of one failure out of three

---

[9] For example, the Zuni Indians, who have no place for struggle and extreme individualism, for heroes who, "fighting, fighting, fighting, die driven against the wall."—Ruth Benedict, *Patterns of Culture* (Penguin edition), p. 119. The Hindus lack tragedy because their ethos prevents them from seeing material misfortune as significant; nor is the individual important enough to them for tragedy to be meaningful.

[10] Especially Joseph Wood Krutch, *The Modern Temper* (New York, 1929). Besides Krutch's brilliant diagnosis, I have used others who have analyzed cultural conditions favorable and unfavorable to tragedy, notably William Van O'Connor, *Climates of Tragedy* (Baton Rouge, 1943), and Willard Farnham, *The Medieval Heritage of Elizabethan Tragedy* (Berkeley, 1936).

or four. A people used to the aspirin of optimism ask, quite reasonably, why should we experience pain in our dramas any more than in our dentist chairs? The best use they can make of tragic pain is didactic: a lesson about how to do better next time.

Optimism belongs, then, among the opiates that soften the awareness of evil and make life look like a set-up especially prepared for man. (Oddly, those who most often use the term "opiate," the Marxists, are themselves equally victims of this optimism, feeling that history is working out some kind of dialectic in favor of the society they want.) Other cultural opiates, not so prevalent in America, include: Puritanism, which tried to ostracize evil as the work of the Devil; fatalism, which takes all the responsibility for evil off man; other worldliness, which denies reality to material misfortunes; and the patriotic sentimentalization of death. It was the Romans, says Edith Hamilton, who thought it sweet to die for one's country; "the Greeks never said it was sweet to die for anything." Clearly, you can't have tragedy when such notions act as buffers to take the edge off the bitterest blows.

Equally unfavorable to the tragic hero is the naturalism which, developed as an artistic technique by European writers, has become an integral part of the American outlook. The American takes this view of things as normally as the medieval man did miracles and the Devil. Coming under a variety of names (mechanism, determinism, environmentalism, behaviorism, materialism, positivism, relativism, amoralism), it is essentially a picture of man submerged in an impersonal and subhuman nature. Naturalism is, of course, not just the realism of the naked eye but a scientific, largely materialistic and mechanical *interpretation* of human phenomena—a model. To be submerged in nature may mean such things as the following: all events have causes; the external causes of human acts are environment and heredity; morals are not metaphysical laws but natural parts of culture; man is not separated from other animals by a gulf, he is just the star performer in the zoo.

Such a view is bound to shape both the kinds of figures made by artists and the way they are interpreted. Stress on meaningless mechanism, external causation, may reduce a tragic hero to a beetle crushed under a rock. Studs Lonigan on a morgue slab is in some sense a symbol of the avalanche of naturalism over tragedy. So also is Clyde Griffiths, who, as depicted by Dreiser, is a puppet of circumstances. A mass of documentation is piled up to prove how social forces—home, education, deprivations, snubs, and denatured American ideals—move him toward his crime and to this extent lessen his freedom and responsibility. The pile-up of environmental forces also dulls the perception of evil, which (as O'Connor has shown) is essential for feeling tragedy. If I may try to explain this, it is because the evil of anything depends on two things: how important is he who suffers and how much of the trouble is due to the will of man. Reduce man either as sufferer or willing agent and it is impossible to have evil. This may lend significance to Krutch's observation that "the idea of nobility is inseparable from the idea of tragedy," and that "no man can conceive it unless he is capable of believing in the greatness and importance of man." What it seems to add up to, then, is that making nature more makes man less.

Yet, for all its threat, naturalism need not be fatal to a hero if, amid the mass of circumstances that seem to overwhelm him, he is allowed some loophole for noble choice. Thus Willy Loman in *Death of a Salesman* is a victim only to the extent that spurious American values—in this case the good-fellow ideal of success—have collapsed for him. But this victimization is not the last word; it becomes an *opportunity*, as Miller himself explains, for that burst of heroic determination in defeat which is the essence of tragedy. So by this play Miller claims that sordid life, for all its relentless pressures, need not be "below tragedy, as often asserted." The common man can take on such stature "to the extent of his willingness to throw all he has into the contest" to maintain his "chosen image" of what and who he is in the world.

A more serious blow to the hero's dignity and volition is to psychologize him, especially to analyze his conflicts in terms of psychopathology to a point where he is neither normal nor in control of what he does. The clinical character of many modern tragedies (such as those by O'Neill and Williams) is too obvious to need emphasis. Let me say only this: when a man becomes a "case," he ceases to be human to some extent. The disease occupies the foreground and, as it were, plays the part. Other writers have described this morbid effect as "converting art into an alienist's notebook," or an "obsession with filth" that obscures dignity. A possible result is disintegration of tragedy into mere horror and sensation.

If naturalism hurts tragedy, there is another element of the American ethos that gives little less than a *coup de grâce* to this kind of hero. It is the inability to make absolute commitments, called by David Riesman other-directedness (by moralists, opportunism). Anyone puzzled by the success of "brain-washing" on soldiers need not be so puzzled if he recognizes that many people today hold their beliefs conditionally, not absolutely. That is, their beliefs are inconsistent, come from all kinds of sources, and need to be upheld by agreement with others in the situation. Remove this condition of group support and there is no strong impulse to maintain them. Now a basic requirement of tragedy is to throw oneself completely into action, to "play the game through." Every great tragic figure has been true to his fault, so to speak. This is his tragic commitment. But the average American, while he may admire a martyr with a clear-cut cause of service, does not like to follow a course through to tragic consequences. He has too much common sense, for one thing. There is in him the spirit of the world, of compromise, of opportunism. He is proud of being flexible, able to start in a new direction when one line of action peters out. In other words, he is not obligated. "Die-hard" is his name for one who sticks too long to a cause. This is both a strength and a weakness. Putting it in terms of Riesman's character-types, a tragic actor must be *inner*-directed; it is commitment to something within and private that makes him tragic. The *other*-directed audience sees this "fault," sympathizes perhaps, but does not follow. For an other-directed person bases conduct on what others want him to do and therefore does not hold to a course of rather obstinate individuality. Theoretically, tragedy is impossible in an other-directed society. The tragic hero finds himself fighting alone—the crowd has deserted him. Now one who throws himself away on a lost cause, we well know, is a fool—so much for tragic dignity.

These ways of looking at things—optimism, naturalism, and other-directedness—seem to be the main elements of the American climate of opinion that stand in the way of the success of the tragic hero and help account for the unenthusiastic response of audiences to him. Bearing in mind the distracting types previously described, we see why it is so easy for him to be mis-cast and a misfit, and why he has such a hard time.

IV

There remains a fact about the hero himself that, regardless of what the climate of opinion and perceptual images may be, is bound to affect the way he is received. I mean that he is not the man he used to be. Partly as a result of the naturalism already described, the tendency among artists is to pick smaller men as subjects of tragedy. The standard of better-than-average, used in the Athenian and Elizabethan classics, has been abandoned. Comparing any fair sample of modern characters with those of earlier periods will show that there has been a decline in the stature of the tragic hero. The thing could be proven in feet and pounds, if need be; Krutch has demonstrated it convincingly by comparing people like Oswald Alving and Hamlet. This means that, regardless of social climate and cultural images, we have a harder time admiring the tragic hero today. He is such an ordinary person, his weaknesses and faults are so evident, that it is often hard to muster more than forgiveness for him. If we are to admire a Clyde Griffiths, a Blanche DuBois, an Emperor Jones, a Native Son, it must be all our own effort, so to speak; the artist has helped us but little—indeed, he may have so alienated us that we are unwilling to stay around for the funeral. Now (while this is entirely speculation), were tragic writers of today to choose clearly superior men as their subjects, we should have at least a favorable attitude toward them before the trouble started.

In short, the objective mediocrity of the modern hero combined with the unfavorable ethos and distracting cultural images make it very unlikely that an impression of grandeur will be produced when a man goes to pieces or blows his brains out before an American audience.

With such conditions working against the tragic hero, it is a wonder, indeed, that so many Americans do occasionally listen to his sombre lesson. While he cannot be said to be a popular type—and shows little signs of becoming one—he may serve by his presence to remind us, like an African mask in a modern living room, of insights that our ethos might otherwise hide. We test our perception on him, finding more often than not that he reflects themes of our own culture. Working like a prism, he scatters popular thought into its elements, showing its tendency to veer away from tragic insight to simpler modes of perception. But in so doing, he has utility for analyzing this thought. Enigma though he is—even if a fool in our eyes— he is, perhaps, capable of playing Touchstone for us.

The Criticism of Greek Tragedy*

WILLIAM ARROWSMITH

My purpose here is to do a little superstitious rapping in the hope of persuading into existence something a little different in the kind of criticism we normally bring to bear upon Greek tragedy. If this seems pretentious, blame the subject in part: Greek tragedy requires, I think, a formidable apparition by way of an adequate criticism and certainly a larger one than I can summon up, though also a larger one than presently attends the scene. What I want to do is to outline the nature of the job to be done, as I see it, and to discuss what seems to me inadequate in both the traditional and contemporary ways of writing about Greek tragedy. I think I see—though vaguely —the kind of criticism to which Greek tragedy points, though I recognize that this may turn out to be merely a mirage made up to answer imaginary needs, or an old familiar ghost in a new murk, or even something that concerns no one but students of Greek tragedy. Whatever the results, I am convinced that the need is real; that we have reached some kind of impasse in the study of Greek tragedy in which neither the older nor the newer criticism, nor any compromise between them, is really adequate; and further, that the need is general.

Impasse is perhaps a strong word, and certainly an easy one. Yet the diagnosis should surprise no one. The inadequacies of the older historical and philological criticism are by now notorious, and we can dispense with a parade of slogans that have more than accomplished their purpose. At the moment, the New Criticism enjoys high academic repute; it has, for the most part, been thoroughly institutionalized; it continues to do striking work in the hands of competent critics, and wherever it has allied itself with true scholarship, it has been an instrument of subtlety and depth. But as a method it is liable to the same distortion as any method; and it has everything to fear from the literalness of its zealots. No one who reads much

* William Arrowsmith, "The Criticism of Greek Tragedy," *Tulane Drama Review*, Vol. III, No. 3 (March, 1959).

recent criticism can be unaware of the carking restiveness among the pioneers of the New Critics as they see their methods turned into formulae and the crucial tact of the good critic expelled by the needs of schematic order. "I want," says R. P. Blackmur in *The Lion and the Honeycomb*, "to protect the methods [of the New Criticism] from its methodologies." I have the same hope here, and it is a hope which I want as much as possible to put in positive terms. But because the field I have in mind is Greek tragedy and classical studies generally, and because the situation of the New Criticism is different in respect to a dead language than what it is to a modern one, these matters deserve a context.

Roughly since the end of the war the traditional methods of classical scholarship as they affected literary criticism have been under attack in our graduate schools by the advocates of the New Criticism. As compared with studies in modern literatures, the attack on the classical front came late, delayed both by the addiction to cultural lag which is almost a point of pride among classicists, and by the extreme penetration of classical studies by the austere and quasi-scientific methodologies of the German *gymnasium*. Unlike scholars of English who never really wholly renounced criticism, classicists in America came to regard criticism as the perverse imp of the subjective in a field they fondly imagined was objective. This suspicion of criticism, it should be noted, was a peculiarly American thing, just as the reaction against it has been, for the most part, American also. If the stimulus to this dislike of criticism derived from Germany, it is also true that the formidable influence of such great scholars as Wilamowitz countered the current there, while elsewhere in Europe the long tradition of humane scholarship kept the activities of critic and scholar in more or less vital relation. One can point with pride, it is true, to American achievements in classical scholarship in the twentieth century, but the achievements occur in just those fields where the refinement of method, and especially scientific method, is crucial: archaeology, epigraphy, papyrology, numismatics, palaeography. Worse yet, all of these dubious sciences were devoted with an appalling single-mindedness to one end, the discovery of fact, in which fact was arbitrarily and with killing literalness reduced to historical or philological fact. Criticism itself was clearly confounded with the journalism of values and pushed to the fringes where it petered out either in limp impressionistic essays on the value of the classics or in the mellow *obiter dicta* of dying scholars. In short, American classical scholarship for forty years effectively renounced literary criticism as an honorable and rational habit of mind, and the results are apparent in the dreary waste of literary studies during those years; at least I can think of no first-rate, nor even second-rate, critical work on Greek tragedy by an American scholar from 1900 to 1940, though there is God's good plenty of works on the stage, conventions, Attic society, resolved *senarii* and the like. But certainly one finds nothing comparable to the real criticism of such European scholars as Sheppard, Wilamowitz or even the much-maligned Gilbert Murray.

When the attack finally came it came with the energy that attends any deep habit of mind that has for a long time been rigorously suppressed. It was slowed, not merely by the entrenchment of the Germanic spirit, but by a factor of considerable but neglected importance: unlike English, both Greek and Latin are dead languages, poorly preserved and poorly documented, lacking precisely that richness of information about language which is everywhere the essential condition of the newer criticism. But in the enthusiasm for a method that had the advantage of being at least literary, that honored the work for itself and not for its historical or informational uses, this crucial limitation was brushed aside. Real excesses, however, were prevented by the salutary insistence of the older generation that the fundamental responsibilities of the scholar be observed. This insistence, because defensive, was both surly and grumpy, but it had its effect: at least no classical critic, to my knowledge, has yet proclaimed that the *Oresteia* is a "hierarchy of epiphanies." Moreover, from the first, the impulse to the restoration of criticism to scholarship in America came as much from the humane tradition of European scholarship as from critics like Empson, Brooks, Ransom and Blackmur. Indeed, it was on the whole European scholars who first appreciated the refinement of verbal techniques offered by the New Criticism. Besides, no critic worth his salt, however belligerent, could honestly deny that the extreme poverty of fact which attends classical studies had long ago forced scholars to adopt in desperation something very like the New Criticism: one thinks of Jebb's monumental close-reading of Sophocles, with its susceptibility to shade and texture; Wilamowitz' great edition of the *Heracles*, and now of Fraenkel's *Agamemnon;* on still another level, verging toward the perverse or crankish, are the strange works of Verrall and Norwood on Euripides and such non-classical oddities as Samuel Butler's *The Authoress of the Odyssey.*

But in the last ten years it is abundantly clear that criticism has returned to classical scholarship; if the New Criticism as such is not yet, in classics, the heavy industry it has become in English studies, its pressure is clearly visible and especially among the younger generation. The direct influence of the critics themselves upon classical studies has mostly been oblique, and, more often than not, unfortunate: Francis Fergusson's able but unconvincing piece on the *Oedipus Rex* is some kind of exception, extraordinary in its perceptivity, but crippled in its too great reliance upon theories of the ritual origins of tragedy. And neither Kenneth Burke's strange essay on the *Oresteia* nor Edmund Wilson's perversion of the *Antigone* provides reliable models. But the New Criticism is writ large in Goheen's study of the imagery of the *Antigone*, diffused throughout Kitto's *Greek Tragedy* and Lattimore's superb introduction to his translation of the *Oresteia*, or Owen's fine commentary on the *Iliad*, and everywhere visible in the spate of dissertations which study single plays or single metaphors or the master-tropes of tragedy, and in the insistent emphasis upon the key terms of the New Critics: irony, ambiguity, symbol, tone, image, texture, formal structure and myth. And finally, even the classical journals and the professional societies have shown in the last few years a grudging willingness to admit the newer critics as at least junior partners in the firm.

From the point of view of the past, these are encouraging signs, and all the more so since critical activity has here been accompanied by extraordinary energy in the field of translation—the new translations of Homer, tragedy, Vergil, Ovid, Hesiod, Pindar and Greek lyric. Good translation is, of course, exemplary and creative criticism: to have an *Iliad* or an *Oresteia* as substantial and moving as we have in Lattimore's translations is to have a guarantee of the fresh and right response of feeling without which criticism is an empty exercise. In this sense translations and criticism work hand in hand, each sponsoring the other's vitality: just as criticism is crippled if it neglects scholarship, so the translator's task is vitiated without the act of criticism. In this connection the difference between Lattimore's *Oresteia* and Pound's *Trachiniae* is illuminating; for what makes Pound's translation incomparably the poorer of the two is the way in which, the scholarship suspended almost altogether, the critical sense is so impaired that it can no longer supervise the adjustment of language to the moral and emotional facts of the play. Talent here, tethered to nothing except Pound's extraordinary sense of music, has gone rough and wild. By which I do not mean, of course, that Lattimore's scholarship makes him an acceptably tame poet; on the contrary, there is an immense turbulence in his translation, but it is a true and Aeschylean turbulence, not an imposed wildness. Good poetry guarantees good turbulence; the work of critic and scholar are required to make that turbulence Aeschylean and true.

Up to now the most conspicuous failure of both the traditional and the new critics in respect to Greek tragedy has been the failure to realize turbulence: turbulence of experience, turbulence of morality in the process of getting made, and the turbulence of ideas under dramatic test. If any one charge can be brought against the older criticism, it would be, I think, that it has seemed to ask too little of Greek tragedy, and asking so little, has rarely discovered much. Its crucial failure has come at the point where all criticism is finally tested: the ability to transfer complex experience from one period or language to another, and to get the substance of that experience—its turbulence as well as its final order—into language. This is, of course, in the end, impossible, but it is the ideal by which we measure the adequacy of any interpretative criticism. Where the older criticism failed was in the deeper skills of the very humanity it professed, the point where passion is used to make the experience from which any great image of humanity, like the Greek one, is made. Intensely obsessed with history and politics, the traditional criticism failed to show how history and politics got into tragedy and what they did there in relation to the humanity of the heroes; concerned with man and his destiny, it could never quite conjure up the complex reality of experience and suffering that in the Greek plays gives human passion its meaning; committed to the task of clarity, it failed on the whole to remove that dense patina of stiffness and strangeness and austerity that makes Greek tragedy so formidable to our first impressions, or translated it into sentimental commonplaces and limp passions.

Who, after all, is really stirred by the standard interpretations of the *Antigone*—that tidy passion of a perfect heroine caught up on the gods' errand and hindered by a brutal Creon, a conforming Ismene, and a dunderheaded chorus with an inexplicable gift of tongues? And who believes the fashionable reverse, with its stubborn and presumptuous Antigone, its tragic Creon and its misunderstood Ismene? These interpretations are, to my mind, not credible because they so clearly violate the emotional experience of the play or reduce its difficulties to the vanishing-point. What has not gotten into them is the play's real turbulence and complexity and what they express is rather the superficial order the play throws up as its terms or its field, not its subject or solution. What is missing is what, to my mind, the play insists upon in both action and character: the way in which Antigone, trying to uphold a principle beyond her own, or human, power to uphold, gradually empties that principle in action, and then, cut off from her humanity by her dreadful heroism, rediscovers herself and love in the loneliness of her death; not the opposition between Antigone and Creon, but the family resemblance which joins them in a common doom; not great heroism justified by great principles, but conduct in the fateful grip of principles, making out of courage and love a deeper principle altogether. And if you look to the *Oedipus Rex* or the *Agamemnon* or the *Bacchae* it seems to me you find the same impoverishment: what is real or turbulent in the life of those plays is for the most part expelled, either because the critic has let his own principles of order usurp the play, or because his own experience is unequal to it, or because he refuses the act of criticism once it gets near the difficult edge of experience. How many interpretations of the *Oedipus Rex* for instance, have come to grief on the fruitless quest for a tragic flaw that will justify the hero's suffering simply in order that Aristotle be justified. How commonly the cry of botching is raised against Euripides because his plays refuse to conform to the critic's expectations of proper organic structure. And how little of the full turbulence of the *Orestes* or *Bacchae*—those great pitiless mirrors of the terrible political and social desperation of late fifth-century Hellas—does our criticism get, largely because we ask so much less of tragedy than it requires.

Thanks to the New Criticism, we can hope to see the turbulence of language and rhetoric restored to tragedy, for the New Critics are nothing if not keen-nosed where verbal subtlety and density are concerned. And we have, I think, everything to hope for from the thorough examination of the rhetorical habits of Greek tragedy. But I sometimes wonder whether a keen nose for metaphor, irony or ambiguity is much to the point when the spoor is as old and crossed as that of Greek tragedy. It is, for instance, extremely difficult in fifth-century literature to distinguish between metaphor that is genuinely fresh and metaphor that has hardened into idiom or *cliché;* we simply do not possess the linguistic evidence that might allow us to tell them apart. How fresh, for instance, are those yoke and ship images which run like master-tropes through all three tragedians? Or are these simply the metaphorical idiom of an agricultural and seafaring people? The answer, of course, lies in a desperately difficult tact, but that tact comes far harder in Greek and Latin than it does in a living literature like English where we understand stress and tone as we never can in Greek. And the chances are high, of course, that tact will disappear before the critic's drive for conceptual consistency: I know of at least one treatment of the symbolism of the *Oresteia* where the interpretation derived more from the itch for conceptual rigor in the imagery than from the emotional experience of the play. And this risk seems to me particularly high for the New Criticism in its academic setting, where the old insistence upon methodology and the student's necessary economies with complexity combine to harden method into mere formula.

I would not, of course, like the consciousness of risk to damage the enterprise: we badly need in Greek tragedy just that refinement of rhetoric which has been the success of the New Criticism. We need to know, for instance, just how those *sententiae* with which Greek tragedy is so lavish and which so embarrass modern producers of Greek plays, arise from the action; the structure of *stichomythia*, that brisk staccato exchange of single lines for up to a hundred lines at a time, is badly in need of work; I suspect that the relation between metaphor and dance-figures is crucially important; we know very little about irony in tragedy, so little that the tone of whole scenes and even whole plays is in question; the language itself, with its curious alternation between stiff archaism and colloquial speech, its habits of rhetorical movement, from the big jaw-breaking, piled-up compounds of Aeschylus to the deceptive simpleness of Euripides, is still *terra incognita;* and I suspect that we have barely started to do the work required by the choral lyrics. Beyond these jobs, it is my personal conviction that the study of tragedy would enormously benefit from a shift in perspective; we need to question, that is, our tacit assumption that Greek tragedy is staged in a religious context or represents a kind of collective worship, for the assumption vitally affects interpretation. And it seems to me that nothing but chaos can come from the fashionable notion that because Greek tragedy begins in ritual, its structure is therefore ritual dramatized, its hero a ritual scapegoat, and its action a shadow play of the death of the *Eniautosdaimon* or god of the year. The more I read of Greek Tragedy, that is, the more I am impressed with its very distance from its ritual origins and its stubborn refusal to behave as honest ritual should. And there is something violently improbable about an image of the Greek theatre which does the kind of damage done by Gilbert Murray's recanted theory of its ritual elements and more recently by Francis Fergusson in his study of the *Oedipus*.

If we require an idea of the Greek tragic theatre at all, it seems to me that the clue might best be taken from the very charge of rhetoric so peristently brought against tragedy, and against Euripides in particular ever since the time of Schlegel. Over and over again, that is, the late fifth-century tragedy seems to suggest as its informing image a theatre shaped more by the law-court than by the altar. In this theatre, the *agon* is viewed essentially as a trial, and the characters, with all the tricks of sophistic rhetoric, put their cases in opposed speeches—often of identical length, as though timed by the waterclock of the Athenian dikastery. The audience in this theatre sits as jurors, not merely a panel of five hundred jurors, but the full *Heliaea*, the sovereign judicial assembly (*ekklesia*). No appeal, no matter how emotional, is debarred, and each character in his plea speaks with the formal passion of a man whose life and fortunes hang upon his words. But it is a formal and rhetorical passion, below which we can glimpse, as the jury must, the personal passion and the real motives glozed by the rhetoric and often exposed in action. Such a theatre, of course, is most appropriate to Euripides, but in some degree, I think, to Sophocles also, especially in later plays. I find tentative confirmation of this not merely in the number of Greek tragedies which openly stage formal trial scenes, but in the very structure of Euripidean drama: its persistent avoidance of the single hero in favor of the *agon* of two chief characters—Pentheus vs. Dionysus, Phaedra vs. Hippolytus, Orestes vs. Menelaus, Ion vs. Creusa—and the corresponding division of so many plays into two almost disparate actions; the flat assertion of the intention to make a formal plea; and, most important, the constant impression of the plays as problem plays in which the judgment is never asserted, but left, as it were, to the audience of jurors. If they understand the play, they make the right decision, or better, understand that no moral decision is relevant because the problems are beyond the reach of moral judgment, i.e. are both tragic and true. If this is correct, it is understandable why the constant imposition upon Euripides of Aristotelian structure and the notion of a religious theatre so regularly distort him. I throw this suggestion out, not as a developed thesis, but merely as a hint. For it seems to me that in the study of tragedy, as in almost any other human study, the discoveries come in that slight shift of perspective which we get when we examine those prejudices and assumptions which are so close to habit that we are almost unaware of them. And both our almost unconscious Aristotelianism and our deep assumption that Greek tragedy is finally religious tragedy are habits which I think need severe scrutiny by any serious critic of Greek drama.

The last charge which I should like to bring against the New Criticism is related to just this refusal to examine one's oldest habits. It is finally full interpretation of the plays and the tragedians that we want, and I find it puzzling that the newer criticism of Greek tragedy so seldom undertakes the full job. This may be modesty, but I suspect it is the old illusion of objectivity in fancy dress; and between *Quellenforschungen* and metaphor-snooping, both uprooted from the values they were intended to discover or reinforce, I can see very little difference. It is not merely that the New Critics have failed to take up the job of full interpretation, however, that I find distressing, but the fact that their analyses proceed more from the habit of old interpretation than the fresh act. I am not by this proposing that the New Critics should make their fortunes by systematically inverting all traditional criticism, but that analysis, wherever possible, should free itself from the immense authority of the standard interpretations. A book I admire, Goheen's analysis of the imagery of the *Antigone* originally written as a dissertation and suffering the handicaps of that impossible genre, ably illustrates just how much the New Critics have to offer in enriching our criticism of tragedy. But unless I am mistaken, Goheen's close analysis is subtly hindered by the authority of the nineteenth-century *Antigone*, whose shape guides the analysis where it needs to go, but not where it might have gone were its destination a little less certain. This is not slyness, of course, but the necessarily blinkered gaze of good conviction: you look where you are going, not askance. But the one metaphor Mr. Goheen overlooks—the metaphor of alienation, Antigone as *metic* or peregrine—a casual sport so far as his theory is concerned, seems to me the one metaphor that most illuminates the key word of the play—*philia* or love. Habit is hard to shed, of course, but in the case of Greek tragedy where critical habit has hardened into cultural habit, I think it is crucial to any hope of a fresh and exacting criticism.

In this connection one point deserves mention. Greek tragedy is, *par excellence*, a sacred cow, even more sacred, I suspect, than Shakespeare, since it is seldom produced or else produced via the atrocious medium of Mr. Robinson Jeffers and Broadway; and most students get introduced to it in the killing atmosphere of reverential hush that attends the reading of any classic in our general humanities courses. Worse, fewer and fewer literary men read Greek nowadays or read it with sufficient security to challenge the scholars on their own ground, as Goethe challenged Schlegel and Matthew Arnold challenged Newman with enormously fruitful results. And in scholarship, as I suggested earlier, unconscious timidity in the face of the accumulated judgments of dead scholars is a deep critical habit. In evidence of this attitude of blind deference to Greek tragedy, let me cite the production not so long ago on Broadway of two Greek plays by a modern Greek repertory troupe: night after night, audiences and dramatic critics, unable to understand a word of the productions, but deeply impressed with the performance of their cultural duties, willfully applauded on the curious assumption that Greek tragedy is mostly gesture anyway, and that a modern Greek company, by virtue of being Greek, somehow must possess the secrets of ancient Greek tragedy. Against adulation like this, it may be beyond the power of criticism to help, and the critic himself may be insensibly drawn into the work of justification rather than criticism. But it needs to be pointed out that we are in real danger of taking over almost intact the canon of Greek tragedy which the nineteenth century established. Who, after all, except classical scholars, now reads any Aeschylus except the *Oresteia* and *Prometheus*, any Sophocles except the Theban plays, and what Euripides besides the *Alcestis*, *Medea*, *Hippolytus* and *Bacchae?* I am not, of course, suggesting that these are not great plays, but that the canonizing of them into a cultural monument damages the chosen eleven as much as the excluded tragedies.

Worse, the difficulty is not merely that we have adopted an old taste, but the habits that accompany that taste as well, and especially the nineteenth century habit of making Sophocles the norm, if not the ideal, of tragedy—a habit which has done great damage to Aeschylus and almost irreparable damage to Euripides. It is no accident, for instance, that the favored plays of Euripides are precisely those which appear to meet the standards of so-called Aristotelian structure, that is, the "organic structure" which critics think they find in Sophocles. Against this tendency, I can only argue that it botches Sophocles as badly as Euripides, and that it cuts off our access to a power in Euripides that meant very little to the nineteenth-century but everything to the twentieth—I mean that part of Euripides that is concerned with political desperation, the corruption of power, and the corrosion of the civilized virtues into a set of specious slogans for demagogic consumption. We need not only the *Bacchae*, but the *Hecuba*, the *Heracles*, the *Orestes*, *Electra*, *Supplices* and *Trojan Women*—all plays in which we should sense the full turbulence of one of the very greatest of dramatists in a context that very easily becomes our own. But this means production as well as criticism, since nothing hinders the critic's right perception of a play more than the perpetual unavailability of his material in living form. At the moment, I can think of no greater service to Greek tragedy than the regular production of those plays that lie outside the canon and are so commonly regarded as undramatic, and particularly the plays of Euripides whose structure is censured by critics who have never seen them performed. But such a service needs to be regular, a continuous repertory production, and not merely those sporadic productions which derive from a duty to the classics; but it is a service I hope some lively academic theatre may be encouraged to perform, since Broadway offers even less to Greek tragedy than it does to the modern playwright.

What, in the meantime, should criticism do? I spoke earlier of the turbulence traditional criticism missed, and, at its most general, the charge I have preferred against the criticism of tragedy is its incompleteness. What was incomplete in the older criticism was that it over-generalized experience and missed whatever was complex and particular in human passion; it took the particular turbulence for granted, that is, and thereby reached its own generalizations of what should have given them life. What the newer criticism missed was meant to be implied by what it got—turbulence of language; but the implications, trapped by the New Criticism's notorious penchant for the autonomy of the work and its deep embarrassment in the face of value, only rarely succeeded; experience got swamped in the generalizing drive of the symbolism or the technique of the dramatist's work. What I want to restore to the criticism of tragedy is a sense, a feel, a look of significantly lived experience, particular before being general, the turbulence of the actual disorder of experience as it moves on to make the dramatist's order. To restore depth and passion to the terms of experience—the notion of a personal fate, responsibility, purpose, the emotions before and after their moralizing, illusion, necessity and reality; to show how values burgeon out of structure and plot; to know again why the plot is the "soul of the play," not its skeleton; to see that any character in a play who lives and uses his passion is prior to anything he may stand for; to refresh the simplicity of reason through the complexity of passion, not the other way around: this is a part of what I mean by turbulence, the turbulence to which both the critic and the producer are responsible. Unless the criticism of tragedy can make itself big enough to talk about experience at the level it proposes, it is doomed to even greater inadequacy than even criticism must normally expect. To talk about literature at the level of experience implies a criticism large enough to contain what is chaotic in experience as well as what is orderly. And it is my conviction that criticism of Greek tragedy, too heavily committed to the criteria of orderly reason and the rhetoric of intelligence, has dehumanized its heroes by cutting them off from the condition in relation to which they win their meaning. The hero, cut off by an inadequate criticism from the actual power and anguish of the condition he can never quite escape without destroying himself, loses the terrible tension and redeeming dignity of his equivocal status.

Nothing comes easier than to ask criticism to become more complete and humane, and nothing is harder to do. Nor can we prescribe methods for doing it without sooner or later ramming our plays into categories which violate them. What we need at this point seems to me not more method, but a refreshment of perspective: and particularly we want perspectives which undercut our old methods as they harden into habit and prevent us from seeing more than they allow. It is by such refreshment of perspective that we are apt to enlarge our criticism. At least this is my hope in the following remarks.

II

I suggested earlier that one refreshment of perspective might be found in a shift in our traditional idea of the Greek theatre, at least as that idea affects Euripides. And I should like to suggest further that we need much more precision in dealing with the hero and a different purchase on that central and elusive concept. What is most urgently needed is some sense of flexibility and variety in the ways heroism is manifested, and more attention to the *dramatic* use of the hero. The difficulty is not merely that we fail to distinguish between generic kinds of heroism or between the heroism of one dramatist and another, but that discussion begs almost all of the questions that affect the *dramatic* status of the hero in relation to his own humanity and also skirts whatever experience is relevant to the earning of heroism. Attempts to meet this problem with a unitary concept, as in Whitman's recent book on Sophocles, have been Procrustean in result: it is, of course, a pleasure to be rid of the view that Sophocles was an enlightened bishop and his heroes Anglicans in trouble, but a Nietzschean Sophocles with a Zarathustrian Antigone hardly helps us much. But most commonly heroism is treated in drastically abrogated moral terms, or made to satisfy the Aristotelian theory of the hero's tragic flaw, or reduced to the protagonist, or hypostatized and used as a critical *deus ex machina*. The crucial questions relevant to heroism, however, seem to me to be the following. First, how is heroism asserted in tragedy and how is it sustained, both morally and dramatically? What skills of experience or reality distinguish the hero from the other characters and from his former self? What is the relation between the achieved dramatic reality of the hero and his symbolic dignity? What is the cost of heroism to the hero in contrast to the values of what his heroism asserts? How does the hero's mortality affect his morality? What are the *legitimate* limits of the hero's responsibility for his nature or his acts? What is the relation between necessity and illusion in the hero's ability to rise to, and even surpass, the meaning of his own experience?

All of these questions are uprooted from the plays that propose them, but they are proposed by the plays at that level where criticism cannot refuse them without really refusing everything. As they affect the *Antigone*, for instance, they seem to me to illuminate the whole moral and experiential fabric of the play. Here if ever, for instance, the tension between the cost of heroism and the values of its assertion is both vivid and crucial. Half of the dynamic horror of Antigone's tragedy is precisely her equivocal status: torn between the cold heroism of her assertion of principle and her humanity, she almost loses her humanity in the fateful grip of her principle. What distinguishes her from Creon? Principle, of course, but look again, and the distinction is replaced by the family resemblance, a stubborn intractable loyalty to principle, and even a resemblance in principle, for both claim to act on behalf of love, *philia*. This principle, it is true, may be translated to another level and replaced by a struggle between family gods and state gods, but both protagonists claim at bottom to be agents of love: Antigone asserts that she was born to love (*sumphilein*) while Creon, in words that have been very strangely neglected, clearly states that he acts on behalf of the state because *philia*, love, can only exist within the context of a stable and orderly society. And this same *philia* is, of course, Ismene's principle too, without Antigone's courage, but *philia* for all that; and when Antigone refuses Ismene the right to die with her, she refuses her sister, her *philē*, both her *own principle and the dignity of a personal fate*. If, then, Antigone is the heroine of *philia*, we have to see, in action, what it means to act for *philia* in a conflict of *philiai;* how fate is here set against fate; how the family resemblance between Creon and Antigone is carried out in action up to the moment of heroism, and only then are they separated in a common doom. If we see these things, I think we cannot help seeing and reporting the turbulence also: the real disorder (but also the tragic symmetry) of a world where the living of love involves the denial of love elsewhere; where morality unmakes itself in conflict and is refreshed by significant passion; where heroism in the end means not surpassing one's humanity but discovering and incarnating its dignity at the moment of agony, and where the hero, finding weakness he never suspected, finds also his greatest strength. The hero, says Plato in one of his wonderfully crazy etymologies, "is born of love [that is, *erōs*]"; or, to put it in other terms, the hero is reduced, but also raised, to the human condition. So, at least, it seems to me with Antigone. What she first accepts as a fate, the principle of love that dooms her to death, is hardened by her desperate plight and her desperate courage and loneliness; and this in turn hardens her—"Great suffering makes a stone of the heart," as Yeats puts it

—making her refuse Ismene the same dignity of fate she claims. As she hardens, so does Creon on behalf of the same principle, denying Haemon in order to hurt Antigone, just as Antigone dishonors Ismene in order to honor Polyneices. Still hardened, but increasingly tormented by a loss she does not understand and yet the fate she chose, Antigone is condemned to her symbolic death, walled alive in a tomb, and thus cut off alike from both the living and the dead, the human being still alive, like Niobe, beneath the cold rock of her heroism. And suddenly, as the chorus compares her to a goddess, she knows what has happened, and cries, "I am mocked, I am mocked!" and the rock falls away, leaving that final warm confusion that makes her so human and so lovely. In all this Creon is left far behind, though he suffers perhaps even worse; he never had Antigone's human skills to begin with; he knows only the horror, Antigone knows the horror and the glory. And that knowledge, or better, merely *being* that knowledge, the final knowledge of tragedy, is Antigone's heroism. Until you come to that point, however, the experience is troubled, criss-crossed with paradox, turbulent with lonely passion and isolated meaning; if simplicity supervenes with heroism, that simplicity owes all of its power to the turbulence it tries to resolve.

Alternatively, in dealing with Euripides, we need to observe how the whole context of heroism has altered; that we are dealing with a world where the senselessness of circumstance may deprive the hero of responsibility, or strike at a point where responsibility is no longer relevant, as in the *Hecuba* or *Heracles*. With such an alteration, the nature of heroism is also altered, since its necessities change. Thus in the *Heracles*, the hero declares his triumph over the amoral powers which afflict him by the simple act of enduring in a world which tells him to die. For Euripides preserves the disorder of actual experience, measuring its horror against the unrequited illusion of order which sustains human beings, and the final dignity of Heracles is that he asserts the human cry for order and meaning almost in the very teeth of his own experience of hideous disorder. And the whole motive of the play is to bring the hero to the point where he shares, for the first time, common ground with the other characters. He discovers, that is, his condition and its anguish, an anguish from which his great strength has hitherto exempted him; in the discovery of anguish comes the discovery of community and love in weakness before necessity. Love is the hope which finally permits Heracles to endure a hideous necessity he never made, and from his discovery of love and helplessness flow acceptance and courage, the courage which asserts the human demand for order in a world which annuls all hope of a *moral* order. So much may be immediately obvious, but the point I should like to make is precisely the profound relationship between the hero's progress and the structure of the play, the way in which the created or assumed reality of each part of the play exactly defines, as challenge and disorder, the growth of heroism and order, forcing Heracles steadily back upon his humanity in order to refresh his heroism. Yet the *Heracles* has been savagely censured for its dislocation of plot, its apparent division into two discrete actions bound together by nothing more than sequence. But unless I am mistaken, everything that seems strange about the play's structure can be explained in terms of its intent, the conversion of heroism via the conversion of reality and necessity. At least it seems to me that, far from being botched, the *Heracles* is one of the most wonderfully constructed plays of Greek tragedy, if we mean by good construction a plot exactly designed to force meaning into action. What hinders us here, however, is the deeply Aristotelian bias of our critical habits and especially the habit of imposing the example of the *Oedipus Rex* upon all other Greek plays. We expect unity to be of one kind, and missing it, we misread or condemn the play in order to salvage our own bad habits.

Heroism is, of course, more difficult to comprehend in those plays—far more common than we like to believe—where we have no central dominating hero in the manner of the *Oedipus Rex* and the *Heracles*. Indeed, in the case of Euripides, the single hero is a comparative rarity. We have, for instance, a group of plays on the order of the *Hippolytus* or the *Phoenissae*, in which heroism is diffused over several characters or the whole human cast, and others, like the *Orestes*, the *Hecuba* and—I believe—the *Bacchae*, where there are protagonists but no heroes, and no heroism either. What you get in the *Orestes* is really like what you get in Shakespeare's *Troilus and Cressida:* an image of heroism seen as botched, disfigured and sick, carried along by the slogans and machinery of heroic tragedy and then exposed in action. This is neither a satire of tragedy, however, nor a melodramatic perversion, but tragedy of total turbulence, without a principle of order in sight except that order implied in the observation that heroism has been botched and all order omitted. Consider the *Bacchae* in this respect. Attempts to make heroes out of Pentheus and even Dionysus have not succeeded for obvious reasons: at least I find it hard to see the stuff of heroism in Pentheus' irritable voyeurism and Dionysus has all the heroism of an earthquake. What we have, of course, is not heroic tragedy but a tragic contest between parties who all claim to act on behalf of the same principle—*sophia*, badly translated as "wisdom"—and who all alike deprave their principle in action. What alone can order the play and judge that depravity to which *sophia* is subjected is an understanding of right *sophia;* but it is important to see that the play omits by merely implying the only order appropriate to its instances of heroism failed.

My point, then, is the simple one that heroism is too complex a term to be handled loosely, and that, if mishandled, it generates trouble in other directions. We need a tact with our terms which can distinguish when a particular concept is demanded and when it is superfluous; so far as heroism is concerned, we particularly need precision when we attempt to relate it to *dramatic* movement, plot, genre, and a particular dramatist. Where our definitions tend to be static rather than dynamic, or uprooted from a single type, or abstracted from one dramatist and imposed upon others, we impoverish tragedy in the critical act.

Likewise, in reading Aeschylus, we need to observe how a shifting or evolving cosmology fundamentally conditions the nature and possibilities of heroism. For surely we cannot alter the basic laws of the world in which men live and suffer without thereby deeply affecting the moral quality of their conduct and the judgments relevant to it. And the *Oresteia* is, of course, just such an evolving cosmology: a dramatic image of the gradual evolution, according to the masterplan of Zeus, of the institution of civilized justice. The progress itself hardly needs documentation. No one can read or see the trilogy and miss those wonderful transfigurations that chart the progress of justice from primitive blood-vengeance to civilized trial by jury: the blood-red tapestries on which Agamemnon goes to his death, suddenly revealed as the holy red robes of the transfigured Furies, or the metamorphosis of Persuasion (*Peitho*) from the sinister abstraction that seduces Helen, to Clytemnestra's coiling rhetoric as she lures Agamemnon to his doom, and finally that patient, crucial argument by which Athena persuades the Furies to accept an honored place in the new dispensation of Zeus. We are witnessing nothing less than the conversion of a world *and*, as the Chorus tells us, the reconciliation of Zeus and the Fates. Throughout the trilogy, from murder to murder to murder, we have been promised a fulfillment, a dawn, a delivery out of this intolerable net of contradictory evils, and finally, after so many false dawns and illusory solutions, we are shown the manifest pattern of Zeus the Fulfiller, the silver strand in the tapestry of blood.

A parable, then, of tragic scope, a passion of men and gods struggling from darkness into the light: so much is obvious. But if no one misunderstands the nature of the light, what do we make of the darkness there in the *Agamemnon* where everything is chaos and contradiction, where men are apparently whirled helplessly from evil to worse evil, with no end in sight ever? What, in other words, is the relation of Zeus of the *Eumenides* to the darker Zeus of the *Agamemnon?* Is he an inscrutable god, secretly at work behind all the apparent contradictions, slowly forcing the whole action toward an inevitable conclusion? A kind of Greek Jehovah, that is, tempting men, out of his enormous bewildering mystery, to cramp him in the small boxes of their own petty theodicies? Or is he like the Zeus of the Prometheus-trilogy, an undeveloped god who once again undergoes a progress from callous indifference to a final moral wisdom tempered by compassion?

Or is he a gradualist, a reforming Fabian demiurge, hampered by a whole host of discordant powers, the still potent heirs of an older dispensation, and by quarrels on Olympus too?

As I see it, the world of the *Agamemnon* is clearly one in which the possibility of moral action is obscured and prevented by a deep discord in the nature of things. We have a prospect of insuperable moral difficulty, a nightmare of justice in which the assertion of any right involves a further wrong, in which fate is set against fate in an intolerable, necessary sequence of violence. There is Zeus, of course, and Zeus is strong; but if the Chorus, in a famous ode, praises Zeus' power and wisdom, we are meant to read that prayer, I think, not as a factual description of a known Zeus, but as a last desperate act of faith, cried in the very teeth of experience: *sorrow, sorrow, but may good win out in the end*. In other words, the *Agamemnon* presents us with a world which is at all points essentially Homeric; nothing, in fact, in the entire *Agamemnon*, including the choral ode on Zeus, is incompatible with the cosmology of Homer. The life of men on earth, torn this way and that by conflict and irresponsibility in heaven, is a tragic hell; and if men and gods jointly share the responsibility for human actions, the choices are irreparably clouded by inconsistency and discord among the gods. In the *Iliad* and the *Odyssey* there is a double standard: divine adultery, for instance, is comic, but human adultery is terribly punished. So too the *Agamemnon* shows us, in conscious juxtaposition, the same double standard: Agamemnon himself is the fatally chosen instrument of Zeus to punish the adultery of Paris, but Apollo callously and with impunity seduces Cassandra and leads her to her death at Clytemnestra's hands. The contrast could hardly be more glaring. And though in the *Eumenides* Apollo may very well incarnate the ruthlessness of the male in a contest with the female Furies, it is an intentional anomaly in the *Agamemnon* that the same ruthlessness should be visited on a helpless human victim. And what are we to make of the fact that Artemis, "angered at the flying hounds of her father," should openly flout the will of Zeus and demand the sacrifice of Iphigeneia before allowing the Greeks to proceed on the Zeus-enjoined conquest of Troy? The only possible conclusion is surely that there is discord in heaven, just as in the *Iliad* we see god set against god in a perpetual attempt to slow or cross the will of Zeus. Anomaly, contradiction, moral irresponsibility on earth and in heaven: this is the world of the *Agamemnon*, and it is, I think, precisely what we should expect. How else, dramatically speaking, could Aeschylus have shown us his gradual progress toward the light? For the light requires a darkness to dispel, and the darkness of the *Agamemnon* is a deliberately constructed one, not the result of the dramatist's confusion or inconsistency.

A related problem: does Agamemnon enjoy freedom of action or was he compelled to sacrifice Iphigeneia? Once again the answer, I think, is the Homeric one, which is to say that Agamemnon freely chose but he was also compelled to choose. So in the *Iliad* we see Agamemnon freely confiscate Achilles' prize and so bring on the fatal wrath; later, however, he declares that it was not he who did it but Zeus and Ate, which is simply Homer's way of sustaining the crucial doubleness of all his action: Agamemnon chose an act which Zeus also chose him to do. To modern ears this may seem an evasion of difficulty by way of paradox, but the notion, I believe, is firmly classical and also commonsensical: we all think we act with freedom though upon reflection it frequently seems that we could not possibly have acted otherwise than we did. So in the *Agamemnon* we find the Chorus declaring that Agamemnon put on the yoke of necessity, but before that it asks: "What course without evils?" Which, at least to my ears, suggests choice, however small in fact that choice may have been. In short, Agamemnon chooses his necessity, but equally Zeus' necessity chose him; being the kind of man he is, he chooses as he does. Consider in this connection the famous Aeschylean fragment: "when Zeus wishes to destroy a man's house utterly, he puts an *aitia* [i.e. a cause or responsibility] in the man." What does this mean except that a man acts from the necessity of his nature *and* as god compels him? Similarly we later find Agamemnon asserting that he and the gods are jointly responsible [*metaitioi*] for the destruction of Troy, and Clytemnestra likewise declares to Orestes that she and Destiny are jointly responsible accomplices [*paraitioi*] in the murder of Agamemnon. And surely it is just this joint responsibility that the action everywhere exhibits and requires. Thus in the famous central scene of the red tapestries, we see Agamemnon, reluctant and wary but also deeply tempted and guilty, finally lured into Clytemnestra's net as his fatal vanity once drove him, with the connivance and foreknowledge of heaven, to sacrifice his daughter. So too we can detect in Clytemnestra's action itself both the deep sources of her own motivation *and* the hand of heaven. She too chooses her revenge, but she is also the instrument chosen of heaven to cut down Agamemnon.

Consider also the deliberate parallel with Orestes. At the opening of the *Choephoroe* we find Orestes suffering under almost the same necessity as Agamemnon earlier: just as Artemis ordered Agamemnon to kill his daughter, so Orestes is commanded by Apollo to murder his mother. Hideous punishment is threatened if he disobeys, and yet Orestes, I think, can be said to choose here because he so clearly acts for motives that are properly his own: vengeance for his father and the recovery of his patrimony. He too chooses, that is, the act he is also constrained to commit. But there is this time a crucial difference: the comparative purity of the motive. Unlike Agamemnon and Clytemnestra, Orestes undertakes his murder with the reluctance and misgiving of an innocent heart and also with the determination of justice. Even Electra explicitly questions the wisdom of a god who could command that a mother be murdered by her son. For the first time, that is, in the history of the house of Atreus, a murder is being undertaken in something like purity of heart, for Orestes' act is clouded neither by his father's fatal vanity nor by his mother's jealousy and guilty hatred. It is revenge pure and simple, reluctant and unhappy and uncertain, but the nearest thing to the spirit of true justice that an age of vendetta-justice can offer. For we must be careful to judge the hero by the standards of the age in which he lives, and this is a world whose only justice as yet is the simple and brutal *lex talionis*.

Great consequences flow from this, I think, for innocence in this play is crucial. Not only does it signify to Zeus that the moment is at last ripe for the institution of civilized justice, but it is because Orestes' heart was pure and his action productive of conscience and remorse that he can, without divine inconsistency, be purged and finally acquitted. But there is more to it than that: precisely because Orestes' innocence is deeply his own, the native reaction of his own heart to the callous command of a god who told him to cut down his father's murderers "in their own fashion, to turn to the bull's fury in the loss of his estates," mankind becomes, through Orestes, partner and accessory [*metaitios*] with Zeus in the great act of justice that closes the trilogy. Orestes' act releases Zeus, but because the act was undertaken in free innocence, men share with Zeus the glory of the new justice which we now see has been Zeus' intent from the beginning. But wisdom on earth *must* precede Zeus' revelation: the condition of justice is the free and rightly motivated collaboration of men, and this could only come about when men discovered both innocence and compassion before necessity. Orestes kills but first he hesitates, and the whole world and the fate of mankind hang in that act of hesitation. For the play is about nothing less than the discovery of wisdom [*sophia*] under the yoke of awful necessity. To us, the heirs of Orestes' act, it may seem a small wisdom that a man who must kill should, for pity's sake, hesitate, but this is the wisdom appropriate to the necessity in question. And it marks, I think, in Aeschylus' eyes, a great moment in the fortunes of mankind, since it is the indispensable prerequisite of civilized justice itself. God sends necessity upon man that he may learn, and learning, become the partner of god in the great drama of the making of a civilized world.

Look back now at the *Agamemnon* from this vantage-point. If I am right, what we see is a world of terrible disorder, fate set against fate, god against god, man against man and god, all entangled in the great net of a justiceless, impossible justice. For this confusion, man and god are jointly responsible, but even the mind of Zeus is hampered and restricted by the still potent necessities of an older and more barbaric world-order. In this world, tragedy can only work itself out through time and suffering, and Zeus himself is powerless to act until the heart of man happens on the beginnings of a truer justice. For justice without the wisdom to sustain it would have been a meaningless gift, and wisdom, as the Chorus tells us, is learned in suffering. And so we see Clytemnestra and Agamemnon caught in a necessity which their own natures as well as the conflicting purposes of heaven have made. But we should not judge them too harshly; true, they do what they do and suffer what they suffer because they are what they are, but unless I am mistaken, we can almost hear Aeschylus saying between the lines, how can we expect men to be better than gods? If Agamemnon has murdered Iphigeneia, how much more brutal is the conduct of Apollo towards Cassandra. We must judge, that is, by the standards appropriate to Agamemnon's world, and if we judge him rightly we shall be in a position to understand the true stature of Orestes' heroism, surpassing in moral skills the god who commanded him to kill. Agamemnon, however proud, however guilty of *hybris*, is a man torn between the necessity of his own nature and the necessities imposed upon him by a world of moral disorder. He is not, I think, a true tragic hero—for Orestes is the hero of the *Oresteia*—but the self-involved tragic victim of a world which is as flawed as he is. He is therefore a candidate for compassion as much as judgment, and so are Clytemnestra and her victim, Cassandra. Only a mind unreceptive to the meaning of Athena's justice can refuse to give these casualties of a great cosmology in the making the human justice of pity and compassion. This, it seems to me, is an essential part of the real complexity and enormous moral turbulence of the *Oresteia*.

III

Unless I am mistaken, tragedy is also in deep need of some new perspectives in the matter of its operative moral terms as well as in structure and plot. And particularly, I think, we need to question again the relevance of Aristotle on at least two points—the so-called tragic flaw and the putative Aristotelian theory of tragic structure, the structure that draws its sanction from the *Oedipus Rex* and is reinforced by our modern preference for the organic. Aristotle is, I know, a rough customer: he has of necessity immense authority, and one is never quite sure whether one is talking about Aristotle or about something that has borrowed the authority of his name. But I have never been able to satisfy myself that the *Poetics* is the purely inductive treatise that scholars claim it is: again and again, that is, what is inductive in the *Poetics* seems to me to be directed by what is not, the pervasive notion of a purposive and rational universe and all that such a notion implies for tragedy and for the structure of tragedy. Thus for Aristotle a tragic fall is grounded in a consistent and harmonious sense of a man's responsibility for his nature and his actions: when the hero falls, he falls for his own failure, and behind the rightness of his fall, working both pity and terror by the precise and relentless nature of its operations, stands the order which society and a god-informed world impose upon the individual. What the law requires, the world requires too, and so the Aristotelian play portrays, like an image of human life, the individual torn and suffering between his nature and an objective world-order.

The tragic fall is, of course, in the common reading of Aristotle, based upon the hero's possession of a tragic flaw; and whether as doctrine or habit, the attempt to find a tragic flaw in Greek plays seems to me a persistent stumbling-block. If you really look at the *Oedipus*, for instance, it is immediately clear that Oedipus' tragic flaw is hard to discover: one wants to know—if you begin with the Aristotelian habit—just what in the hero's nature or his acts makes him suffer as hideously as he does, and the obvious answers—his anger, his treatment of Creon and Teiresias, his attempt to avoid his fate—are all unsatisfactory, or if satisfactory, indict the gods that could afflict a man so grievously for such offense. One recent critic of the play, an Aristotelian by conviction as well as habit, recognized his dilemma immediately and proceeded to solve it by the suggestion that Sophocles in this play has generalized *hamartia* into something like original sin: Oedipus has no particular flaws but suffers in the very flaw of his humanity. I suspect that very few classicists, whatever their religious color, will be happy with this theory, and I hope that even Aristotelians might object. But I use it to illustrate the kind of trouble that the expectation of a tragic flaw can create even in the treatment of a play which Aristotle regarded as the paradigm of his theories.

I cannot myself pretend to understand that mysterious play, but I wonder if we are perhaps not the better off for proceeding from the play rather than from Aristotle. Freed from our own *a prioris*, the experience of the play may at least propose itself in different terms. Thus it has always seemed to me that the single most pertinent fact of the *Oedipus* was not the hero's flaw, but his refusal to accept a ready-made fate: he wants his own fate, not the gods', and though his personal fate may be cut short by his doom, Oedipus at the close of the play insists upon distinguishing his own responsibility by blinding himself. It is the magnificence of his own declaration of responsibility that makes him so heroic: his fate is *his* and no one else's. His anger is anger, neither more nor less; it is not the source of his doom, but the irritant that he exhibits on the road to doom; and if he has a *hamartia*, it is not sin or flaw but the ungovernable tragic ignorance of all men: we do not know who we are nor who fathered us but go, blinded by life and hope, toward a wisdom bitter at the gates of hell. The cost of action is suffering, and heroism is the anguished acceptance of our own identities and natures, forged in action and pain in a world we never made. Whatever the final merits of this suggestion, it at least, I think, preserves the dignity of human passion in the play without violating in the name of a crude automatic justice the mysterious destiny that rules the play.

But crude or vulgar Aristotelianism [1] has hurt all three dramatists, and Euripides in particular, and one of the most urgent tasks for the criticism of tragedy is the thorough re-examination of Euripidean structure; once we get Euripides straight, we may be in a position to see just where we have subtly distorted Aeschylus and Sophocles in the name of a misunderstood Aristotle. But here again, I think, criticism might best begin from the obvious—the long insistence of critics that Euripidean plays lack unity, fall into disparate actions or are merely episodes strung together. We start, that is, from the fact of dislocation and attempt to see whether dislocation might not be deliberate method rather than the hit-or-miss *ad hoc* work of a genius who consistently botched. What is immediately apparent if we start from this point is the real coherence of the plays so far as structure is concerned; what is most obvious in the *Heracles* or *Hecuba* is true also of the *Bacchae, Hippolytus* and *Medea:* all lack the kind of unity which the organic theory requires, all exhibit dislocation. If we ask why this is so, I think we find it mirrored by a curious doubleness in the action or in the given and created realities of the plays. Thus the *Heracles* shows two successive plateaus, the first a reality appropriate to legend and old convention, i.e. a world of

---

[1] Much of contemporary dogmatizing about what Aristotle did or did not mean seems to me to rest squarely upon uninformed or unimaginative interpretation of what Aristotle actually said. I am encouraged in this opinion by Professor Gerald F. Else's magisterial *Aristotle's Poetics: The Argument* (Harvard University Press, 1957), surely the most important book on Aristotelian criticism in the twentieth century and one which will inevitably shape and alter the whole tenor of modern explication of Aristotle.

At my request, Professor Else has provided me with a brief statement of his views of what Aristotle actually said, and I quote him verbatim in the conviction of complete agreement. He writes: "There is no doubt that the root and center of Aristotle's theory of tragedy, indeed of all poetry, is the idea of an action (N.B. "*an* action," not simply "action"). It should be easy to say what he means by an action, since he talks about it so much; but there are obscurities and ambiguities. Perhaps the key is that an action is a *trans*action, the living out of a decisive turn of events by a significant human being. Aristotle seems to say that neither *people* nor *situations*—suffering, hopelessness, demoniacal possession, or whatever—are tragic in themselves. Involvement in action is the sign-manual of our human condition and our passport to happiness; it is also the warrant of our possible ruin. Without action a man can be, but he can neither win nor lose; and the winning or losing (not having-lost or being-about-to-lose, or even being-such-as-to-lose) is the tragedy. What is tragic is neither the potentiality nor the actuality of suffering, but its actualization. Tragedy cannot be *displayed*, but only *enacted*. It would seem to follow that the tragic action, though involved with universals—character (type), characteristic acts, pattern of events—is irreducibly a particular. Whether or not Oedipus is a type, the hell into which he enters is his individually, for *only he has entered it through this action*. But it is not clear whether Aristotle is aware of this further corollary. What he does do, beyond any ambiguity, is to insist on the primacy of the action."

mythical illusion, the second the full created tragic reality out of which heroism is born. If we look, say, at the *Orestes*, we discover a play which freely invents its own reality and then confronts the action so created with an epiphany of Apollo in which the whole motion of the play up to that point is flatly contradicted. We get a head-on collision, that is, between the action of the play and the traditionalizing impossible *deus ex machina*, and no attempt is made to modulate or explain these incompatible sequences. The same is true of the *Iphigeneia at Aulis*, and also, I think, of the *Medea* and *Electra:* their conclusions are simply at variance, as real events, from the whole tenor of the action. In the *Hippolytus* and *Bacchae* this doubleness is used in a different and less violent way: both plays dramatize the full incredibility of a traditional account of Olympian anthropomorphism—it is incredible that gods, real gods, should act as Dionysus and Aphrodite do. But once the familiar reality has been exposed and displaced, both plays proceed, in a symbolic manner, to hint at a deeper meaning and a different reality for these displaced gods. What I am trying to suggest is that again and again in Euripides, what makes the plays dislocated in structure is a deliberate juxtaposition of antithetical realities—the reality of the material which the play takes from legend and myth, and the new reality which the dramatist forces, as action, from his old material. We get the same kind of jar, that is, that our lives receive when they proceed upon inadequate conviction and are suddenly confronted with difficulty too great for the old conviction. But to my mind our understanding of Euripidean structure rests firmly upon our ability to understand the dramatic experience that bridges the two or even three plateaus of reality that most Euripidean plays exhibit. In the *Heracles*, for instance, we get between the two actions no *propter hoc* connection of the kind Aristotelians insist upon, and yet the connection seems to me, if not quite necessitous, at least valid with whatever validity the conversion of human experience possesses.

If heroism happens to arise from a fortuitous and accidental eruption of the irrational in the nature of things—as in the *Heracles* or the *Hippolytus*— the very fact that it is in the nature of things makes the eruption necessary or probable: we tend to disbar it only because our Aristotelian habits predispose us to a dramatic world like that of Sophocles, where the apparent irrationalities of experience are explained by a divine order we cannot comprehend. But as applied to Euripides, these habits and their corollary in a crude notion of the tragic flaw can only complicate chaos further. We need rather a theory of Euripidean structure which starts from dislocation and attempts to show the relation of this form to a world of moral disorder. Unless I am mistaken, such examination must also show the irrelevance of *propter hoc* structure to Euripides, whose sense of necessity in drama derives more from the motion of the human mind under stress and the patterns which men's convictions make when confronted by adventitious realities. A man's character may be his destiny, but for Euripides destiny is often dependent upon and defined by circumstances the hero never made, nor the gods either. Unless we can restore an understanding of the importance of the dramatist's assumed world for his form, Euripides must stand perpetually condemned or be explained with all the willful improbability of Verrall. At least the latest book on Euripidean structure—Gilbert Norwood's *Essays on Euripidean Drama*—makes the implicit claim that these dislocations of plot and internal inconsistencies in the plays are best explained as the work of fourth century redactors. This seems both unfortunate and unnecessary.

One final point. Nothing, I think, more effectively hinders our understanding of the experience of Greek tragedy than the inadequacy and crudity of meaning which critics and translators assign to the operative moral terms of Greek tragedy—*sophia, hybris, anankeē, sōphrosunē, aristeia, timē, authadia* and the like. For in much criticism of tragedy these terms are used as though they possessed simple English equivalents, without, I think, adequate reference to the experience with which they were meant to cope. Alternatively, they are exposed to static definition without regard to the transformations which tragedy may force upon them as the hero moves from a situation of conventional morality and reality to an ordeal for which the traditional wisdom of the Chorus may be utterly inadequate. In such situations it is my conviction that the old moral terms are employed with a meaning so turbulent with fresh or restored experience that they are no longer the same terms, nor the hero to whom they apply the same man. *Timē*, for instance, is normally translated as *honor*, but its root meaning is price, or valuation, and in most tragedies where the concept is important—the *Antigone*, for instance—the word operates very much like the deep sense of our word "respect." Thus when Ismene claims that Antigone has not shown *timē* to her, and that Creon has not shown *timē* to Haemon, she means, not that she and Haemon have been dishonored, or insulted, but that they have not been respected: they have been disallowed the dignity of a fate and their dignity as individuals. They have, as it were, been priced all wrong, and this charge is, of course, central to the play, since Antigone claims to act for *philia* because she wishes to give *timē* to Polyneices. What, the play seems to suggest, is the assertion of *philia* worth without *timē* too? And what is a *philia* which, in order to respect one person, shows disrespect to another, both equally claiming the rights of *philia?*

Or consider the word *sophia*, which we badly translate as "wisdom," as it gets into the *Bacchae*. Among other things, *sophia* means a knowledge and acceptance of one's nature and therefore of one's place in the scheme of things. It presupposes, that is, self-knowledge, an acceptance of those necessities that compose the limits of human fate. It also means the consequent refinement of feelings by which a man recognizes and respects the sufferings of others before necessity: it issues in compassion.[2] *Sophia* is further contrasted with its opposite, *amathia*, a deep, brutal, unteachable, ungovernable self-ignorance which breaks out in violence and cruelty. If the *sophos* is by definition susceptible to the feelings of civilized humanity, a compassion learned in fellow-suffering, the *amathēs* is callous and merciless, a barbarian by nature. But it is these meanings which crowd into the *Bacchae* and everywhere provide, through dramatic action and testing, the play's missing principle of order. For in the course of the action, through the very brutality which they use to support their claims to *sophia*, both Pentheus and Dionysus utterly expose their own *amathia*.

But more than the self-indictment of Pentheus or Dionysus is involved here. For Euripides has taken elaborate pains to show in Pentheus something more than the man who does not know the deep Dionysiac necessity of his own nature: he is also the proud iconoclastic innovator, the rebel at war with tradition, standing outside of the community's *nomos* [custom as law] and as *theomachos*, disdainful of any power above man. Ranged against him are Cadmus, Teiresias and the chorus, who all alike appeal to the massive tyranny of tradition and folk-belief, and constantly invoke as the sanction of society against the rebellious or anti-traditional man the words *sōphrosunē* and *dikē*. Thus in flat opposition to Pentheus' lonely arrogance of the "exceptional" (*perissos*) man, defying the community's *nomos* in the name of his own self-will, is set the chorus' tyrannous tradition: "Beyond the old beliefs, no thought, no act shall go (891–2)." We have, that is, a head-on collision between the forces which represent a brutally depraved conservative tradition and the arrogant exemplar of the ruthlessly anti-traditional mind. Both positions are alike in the cruel and bigoted violence with which they meet opposition, and the *sophia* and *sōphrosunē* and *dikē* which they both claim mock their pretensions and condemn their conduct. If the conduct of the chorus and Dionysus outrage our sympathies and finally enlist them on Pentheus' behalf, it is because, in the nature of things, the *amathia* of a man is less heinous than that of a god. But both are *amatheis*, Pentheus no less than the chorus, and the play as a whole employs them and their struggle as a bitter image of both Athens and Hellas terribly divided between the forces that, in Euripides' mind, more than anything else destroyed them: on the one side, the conservative and aristocratic tradition in its extreme corruption, disguising avarice for wealth and power with the fair professions of the traditional *aretai*, meeting all attempts at change or moderation with the tyranny of popular piety, and disclosing in its actions the callousness and

---

[2] Cf. *Electra*, 11. 294–5, where Orestes states that pity (*to oiktos*) is never to be found among the *amatheis* but only among the *sophoi* i.e. compassion is a true component of "wisdom."

refined cruelty of civilized barbarism; on the other side, the exceptional individual, selfish and egotistical, impatient of public welfare and tradition alike, opportunistic, demagogic and equally brutal in action. In saying this, I do not intend to dispute the obvious religious concerns of the *Bacchae*, but to stress what, to my knowledge, has not been emphasized, that the play is, like the *Heracles*, the *Electra* and the *Orestes*, a composite of discrete conversions, social and political as well as religious. And all of these concerns meet in the term *sophia* and its opposite, *amathia*, which at their widest enclose most of what we mean by "civilized" and "uncivilized," both morally and politically. Thus when Euripides has his chorus assert that *to sophon* is not the same as *sophia* he means that the pretensions and conventions and habits of civilization are by no means equivalent to civilized practices.

But in my opinion the same widening and deepening of the operative moral terms of Greek culture is to be found everywhere in tragedy—*philia* in *Antigone*, *sōphrosunē* in *Hippolytus*, *eugeneia* in *Heracles*, *aristeia* in *Orestes*, etc.—and it would be surprising if it were not so. But upon our sense of the play of the traditional or lazy meanings of these words and the definitions which the tragic action makes lies, I think, much of the turbulence now missing from the criticism of tragedy.

Let me close with a brief note on necessity, for necessity seems to me the crucial center of Greek tragedy, just as Greek tragedy seems to me unique in the firmness and sharpness with which it follows necessity into human action. In its basic aspect, necessity (*anankē*) is that set of unalterable, irreducible, unmanageable facts which we call the human condition. Call it destiny, call it fate, call it the gods, it hardly matters. Necessity is, first of all, death; but it is also old age, sleep, the reversal of fortune and the dance of life; it is thereby the fact of suffering as well as pleasure, for if we must dance and sleep, we also suffer, age and die. It is also sex, the great figure of amoral Aphrodite who moves in the sea, land and air and as an undeniable power in the bodies of men, compelling and destroying those who, like Hippolytus, refuse to accept her. Or it is Dionysus, the terrible ambiguous force of the *Bacchae*, "the force that through the green fuse drives the flower," and who destroys Pentheus who lacks the *sophia* that accepts him. It is the great god-sprung trap of the *Oedipus* and also the nature of Oedipus himself, that stubborn human courage of pride that drives him relentlessly into the trap. It is the necessity of political power which, in corruption, destroys Hecuba and Iphigeneia and Cassandra and Polyxena. It is the inherent hostility of blind chance, the incalculable daemonic malice which in the Euripidean *Heracles* calls out to the hero to die and tells him that there is no hope and no moral order in the world at all. Suspend necessity in the form of the play, and you get such charming, romantic plays as *Iphigeneia at Tauris* and the *Helen*. Romantic, that is, because not tragic; and not tragic because necessity, the mainspring of tragedy, has been, for fun, for entertainment and experiment, removed. Where men are freed from the yoke of necessity, their lives cease to be tragic, and with the loss of suffering comes also the loss of dignity and *sophia*.

For it is in the *struggle* with necessity that heroism is born, and even the hero, if he is to retain his humanity, must accept necessity. Ripeness is all. And so we see Orestes discover purity and compassion in the face of a necessity that threatens to deform him as it has already deformed his father and mother and as it inevitably deforms the weak, the flawed, the average human nature. So too Antigone accepts her necessity, the consequence of her own act, humanity pushed to the extreme, and thereby comes again upon her humanity in the very act of acceptance and recognition of loss. So Oedipus by asserting his total utter responsibility for his own fate, wins the victory over a necessity that would have destroyed a lesser man. And so Heracles claims a moral dignity forever out of reach of the amoral powers that persecute him. There is a magnificence here in the power to rise, in the anguished acceptance that must always, in Greek tragedy, precede the winning of dignity. For it is here before necessity that old morality is unmade and then remade into a new thing. Thus Orestes, having discovered at least that compassion that made him hesitate, enables justice to be born. And so too at the close of the *Hippolytus* and *Bacchae* we see the suffering human survivors of the play discover, under the awful yoke of an intolerable necessity, the love and *compassion*, the shared suffering that makes men endure with love in a world which shrieks at them to die. Learn wisdom through suffering, says Aeschylus, and if we are loyal to the turbulence of Greek tragedy, we can see what he means. For, stripped to the bone, the essential *action* of the greatest of the Greek tragedies is an enactment of lives lived out under the double yoke of man's own nature and a world he did not make; the weaker fail or are deformed; the strong survive, and by surviving and enduring, liberate the dignity of significant suffering which gives man the crucial victory over his own fate.

The Implications of Tragedy[*]

CLIFFORD LEECH

The gulf between the learned use and the popular use of the same word is nowhere better illustrated than in "tragedy." The term is used from day to day in referring to incidents of a distressful nature, and, in so far as it is popularly used as the name of a literary type, it is applied to any play or story with an unhappy ending. This is unfortunate, for the widespread vague use of the term makes it more difficult for students to clarify their ideas on the significance of *King Lear* and the *Agamemnon:* if our labels are smudged, we are forced to make a continual effort to remind ourselves of the contents of each package. Yet here we cannot blame the journalist for the blurring of the word's meaning, for the vague use of "tragedy" goes back to medieval times. Moreover, even those who have aimed at using the word precisely have not reached agreement concerning the nature of the literary type to which the word is, by them, applied.

The most famous definition of tragedy in medieval times is given by Chaucer in the Prologue to *The Monk's Tale:*

> Tragedie is to seyn a certeyn storie,
> As olde bokes maken us memorie,
> Of him that stood in greet prosperitie
> And is y-fallen out of heigh degree
> Into miserie, and endeth wrecchedly.

He adds that tragedies are commonly written in hexameters, but that "many oon" has been written in prose as well as in other metres. Similarly in his translation of Boethius he adds the gloss:

Tragedie is to seyn, a ditee of a prosperitie for a tyme, that endeth in wrecchednesse.

It is evident that, in Chaucer's view, a tragedy need not be written in dramatic form. This arose out of the break in continuity between the drama

* Clifford Leech, "The Implications of Tragedy," from *Shakespeare's Tragedies and Other Studies in 17th Century Drama* (Chatto & Windus, Ltd., 1950), pp. 3–20.

of antiquity and the drama of the medieval church, and indeed most medieval references to tragedy similarly make no mention of dramatic representation. But this is not the only omission which strikes us in Chaucer's definition, for he indicates no cause for the fall from high degree. This, however, he had to consider when writing the "tragedies" of *The Monk's Tale:* he could not pen tales of woe without implying why the woe came about. In the opening lines of *The Monk's Tale* he averred that it was Fortune who was responsible for the change in a man's estate: capriciously she might turn her back, and man should steel himself for these methodless reversals. On the other hand, in some of the Monk's "tragedies" a totally different idea is put forward: man is there frequently robbed of his prosperity on account of sin: Adam, for example, is turned out of Paradise "for misgovernaunce." Chaucer, in fact, hesitates in his conception of tragedy in much the same way as do most people who tell sad tales: at times they believe that misfortunes come because they are merited, at times they feel that there is such a thing as bad luck: they waver between a planned universe of rewards and punishments and a chaotic universe in which chance operates without motive.

Yet if Chaucer's use of the term is the common one, we should recognize that literary theorists have been justified in trying to use the term more precisely. They have felt that certain pieces of dramatic literature are of a special kind, leaving an impression on our minds which is peculiar to themselves, and thus demanding a special label. Aristotle in Chapter VI of *The Poetics* produced a definition of tragedy which has served as a starting-point for every modern critic who has attempted to describe the effect of plays of this kind; and though the definition is obscure in the crucial point, that of *catharsis*, it provides clear evidence that Aristotle recognized tragic plays as constituting a special *genre*. At the same time Aristotle illustrates how difficult it is to be precise concerning the nature of his *genre:* in Chapter XIII he claims that the tragic hero, "a man not pre-eminently virtuous and just," should fall from prosperity to misery through a fatal flaw in his character or an error of judgment, and thus he defends the unhappy ending in tragedy; in Chapter XIV, however, he gives especial praise to that type of tragedy in which disaster is avoided at the last moment through the revelation of something previously unknown. The contradiction may well be due to the conflicting claims of philosophic theory and dramatic effectiveness. In any event, it may serve as a warning of the difficulty of achieving consistency in a theory of tragedy, and of deciding exactly which plays are to be accepted as tragic.

It is not my purpose here to consider the many explanations of *catharsis* that have been put forward from the time of the Italian Renaissance critics. In all likelihood Aristotle's notion was that tragedy served as a safety-valve, a means of freeing the mind from the pity and the fear that might otherwise enter public or private life, and Mr F. L. Lucas may be right in his belief that Aristotle claimed this cathartic effect for tragedy as a defence against the charges of Plato.[1] But that the emotions of pity and fear are concerned in the tragic effect has not been disputed by any subsequent theorist. Dr I. A. Richards, indeed, has seen these two emotions as opposing forces which tragedy brings into a state of equilibrium. For him the tragic effect is the achievement of a state of repose in the nervous system, a repose without inertia because it is the result of a perpetual opposition:

Pity, the impulse to approach, and Terror, the impulse to retreat, are brought in Tragedy to a reconciliation which they find nowhere else, and with them who knows what other allied groups of equally discordant impulses. Their union in an ordered single response is the *catharsis* by which Tragedy is recognised, whether Aristotle meant anything of this kind or not. This is the explanation of that sense of release, of repose in the midst of stress, of balance and composure, given by Tragedy, for there is no other way in which such impulses, once awakened, can be set at rest without suppression.[2]

But the difficulty about this is that Dr Richards does not tell us what it is that we feel an impulse to approach and a simultaneous impulse to retreat from. We feel pity—or perhaps sympathy would be the better word—with reference to the tragic hero and to other characters who are involved in disaster, but we are not terrified by him or them. Even where the tragic hero, like Orestes or Macbeth, causes fear to the other characters, we do not share their feelings. Our fear is aroused by the picture of the universe that the tragic writer presents, we are impelled to retreat from the contemplation of evil, we should like to shut our eyes if we could. If, therefore, the pity and the fear are aroused by different stimuli, it is difficult to see how any balancing of them can be other than fortuitous. Our sympathy with Hamlet is greater than our sympathy with Othello, because most of us find Hamlet the more attractive character: yet it would be a rash assumption that the play of *Hamlet* arouses more terror than the play of *Othello*. Moreover, Dr Richards's view of tragedy is weighted on the therapeutic side. He claims that it makes us feel that "all is right . . . in the nervous system,"[3] but he neglects that part of our experience which is the recognition that the dramatist's view of the universe is terrible as well as strengthening.

Yet the idea that the tragic effect resides in an equilibrium of opposing forces does seem to correspond with our experience. After witnessing a successful performance of one of Shakespeare's four great tragedies, or of Webster's *The Duchess of Malfi*, or of the *Agamemnon*, our state of mind is

---

[1] *Tragedy in Relation to Aristotle's Poetics*, 1927, p. 33.
[2] *Principles of Literary Criticism*, 1934, pp. 245 and 246.
[3] *Op. cit.*, p. 246.

active, and yet active to no immediate end: we are in a state of unusual stimulation, and yet we are more inclined to contemplate the experience than to plan our future conduct: we have seen a picture of evil, but it has neither palsied our faculties nor aroused us to struggle against it.

It is not surprising, therefore, that Professor Una Ellis-Fermor has also seen a balance of opposing forces in the effect of tragedy.[4] For her the balance is between the view that the world is controlled by an alien and hostile destiny and the view that somehow this apparent evil may be explained in terms of good. She points out that in the *Agamemnon* and the *Choëphore* Aeschylus presents the evil of things through the actions and the words of the actors, and through the speeches of the Chorus suggests that outside the human world there is a divine organisation of things. In Shakespeare, she suggests, the fact that such characters as Cordelia and Kent can exist must lead to what she calls a "positive" interpretation—that is, an idea that the universe is under benevolent direction. Feeling, perhaps, that the indications of goodness are in some indubitable tragedies rather too slight, Professor Ellis-Fermor adds that the very principle of order apparent in the formal articulation of tragic plays acts as a counterpoise to the evil chaos that seems to prevail. Her view, in brief, is that the tragic equilibrium consists in the simultaneous holding in the mind of the two conflicting ideas: that the universe is divinely directed and that it is devil-ridden. She implies, however, that this equilibrium is impermanent, that the tragic writer may find his way beyond it to an acceptance of the idea of divine control, and she refers here to Shakespeare's final romances as evidence that Shakespeare escaped from the dark vision of *Othello* and *Lear*.

The difficulty in Professor Ellis-Fermor's position is that the indications of a divinely controlled universe are in many tragedies scarcely sufficient to counterpoise the presentation of evil. It is not enough that in *Othello* we have characters who mean no harm: Othello and Desdemona are well-intentioned enough, but their disaster comes upon them through his credulity and her lack of directness: in view of the magnitude of the suffering that is brought about by these comparatively minor faults, it is difficult to see that their good qualities point to a divinely controlled universe. And the control of art need suggest nothing more than that man has a certain faculty for ordering part of his experience: it does not transform the nature of that experience, and it does not necessarily suggest that either he or a creator can control the totality of experience.

That there is an equilibrium of forces in the tragic effect I think we can admit, but Professor Ellis-Fermor has looked too far in trying to reconcile the tragic and the Christian pictures of life. We need to examine the tragic picture in more detail—to consider, banishing presuppositions as far as we

---

[4] *The Frontiers of Drama*, 1945, pp. 127–147.

can, the view of life offered to us by plays that we will all agree to have a similar effect on us, plays that we will not hesitate to call "tragic."

Not only are great evil and suffering presented in such plays but there is no comprehensible scheme of rewards and punishments suggested. Oedipus sins, as Aristotle puts it, through an error of judgment, yet he is led to a state of mind where even the thought of death is no escape from the horror; Othello is induced to murder his innocent wife and then to realise his mistake: only suicide offers itself as a way out; Desdemona and Ophelia are guilty of nothing more than weakness, yet they are destroyed; Lear is hot-tempered and foolish, yet no one will claim that he deserved to endure madness and the storm on the heath; Cordelia refuses to play her father's game, and is hanged for it; Gloucester begets Edmund, and his eyes are plucked out; Webster's Duchess of Malfi loves and marries her steward Antonio, and on that account is slowly tortured to death. Moreover, the plays frequently include a number of minor characters whose sudden and cruel deaths do not arise out of any fault of their own: Lady Macduff and her son, Polonius, Rosencrantz and Guildenstern, the brave servant in *King Lear* who tries to save Gloucester from blindness, the virtuous Marcello in Webster's *The White Devil*—all these can hardly be said to get their deserts. It is true that in some tragedies the final disaster springs from an evil act on the part of the hero—*Macbeth* and the plays of Marlowe come quickly to the mind—but even there we feel no satisfaction in the hero's punishment. Rather, we have a feeling that his initial conduct was hardly within his own control: Macbeth was singularly unfortunate in the joint temptation from the witches and his wife, and the witches' prophecy suggests from the beginning that his crime was predetermined; Marlowe's heroes are felt to act as they do because the world is what it is, a world which presents a perpetual challenge to the man of high courage. Thus we feel no desire to rejoice when the perpetrator of evil is brought to his doom, and at the same time we are aware that many characters in these plays are subjected to an evil for which they are in no way responsible.

Nor is there in great tragedy the suggestion that these things will be put right in another world. It is true that in comparatively minor works like Kyd's *The Spanish Tragedy* we are assured in an epilogue that the hero and his supporters will find their way to the Elysian Fields while their adversaries will know infernal tortures, but in *Othello* and *Lear* and *Macbeth* there is no such emphasis on a compensatory future life. Othello contemplates immortality only with horror:

> O ill-starr'd wench!
> Pale as thy smock! when we shall meet at compt,
> This look of thine will hurl my soul from heaven,
> And fiends will snatch at it. (V. ii.)

Cleopatra assumes a heavenly encounter with Antony, and fears that Iras
will get to him first:

> This proves me base:
> If she first meet the curled Antony,
> He'll make demand of her, and spend that kiss
> Which is my heaven to have. (V. ii.)

Her speech is no consolation to the audience, who are made to feel only the
strange limitations of this late tragic figure. In *Hamlet* heavenly joys are on
occasion referred to: Horatio's

> Good night, sweet prince,
> And flights of angels sing thee to thy rest! (V. ii.)

and Laertes'

> I tell thee, churlish priest,
> A ministering angel shall my sister be,
> When thou liest howling. (V. i.)

are, however, pieces of embroidery on the situation of the moment rather
than functional utterances in the play. Indeed, *Hamlet* is essentially a play
of doubt concerning what happens after death, and we are likely to agree
that in no Shakespearian tragedy are we made to think of the characters as
emerging from their suffering into the beatific vision: the stresses they encounter are not preparations for a future life but are inescapable conditions
of the only world in which they certainly have an existence. What may or
may not happen after death is something that the tragic dramatist normally
leaves out of consideration: on the rare occasions when he does consider it,
as Marlowe does in *Faustus*, it is to see it as part of the evil which his tragic
hero must endure.

Because of the apparent absence of a kindly or just disposition of things
in the world and because of his disregard of a future life, the tragic dramatist
inevitably sees the gods as remote, if not as beings actively hostile to man.
Perhaps the remoteness of the gods is given most succinct expression in
Webster's *The Duchess of Malfi*, where the Duchess is subjected to intense
mental torture before she is finally killed. Hearing false news of the death
of her husband and children, she cries out that she could curse the stars:
Bosola, her enemies' instrument, let her tongue run on in grief for a few
moments and then bids her look heavenward:

> Look you, the stars shine still. (IV. i.)

All seventeenth-century English tragedy is, indeed, marked by a feeling
that, if there are gods who control the universe, they are far away from
men, and indifferent to the individual's fate. Sometimes this sense of re-

moteness becomes sharpened into a belief that the gods are malicious, enjoying the impotence and the suffering in the world beneath them. Gloucester's cry in his despair:

> As flies to wanton boys, are we to the gods,
> They kill us for their sport. (IV. i.)

is almost paralleled by this piece of bitterness from *The Duchess of Malfi:*

> We are merely the stars' tennis-balls, struck and bandied
> Which way please them. (V. iv.)

But these are dramatic utterances, mere exclamations of the characters' despair, and are no more to be taken as expressing the totality of the playwright's attitude than are the words of Horatio and Laertes, already quoted, envisaging post-lethal joys. In the tragedies of the Greeks the gods intervene more directly than in Elizabethan tragedy, but there, too, there is no assurance of an evenhanded justice in the fates of men, and no suggestion that man can find his compensation in an after-life. When, as in the *Eumenides*, the dramatist tries to humanise the justice of the gods, the play becomes more of a civic pageant than a tragedy: the acquittal of Orestes through the casting-vote of Pallas answers no questions but diverts the spectators' emotions into a new, and non-tragic, direction. But when a play is consistently tragic, the Greek writer does not see a man's problems as solved by a mere appeal to the Gods.

Nevertheless, it is noticeable that tragedy does not necessarily or even normally present an indictment of the divine powers. Professor Ellis-Fermor is certainly right in claiming for the choric utterances in the *Agamemnon* an expression of faith in the divine plan: here, indeed, is a passage which simultaneously brings out the remoteness of Zeus and the divine guidance of man through suffering to wisdom:

> Zeus, whoever He is, if this
> Be a name acceptable,
> By this name I will call him.
> There is no one comparable
> When I reckon all of the case
> Excepting Zeus, if ever I am to jettison
> The barren care which clogs my heart.
>
> Not he who formerly was great
> With brawling pride and mad for broils
> Will even be said to have been.
> And He who was next has met
> His match and is seen no more,
> But Zeus is the name to cry in your triumph-song
> And win the prize for wisdom.

> Who setting us on the road
> Made this a valid law—
>   'That men must learn by suffering.'
> Drop by drop in sleep upon the heart
> Falls the laborious memory of pain,
> Against one's will comes wisdom;
> The grace of the gods is forced on us
>   Throned inviolably.[5]

Man thus has no certain knowledge even of God's name, and God is without pity in his hard discipline. So, too, it is remarkable that in *King Lear* there are repeated references to divine justice. When Albany hears that Cornwall was killed immediately after he had plucked out Gloucester's eyes, his comment is:

>   This shows you are above,
>   You justicers, that these our nether crimes
>   So speedily can venge! (IV. ii.)

And the deaths of Goneril and Regan bring from him these words:

>   This judgment of the heavens, that makes us tremble,
>   Touches us not with pity. (V. iii.)

Most striking of all is Edgar's comment to his dying brother Edmund: he sees the misery of their father as springing from the dissolute begetting of Edmund, and pronounces that

>   The gods are just, and of our pleasant vices
>   Make instruments to plague us:
>   The dark and vicious place where thee he got
>   Cost him his eyes. (V. iii.)

This terrible sentence seems as outrageous to our moral sense as the hanging of Cordelia or the torture of Webster's Duchess. What kind of justice, we wonder, is this, which will seize on so small a fault and inflict so terrible a punishment? The "justice" of the gods, as seen in tragedy, is as terrible as their indifference: in fact, we shall not see tragedy aright unless we recognize that the divine justice mirrored in it is an indifferent justice, a justice which cares no whit for the individual and is not concerned with a nice balance of deserts and rewards.

This justice operates like an avalanche or an echo in an enclosed space. If an evil act is committed, no matter how trifling, it will bring consequences which are far more evil than the original act. Lear, vain and delighting in power and its display, indecently demands a public profession of

---

[5] *The Agamemnon of Aeschylus*, translated by Louis MacNeice, 1936, pp. 18 and 19. Reprinted by permission of Faber & Faber, Ltd., and Harcourt, Brace & World, Inc.

love from his daughters: that leads to the events of the heath, the hanging of Cordelia, the loss of Gloucester's eyes, civil war, and Lear's own death. Thyestes seduces his brother's wife, and the long train of disasters begins for the house of Atreus. Sometimes, however, it is a neutral act which provides the starting-point: the marriage of Webster's Duchess to her steward Antonio shows only a mild disregard for "degree," but it releases the evil forces which have been stored up in the minds of her brothers. The justice of the gods consists simply in the natural law that every act must have its consequence and that the consequence will be determined by the act and its context. If the act is in any way evil or if the situation is one with evil potentialities, then a train of evil will be the result. The tragic writer believes in causation, in the doctrine that means determine ends, and in the powerlessness of the human will to interrupt a chain of disasters.

We may therefore easily understand why the revenge-motive is so common in Greek and Elizabethan tragedy: the blood-feud is the most obvious example of the kind of situation in which wrong inevitably succeeds to wrong.

In such a world-picture as the tragic writer presents to us, it may appear difficult to see how an equilibrium of forces can exist. The impact on our minds of such inhuman justice would at first sight appear only terrible and paralysing. Yet it remains true that our experience of tragic drama is not like that. When we think of Shakespeare's tragedies, of Webster's, of Marlowe's, or of modern tragedies like Mr Eugene O'Neill's *Mourning Becomes Electra*, or Mr Sean O'Casey's *Juno and the Paycock*, what we recall is made up of an indifferent universe and certain characters who seem to demand our admiration. Whether the characters are comparatively blameless, like Hamlet or Webster's Duchess, or deeply guilty, like Macbeth, we feel that they have a quality of mind that somehow atones for the nature of the world in which they and we live. They have, in a greater or lesser degree, the power to endure and the power to apprehend: ultimately they are destroyed, but in all their sufferings they show an increasing readiness to endure, an ever greater awareness. As the shadows gather around them, they stand up the more resolutely, they see the human situation with clearer eyes. Webster's Duchess is at the beginning of the play merely an attractive and enterprising woman, but it is when she cries, in the midst of torment: "I am Duchess of Malfi still," that we recognise her full stature. Lear develops even more remarkably from a vain, hot-tempered tyrant to a man who sees the omnipresence of social wrong and the bodily distress of the poor. So, too, our attitude to Electra and Orestes and Oedipus is inevitably one of growing admiration. Because, moreover, the dramatist has made it clear that his tragic hero is human, a man with weaknesses like our own, we feel not merely admiration but pride: we are proud of our human nature because in such characters it comes to fine flower. In a planned but terrible universe we see man justifying his existence.

Thus the equilibrium of tragedy consists in a balancing of Terror with Pride. On the one hand, we are impelled to withdraw from the spectacle, to try to forget the revelation of evil methodised; on the other, we are roused to withstand destiny, to strive to meet it with the fortitude and the clear eyes of the tragic figure. This feeling of Pride comes into full existence when the hero knows his fate and contemplates it: it is essentially distinct from the *hubris* which he may display, but which we cannot share in, before his eyes are opened.

The tragic picture of the universe postulates a limited free will. Man cannot determine the pattern of event, but he is frequently responsible either for the initiation of an evil chain or for the release of evil forces latent in a situation. Moreover, his thoughts and feelings, his attitude to the enveloping situation, are in his own control: like Orestes, he can see the horror of the matricide he must commit; like Macbeth, he can recognise his own weakness and ultimately his own insignificance in the universal scheme. Some degree of free will is, indeed, essential in tragedy, for we could hardly feel proud of an automaton.

Because of its closer approximation to the everyday appearance of things, there seems to be a greater degree of free will in Elizabethan than in Greek tragedy: it seems as if Hamlet could deflect the course of the action at almost any point if he wished, while clearly Orestes and Oedipus are bound to an established pattern. But Shakespeare and his contemporaries have gone out of their way to make us realise that the pattern is preordained for their characters too: in some plays Shakespeare uses supernatural devices to indicate the course of future events—for example in *Macbeth, Julius Caesar* and *Antony and Cleopatra*—and always he draws his characters in such a way that there is clearly only one line of conduct possible for them in the particular situation in which they find themselves: for them it is the doom-in-the-character rather than the doom-on-the-house. Hamlet must be killed because Hamlet in his particular situation can have no other end: his fate is as inevitable as that of a man lost in the heart of a desert.

Dr E. M. W. Tillyard has put forward an idea of tragedy that must be considered. This has, indeed, often been suggested by writers who have tried to dilute the element of Terror in tragic plays, asserting that in tragedy, as in real life, we see how man can learn and be redeemed through suffering. Dr Tillyard's presentation of this idea is linked up with his view of the *Oresteia* and of Shakespeare's final romances. He sees tragedy as a picture of life disturbed by the intrusion of a disruptive evil force, the apparent triumph of that force, and then the reassertion of a normality which has been strengthened through trial.[6] He points to Othello's last speech, to Lear's wider sympathy near the close of his drama, to Shakespeare's own passage through the despondency of *Timon* to the serenity of *The Tempest*. Certainly our pride in Lear grows as the play proceeds, he emerges as a great figure through the increasing darkness of the situation, but this is not to say that normality resumes her reign, all the better for the testing-time. Lear dies, defeated: that is the essential reason for our Terror; our Pride comes from his acceptance and full knowledge of the situation. The potentialities of evil and suffering are as strong as ever, the gods as ruthless, man's will as powerless. At the end of a Shakespearian tragedy, as at the end of Marlowe's *Faustus* or of *Oedipus at Colonus*, we have a quiet close: words of peace are spoken, and we are conscious that the evil situation no longer exists: the forces of evil have worked themselves out: Hamlet and all his kin are dead. There is nothing reassuring in the new situation, no promise that a new chain of evil will not quickly ensue, no lesson that men or the gods have learned. No message of hope for the future has been brought. The tragic situation, it is implied, is recurrent in human life: that is why we feel Terror; because we have seen men like ourselves yet stronger than we could expect to be, we feel also Pride.

Thus the tragic picture is incompatible with the Christian faith. It is equally incompatible with any form of religious belief that assumes the existence of a personal and kindly God. For that reason we should not be surprised at the rarity of tragedy. Chaucer's view of it as a story of a fall from prosperity to wretchedness, either at the bidding of Fortune or through divine retribution, is a mixture of unconscious paganism with Christian tradition: we cannot expect to find true tragedy anywhere in the Middle Ages, except here and there in early times when literature was not thoroughly Christianised. We can indeed recognize something of the tragic spirit in English poetry before the Conquest, from *Beowulf* to *The Battle of Maldon*. But we should not look for tragedy in the drama of seventeenth-century Spain, for always there the spirit of religion burned brightly: Calderón and Lope de Vega might show evil in their plays, but it was an evil which attended on divine forgiveness or on an acceptable retribution; they might show suffering, but with them indeed it was the suffering of purgatorial fire. Nor should we look for tragedy in the classical drama of India: the gods there are seen as close to man, as his friends and teachers, ready to test human beings but ultimately to reward virtue wherever it should show itself. We can, however, find tragedy in those European countries which were brought most fully under Renaissance influences, with a weakening of medi-

---

[6] *Shakespeare's Last Plays*, 1938, pp. 16–18.

eval faith and some return to stoicism. In the atmosphere of comparative
toleration under Elizabeth and James, English tragedy was especially free to
develop. In seventeenth-century France, Racine could write tragically,
though the form of his plays makes them appear almost like careful exercises
in imitation of the classics: there is a lack of immediacy, of direct relation
to the life around him, which perhaps made both the author and his audience
feel safer: there was no compulsion for them to take too seriously the tragic
view of things there presented. But from the seventeenth century until comparatively recent years the tragic form has been exceedingly rare, not because of a revival of religious faith, but because in these years men have not
often combined a sharp sense of evil, a faith in man, and a sense of the imper-
sonality of divine justice. In later days it is the faith in man that has been
most difficult to come by, though tragedy has made an occasional appearance
in modern European and American drama, and the tragic spirit has not infrequently found nondramatic expression in the modern novel.

But whenever tragedy has come into being, its customary and right dress
has been poetry. The equilibrium of Pride and Terror is, as we have seen,
an opposition of persistent forces, and consequently the tragic play is char-
acterised by strong tension. An appearance of casualness in the play will
weaken the tension, and contradict the implication of a preordained pattern
of event. Moreover, in order that the spectator's mind may more fully respond to the vision of evil and of human strength in defeat, the language must
be finely turned. The medium of tragedy must be poetry, or at least a kind of
prose which in its formal properties is clearly distinguished from the prose
of the everyday, haphazard situation—not because the beauty of the words
will atone for the presentation of evil, soothing our nerves and dulling our
perceptions, but because only by a co-ordination of our faculties can we
reach a full realisation of any complex picture of the world. Tragedy offers
us a view of things which aims at comprehensiveness, and thus in its scope
resembles the great religions of east and west. Like them, therefore, it needs
all the resources of language for communication with men.

The Fate of Athaliah—
and Racine[*]

LIONEL ABEL

I

A figure shaped to the purpose of tragedy—such is Athaliah, Queen of Judah, daughter of Ahab and Jezebel, even as she appears, set violent before us, strictly judged and summarily disposed of, in the Second Book of Kings.[1]

A faithful daughter and a monstrous grandmother, Athaliah fell victim to the only grandson whom she had failed to kill. Except for this grandson, Joash, and her father, Ahab, every male member of Athaliah's immediate family was either destroyed by God or slain by her. God, having avenged Himself on Athaliah's mother, Jezebel, encompassed the ruin of Athaliah's brothers, of her husband, Joram, and of all her sons, including Ahaziah, King of Judah. The Lord, not satisfied with vengeance on Jezebel, was interested, it seems, in wiping out the posterity of Ahab,[2] who were an offense to Him. But Athaliah, equal to her terrible Opponent, was ready to match Him murder for murder, life for life. She undertook to wipe out the posterity of David, though this meant slaughtering her own grandsons. In their veins the blood of David mingled with the blood of Ahab. To extirpate the one race meant to sacrifice the other. Before this atrocity, Athaliah, headlong and sanguinary, did not flinch. At the eleventh hour it was God who did. (From a theological view, had He not wavered, humanity would have lost. Was not

---

[1] Athaliah's story is recounted with like brevity in the Second Book of Chronicles.

[2] Ahab appears to have escaped God's wrath, which is undoubtedly why God was so vengeful toward his descendants. In any case, Ahab's escape from God's anger seems to have made his name the appropriate one for Herman Melville's impious hero in *Moby Dick*.

[*] Lionel Abel, "The Fate of Athaliah—and Racine," from *Methatheatre: A New View of Dramatic Form* (Hill and Wang, 1963), pp. 11–38. [Footnotes in this selection in French have been omitted and the others are numbered.]

355

the promised Messiah ordained to come from David's seed?) Suddenly the
Lord bethought Him that He would have to save some of the blood of Ahab
in order not to lose all of David's. Thus, from the cruel Queen's assault upon
her grandsons, the infant Joash was by miracle preserved. The boy, found
and hidden by Jehosheba, wife to the High Priest Jehoiada, was raised secretly by them, and in time was revealed to the people as David's descendant. After a palace revolution Joash assumed the throne. His grandmother
was put to the sword.

These facts are sufficient to justify our judgment that Athaliah is tragic—
to the most eminent degree. And in how many meanings of the word! First,
for the greatness of her Opponent (could there be a greater?); then, for being even more uncompromising than He, and again, for the grandeur of the
aim which she refused to compromise. And when we think about that aim,
we see that she is tragic in still another and—to a modern mind—especially
interesting sense: her aim was precisely tragedy; her purpose was to bring
the epic history of the Jews to a bloody close. If it was God who began the
tragedy, it was Athaliah who continued it from the point where He left off,
so that He was finally forced to intervene and prevent her from accomplishing what had originally been His own design. Thus Athaliah's action, until
the very end, is indistinguishable from God's. We may even say that God
realized His vengeance by means of her: in her appeared the rigor He Himself had to renounce. So if the Queen was accursed, all of her acts were
sacred.

II

Seen thus, Athaliah surely merits our respect; yet she does not appear to
have greatly impressed the writers of the Book of Kings (or Chronicles).
It is not surprising that this rebel against God elicited little admiration from
those who wrote the Scriptures; but one wonders that the writers did not
take some lyrical note of the Queen's quality. They had, after all, written
wonderfully of her scarcely better mother, Jezebel, fashioning in their best
rhythms an imperishable image of flaming iniquity. Jezebel's fate is prophe-
sied: "In the portion of Jezreel shall the dogs eat the flesh of Jezebel, and the
body of Jezebel shall be as dung on the face of the field in the portion of
Jezreel, so that they shall not say 'This is Jezebel.'" This marvelous male-
diction—pronounced by a prophet with the oddly delightful name of Elijah
the Tishbite—has surely helped to make Jezebel remembered. But Athaliah
is scarcely depicted in the Book of Kings. We hear nothing that she says;
she is never characterized; only her deeds are told. The only poetry she has
comes from the facts of her story. The figure of Athaliah, as the Bible presents her, is purely, exclusively tragic. And for centuries the Queen remained imaginatively, poetically unknown. But in 1691, Jean Racine pre-

sented *Athalie*,[3] his last and one of his most original tragedies, at Saint-Cyr. This play may be said to do more than remedy the neglect suffered by the Queen at the hands of the writers of Kings and Chronicles. Sainte-Beuve called *Athalie* "as beautiful as *King Oedipus*, and with the true God to boot." Voltaire judged it "the masterpiece of the human mind."

III

Athaliah's epiphany, so long delayed, so perfect when it came, required, of course, some help from chance. I shall review briefly the favoring, well-known circumstances. Jean Racine, brought up at Port Royal, learned the Greek classics together with the Bible; his understanding of the Greek conception of fate blended with his awe at the implacable acts of the Old Testament God. Evidently the writing of *Athalie* required a sensibility formed both by Jansenism and the Greek dramatists; the very same sensibility, though, was essential for the writing of *Phèdre*. It would seem to me, too, that simply to compare Racine the orphan, brought up by the nuns at Port Royal, and the grandson of Athaliah, raised by the High Priest, Jehoiada, can tell us little about *Athalie* or the likelihood that Racine would write it. Let us note, instead, everything that might have prevented him from writing that play.

Racine began his career as a court poet. His subjects were taken from Roman history and Greek mythology, and while he was, no doubt, influenced in his bent for tragedy by the religious education he had received at Port Royal, still the themes of his first plays had been almost exclusively erotic. Nothing surprising in this: the new young court of Louis XIV was almost exclusively interested in erotic relations. However, in 1677, *Phèdre* failed, as the result of an intrigue against Racine. The dramatist had considered this play his greatest work. His judgment may be questioned; but certainly *Phèdre* contains the most wonderful poetry Racine was capable of writing. Had the play succeeded, it is likely that Racine would have continued to make dramatic poetry out of Greek and Roman stories; we might have had an *Alceste* by him and an *Iphigénie en Tauride*. We might not have had *Esther* or *Athalie*. But *Phèdre* failed, and Racine stopped writing plays, embarking on his new career as court memorialist. Twelve years later Madame de Maintenon asked him to write a dramatic poem to be played by the

---

[3] Georges Mongredian, in his book *Athalie*, claims there were no literary sources for Racine's play besides the Old Testament. But Professor Meyer Schapiro has shown me a brief text on Athaliah in Boccaccio's book on the misfortunes of celebrated persons. Translated into French, Boccaccio's work appeared with a medallion of Athaliah by Fouquet. Racine must have read the book. Boccaccio's book contains texts on two other famous persons treated by Racine: Agrippina and Berenice. However, the text of Boccaccio on Athaliah is quite brief, not especially penetrating, and tells us little not already known from the Bible.

girls of Saint-Cyr. She specified that the work should be without erotic interest. Racine hesitated. Madame de Quellus, who knew of the affair, notes in her memoirs: "He wanted to please Madame de Maintenon. Refusal was impossible for a courtier, but the commission was a delicate one for a man who had a great reputation to maintain and who, while he had abandoned writing for the theatre, nevertheless did not want to diminish the reputation his works had gained." We know that Boileau himself advised Racine against accepting. But Racine accepted, and *Esther* was presented before the King and court at Saint-Cyr in 1689. The play was a success and Madame de Maintenon requested another. Racine wrote *Athalie*. It was produced in 1691, and did not find favor; in fact, Louis XIV is said to have left in a rage. Racine wrote no more plays. If *Esther* had not succeeded and if *Phèdre* had not failed, Racine would probably not have written *Athalie*.

Yet how could he not have written *Athalie?* What, from the facts, seems like a wonderfully lucky chance, appears as indispensable and necessary when we take into account Racine's special qualities as a writer of tragedy, and the value of his last work. Of all the authors of tragedy since Aeschylus, Racine, by temperament, training, and resolve, was probably the most gifted for making murder meaningful on the stage. Athaliah, in Racine's last play, is put to death more perfectly than any character in all dramatic literature, and I do not exclude the deaths of Agamemnon and Clytemnestra in the *Oresteia*, the death of King Pentheus in the *Bacchae*, the deaths of Antony and Cleopatra, and of Macbeth. Yet before he wrote *Athalie*, Racine, with some six or seven dramatic masterpieces behind him, had not yet killed anyone on the stage adequately, let alone perfectly.

IV

Thierry Maulnier and Jean Giraudoux have underscored Racine's capacities as a killer of his characters; but they never saw how dependent this estimate of him is on what he achieved in his last work. Certainly their estimate is not justified by his prior works alone.

Andromaque, for example—which French critics from La Harpe to Maulnier have regarded as a tragedy—is far too psychological and romantic a melodrama for the deaths of two of its main characters, at the climax, to strike us tragically. The loves of Orestes for Hermione, of Hermione for Pyrrhus, and of Pyrrhus for Andromache, are frankly presented by Racine himself as sentiments not quite worthy of persons of their rank and station. In fact, Racine's judgment of the sentiments of his own characters does not differ much from that of his rival, Corneille, who disliked *Andromaque*, nor from that of Madame de Sévigné, who liked it, but thought that it fell short of the sublimity Corneille had taught the French court to admire. The passions of Pyrrhus, Orestes, and Hermione are not to be admired, nor did Racine intend them to be.

Let us note, though, that these three characters are the children of the great figures whose exploits Homer had celebrated: Orestes is the son of Agamemnon; Pyrrhus the son of Achilles; Hermione the daughter of Helen. The one character in the drama who comes directly from Homer's *Iliad* is Andromache, the widow of Hector. Now her feeling for her dead husband is sublime. Andromache's passion, which we cannot but admire, is more natural than that exhibited by any character in any play by Corneille. She is the prisoner of Pyrrhus, Achilles' son. Achilles had killed her husband, and Pyrrhus, conqueror of Troy, had slain her father and brothers. Now Pyrrhus, who is in love with her, has the power of life and death over her son by Hector, the boy Astyanax:

So young, so to be pitied, but yet the one link remaining between any still living Trojan and all the kings dead and buried under the ruins of Troy.

If Andromache refuses Pyrrhus she will betray Hector, for Pyrrhus will kill Hector's son and heir. But if she accepts Pyrrhus' love in order to save Hector's son, she will be unfaithful to Hector. From this tragic dilemma no happy outcome is conceivable, except by chance. Racine in his play provided just that chance. The tragically conceived Andromache does not die, is not forced to marry Pyrrhus, and yet saves her son. The romantically conceived Pyrrhus dies at the hand of Orestes, and the equally romantic (and very modern) Hermione takes her own life. Certainly there is a tragic tonality in the play: the events express the just revenge of Troy on Greece for the brutal excesses of the Greek victors; yet the one really tragic figure succeeds, and comes through the action safely. The pathetic, somewhat comical and modernly complicated characters are ill-starred, and fail or die. This is an extraordinary work; it is not a true tragedy.

In *Bajazet*, which, too, has been called a tragedy, all the principal characters are killed at the end, strangled by the gigantic Negro executioner in the harem where the drama takes place. There are many deaths, but after reading and rereading the play, and after having seen it on the stage, one must agree with the seventeenth-century judgment: there is no reason for so much butchery. Racine, in this play, does demonstrate his temperament for killing, but he does not reveal himself as one with the *right* to kill, which, on the stage, means the ability to inflict death tragically.

No, *Bajazet* is no tragedy. Roxanne, the favorite of the absent Sultan, whom she is planning to depose, orders Bajazet to marry her. He, being in love with Atalide, after much hesitation, finally refuses. Roxanne brutally sends him to the strangler. But had Bajazet accepted Roxanne's offer of love, his end would have been the same, for Acomat, the Sultan's grand vizier, returning to take charge of the harem, would certainly have meted out the same fate to Bajazet that he does to Roxanne. Moreover, there is something commonplace in Bajazet's character, and something comical about his trying to be heroically true to his sentiment for one woman while living in a harem.

One character is indeed touched by tragedy: Atalide. She loves Bajazet, and knowing Roxanne will be unmerciful if he refuses her, implores him to accept her rival's offer. The scene in which she makes this plea is touching and beautiful, perhaps all the more so because Atalide, urging her own lover to be unfaithful to her, is realistic, not idealistic. Bajazet, as I have already noted, in preferring death to infidelity, seems, given the circumstances, not to know where he is. The movement of the play is pure melodrama; nothing great is at issue, and Bajazet is not really a romantic lover. Some French critics have called him a Christian gentleman who had wandered by chance into a harem; this judgment, far from justifying the play, makes it seem, for all its brilliance, somewhat absurd.

Neither *Britannicus* nor *Mithridate* need be considered at length. In the latter play there is a lovely woman, Monine, whom Voltaire thought a great creation. With her, he said, Racine "introduced taste into heroism." It is a fine remark. Yet Voltaire did not consider the play a tragedy. How could he have? It ends happily. Voltaire, however, did think *Britannicus* a tragedy. In this drama, Nero begins his career as a monster by killing his half-brother, Britannicus, in order to defeat the political intrigues of his mother, Agrippina. Evil is triumphant in the beautifully structured and eloquent drama. The true antagonists are Nero and Agrippina, between whom there is no moral issue, only a question of power. The young Britannicus and Junie, who love each other, are children. Whether they live or die, the fate of Rome will be unaltered. Britannicus is killed and Junie escapes from Nero by becoming a vestal virgin. Rome will be controlled by one or the other of the two evil persons in the drama, and it is hardly thinkable that Rome under Agrippina would be different from Rome under Nero. How can the death of Britannicus affect us tragically, then? The play, in its psychology and rhetoric, is "for connoisseurs," as Voltaire noted, but certainly not for connoisseurs of tragedy.

Consider Racine's first and probably most perfect tragedy, *Bérénice*. This is one of the most simply constructed and beautiful plays ever written. It is tragic throughout, yet it does not end with the death of its protagonists, Titus, Emperor of Rome, and Berenice, the Jewish queen who loves him and is loved by him. They are unable to marry because Roman republican law, surviving under the Empire, forbids an emperor to marry a queen. As long as Augustus, the father of Titus, lived, Titus and Berenice expected to marry. When the play begins, Augustus has just died, and Titus realizes at last that he cannot defy the law of the state over which he hopes to rule. Titus sends Antiochus, a visiting king from the East, who also is in love with Berenice, to inform her that the new Emperor of Rome cannot marry her. Antiochus is eager to bear the message; he sees a chance to plead his own

case. But when he has told Berenice of the decision of Titus, she peremp-
torily dismisses him, forbidding him even to see her again. Antiochus is almost comical in this scene, and would indeed be, if Racine, with extraordinary finesse, had not saved him for tragedy by endowing him with a wonderful discretion. Racine also gave him one of his greatest, saddest, and most
admired lines:

> What shape could my grief take in the all-vacant East?
> (*Bérénice:* Act 1, scene 4)

At last Berenice confronts Titus, and he tells her in his own words that he
cannot marry her. Is he not the Emperor? she wants to know. He is the
Emperor, and that is why he cannot obey his heart. Titus even considers
giving up his empire for Berenice, but would she love him if he were not the
Emperor of Rome? They part forever, and the last word of the play, spoken
by Antiochus, is "alas."

The movement of this play has the sureness of the very greatest tragedies.
The mechanism is flawless. Rome, which decrees the separation of the
lovers, is identical with the civilized world. It is the world at its best which
denies what is best in the lovers: their feeling for each other. In the end they
both recognize this. All the same, they choose to live. Moreover, the plot
allows them to live, and we do not have to believe completely their protests that they would rather die than part. Racine himself, feeling that the
absence of death from his play might be regarded as a fault, argued in his
preface to it that death is not essential in tragedy. His argument is interesting:

I grant that I did not push Berenice to the point of a suicide like Dido's, for
Berenice was not bound as irrevocably to Titus as Dido to Aeneas; thus she was not
obliged, like Dido, to refuse to live at all. Nevertheless, her final farewell to Titus,
and her struggles to give him up, are not, I think, the least tragic moments of my
play; I shall even go so far as to say that the emotion which the play had already excited is intensified in these moments. Blood and corpses are, after all, not essential to
tragedy: enough if the action be great, the characters heroic, their emotions real;
enough if the work provokes by its every detail, that majestic sadness wherein lies
the whole pleasure of tragedy.

Racine's argument for not having pushed Berenice to the point of a death
like Dido's is not strong. It is conventional and one may doubt that it was
written with full conviction. What is interesting about the passage—aside
from the beautiful phrase explaining "the whole pleasure of tragedy"—is
the fact that Racine, so praised as an *ange exterminateur* (angel of death),
should here be arguing that death is not essential to the main purpose of the
tragic poet.

In his *Iphigénie à Aulis*, there is death, blood is shed, but not the blood of
Iphigenia. Death is meted out to Eriphilia, substituted at the last moment on

the sacrificial altar for Iphigenia, and Eriphilia is too calculating and vicious for her death to touch us. As Racine noted in his preface, he chose that variant of the Greek story in which the daughter of Theseus and Helen is sacrificed, suffering the fate the gods demanded for Iphigenia, the daughter of Agamemnon. Racine argues that it would have been in bad taste to have Iphigenia sacrificed, since she was innocent and virtuous. According to Aristotle, he is right, and Racine understood Aristotle better than any other dramatic author of his time. It is, therefore, all the more surprising that Racine did not wish to see that the sacrifice of Eriphilia—in view of her character—was just as contradictory to Aristotle's conception of tragedy as the sacrifice of Iphigenia would have been. For while the Greek philosopher held that the death of a good person is untragic, causing the spectator to suffer too much, he maintained also that the death of a bad person is equally untragic, since it cannot but gladden the one witnessing it. The true tragic emotion is more complicated.

In fact, Racine's whole argument is disingenuous. Iphigenia, though virtuous, could die in a properly Aristotelian tragedy if she were not the protagonist of the play—if, for instance, this role were reserved for her father, Agamemnon, who, in every variant of the story, agrees to her sacrifice so that the winds can blow and the Greek fleet sail. Like Hegel, Kierkegaard understood that the protagonist in any tragedy about the sacrifice of Iphigenia would have to be Agamemnon. And when Kierkegaard resolved to oppose a hero of religion to a hero of tragedy, he elected for Abraham, intent on sacrificing Isaac, as against Agamemnon, prepared to kill his daughter.

The truth is that Racine wanted Iphigenia as his protagonist because he wanted a play with erotic interest. In *Iphigénie à Aulis*, Eriphilia is the rival of Iphigenia for the love of Achilles; Iphigenia gets Achilles and Eriphilia is sacrificed in her place. The winds blow, the ships sail, the evil character has been punished, the good girl saved, and what makes this consummation so utterly untragic is that the army of Agamemnon can now head, without a pang of conscience, for the brutal ten years of carnage on the plains of Troy.

The art of inflicting tragic death on the stage is a difficult one, and even with his ninth play, Racine had not yet mastered it. Did he succeed in *Phèdre?*

This play is considered by most critics to be Racine's greatest. It is his most famous, the one most universally known, and the role of Phaedra is as prized by French actresses as that of Hamlet by actors on the English-speaking stage. I do not wish to examine this judgment here. Surely, the play is great; as certainly, it is faulty. But the point I want to insist on here is that with *Phèdre*, Racine for the first time in his career succeeds in constructing a tragedy that ends with tragic death. *Bérénice*, his first real tragedy, did not.

Yet as has been pointed out by French critics, Phaedra is almost dead at the moment the play begins. She loves her stepson Hippolytus, but she is not reconciled to the sinfulness of an adulterous and incestuous passion; she never forgets that she is the daughter of Pasaphaë, queen of the pure sky, and of Minos, king of Hades, who sits in judgment on the dead. Her first words on her entrance express her hatred for life and her desire to die:

> No, not another step. I need your arm.
> I can scarcely stand erect. My strength is gone.
> My eyes shut on that sun I have not seen so long.
> My knees give way. Oenone, stay. You be strong.

Oenone, after long questioning, succeeds in making Phaedra confess to the cause of her torment and of her desire to die. When Phaedra finally admits to her passion for Hippolytus, she does so with a relentless exactitude. There is nothing comparable to the truthfulness of this confession by any character in Shakespeare:

> The ill, the ache, come from farther off. I was
> The bride of Theseus, happy, or without cause
> For any unhappiness. My mind was free,
> When in Athens I came on my great enemy.
> I saw him, I blushed, I paled, incredulous, dazed—
> I had not thought I could be so amazed.
> I could scarcely see. I could not speak. I stood,
> Rigid, frozen, burning, flesh and blood!
> I knew then the power of Venus to subjugate
> With love whoever has incurred her hate.
> She had shown her power. For me to circumvent it!
> I built her a temple, richly ornamented.
> I ordered sacrifice made. Myself I picked the beasts!
> I searched for my lost reason in their flesh.
> Weak remedies for love that will not die!
> Vainly I lit the altar fires, I
> Spoke the name of the Goddess reverently,
> But still loved Hippolytus, saw him constantly.

*   *   *

> I avoided him yet found him. Fateful chance!
> The son's features were in his father's countenance! . . .
> I turned against every throb in me that wooed him
> And took heart from a plan: it was to persecute him!

*   *   *

> I demanded his exile and my continual plea
> At last banished him to Troezene and far from me.

> I breathed again, Oenone, once again,
> My days were guiltless though not without pain.
> I tried to be faithful to my marriage vows,
> Submissive to my husband, a dutiful spouse.
> Vain effort. Cruel stroke! Venus the cause!
> I was brought to Troezene, and by Theseus.
> I saw Hippolytus. I knew my fate. It was—
> It is no fugitive passion to hide, confide, betray!
> It's the whole length of Venus, stretched out over her prey!
> (*Phèdre:* Act I, scene 3)

Phaedra, resolved to die, is kept alive by the rumor that Theseus, her husband, is dead, which makes her love for her stepson as Oenone interprets it, "not so extraordinary." Brunetière thought the action of the play invalidated by the fact that it is based on Phaedra's belief in a false rumor. But surely this is captious criticism. Phaedra wants to believe that Theseus is dead; a woman in her state of mind would believe such a rumor, especially when it is believed by others. Why should Brunetière have assumed that characters inflamed by passion generally act on sound assumptions? No, there is no flaw in Phaedra's acceptance of the report that her husband is dead. Taking counsel from Oenone, she confesses her passion to Hippolytus. It was not her intention to do so; she had meant, instead, to proclaim her continuing love for Theseus. But Phaedra's passion is more truthful than she wants to be. Her confession, heard on the stage, has an absolute magic. We see what is most inward in a character, expressed against the character's own wish. She says:

> Yes, Prince, I long for, yearn for Theseus.
> For him, yet not for him. Not as he was
>
>   *   *   *
>
> But as he might be, faithful, even fierce,
> Young, charming, proud of head, and pure of brow,
> As one depicts a god, or as I see you now.
> He had your glance, your bearing, turn of phrase,
> That proud reserve I see as yours was his
> When he strode up our shore, bright, worthy of
> The daughters of King Minos, ripe for love.
> Where were you then, Hippolytus? Theseus brought with him
> All the brave youth of Greece. Why were not you with them?
>
>   *   *   *
>
> You might have slain the fabled minotaur,
> Conquered the cunning maze of his vast lair.
> My sister Ariadne would to you

Have given the fate-spun thread, and brought you through.
No! I would have given it you! Love would have taught me
That the whole circumstance of your victory
Hung on a thread! No, No! I would have gone down into
That labyrinth, shown each twist of it to you,
Myself, not trusting to a thread so easily
Snapped, to bring you safely back to me!
I would have shared the danger that lay hid
In those dark turns, and run the risks you did.
Yes, Phaedra in the labyrinth would go first
To emerge from it with you—or with you be lost.

(Act II, scene 5)

Hippolytus is shocked, morally outraged by this avowal; he is himself in love with Aricia, Theseus' ward. Rebuffed, Phaedra has to endure, besides, the return of Theseus. She permits Oenone to tell her husband that his son has made advances to her. In a great scene, Theseus vents his rage on Hippolytus and calls on Poseidon to kill the youth. Poseidon obliges: Hippolytus is killed by a monster from the sea, whereupon Theseus realizes he had never completely believed Phaedra's story. He tells her, not without bitterness, of his son's death. She admits the truth and dies, a suicide, offstage.

Why diminish a work so splendid? But why praise, beyond its evident merit, a work so great? In *Phèdre* Racine created a true tragedy, and dealt death to two of his main characters. Nevertheless, the play is not without fault. First of all, as we have seen, Phaedra *wanted* to die from the beginning. Her death, when it comes, is therefore less pathetic and less terrible than would be the death of someone who had all along desired life. Another, very serious fault: the gods are involved in the action but not in a way that is clear. As Phaedra says, she is the victim of Aphrodite. And it is Poseidon who executes on Hippolytus the curse pronounced by Theseus. A god and a goddess are involved, but there is no logical or ideological relation between them.

In the Euripides play, from which Racine took his story, Hippolytus was a worshiper of Artemis and Phaedra was submissive to Aphrodite: Artemis and Aphrodite were at odds, even at war. Hence, for Euripides, the deaths of Phaedra and Hippolytus followed from an irreconcilable dispute between two goddesses, one representing spiritual power against sex, the other the force of sex as such. Hippolytus refuses Phaedra, not because he loves another woman, but because he does not and cannot love at all, being vowed to Artemis. Racine's play is undoubtedly greater than the play of Euripides; yet its construction is less logical, its final meaning less clear.

Racine had finally killed a sympathetic character in a great but faulty tragedy.

V

In a novel, characters can grow old and die; on the stage a character, whose dying is to interest us, must be put to death. There is a most interesting recognition of this in Shakespeare's *Henry IV*, Part II. Henry IV is dying. He has fallen asleep. Prince Hal enters, thinks his father already dead, removes the crown from his head, and speaks as if he, Prince Hal, were already Henry V. Henry IV awakes, accuses Prince Hal of wanting to kill him. In a subsequent scene we learn that Henry IV has died. The cause of death is, of course, old age and exhaustion; yet, Henry IV has been killed symbolically by his son, and thus has had a proper theatrical end.

The taking of a person's life is the most drastic, the most dramatic act there is. Obviously the most fundamental sanctions are involved. To kill—to destroy a life one has not created—is an *imitatio dei*, even when committed by an atheist. What about the infliction of death on an imaginary person, a fiction, a character in a play?

In my view—I am aware it may strike the reader as a paradox—it is as difficult to justify inflicting death on a character as to justify killing a real person. Perhaps the difficulty will be best understood if one thinks in purely rational terms of passing judgment on another life. One will then realize that no reason is sufficient. Also, there is this fact: The best and most convinced assassins have always been fanatics. Has one the right to kill without being fanatical? And does the dramatist who wants to bring his protagonist to a tragic end also have to be a fanatic in some sense?

In his fine book *Death in the Afternoon*, Hemingway pointed out that the best killers of bulls have never been the best or most skilled matadors. Those bullfighters whom Hemingway most admired as artists, he did not admire most for their manner of killing. On the contrary, he claims, the men who killed best were fairly simple, uncomplicated persons, rather unskilled in the earlier passes, and deft only when it came to the ultimate blow. May this hold, too, for the infliction of death on the stage? Does the great writer of a great tragedy have to be a fairly simple, rather religious fellow, to deliver with sureness the final and culminating stroke?

Or is it sheer skill in dramaturgy which justifies the playwright in putting a character to death when death is required by his plot? Yet Corneille, in so many ways a more skillful playwright than Racine, was inept at inflicting death. In fact, his plays, so well plotted, become disorganized once death occurs. Corneille, the dramatist of the rational will, thought he could clarify everything, but he could not impose death purposefully. Once *Le Cid* has killed the father of Chimène, the play collapses. Chimène, though she loves the man who has killed him, must avenge her father's death. If she does not, she is unworthy to be the wife of Rodrigue, or a heroine of Corneille. On the other hand, Corneille has plotted his play so that Chimène and Rodrigue must marry, and he is unable to resolve this contradiction. Something similar occurs in *Horace*. The younger Horatius has seen his two brothers die at the hands of the three Curiations. He succeeds in killing the three, one of whom is the husband of his sister. She curses her brother and Rome. Whereupon Corneille's hero kills her. This was intended to be an exalted moment, expressing patriotic emotion. But one imagines that Corneille was a bit sickened by his own hero's action. In fact, the old Horatius, the hero's father, does not admire what his son has done. Nor do the Roman leaders, who have the problem of hailing the young Horatius as the savior of Rome, and of justifying his murder of his own sister. The play is never a tragedy, and it ends in what is very close to farce. The hero is acclaimed, but those who applaud him would prefer to try him for murder.

One needs something better than reasons to justify killing. This holds both in real and in imagined action.

What can justify killing on the stage? The feeling that the death of the character is destined. But what is meant by the word *destiny*?

If a rational meaning could be assigned to this term, there would be no such thing as tragedy. Yet how can the term *destiny* be understood, if not rationally?

Francis Bradley and Henri Bergson have pointed out that certain truths appear evident to consciousness when felt with a certain intensity, and that at a lesser intensity, these truths appear as contradictions. Does this notion apply here?

Let us take a play of Shakespeare's, commonly regarded as a tragedy, but in which the death of each significant and appealing character disgusts us with life and with the play, too. In *King Lear*, the deaths of Gloucester, Lear, and Cordelia are all horrible and unjustifiable in aesthetic terms. There are two remarks in *Lear* which relate to destiny, and they contradict each other:

> As flies to wanton boys, are we to th' gods,
> They kill us for their sport.

and

> The gods are just, and of our pleasant vices,
> Make instruments to plague us.

Clearly, these remarks refute each other. The difficulty of thinking that both are true is the chief problem of Shakespeare's play and prevents it from being a true tragedy. We cannot accept or be exalted by the deaths of Gloucester, Cordelia, or Lear himself. There is no destiny in any of these deaths, for in a true vision of destiny, the contradiction implied by the two views that (1) the gods are wanton in their treatment of us, and (2) the gods are just in their treatment of us, would be transcended. The deaths of Lear and Gloucester seem to follow from the proposition that the gods are just. The death of Cordelia—which Samuel Johnson found so objectionable, and which prompted him to suggest that Shakespeare was never at his best but always somewhat labored when it came to writing tragedy—seems to follow from the proposition that we are to the gods like flies to wanton boys. So that the deaths in *King Lear* follow from conflicting principles. The work is simply not unified. And this is one reason it tends to be ineffective on the stage.

Shakespeare did, of course, write *Macbeth*. When he wrote *King Lear* he did not, I think, have the single vision which tragedy requires. "Let your eye be single, and your body will be filled with light." Altered to our purpose, and addressed to the dramatist, these words of the New Testament would read: Let your eye be single and you will be able to bring the darkness of death tragically to the stage.

Shakespeare must have felt at some moment in his career that his interests were too varied, his skepticism too acute, for him to kill his own characters tragically. Even as the Duke of Vienna, in *Measure for Measure*, questions his fitness for punishing his subjects severely, so, I suggest, Shakespeare questioned his right to kill dramatically. He did not lack the technical means, to be sure; neither, of course, did Corneille. But Corneille, great playwright and poet though he was, did not have the kind of conscience we have a right to assume Shakespeare had, in giving up tragedy altogether to create an entirely new kind of drama.

The vision of the tragedian has to be single and simple. Are we back then with the thought that the tragic artist has to be an uncomplicated person? Religious if not devout? Or not unlike those men Hemingway described as the best killers in the bull ring? Now I would not altogether reject the notion, often held, that the great tragic artists have been religious persons. Dostoyevsky was one of the most complicated of men; perhaps he was not a believer, but certainly he wanted to believe. In his sophistication, he desired to be naïve. Though not a playwright, he was the most dramatic of all novelists—and the most tragic, too. In the *Brothers Karamazov*, Fyodor Karamazov is killed, in fact, by his illegitimate and epileptic son Smerdyakov. The real murderer, of course, is his eldest son Ivan, who has indicated by certain signs—though not in so many words—to Smerdyakov, who admires him, that he, Ivan, would be pleased by the old man's death. Can we say that Ivan killed his father knowingly? We cannot. Can we say he killed his father without knowing? We cannot say that either. The murder of the old Karamazov would have satisfied Aristotle completely. There is nothing more sophisticated in all of ancient or modern dramaturgy. No simple-minded dramatist could have brought off such an effect.

Dostoyevsky was able to feel Fyodor Karamazov's death as wanton and yet as justified. From the outset of the novel, Dostoyevsky had presented

Fyodor as hated by his sons—all except the near-saint, Alyosha. The inability of Fyodor's sons to love him doomed him; they would have had to be saints for him not to have been murdered.[4] Thus his murder is inevitable, and yet his sons are responsible. This seems to us a paradox on reflection, not when we read the *Brothers Karamazov*.

Could Dostoyevsky have so succeeded without being or wanting to be religious? It is doubtful. The desire for a simple faith can be the equivalent, in art at least, of faith itself. Of course, such desire must be genuine. In whom could it be more genuine than in a man tormented by his own complexity? There are many art forms which admit personal complexity as a value. The art of tragedy is quite different. Here complexity is of value only as something to be overcome.

To avoid any misunderstanding, I wish to make clear that religious belief is not the only kind of belief necessary for that simplification and purity of vision that tragedy requires. Shakespeare, who we tend to think was not religious, did write *Macbeth*. (It is to be noted, though, that this play is the one work of his which projects a necessary order beyond nature's.) Let us put the matter this way: the single view necessary for the tragic poet cannot go without a certain humiliation of the mind, through its acceptance of an inflexible order. Such acceptance was not at all characteristic of Shakespeare. It would be surprising, though, if a man who sympathized with so many postures of consciousness did not, at some time in his career, yield completely to a feeling for fatality.

VI

Racine's life and career can be described as a voluntary yielding to different but always inflexible orders: first to that of the Jansenists, who educated him at Port Royal; then to that of classical Greek tragedy, which he never questioned, though his predecessor in the theatre, Corneille, had; finally to that of the court of Louis XIV. In his excellent book, *Racine and Poetic Tragedy*, Eugene Vinaver writes: "The classical doctrine left the poet the choice of sentiments. Yet, there again Racine forbids himself any boldness and, even in his predilection for certain moral states, does nothing but follow the tastes and tendencies of the century, accommodated to his manner." Vinaver denies that Racine was ever original in his understanding of classical tragedy, but insists that such originality as he shows—and at times this is very marked—was the inevitable result of a good mind yielding to an order which it had merely tried to understand, but not to change.

There was no criticism of the monarchy in Racine's plays—as there is in

---

[4] Alyosha tried to be a saint. His motive may have been to be capable of not killing his father. As matters turned out, though, his interest in the death of the saint, Zossima, prevented him from intervening when he might have saved his father and his brothers.

the works of Molière and Corneille. For most of Racine's life, no doubt, the authority of Louis XIV over Racine was absolute. There is a story that once Racine formulated a program to help the poor and presented it to the King, who is said to have replied: "Just because you're a great poet, don't think you can be a minister." Racine at once put his project aside and is not known to have ever again directly intervened in politics.

How are we to understand this voluntary submission of Racine to religious, classical, and royal authority? It is precisely what makes him exceptional in his own century; and among all the great dramatists of the age, taking into account those of England and Spain as well as of France, Racine was the only one who really tried to be faithful to Aristotle, who never criticized the figure of his king, and who never questioned the religion in which he was indoctrinated as a child. How different he was, not only from his contemporaries, Corneille and Molière, but from Marlowe and Shakespeare, and also from the great Spaniards, Lope de Vega and Calderón!

In the conduct of his life, Racine exhibits a conspicuous purposefulness in advancing his career. Was this dramatist of such poetic purity fundamentally a careerist? Why was there in him no feeling of rebellion, no violence against what was already canonized in religion, politics, and art? I would suggest that Racine concerned himself in the main with the perfect fulfillment of his role, which was to write tragedy. What did not help him in that role was inessential; he must have intuitively felt that the acceptance of the various orders to which he did submit—at times in the interest of his career —was helpful to him in his life task. There is something wonderfully adroit in his inner knowledge of what he needed in order to fulfill himself and to perfect the image we have of him. But we would not have had this image without his last play.

VII

Racine was writing *Athalie*. He had succeeded with *Esther*. His choice of a subject for the new work to be given at Saint-Cyr was the story of Athaliah, who had now found the perfect poet to describe her fate. It is interesting to consider how the two destinies, those of the poet and of the biblical Queen intersect. Athaliah, who had remained fairly insignificant for two thousand years, was now to express herself in one of the greatest tragedies ever written. Racine, who had trained himself to kill tragically on the stage, was for the first time in his career to do so perfectly.

But there were many practical reasons why Racine should not have chosen the subject. Had he been concerned at this point with Louis XIV's opinion of him, and not with faithfully completing his own image, he would surely have elected for some other story. As a courtier, Racine could not but have been aware that Louis XIV, having destroyed Port Royal and imprisoned

the leading Jansenists—including the niece of the great Arnaud himself—
would not take kindly to a religious play based on the Old Testament, in
which a ruling monarch was presented as the enemy of God and overthrown
in a revolution led by a priest. Surely Racine knew this. Why then did he
risk for the first time in his life the King's displeasure?

Racine was older now. He had a career behind him, one which the court
had favored and finally frustrated. Without the support of the court, he
would not have written *Andromaque* or *Bérénice*. But it was a court intrigue
which had led to the failure of what he considered his greatest work, *Phèdre*.
There is something else, too, to be considered. In *Iphigénie à Aulis*, which
has been called Racine's "royal tragedy" but is no tragedy at all, Racine, the
orphan, had made the villain an orphan, killed her off at the play's close, and
thereby destroyed any chance of the work ending tragically. In writing
Athalie, Racine again chose to deal with an orphan, Joash. This time an
orphan would be the hero—backed by the greatest king of all: the Lord. So
supported, Racine could risk displeasing Louis XIV. Though he was still
submissive to authority, this time Racine would do the one thing which as a
writer of tragedy he had thus far left undone.

He also felt free to violate the unities of time and place. In *Esther* he had
violated the Aristotelian canon calling for a definite and single place; in
Athalie both time and place are left undefined. Moreover, as in *Esther*, in
Athalie he introduced a chorus. What is the reason for the Chorus in his last
play?

As Aristotle pointed out, the Chorus must be functional. This is not always the case, even in the works of Sophocles. It is hard to see what function the Chorus has in *The Women of Trachis*. Greek scholars have noted,
too, the purely conventional character of the Chorus in *Philoctetes*. Apparently Sophocles himself was not incapable of falling into neoclassicism.
But in *Athalie* the Chorus, composed of young girls, in words taken from the
Psalms and put by Racine into the very purest French, chants a continuous
paean to the majesty, might, and love of the Old Testament God. Since it is
fundamentally God who is the victor over Athaliah, the verses of the young
girls, in adoration of His glory, have the further purpose of indicating how
weak Athaliah is, how certain her destruction. I have the impression in reading the play that after each chorus—unheard by Athaliah; she is never present while the Chorus speaks—she bleeds a little. The verses are like the
banderillas placed in the side of the bull by the matador to weaken and
madden him, preparing him for death.

Athaliah begins to die with the first line of the play uttered by the slightly
comical Abner, her military chief, who is faithful to the true God at
the same time that he is loyal to Athaliah as the legitimate Queen of
Judah. Abner does not suspect that a male descendant of David still lives.

And, although he does not approve Athaliah's worship of Baal, he will not, for religious reasons, violate the monarchical principle. His first words are:

> I've come to spend a little while with God.

The dropping in on God by Abner, the main support of Athaliah, sets the tone for each subsequent happening. Jehoiada, the High Priest, protests to Abner against the worship of Baal in the kingdom, which has the Queen's backing. Abner would like to be indignant too, but does not think it proper to be critical of his sovereign. He suggests that the time of miracles is past and brings down on himself a ringing denunciation by the High Priest Jehoiada, who accuses him of lacking faith. However, the priest knows that there is a living male descendant of David; Abner does not. After their interview the High Priest confides to his wife, Jehosheba, that the time has come to reveal Joash to the people.

Athaliah has a premonition that Joash exists. She has had a dream, which she recounts to her advisers: her mother, Jezebel, has appeared to her

> In the dead vast and middle of the night

and told her that she, too, is about to be overwhelmed by the cruel Old Testament God. Immediately afterward, Athaliah, still dreaming, sees a young boy in priest's dress. The sight of him raises her spirit; she admires his noble and modest air, his gentleness; whereupon the boy plunges a dagger into her breast. She dreams of the boy again and he repeats his action. Deeply troubled on awakening, she thinks of propitiating the God her mother's specter has warned her against. She goes to the temple and sees a young boy in every respect exactly like the boy who has killed her in her dream. Who is this boy? Neither Abner nor Mathan, the High Priest of Baal, know.

Athaliah has already foreseen her own execution. On the point of being destroyed by God, she seems to absorb, by a kind of divine contagion, God's mercy, even as prior to this she had absorbed God's wrath. She goes again to the temple, sees Joash, is again struck by his nobility, pride, and grace; and in an astonishing scene offers to take him to her palace and treat him as her son; she remarks that she has no son and suggests that he might become her heir. The boy rejects her overtures. The extraordinary thing about the scene is the fascination of Athaliah with the boy who, her dream has already informed her, is to be her executioner. Lucien Goldmann interprets Athaliah's attraction to Joash as springing from that uncertainty of judgment noted by most historians in ruling groups about to be overthrown, and I think Goldmann is right in this observation—which points up the extraordinary realism of Racine. All the same, in tragedy, psychological acuteness has mainly a negative value. It aids the dramatist in avoiding error. In other words, Athaliah's weakness for Joash is psychologically plausible, but we are not touched because it is psychologically plausible; we are touched because she loves her grandson, not knowing him to be her grandson, and because his victory over her will mean her death.

She has already died four preparatory deaths by the end of scene VII of the second act: twice in her dream, again when she sees Joash in the temple for the first time, then again in the temple when he repudiates her offer to take him to her palace.

Of course, it is the High Priest who actually plots Athaliah's destruction. After her first two visits to the temple, he induces her to return a third time on the pretext of revealing to her David's "secret treasure." This is not, as Athaliah thinks, gold, but Joash, whose ascent to power will mean her death. She comes with Abner and finds that the assembled Levites have made obeisance to Joash: the High Priest has revealed him as their legitimate king. Abner turns against Athaliah, and her doom is sealed.

Some have questioned whether the High Priest is truly noble. If he is not, then, of course, my claim that Athaliah is killed perfectly, dramatically speaking, would be invalid. Voltaire, having praised the play above all other tragedies, finally elected to attack it as a piece of monumental superstition. He saw at once that the way to attack it was to diminish the character of Jehoiada, whom he called a "bloody, authoritarian priest."

If one has no sympathy for Jehoiada, then *Athalie* is no tragedy. For the form of tragedy requires that we sympathize with both the executioner and the victim. This was suggested by Aristotle when he said that tragedy relieves us of pity and terror, and made still clearer by James Joyce in *The Portrait of the Artist as a Young Man*, when Stephen Daedalus, commenting on Aristotle's *Poetics*, says that in tragedy pity unites us with the sufferer, terror with the cause of suffering. The difficulty of most dramatists trying to produce tragedy is not so much to create a sympathetic victim as to create a sympathetic executioner. After the Greeks, it was probably Racine who did this best, and I have said that he only did it perfectly in his last play, *Athalie*.

But *did* he in *Athalie?* Is Jehoiada ignoble or unsympathetic? One can answer by saying that he does nothing by himself, that all his actions are determined by God. Such was Sainte-Beuve's view:

> The great, or rather the only character in *Athalie*, from its first to its last line, is God. The Lord is there, above the high priest and the boy, and at every moment of this powerful and simple story they are controlled by Him. He Himself remains invisible and immutable; always His presence is felt, although hidden by that Holy of Holies to which Jehoiada goes once each year, always returning stronger because of Him whose strength cannot be measured. This unity, this omnipotence of the Eternal

Character, far from destroying the drama, or reducing it to a continuous paean, becomes the dramatic action itself, and rising above all characters in the play, acts on everyone of them. . . .

Nevertheless, Jehoiada must be justified in his human personality. He is a fanatic, and one can say against him that being fanatical he is incapable of moral experience. Jehoiada has of course dignity, courage, and faith. He belongs to an oppressed minority; and he is an instrument of God's purpose. But these facts are not sufficient, as Racine must have known, to make him sympathetic enough for us to accept him as the executioner of Athaliah. One of the most brilliant moments of the play occurs when the High Priest has a prophetic vision and sees that his own son will be put to death by Joash, when the latter is King. Because Jehoiada accepts the death of his son for the sake of God, we can accept him humanly as Athaliah's executioner.

Athaliah is caught in the temple. The Levites surround her. She sees Joash crowned. Abner deserts her. The Queen knows she is doomed, and dooms herself once again:

> Then let the boy be King . . .
> And may the symbol of God's victory
> Be my own grandson's dagger stuck in me!
> (Act V, scene 6)

The Queen, about to die, foresees, though, that her grandson will eventually desert David and act as if he were Ahab's heir:

> Rebellious to Your wish, indifferent to Your will
> This grandson of Ahab shall confound You still!
> He'll flee Your law—I see it—even toward Hell!
> The avenger of Athaliah, Ahab, and Jezebel!
> (Act V, scene 6)

Athaliah, who grows weaker throughout the play wooing her own destruction, at the last foresees and boldly asserts the future treachery to the God of her destroyer. Having died so many times in her imagination, when she finally is about to be executed, she prophesies her future vengeance.

With Athaliah's last speech, Racine completed the old Queen's life in tragedy, and his own career as a tragic poet.

Goethe and the

Avoidance of Tragedy*

ERICH HELLER

Wenn ein moderner Mensch . . . an einem so grossen Alten Fehler zu rügen hätte, so sollte es billig nicht anders geschehen als auf den Knien. [*If a man of our time were to find fault with such a great man of the past, then, to be just, he should do so on his knees.*]—GOETHE TO ECKERMANN, *March 28th, 1827*

1

In 1797, after a lapse of seven years following the publication of the *Fragment: Faust*, and more than twenty years after the completion of the first draft of the dramatic poem, the *Urfaust*, Goethe announced in a letter to Schiller (June 22nd) that, finding himself in a state of acute unrest, he was preparing, as a kind of spiritual sedative, to take up *Faust* once more and to retreat 'into that world of symbols, ideas and mists' (June 24th). He begged his friend 'to think it over in a sleepless night', and to tell him what he would expect of the whole work and, as it were, 'interpret, as a true prophet, his [Goethe's] own dreams' (June 22nd). Goethe must have known that he would arouse some uneasiness in Schiller's methodical mind when he added: 'As the various parts of the poem can be treated in different modes if only they fall in with the spirit and the tone of the whole, and as, moreover, this creation is subjective in kind, I shall be able to work at it in odd free moments now and then'. Schiller's reply was as prompt as it was suggestive of misgivings. 'With all its poetic individualism,' he said, 'this play cannot escape the demand for symbolic significance. . . . The duality of human

* Erich Heller, "Goethe and the Avoidance of Tragedy," from *The Disinherited Mind* (Farrar, Straus & Company, 1957), pp. 37–63. [Footnotes for this selection have been omitted.]

nature and the unsuccessful striving for a reconciliation in man between what is divine and what is physical—this is something one cannot lose sight of; and just because the story tends towards shrillness and formlessness one does not wish to be arrested within the subject itself, but to be guided by it towards ideas. In brief, the claims made upon *Faust* are at the same time philosophical and poetical, and in whatever direction you may turn, the very nature of the subject will impose upon you a philosophical treatment, and the imagination will have to put up with a period of employment in the service of an idea' (June 23rd).

It is, once again, the issue raised by *Naive und sentimentalische Dichtung*. In that essay, which had appeared in the preceding year, Schiller defended the workings of his own reflective genius against the overpowering spontaneity of Goethe's. This time, Schiller seems to imply, Goethe will have to leave behind the state of innocence, submitting himself to a more complex, more philosophically disciplined inspiration. If it appeared to Schiller that in *Werther*, in *Tasso*, a miraculously preserved innocence, a poetic imagination of almost terrifying integrity, had told the story of a world divided and coming to grief—as though the genius of the tree in Paradise had opened its mouth to announce to the world the news of the Fall—then the continuation of that record could only come from the creature that had eaten the apple. For the hero of *Faust* was no longer the kind of person that Werther was, or Egmont, or Tasso, or Iphigenie, who are all profoundly 'naïve'—the word to be understood with its German connotations. One might be tempted to apply to them Pascal's reflection that 'the heart has reasons of which the reason knows nothing', were it not for the fact that Pascal meant *reasons* of the heart (Hölderlin had them), tools of the highest *understanding* of the world, whereas Werther, Egmont, Tasso and even Iphigenie, live, with regard to the world, in a state of fundamental incomprehension, varying between the raptures of bliss ('himmelhoch jauchzend') when the heart, wholly immaculate, to use Iphigenie's phrase, enjoys itself, and the agonies of woe ('zu Tode betrübt') when the uncomprehended world interferes. *They do not know*—in the sense in which knowledge means the knowledge of good and evil; they live, not beyond, but before that fatal rift, and thus reflect an essential characteristic of their creator's genius and sensibility. Here is at least one of the roots of Goethe's uniqueness within the European tradition, a uniqueness revealed in achievement as well as in failure. This also accounts for the extremes of Goethe worship (mostly inside Germany) and Goethe rejection (mostly outside Germany, and by critics of the stature of, for instance, Irving Babbitt, Ortega y Gasset, George Santayana, T. S. Eliot).

Any criticism of Goethe requires the utmost tact. Not only is the man so immense—and nothing is more difficult in criticism than to keep alive at every moment that sense of proportion which the very difference in level between creativeness and critical judgment demands; criticism is, alas, an unaristocratic habit, easily tempted into a false intimacy, in praise and negation alike—but also so much of the perennial discussion about Goethe is so massively wrongheaded, and so passionate, that it has filled the atmosphere around him with an abundance of electrical charges, making it all too easy to produce short circuits. I am saying this because I wish to speak of a limitation in Goethe's range of awareness and of a defect in his sensibility, and because I believe, paradoxically enough, that this limitation lies in the very boundlessness of his genius, and the defect in the inexhaustible richness of his sensitivity. It would be preposterous to derive the standards for an assessment of Goethe's achievements from anywhere else but the great classics of European civilization. Yet it would be futile to seek a place for him in a pattern determined by Homer, or Sophocles, or Virgil, or Dante, or Shakespeare. His range is too wide, and his gifts too universal ever to find full realization in one type of work alone, and his genius too diffused ever to concentrate on a single exemplary, classical achievement; and while in scope he is too vast ever to represent the character of an age, the mode of his imagination, its susceptibilities and idiosyncrasies, partake, at the same time, too definitely of the unresolved problems of the late eighteenth century for him easily to be acknowledged as being for all times and all places. With regard to Goethe's position within his own nation, it is very revealing that it could be said with some justice—as it was said immediately after the Second World War by Karl Jaspers—'that we came face to face with experiences in which we had no inclination to read Goethe, but took up Shakespeare, or the Bible, or Aeschylus, if it was possible to read at all'.

What was the nature of the experience in the face of which Goethe offered no help? It was the very kind of experience before which Goethe himself always proved helpless: the exposure to the manifestations of evil and sin. 'The mere attempt to write tragedy might be my undoing', he once said, and it was the truth—at least for the greatest part of his life. Among his dramas there are three dramatic poems which, more than any other dramas he wrote, established his fame: *Iphigenie, Tasso, Faust*. All of them are potential tragedies, indeed so much so that one may feel that the tragic conclusion could only be avoided at the price of complete artistic conclusiveness. They show a moving and yet unsatisfactory reluctance of mind and imagination to accept the rule of the road leading to the very centre of human destiny. This is not to imply that in that very centre there dwells, inescapably, tragedy. But once a man is compelled to penetrate to that central point in all seriousness, then there is only one region left that stretches, for the European, beyond tragedy. Beyond Hamlet and the rest that is silence, there stands only Prospero:

And my ending is despair,
Unless I be reliev'd by prayer,
Which pierces so that it assaults
Mercy itself, and frees all faults.

And frees all faults; the German translation of this is: *Alle menschliche Gebrechen*, which, we are told by Goethe, are redeemed by 'pure humanity', of which Iphigenie is the embodiment.

Anyone who has ever come under the spell of Goethe's *Iphigenie* knows its power to persuade, to convince and to move. There seems to be no doubt that it is poetically true. But which aspect of poetic truth do we mean? The same that applies to *Antigone* or *King Lear?* No, certainly not. *Iphigenie* is lyrically, but not dramatically true, which is as much as to say that it has the truth of a vision of what life and the world could be if they corresponded to what is best in a great and good soul. It is dramatically not true because the objective world which is the scene of the play is not real enough to offer serious resistance to the realization of that vision. In other words, there is no real evil in that world. All the evil inherent in the mythological pattern taken over from the Greeks is considerably reduced in stature so as to lose an essential degree of reality. The reality of evil asserts itself poetically on only three occasions, which are scattered about the play like three erratic blocks in the gentle groves of human kindness: Iphigenie's story of the horrible deeds perpetrated in her family, Orestes' account of the murder of his mother with the rage of madness that follows, and the *Parzenlied* (the song of the goddesses of Fate). For the rest—and it is all but the whole play—the inexorable hardness of the Greek myth is dissolved into the softer substance of the goodness of human nature.

From the opening monologue of the first act onwards we are sure that, unless the poem were to become grossly incongruous, Iphigenie could not seriously be asked to perform, or indeed seriously consider, human sacrifices, let alone the sacrifice of her own brother. And the much-discussed question of the 'cure' of Orestes reveals, through the very wording of the question as suggested by the play, the surprising shift of emphasis from what was once, and is again, the centre of the problem, to a more humane periphery. Cure? Of what? Of a temporary fit of madness? For surely there is no 'cure' for the murder of a mother. There is, for the Greeks, only the supreme sacrifice to atone for it, or else the direct intervention of the gods to lift the curse—which is, in spite of all the fundamental differences, nearer the Christian repentance and the forgiving grace than the administering of pure humanity. If the curse on the house of Tantalus and the deed of Orestes are to be taken as real—as real, say, as the murder committed by Macbeth —then Goethe's solution is not dramatically true. We simply have to discard the reality of curse and murder—and, indeed, this oblivion is granted to us by the lyrically soothing climate of Arcadian Tauris itself—we have to accept curse and murder as mythological names for a less spectacular kind of guilt, and finally allow a more vaguely general state of spiritual restlessness to assume the place of any articulate guilt if we are to remain convinced of the effectiveness of a purely human redemption.

Schiller's dramatic instinct sensed this defect of Goethe's Orestes; in criticizing him in terms of purely dramatic considerations, he yet pointed to the profounder issue when he wrote to Goethe (January 22nd, 1802): 'Orestes is the most doubtful figure of the drama. There is no Orestes without Furies; and when the cause of his condition does not strike the senses but lies hidden in his mind and emotions, his is too long and monotonous an agony—without an object. Here we are up against one of the limitations of modern drama as compared with ancient tragedy. I wish you could think of a remedy; but bearing in mind the economy of the play, I do not think it likely that you will; for you have indeed done everything that is possible without gods and spirits.'

I have said that the theme of *Iphigenie* would lend itself to, indeed invite, a tragic treatment. The reply that the play of Euripides, from whom the story is borrowed, is not a tragedy either would be beside the point, for it is too obvious that Goethe's heroine is a person totally different from Euripides' Iphigenia. Yet there is one Greek tragedy which, in situation and aspects of the main character, is related to Goethe's *Iphigenie:* the *Antigone* of Sophocles. In both plays it is a loving sister who has determined in her soul to abide by the divine law as it is given to her, and to remain, as Antigone says, 'imprisoned in the fear of the gods', and thus to defy all worldly power and the rules of common sense. In both plays the conflict involves death—or, at least, potentially death—not merely for the one who is so madly resolved, but for those whom she loves as well: in *Antigone* for Ismene, perhaps, the sister, and for Haemon, the lover, and in *Iphigenie* for Orestes, the brother, and Pylades, the friend. In the one play as much as in the other, the heroine is bound by bonds of gratitude to him whom she has decided to disobey; in both plays the king has provided a home for the child of a cursed race after her great tribulations. For Antigone as well as for Iphigenie it is not merely the wish for full moral realization of her own character that inspires her deed, but the hope of redeeming the guilt of ancestors. Moreover, in both plays the king is finally moved to revoke his own law and to yield to an overriding commandment. Thus it is through the contrast between Sophocles' *Antigone* and Goethe's *Iphigenie* (and not in comparison with the play of Euripides, where such problems never enter) that one can see most clearly the limitations of the Iphigenie faith.

These limitations might be artistically irrelevant were the play not such

that its subject could not be dealt with on the level which Goethe set himself, without implicitly giving a comprehensive vision (a vision, not a discussion) of the ultimate nature of the moral problem involved. Also one
cannot state these limitations by simply drawing attention to the tragic ending of *Antigone* and the happy solution of *Iphigenie*. But perhaps one can
bring home the point that matters by saying that Iphigenie would not do
what she does—or rather, would not be what she is—if her vision of life
really comprehended the possibility of her having to put her brother to
death; whereas Antigone, whether or not she is to die herself and bring
death to others, *is* the realization of the truth that the triumph of divine law
may involve at every point disaster in terms of human aspirations. In other
words, there is in Goethe's *Iphigenie* an incongruity between the radicalism
with which the moral problem is posed, and the certainly lovable gentleness
of the spiritual nature that has to carry it. The *dramatic* flaw of Goethe's
other great poetic drama, *Torquato Tasso*—lyrically as supremely successful
as *Iphigenie*—is that the spiritual excitement of the hero is in excess of the
moral facts of his situation, while in *Iphigenie* the moral situation outweighs
the spiritual stature of the protagonist. It is because in the dramatic order of
things natures like Iphigenie must not be made to encounter such situations
(which could only crush them without affording them even the semblance of
spiritual triumph) that, in this case, the moral problem is identical with the
problem of dramatic integrity.

At the root of this problem there is not merely the time-honoured and, in
this form, interminable antithesis between the belief in the fundamental
goodness and the dogma of the essential corruption of the human heart.
Not one of the characters of *Antigone* is 'bad'. If Creon were a wicked man
there would still be catastrophe, but no tragedy. For both Greeks and Chris-
tians it is not in terms of morality that the moral problem can be solved.
Once more, it is not the belief in man's readiness to be persuaded and moved
into goodness that limits the spiritual scope of Goethe's *Iphigenie*. The uneasiness springs from a different question, which is, I think, implicitly answered by Goethe; the question: what would happen to the human spirit if
all human goodness were of no avail on this earth, as happens to be the case
in *Antigone?* Would the ending be despair then, or a faith beyond despair?
The light and the beauty which emanate from Iphigenie have their source in
her (or Goethe's) conviction that in the final reckoning such questions will
not be asked. Yet as it happens, Iphigenie actually does ask the question.
From the depth of her conflict she implores the gods that good should prevail
on the shores of Tauris, that they should save her and thus '*save their image
in her soul*'. In other words, the image of the gods in Iphigenie's soul is such
that it would be undone by catastrophe and her faith would crumble. But
this is an extraneous and somewhat illegitimate consideration; it would be

better to say that Iphigenie simply embodies the belief that the gods cannot fail her by contradicting her own convictions of what is good and necessary. Thus she stands for the impossibility of tragedy. Antigone, on the other hand, knowing that she is to die and lamenting her fate, asks on which right of the gods she might have trespassed. Why should she in her wretchedness still raise her eyes to the heavenly powers? 'My lot was godlessness received in exchange for piety. But if this is good before the gods then I shall suffer, and in suffering come to know my sin.'

If it can be said that Goethe's limitations have their origin in the apparently limitless scope of his genius, then what is meant is his *genius*, not his talents; on the contrary, he always used his talents to defend himself against his genius. In the deployment of his extrapoetic talents he often seems to insist stubbornly on a playfully cultivated mediocrity. This we can see at work in his unsophisticated taste for rather dull drawings, in his 'classical' preoccupation with the most uninspired examples of Roman sculpture, in his preferring Zelter's innocuous music to Beethoven's and, above all, in the all but philistine pedantry betrayed by his endless collecting, cataloguing, describing and displaying of all manner of objects, documents and instruments. People lacking in a sense of humour have often blamed Goethe for so irresponsibly scattering his interests and wasting his time. Their insatiable desire for still more and still greater poetry is sadly frustrated by the Herr Geheimrat's habits of painstaking theatrical management and time-squandering mineralogical meticulousness.

Yet there is, of course, in all seriousness something puzzling in those radical defensive manoeuvres of Goethe, and I think that only by understanding them as necessary defences can one hope to arrive at some comprehension of Goethe's genius. Only then may one see a little more clearly why his lyrical achievements should have been so truly incomparable, his embarrassment in the face of tragedy so conspicuous, the moral solutions offered by some of his works such anti-climaxes that Irving Babbitt could speak of them as 'sham solutions', and, incidentally, his science so aggressively anti-Newtonian. It may also help to explain why his greatest work, *Faust*, had to remain so ambiguous (and I mean an ambiguity falling short of the essential ambiguity of all great art, an ambiguity not in terms of unresolvable paradox, but of plain contradiction)—so ambiguous that throughout the message-ridden German nineteenth century it could, with the support of what were quite unambiguous quotations, be interpreted as the high-poetical celebration of restlessly active striving and of a freedom that resides in conquest; whereas now, with the ethos of action and aggrandizement deflated, and again with quite unequivocal support from the text, it can be shown to proclaim the hope in the inscrutable workings of divine grace which may descend upon the greatest sinner.

2

Critics have always tried to account in various ways for Goethe's more baffling waverings and uncertainties. Some say that at times he jeopardized his genius by occupying himself with the wrong things; others, that he allowed himself too easily to get entangled in the wrong emotions. Yet it is difficult to be convinced by the standards such critics apply in their assessments of what was 'right' for Goethe. Is it what Ortega y Gasset calls the 'realized *Existenz*' of Goethe the man? This might only have been attained by the sacrifice of Goethe the poet. Or is it the idea of contented equilibrium and psychological balance which Barker Fairley's *Study of Goethe* appears to put forward? But surely this therapeutic approach is most unbecoming for the literary critic, who would soon be out of his job if poets decided to accept for the conduct of their lives the rules of mental health. To say that Goethe was pathologically introspective in his youth is to say that we should be prepared to dispense with *Werther* and the original design of *Faust;* and to imply that Frau von Stein was bad for Goethe is equal to holding that it would have been just as well if Goethe had not written *Iphigenie* or *Tasso* or *Erhabner Geist, du gabst mir, gabst mir alles* or *Warum gabst du uns die tiefen Blicke.* This kind of criticism implicitly pretends to possess the secret of an ideal pattern of creative life which, had it only been adopted by Goethe, would have made him into a still greater poet and a better and happier man.

The paradox of limitations caused by universality, with which Goethe confronts us, originates in a violent clash between the nature of Goethe's genius and his historical situation. In the spiritually barren climate of eighteenth- and nineteenth-century society, amidst that vanity fair of conflicting values and self-contradictory aspirations, a genius apparently so chaotic and yet so profoundly organized as that of Goethe's will easily seem to itself (and to others) to be something almost monstrous, demonic, extra-human —in fact, the spirit of *Nature* itself. And this is what, set up against the spiritual character of his age, Goethe's genius was. If Goethe is not a *European* classic, this is due to the fact that his society was lacking in a fundamentally accepted and generally valid spiritual mould in which alone a classic can be cast.

In spite of all the unavoidable cleavages, disharmonies, animosities and antagonisms which are the perennial lot of human beings and human societies, there is a possibility—and this possibility is called culture when it is realized—of a community of men living together, and maybe fighting one another, in a state of tacit agreement on what the nature and meaning of human existence really is. This unity will then show itself to be at work beyond, or beneath, or despite all differences of actually proclaimed beliefs and articulate opinions. Such must have been the society for which the performances of the tragedies of Aeschylus and Sophocles were national celebrations; such were wide stretches of what we rather vaguely call the Middle Ages; such were, to judge by their artistic creations, the days of the Renaissance and of Elizabeth. The age of Goethe, however, was not of this kind. Its true representatives were the twin creatures of spiritual chaos: rationalism and romanticism, the one abhorring, the other worshipping the irrational aspect of man. In the absence of a genuine supranatural order human beings were thrown back on their purely naturalistic resources, with analytical sceptical reason on the one hand, and disorganized emotions on the other. Pascal's reasons of the heart degenerated into sheer emotionalism, which was mistaken for spirituality, and Plato's reason of understanding into the crudest empiricism, which prided itself upon its 'realistic' outlook. In vain had Kant fought his lonely battle. Those who came after him, the great philosophers of the age of Goethe, who, of course, felt and knew the disaster that had befallen the spirit, raised their arbitrary, 'exciting', 'interesting' metaphysical towers above the heads of a society that had become Babel in its mutual incomprehension.

Into such a situation there was born a genius who, more than any other of his time (with the possible exception of Blake), seemed to have been sent to fill with precious life whatever order of the spirit, whatever tradition he may have found upon his arrival—as Sophocles had done with the religious tradition of Greece, and Dante with the scholastic order of the Middle Ages. But, alas, 'the day was so absurd and confused', as Goethe himself put it in his last letter to Wilhelm von Humboldt, and his genius, being a perpetual source of light to the world, had itself to grope in darkness. What, I think, is correct in Ortega y Gasset's and—in some measure—Karl Jasper's thesis of Goethe's *Existenz* having remained unfulfilled is the fact that his own genius was an unending puzzle to him. For the very nature of this genius deprived Goethe of that particular kind of historical sense, that intuitive grasp of the historical character of his age and his own position in it, which Schiller had and, above all, Hölderlin, who wrote:

> . . . *Indessen dünket mir öfters*
> *Besser zu schlafen, wie so ohne Genossen zu seyn,*
> *So zu harren und was zu thun indess und zu sagen,*
> *Weiss ich nicht und wozu Dichter in dürftiger Zeit?*

> . . . Meanwhile, it seems to me often,
> Better to slumber than live without companions, like
>   this,
> So to linger, and know not what to begin or to utter,
> Or, in such spiritless times, why to be poet at all?

Goethe too knew that question, and there were periods in his life when he actually did answer it in the negative and all but behaved accordingly. But for him the question was not an historical one; not 'why to be poet at all in spiritless times', but solely whether he himself *was* a poet. True, he once wrote (and just when he was about to resume his work on *Faust*) : 'We are compelled to step out of our century if we wish to work according to our convictions' (to Schiller, November 25th, 1797); but such statements are extremely rare. Unaware of the deeper historical perspective of his situation, he merely perceived through his own agonies and through his spontaneous hostility towards almost all and everything that represented the spiritual character of his century—its rationalism, its romanticism, its unnatural hysterias, its cold empiricism, its idealistic philosophies, its tempestuous music—that there was a gulf fixed between what he himself was in his inmost being and the world in which he lived as a citizen. Yet, unlike Hölderlin, he would not allow his genius to burden and destroy him with the historical mission of poetic prophet-martyr. He continually tried to 'do the duty of the day' by seeking a compromise between opposition and collaboration. Within his genius (which is never the whole man) he was undivided, in the sense in which a genuine pattern of nature and spirit fused, or any vital religious and cultural order, is undivided; but in the absence of any such valid order of human life outside himself he came to identify the inner order, inherent in his genius, with the spirit of nature itself.

'Unnatural,' in the mouth of Goethe, was one of the strongest invectives. 'Diese verdammte Unnatur!' he exclaimed, faced with the productions of Kleist, and Kleist was judged. Thus pantheism, God in nature, became his natural religion, and Spinoza his chosen prophet. 'This philosopher,' he wrote in a letter to Jacobi (June 9th, 1785), 'does not prove the being of God; God is being. And if others, because of this, blame him as an atheist, then I feel like praising him as *theissimum*, indeed *christianissimum*.' In the same letter, however, he confesses, in a rather touchingly ingenious fashion, that he had never read systematically what the philosopher wrote (if he had, there is reason to think that he would occasionally have felt rather sadly disappointed) : 'My way of living and thinking does not permit it. But whenever I cast a glance into his books, I believe I understand him, that is, he never seems to be self-contradictory, and I can derive from him something that affects my own feelings and doings in a very salutary manner.' How amazingly self-assured was Goethe's conviction that he represented, as it were, nature in her own right! And what a wonderful intimacy with all the disguises of the godhead is displayed in the following lines (from a very much later letter to Jacobi, January 6th, 1813) : 'With all the manifold facets of my being, one way of thinking is not sufficient for me; as a poet and artist I am a polytheist, but a pantheist as a student of Nature, and either belief I hold with equal determination. And if I need a divinity for my personal being, my moral existence—well, this need too is promptly catered for.'

Goethe, having to express the whole order of spirit and nature through his own genius, was limited in the performance of such an impossible duty by the absence of anything corresponding to that order within the society to which he belonged. Goethe's genius is miraculously 'natural' and 'un-civilized', in the sense that he has no support from a society civilized in the mould of the spirit that was his. And this is why, as a member of this society which had so little use for his genius, he could be so amazingly 'civilized', often to the point of cold formality and embarrassed stiffness, and even to the point of saying that he would rather commit an act of injustice than tolerate disorder. And this is also why his genius seems so boundless and its limitations, at the same time, so striking; for within his own contem-porary situation such genius as his hovers perpetually on the precarious dividing-line between greatness and excess. (His counterpart, in the sphere of political genius, was Napoleon.) In the absence of a tradition to feed and educate his genius, the umbilical cord between it and nature was, as Goethe himself once put it, never severed.

Schiller, while admiring this fascinating spectacle of an undivided poetic nature, yet ceaselessly strained to play the part of midwife. In the letters about *Faust*, and still more in the correspondence about *Wilhelm Meister*, he makes the ever-renewed and ever-frustrated attempt to civilize, educate and discipline what seemed to him a too luxurious production of genius. Yet he was bound to fail, in spite of the fact that he had a profounder under-standing of Goethe than anyone else. In one of the very first letters he wrote to him (August 23rd, 1794) he said that if Goethe had been born a Greek or in any other civilization where he would have been surrounded by 'an exquisite nature and an ideal art,' his struggle 'would have been shortened or even been superfluous'. At least in the creation of certain types of work— *Faust* and *Wilhelm Meister* for instance—Goethe, he thought, ought to resign himself to the rigours of a more philosophical discipline. It was no good. Ideas were not embodied in the society of his time, and in the abstract terms of philosophical speculation Goethe had no use for them. He had to *see* and feel them; but when he did see and feel them they became so real to him that he was even surprised that to others they appeared to be mere 'ideas'.

The impression that Goethe's genius is 'wholly nature' is partly due to an optical illusion caused by the refraction in the medium of a 'spiritless time' where the spiritual had ceased to be incarnate, having evaporated into vague abstractions. The anaemic and artificial civilization of his day drove Goethe again and again into a realm where the 'real thing' could be found. This is why Italy was such a revelation to Goethe. There, set up against a clearer sky and the memory of a clearer realization of the human destiny, he found a vision of life in which nature and humanity were merged in a 'natural civilization'.

It would be inadequate to the point of idiocy to approach Goethe in a moralizing fashion; but there is no reason why one should not see that, with such a predominance of nature within him and such a lack of civilized tradition around him, he had to fail when faced with the tragic or religious aspect of the moral problem as it is inherent in the very plots of both *Iphigenie* and *Faust*. No human being can come to grips with such a problem unaided by tradition and traditional teaching. As it happened, within the 'tradition' of Goethe's day it was precisely this problem that had been deformed and dwarfed beyond recognition. The practical, 'lived' side of it was indeed, after all is said (and said with great affection) about Fräulein von Klettenberg and other beautiful souls, too pietistically mediocre ever really to mean anything to Goethe; and its philosophical side too speculative, abstract and metaphysical not to be discarded by Goethe's passion for 'reality'. In the spiritual climate of the eighteenth and the beginning of the nineteenth centuries the terror of a man's exposure to the need for ultimate moral or religious decisions could not be creatively grasped, either on the level of Greek tragedy or on that of undiluted Christianity, or indeed even on the level of that unique encounter of both which took place in the Elizabethan drama. And Goethe was of his age in failing to grasp it in either of these spheres.

We have seen what happened in his dealings with a classically tragic subject; how he missed the meaning of the cross of Christianity is best illustrated by that passage from *Wilhelm Meisters Wanderjahre* where he 'draws a veil over this suffering' just because he 'reveres it so deeply', and because he 'regards it as a damnable insolence to expose the agonies of the saint to the sun which had hidden its face when an infamous world obtruded upon it this sight'. (It happened to be Weimar where an American commandant very wisely decreed that Hitler's electorate in what was once Goethe's city were to be shown the horrors of Buchenwald concentration camp.) And summing up the meaning of *Hamlet*, Goethe defines it as the tragedy of a man who was too weak to carry the burden of his mission. Stating the problem in terms of strength and weakness, he once more fails to be impressed by the moral aspect of *Hamlet* and the all-pervasive, all-corroding power of evil, the 'morbid' preoccupation of Elizabethan tragedy. For to be able to perceive and creatively to articulate this problem, that is, to form a vision of it rather than to discuss it, presupposes a theology underlying, however dispersedly, the picture of reality that an age possesses; and this is something different from a philosophy of nature and from even the highest human wisdom. Goethe's genius soared gloriously above the flat expanses of contemporary religious sentimentality and mediocre morality, in triumphant opposition to all puritan gloom, moral suspicion and tearful piety, asserting that life, whatever it be, is good and beautiful: 'wie es auch sei, das Leben, es ist gut', and

> *Ihr glücklichen Augen,*
> *Was je ihr gesehn,*
> *Es sei wie es wolle,*
> *Es war doch so schön!*

It is this finality in his assertion of life that makes it possible to claim for Goethe the position of the greatest lyrical genius of Europe. But though it is *his* final assertion, it is not ultimate. It indeed transcends all sorrows of Werther, Tasso and Ottilie, and endless conflicts most deeply felt and suffered. But would it transcend, one wonders, tragedy fully realized? And only there is the place of an ultimate 'Es ist gut'.

3

Under such auspices what was to become of a dramatic plot in which a man enters into a contract with the Devil, signing away, on certain conditions, the fate of his soul? What was to become of *Faust?* One may well ask. It took Goethe, all in all, sixty years to decide, or rather to decide that he would not quite decide. Certain things, however, the play decided for him. For instance, that it would, being Goethe's, become a lyrical masterpiece. There is no greater and no more varied lyrical poetry to be found within the German language. And more: *Faust* became a pageant of the human spirit on its voyage throughout the ages. An extraordinary wealth of mythological creatures, Teutonic, Greek, Christian, populate the scene, all testifying to their creator's inexhaustible imaginative power. And still more: the hero of the play was to become the representative of a whole epoch of history, its lust for knowledge, for power over nature, its intellectual and emotional instability, its terrible failure in love, humility and patience. And still more: the first part of the play, dominated by what is usually called the Gretchen tragedy, was to bring out most movingly the undoing, by the Faustian manoeuvres, of what was left in the world of simplicity of heart, devotion of love and innocence of feeling. This part of what is, after all, called the tragedy of Faust, developed by its own momentum into a poetic and dramatic achievement so immaculate that it will, I think, for ever hold its place by the side of what is great in the literature of the world— and this precisely because in its design it is not, in the traditional sense, tragic but lyrical. It is what might have become of the play *Hamlet* if Ophelia and not the Prince of Denmark were to be its protagonist. In other words, Goethe may have succeeded in creating a new genre: sentimental tragedy, or the tragedy of human *feelings:* Werther, Gretchen, Ottilie. What he could not write was the tragedy of the human *spirit*. It is here that the tragedy of Faust fails and becomes illegitimately ambiguous, because there is for Goethe in the last analysis no specifically *human* spirit. It is fundamentally at one with the spirit of nature. Hence it is He, the Spirit of Nature, or the Spirit of Earth, not God or the Devil, who holds in his hands the final decision over Faust's bliss or damnation. Had He, when He appeared to Faust in the first scene of the play, not rejected him, neither God in Heaven nor the Devil in Hell would have had a chance. And one of the only two scenes in which Faust really regrets that he has committed himself to his satanic company is the great monologue *Wald und Höhle:*

> *Erhabner Geist, du gabst mir, gabst mir alles . . .*

> Oh thou great Spirit, thou has given me all . . .

when it appears that this Spirit did not crush him after all.

There are in this vast display of demons great and small only two that affect Faust demonically; certainly not God, who is a jovial old gentleman, enlightened and rather commonplace in some of his utterances ('Ein guter Mensch, in seinem dunklen Drange, Ist sich des rechten Weges wohl bewusst', which really means not more than that a good man will not altogether go astray; a conviction not so difficult to hold that it would need a divinity to persuade one), and certainly not Mephistopheles, a Voltairean spirit, with whom Faust is from the very beginning on terms of great familiarity. Goethe himself, in a conversation with Eckermann (March 2nd, 1831), has denied him all demonic properties: 'He is altogether too negative,' he said, and has explicitly stated in the play itself that he is of lesser rank than the Spirit of Earth. But the two which teach Faust what a real demon is are the Earth Spirit and the Mothers, the innermost spirits of nature and life. They represent the demonic element in Goethe's genius. It is in union with this element that Faust seeks his happiness from beginning to end, or *almost* to the very end, and not in the realization of a specifically human spirit. And Faust has been in contact with those demons before Mephistopheles enters the scene. This contact means black magic, and Faust is a magician when the curtain rises. It is this that reduces the *dramatic* stature of Mephistopheles to all but nil, and not the rather naïve consideration that Goethe has forestalled all dramatic tension in this respect by making, in the Prologue, the Lord himself, a sure winner, as it were, party to the wager. All that Mephistopheles can do for Faust is to give him a hand in a job of which he already knows the essential tricks of the trade. And throughout the play the Devil performs hardly any magical feats with which one would not willingly credit the magician himself who had already succeeded in establishing contact with the very spirit of life.

All this would be rather irrelevant if it were not at the centre of the essential ambiguity of *Faust*—the most striking outcome of Goethe's avoidance of tragedy. What does Faust *really* expect of Mephistopheles? Still more magic? No; but contentment, rest, peace; to be able to say to the moment: 'Verweile doch, du bist so schön'. [Stay, thou art so fair.] In other words, life is good. True, this is preceded by Faust's contemptuous identification of such a state with self-complacency. But it is the words themselves, not what leads up to them, which become the condition of the wager. And their poetic truth gives the lie to the preamble. They are made of the same stuff as 'Es sei, wie es wolle, Es war doch so schön!' And this the devil is to provide? The very same devil whom Faust, a few scenes later, when he has found temporary peace in the company of the Spirit of Nature, knows to be the spirit responsible for

> *So tauml' ich von Begierde zu Genuss*
> *Und im Genuss verschmacht' ich nach Begierde*

Thus I tumble from desire to fulfilment
And in fulfilment I crave for more desire

for ever destroying that very peace which communion with the Spirit of Nature gives him. With the Devil defined as the spirit of negation and unrest, this becomes indeed a very strange condition meaning in fact that the Devil is to have Faust if Faust ever escapes the Devil.

What, on the other hand, is the condition of the wager between the Lord and Mephistopheles?

> *Zieh diesen Geist von seinem Urquell ab*

Drag this spirit away from the very source of his life

The Lord, that is, challenges Mephistopheles to alienate Faust from the springs of life, to uproot him. If he succeeds, Faust will be his. This sounds more like 'Deprive him of all peace, if indeed you can' than 'Make him contented with the moment'. And in the end, when Faust, anticipating this peace and contentment, blinded by anxiety, deluded into the belief that the great work of colonization has begun while, in actual fact, the busy noise is merely the sound of shovels digging his own grave, utters the fatal words, in the face of a vision so totally unconvincing in its meagre guilt-burdened town-and-country-planning bliss that one cannot but agree with Mephistopheles that it is the emptiest moment of his life, then the Devil is cheated of his apparently well-deserved prey by the feeble trick of a future tense ['Im Vorgefühl von solchem hohen Glück'], and by the intervention of divine grace called down upon him by the only human love Faust ever received and experienced.

How is this? Faust has indeed promised that he would content himself, even anticipated the enjoyment of peace ['Geniess' ich jetzt . . .'] in his vision of the contented future. He has satisfied the Devil who has never been found wanting in the shrewd judgment of any situation, and is, having faithfully renounced his programme of eternal striving, carried into Heaven in reward for his determination to strive eternally:

> *Wer immer strebend sich bemüht,*
> *Den können wir erlösen.*

> It is the struggling, striving man
> Whom we are free to save.

What is at the root of such confusion, which has indeed defeated four generations of interpreters of *Faust*, and, if we are to trust Eckermann's report, Goethe's own faculties as a commentator? It would be tempting to relegate it to the place where many an impenetrable mystery is stored, were it not for the persistent suspicion that we are faced here not so much with a genuine poetic paradox as with a plain contradiction. It is the inevitable contradiction of the undedicated mind and heart. In Faust's world there are no real loyalties to be realized and no real commitments to be broken. Both his eternal striving and his desire for peace are merely the extreme stations of his mind and heart in their never-ending voyage of self-exploration. His 'tragedy' is that he is incapable of tragedy. For tragedy presupposes the belief in an external order of things which is indeed incomplete without the conformity of the human soul, but would be still more defective without the soul's freedom to violate it. Yet Faust's dilemma is different. His 'two souls' are merely the one soul divided in itself because it knows of no independent external reality to which it is related as a free agent. Faust is in every essential respect Goethe's *alter ego*, the embodiment of that part of his self which remained unprotected by his apparently fondest trust and belief: that he belonged to Nature as her most precious possession. Faust, outside this zone of safety, is therefore torn between the belief in a world to which, strive as he may, he has no access whatever, and the belief in himself as the creator of his own world. Thus the spiritual extremes of his existence are not guilt and atonement, but despair and titanism. It is a situation unresolvable in tragedy.

Nature is fundamentally innocent, and Goethe's genius is in communion with Nature. Hence there can be, for Goethe, no catharsis, only metamorphosis. It is never with the spirit of a transcendent God or with the spirit of Man that Goethe's potentially tragic heroes are reunited after their dramatic crises. When the crisis is over, they are at one again with the spirit of Nature. They are not purified in a tragic sense, not raised above their guilt through atonement, but enter, as it were, a biologically, not morally, new phase of life, healed by oblivion and restored to strength through the sleep of the just. This is what happens to Orestes, and what happens to Faust at the beginning of Part II. Both put down their cup of Lethe and burst into magnificent praises of Nature. But such, clearly, could not have been the conclusion of Faust. He had to be saved or damned, for Heaven and Hell had become involved by virtue of the legendary pattern. But it is *only* by virtue of the legendary pattern that they have become involved at all. For the world of Faust is only just Christian enough to have room for purgatory. It is a purgatory suspended between two half unreal spheres. Hence 'Mephistopheles must only half win his wager', and Faust be 'only half guilty', as Goethe himself put it in a letter which looks forward to the play's 'most serene conclusion' when 'the old Lord may exercise his privilege of mercy'.

What is Faust's sin? Restlessness of spirit. What is Faust's salvation? Restlessness of spirit. The confusion lies in a perpetual criss-crossing of restless strivings of different qualities: the striving for peace, and the striving for sensation; or, to put it differently, and in terms of the quality of the contentment sought, the striving for that peace that passeth all understanding, and the striving for a state of calm, an 'enough' which is merely a state of emotional exhaustion. What the heavenly powers mean by that striving which carries its own salvation must surely be different from the striving the goal of which Faust hopes to achieve with the help of black magic and the Devil. Yet these two kinds of striving perpetually get into each other's way throughout the poem, and the entanglement is at its worst in the crucial last scene of Faust's life when his desire for doing good and for the realization of his humanity within its decreed limits is inextricably bound up with the delusion and madness of titanism. Of these two strivings the one desires the attainment of the superman, the alchemist heightening of all human faculties, whereas the other aims at renunciation and resignation to the simple state of man. The first is the native element of Goethe's genius, the second the longing of Goethe's moral existence.

> *Könnt' ich Magie von meinem Pfad entfernen,*
> *Die Zaubersprüche ganz und gar verlernen,*
> *Stünd ich, Natur, vor dir ein Mann allein,*
> *Da wär's der Mühe wert, ein Mensch zu sein.*

[Could I forget my sorcery, and ban my magic, stand, stripped of it utterly, oh Nature, face to face with thee, it would be worth while then to be a man.]

This outcry of Faust's, towards the end of the play when he is visited by *Sorge*—and this is the second place where Faust is prepared to renounce the

Devil—reveals perhaps Goethe's deepest secret. To cut the umbilical cord joining him with Nature and her magic power, not to remain what he once called 'a magic oyster over which there pass mysterious waves', to be face to face with Nature and escape the fate of Proteus—this only would be human happiness. Over and over again he sought deliverance from his genius in work, in the practical jobs of everyday life, through Wilhelm Meister's, through Faust's solution, and so desperately that as a man of fifty he confessed to Schiller (January 6th, 1798) that he owed it to him if he had learned to 'look at the manysidedness of my own inner being with more justice. . . . *You* have made me a poet again which I had all but ceased to be.' Such was the nature of his genius and the character of his age that the spirit could only live at the expense of life, and life only at the expense of the spirit. Thus the meaning of creative genius as well as the meaning of doing the sober work of the day, inwardness as well as action, had to remain puzzles to each other, anonymous, undefined strangers. They never met in a common dedication and could not be at peace with each other because they knew no will other than their own. And at such distance from 'la sua volontate è nostra pace' neither divine comedy nor human tragedy can be written.

It was impossible for Goethe to accept this situation, and impossible, by the very nature of things, to solve it. Hence his perpetual oscillation between the precarious magic of the inner communion with the deep where the Earth Spirit dwells, and the moral determination to reconcile himself to the cruder demands made on human existence by society, with the emphasis of approval shifting to and fro between the two: Egmont and Oranien, Tasso and Antonio, Prometheus and *Grenzen der Menschheit*, elective affinities and legal bonds. Was harmony ever to be achieved? The answer may be found in the ambiguity of *Faust*.

The Sun Always Rises:

Ibsen's *Ghosts* as Tragedy?*

ROBERT W. CORRIGAN

What profit has man of all his labour wherein he laboureth under the sun? One generation passeth away, and another generation cometh; but the earth abideth forever. . . . The sun also ariseth, and the sun goeth down, and hasteth to the place where he arose.—Ecclesiastes

Ghosts created the biggest stir in Europe of all of Ibsen's plays. It was the hallmark of the Free Theatre movement. Antoine at the Théâtre Libre, Brahm at the Freie Buehne, and Grein at the Independent Theatre in London all produced this play as a symbol and a harbinger of their freedom. But the play was violently received. It shocked respectable middle-class audiences everywhere; it was condemned and banned; for the young turks of liberalism it was a banner to be waved on high. From the beginning the play had a notoriety that Ibsen only partially intended.

Fortunately, *Ghosts* is now seen in clearer perspective and we tend to be amused by the critical reaction of the Nineties. But *Ghosts* is still a controversial play. The number of respectable interpretations currently making the rounds is large and when you get on the subject of *Ghosts* as tragedy—well, it is one of those plays, like *Death of a Salesman*, it just won't stay settled and is always good for an argument. The four major interpretations of the play usually advanced are: First, Ibsen wrote *Ghosts* as an answer to the objections raised by Nora's flight from her husband and children in *A Doll's House*. Tied to a worse husband than Helmar, Mrs. Alving, instead of leaving him, had decided to stay, and to cover up the "corpse" of her married life with re-

---

* Robert W. Corrigan, "The Sun Always Rises: Ibsen's *Ghosts* as Tragedy?" *Educational Theatre Journal*, 1959, pp. 171–180.

spectable trappings.[1] Second: Mrs. Alving and Oswald are the victims of a two-fisted fate which takes the form of the laws of heredity in a mechanistic world and the stultifying and debilitating conventions of respectability. Third: Hereditary disease was for Ibsen the symbol of all the determinist forces that crush humanity, and, therefore, he sought to put in opposition to these forces the strongest of all instincts—maternal passion. And, finally, there is a fourth group of critics who dismiss the play as irrelevant except as an historical landmark. They argue that although the play may have been revolutionary in its day, today any dramatic conflict which presents suffering and a shot of penicillin as its alternatives is not very convincing. All of these interpretations—and they have been persuasively argued by responsible critics—seem to me to be either misreadings of the play or beside the point. They are comments about the play, but they are ancillary and fail to recognize the underlying conflict of the play. For this reason most modern commentaries on *Ghosts* fail to describe and interpret the central action which Ibsen is imitating, and this has resulted in many limited or erroneous discussions of the play as a tragedy. It is this central action and its tragic implications which I wish to discuss, and this can best be done by first turning to Ibsen the man and the artist.

I

Ibsen's biography is a study in conflict and contradiction. The gadfly of bourgeoisie morality was helplessly bourgeois; the enemy of pietism was a guilt-ridden possessor of the worst kind of "Lutheran" conscience; the champion of the "love-life of the soul" was incapable of loving; the militant spokesman against hypocrisy and respectability was pompous and outraged at any breach of decorum. Ibsen's life is the contradiction of those values affirmed in his plays. This should not confuse us, however, if we will look even briefly at some of the significant events in a life that was really quite dull.

Ibsen was born into an atmosphere of fairly prosperous parochial respectability. His father was a small-time shipping tycoon in the little town of Skien. In 1836, when Ibsen was eight years old, his father went bankrupt and was accused of embezzlement and forgery. The charges were never proved, but the family was ostracized and reduced to a grubbing kind of poverty. When Ibsen was sixteen he left his family, amidst bitter renunciations on both sides, never to see or correspond with them again. Even when his parents died he failed to return or write. He wrote to a friend on the occasion of his father's death that he was "unable to offer assistance of any kind." So at sixteen Ibsen went to the dismal town of Grimstead as an ap-

---

[1] Janko Lavrin, *Ibsen*, London, 1950, p. 81.

prentice in pharmacy. Here he had an illegitimate son, Hans Jakob, and once again was "run out of town." He left Grimstead, leaving mother and child stranded, and never took the slightest interest in them. He went to Christiana (now Oslo) to begin his career as a writer and failed. In 1851 he was hired as director and dramaturg of the new Bergen National Theatre. Again, Ibsen was a failure. Letters and memoirs of actors in his company show him to have been incompetent as both a director and as a manager; and the plays written expressly for the theatre in his role as dramaturg were all miserable flops. Furthermore, he must have felt failure in his personal life. He fell in love three times in Bergen, and in each instance the girl's father broke off the affair because Ibsen was not suitable as a son-in-law. By 1857 he was on the verge of being fired; friends stepped in and got him a job as director of the newly organized Norwegian Theatre in Christiana. But failure followed him and by 1862 the National Theatre was bankrupt both artistically and financially and Ibsen was bitterly denounced by the press. Once again, friends came to his aid and he was given a small dole in the form of a literary scholarship to study abroad.

The story of Ibsen's success as an international playwright is well-known and in 1891 he returned to Norway as a celebrity. In Christiana, where he settled for good, he became something of a national institution and was far from disliking such a status. All the frustration, humiliation, and rejection he had endured in youth and early manhood were now amply compensated for. He was wealthy and internationally famous. As if anxious to do full justice to his literary and social position, Ibsen increased his air of excessively dignified respectability. So much so that in all his external habits he was even more strict and methodical than those philistines whom he had ridiculed so aggressively in his plays. Immaculately dressed in his frock-coat, and silk top-hat, he took his daily walks along the same streets, sat at the same table in the same cafe (where the customers all respectfully rose whenever he entered), and went home at the same time—with the regularity of clockwork. He was also fond of displaying his numerous decorations and medals, which he used to collect and covet with the relish of a *nouveau riche* enjoying all the external insignia of his own importance.

In short, Ibsen became a "pillar of society" in his last days; he was a regular speaker at the Norwegian equivalents of the Rotary Club, the AAUW, Labor Unions, and the Better Business Bureau. In his speeches he praised all of these groups and gratefully accepted their adulation and honors. His study walls were covered with plaques and certificates from civic organizations and only a bust of Strindberg—a bust that captured the penetrating and demonic quality of Strindberg's gaze—acted as an antidote to this display of middle-class self-righteousness. On March 15th, 1900 Ibsen had a stroke, and another in the following year. These paralytic strokes were followed by amnesia and for six years he lay helplessly senile. He died on May 23rd, 1906, at the age of seventy-eight.

The clue to the meaning of all Ibsen's plays lies in this strange biography. Ibsen's plays are a continuous act of expiation. Certainly, it is significant that bankruptcy and the resultant rejection by society appears in four of his plays; the desire to restore the family honor is central to two more; and there are illegitimate children in eight plays. Thematically, the plays are, almost without exception, patterned in a similar way: a hidden moral guilt and the fear of impending retribution. Structurally, the plays are epilogues of retribution. All of the plays after *Peer Gynt* begin on a happy note late in the action. In each case the central figure has a secret guilt which is soon discovered. As the play progresses, by series of expository scenes (scenes which delve into the past and are then related to the present condition of the characters), a sense of the foreboding doom of impending retribution envelops the action and each of the plays ends with justice, in the form of moral fate having its way. And finally, beginning with *Ghosts*, Ibsen introduces the theme of expiation. In every play following *Ghosts*, at least one of the central characters feels the need to exorcise his guilt, doubt, or fear by some form of renunciation.

Perhaps more important is the fact, that as Ibsen's art developed these themes and attitudes changed in tone and form. The guilt, which had been specific in the early plays—Bernick's lie, Nora's forgery, Mrs. Alving's return—becomes more and more abstract, nebulous, and ominous as best evidenced in the nameless guilt of Solness and Rosmer. The fear, which in the early plays had been the fear of discovery, becomes a gnawing anxiety. Self-realization, which in *Brand* is presented in terms of the Kierkegaardian imperative of either/or is realized in the later plays in an ambiguous kind of self-destruction. And finally, significant action on the part of the characters has tendencies towards becoming a frozen stasis of meaningless activity and contemplation.

Ibsen's life and his work are closely interwoven. Ibsen, rejected from society as a young man, had good reason to see the blindness of bourgeois respectability in his exile. And yet his sharp criticism of society is always balanced by his desire to be a part of that very society he saw and knew to be false. Over and over again in his plays and letters he condemns the hypocrisy, the intellectual shallowness, and the grim bleakness of his Scandinavian homeland. But he returned to it in pomp and circumstance. Herein lies the crux to an understanding of Ibsen's art in general and *Ghosts* in particular. More and more we see that both in Ibsen the man and in the characters of his plays the basic struggle is within.

Ibsen lived in a time of revolution; he was a maker of part of that revolution; and he knew full well that all the things he said about bourgeois society were true. But despite his rational understanding, his intellectual comprehension of this fact, he was driven by deeper forces within him not only to justify himself to that false society, but to become a part of it. It is this struggle within himself between his rational powers and the Trolls of the Boyg that best explains his life and work. Ibsen's plays are his attempts to quell the guilt he felt for desiring values which he knew to be false. In support of this point, I call attention to two important bits of evidence: the first is a letter written by Ibsen to Peter Hanson in 1870:

While writing *Brand*, I had on my desk a glass with a scorpion in it. From time to time the little animal was ill. Then I used to give it a piece of soft fruit, upon which it fell furiously and emptied its poison into it—after which it was well again. Does not something similar happen to us poets? The laws of nature regulate the spiritual world also. . . .

The second is a short poem entitled "Fear of Light" (presently, I shall relate the significance of that title to *Ghosts*):

> What is life? a fighting
> In heart and brain with Trolls.
> Poetry? that means writing
> Doomsday-accounts of our souls.

I contend that Ibsen's plays were attempts—attempts that were bound to fail, just as Mrs. Alving's attempts were bound to fail—to relieve Ibsen of his guilt and at the same time were judgments of his failure to overcome the Trolls (which first appear as Gerd in *Brand*), those irrational forces and powers within man over which he has no control.

Keeping these facts in mind, let us now turn to *Ghosts*. One does not have to be a very perceptive student of the theatre to realize that the "ghosts" Ibsen is talking about are those ghosts of the past that haunt us in the present. In fact, Ibsen has often been criticized for using his ghost symbolism with such obviousness, such lack of subtlety, and so repetitiously. Certainly, when reading the play we feel this criticism is justified. Oswald's looking like Captain Alving; his interest in sex and liquor; his feelings toward Regina; his syphilitic inheritance; Pastor Mander's influence over Mrs. Alving, the orphanage, and the fire are only a few of the "ghosts" that Ibsen uses as analogues to his theme. Alrik Gustafson puts it this way:

Symbols are, of course, a commonplace in Ibsen's dramas, but in his early plays before *The Wild Duck* he uses symbolistic devices somewhat too obviously, almost exclusively to clarify his themes. Any college sophomore can tell you after a single reading of *Pillars of Society*, *A Doll's House*, or *Ghosts* what the symbols expressed in these titles mean. The symbols convey *ideas*—and little else. They have few emotional overtones, are invested with little of the impressive mystery of life, the tragic poetry of existence. They tend to leave us in consequence cold, uncommitted, like after a debate whose heavy-handed dialectic has ignored the very pulse-beat of a life form which it is supposed to have championed.[2]

But *Ghosts* is concerned with more than the external manifestations of an evil heritage. In those oft-quoted lines that serve as a rationale for the play, Mrs. Alving says:

I am half inclined to think we are all ghosts, Mr. Manders. It is not only what we have inherited from our fathers and mothers that exists again in us, but all sorts of old dead ideas and all kinds of old dead beliefs and things of that kind. They are not actually alive in us; but there they are dormant, all the same, and we can never be rid of them. . . . There must be ghosts all over the world. . . . And we are so miserably afraid of the light, all of us . . . and I am here, fighting with ghosts both without and within me.

The ghosts of plot and symbol are the manifestations of Mrs. Alving's struggle with the ghosts within. It is this internal conflict, a conflict similar to Ibsen's personal struggle, that is the play's central action.

To define this action more explicitly, I would say that Ibsen is imitating an action in which a woman of ability and stature finds her ideals and her intellectual attitudes and beliefs in conflict with an inherited emotional life determined by the habitual responses of respectability and convention. As the play's form evolves it becomes apparent that the values Mrs. Alving affirms in intellectual terms are doomed to defeat because she has no control over her emotional inheritance—an inheritance of ghosts which exists, but which cannot be confined to or controlled by any schematization of the intelligence. Every significant choice that Mrs. Alving has ever made and the resultant action of such a decision is determined by these ghosts of the past rather than by intellectual deliberation. To mention but a few instances: Her marriage to Captain Alving in conformity to the wishes of her mother and aunts; her return to her husband; her reaction to the Oswald-Regina relationship; her acceptance of Manders after she has seen and commented upon the hypocrisy of the scene with Engstrand; her failure to tell Oswald the "straight" truth about his father; the horror of her reaction when Oswald is indifferent to his father's life; and finally, the question mark with which the play ends. All of these scenes are evidence that Mrs. Alving's ideals of freedom and her rhetorical flights into intellectual honesty are of no use to her when it comes to action. Perhaps, I can make my point more clear by briefly developing two of the above mentioned episodes.

As the second act opens, Mrs. Alving comes to a quick decision about Oswald's relationship with Regina: "Out of the house she shall go—and at once. That part of it is clear as daylight." I will return to the relationship of

---

[2] Alrik Gustafson, "Some Notes on Theme, Character, and Symbol in *Rosmersholm*," *The Carleton Drama Review*, Vol. I, No. 2, pp. 9–10.

light to enlightenment, but for the moment we see that Mrs. Alving's decision is based upon an emotional response determined by her inheritance of respectability. Then, Mrs. Alving and the pastor begin to talk; and Mrs. Alving always talks a good game. After better than four pages of dialogue, Mrs. Alving is finally able to exclaim: "If I were not such a miserable coward, I would say to him: 'Marry her, or make any arrangement you like with her—only let there be no deceit in the matter.' " The pastor is properly shocked when Mrs. Alving gives him the "face the facts of life" routine; but her liberation, which is only verbal, is short lived! Manders asks how "you, a mother, can be willing to allow your . . . " This is Mrs. Alving's reply: "But I am not willing to allow it. I would not allow it for anything in the world; that is just what I was saying."

Or to take another situation. In Act I, Mrs. Alving tells Manders what her husband was really like: "The truth is this, that my husband died just as great a profligate as he had been all his life." In Act II, she is telling Manders of all the things she *ought* to have done and she says: "If I had been the woman I ought, I would have taken Oswald into my confidence and said to him: 'Listen, my son, your father was a dissolute man.' " In the third act circumstances have forced Mrs. Alving to tell Oswald the truth about his father: "Your poor father never found any outlet for the overmastering joy of life that was in him. And I brought no holiday spirit into his house, either; I am afraid I made your poor father's home unbearable to him, Oswald."

When we come to see the big scenes in this way, we then recall the numerous small events that create the network of the action and give the play its texture. Such things come to mind as Mrs. Alving's need of books to make her feel secure in her stand, and the neat little bit in the first act where Mrs. Alving reprimands Oswald for smoking in the parlor, which Ibsen then underscores by making it an issue in the second act.

Ibsen's plays are filled with such incidents; those little events that tell so much. I am of the persuasion that Ibsen is not very good at making big events happen; as appealing as they may be to a director, they tend to be theatrically inflated; they are melodramatic in the sense that the action of the plot is in itself larger than the characters or the situation in the play which create such events. Ibsen is the master of creating the small shocking event, or as Mary McCarthy puts it: "the psychopathology of everyday life." Nora's pushing off the sewing on the widow Christine; Hjalmer letting Hedwig do the retouching with her half-blind eyes as he goes off hunting in the attic; his cutting of his father at Werle's party and the moment when Hedda intentionally mistakes Aunt Julia's new hat for the servant's, are all examples of this talent. These are the things we know we are capable of! This is the success (and the limitation) of the naturalistic convention "which implies a norm of behavior on the part of its guilty citizens within their box-like living rooms."

But to return to the main business at hand: the conflict for Mrs. Alving, then, is not how to act. She just acts; there is no decision, nor can there be, for she has no rational control over her actions. Herein lies the conflict. Just because Mrs. Alving has no control over her actions, does not mean she escapes the feelings of guilt for what she does and her inability to do otherwise. Her continual rhetoricizing about emancipation and her many acts of renunciation are attempts to satisfy these feelings of guilt. For example, and I am indebted to Weigand here,[3] the explicit reasons she gives for building the orphanage do not account sufficiently for her use of the expression, "the power of an uneasy conscience." There is a big difference between fear that an ugly secret will become known and an evil conscience. Mrs. Alving's sense of guilt is the result of an intellectual emancipation from the habits of a lifetime; it is an emancipation from those values which she emotionally still accepts. It is precisely for this reason that her attempts at expiation are never satisfactory—they are not central to and part of her guilt.

To put it another way, Mrs. Alving's image of herself as liberated from out-worn ideas is at odds with what in fact she is, a middle-aged woman bound by the chains of respectability and convention. It is for this reason, in a way similar to Sartre's characters in the hell of *No Exit*, that she suffers. She is aware of the disparity between image and fact: "I ought" is a choric refrain that runs through her conversation; and she constantly looks for ways to affirm her image and assuage her guilt. And yet, the very fact that she accepts the image of herself as free, when experience has proven otherwise time and time again, explains why she is defeated in every attempt at atonement.

The sun finally rises. Ibsen has been preparing for this from the beginning. As the past is gradually revealed in the play and as the issues of the action come into sharper focus, "light" becomes more and more important in Ibsen's design. The play opens in the gloom of evening and rain; Mrs. Alving, at least according to Ibsen's stage directions, plays most of her important revelation scenes at the window, the source of light; as Mrs. Alving decides to quell Oswald's "gnawing doubts," she calls for a light; Oswald's big speech about the "joy and openness of life" uses the sun as its central metaphor; the light that reveals—tells the truth—how impossible it is for Mrs. Alving to atone for her guilt has its source in the flames of the burning orphanage; and, finally, it is the sun, the source of all light, that reveals the meaning of the play's completed action. Mrs. Alving is still trapped within the net of her own inheritance. She, as she has already told us and as Ibsen tells us in his poem, "Fear of Light," is afraid to face the real truth about herself. This fear is something over which she has no control.

If we can empathize with Mrs. Alving, and I think we can, we have been

---

[3] Hermann Weigand, *The Modern Ibsen*, New York, 1925, p. 82.

led to feel, as she believes, that as the light comes out of darkness, as the pressures of reality impinge upon her with unrelenting force, she will be capable of an act of freedom. We want to believe that she will affirm the image that she has of herself as a liberated human being by an action that is expressive of that freedom, even if that action is the murder of her own son. We want to feel that the light and heat of the sun will have the power to cauterize the ghosts of her soul. But if we have been attentive to the developing action, if we but recall what events followed the "lesser lights"; then we realize that there can be no resolution. Mrs. Alving can give only one answer, "No!"

Mrs. Alving, like Oswald, who is the most important visible symbol of the ghosts, is a victim of something over which she has no control. We are reminded of Oswald's famous speech in the second act: "My whole life incurably ruined—just because of my own imprudence. . . . Oh! if only I could live my life over again—if only I could undo what I have done! If only it had been something I had inherited—something I could not help." We have known all along that Oswald is a victim, so Ibsen is telling us for a purpose. The reason, as a study of his other plays will attest, is that for Ibsen the external is always the mirrored reflection of what's within. Mrs. Alving is also a victim! Like Oswald, she is doomed just by being born. And since she never comes to understand herself; since she never realizes and accepts the disparity of her image of herself and the truth about herself, she can never—in a way that Oedipus, a similar kind of victim, can—resolve the conflict.

For Mrs. Alving the sun has risen and just as she cannot give Oswald the sun, so the light of the sun has not been able to enlighten her. This, I believe is the conflict in the play and the developed meanings of this conflict form the play's central action.

II

But is this action tragic? How, if at all, is *Ghosts* a tragedy? It seems to me that there are two possible answers to these questions and the answer will depend largely on which interpretation of the play one accepts. The prevelant interpretation is the one which claims that this is a play of social protest and reform. The adherents of such a view can gather together a great deal of evidence in support of their case: all of Ibsen's plays from *League of Youth* to *The Wild Ducks* passages from the plays themselves, like Oswald's speech on the freedom of Europe; numerous of Ibsen's public speeches, and several of his letters. With this interpretation the play is saying that if man would only see how hypocritical and outmoded his values were then the disasters that occur in the play need never have taken place. This view has as its fundamental premise that social evils can be cured and that when they are man is capable of living with a "joy of life." But if this is true, if all you have to do

is be honest with yourself—and such a view assumes this is possible—and
if men would see the falseness of social conventions and change them, then
it seems to me the eternal elements of tragedy are dissolved in the possibility
of social reform. Tragedy is concerned with showing those destructive conflicts within man that exist because man is a man no matter what age he may
happen to be a part of, and no matter what kind of a society he may live in.
John Gassner puts it this way:

Tragedy requires an awareness of "life's impossibilities," of limitations imposed
upon man by the nature of things and by the nature of man, which cannot be poetically dissolved by sentiment or "reformed" out of existence.[4]

In some ways, I think Ibsen did intend *Ghosts* to be a play of social reform,
but if this is the case, he created more than he planned. In all of his early
plays, the plays we think of as the social reform plays, Ibsen is much like
Mrs. Alving; he believed intellectually in freedom and wrote and talked a
good deal about it, but is this the whole story? The disassociation of the
ideals men live by and the facts of their living is a central theme in Ibsen's
work, but it is interesting to note that even in *Ghosts* the possibility of the
"happy illusion" is presented. It is a hint that Ibsen is coming to feel that the
conflict between truth and ideals can never be reconciled. By the time of
Rosmersholm, even the free souls are tainted, the reformers are corrupt, and
the man trying to redeem himself is shown to be capable only of realizing
that he cannot be redeemed. Rosmer's death is an act of expiation, but suicide is decided upon only after Rosmer discovers the impossibility of redemption within society by means of freer and more honest views and relations.

Thus, while it is true that Ibsen, both in his public pronouncements and in
his plays prior to *Ghosts*, gives us evidence that he believes optimistically in
the possibility of social reform; that he believes that finally the sun will rise
and continue to shine if man works long and diligently at facing the truth, I
wonder if Ibsen is in fact whistling as he walks in the night through a grave-
yard. I wonder if Ibsen, even as early as *Ghosts*, isn't being a Mrs. Alving.
Certainly this passage from a letter written during the composition of *Ghosts*
permits us to wonder:

The work of writing this play has been to me like a bath which I have felt to leave
cleaner, healthier, and freer. Who is the man among us who has not now and then felt
and acknowledged within himself a contradiction between word and action, between
will and task, between life and teaching on the whole? Or who is there among us
who has not selfishly been sufficient unto himself, and half unconsciously, half in
good faith, has extenuated this conduct both to others and to himself?

---

[4] John Gassner, *The Theatre In Our Times*, New York, 1954, p. 67.

The alternative interpretation of *Ghosts* is the one which I have outlined in this essay. Mrs. Alving is a victim in a conflict over which she has no control. What are the implications of such a view to tragedy?

In 1869 Ibsen wrote a significant letter to the critic George Brandes. In this letter he says:

> There is without doubt a great chasm opened between yesterday and today. We must continually fight a war to the knife between these epochs.

What Ibsen meant in this letter was that to live in the modern world is to be, in many important ways, different from anyone who ever lived before. Now this doesn't mean that man has changed; human nature is still the same, but Ibsen felt that the modern way of looking at man had changed in a way that was significantly new.

Joseph Wood Krutch pursues this problem in his recent book, *"Modernism" in the Modern Drama*. Krutch develops his argument by pointing out that since Greek times the Aristotelian dictum that "man is a reasoning animal" had been pretty universally accepted. This view did not deny man's irrationality, but it did assert that reason is the most significant human characteristic. Man is not viewed as pre-eminently a creature of instincts, passions, habits, or conditioned reflexes; rather, man is a creature who differs from the other animals precisely in the fact that rationality is his dominant mode.

The modern view assumes the opposite premise. In this view men are not sane or insane. Psychology has dissolved such sharp distinctions; we know that normal people aren't as rational as they seem and that abnormal people don't act in a random and unintelligible way. In short, the dramatist of our age has had to face the assumption that the rational is relatively unimportant; that the irrational is the dominant mode of life; and that the artist must realize, therefore, that the richest and most significant aspects of human experience are to be found in the hidden depths of the irrational. "Man tends to become less a creature of reason than the victim of obsessions, fixations, delusions, and perversions." [5]

It is this premise that all of the great dramatists at the end of the 19th century, beginning with Ibsen, had to face. How is one to live in an irrational world! How is one to give meaning to life in a world where you don't know the rules? How are human relationships to be meaningfully maintained when you can't be sure of your feelings and when your feelings can change without your knowing it? Ibsen's plays, beginning with *Ghosts*, dramatize man destroyed by trying to live rationally in such a world. But to accept irreconcilable conflict as the central fact of all life; to make dissonance rather

---

[5] J. W. Krutch, *"Modernism" in Modern Drama*, Ithaca, N. Y., 1953, p. 22.

than the harmony of reconciliation the condition of the universe is to accept
as a premise a view of life which leads in drama, as in life, to a world in
which men and women, heroes and heroines, become victims in a disordered
world which they have not created and which they have no moral obligation
to correct.

It is this process, which began in the drama when Ibsen came to see man
as a victim of irrational powers, of the Trolls, over which he has no control,
that leads to the sense of futility that so completely dominates a great deal of
modern drama. This is the kind of futility that is expressed in our text from
Ecclesiastes (as it is in Hemingway's novel); but is this sense of futility
generative of what we traditionally associate with tragedy?

The traditional forms of tragedy have been affirming in the sense that
they celebrated man's ability to achieve wisdom through suffering. Such
tragedy saw man as a victim, to be sure, but it also saw man as having those
heroic qualities and potentialities which permitted him to endure his suffering and be significantly enlightened by them in such a way that victory was
realized even in defeat.

The central conflict of *Ghosts* is not peculiar to the modern world. The
disassociation of fact and value is a common theme in all tragedy. But there
is a significant difference when this theme is used before Ibsen. Traditional
tragedy celebrates the fact that, although most of us are incapable of it, the
values men wish to live by can, if only for a moment, be realized through
the actions of the tragic hero. It celebrates the fact that man's capacity for
greatness is often expressed in the committing of an action which is horrify-
ing and ought not to happen and yet which must happen. In this way the
possibility that man's actions and his values can be in harmony is realized.
This is the affirmation of tragedy; this is the meaning of the sun that resolves
so many traditional tragedies. In this kind of tragedy the hero goes through
the "dark night of the soul" with all its pain, suffering, doubt, and despair;
but man is viewed as one responsible for and capable of action, even if that
action is a grasping for the sun. Because of this fundamental difference in
view, in traditional tragedy the dark night passes away and the sun also
rises on the rebirth and affirmation of a new day.

This sunrise of traditional tragedy, which celebrates the "joy and meaning of life," is not the sunrise of futility. It is not the sunrise which sheds its
rays as an ironic and bitter joke on a demented boy asking his equally helpless mother: "Mother, give me the sun, The sun—the sun!"

Perhaps Mrs. Alving is more tragic than Oedipus, Hamlet, or Lear; but
if she is, her tragedy must be evaluated by new canons of judgment; for she
differs from her predecessors in kind and not degree.

The Possibilities and Perils of Modern Tragedy*

JOHN GASSNER

I

A question that continues to agitate literary circles is whether it is possible to write tragedy in modern times and whether indeed it has been possible to produce tragedies at all ever since Ibsen's generation abandoned romanticism. The subject has become a veritable vested interest of academic criticism, but has also involved non-academic critics and creative writers. It has been impossible to declare a moratorium on the question because it thrusts itself into the foreground of discussions of the worth and pretensions of the modern theatre. Playwrights and critics who deplore the vogue of realism or the absence of poetry on the stage are especially inclined to make the impossibility of writing tragedy for the commercial theatre an article of faith. And it appears to be an absolute conviction on the part of some commentators that modern drama should be excluded from the aristocracy of letters altogether. Since tragedy is the most aristocratic of dramatic genres, it is a foregone conclusion of the literary mandarins that a tragic playwright cannot thrive in the theatre of the populace.

It is not the theatre, however, but the modern world that receives criticism's first and most devastating fire. How indeed should the exalted art of tragedy, which has traditionally dealt with the fate of singular individuals, flourish in the age of the common man? How should the grandeur of the tragic hero and the splendor of tragic vision survive in a world leveled down by democracy and cheapened by mass-production and mass-consumption, a world in which even emotions and ideas have been converted into commodities gaudily packaged for the buyer? At the same time, the leaders of

* John Gassner, "The Possibilities and Perils of Modern Tragedy," *Tulane Drama Review*, Vol. 1, No. 3 (June, 1957), pp. 3–14.

this mandarin brand of criticism, many of whom have cherished ideals of classic or medieval unity, have been wont to observe that this world characterized by a distressing sameness is paradoxically a divided one. It is said to be incapable of providing the individual with a coherent view of himself and of his place in the universe. The same critics who disdain a world grown irrevocably common are apt to deplore the absence of communion in it. They regret the absence of tradition and belief in our mongrel culture. With no myth or cult to assure the continuity of time-honored values, with no religion to relate the individual unequivocally to the universe, with no fixity of class structure to bind men to their place, we presumably cannot have significant dramatic action: it cannot be significant because it cannot be communally meaningful. The high concern with human fate that has characterized tragic art in past ages must therefore make way for considerations of temporary and local conflict between ant-men who are paradoxically common without being representative.

A commonplace realism, then, takes the place of the ideality to which the art of tragedy aspires by historical example since the time of Aeschylus and by critical prescript since the time of Aristotle. And it is a rare event indeed when the language of the modern stage does not reflect the commonplace view of mankind. The plot may pulsate with exciting events, as in the plays of O'Neill, but the language limps behind the action and limits its tragic resonance. The inarticulateness so often postulated by realism as a result of its idolatry of verisimilitude dooms the characters to a level of consciousness too low to sustain an impressive personality and a significant action. And that inarticulateness is itself mainly a concomitant of the selection of low-grade personalities for dramatic representation as well as of a low view of humanity. Rarely do the modern plays assume or demonstrate that greatness of spirit we discover in an Antigone and Oedipus or a Hamlet, Othello, and Lear. Henry James was surely correct when he declared in one of his prefaces that "the agents in any drama are interesting only in proportion as they feel their respective situations," and feeling communicates itself mainly through language. The prose of modern drama, often commonplace if not indeed barbarically colloquial, is both a symptom of the absence of tragic art and a cause of its absence.

So runs the argument, which is fortified by the critics' dismal view of modern liberalism, which entertains nontragic premises in so far as it puts its trust in rationalism, science, and sociology. When behavior is explained largely by heredity, instinct, and environment man is deprived of any genuine responsibility for his actions that would make dramatic conflict humanistically relevant and calamity morally significant. There can be no tragic heroes in the bleak commonwealth of conditioned animals. Nor is the individual given materially greater significance when he is treated as a psychological case history. His writhings in the grip of a neurosis or psychosis may gratify our curiosity but not our moral sense. He may be interesting as a specimen of morbidity, but his plight—his error and his suffering—will exalt neither the character nor spectator. A heroic view of man, then, is the last thing that sociology and psychopathology can supply whereas it has been the peculiar triumph of tragic art in the past to affirm the wonder of man. For ages, tragedy has been a high mystery by means of which defeat has been transformed into victory for the human spirit. In this mystery which converts despair over the human condition into reconciliation with fate and leaves us exhilarated rather than dismayed, the protagonist is the sacrifice, and the sacrifice must be worthy of the rite. With respect to both the protagonist or sacrificial victim and the humanity which the rite redeems modern rationalistic inquiry is held to be altogether too disillusioning. But if the modern viewpoint is too depressing, it is also too optimistic for tragedy, for modern liberalism has been inveterately melioristic. Denying that evil and suffering are absolute and unalterable, the liberal viewpoint has proposed to remove or moderate the very conditions that make tragedy possible and its ministrations welcome, if not indeed imperative. The modern viewpoint, then, appears to be both too hard and not hard enough for tragedy.

The critics of liberal modernism cannot, however, be completely represented by the above-given arguments, for they have set up their batteries not only on the literary heights but on the summits of theological disputation. They have wondered, for example, how a modern writer of the liberal persuasion can expect to write tragedy while rejecting the doctrine of original sin, failing to make characters feel accountable to God, or depriving man of an inviolable ethos and of the solace of belief that his suffering has spiritual significance. And some critics have also become amateur anthropologists in emphasizing the ritualistic character of a tragic performance. They seem to believe that because tragedy developed out of religious ritual in Greece, the modern theatre, which is not at all pyramided upon any religious rites, is unable to engender tragic art. The error in this kind of reasoning is the familiar "genetic fallacy," which assumes that a thing must remain what it was at its inception. The proponents of this view are also inconsistent: they certify many Elizabethan and seventeenth-century plays as true tragedies, although neither the Elizabethan nor the neo-classic French theatre had any marked ritualistic basis or character.

The genetic fallacy, however, is not always conspicuously advanced. It is apt to be screened from view by the argument that a community of values (as best expressed in religion and ritual) is essential to the development of tragedy, and this is, on the surface, a reasonable belief. If the tragic experience demonstrates the calamitous results of a character's conduct, that conduct must obviously constitute a violation of a more or less accepted norm. In a community which sanctioned parricide and incest, for example, Oedipus would not be a tragic character. And if a tragically misguided character is to arrive at restorative perceptions or redeeming realizations in the course of his suffering, these must meet with agreement from the public. The emphasis upon the need for a community of values, however, becomes an argument against the possibility of writing tragedy today as soon as the critic implies that the agreement must be strict enough to disallow modern diversity and scepticism, if not strict enough indeed to constitute a religious or quasi-religious sanction. It is doubtful that such "communion" was ever absolute in the individualistic Athenian and Elizabethan periods, and it might be contended that communion is a religious experience that ought not to be confused with social conformity. History indeed supplies many examples of ancient despotisms and modern totalitarian societies that failed to produce tragic art. Conformity, however, does not seem to disturb contemporary neo-ritualists, provided the commonly held values are approvable; and they are apt to be approved if only they are pre-modern and traditional. The neo-conservative position, as laid down in previous decades by Hulme and T. S. Eliot, is indeed the final emplacement from which traditionalists offer resistance to the idea that playwrights whose thought has been contaminated by modern science or sociology can compose tragedy.

The position of the traditionalists on this issue tends to be inflexible. They rarely admit that any modern dramatist has written a true tragedy, and a play dealing "tragically" with a commoner's fate such as *Death of a Salesman* is treated as pretentious vulgarity. A more moderate position grants a few deviations into tragedy by Ibsen, O'Neill, and perhaps a few other writers. But the advanced and more persistent traditionalist view holds that realistic dramaturgy and prose are incompatible with tragedy, as are liberalism, meliorism, sympathy with ordinary persons, scepticism, and modern individualism. According to this view, the would-be tragedian, unless he renounces the ambience of modern thought and popular art, will end up only with melodrama, propaganda, pathology, pathos and sentimentality, or just plain nastiness and bathos. Tragic art, according to this view, has been achieved in the modern age by only two species of writers—the primitive and the ultra-sophisticated: by a Synge and Lorca, on the one hand, or a Cocteau, Yeats, and Eliot, on the other. The primitives have escaped modernity while the ultra-sophisticated have passed beyond it and returned to mystery, legend, ritual, and the racial unconscious.

II

That, in brief, is one side of the argument concerning tragedy in the modern theatre, and it is not difficult to understand why it should be punctuated with so much intellectual artillery. The fire is directed at the modern spirit, which presumably cannot have much worth if it does not produce tragic art—an assumption which would of course invalidate all but the three brief periods of human history which produced Attic, Elizabethan, and neo-classic French tragedy of the latter part of the seventeenth century.

But the other side of the argument, though less often maintained, has also been vigorously advanced. Implicit in the theatre's hopes and endeavors for the past three quarters of a century has been the conviction that tragedy could be revitalized by sinking its roots deeper in modern consciousness and by relating it more closely to the immediate life of the times. I do not know of any comprehensive statement that adequately presented this viewpoint until Herbert J. Muller published his vigorous book *The Spirit of Tragedy* late in 1956. Presentations of the modern liberal position have been scattered in a variety of prefaces, letters, diaries, and reviews; and liberal doctrine concerning tragedy has never been particularly impressive, even though such important writers as Hebbel, Zola, Strindberg, Galsworthy, and Arthur Miller have contributed to it. The real force of the argument must be sought in the works to which the theories were prefatory or supplementary; it resides in whatever realizations of modern tragedy can be found in the plays of Ibsen, Strindberg, Tolstoy, Curel, Hauptmann, O'Neill, Galsworthy, O'Casey, and other playwrights.

A fundamental premise has been the opinion that a great deal of the tragic art of the past, while excellent as far as it went, belongs to the past. The pagan beliefs that served Attic tragedy twenty-five centuries ago are no longer acceptable to modern man. Neither are the beliefs of the Elizabethan period and the age of Louis XIV. There is simply no single true philosophy of tragedy any more than there is a single inviolable tragic form. Tragic art is subject to evolutionary processes, and tragedy created in modern times must be modern. The fact that it will be different from tragedy written three, five, or twenty-five centuries ago does not mean that it will no longer be tragedy; it will merely be different. It will be as different from earlier tragic literature as *Hamlet*, let us say, is different from *Oedipus Rex*, or as *Phaedra* is different from Euripides' *Hippolytus*. Aristotle himself did not presume to legislate on tragedy for all time, but spoke modestly about tragic art as he knew it from the works of a handful of Athenian playwrights. He spoke of tragedy as it had developed up to his time in Greece, rather than of an everlasting and invariable type of drama. In generalizing about tragic method he spoke of optimal approaches rather than of absolutes; in the *Poetics*, he even countenanced a turn of fortune from bad to good as a possible, though not as the most effective, pattern of a tragedy. It was apparent to him that the Greek plays differed in kind and degree of tragic artistry, whatever their external structural similarities. It could be apparent to us, too, if we did not invite the hobgoblin of consistency into literary theory and attributed to Greek tragedy a single form, quality, and effect. The leaders of the modern theatre after 1870 rejected esthetic absolutism. They envisaged not only the possibility of writing tragedy with modern minds, but of extending its range and enlarging its potentialities as a study of man and his world.

The modern view started, sensibly enough, with considerations of character and environment. Tragic art was allowed to focus on all, rather than on only class-privileged, representatives of the human race. By 1870, the destiny of nations was no longer being shaped exclusively or even predominantly by a dynasty or an aristocracy. It was virtually granted by then that a character's station in society was secondary in importance to his stature as a human being. Of first importance was his capacity to manifest desires and engage in actions that could reveal human nature and its strivings significantly. Ibsen and his successors did not intend to repeat the error of early writers of "bourgeois tragedy" such as Diderot and Lillo who made common characters commonplace in feeling, will, and destiny. Many writers proceeded to endow them with passion-charged personalities, as Ibsen proved himself capable of doing when he created Hedda Gabler and O'Neill when he created Christine and Lavinia, the modern Clytemnestra and Electra of his *Mourning Becomes Electra*. Moreover, even examples from the past favored latitude. It had been possible for Shakespeare to plumb human destiny with so hesitant and divided a character as Hamlet. It had even proved possible to create tragedy with essentially anti-heroic figures such as Richard II and Euripides' Orestes and Electra. If the modern playwright tended more and more to focus on characters of divided will and thwarted desire, he was under no necessity to renounce all intention of giving them tragic prominence. The generally non-heroic character could be revealed as heroic in some central aspect. Strindberg's mentally tormented Captain in *The Father*, for example, is a clinical case. Yet he could be fully analyzed without lessening the force of his defense of masculinity in an overfeminized society. His personality and experiences were too intensely realized by Strindberg to generate pity without also producing fear; he, the protagonist, fought too strenuously against his wife Laura, his antagonist, and he resisted his fate too forcefully to engender pathos rather than passion. Thus, too, the Willy Loman of *Death of a Salesman* could be tethered to the satchel of a traveling salesman, could be made to swallow the mental garbage of a materialistic society, could be drawn in all his littleness as a business failure, and yet be allowed to draw attention to the soaring part of his personality. His self-regard or ideal of himself wills him to assert his sense of worth against his own littleness and makes him rage like a caged lion in his suburban home—and suburban mind. According to liberal doctrine, indeed, modern dramatists could reveal more, rather than fewer, facets of humanity.

That communication with modern audiences was henceforth to be attained on the maximum levels of understanding available to modern consciousness was indeed the ruling conviction of Ibsen, Strindberg, Shaw, Hauptmann, Curel, and other pioneers of the late nineteenth-century theatre, to which our own is still very largely bound. In their view it was preposterous to compose tragedy according to histrionic notions of heroism, and they consequently broke with romanticism as firmly as romantic writers had broken with neo-classicism. The moderns, moreover, could admire Shakespeare without believing that the Elizabethan world-picture was correct or meaningful for the modern world; and they could find merit in classic tragedy or even employ its retrospective dramatic structure, as Ibsen did in *Ghosts*, without subscribing to Greek notions of Fate. It seemed sounder as well as more honest to attempt to translate ancient concerns into present ones and old concepts into new ones. Aeschylus and Euripides had not hesitated to do so, and there was no particular reason why Ibsen and Strindberg or O'Neill and Arthur Miller, after them, should.

The proponents of modern drama, moreover, could contend that they met the fundamental requirements of tragic art with considerable fidelity. They approached their subject with high seriousness, motivated human conduct, refrained from mere pathos by studying social and psychological causation, avoided melodrama, and made calamity a means for achieving significant revelations concerning the individual and his milieu. For them error, evil, and suffering were never ends in themselves, useless in providing the audience with a *frisson* and the playwright with an income. They knew that perception was a necessary element in the tragic experience and proposed to provide realization not by rote but by critical inquiry and by a realistic testing of the alternatives of action. Sometimes it was the main character who was led from passion to perception or from suffering to understanding; sometimes the final comprehension belonged to a group of secondary characters whose role was not radically different from that of a Greek chorus; sometimes it was the audience that was expected to understand what the characters could not express. The means might differ in respect to the situation and the intelligence of the character, but suffering was not allowed to be devoid of meaning. In one way or another, some means was to be found for compensating calamity with insight. And direct or indirect means were sought for supplying the tragic awareness that the protagonist of a modern play could not articulate because he could not be convincingly given the self-conscious intelligence of a Hamlet or the eloquence of persons in the more formal tragedies of the past.

Articulateness on the part of the characters was indeed very much the concern of the modernists, for, as critics impatient with prose in the theatre tend to forget, verse-drama had become quite decadent in the nineteenth century before it was abandoned. (Nor was it abandoned so absolutely that an Ibsen, Hauptmann, or Maxwell Anderson would not go back to verse.) Pioneers of the modern theatre found it necessary to reject verse and rhetorical prose not merely for the sake of "fourth-wall" verisimilitude, but for the sake of simple artistic integrity. They could not countenance the customary use of eloquence as a screen for hollow content and commonplace feeling and thought. The decision to write prose-drama was the result of clear deliberation on Ibsen's part. The author of *Brand* and *Peer Gynt* laid aside a considerable reputation as a poet and a hard-won success as a playwright when he entered upon the realistic and prose part of his career in his fiftieth year. That his prose in *A Doll's House* and the plays that followed became a very powerful instrument demonstrating the mental and emotional processes of his characters is evident even in translation. The planning of the dialogue, the verbal exchanges between the speakers, the innuendo or double-meaning of many a line, and the stress on key words and phrases do not indicate indifference to the role of language in the drama. The cumulative effect of his and other writers spare dialogue could provide the articulateness that had previously been allocated to the set speeches, harangues, and soliloquies of characters in the pre-realistic drama. Motivations could be found, moreover, for some distinctly infectious speeches when characters addressed an assembly or summarized a passionately held conviction. Ibsen's successors, among whom there were such masters of dialogue as Shaw and O'Casey, continued to prove that prose could be written for the theatre with compelling *brio*. Many a verse-drama of the past three centuries sounds exceedingly flat with its familiar tropes and metronomic regularity by comparison with the verbal explosions of modern realistic and expressionist plays. And to dramatic excitement could be added a variety of effects capable of lending nuance, poetic reverberation, and Chekhovian counterpoint. Peasant dialect, as in the plays of Synge, could be relied upon to yield a new music and a new imagery for the theatre, as could even the colloquialism of the city-streets. And symbolism could be imbedded in the soil of realism whenever a playwright was capable of composing a *Rosmersholm* and *The Master Builder*.

Nor does the search for a poetically charged prose exhaust the effort to ensure expressiveness on the modern stage. Developments in physical production and in the art of acting have contributed imaginativeness and power to the stage. We have supplemented the verbal element of the drama with the so-called *poésie de théatre*, ever since the turn of the century when Gordon Craig called for expressive stage design and Stanislavsky for *inner* realism in acting. The masters of this "poetry of the theatre" could give scenic atmosphere and visual symbolization to a tragic action. "A good scene design should not be a picture but an image," wrote Craig's American disciple Robert Edmond Jones, and it could create "an expectancy, a foreboding, a tension" in the theatre. That acting could add emotional depth and dramatic stature to a playwright's character was evident, of course, whenever a Duse or Nazimova played an Ibsen part.

Finally, we should not overlook the modern playwright's search for new dramatic form, especially in the turbulent expressionist mode which is marked by fantastic invention, explosive dialogue, and expressive distortion of scenes and characters. There have been expressionist attempts to write tragedy as well as realistic ones, ever since the turn of the century. Playwrights who gravitated toward expressionism tended to concern themselves with such contemporary themes as the Oedipus complex, the alienation of the individual in a cheapened world, and the crises of war and revolution. One could maintain indeed that the boundaries of tragic art were extended by the adoption of modern expressionist technique in such plays as *The Spook Sonata*, *The Hairy Ape*, and *Death of a Salesman*, as well as by naturalistic presentations of character and environment that closed a ring of inevitability around the dramatic action of the individual. If this argument does not at all prove that modern playwrights have written better tragedies than Sophocles and Shakespeare did (and the reverse is obviously the case), it does suggest that modernity may be relieved of the charge that it has extinguished the art of tragedy—which is one more charge added to the general indictment of our civilization or, rather, of the democratic and scientific spirit.

III

To mediate between the conflicting claims of the pro-modern and anti-modern factions is no easy matter. The value we place on specific works is the first and last consideration. There is no difficulty in claiming that the modern age can produce tragedy if we are prepared to qualify a considerable number of modern plays as "tragedies." And, conversely, it is easy enough to maintain that the modern spirit cannot support tragic writing once we disqualify them.

An agile disputant can easily sustain his aristocratic distaste for the world of the common man by invalidating almost any modern play. All he has to do is to insist on absolute standards of high tragedy derived from a few masterpieces of the past and prove that the modern work deviates from them. He can then protest, often with good reason, that the hero of some particular play written since *A Doll's House* lacks the magnitude of mind or spirit that could give him the "tragic stature" needed to dignify humanity even in the character's descent from grace and fall from good fortune. With respect to many a modern stage character from Ibsen's Oswald Alving to

O'Neill's "Yank" and Miller's Willy Loman it has been possible for very intelligent critics to say, with Henry James, that "Our curiosity and our sympathy care comparatively little for what happens to the stupid, the coarse, and the blind." The critic may indeed multiply his strictures without ever being entirely wrong. The plays may impress him as depressing rather than exalting, and as topical rather than universal. They may also strike him as too prosaic, too intellectual or too unintellectual, too active or too passive, too optimistic or two pessimistic. Any one of these attributes can be easily identified, torn out of context, and used to invalidate the tragic status of such modern pieces as *Ghosts*, *Hedda Gabler*, *The Father*, *The Power of Darkness*, *The Lower Depths*, *The Hairy Ape*, *Desire Under the Elms*, *Mourning Becomes Electra*, *The Iceman Cometh*—and even *Saint Joan*. Advocates of a scrupulously restricted category of tragedy would probably certify only plays produced at some remove from the liberal-scientific spirit or deliberately set against it. They would certify peasant drama set in regions remote from our industrial civilization such as Synge's Aran Islands, off the west coast of Ireland, or Lorca's Spanish countryside. They would also qualify formally structured plays, preferably suggestive of ritual and rooted in theology or in myth: Among these would be Eliot's *Murder in the Cathedral* and *Family Reunion*, some short poetic pieces by Yeats patterned after medieval Japanese drama, and a few antirealistic French plays such as Giraudoux' *Electra* and Cocteau's *The Infernal Machine*, which one young American enthusiast recently recommended to us as *the* model for modern tragedy. To this, one may add a genre of neo-romantic verse-drama represented by Maxwell Anderson's Elizabethan trilogy, *Elizabeth the Queen*, *Mary of Scotland*, *Anne of the Thousand Days*, and his *Winterset*—plays well patterned after a conventional tragic blueprint.

A strenuous exponent of the realistic and more or less liberal persuasion, however, could, in turn, cut a good deal of the ground from under the literary opposition. Turning to specific works, he could show, for instance, that Anderson's achievement in the historical field, and similar achievements in other countries, are tragic only by rote, posture, and imitation. He could maintain, too, that *Winterset*, despite its powerful second act, was only factitiously tragic; that it consists of a forced marriage between poetic rhetoric and gangster melodrama, and that the playwright evades his Sacco and Vanzetti theme with rather transparent borrowings from *Hamlet* and *Romeo and Juliet*. These animadversions would probably win the endorsement of members of the literary élite of our day, since they have even less use than the liberal realists for popular romanticism. But the latter would promptly turn on their allies to remind them that literary formalism, too, has proved vain. On the one hand, we have had the example of so great a poet as Yeats withdrawing from the modern drama in order to compose tragic one-act plays intended for private performance, an admittedly thin harvest for the man who had helped to establish the Abbey Theatre and had discovered Synge and O'Casey for the Irish national stage. On the other hand, we have had the example of Cocteau and other French sophisticates leaning toward contrived tragicality and arriving at cleverness or virtuosity in the theatre much more conclusively than they have arrived at tragedy. And the argument would gravitate toward T. S. Eliot, the high priest of anti-modernism in our time, who abandoned the rigors of high tragedy with *The Cocktail Party* and edged closer to Noel Coward than Sophocles with drawing-room lines and scenes. This after having composed two tragedies with a marked ritualistic and a theological basis, *Murder in the Cathedral* and *Family Reunion*, which owed a good deal to Shaw and Coward respectively in virtually all scenes in which the plays came to life as theatre. It will be apparent, then, that the uncertainties of tragic writing in the present world are not altogether on one side. And if the peril of trying to write tragedies under the modern liberal dispensation is an unliterary descent into *banality*, the peril of creating it under any other dispensation is a literary ascent into *futility*.

Which is the greater evil cannot be determined, I suppose, without bias. (My own is, on the whole, democratic, while that of some men of letters for whom I have entertained the greatest admiration is largely aristocratic.) Nevertheless the two factions are not fated to remain completely apart, and there are areas of agreement available to reasonable exponents of either viewpoint. The "liberals" can agree that variable degrees of inadequacy have attended the efforts of O'Neill, Ibsen, and the sociological playwrights to produce tragic literature, while "conservatives" have been known to concede some measure of tragic power to Ibsen, Strindberg, and O'Casey. It would certainly appear from the divergent enthusiasms of the partisans that, in one way or another, it has been possible to write tragic drama— that is, some clearly definable tragedies and many plays more or less tragic in feeling such as Chekhov's *The Three Sisters*.

Agreement could be reached especially if we first noted that there are degrees of tragic ascent today and that some are more favored than others. And this should not disturb us particularly, for there were, after all, degrees of tragic ascent even in the great ages of tragic literature—as we may observe, for instance, by comparing Sophocles' *Electra* with Euripides' *Electra* or *Macbeth* with *Richard II*. Modern playwriting is apt to fall into a category of "middle tragedy" or perhaps "low tragedy" instead of "high tragedy," a term suitable for some (and only for some) of the tragic pieces of the Attic, Elizabethan, and French neo-classic periods of the theatre. With agreement on this subject, we could then settle down to the essential business of encouraging and creating the plays, regardless of degree, that may best express the tragic and near-tragic understanding of which we are capable in our time and place.

We may also arrive at the conclusion that there is really no compelling reason for the modern stage to *strain* toward tragedy. There are other ways of responding to the human condition. There is, for one thing, the time-honored way of comedy. Shaw followed it so creditably in his so-called comedies of ideas that his plays have overshadowed the work of many a tragedian of modern, Victorian, or Elizabethan times. The writing of comedies is as serious a business as the writing of tragedies; comedy, too, constitutes a criticism of life, incorporates values, and affords a catharsis. The comic viewpoint is at least as relevant as the tragic to man's life in society and perhaps even more representative of human conduct. Nor does the comic playwright have to spare us glimpses into the abyss of human nature or encounters with what Nietzsche called "the terrible wisdom of Silenus." Comedy is an art of notable variety, and its complexion runs from light to dark and from sweet to bitter.

There is also the way of *drame*, of serious drama without tragic pretensions. Many provocative social and psychological dramas as diversified as *Awake and Sing* and *The Children's Hour*, as well as imaginative works such as *Our Town* and *The Skin of Our Teeth*, have filled a place in our theatre without conveniently fitting into pigeonholes of tragedy. Generally, indeed, our age has found its sensibility and mood most adequately expressed by amalgamations of grave and comic writing. We have been partial to a mixed genre represented at its best, perhaps, by several of Chekhov's masterpieces, although "mixed drama" is not at all exhausted by Chekhov's highly individual style. We can only conclude that if plays such as *The Cherry Orchard*, *Heartbreak House*, *Juno and the Paycock*, *The Glass Menagerie*, and *Six Characters in Search of an Author* have not conformed to any blueprints of tragedy (and there was no intention on their author's part to achieve such conformity), this has been no loss to the theatre of our century. It is the value of the specific work and not the *genre* that really and finally matters to the playgoer, and not to prefer a distinguished non-tragic composition to an undistinguished tragic one would be pedantry rather than responsible criticism.

Tragedies of one kind or another have been contributory to the interest and power of the modern theatre. But the creative spirit of an age should be allowed, and indeed expected, to engender its own dramatic forms or to modify existent ones. Overawed, it would seem, by premises and promises of tragic grandeur, playwrights from D'Annunzio to Maxwell Anderson (nor would I acquit O'Neill when he composed *Dynamo* and *Lazarus Laughed* or Miller when he wrote *A View from the Bridge*) have strained too much to produce standardized high tragedy with a contemporary fillip of interest. They would have been well advised to leave some tragic motifs and trappings alone, and they should have refrained from endeavoring to lift some of their characters and situations out of the non-tragic categories that would have suited them better. Critics and scholars have been prone to compound confusion for playwrights by harping on categories of drama, glorifying one of these above all others, and paying insufficient heed to the fact that tragedy has been infrequently produced throughout the ages and rarely in pure form. And since everybody has been infected at some time or other with the desire to see the modern drama live beyond its spiritual income, it may yet become necessary to stress the perils rather than the possibilities of tragedy.

Part Ten

SOME CLASSICS OF TRAGIC THEORY

Aristotle
From THE POETICS

Friedrich Hegel
From THE PHILOSOPHY OF FINE ART

Friedrich Nietzsche
From THE BIRTH OF TRAGEDY

Søren Kierkegaard
THE ANCIENT TRAGICAL MOTIF AS REFLECTED IN THE MODERN

From *The Poetics**

ARISTOTLE

A Tragedy, then, is an artistic imitation of an action that is serious, complete in itself, and of an adequate magnitude; so much for the object which is imitated. As for the medium, the imitation is produced in language embellished in more than one way, one kind of embellishment being introduced separately in one part, and another kind in another part of the whole. As for the manner, the imitation is itself in the form of an action directly presented, not narrated. And as for the proper function resulting from the imitation of such an object in such a medium and manner, it is to arouse the emotions of pity and fear in the audience; and to arouse this pity and fear in such a way as to effect that special purging off and relief (*catharsis*) of these two emotions which is the characteristic of Tragedy.

By 'language embellished in more than one way' is meant language which is simply rhythmical or metrical, language which is delivered in recitative, and language which is uttered in song. And by the separate introduction of one kind of embellished language in one part, and of another kind in another part, is meant that some portions of the tragedy (e.g., prologue and episode) are rendered in verse alone, without being sung or chanted, and other portions again (e.g., parode and stasimon) in the form of singing or chanting.

[The several elements in Aristotle's definition of tragedy are gathered from his previous remarks, as he says; save that hitherto the only possible reference to the function of tragedy, its effect upon the audience, or reader, is contained in the opening words of the treatise, where he promises to discuss the specific function of each kind of poetry. In the definition, he implies that other forms of art—we might instance comedy—have as their special end or pleasure the relief of others of the general class of disturbing emotions to which pity and fear belong.

---

* Aristotle, from *The Poetics* in *Aristotle on the Art of Poetry* [335–322 B.C.], Lane Cooper, tr. (Cornell University Press, 1947), pp. 17–31. [An amplified version with supplementary illustrations. Brackets enclose amplifications.]

The effect of tragedy upon the emotions is not merely something that took place in a former age, or among the Greeks alone; it may be observed at all times, and in virtually all persons, including the reader of this sentence. However much the malign influence of a narrowly intellectual education may check the native motions of the heart, few indeed must be they who are hopelessly bereft of all pleasure in the tragic *catharsis*. For generations, it is true, there has been a debate over the precise meaning one should attach to Aristotle's phrase—a debate that frequently has turned upon the study of words apart from things, and on the whole has not been sufficiently concerned with the actual experience of audiences, or rather of specially qualified judges, during the presentation of good tragedy and immediately thereafter. But if the words of Aristotle describe an effect which really occurs, it must be that a person of intelligence and normal sympathies will undergo, and be able to mark, the experience, not only in witnessing the best tragedy, but even in reading it. The student of the *Poetics* might render his notion of the tragic *catharsis* more exact by an attempt to observe his own emotions when he reads, or re-reads, Sophocles' *Oedipus the King* or Shakespeare's *Othello*.

Furthermore, one might collect and examine the utterances of poets and other men of unusual sensibility on the feelings which tragic stories have aroused in them;—not primarily such conscious explanations of the Aristotelian *catharsis* as that of Milton in his preface to *Samson Agonistes*. This, though important, is a different kind of evidence from the lines in the first of Milton's Latin Elegies—thus translated by Cowper:

> I gaze, and grieve, still cherishing my grief;
> At times, e'en bitter tears yield sweet relief.

Similar spontaneous illustrations of the tragic pleasure have come from other English poets; for example, Wordsworth, in the Dedication preceding *The White Doe of Rylstone*:

> Pleasing was the smart,
> And the tear precious in compassion shed;

and Coleridge, in *Love*:

> She wept with pity and delight.

It is probable also that a study of emotional suspense and its relief in the audience, by an experimental psychologist, would throw light upon the passage in Aristotle. For the present, however, no explanation could prove more helpful to the general reader than a part of Bywater's note, his language being followed almost verbatim:

In Greek physiology and pathology, *catharsis* is a very general term for a physical clearance or discharge, the removal by art or an effort of nature of some bodily product, which, if allowed to remain, would cause discomfort or harm. The *catharsis* of the soul as described in the *Politics* of Aristotle is a similar process in reference to certain emotions—the tacit assumption being apparently that the emotions in question are analogous to those peccant humors in the body which, according to the ancient humoral theory of medicine, have to be expelled from the system by the appropriate *catharsis*. With some adaptation of the statements and hints in *Politics* 8. 7, as thus interpreted, it is not difficult to recover the outlines at any rate of the Aristotelian theory of the cathartic effect of tragedy: Pity and fear are elements in human nature, and in some men they are present in a disquieting degree. With these latter the tragic excitement is a necessity; but it is also in a certain sense good for all. It serves as a sort of medicine, producing a *catharsis* to lighten and relieve the soul of the accumulated emotion within it; and as the relief is wanted, there is always a harmless pleasure attending the process of relief.

It must be added that pleasure, to Aristotle, signifies, not a passive state of being, but a form of activity.

In his working definition he does not allude to the element of pleasure in the tragic relief. As he develops his thought, we become aware that the relief is itself a form of pleasure; so that the characteristic effect of tragedy may be referred to as either one or the other. We discover, too, that there are certain satisfactions contributory to the main effect; for example, the pleasure of discovery or recognition, when we learn the author of a deed or the upshot of an incident; the pleasure of astonishment, when the outcome of a series of events is unexpected, yet is seen to be inevitable; and the pleasure derived from 'embellished language,' that is, from the rhythm and music of tragedy. Furthermore, the pleasure is explained negatively: the play must not offend us with effects that are revolting, or with events that run counter to our sense of what is reasonable and likely.]

Advancing now from the synthetic definition of Tragedy, we proceed to analyze the elements that separately demand the attention of the tragic poet. Since there are *dramatis personae* who produce the author's imitation of an action, it necessarily follows that (1) everything pertaining to the appearance of the actors on the stage—including costume, scenery, and the like—will constitute an element in the technique of tragedy; and that (2) the composition of the music ('Melody'), and (3) the composition in words ('Diction'), will constitute two further elements, as Melody and Diction represent the medium in which the action is imitated. By Diction is meant, in this connection, the fitting together of the words in metre; as for Melody (= 'Song'), the meaning is too obvious to need explanation.

But furthermore, the original object of the imitation is an action of men. In the performance, then, the imitation, which is also an action, must be carried on by agents, the *dramatis personae*. And these agents must necessarily be endowed by the poet with certain distinctive qualities both of (4) Moral Character (*ethos*) and (5) Intellect (*dianoia*)—one might say, of heart and head; for it is from a man's moral bent, and from the way in which he reasons, that we are led to ascribe goodness or badness, success or failure, to his acts. Thus, as there are two natural causes, moral bent and thought, of the particular deeds of men, so there are the same two natural causes of their success or failure in life. And the tragic poet must take cognizance of this.

Finally, the action which the poet imitates is represented in the tragedy by (6) the Fable or Plot. And according to our present distinction, Plot means that synthesis of the particular incidents which gives form or being to the tragedy as a whole; whereas Moral Bent is that which leads us to characterize the agents as morally right or wrong in what they do; and Intellect (or 'Thought') is that which shows itself whenever they prove a particular point, or, it may be, avouch some general truth.

In every tragedy, therefore, there are six constitutive elements, according to the quality of which we judge the excellence of the work as a whole: Plot (6); Moral Disposition (4); Diction (3); Intellect (5); Spectacle (1); Melody (2). Two of them, Melody and Diction, concern the medium of imitation; one, Spectacle, the manner; and three, Plot, Moral Disposition, and Intellect, the objects. There can be no other elements. These constitutive elements, accordingly, not a few of the tragic poets, so to speak, have duly employed [in spite of what adverse critics may assert]; for, indeed, every drama must contain certain things that are meant for the eye, as well as the elements of Moral Disposition, Plot, Diction, Melody, and Intellect.

[That element of a drama which is here called moral bent or disposition (*ethos*) is often rendered into English by the word 'character.' There is a danger, which Aristotle himself does not always avoid, of confusing character in this narrower sense with personality, and hence of identifying character with agent. From this confusion there often results a misunderstanding of Aristotle's subsequent remarks upon the relative importance of plot and moral bent (character in the narrower sense). In dealing with this point it is undesirable to refer to the *dramatis personae* as 'characters'; one would do well to use the word 'agents' instead, and to bear in mind that the personality of the agents is divided by Aristotle into two separate elements, corresponding to qualities of heart and head respectively. If at first we make the most of this distinction, we shall not go far astray in later passages where it is not so carefully preserved. What Aristotle next specifically maintains is that, among the six elements, plot or action is of greater importance than the moral bent of the agents; he might equally well have said it was of greater importance than their faculty of reason, i.e., than 'Thought.']

The most important of the constitutive elements is the Plot, that is, the organization of the incidents of the story; for Tragedy in its essence is an imitation, not of men as such, but of action and life, of happiness and misery.

And happiness and misery are not states of being, but forms of activity; the end for which we live is some form of activity, not the realization of a moral quality. Men are better or worse, according to their moral bent; but they become happy or miserable in their actual deeds. In a play, consequently, the agents do not perform for the sake of representing their individual dispositions; rather, the display of moral character is included as subsidiary to the things that are done. So that the incidents of the action, and the structural ordering of these incidents, constitute the end and purpose of the tragedy. Here, as elsewhere, the final purpose is the main thing.

Such is the importance of this element that, we may add, whereas Tragedy cannot exist without action, it is possible to construct a tragedy in which the agents have no distinctive moral bent. In fact, the works of most of the modern tragic poets, from the time of Euripides on, are lacking in the element of character. Nor is the defect confined to tragic poets: it is common among poets in general. And there is a similar defect among the painters—in Zeuxis, for example, as contrasted with Polygnotus; for Polygnotus excels in the representation of the ethical element, whereas the pictures of Zeuxis are in this respect wholly deficient. [In the same way, one might compare the vigorous delineation of ethical qualities in Rembrandt with the absence of this power in Rubens. Among English poets of all sorts, Chaucer, Shakespeare, Milton, and Wordsworth serve to exemplify the presence of this quality; it is relatively lacking in Dryden, Shelley, and Byron.]

Again, one may string together a series of speeches in which the moral bent of the agents is delineated in excellent verse and diction, and with excellent order in the thoughts, and yet fail to produce the essential effect of Tragedy as already described. One is much more likely to produce this effect with a tragedy, however deficient in these respects, if it has a plot—that is, an artistic ordering of the incidents. In addition to all this, the most vital features of Tragedy, by which the interest and emotions of the audience are most powerfully aroused—that is, reversals of fortune, and discoveries of the identity of agents—are parts of the plot or action. It is significant, too, that beginners in the art become proficient in versification and in the delineation of personal traits before they are able to combine the incidents of the action into an effective whole. Herein the progress of the individual dramatist repeats the history of the art; for almost all the early poets succeeded better with these two elements than in the formation of plots.

(1) The Plot, then, is the First Principle, and as it were the very Soul of Tragedy.

(2) And the element of Character is second in importance.—There is a parallel in the art of painting: the most beautiful colors, laid on with no order, will not give as much pleasure as the simplest figure done in outline.—

Tragedy is an imitation of an action: mainly on account of this action does it become, in the second place, an imitation of personal agents.

(3) Third in importance comes the Intellectual element. This corresponds to the power of the agent to say what can be said, or what is fitting to be said, in a given situation. It is that element in the speeches of a drama which is supplied by the study of Politics and the art of Rhetoric; for the older tragic poets [e.g., Sophocles] made their heroes express themselves like statesmen, whereas the modern [including Euripides] make theirs use the devices of the rhetoricians. This Intellectual element must be clearly distinguished from the Ethical element in the drama, for the latter includes only such things as reveal the moral bias of the agents—their tendency to choose or to avoid a certain line of action, in cases where the motive is not otherwise evident. And hence the poet has no call to employ the ethical element in speeches where the agent is neither choosing nor avoiding a line of action. The Intellectual element, on the other hand, is manifested in everything the agents say to prove or disprove a special point, and in every utterance they make by way of generalization.

(4) Next in importance among the four essential constituents comes the Diction. This, as has been explained, means the interpretation of the sentiments of the agents in the form of language, and is essentially the same thing whether the language is metrical or not.

(5) Of the two elements remaining, Melody is the more important, since it occupies the chief place among the accessory pleasures of Tragedy.

(6) The element of Spectacle, though it arouses the interest of the audience, is last in importance, since it demands the lowest order of artistic skill, and is least connected with the art of poetry as such. A tragedy can produce its effect independently of a stage-performance and actors—that is, when it is read; and besides, the business of preparing the stage and the actors is the affair of the costumer rather than of poets.

Having thus distinguished the six constitutive elements, we are now to discuss, as the first and most important consideration in the art of Tragedy, the proper organization of the incidents into a plot that will have the ideal tragic effect. According to the definition, a tragedy is an imitation of an action that is complete in itself, forming a whole of a sufficient magnitude or extent; for a thing may be a whole and yet wanting in magnitude.

Now a Whole is that which has (1) a Beginning, (2) a Middle, and (3) an End.

(1) A Beginning (= X) is that which does not itself come after anything else in a necessary sequence, but after which some other thing (= Y) does naturally exist or come to pass.

(3) An End (= Z), on the contrary, is that which naturally comes after something else (= Y) in either a necessary or a usual sequence, but has nothing else following it.

(2) A Middle (= Y) is that which naturally comes after something else (= X), and is followed by a third thing (= Z).

A well-constructed plot, therefore, can neither begin nor end where and when the poet happens to like. It must conform to the principles just enunciated.

And further, as to Magnitude: to be beautiful, a living organism, or any other individual thing made up of parts, must possess not only an orderly arrangement of these parts, but also a proper magnitude; for beauty depends upon these two qualities, size and order. Hence an extremely minute creature cannot be beautiful to us; for we see the whole in an almost infinitesimal moment of time, and lose the pleasure that comes from a distinct perception of order in the parts. Nor could a creature of vast dimensions be beautiful to us—a beast, say, one thousand miles in length; for in that case the eye could not take all of the object in at once—we should see the parts, but not the unity of the whole. In the same way, then, as an inanimate object made up of parts, or a living creature, must be of such a size that the parts and the whole may be easily taken in by the eye, just so must the plot of a tragedy have a proper length, so that the parts and the whole may be easily embraced by the memory. The artificial limits, of course, as these are determined by the conditions of stage-presentation, and by the power of attention in an audience, do not concern the art of poetry as such. If it were necessary to present one hundred tragedies in succession [an exaggerated illustration], they would doubtless have to be timed with water-clocks—as some say was formerly the custom. The artistic limit, set by the nature of the thing itself, is this: So long as the plot is perspicuous throughout, the greater the length of the story, the more beautiful will it be on account of its magnitude. But to define the matter in a general way, an adequate limit for the magnitude of the plot is this: Let the length be such that the story may pass from happiness to misfortune, or from misfortune to happiness, through a series of incidents linked together in a probable or inevitable sequence.

The Unity of a Plot does not consist, as some suppose, in having one man as subject; for the number of accidents that befall the individual man is endless, and some of them cannot be reduced to unity. So, too, during the life of any one man, he performs many deeds which cannot be brought together in the form of a unified action. . . . For, as in the other imitative arts, painting and the rest, so in poetry, the object of the imitation in each case is a unit; therefore in an epic or a tragedy, the plot, which is an imitation of a dramatic action, must represent an action that is organically unified, the structural order of the incidents being such that transposing or removing any one of them will dislocate and disorganize the whole. Every part must be necessary, and in its place; for a thing whose presence or absence makes no perceptible difference is not an organic part of the whole.

From *The Philosophy of Fine Art**

FRIEDRICH HEGEL

The genuine content of tragic action subject to the *aims* which arrest tragic characters is supplied by the world of those forces which carry in themselves their own justification, and are realized substantively in the volitional activity of mankind. Such are the love of husband and wife, of parents, children, and kinsfolk. Such are, further, the life of communities, the patriotism of citizens, the will of those in supreme power. Such are the life of churches, not, however, if regarded as a piety which submits to act with resignation, or as a divine judicial declaration in the heart of mankind over what is good or the reverse in action; but, on the contrary, conceived as the active engagement with and demand for veritable interests and relations. It is of a soundness and thoroughness consonant with these that the really tragical *characters* consist. They are throughout that which the essential notion of their character enables them and compels them to be. They are not merely a varied totality laid out in the series of views of it proper to the epic manner; they are, while no doubt remaining also essentially vital and individual, still only the one power of the particular character in question, the force in which such a character, in virtue of his essential personality, has made himself inseparably coalesce with some particular aspect of the capital and substantive life-content we have indicated above, and deliberately commits himself to that. It is at some such elevation, where the mere accidents of unmediated individuality vanish altogether, that we find the tragic heroes of dramatic art, whether they be the living representatives of such spheres of concrete life or in any other way already so derive their greatness and stability from their own free self-reliance that they stand forth as works of sculpture, and thus the lofty tragic characters of the Greeks also interpret the essentially more abstract statues and figures of gods more completely than is possible for any other kind of elucidation or commentary.

* Friedrich Hegel, from *The Philosophy of Fine Art*, F. P. B. Osmaston, tr. (G. Bell & Sons, Ltd., 1920). [Footnotes in this selection have been renumbered.]

Broadly speaking, we may, therefore, affirm that the true theme of primitive tragedy is the godlike. But by godlike we do not mean the Divine, as implied in the content of the religious consciousness simply as such, but rather as it enters into the world, into individual action, and enters in such a way that it does not forfeit its substantive character under this mode of realization, nor find itself converted into the contradiction of its own substance. In this form the spiritual substance of volition and accomplishment is ethical life. For what is ethical, if we grasp it, in its direct consistency—that is to say, not exclusively from the standpoint of personal reflection as formal morality—is the divine in its secular or world realization, the substantive as such, the particular no less than the essential features of which supply the changing content of truly human actions, and in such action itself render this their essence explict and actual.

(b) These ethical forces, as also the characters of the action, are *distinctively defined* in respect to their content and their individual personality, in virtue of the principle of differentiation to which everything is subject, which forms part of the objective world of things. If, then, these particular forces, in the way presupposed by dramatic poetry, are attached to the external expression of human activity, and are realized as the determinate aim of a human pathos which passes into action, their concordancy is cancelled, and they are asserted *in contrast* to each other in interchangeable succession. Individual action will then, under given conditions, realize an object or character, which, under such a presupposed state, inevitably stimulates the presence of a pathos opposed to itself, because it occupies a position of unique isolation in virtue of its independently fixed definition, and, by doing so, brings in its train unavoidable conflicts. Primitive tragedy, then, consists in this, that within a collision of this kind both sides of the contradiction, if taken by themselves, are *justified*; yet, from a further point of view, they tend to carry into effect the true and positive content of their end and specific characterization merely as the negation and *violation* of the other equally legitimate power, and consequently in their ethical purport and relatively to this so far fall under *condemnation*.

I have already adverted to the general ground of the necessity of this conflict. The substance of ethical condition *is*, when viewed as concrete unity, a totality of *different* relations and forces, which, however, only under the inactive condition of the gods in their blessedness achieve the works of the Spirit in enjoyment of an undisturbed life. In contrast to this, however, there is no less certainly implied in the notion of this totality itself an impulse to move from its, in the first instance, still abstract ideality, and transplant itself in the real actuality of the phenomenal world. On account of the nature of this primitive obsession, it comes about that mere difference, if conceived on the basis of definite conditions of individual personalities, must inevitably associate with contradiction and collision. Only such a view can pretend to deal seriously with those gods which, though they endure in their tranquil repose and unity in the Olympus and heaven of imagination and religious conception, yet, in so far as they are actual, viewed at least as the energic in the definite pathos of a human personality, participate in concrete life, all other claims notwithstanding, and, in virtue of their specific singularity and their mutual opposition, render both blame and wrong inevitable.

(c) As a result of this, however, an unmediated contradiction is posited, which no doubt may assert itself in the Real, but, for all that, is unable to maintain itself as that which is wholly substantive and verily real therein; which rather discovers, and only discovers, its essential justification in the fact that it is able to *annul* itself as such contradiction. In other words, whatever may be the claim of the tragic final purpose and personality, whatever may be the necessity of the tragic collision, it is, as a consequence of our present view, no less a claim that is asserted—this is our *third* and last point —by the tragic resolution of this division. It is through *this* latter result that Eternal Justice is operative in such aims and individuals under a mode whereby it restores the ethical substance and unity in and along with the downfall of the individuality which disturbs its repose. For, despite the fact that individual characters propose that which is itself essentially valid, yet they are only able to carry it out under the tragic demand in a manner that implies contradiction and with a one-sidedness which is injurious. What, however, is substantive in truth, and the function of which is to secure realization, is not the battle of particular unities, however much such a conflict is essentially involved in the notion of a real world and human action; rather it is the reconciliation in which definite ends and individuals unite in harmonious action without mutual violation and contradiction. That which is abrogated in the tragic issue is merely the *one-sided* particularity which was unable to accommodate itself to this harmony, and consequently in the tragic course of its action, through inability to disengage itself from itself and its designs, either is committed in its entire totality to destruction or at least finds itself compelled to fall back upon a state of resignation in the execution of its aim in so far as it can carry this out. We are reminded of the famous dictum of Aristotle that the true effect of tragedy is to excite and purify *fear* and *pity*. By this statement Aristotle did not mean merely the concordant or discordant feeling with anybody's private experience, a feeling simply of pleasure or the reverse, an attraction or a repulsion, that most superficial of all psychological states, which only in recent times theorists have sought to identify with the principle of assent or dissent as ordinarily expressed. For in a work of art the matter of exclusive importance should be the display of that which is conformable with the reason and truth of Spirit; and to discover the principle of this we have to direct our attention to wholly different points of view. And consequently we are not justified in restricting the application of this dictum of Aristotle merely to the emotion of fear and pity, but should relate it to the principle of the *content*, the appropriately artistic display of which ought to purify such feelings. Man may, on the one hand, entertain fear when confronted with that which is outside him and finite; but he may likewise shrink before the power of that which is the essential and absolute subsistency of social phenomena. That which mankind has therefore in truth to fear is not the external power and its oppression, but the ethical might which is self-defined in its own free rationality, and partakes further of the eternal and inviolable, the power a man summons against his own being when he turns his back upon it. And just as fear may have two objectives, so also may compassion. The first is just the ordinary sensibility —in other words, a sympathy with the misfortunes and sufferings of another, and one which is experienced as something finite and negative. Your countrified cousin is ready enough with compassion of this order. The man of nobility and greatness, however, has no wish to be smothered with this sort of pity. For just to the extent that it is merely the nugatory aspect, the negative of misfortune which is asserted, a real depreciation of misfortune is implied. True sympathy, on the contrary, is an accordant feeling with the ethical claim at the same time associated with the sufferer—that is, with what is necessarily implied in his condition as affirmative and substantive. Such a pity as this is not, of course, excited by ragamuffins and vagabonds. If the tragic character, therefore, just as he aroused our fear when contemplating the might of violated morality, is to awake a tragic sympathy in his misfortune, he must himself essentially possess real capacity and downright character. It is only that which has a genuine content which strikes the heart of a man of noble feeling, and rings through its depths. Consequently we ought by no means to identify our interest in the tragic *dénouement* with the simple satisfaction that a sad story, a misfortune merely as misfortune, should have a claim upon our sympathy. Feelings of lament of this type may well enough assail men on occasions of wholly external contingency and related circumstance, to which the individual does not contribute, nor for which he is responsible, such cases as illness, loss of property, death, and the like. The only real and absorbing interest in such cases ought to be an eager desire to afford immediate assistance. If this is impossible, such pictures of lamentation and misery merely rack the feelings. A veritable tragic suffering, on the contrary, is suspended over active characters entirely as the consequence of their own act, which as such not only asserts its claim upon us, but becomes subject to blame through the collision it involves, and in which such individuals identify themselves heart and soul.

Over and above mere fear and tragic sympathy we have therefore the feeling of *reconciliation*, which tragedy affords in virtue of its vision of eternal justice, a justice which exercises a paramount force of absolute constrin-

gency on account of the relative claim of all merely contracted aims and passions; and it can do this for the reason that it is unable to tolerate the victorious issue and continuance in the truth of the objective world of such a
conflict with and opposition to those ethical powers which are fundamentally
and essentially concordant. Inasmuch as then, in conformity with this
principle, all that pertains to tragedy pre-eminently rests upon the contemplation of such a conflict and its resolution, dramatic poetry is—and its
entire mode of presentation offers a proof of the fact—alone able to make
and completely adapt the tragic, throughout its entire course and compass,
to the principle of the art product. And this is the reason why I have only
now found occasion to discuss the tragic mode of presentation, although it
extends an effective force, if no doubt one of subordinate degree, in many
ways over the other arts.

                         *   *   *   *

In the tragic drama we are now considering, the general basis or background for tragic action is supplied, as was also the case in the Epos, by that
world-condition which I have already indicated as the *heroic*.[1] For only in
heroic times, when the universal ethical forces have neither acquired the independent stability of definite political legislation or moral commands and
obligations, can they be presented in their primitive jucundity as gods, who
are either opposed to each other in their personal activities, or themselves
appear as the animated content of a free and human individuality. If, however, what is intrinsically ethical is to appear throughout as the substantive
foundation, the universal ground, shall we say, from which the growth of
personal action arrests our attention with equal force in its disunion, and is
no less brought back again from such divided movement into unity, we shall
find that there are two distinct modes under which the ethical content of
human action is asserted.

First, we have the simple consciousness, which, in so far as it wills its
substantive content wholly as the unbroken identity of its particular aspects,
remains in undisturbed, uncriticized, and neutral tranquillity on its own account and as related to others. This undivided and, we may add, purely
formal state of mind in its veneration, its faith, and its happiness, however,
is incapable of attaching itself to any definite action; it has a sort of dread
before the disunion which is implied in such, although it does, while remaining itself incapable of action, esteem at the same time that spiritual courage
which asserts itself resolutely and actively in a self-proposed object, as of
nobler worth, yet is aware of its inability to undertake such enterprise, and
consequently considers that it can do nothing further for such active personalities, whom it respects so highly, than contrast with the energy of their

---

[1] See Chapter II [of *The Philosophy of Fine Art*].

decision and conflict the object of its own wisdom, in other words, the substantive ideality of the ethical Powers.

The *second* mode under which this ethical content is asserted is that of the
individual pathos, which urges the active characters with moral self-vindica-
tion into opposition to others, and brings them thereby into conflict. The
individuals subject to this pathos are neither what, in the modern use of the
term, we describe as characters, nor are they mere abstractions. They are
rather placed in the vital midway sphere between both, standing there as
figures of real stability, which are simply that which they are, without aught
of collision in themselves, without any fluctuating recognition of some other
pathos, and in so far—in this respect a contrast to our modern irony—
elevated, absolutely determinate characters, whose definition, however, discovers its content and basis in a particular ethical power. Forasmuch as,
then, the tragic situation first appears in the *antagonism* of individuals who
are thus empowered to act, the same can only assert itself in the field of
actual human life. It results from the specific character of this alone that a
particular quality so affects the substantive content of a given individual,
that the latter identifies himself with his entire interest and being in such a
content, and penetrates it throughout with the glow of passion. In the
blessed gods, however, it is the divine Nature, in its indifference, which is
what is essential; in contrast to which we have the contradiction, which in
the last instance is not treated seriously, rather is one which, as I have already noticed when discussing the Homeric Epos, becomes eventually a
self-resolving irony. These two modes or aspects—of which the one is as
important for the whole as the other—namely, the unsevered consciousness
of the godlike, and the combating human action, asserted, however, in godlike power and deed, which determines and executes the ethical purpose—
supply the two fundamental elements, the mediation of which is displayed
by Greek tragedy in its artistic compositions under the form of *chorus* and
heroic figures respectively.

In modern times, considerable discussion has been raised over the significance of the Greek chorus, and the question has been raised incidentally
whether it can or ought to be introduced into modern tragedy. In fact, the
need of some such substantial foundation has been experienced; but critics
have found it difficult to prescribe the precise manner in which effect should
be given to such a change, because they failed to grasp with sufficient penetration the nature of that in which true tragedy consists and the necessity of
the chorus as an essential constituent of all that Greek tragedy implies.
Critics have, no doubt, recognized the nature of the chorus to the extent of
maintaining that in it we find an attitude of tranquil meditation over the
whole, whereas the characters of the action remain within the limits of their
particular objects and situations, and, in short, receive in the chorus and its

observations a standard of valuation of their characters and actions in much the same way as the public discovers in it, and within the drama itself, an objective representative of its own judgment upon all that is thus represented. In this view we have to this extent the fact rightly conceived, that the chorus is, in truth, there as a substantive and more enlightened intelligence, which warns us from irrelevant oppositions, and reflects upon the genuine issue. But, granting this to be so, it is by no means, like the spectator, a wholly disinterested person, at leisure to entertain such thoughts and ethical judgments as it likes which, uninteresting and tedious on its own account, could only be attached for the sake of such reflections. The chorus is the actual substance of the heroic life and action itself: it is, as contrasted with the particular heroes, the common folk regarded as the fruitful earth, out of which individuals, much as flowers and towering trees from their native soil, grow and whereby they are conditioned in this life. Consequently, the chorus is peculiarly fitted to a view of life in which the obligations of State legislation and settled religious dogmas do not, as yet, act as a restrictive force in ethical and social development, but where morality only exists in its primitive form of directly animated human life, and it is merely the equilibrium of unmoved life which remains assured in its stability against the fearful collisions which the antagonistic energies of individual action produces. We are made aware of the fact that an assured asylum of this kind is also a part of our actual existence by the presence of the chorus. It does not, therefore, practically co-operate with the action; it executes no right, actively, as against the contending heroes; it merely expresses its judgment as a matter of opinion; it warns, commiserates, or appeals to the divine law, and the ideal forces imminent in the soul, which the imagination grasps in external guise as the sphere of the gods that rule. In this self expression it is, as we have already seen, lyrical; for it does not act and there are no events for it to narrate in epical form. The content, however, retains at the same time the epic character of substantive universality; and its lyric movement is of such a nature that it can, and in this respect in contrast to the form of the genuine ode, approach at times that of the paean and the dithyramb. We must lay emphatic stress upon this position of the chorus in Greek tragedy. Just as the theatre itself possesses its external ground, its scene and environment, so, too, the chorus, that is the general community, is the spiritual scene; and we may compare it to the architectural temple which surrounds the image of the god, which resembles the heroes in the action. Among ourselves, statues are placed under the open sky without such a background, which also modern tragedy does not require, for the reason that its actions do not depend on this substantive basis, but on the personal volition and personality, no less than the apparently external contingency of events and circumstances.

In this respect it is an entirely false view which regards the chorus as an accidental piece of residuary baggage, a mere remnant from the origins of Greek drama. Of course, it is incontestable that its source is to be traced to the circumstance that, in the festivals of Bacchus, so far as the artistic aspect is concerned, the choral song was of most importance until the introduction and interruption of its course by one reciter, whose relation finally was transformed into and exalted by the real figures of dramatic action. In the blossoming season of tragedy, however, the chorus was not by any means merely retained in honour of this particular phase of the festival and ritual of the god Bacchus; rather it became continuously more elaborate in its beauty and harmonious measures by reason of the fact that its association with the dramatic action is essential and, indeed, so indispensable to it that the decline of tragedy is intimately connected with the degeneration of the choruses, which no longer remain an integral member of the whole, but are degraded to a mere embellishment. In contrast to this, in romantic tragedy, the chorus is neither intrinsically appropriate nor does it appear to have originated from choric songs. On the contrary, the content is here of a type which defeats from the first any attempt to introduce choruses as understood by Greek dramatists. For, even if we go back to the most primitive of those so-called mysteries, morality plays, and farces of a similar character, from which the romantic drama issued, we find that these present no action in that original Greek sense of the term, no outbreak, that is, of opposing forces from the undivided consciousness of life and the godlike. To as little extent is the chorus adapted to the conditions of chivalry and the dominion of kings, in so far as, in such cases, the attitude of the folk is one of mere obedience, or it is itself a party, involved together with the interest of its fortune or misfortune in the course of the action. And in general the chorus entirely fails to secure its true position where the main subject-matter consists of particular passions, ends, and characters, or where any considerable opportunity is admitted to intrigue.

In contrast to the chorus, the *second* fundamental feature of dramatic composition is that of the *individuals* who act in *conflict* with each other. In Greek tragedy it is not at all bad will, crime, worthlessness, or mere misfortune, stupidity, and the like, which act as an incentive to such collisions, but rather, as I have frequently urged, the ethical right to a definite course of action. Abstract evil neither possesses truth in itself, nor does it arouse interest. At the same time, when we attribute ethical traits of characterization to the individuals of the action, these ought not to appear merely as a matter of opinion. It is rather implied in their right or claim that they are actually there as essential on their own account. The hazards of crime, such as are present in modern drama, the useless, or quite as much the so-called noble criminal, with his empty talk about fate, we meet with in the tragedy of ancient literature, rarely, if at all, and for the good reason that the decision and deed depends on the wholly personal aspect of interest and character, upon lust for power, love, honour, or other similar passions, whose justification has its roots exclusively in the particular inclination and individuality. A resolve of this character, whose claim is based upon the content of its object, which it carries into execution in one restricted direction of particularization, violates, under certain circumstances, which are already essentially implied in the actual possibility of conflicts, a further and equally ethical sphere of human volition, which the character thus confronted adheres to, and, by his thus stimulated action, enforces, so that in this way the collision of powers and individuals equally entitled to the ethical claim is completely set up in its movement.

The sphere of this content, although capable of great variety of detail, is not in its essential features very extensive. The principal source of opposition, which Sophocles in particular, in this respect following the lead of Aeschylus, has accepted and worked out in the finest way, is that of the *body politic*, the opposition, that is, between ethical life in its social universality and the family as the natural ground of moral relations. These are the purest forces of tragic representation. It is, in short, the harmony of these spheres and the concordant action within the bounds of their realized content, which constitute the perfected reality of the moral life. In this respect I need only recall the "Seven before Thebes" of Aeschylus and, as a yet stronger illustration, the "Antigone" of Sophocles. Antigone reverences the ties of blood-relationship, the gods of the nether world. Creon alone recognizes Zeus, the paramount Power of public life and the commonwealth. We come across a similar conflict in the "Iphigenia in Aulis," as also in the "Agamemnon," the "Choephorae," and "Eumenides" of Aeschylus, and in the "Electra" of Sophocles. Agamemnon, as king and leader of his army, sacrifices his daughter in the interest of the Greek folk and the Trojan expedition. He shatters thereby the bond of love as between himself and his daughter and wife, which Clytemnestra retains in the depths of a mother's heart, and in revenge prepares an ignominious death for her husband on his return. Orestes, their son, respects his mother, but is bound to represent the right of his father, the king, and strikes dead the mother who bore him.

A content of this type retains its force through all times, and its presentation, despite all difference of nationality, vitally arrests our human and artistic sympathies.

Of a more formal type is that second kind of essential collision, an illustration of which in the tragic story of Oedipus the Greek tragedians especially favoured. Of this Sophocles has left us the most complete example in his "Oedipus Rex," and "Oedipus at Colonus." The problem here is concerned with the claim of alertness in our intelligence, with the nature of the obligation implied in that which a man carries out with a volition fully aware of its acts as contrasted with that which he has done in fact, but unconscious of and with no intention of doing what he has done under the directing providence of the gods. Oedipus slays his father, marries his mother, begets children in this incestuous alliance, and nevertheless is involved in these most terrible of crimes without active participation either in will or knowledge. The point of view of our profounder modern consciousness of right and wrong would be to recognize that crimes of this description, inasmuch as they were neither referable to a personal knowledge or volition, were not deeds for which the true personality of the perpetrator was responsible. The plastic nature of the Greek on the contrary adheres to the bare fact which an individual has achieved, and refuses to face the division implied by the purely ideal attitude of the soul in the self-conscious life on the one hand and the objective significance of the fact accomplished on the other.

For ourselves, to conclude this survey, other collisions, which either in general are related to the universally accepted association of personal action to the Greek conception of Destiny, or in some measure to more exceptional conditions, are comparatively speaking less important.

In all these tragic conflicts, however, we must above all place on one side the false notion of *guilt* or *innocence*. The heroes of tragedy are quite as much under one category as the other. If we accept the idea as valid that a man is guilty only in the case that a choice lay open to him, and he deliberately decided on the course of action which he carried out, then these plastic figures of ancient drama are guiltless. They act in accordance with a specific character, a specific pathos, for the simple reason that they are this character, this pathos. In such a case there is no lack of decision and no choice. The strength of great characters consists precisely in this that they do not choose, but are entirely and absolutely just that which they will and achieve. They are simply themselves, and never anything else, and their greatness consists in that fact. Weakness in action, in other words, wholly consists in the division of the personal self as such from its content, so that character, volition and final purpose do not appear as absolutely one unified growth; and inasmuch as no assured end lives in the soul as the very substance of the particular personality, as the pathos and might of the individual's entire will, he is still able to turn with indecision from this course to that, and his final decision is that of caprice. A wavering attitude of this description is alien to these plastic creations. The bond between the psychological state of mind and the content of the will is for them indissoluble. That which stirs them to action is this very pathos which implies an ethical justification and which, even in the pathetic aspects of the dialogue, is not enforced in and through the merely personal rhetoric of the heart and the sophistry of passion, but in the equally masculine and cultivated objective presence, in the profound possibilities, the harmony and vitally plastic beauty of which Sophocles was to a superlative degree master. At the same time, however, such a pathos, with its potential resources of collision, brings them to deeds that are both injurious and wrongful. They have no desire to avoid the blame that results therefrom. On the contrary, it is their fame to have done what they have done. One can in fact urge nothing more intolerable against a hero of this type than by saying that he has acted innocently. It is a point of honour with such great characters that they are guilty. They have no desire to excite pity or our sensibilities. For it is not the substantive, but rather the wholly personal deepening of the personality which stirs our individual pain. His securely strong character, however, coalesces entirely with his essential pathos, and this indivisible accord inspires wonder, not compassion. The drama of Euripides marks the transition to that.

The final result, then, of the development of tragedy conducts us to this issue and only this, namely, that the twofold vindication of the mutually conflicting aspects is no doubt retained, but the *one-sided* mode is cancelled, and the undisturbed ideal harmony brings back again that condition of the chorus, which attributes without reserve equal honour to all the gods. The true course of dramatic development consists in the annulment of *contradictions* viewed as such, in the reconciliation of the forces of human action, which alternately strive to negate each other in their conflict. Only so far is misfortune and suffering not the final issue, but rather the satisfaction of spirit, as for the first time, in virtue of such a conclusion, the necessity of all that particular individuals experience, is able to appear in complete accord with reason, and our emotional attitude is tranquillized on a true ethical basis; rudely shaken by the calamitous result to the heroes, but reconciled in the substantial facts. And it is only in so far as we retain such a view securely that we shall be in a position to understand ancient tragedy. We have to guard ourselves therefore from concluding that a *dénouement* of this type is merely a moral issue conformably to which evil is punished and virtue rewarded, as indicated by the proverb that "when crime turns to vomit, virtue sits down at table." We have nothing to do here with this wholly personal aspect of a self-reflecting personality and its conception of good and evil, but are concerned with the appearance of the affirmative reconciliation and the equal validity of both powers engaged in conflict, if the collision is complete. To as little extent is the necessity of the issue a blind destiny, or in other words a purely irrational, unintelligible fate, identified with the classical world by many; rather it is the rationality of destiny, albeit it does not as yet appear as self-conscious Providence, the divine final end of which in conjunction with the world and individuals appears on its own account and for others, depending as it does on just this fact that the highest Power paramount over particular gods and mankind cannot suffer this, namely, that the forces, which affirm their self-subsistence in modes that are abstract or incomplete, and thereby overstep the boundary of their warrant, no less than the conflicts which result from them, should retain their self-stability. Fate drives personality back upon its limits, and shatters it, when it has grown overweening. An irrational compulsion, however, an innocence of suffering would rather only excite indignation in the soul of the spectator than ethical tranquillity. From a further point of view, therefore, the reconciliation of *tragedy* is equally distinct from that of the *Epos*. If we look at either Achilles or Odysseus in this respect we observe that both attain their object, and it is right that they do so; but it is not a continuous happiness with which they are favoured; they have on the contrary to taste in its bitterness the feeling of finite condition, and are forced to fight wearily through difficulties, losses and sacrifices. It is in fact a universal demand of truth that in the course of life and all that takes place in the objective world the nugatory character of finite conditions should compel attention. So no doubt the anger of Achilles is reconciled; he obtains from Agamemnon that in respect of which he had suffered the sense of insult; he is revenged upon Hector; the funeral rites of Patroclus are consummated, and the character of Achilles is acknowledged in all its glory. But his wrath and its reconciliation have for all that cost him his dearest friend, the noble Patroclus; and, in order to avenge himself upon Hector for this loss, he finds himself compelled to disengage himself from his anger, to enter once more the battle against the Trojans, and in the very moment when his glory is acknowledged receives the prevision of his early death. In a similar way Odysseus reaches Ithaca at last, the goal of his desire; but he does so alone and in his sleep, having lost all his companions, all the war-booty from Ilium, after long years of endurance and fatigue. In this way both heroes have paid their toll to finite conditions and the claim of nemesis is evidenced in the destruction of Troy and the misfortunes of the Greek heroes. But this nemesis is simply justice as conceived of old, which merely humiliates what is everywhere too exalted, in order to establish once more the abstract balance of fortune by the instrumentality of misfortune, and which merely touches and affects finite existence without further ethical signification. And this is the justice of the Epic in the field of objective fact, the universal reconciliation of simple accommodation. The higher conception of reconciliation in tragedy is on the contrary related to the resolution of specific ethical and substantive facts from their contradiction into their true harmony. The way in which such an accord is established is asserted under very different modes; I propose therefore merely to direct attention to the fundamental features of the actual process herein involved.

First, we have particularly to emphasize the fact, that if it is the one-sidedness of the pathos which constitutes the real basis of collisions this merely amounts to the statement that it is asserted in the action of life, and therewith has become the unique pathos of a particular individual. If this one-sidedness is to be abrogated then it is this individual which, to the extent that his action is exclusively identified with this isolated pathos, must perforce be stripped and sacrificed. For the individual here is merely this single life, and, if this unity is not secured in its stability on its own account, the individual is shattered.

The most complete form of this development is possible when the individuals engaged in conflict relatively to their concrete or objective life appear in each case essentially involved in one whole, so that they stand fundamentally under the power of that against which they battle, and consequently infringe that, which, conformably to their own essential life, they ought to respect. Antigone, for example, lives under the political authority of Creon; she is herself the daughter of a king and the affianced of Haemon, so that her obedience to the royal prerogative is an obligation. But Creon also, who is on his part father and husband, is under obligation to respect the sacred ties of relationship, and only by breach of this can give an order that is in conflict with such a sense. In consequence of this we find immanent in the life of both that which each respectively combats, and they are seized and broken by that very bond which is rooted in the compass of their own social existence. Antigone is put to death before she can enjoy what she looks forward to as bride, and Creon too is punished in the fatal end of his son and wife, who commit suicide, the former on account of Antigone's death, and the latter owing to Haemon's. Among all the fine creations of the ancient and the modern world—and I am acquainted with pretty nearly everything in such a class, and one ought to know it, and it is quite possible —the "Antigone" of Sophocles is from this point of view in my judgment the most excellent and satisfying work of art.

The tragic issue does not, however, require in every case, as a means of removing both over-emphasized aspects and the equal honour which they respectively claim, the downfall of the contestant parties. The "Eumenides" ends, as we all know, not with the death of Orestes, or the destruction of the Eumenides, these avenging spirits of matricide and filial affection, as opposed to Apollo, who seeks to protect unimpaired the worth of and reverence for the family chief and king, who prompted Orestes to slay Clytemnestra, but with Orestes released from the punishment and honour bestowed on both divinities. At the same time we cannot fail to see in this adjusted conclusion the nature of the authority which the Greeks attached to their gods when they presented them as mere individuals contending with each other. They appear, in short, to the Athenian of everyday life merely as definite aspects of ethical experience which the principles of morality viewed in their complete and harmonious coherence bind together. The votes of the Areopagus are equal on either side. It is Athene, the goddess, the life of Athens, that is, imagined in its essential unity, who adds the white pebble, who frees Orestes, and at the same time promises altars and a cult to the Eumenides no less than Apollo. As a contrast to this type of objective reconciliation the settlement may be, *secondly*, of a more personal character. In other words, the individual concerned in the action may in the last instance surrender his one-sided point of view. In this betrayal by personality of its essential pathos, however, it cannot fail to appear destitute of character; and this contradicts the masculine integrity of such plastic figures. The individual, therefore, can only submit to a higher Power and its counsel or command, to the effect that while on his own account he adheres to such a pathos, the will is nevertheless broken in its bare obstinacy by a god's authority. In such a case the knot is not loosened, but, as in the case of Philoctetes, it is severed by a *deus ex machina*.

But as a *further* and final class, and one more beautiful than the above rather external mode of resolution, we have the reconciliation more properly of the soul itself, in which respect there is, in virtue of the personal significance, a real approach to our modern point of view. The most perfect example of this in ancient drama is to be found in the ever admirable "Oedipus at Colonos" of Sophocles. The protagonist here has unwittingly slain his father, secured the sceptre of Thebes, and the bridal bed of his own mother. He is not rendered unhappy by these unwitting crimes; but the power of divination he has of old possessed makes him realize, despite himself, the darkness of the experience that confronts him, and he becomes fearfully, if indistinctly, aware of what his position is. In this resolution of the riddle in himself he resembles Adam, losing his happiness when he obtains the knowledge of good and evil. What he then does, the seer, is to blind himself, then abdicate the throne and depart from Thebes, very much as Adam and Eve are driven from Paradise. From henceforward he wanders about a helpless old man. Finally a god calls the terribly afflicted man to himself, the man, that is, who refusing the request of his sons that he should return to Thebes, prefers to associate with the Erinyes; the man, in short, who extinguishes all the disruption in himself and who purifies himself in his own soul. His blind eyes are made clear and bright, his limbs are healed, and become a treasure of the city which received him as a free guest. And this illumination in death is for ourselves no less than for him the more truly visible reconciliation which is worked out both in and for himself as individual man, in and through, that is, his essential character. Critics have endeavoured to discover here the temper of the Christian life; we are told we have here the picture of a sinner, whom God receives into His grace; and the fateful misfortunes which expire in their finite condition are made good with the seal of blessedness in death. The reconciliation of the Christian religion, however, is an illumination of the soul, which, bathed in the everlasting waters of salvation, is raised above mortal life and its deeds. Here it is the heart itself, for in such a view the spiritual life can effect this, which buries that life and its deed in the grave of the heart itself, counting the recriminations of earthly guilt as part and parcel of its own earthly individuality; and which, in the full assuredness of the eternally pure and spiritual condition of blessedness, holds itself in itself calm and steadfast against such impeachment. The illumination of Oedipus, on the contrary, remains throughout, in consonance with ancient ideas, the restoration of conscious life from the strife of ethical powers and violations to the renewed and harmonious unity of this *ethical content itself*.

From *The Birth of Tragedy**

FRIEDRICH NIETZSCHE

We have tried to illustrate by this historical example how tragedy, being a product of the spirit of music, must surely perish by the destruction of that spirit. In order to moderate the strangeness of such an assertion and at the same time to demonstrate how we arrived at it, we must now frankly confront certain analogues of our own day. We must step resolutely into the thick of those struggles which are being waged right now between the insatiable thirst for knowledge and man's tragic dependency on art. I will not speak in this connection of those lesser destructive instincts which have at all times opposed art, and especially tragedy, and which in our own day seem to triumph to such an extent that of all the theatrical arts only the farce and the ballet can be said to thrive, with a luxuriance which not all find pleasing. I shall deal here only with the distinguished enemies of the tragic view, that is to say with the exponents of science, all dyed-in-the-wool optimists like their archetype, Socrates. And presently I shall name those forces which seem to promise a rebirth of tragedy and who knows what other fair hopes for the German genius.

Before rushing headlong into the fight let us put on the armor of such perceptions as we have already won. In opposition to all who would derive the arts from a single vital principle, I wish to keep before me those two artistic deities of the Greeks, Apollo and Dionysos. They represent to me, most vividly and concretely, two radically dissimilar realms of art. Apollo embodies the transcendent genius of the *principium individuationis;* through him alone is it possible to achieve redemption in illusion. The mystical jubilation of Dionysos, on the other hand, breaks the spell of individuation and opens a path to the maternal womb of being. Among the great thinkers there is only one who has fully realized the immense discrepancy between the plastic Apollonian art and the Dionysiac art of music. Independently of

* Friedrich Nietzsche, from *The Birth of Tragedy and the Genealogy of Morals* [1870–1871], Francis Golffing, tr. (Doubleday, 1956).

Greek religious symbols, Schopenhauer assigned to music a totally different character and origin from all the other arts, because it does not, like
all the others, represent appearance, but the will directly. It is the metaphysical complement to everything that is physical in the world; the thing-
in-itself where all else is appearance (*The World as Will and Idea, I*). Richard Wagner set his seal of approval on this key notion of all esthetics when
he wrote in his book on Beethoven that music obeys esthetic principles
quite unlike those governing the visual arts and that the category of beauty
is altogether inapplicable to it—although a wrongheaded esthetic based on a
misguided and decadent art has attempted to make music answer to criteria
of beauty proper only to the plastic arts, expecting it to generate *pleasure
in beautiful forms*. Once I had become aware of this antinomy I felt strongly
moved to explore the nature of Greek tragedy, the profoundest manifestation of Hellenic genius. For the first time I seemed to possess the key
enabling me to inspect the problem of tragedy in terms that were no longer
derived from conventional esthetics. I was given such a strange and un-
familiar glimpse into the essence of Hellenism that it seemed to me that our
classical philology, for all its air of triumphant achievement, had only dealt
with phantasmagorias and externals.

We might approach this fundamental problem by posing the following
question: what esthetic effect is produced when the Apollonian and Dionysiac forces of art, usually separate, are made to work alongside each
other? Or, to put it more succinctly, in what relation does music stand to
image and concept? Schopenhauer, whose clarity and perspicuity on that
point Wagner praises, has, in *The World as Will and Idea, I*, the following
passage, which I shall quote entire: "According to all this, we may regard
the phenomenal world, or nature, and music as two different expressions
of the same thing, which is therefore itself the only medium of the analogy
between these two expressions, so that a knowledge of this medium is required in order to understand that analogy. Music, therefore, if regarded as
an expression of the world, is in the highest degree a universal language,
which is related indeed to the universality of concepts, much as these are
related to the particular things. Its universality, however, is by no means
the empty universality of abstraction, but is of quite a different kind, and is
united with thorough and distinct definiteness. In this respect it resembles
geometrical figures and numbers, which are the universal forms of all possible objects of experience and applicable to them all *a priori*, and yet are not
abstract but perceptible and thoroughly determinate. All possible efforts,
excitements and manifestations of will, all that goes on in the heart of man
and that reason includes in the wide, negative concept of feeling, may be
expressed by the infinite number of possible melodies, but always in the
universality of mere form, without the material; always according to the

thing-in-itself, not the phenomenon—of which melodies reproduce the very soul and essence as it were, without the body. This deep relation which music bears to the true nature of all things also explains the fact that suitable music played to any event or surrounding seems to disclose to us its most secret meaning and appears as the most accurate and distinct commentary upon it; as also the fact that whoever gives himself up entirely to the impression of a symphony seems to see all the possible events of life and the world take place in himself. Nevertheless, upon reflection he can find no likeness between the music and the things that passed before his mind. For, as we have said, music is distinguished from all the other arts by the fact that it is not a copy of the phenomenon, or, more accurately, the adequate objectivity of the will, but is the direct copy of the will itself, and therefore represents the metaphysical of everything physical in the world, and the thing-in-itself of every phenomenon. We might, therefore, just as well call the world embodied music as embodied will: and this is the reason why music makes every picture, and indeed every scene of real life and of the world, at once appear with higher significance; all the more so, to be sure, in proportion as its melody is analagous to the inner spirit of the given phenomenon. It rests upon this that we are able to set a poem to music as a song, or a perceptible representation as a pantomime, or both as an opera. Such particular pictures of human life, set to the universal language of music, are never bound to it or correspond to it with stringent necessity, but stand to it only in the relation of an example chosen at will to a general concept. In the determinateness of the real they represent that which music expresses in the universality of mere form. For melodies are to a certain extent, like general concepts, an abstraction from the actual. This actual world, then, the world of particular things, affords the object of perception, the special and the individual, the particular case, both to the universality of concepts and to the universality of the melodies. But these two universalities are in a certain respect opposed to each other; for the concepts contain only the forms, which are first of all abstracted from perception—the separated outward shell of things, as it were—and hence they are, in the strictest sense of the term, *abstracta;* music, on the other hand, gives the inmost kernel which precedes all forms, or the heart of things. This relation may be very well expressed in the language of the schoolmen by saying: the concepts are the *universalia post rem,* but music gives the *universalia ante rem* and the real world the *universalia in re.* That a relation is generally possible between a composition and a perceptible representation rests, as we have said, upon the fact that both are simply different expressions of the same inner being of the world. When now, in the particular case, such a relation is actually given—that is to say, when the composer has been able to express in the universal language of music the emotions of will which constitute the heart of an event—then the melody of the song, the music of the opera, is expressive. But the analogy discovered by the composer between the two must have proceeded from the direct knowledge of the nature of the world unknown to his reason and must not be an imitation produced with conscious intention by means of conceptions; otherwise the music does not express the inner nature of the will itself, but merely gives an inadequate imitation of its phenomenon: all specially imitative music does this."

In accordance with Schopenhauer's doctrine, we interpret music as the immediate language of the will, and our imaginations are stimulated to embody that immaterial world, which speaks to us with lively motion and yet remains invisible. Image and concept, on the other hand, gain a heightened significance under the influence of truly appropriate music. Dionysiac art, then, affects the Apollonian talent in a twofold manner: first, music incites us to a symbolic intuition of the Dionysiac universality; second, it endows that symbolic image with supreme significance. From these facts, perfectly plausible once we have pondered them well, we deduce that music is capable of giving birth to myth, the most significant of similitudes; and above all, to the tragic myth, which is a parable of Dionysiac knowledge. When I spoke earlier of the lyric poet I demonstrated how, through him, music strives to account for its own essence in Apollonian images. Once we grant that music raised to its highest power must similarly try to find an adequate embodiment, it stands to reason that it will also succeed in discovering a symbolic expression for its proper Dionysiac wisdom. And where should we look for that expression if not in tragedy and the tragic spirit?

It is vain to try to deduce the tragic spirit from the commonly accepted categories of art: illusion and beauty. Music alone allows us to understand the delight felt at the annihilation of the individual. Each single instance of such annihilation will clarify for us the abiding phenomenon of Dionysiac art, which expresses the omnipotent will behind individuation, eternal life continuing beyond all appearance and in spite of destruction. The metaphysical delight in tragedy is a translation of instinctive Dionysiac wisdom into images. The hero, the highest manifestation of the will, is destroyed, and we assent, since he too is merely a phenomenon, and the eternal life of the will remains unaffected. Tragedy cries, "We believe that life is eternal!" and music is the direct expression of that life. The aims of plastic art are very different: here Apollo overcomes individual suffering by the glorious apotheosis of what is eternal in appearance: here beauty vanquishes the suffering that inheres in all existence, and pain is, in a certain sense, glossed away from nature's countenance. That same nature addresses us through Dionysiac art and its tragic symbolism, in a voice that rings authentic: "Be like me, the Original Mother, who, constantly creating, finds satisfaction in the turbulent flux of appearances!"

Dionysiac art, too, wishes to convince us of the eternal delight of existence, but it insists that we look for this delight not in the phenomena but behind them. It makes us realize that everything that is generated must be prepared to face its painful dissolution. It forces us to gaze into the horror of individual existence, yet without being turned to stone by the vision: a metaphysical solace momentarily lifts us above the whirl of shifting phenomena. For a brief moment we become, ourselves, the primal Being, and we experience its insatiable hunger for existence. Now we see the struggle, the pain, the destruction of appearances, as necessary, because of the constant proliferation of forms pushing into life, because of the extravagant fecundity of the world will. We feel the furious prodding of this travail in the very moment in which we become one with the immense lust for life and are made aware of the eternity and indestructibility of that lust. Pity and terror notwithstanding, we realize our great good fortune in having life —not as individuals, but as part of the life force with whose procreative lust we have become one.

Our study of the genesis of Greek tragedy has shown us clearly how that tragic art arose out of music, and we believe that our interpretation has for the first time done justice to the original and astounding meaning of the chorus. Yet we must admit that the significance of the tragic myth was never clearly conceptualized by the Greek poets, let alone philosophers. Their heroes seem to us always more superficial in their speeches than in their actions: the myth, we might say, never finds an adequate objective correlative in the spoken word. The structure of the scenes and the concrete images convey a deeper wisdom than the poet was able to put into words and concepts. (The same may be claimed for Shakespeare, whose Hamlet speaks more superficially than he acts, so that the interpretation of *Hamlet* given earlier had to be based on a deeper investigation of the whole texture of the play.) As for Greek tragedy, which we experience only through the printed word, I have already indicated that the incongruence between myth and word may lead us to think it more trivial than it actually is and to presume for it a more superficial effect than, according to the ancients, it must have had. It is so easy to forget that what the poet *qua* poet was unable to achieve, namely the supreme spiritualization of myth, might be achieved by him at any moment in his character of musician. . . .

Tragedy absorbs the highest orgiastic music and in so doing consummates music. But then it puts beside it the tragic myth and the tragic hero. Like a mighty titan, the tragic hero shoulders the whole Dionysiac world and removes the burden from us. At the same time, tragic myth, through the figure of the hero, delivers us from our avid thirst for earthly satisfaction and reminds us of another existence and a higher delight. For this delight the hero readies himself, not through his victories but through his undoing. Tragedy interposes a noble parable, *myth*, between the universality of its music and the Dionysiac disposition of the spectator and in so doing creates the illusion that music is but a supreme instrument for bringing to life the plastic world of myth. By virtue of this noble deception it is now able to move its limbs freely in dithyrambic dance and to yield without reserve to an orgiastic abandon, an indulgence which, without this deception, it could not permit itself. Myth shields us from music while at the same time giving music its maximum freedom. In exchange, music endows the tragic myth with a convincing metaphysical significance, which the unsupported word and image could never achieve, and, moreover, assures the spectator of a supreme delight—though the way passes through annihilation and negation, so that he is made to feel that the very womb of things speaks audibly to him.

Since, in this last passage, I have tentatively set forth a difficult notion, which may not be immediately clear to many, I would now invite my friends to consider a particular instance that is within our common experience and which may support my general thesis. I shall not address myself to those who use the scenic representation and the words and emotions of the actors to help them respond to the music. To none of these is music as a mother tongue, and, notwithstanding that help, they never penetrate beyond the vestibule of musical perception. Some, like Gervinus, do not even attain the vestibule by this means. I address myself only to those having immediate kinship with music, who communicate with things almost entirely through unconscious musical relations. To these genuine musicians I direct my question: 'how can anyone experience the third act of *Tristan and Isolde*, apart from either word or image, simply as the movement of a mighty symphony, without exhausting himself in the overstretching of his soul's pinions?' How is it possible for a man who has listened to the very heartbeat of the world-will and felt the unruly lust for life rush into all the veins of the world, now as a thundering torrent and now as a delicately foaming brook—how is it possible for him to remain unshattered? How can he bear, shut in the paltry glass bell of his individuality, to hear the echoes of innumerable cries of weal and woe sounding out of the "vast spaces of cosmic night," and not wish, amidst these pipings of metaphysical pastoral, to flee incontinent to his primordial home? And yet the reception of such a work does not shatter the recipient, the creation of it the creator. What are we to make of this contradiction?

It is at this point that the tragic myth and the tragic hero interpose between our highest musical excitement and the music, giving us a parable of those cosmic facts of which music alone can speak directly. And yet, if we reacted wholly as Dionysiac beings, the parable would fail entirely of effect, and not for a single moment would it distract our attention from the reverberations of the *universalia ante rem*. But now the Apollonian power, bent upon reconstituting the nearly shattered individual, asserts itself, proffering the balm of a delightful illusion. Suddenly we see only Tristan, lying motionless and torpid, and hear him ask, "Why does that familiar strain waken me?" And what before had seemed a hollow sigh echoing from the womb of things now says to us simply, "Waste and empty the sea." And where, before, we had felt ourselves about to expire in a violent paroxysm of feeling, held by a most tenuous bond to this our life, we now see only the hero, mortally wounded yet not dying, and hear his despairing cry: "To long, even in death, and be unable to die for longing!" And where, before, the jubilation of the horn after such an excess of feeling and such consuming pains would have cut us to the quick, as though it had been the crowning pain, now there stands between us and this absolute jubilation the rejoicing Kurwenal, turned toward the ship which brings Isolde. No matter how deeply pity moves us, that pity saves us from the radical "pity of things," even as the parable of myth saves us from the direct intuition of the cosmic idea, as idea and word save us from the undammed pouring forth of the unconscious will. It is through the workings of that marvelous Apollonian illusion that even the realm of sound takes plastic shape before us, as though it were only a question of the destinies of Tristan and Isolde, molded in the finest, most expressive material.

Thus the Apollonian spirit rescues us from the Dionysiac universality and makes us attend, delightedly, to individual forms. It focuses our pity on these forms and so satisfies our instinct for beauty, which longs for great and noble embodiments. It parades the images of life before us and incites us to seize their ideational essence. Through the massive impact of image, concept, ethical doctrine, and sympathy, the Apollonian spirit wrests man from his Dionysiac self-destruction and deceives him as to the universality of the Dionysiac event. It pretends that he sees only the particular image, e.g., Tristan and Isolde, and that the music serves only to make him see it more intensely. What could possibly be immune from the salutary Apollonian charm, if it is able to create in us the illusion that Dionysos may be an aid to Apollo and further enhance his effects? that music is at bottom a vehicle for Apollonian representations? In the pre-established harmony obtaining between the consummate drama and its music, that drama reaches an acme of visual power unobtainable to the drama of words merely. As we watch the rhythmically moving characters of the stage merge with the independently moving lines of melody into a single curving line of motion, we experience the most delicate harmony of sound and visual movement. The relationships of things thus become directly available to the senses, and we realize that in these relationships the essence of a character and of a melodic line are simultaneously made manifest. And as music forces us to see more, and more inwardly than usual, and spreads before us like a delicate tissue the curtain of the scene, our spiritualized vision beholds the world of the stage at once infinitely expanded and illuminated from within. What analogue could the verbal poet possibly furnish—he who tries to bring about that inward expansion of the visible stage world, its inner illumination, by much more indirect and imperfect means, namely word and concept? But, once musical tragedy has appropriated the word, it can at the same time present the birthplace and subsoil of the word and illuminate the genesis of the word from within. And yet it must be emphatically stated that the process I have described is only a marvelous illusion, by whose effects we are delivered from the Dionysiac extravagance and onrush. For, at bottom, music and drama stand in the opposite relation: music is the true idea of the cosmos, drama but a reflection of that idea. The identity between the melodic line and the dramatic character, between relations of harmony and character, obtains in an opposite sense from what we experience when we witness a musical tragedy. However concretely we move, enliven, and illuminate the characters from within, they will always remain mere appearance, from which there is no gateway leading to the true heart of reality. But music addresses us from that center; and though countless appearances were to file past that same music, they would never exhaust its nature but remain external replicas only. Nothing is gained for the understanding of either music or drama by resorting to that popular and utterly false pair of opposites, body and soul. Yet this contrast, crude and unphilosophical as it is, seems to have developed among our estheticians into an article of faith. About the contrast between the phenomenon and the thing-in-itself, on the other hand, they have never learned anything nor, for some obscure reason, wanted to learn.

If our analysis has shown that the Apollonian element in tragedy has utterly triumphed over the Dionysiac quintessence of music, bending the latter to its own purposes—which are to define the drama completely—still an important reservation must be made. At the point that matters most the Apollonian illusion has been broken through and destroyed. This drama which deploys before us, having all its movements and characters illumined from within by the aid of music—as though we witnessed the coming and going of the shuttle as it weaves the tissue—this drama achieves a total effect quite beyond the scope of any Apollonian artifice. In the final effect of tragedy the Dionysiac element triumphs once again: its closing sounds are such as were never heard in the Apollonian realm. The Apollonian illusion reveals its identity as the veil thrown over the Dionysiac meanings for the duration of the play, and yet the illusion is so potent that at its close the Apollonian drama is projected into a sphere where it begins to speak with Dionysiac wisdom, thereby denying itself and its Apollonian concreteness. The difficult relations between the two elements in tragedy may be symbolized by a fraternal union between the two dieties: Dionysos speaks the language of Apollo, but Apollo, finally, the language of Dionysos; thereby the highest goal of tragedy and of art in general is reached.

The Ancient Tragical Motif as Reflected in the Modern[*]

SØREN KIERKEGAARD

AN ESSAY IN THE FRAGMENTARY READ BEFORE A MEETING OF THE SYM-
PARANEKROMENOI

Should anyone feel called upon to say that the tragic always remains the tragic, I should in a sense have no objection to make, insofar as every historical evolution always remains within the sphere of the concept. Supposing, namely, that the word had a meaning, and that the two-fold repetition of the word tragic should not be regarded as constituting a meaningless parenthesis about a contentless nothing, then the meaning must be this, that the content of a concept does not dethrone the concept, but enriches it. On the other hand, it can scarcely have escaped the attention of any observer, and it is something that the reading and theater-going public already believes itself to be in lawful possession of, as its share dividend in the labors of the experts, that there is an essential difference between the ancient and modern tragedy. If one were again to emphasize this distinction absolutely, and by its aid, first stealthily, then perhaps forcibly, separate the conceptions of the ancient and modern tragical, his procedure would be no less absurd than that of the first, since he would forget that the foothold necessary for him was the tragic itself, and that this again was so far from being able to separate, that it really bound the ancient and modern together. And it must be regarded as a warning against every such prejudiced attempt to separate them, that aestheticians still constantly turn back to established Aristotelian determinations and requirements in connection with the tragical, as being exhaustive of the concept; and the warning is needed so much the more, as no one can

* Søren Kierkegaard, "The Ancient Tragical Motif as Reflected in the Modern," from *Either/Or; A Fragment of Life*, Vol. I [1843], David and Lillian M. Swenson, trs. (Princeton University Press, 1944), pp. 111–133.

escape a feeling of sadness in observing that however much the world has changed, the conception of the tragic is still essentially unchanged, just as weeping is still natural to all men alike.

Reassuring as this may seem to him who desires no such separation, least of all a breach, the same difficulty which has just been rejected reappears in another and almost more dangerous form. That we still constantly go back to the Aristotelian aesthetics, not merely from a dutiful sense of respect, or because of old habits, no one will deny who has any knowledge of modern aesthetics, and thus perceives how exactly this latter follows Aristotle in all the main points. But as soon as we view these a little more in detail, the difficulties immediately become evident. The qualifications are very general, and one may in one sense be quite in agreement with Aristotle, and in another sense wholly disagree with him. In order not to anticipate the following essay by mentioning at once the subject which will constitute its content, I prefer to illustrate my meaning by citing the corresponding observation with respect to comedy. If an old aesthetician had said that comedy presupposes character and situation, and has for its purpose the arousal of laughter, one might indeed turn back to this again and again; but when one reflects upon how widely different are the things which can make a human being laugh, then one soon becomes convinced of how tremendously inclusive this requirement was. Whoever has at any time made his own laughter and that of others the subject of his observation; whoever, as in this study, has had his eye not so much on the accidental as on the general; whoever has observed with psychological interest how different are the things which in each generation arouse laughter, will readily be convinced that the invariable requirement that comedy ought to arouse laughter contains a high degree of variability relative to the different conceptions of the ridiculous entertained in the world consciousness, without the variability becoming so diffuse that the corresponding somatic expression would be that the laughter expressed itself in tears. So also in relation to the tragic.

That which will here constitute the principal content of this little inquiry, is not so much the relation between ancient and modern tragedy, as it will be an attempt to show how the characteristic of ancient tragedy is embodied within the modern, so that the true tragedy appears therein. But however much I may endeavor to make this evident, I shall still refrain from every prophecy about this being what the age demands, so that its appearance becomes entirely without result, more especially so as the entire tendency of the age is in the direction of the comic. Existence is more or less undermined by doubt on the part of the subjects, isolation constantly gets more and more the upper hand, something one can best be convinced of by giving attention to the multitudinous social exertions. These movements show just as much about the isolated endeavors of the age that they seek to counteract, as they show that they are trying to counteract it in an irrational manner. The isolationist idea consists in one stressing oneself as number; when one will stress himself as one, then this is isolation; in this may all the friends of the Association grant me leave, even if unable or unwilling to see that there is quite the same isolation, if hundreds stress themselves exclusively as hundreds. The number is always a matter of indifference, whether it be one or a thousand, or the population of the whole world numerically determined. This spirit of the Association that stresses number, is, therefore, just as revolutionary as the spirit it would counteract. When David would rightly savor his power and glory, he took a census of the people; in our age, on the other hand, one might say that the people, in order to feel their importance in comparison with a higher power, count themselves. Hence, all these associations bearing the stamp of the arbitrary are most frequently created for some accidental purpose, naturally governed by the associations.

The many associations thus prove the disorganization of the age, and themselves contribute toward hastening that dissolution; they are the infusoria in the organism of the state, which indicate that it is disorganized. When was it that political clubs began to be general in Greece, if not at the very moment when the state was in process of dissolution? And has not our own age a remarkable similarity to that one, which not even Aristophanes could make more ludicrous than it actually was? Is not the invisible and spiritual bond which held the state together politically, lost; is not the power of religion which held fast to the invisible, weakened and annihilated; have not the statesmen and clergy this in common, that they, like the augurs of old, can scarcely look at one another without smiling? One characteristic our age certainly has to a greater degree than Greece, this, namely, that it is more melancholy, and hence it is more profoundly in despair. Thus, our age is melancholy enough to realize that there is something which is called responsibility, and this indicates something significant. While, therefore, everyone wishes to rule, no one wishes to accept responsibility. There is even yet a story fresh in our memories, that a French statesman, when a portfolio was offered to him for a second time, declared that he would accept it, but only on the condition that the secretary of the council should become responsible. It is well known that the king of France is not responsible, while his ministers are; the minister does not wish to be responsible, but will be minister on condition that the secretary of state become responsible; it finally results naturally in the watchmen or street commissioners becoming responsible. Would not this story of shifted responsibility really be a proper subject for Aristophanes! And on the other hand, why are the government and rulers so afraid of accepting responsibility, unless because they fear an attack from an opposition, which equally seeks to evade responsibil-

ity? When, then, one considers these two powers in opposition to one another, but not able to come to grips with each other, because the one
constantly vanishes from the other, the one only a duplicate of the other,
then such a lay-out is certainly not without its comic effect. This is sufficient
to show that the bond which essentially holds the state together is disorganized, but that it should thereby result in isolation is naturally comic,
and the comic lies in trying to stress the *subjective as mere form*. Every isolated individual always becomes comic by stressing his own accidental individuality over against necessary development. It would undoubtedly be
most deeply comic for some accidental individual to get the universal idea of
wishing to be the savior of the world. On the other hand, the appearance of
Christ is in a certain sense (in another sense it is infinitely more) the deepest
tragedy, because Christ came in the fullness of time, and, what I must later
particularly emphasize, He bore the sins of the world.

It is well known that Aristotle mentions two things, thought and character, as the source of action in tragedy, but he notes also that the main
thing is the plot, and the individuals do not act in order to present characters,
but the characters are included for the sake of the action. Here one readily
notices a divergence from modern tragedy. The peculiarity of ancient tragedy is that the action is not only the result of the character, that the action is
not reflected sufficiently into the subject, but that the action itself has a relative addition of suffering. Hence the ancient tragedy has not developed the
dialogue to the point of exhaustive reflection, so that everything is absorbed
in it; it has in the monologue and the chorus exactly the factors supplemental
to the dialogue. Whether the chorus approaches nearer the epic substantiality or the lyric exaltation, it thus still indicates, as it were, the more
which will not be absorbed in the individuality; the monologue again is more
the lyric concentration and has the more which will not be absorbed in action
and situation. In ancient tragedy the action itself has an epic moment in it, it
is as much event as action. The reason for this naturally lies in the fact that
the ancient world did not have the subjectivity reflected in it. Even if the individual moved freely, he still rested in the substantial categories of state,
family, and destiny. This substantial category is exactly the fatalistic element in Greek tragedy, and its exact peculiarity. The hero's destruction
is, therefore, not only a result of his own deeds, but is also a suffering,
whereas in modern tragedy, the hero's destruction is really not suffering, but is action. In modern times, therefore, situation and character
are really predominant. The tragic hero is subjectively reflected in himself,
and this reflection has not only reflected him out of every immediate relation
to state, race, and destiny, but has often even reflected him out of his own
preceding life. We are interested in a certain definite moment of his life,
considered as his own deed. Because of this the tragedy can be exhaustively

represented in situation and dialogue, since nothing of the more immediate is left behind. Hence, modern tragedy has no epic foreground, no epic heritage. The hero stands and falls entirely on his own acts.

This brief but adequate analysis may be useful in illuminating the difference between ancient and modern tragedy, which I regard as having great significance, the difference, namely, in the nature of tragic guilt. It is well known that Aristotle requires the tragic hero to have guilt. But just as the action in Greek tragedy is intermediate between activity and passivity (action and suffering), so is also the hero's guilt, and therein lies the tragic collision. On the other hand, the more the subjectivity becomes reflected, the more one sees the individual left Pelagianally to himself, the more his guilt becomes ethical. The tragedy lies between these two extremes. If the individual is entirely without guilt, then is the tragic interest nullified, for the tragic collision is thereby enervated; if, on the other hand, he is absolutely guilty, then he can no longer interest us tragically. Hence, it is certainly a misunderstanding of the tragic, when our age strives to let the whole tragic destiny become transubstantiated in individuality and subjectivity. One would know nothing to say about the hero's past life, one would throw his whole life upon his own shoulders, as being the result of his own acts, would make him accountable for everything, but in so doing, one would also transform his aesthetic guilt into an ethical one. The tragic hero thus becomes bad, the evil becomes precisely the tragic subject, but evil has no aesthetic interest, and sin is not an aesthetic element. This mistaken endeavor certainly has its cause in the whole tendency of our age toward the comic. The comic lies exactly in isolation; when one would maintain the tragic within this isolation, then one gets evil in all its baseness, not the truly tragic guilt in its ambiguous innocence. It is not difficult when one looks about in modern literature, to find examples. Thus, the very ingenious work of Grabbe, *Faust and Don Juan*, is precisely constructed around this evil. However, in order not to argue from a single work, I prefer to show it in the whole general consciousness of the age. If one wished to represent an individual whom an unhappy childhood had influenced so disturbingly that this impression occasioned his downfall, such a defense would simply not appeal to the present age, and this naturally not because it was wrongly handled, for I have a right to assume that it would be handled with distinction, but because our age employs another standard. It would know nothing about such coddling; without knowing, it holds every individual responsible for his own life. Hence, if he goes to the dogs, it is not tragic, but it is bad. One might now believe that this must be a kingdom of the gods, this generation in which I have the honor to live. On the contrary, this is by no means the case; the energy, the courage, which would thus be the creator of its own destiny, aye, its own creator, is an illusion, and when the age loses the tragic, it gains despair. There lies a sadness and a healing power in the tragic, which one truly should not despise, and when a man in the extraordinary manner our age affects, would gain himself, he loses himself and becomes comical. Every individual, however primitive he may be, is still a child of God, of his age, of his family and friends, herein lies its truth; if in this relativity he tries to be the absolute, then he becomes ridiculous.

One sometimes finds in the language a word which, because of its form, has been used so often in a certain case that at last it is used independently, like an adverb perhaps. Then for the experts such a word acquires an emphasis and a weakness that it never loses. If, in spite of this, it should attempt to change into a substantive and to be inflected in all five cases, it would be truly comic. And so it is, too, with the individual, when perhaps with great difficulty he issues from the womb of time, he will in this tremendous relativity be absolute. If, however, he renounces this claim of the absolute in order to become relative, then he has *eo ipso* the tragic, even if he was the happiest of individuals; indeed I might say that an individual does not become happy until he has the tragic. The tragic has in it an infinite gentleness; it is really in the aesthetic sense with regard to human life, what the divine love and mercy are; it is even milder, and hence I may say that it is like a mother's love, soothing the troubled. The ethical is strict and harsh. If a criminal should therefore plead before the judge that his mother had a propensity for stealing, especially at the time she was carrying him, then the judge might secure the opinion of the health commissioner about his mental condition, and decide that he was dealing with a thief, and not with a thief's mother. Since we are talking about a criminal, the sinner can hardly flee to the temple of aesthetics, but yet the aesthetic will provide an extenuating phrase for him. However, it would be wrong for him to resort to this, for his path leads him not to the aesthetic but to the religious. The aesthetic lies behind him, and it would be a new sin for him now to grasp at the aesthetic. The religious is the expression of a paternal love, since it contains the ethical, but it is softened, and so without being just the same, it gives mildness to the tragic through its continuity. But while the aesthetic gives this rest of continuity before the contrast of sin is stressed, the religious does not give it until this contrast is seen in all its frightfulness. Just at the moment when the sinner almost faints under the universal sin that he has taken upon himself, because he felt that only by becoming more guilty would the prospect of salvation be greater—in that same moment of terror, the consolation shows him that it is a universal sin which has also manifested itself in him. But this consolation is a religious consolation, and he who thinks to gain this in some other way, e.g., by aesthetic vaporings, has accepted this consolation in vain, and has not really gained it. In a certain sense, therefore, it is quite properly tactful of the age to hold the individual responsible for everything, but the unfortunate thing is that it does not do it deeply and intensively enough, and hence its vacillation. It is self-complacent enough to reject the tears of tragedy, but it is also self-complacent enough to dispense with the divine mercy. But what is human life when we take these two things away, what is the human race? Either the sadness of the tragic, or the profound sorrow and joy of the religious. Or is that not the characteristic of everything that proceeds from that happy people—a heaviness, a sadness, in its art, in its poetry, in its life, and in its joy?

In the preceding I have principally attempted to emphasize the difference between ancient and modern tragedy, insofar as this is illustrated in the guilt of the tragic hero. This is precisely the focus from which everything radiates in its peculiar difference. If the hero is unambiguously guilty, the monologue disappears and there is no destiny; the thought is transparent in the dialogue, and the action in the situation. The same thing may also be explained from another side, with regard to the mood which the tragedy evokes in the spectator. It may be remembered that Aristotle requires that tragedy should arouse fear and compassion in the spectator. I recall that Hegel in his *Aesthetics* adopted this view, and indulged in a double reflection about each of the points, which was not, however, particularly exhaustive. When Aristotle separates fear and compassion, then one might interpret fear as the mood which accompanies the individual idea, compassion as the mood which is the definitive impression. This latter mood is the one that appeals to me most, because it is the one which corresponds to the tragic guilt, and therefore, it has the same dialectic as this concept of guilt. Hegel observes that there are two kinds of sympathy, the ordinary kind which is concerned with the finite aspect of suffering, and the true tragic pity. This observation is indeed quite correct, but to me it is of less importance, since this common emotion is a misunderstanding which can just as well apply to ancient as to modern tragedy. True and powerful, however, is what Hegel adds regarding true compassion: "True compassion is, on the contrary, a synthesis of sympathy and the moral justification of the sufferer." While Hegel rather considers sympathy in general and its differences in the variations of the individualities, I prefer to emphasize the different kinds of sympathy in relation to the different kinds of tragic guilt. Before proceeding to indicate this immediately, I shall allow the word sympathy to split itself into the *suffering* (passion, *pathikos*), and add particularly the sympathetic which lies in the word *sym* and yet in such a manner that I do not seem to assert something about the spectator's mood, which might show his arbitrariness, but in such a way that when I explain the difference in his mood, I also express the difference of the tragic guilt.

In ancient tragedy the sorrow is deeper, the pain less; in modern, the pain is greater, the sorrow less. Sorrow always contains something more substantial than pain. Pain always implies a reflection over suffering which sorrow does not know. From a psychological standpoint it is always interesting to watch a child when it sees an older person suffer. The child is not reflective enough to feel grief, and yet its sorrow is infinitely deep. It is not reflective enough to have any conception about sin and guilt; when it sees an older person suffer, it does not occur to it to reflect upon it, and yet when the cause of the suffering is concealed from it, there is a dim suspicion about it in its sorrow. Such, but in complete and profound harmony, is the Greek sorrow, and therefore it is at one and the same time so gentle and so deep. When an older person sees a child suffer, his pain is greater, his sorrow less. The more clearly the conception of guilt stands out, the greater is the pain, the less profound the sorrow. If one now applies this to the relation between ancient and modern tragedy, then must one say: in the ancient tragedy, the sorrow is deeper, and in the consciousness which corresponds to this, the sorrow is deeper. It must in fact be constantly remembered that the sorrow does not lie in myself, but it lies in the tragedy, and that I, in order to understand the deep sorrow of the Greek tragedy, must myself live in the Greek consciousness. Hence, it is certainly often only an affectation when so many profess to admire the Greek tragedies; for it is very evident that our age, at least, has little sympathy for that which precisely constitutes Greek sorrow. The sorrow is deeper because the guilt has the aesthetic ambiguity. In modern times, the pain is greater. It is a fearful thing to fall into the hands of the living God. One might say this about Greek tragedy. The wrath of the gods is terrible, but the pain is not so great as in modern tragedy where the hero bears the whole weight of his guilt, is himself transparent in his suffering of his guilt. Here it is relevant in conformity with the tragic guilt, to show which sorrow is the true aesthetic sorrow, and which the true aesthetic pain. The bitterest pain is manifestly remorse, but remorse has ethical not aesthetic reality. It is the bitterest pain because it has the total transparency of the entire guilt, but just because of this transparency, it does not interest us aesthetically. Remorse has a sacredness which obscures the aesthetic, it may not be seen, least of all by the spectator, and it requires quite a different kind of self-activity. Modern comedy has sometimes presented remorse on the stage, but this only shows a lack of judgment on the part of the author. One may indeed be reminded of the psychological interest it can have to see remorse delineated on the stage, but again the psychological interest is not the aesthetic. This is part of the confusion which in our age asserts itself in so many ways: we look for a thing where we ought not to look for it, and what is worse, we find it where we ought not to find it; we wish to be edified in the theater, aesthetically impressed in church, we would be converted by novels, get enjoyment out of books of devotion, we want philosophy in the pulpit, and the preacher in the professorial chair. This pain of remorse is consequently not the aesthetic pain, and yet it is apparently this which the modern age tends toward as the highest tragic interest. This is also true with regard to the tragic guilt. Our age has lost all the substantial categories of family, state, and race. It must leave the individual entirely to himself, so that in a stricter sense he becomes his own creator, his guilt is consequently sin, his pain remorse; but this nullifies the tragedy. Also, in a stricter sense, the tragedy of suffering has exactly lost its tragic interest, for the power from which the suffering comes has lost its significance, and the spectators cry: "Help yourself, and heaven will help you!" or, in other words, the spectator has lost his compassion, but compassion is in a subjective as well as an objective sense, the precise expression for the tragic.

For the sake of clarity I shall now, before carrying this explanation farther, define a little more carefully the true aesthetic sorrow. Sorrow has the opposite movement from that which pain has; when one does not spoil this by means of a wretched consistency—something I, too, shall avoid in another way—one may say: the more innocent, the more profound the sorrow. If one insists on that, then one destroys the tragic. An element of guilt always remains, but this element is never really subjectively reflected; hence the sorrow in the Greek tragedy is so deep. In order to prevent ill-timed consequences, I shall only note that all the exaggerations only succeed in carrying the matter over into another sphere. The synthesis of absolute innocence and absolute guilt is not an aesthetic category, but a metaphysical one. This is the real reason why one has always been ashamed to call the life of Christ a tragedy, because one instinctively feels that aesthetic categories do not exhaust the matter. Then, too, it shows in another way, that Christ's life is something more than can be exhausted in aesthetic categories: that is, that these neutralize themselves in this phenomenon, and are hushed in indifference.

The tragic action always has an element of suffering in it, and the tragic suffering an element of action, the aesthetic lies in the relativity of these. The identity of an absolute action and an absolute suffering is beyond the powers of aesthetics, and belongs to metaphysics. This identity is exemplified in the life of Christ, for His suffering is absolute because the action is absolutely free, and his action is absolute suffering because it is absolute obedience. Hence the element of guilt which remains in the tragic consciousness is not subjectively reflected, and this makes the sorrow profound. The tragic guilt is something more than merely subjective guilt, it is an inherited guilt; but inherited guilt, like inherited sin, is a substantial category, and it is exactly this substantiality which makes the sorrow deeper. The ever admired tragic trilogy of Sophocles, *Oedipus Coloneus*, *Oedipus Rex* and *Antigone*, essentially centers about this true tragic interest. But inherited guilt contains the self-contradiction of being guilt, and yet not being guilt.

The bond which makes the individual guilty is precisely piety, but the guilt which he thus draws down upon himself, has every possible aesthetic ambiguity. One might readily conclude that the people who developed profound tragedy must have been the Jews. Thus, when they say about Jehovah that He is a jealous God who visits the sins of the fathers upon the children unto the third and fourth generations, or when one hears those terrible imprecations in the Old Testament, then one might easily be tempted to seek here for tragic material. But Judaism is too ethically developed for this; Jehovah's curses are, even though terrible, still also righteous punishment. This was not the case in Greece; the wrath of the gods had no ethical character, but only aesthetic ambiguity.

In Greek tragedy a transition is found from sorrow to pain, and as an example of this I might mention *Philoctetes*. This, in the stricter sense, is a tragedy of suffering. But, too, a high degree of objectivity obtains here. The Greek hero rests in his fate, it is unchangeable, there is nothing farther to be said about it. This element furnishes the precise moment of sorrow in the pain. The first doubt with which pain really begins is this: why has this befallen me, why can it not be otherwise? There is, indeed, in Philoctetes a high degree of reflection, which has always seemed remarkable to me, and which essentially separates him from that immortal trilogy: there is the masterly depicting of the self-contradiction in his pain, which contains so deep a human truth, but there is still an objectivity which sustains the whole. Philoctetes' reflection is not absorbed in itself, and it is genuinely Greek when he complains that no one knows about his pain. There is an extraordinary truth in this, and there also appears here the precise difference between his pain and the precise reflective pain which always wants to be alone with its pain, which seeks a new pain in this solitude of pain.

The true tragic sorrow consequently requires an element of guilt, the true tragic pain an element of innocence; the true tragic sorrow requires an element of transparency, the true tragic pain an element of obscurity. This I believe best indicates the dialectic wherein there is a synthesis of the categories of sorrow and pain, as well as also the dialectic which lies in the concept of tragic guilt.

Since it is contrary to the spirit of our organization to produce closely coherent works or greater wholes, since it is not our purpose to labor upon a Tower of Babel, which God in His righteousness can descend upon and destroy, since we are conscious of the fact that this confusion of tongues happened justly, recognizing it as a characteristic of all human striving in its truth, that it is fragmentary, and that it is precisely this which separates it from Nature's infinite coherence; that the wealth of an individual consists precisely in the energy he shows in producing the fragmentary, and that that which brings enjoyment to the producing individual also brings enjoyment to the receiving individual, not the troublesome and meticulous execution, nor the tedious apprehension of this execution, but the production and enjoyment of the gleaming transitoriness, which for the producer contains something more than the thorough execution, since it is the appearance of the Idea, and for the recipient, it contains something more, since its fulguration awakens his own productivity—since, I say, all this is contrary to the purpose of our Association, moreover, since the period just read must be regarded as a serious attempt in the interjectory style, wherein the ideas break out without breaking through, which in our society has an official status: then I shall, after having called attention to the fact that my procedure still cannot be called rebellious, since the bonds which hold the sentence together are so loose that the intermediary clauses stand out aphoristically and arbitrarily enough, merely call to mind that my style has made an attempt apparently to be what it is not—revolutionary.

Our society needs in every way a renewal and rebirth, to the end that its inner activity may be renewed by a new description of its productivity. Let us then describe our purpose as an attempt in fragmentary pursuits, or in the art of writing posthumous papers. A completely finished work has no relation to the poetic personality; in the case of posthumous papers one constantly feels, because of the interruption, the desultoriness, a need to romance about the personality. Posthumous papers are like a ruin, and what haunted place could be more natural for the interred? The art, then, is artistically to produce the same effect, the same appearance of carelessness and the accidental, the same anacoluthonic flight of thought; it consists in producing an enjoyment which naturally never actually becomes present, but always has an element of the past in it, so that it is present in the past. This has already been expressed in the word: posthumous. In a certain sense, everything which a poet has produced is posthumous; but one would never think of calling a completed work posthumous, even though it had the accidental quality of not having been published in the poet's lifetime. Also, I assume that this is the true characteristic of all human productivity, as we have apprehended it, that it is a heritage, since men are not permitted to live eternally in the sight of the gods. Hence, I shall call the effects that are produced among us an artistic heritage; the negligence and the indolence, I shall call the genius we appreciate; the *vis inertia* the natural law that we worship. By this explanation I have now complied with our sacred customs and rules.

So draw nearer to me, dear brothers of Symparanekromenoi; close around me as I send my tragic heroine out into the world, as I give the daughter of sorrow a dowry of pain as a wedding gift. She is my creation, but still her outline is so vague, her form so nebulous, that each one of you is free to imagine her as you will, and each one of you can love her in your own way. She is my creation, her thoughts are my thoughts, and yet it is as if I had rested with her in a night of love, as if she had entrusted me with her deep secret, breathed it and her soul out in my embrace, and as if in the same moment she changed before me, vanished, so that her actuality could only be traced in the mood that remained, instead of the converse being true, that my mood brought her forth to a greater and greater actuality. I place the words in her mouth, and yet it is as if I abused her confidence; to me, it is as if she stood reproachfully behind me, and yet, conversely, it is in her mystery that she becomes ever more and more visible. She is my possession, my lawful possession, and yet sometimes it is as if I had slyly insinuated myself into her confidence, as if I must constantly see myself standing back of her; and yet, conversely, she lies constantly before me, she constantly comes into existence only as I bring her forth. She is called Antigone. This name I retain from the ancient tragedy, as I connect the whole development with that, although, from another point of view, everything is modern. First, however, a remark. I use a feminine figure because I firmly believe that a feminine nature will be most successful in showing the difference. As woman she will have substantiality enough to show sorrow, but as belonging in a reflective world, she will have reflection enough to feel pain. In order to experience sorrow, the tragic guilt must vacillate between guilt and innocence; that whereby the guilt passes over into her consciousness must always be a determination of substantiality. But since in order to experience sorrow, the tragic guilt must have this vagueness, so reflection must not be present in its infinitude, for then it would reflect her out of her guilt, in that the reflection in its infinite subjectivity cannot let the element of inherited guilt remain, which causes the sorrow. Since, however, her reflection is awake, it will not reflect her out of her sorrow, but into it, each moment transforming her sorrow into pain.

Labdakos' family is, then, the object of the indignation of the angry gods. Oedipus has slain the sphinx, liberated Thebes; he has murdered his father, married his mother, and Antigone is the daughter of this marriage. Thus goes the Greek tragedy. Here I diverge from the Greek. Everything is contained in mine, and yet everything is different. That he has slain the sphinx and liberated Thebes is known to everyone, and Oedipus lives honored and admired, happy in his marriage with Jocasta. The rest is concealed from the eyes of men, and no suspicion has ever called this horrible nightmare into actuality. Only Antigone knows it. How she has come to know it lies outside the tragic interest, and everyone is free to work out his own explanation in regard to it. At an early age, before she was fully developed, dim suspicions of this horrible secret had at times gripped her soul, until certainty with a single blow cast her into the arms of anxiety. Here we have at once a category of modern tragedy. Anxiety is, namely, a reflection, and insofar is essentially different from sorrow. Anxiety is the means by which the subject appropriates his sorrow and assimilates it. Anxiety is the energy of the movement by which sorrow burrows into one's heart. But the movement is not swift like the thrust of a dart, which is continuous, it is not once for all, but it is constantly continuing. As a passionate, erotic glance desires its object, so anxiety looks upon sorrow to desire it. As the quiet, incorruptible glance of love is preoccupied with the beloved object, so anxiety occupies itself with sorrow. But anxiety has another element in it which makes it cling even more strongly to its object, for it both loves and fears it. Anxiety has a two-fold function, partly it is the detective instinct which constantly touches, and by means of this key, discovers sorrow, as it goes round about the sorrow. Or anxiety is sudden, posits the whole sorrow in the present moment, yet so that this present moment instantly dissolves in succession. Anxiety is in this sense a truly tragic category, and the old saying: *quem deus vult pardere, primum dementat*, in truth rightfully applies here. The language itself proves that anxiety is a reflective determination; for I always say: my anxiety, about something in which I separate the anxiety from that for which I am anxious, and I can never use anxiety in an objective sense; whereas when I say: my sorrow, it can just as well express that which I sorrow over, as my sorrow over it. In addition, anxiety always contains a reflection in time, for I cannot be anxious about the present, but only about the past or the future; but the past and the future so resisting one another that the present vanishes, are reflective determinations. The Greek sorrow, on the contrary, like the whole of Greek life, is a present thing, and therefore, the sorrow is deeper, but the pain less. Anxiety therefore belongs essentially to the tragic. Hence, Hamlet is deeply tragic because he suspects his mother's guilt. Robert, the devil, asks how it could happen that he caused so much evil. Høgne, whom his mother had begotten by a troll, happens accidentally to see his image in the water, and asks his mother how his body had acquired such a shape.

The difference is now easily perceptible. In the Greek tragedy Antigone is not at all concerned about her father's unhappy destiny. This rests like an impenetrable sorrow over the whole family. Antigone lives as carefree as any other young Grecian maiden, indeed the chorus pities her, since her death is foreordained, because she must quit this life at so early an age, quit it without having tasted its most beautiful joys, evidently forgetting the family's own deep sorrow. However, it should by no means be said that it is thoughtlessness, or that the particular individual stands alone by himself, without worrying about his relationship to the family. But that is genuinely Greek. The life-relationships when once assigned to them are like the heaven under which they live. If this is dark and cloudy, it is also unchangeable. This furnishes the keynote of the Greek soul, and this is sorrow, not pain. In Antigone the tragic guilt concentrates itself about one definite point, that she had buried her brother in defiance of the king's prohibition. If this is seen as an isolated fact, as a collision between sisterly affection and piety and an arbitrary human prohibition, then *Antigone* would cease to be a Greek tragedy, it would be an entirely modern tragic subject. That which in the Greek sense affords the tragic interest, is that Oedipus' sorrowful destiny re-echoes in the brother's unhappy destiny, in the sister's collision with a simple human prohibition; the tragic fate of Oedipus is, as it were, the after effects which ramify from a single branch of his family. This is the totality which makes the sorrow of the spectator so infinitely deep. It is not an individual who goes down, it is a small world, it is the objective sorrow, which, released, now advances in its own terrible consistency, like a force of nature, and Antigone's unhappy fate is but an echo of her father's, an intensified sorrow. When, therefore, Antigone in defiance of the king's prohibition resolves to bury her brother, we do not see in this so much a free action on her part as a predestined necessity, which visits the father's crime upon the children. There is indeed enough freedom of action to make us love Antigone for her sisterly affection, but in the necessity of fate there is also, as it were, a higher refrain which not only includes Oedipus, but also his family.

While, then, the Greek Antigone lives so carefree that were it not for the disclosure of this new fact, we might imagine her life as very happy in its gradual unfolding, our Antigone's life, on the contrary, is essentially over. I have not endowed her stingily, and as we say that a good word is like apples of gold in pictures of silver, so I have placed the fruit of her sorrow in a cup of pain. Her dowry is not a vain magnificence which moth and rust can corrupt, it is an eternal treasure. Thieves cannot break in and steal it; she will herself be too vigilant for that. Her life does not unfold like that of the Greek Antigone, it is not turned outward but inward, the scene is not external but internal, it is an invisible scene. Should it not make me happy, dear Symparanekromenoi, to arouse your interest in such a maiden, or shall I resort to a *captatio benevolentiae?* Then, too, she does not belong to the world she lives in; even though her life is flower-strewn and healthy, it is still really a secret life. Although she is living, she is in another sense dead; quiet is her life and secretive, the world does not even hear her sigh, for her sigh is buried in the depths of her soul. I do not need to remind you that she is by no means a weak and sickly woman, rather she is proud and vigorous. There is nothing, perhaps, which ennobles a human being so much as keeping a secret. It gives a man's whole life a meaning which it can have only for himself. It saves him from every vain consideration about his environment, self-contained he rests, blessed in his secret—that one could almost say even if his secret was most reprehensible.

Such was our Antigone. She is proud of her secret, proud that she has been selected in a peculiar manner to be the savior of her father's honor and renown, and of that of her family; and when the grateful people acclaim Oedipus with praise and gratitude, then she feels her own importance, and her secret sinks ever deeper into her soul, more inaccessible to every living being. She feels how much responsibility is placed in her hands, and this gives her a supernatural greatness, which is necessary if she is to engage our attention as a tragic personality. As an individual figure she must be able to interest us. She is more than a young girl in general, and yet she is a young girl; she is a bride, and yet she is all innocence and purity. As a bride, woman achieves her destiny, and hence a woman can ordinarily interest us only to the degree that she is brought into relation to her destiny. However, there is an analogy here. One says of a bride of God that she has the inward faith and spirit in which she rests. Our Antigone I should call a bride in a perhaps even more beautiful sense, indeed she is almost more, she is mother, she is in the purely aesthetic sense *virgo mater*, she carries her secret under her heart, hidden and concealed. She is silence, precisely because she is secretive, but this retrospection which lies in silence, gives her a supernatural bearing. She is proud of her sorrow, she is jealous for it, for her sorrow is her love. But still her sorrow is not a dead, immovable possession; it moves constantly, it gives birth to pain, and is born in pain. When a girl resolves to dedicate her life to an idea, when she stands there with the sacrificial wreath upon her brow, she stands as a bride, for the great inspiring idea transforms her, and the votive wreath is like a bridal garland. She knows not any man, and yet she is a bride; she does not even know the idea which inspires her, for that would be unwomanly, and yet she is a bride.

Such is our Antigone, the bride of sorrow. She dedicates her life to sorrow over her father's destiny, over her own. Such a misfortune as has overtaken her father calls for sorrow, and yet there is no one who can grieve over it, because there is no one who knows about it. And as the Greek Antigone cannot bear to have her brother's corpse flung away without the last honors, so she feels how hard it would have been if no man had known this; it worries her that no tears should be shed; she almost thanks the gods because she is selected as this instrument. So is Antigone great in her pain. Here again I can show a difference between Greek and modern tragedy. It is genuinely Greek for Philoctetes to complain that there is no one who knows what he suffers; it is a deep human need to wish that others should realize this; reflective grief, however, does not desire this. It does not occur to Antigone to wish that anyone should understand her grief, but on the other hand, in relation to her father, she feels it to be as aesthetically just that she should sorrow as that a man should suffer punishment when he has done wrong. While, therefore, the very conception that it is predestined that the living should be buried alive, wrings from Antigone in the Greek tragedy, the outburst of sorrow:

> O mockery of my woe!
> I go to the strong mound of yon strange tomb
> All hapless, having neither part nor room
> With those who live or those who die,

our Antigone can say it about her whole life. The difference is extraordinary; there is a factual truth in her assertion which makes the pain less. If our Antigone should say the same, then it would be unreal, but this unreality is the real pain. The Greeks do not express themselves precisely, just because the reflection which goes with this was not present in their lives. So when Philoctetes complains that he lives solitary and forsaken on a desert island, his assertion has in it an external truth; when, on the other hand, our Antigone feels pain in her solitude, then is the fact that she is alone figurative, but just because of this, her pain is real pain.

As far as tragic guilt is concerned, it consists partly in the fact that she buries her brother, partly in connection with her father's sorry fate, which was understood from the two preceding tragedies. Here again I come to the peculiar dialectic which posits the guilt of the family in relation to the individual. This is the hereditary guilt. If one generally considers dialectics fairly abstractly, one thinks more particularly of the logical movement. However, life will soon teach one that there are many kinds of dialectics, that almost every passion has its own. The dialectic, therefore, which posits the guilt of the race or the family in connection with a particular subject, so that he not only suffers under it—for this is a natural consequence against which one would vainly try to harden himself—but bears the guilt, participates in it, this dialectic is foreign to us, has nothing compelling for the modern mind. If a man, however, were to contemplate regeneration in terms of ancient tragedy, then must every individual contemplate his own regeneration, not merely in a spiritual sense, but in the finite sense of the rebirth of family and race. The dialectic which posits the individual in connection with family and race, is not a subjective dialectic, for this, on the contrary, raises the connection and the individual out of the continuity; it is an objective dialectic. It is essentially piety. To preserve this cannot be regarded as something injurious to the individual. In our age one permits something in a natural relation which he will not permit in a spiritual relation. Still, one would not wish to be so isolated, so unnatural, that one would not regard the family as a whole, of which one might say that when one member suffers, then all suffer. One does this involuntarily, otherwise why is a particular individual so afraid that another branch of the family may bring disgrace upon him, unless because he feels that he will suffer from it? This suffering the individual must obviously take with him, whether he will or not. But since the point of departure is the individual, not the family, this forced suffering becomes maximum; he feels that a man cannot become master over his own nature, but he desires this as far as possible. On the other hand, if the individual sees nature as a factor in his truth, this expresses itself in the spiritual world so that the individual becomes a participant in the guilt. This is a result many, perhaps, fail to understand, but then neither do they apprehend the tragic. If an individual is isolated, then he is either absolutely the creator of his own destiny, in which case nothing tragic remains, but only the evil—for it is not even tragic that an individual should be blindly engrossed in himself, it is his own fault—or the individuals are only modifications of the eternal substance of existence, and so again the tragic is lost.

With regard to the tragic guilt, the difference in the modern is readily apparent, after this has assimilated the ancient, for there something can really be said about this. The Greek Antigone participates with a filial piety in her father's guilt, as does also our modern one; but to the Greek Antigone her father's guilt and suffering is an external fact, a disquieting fact, which her sorrow does not alter (*quod non volvit in pectore*); and insofar as she herself personally, as a natural consequence, suffers under her father's guilt, this is again on the whole an external fact. It is otherwise with our Antigone. I assume that Oedipus is dead. Even while he lived Antigone had been aware of this secret, but she had not had courage to confide in her father. By his death she is deprived of the only way by which she could be freed from her secret. To confide it now to any living being would be to disgrace her father; her life acquires meaning for her, which she dedicates by her inviolable silence, daily almost hourly, in showing him the last honors. Of one thing, however, she is ignorant, whether her father himself had known this secret or not. In the modern tragedy this causes the unrest in her sorrow, the ambiguity in her pain. She loves her father with all her soul, and this love transports her out of herself and into her father's guilt; as the fruit of such a love, she feels herself alienated from mankind; she feels her own guilt the more she loves her father; only with him could she find rest, as equally guilty they would sorrow together. But while her father lived she had not been able to confide her sorrow to him, for she did not know whether he knew about it, and consequently there was a possibility of depressing him in a similar pain. And yet, was his guilt less if he had not known about it? The movement here is constantly relative. If Antigone had not known with certainty the actual relationship, then she would be insignificant, then she would have had nothing more than a suspicion to fight against, and that contains too little of the tragic to interest us. But she does know everything; yet even in this knowledge there is still an ignorance which can always keep sorrow in movement, always transform it into pain. Then, too, she is constantly at odds with her environment. Oedipus lives in the popular estimation as a fortunate king, honored and acclaimed; Antigone herself has admired as well as loved her father. She participates in every celebration and festival in his honor; she is more enthusiastic about him than any other young girl in the realm; her thoughts constantly turn back to him; she is praised throughout the kingdom as a model, loving daughter, and yet this enthusiasm is the only way in which she can give her sorrow any relief. Her father is always in her thoughts, but in what way is her painful secret. And yet she dares not give way to her sorrow, dares not grieve; she feels how much depends on her; she fears if anyone saw her suffering that people would begin to ask questions, and so, on this side too, she knows not sorrow but pain.

Considered in this way, I think that Antigone can really interest us; I think you will not reproach my extravagance nor my paternal partiality when I believe that she dares attempt this tragic subject, and dares appear in a tragedy. So far she is only an epic figure, and the tragic in her is only an epic interest.

It is not so difficult to discover a connection into which she might fit; in this respect we may readily be content with what the Greek tragedy gives. She has a sister living, who is, I assume, older than herself and married. Her mother might also be living. That these are naturally always subordinate characters is self-evident, as is the fact that the tragedy acquires an epic moment at all, such as the Greek has, without its needing to be so conspicuous; still, the monologue will here always play the principal role, even if it must be assisted by the situation. One must imagine everything united about this one chief interest which constitutes Antigone's life content, and when the whole is set in order, then the question arises as to how the dramatic interest is brought about.

Our heroine, as she has been presented in the foregoing, is on the point of passing over a moment of her life, she is about to become wholly spiritual, something nature does not tolerate. With the depth of soul she possesses, she must necessarily love with an extraordinary passion, if she does fall in love. Here, consequently, I encounter the dramatic interest—Antigone is in love, and, I say it with pain, Antigone is head over heels in love. Here manifestly is the tragic collision. One ought generally to be a little more particular about what one calls a tragic collision. The more sympathetic the colliding forces are, the deeper but also the more homogeneous they are, the more important the collision. Hence she is in love, and he who is the object of her affections knows that she loves him. My Antigone is no ordinary woman, and consequently her dowry is unusual—it is her pain. She cannot belong to a man without this dowry, she feels that would be very hazardous; to conceal it from such an observer would be impossible, to wish to conceal it would be a betrayal of her love; but can she marry him with it? Dare she confide it to any human being, even to the beloved? Antigone has strength; the question is not whether for her own sake, to relieve her heart, she should reveal something of her pain, for she can indeed bear this without assistance; but the question is, can she justify this to the dead, even if she really suffers in a way by revealing her secret; for her own life, too, is sorrowfully interwoven with this. This, however, does not trouble her. The question is only concerning her father. Consequently the collision from this side is of a sympathetic nature. Her life which was formerly peaceful and quiet, now becomes violent and passionate, always of course within herself, and her speech here begins to be pathetic. She struggles with herself, she has been willing to sacrifice her life to her secret, but now she must sacrifice her love. She conquers, that is to say, the secret conquers, and she loses. Now comes the second collision, for in order that the tragic collision should really be profound, the colliding forces must be homogeneous. The collision just described had not this quality; for the collision is really between her love for her father and for herself, and not whether her own love is too great a sacrifice. The other colliding force is the sympathetic love for her beloved. He knows he is loved, and boldly risks his attack. Her reserve seems admirable to him; he notices that there must be quite peculiar difficulties, but he thinks they cannot be insurmountable to him. What is all important to him is to be able to convince her of how much he loves her, to persuade her that his life is over if he is obliged to relinquish her love. His passion at last becomes something almost unfair, but only the more ingenious because of her resistance. With every assurance of his love, he increases her pain, with every sigh he sinks the dart of sorrow deeper and deeper into her heart. He leaves no means untried to influence her. He knows, as did everyone, how deeply she had loved her father. He meets her at the grave of Oedipus, where she had gone to find relief for her emotion, where she surrenders herself to her longing for her father, even though this longing is mingled with pain because she does not know how she would meet him again, whether he was conscious of his own guilt or not. Her lover surprises her, and he adjures her by the love she bore her father; he notes that he makes an unusual impression upon her; he persists, he hopes for everything by this means, and he does not know that he has really worked against himself. *ain*

Consequently, the interest centers about his being able to secret from her. To allow her to become momentarily de to betray her secret, would not help. The colliding matched that action becomes impossible for the is now increased by her love, by her sympathetic suffering with him she loves. Only in death can she find peace; so her whole life is dedicated to sorrow, and she has, as it were, established a limit, a dam, for the evil destiny, which might perhaps fatally have transmitted itself to succeeding generations. Only in the moment of death can she admit the intensity of her love, only admit that she belongs to him in the moment that she does not belong to him. When Epaminondas was wounded in the battle of Mantinea, he left the arrow sticking in the wound until he heard that the battle was won, because he knew that the instant it was drawn out, he would die. So our Antigone bore her secret in her heart like an arrow, life constantly plunged it deeper and deeper within, without depriving her of life, for as long as it remained in her heart she could live, but in the moment it was drawn out, she must die. The beloved must constantly strive to wrest her secret from her, and yet this means her certain death. Who, then, is responsible for her death, the living or the dead? In a certain sense, the dead, and just as Hercules had predicted that he would not be slain by the living but by the dead, so this applies to her, insofar as the memory of her father is the cause of her death; in another sense it was caused by the living, insofar as her unhappy love is the occasion for her memory destroying her.

Selected Bibliography

There has been no attempt to make this bibliography as inclusive as possible. To do so would require a volume in itself. The books and articles listed here, in addition to the sources used for the text (listed elsewhere), constitute a basic working bibliography for all students interested in the subject of tragedy. I have divided the bibliography so that it more or less corresponds to the divisions which I have established in the text. The single entry under Section VII indicates how little serious work has been done on the general subject of the relationship of melodrama and tragedy. For a more extensive bibliography the student is advised to check those included in several of the books listed under the heading of "General Books on Tragedy" and also Chapter 15 of *Contemporary Literary Scholarship* edited by Lewis Leary.

General Books on Tragedy

Dixon, Macneile. *Tragedy*, London, 1924.
Frye, Prosser. *Romance and Tragedy*, Lincoln, Neb., 1961.
Gassner, John. *The Theater in Our Times*, New York, 1954.
Hallman, Ralph. *Psychology and Literature*, New York, 1961.
Henn, T. R. *The Harvest of Tragedy*, London, 1956.
Mandel, Oscar. *A Definition of Tragedy*, New York, 1961.
McCollom, William G. *Tragedy*, New York, 1957.
Michel, Laurence, and Richard B. Sewall (eds.). *Tragedy: Modern Essays in Criticism*, New York, 1963.
Muller, Herbert. *The Spirit of Tragedy*, New York, 1956.
Steiner, George. *The Death of Tragedy*, New York, 1961.

The Tragic View of Life

Berdyaev, Nicolas. *The Destiny of Man*, London, 1948.
Brereton, Geoffrey. "The Hidden God: Some Comments on the Problem of Tragedy," B.B.C. Third Program, Jan. 29, 1951.
Greene, W. C. *Moira*, Cambridge, Mass., 1944.
Niebuhr, Reinhold. *Beyond Tragedy*, New York, 1938.
Santayana, George. "Tragic Philosophy," *Scrutiny*, 1936.

Scott, Nathan (ed.). *The Tragic Vision and the Christian Faith*, New York, 1957.
Unamuno, Miguel de. *The Tragic Sense of Life*, London, 1921.
Weisinger, Herbert. *Tragedy and the Paradox of the Fortunate Fall*, East Lansing, Mich., 1953.
Yeats, W. B. *The Cutting of an Agate*, New York, 1912.

CHARACTERISTICS OF THE TRAGIC

Adolf, Helen. "The Essence and Origin of Tragedy," *Journal of Aesthetics and Art Criticism*, Dec., 1951.
Anderson, Maxwell. *The Essence of Tragedy*, Washington, 1939.
Bell, C. G. "Tragedy," *Diogenes*, 1954.
DeWitt, Norman J. "Tragedy and Personal Humanism," Introduction to *Renunciation as a Tragic Focus* by E. H. Falk, Minneapolis, 1954.
Hathorn, Richmond Y. *Tragedy, Myth and Mystery*, Bloomington, Ind., 1962.
Jarrett, J. L. "Tragedy, a Study in Explication," ETC., 1955.
Leavis, F. R. *The Common Pursuit*, London, 1952.
Philipson, M. H. "Some Reflections on Tragedy," *Journal of Philosophy*, 1958.
Richards, I. A. *Principles of Literary Criticism*, London, 1925.
Tillich, Paul. *The Protestant Era*, Chicago, 1948.

THE FORM OF TRAGEDY

Brooks, Cleanth, and R. B. Heilman. *Understanding Drama*, New York, 1945.
Burke, Kenneth. *A Grammar of Motives*, New York, 1945.
Eberhart, Richard. "Tragedy as Limitation: Comedy as Control and Resolution," *Tulane Drama Review*, 1962.
Fergusson, Francis. *The Idea of a Theater*, Princeton, 1949.
Fergusson, Francis. "*Macbeth* as the Imitation of an Action," *English Institute Essays: 1951*, New York, 1952.
Kitto, H. D. F. *Form and Meaning in Drama*, London, 1956.
Sebeok, A. (ed.). *Myth: A Symposium*, Philadelphia, 1955.
Snell, Bruno. *The Discovery of the Mind*, Cambridge, Mass., 1953.
Watts, Harold H. "Myth and Drama," *Cross Currents*, 1955.

THE TRAGIC HERO

Campbell, Joseph. *The Hero with a Thousand Faces*, New York, 1949.
Camus, Albert. *The Rebel*, New York, 1956.
Falk, Eugene H. *Renunciation as a Tragic Focus*, Minneapolis, 1954.
Fowlie, Wallace. "Swann and Hamlet: A Note on the Contemporary Hero," *Partisan Review*, 1942.
Klapp, Orrin E. *Heroes, Villains, and Fools*, New York, 1962.
Maeterlinck, Maurice. *The Treasure of the Humble*, New York, 1897.

Miller, Arthur. "Introduction," *Collected Plays*, New York, 1957.
Raglan, Lord. *The Hero*, New York, 1937.
Rank, Otto. *Myth and the Birth of the Hero*, New York, 1952.

THE LANGUAGE OF TRAGEDY

Downer, Alan. "The Life of Our Design," *Hudson Review*, 1949.
Eliot, T. S. *On Poetry and Poets*, New York, 1957.
Goheen, Robert F. "Aspects of Dramatic Symbolism: Three Studies of the *Oresteia*," *American Journal of Philology*, 1955.
Goheen, Robert F. *The Imagery of Sophocles' Antigone*, Princeton, 1951.
Prior, Moody. *The Language of Tragedy*, New York, 1947.
Wheelwright, Philip. *The Burning Fountain*, Bloomington, Ind., 1954.

THE EFFECTS OF TRAGEDY

Jekels, Ludwig. "The Psychology of Pity," *Selected Papers*, New York, 1952.
Koestler, Arthur. *The Age of Longing*, New York, 1951.
Moravia, Alberto. "The Sterility of Suffering," *Yale Review*, 1958.
Pottle, F. A. "Catharsis," *Yale Review*, 1951.
Ransom, J. C. *The World's Body*, New York, 1938.
Roberts, Preston T. "Bringing Pathos into Focus," *University of Chicago Magazine*, 1954.
Wasserman, E. H. "The Pleasures of Tragedy," *ELH*, 1947.

TRAGEDY AND MELODRAMA

Shaw, George Bernard. *Our Theatre in the Nineties*, London, 1932.

THE CLIMATES OF TRAGEDY

Barrett, William. *Irrational Man*, New York, 1958.
Bredvold, Louis I. "The Modern Temper and Tragic Drama," *The Quarterly Review*, 1955.
Camus, Albert. *The Myth of Sisyphus and Other Essays*, New York, 1955.
Drucker, Peter. "The Unfashionable Kierkegaard," *Sewanee Review*, 1949.
Fiedler, Leslie. "Our Country and Our Culture," *Partisan Review*, 1952.
Gassner, John. *Theatre at the Crossroads*, New York, 1960.
Gold, Herbert. *The Age of Happy Problems*, New York, 1962.
Harris, Mark. *The Case for Tragedy*, New York, 1932.
Krutch, Joseph Wood. *"Modernism" in Modern Drama*, Ithaca, 1953.
Michel, Laurence. "The Possibility of a Christian Tragedy," *Thought*, 1956.
O'Connor, William Van. *Climates of Tragedy*, Baton Rouge, 1943.

THE CRITICISM OF TRAGEDY

Arestad, S. "Ibsen's Concept of Tragedy," *PMLA*, 1959.

Bentley, Eric. *The Playwright as Thinker*, New York, 1947.

Bradley, A. C. *Oxford Lectures on Poetry*, London, 1909.

Bradley, A. C. *Shakespearean Tragedy*, London, 1904.

Brooks, Cleanth (ed.). *Tragic Themes in Western Literature*, New Haven, 1955.

Dean, Leonard T. (ed.). *Shakespeare: Modern Essays in Criticism*, New York, 1957.

Dodds, E. R. *The Greeks and the Irrational*, Berkeley, 1951.

Else, Gerald F. *Aristotle's Poetics: The Argument*, Cambridge, Mass., 1957.

Falk, Doris V. *Eugene O'Neill and the Tragic Tension*, New Brunswick, N. J., 1958.

Farnham, Willard. *Shakespeare's Tragic Frontier*. Berkeley, 1950.

Fergusson, Francis. *The Human Image in Dramatic Literature*, New York, 1957.

Fluchère, Henri. *Shakespeare and the Elizabethans*, New York, 1956.

Jones, Ernest. *Hamlet and Oedipus*, New York, 1949.

Kimmelman, George. "The Concept of Tragedy in Modern Criticism," *Journal of Aesthetics and Art Criticism*, 1946.

Kitto, H. D. F. *Greek Tragedy: A Literary Study*, London, 1939.

Kott, Jan. *Shakespeare Our Contemporary*, New York, 1964.

Spencer, Theodore. *Shakespeare and the Nature of Man*, New York, 1942.

Vinaver, Eugène. *Racine and Poetic Tragedy*, New York, 1959.

Weisinger, Herbert. "The Myth and Ritual Approach to Shakespearean Tragedy," *Centennial Review*, 1957.

Whitman, Cedric. *Sophocles: A Study of Heroic Humanism*, Cambridge, Mass., 1951.